Readings for
Reflective Teaching

**Also available from Continuum:**

Beck, J. and Earl, M. (editors), *Key Issues in Secondary Education* 2nd edition

Cashdan, A. and Overall, L. (editors), *Teaching in Primary Schools*

Fisher, R., *Teaching Thinking*

Hillier, Y., *Reflective Teaching in Further and Adult Education*

Matheson, C. and Matheson, D. (editors), *Educational Issues in the Learning Age*

Pollard, A., *Reflective Teaching*

# Readings for Reflective Teaching

Edited by Andrew Pollard

continuum
LONDON • NEW YORK

**CONTINUUM**
The Tower Building, 11 York Road, London SE1 7NX
15 East 26th Street, New York, NY 10010
www.continuumbooks.com

First published 2002
Reprinted  2003, 2004 (twice)

**British Library Cataloguing-in-Publication Data**
A catalogue record for this book is available from the British Library.

   ISBN 0-8264-5114-4 (hardback)
   ISBN 0-8264-5115-2 (paperback)

Typeset by SetSystems Ltd, Saffron Walden, Essex
Printed and bound in Great Britain by
CPI Bath

# CONTENTS

# PART 2: BEING A REFLECTIVE TEACHER

# ACKNOWLEDGEMENTS

The most important issue that any editor faces is, 'What should be included?' I have worried away at this and have imposed myself on a large number of people in discussing possible selections for various chapters. I have also had a great deal of advice from colleagues in many parts of the UK who responded to a consultative questionnaire – and I must mention the exceptional responses from Karen Carter, then at MMU, and Elizabeth Bird of UNL. Additionally, I would particularly like to thank the Editorial Board for the Reflective Teaching textbook and website, who offered advice on many selections. They are: Janet Collins (Open University), Neil Simco (St Martin's College, Ambleside), Sue Swaffield and Paul Warwick (University of Cambridge) and Jo Warin (University of Lancaster).

The administrative complexity of obtaining permissions has been very considerable. This was completed with great efficiency by Jo Yates; Christina Parkinson and Zoë Reeve. I am also extremely grateful to Suzanne Fletcher and other secretarial colleagues at the Cambridge University Faculty of Education for their work on the production of the manuscript.

I would like to thank all the publishers, editors and other publishers' representatives who were kind enough to grant permission for material to be reprinted. An acknowledgements listing for all permissions for the reproduction of extracts is formally provided at the end of the book. Attempts to trace permission holders have been sustained, though a few cases remain where replies to our enquiries have not yet been received. Any enquiries on such matters should be sent, in the first instance, to the Permissions Editor at Continuum.

Finally, I would like to thank all the authors whose work features in this book – and apologize to the many other researchers and educationists whose high-quality material does not! Some, of course, may be delighted to have escaped, for word-length constraints have occasionally forced detailed editing. I sincerely apologize if any authors feel that their work has suffered in that process.

Having reviewed a wide range of publications for possible inclusion in the book, I remain enormously impressed by the richness of research and thinking available to teachers, mentors and trainee teachers. The collection can be seen as a representation of the work of several generations of educational researchers – though, even with 120 readings, it has not been possible to include all the excellent material which is available. In a sense though, the book remains a collective product and I would like to pay tribute to the many academic colleagues and educationalists who remain obsessed enough to keep on trying to describe, analyse and understand education in so many diverse ways.

Andrew Pollard
University of Cambridge, January 2002

# INTRODUCTION

This book is part of a set of professional resources. It links directly to an established textbook, *Reflective Teaching*, and to a website, *RTweb*. We thus now offer three fully integrated and complementary sources of materials:

- *Reflective Teaching* (the core handbook for school-based professional development);

- *RTweb* (a website for supplementary, updatable 'Notes for Further Reading', 'Reflective Activities', links, downloads, etc.);

- *Readings for Reflective Teaching* (a portable library with 120 integrated and linked readings).

*Reflective Teaching* considers a very wide range of professionally relevant topics, presents key issues and research insights, suggests 'Reflective Activities' for classroom work, and offers notes for a small number of 'Key Readings'. The text is used to support professional development by many schools, local education authorities, colleges and universities, and has become a central textbook supporting school-based practice for initial teacher education courses across the UK. In its 2002 version, it has been specifically shaped to support school mentors in their work with initial trainees and newly qualified teachers, and to reflect current training requirements in England, Wales, Scotland and Northern Ireland.

*RTweb* has been established to supplement the two books. In particular, the web enables the Editorial Board to update material regularly. This is particularly relevant for 'Notes for Further Reading', a more extensive and current source of ideas than is possible in a printed book. There is also a glossary of terms, additional 'Reflective Activities' and download facilities for diagrams. Other ideas are being considered.

*Readings for Reflective Teaching*, the present book, has been extensively updated since the 1996 version. Whilst many classic papers remain, almost half of the 120 readings are new. Material from important recent research has been added, and the balance of the book has been adjusted to reflect current issues and concerns.

Three major aims have guided the production of *Readings*.

First, it is intended as a resource for busy teachers, mentors and trainee teachers who appreciate the value of educational thinking and research, and who wish to have easy access to key parts of important publications. The focus remains on primary education, but there are also papers which reflect important issues for the Foundation Stage and at the beginning of Key Stage 3.

Second, the book provides an opportunity to 'show-case' some of the excellent educational research that has been conducted in recent years. Readers may then wish to consult the full accounts in the original sources, each of which is carefully referenced.

Together, these materials provide a unique resource for professional development activities and for teacher training courses. The structure of the three sources is identical, so that the chapters map across from one book to the other and to the web. Thus, whether used in classroom activities, private study, mentoring conversations, workshops, staff-meetings, seminars or action-research projects, the materials should be easily accessible.

Reflective activity is of vital importance to the teaching profession. It underpins professional judgement and its use for worthwhile educational purposes. It provides a vehicle for learning and professional renewal – and thus for defending the independence and integrity of teachers. We hope that you will find these materials helpful in your professional work and as you seek personal fulfilment as a teacher.

### A note for students on citation

If wishing to reference a reading from this book in a piece of written coursework or for a professional publication, you will need to cite your source. Using the Harvard Convention and drawing only on this text, you should provide a bibliography containing details of the *original* source. These are provided following the introduction to each reading. You should then put: 'Cited in Pollard, A. (ed.) (2002) *Readings for Reflective Teaching*. London: Continuum'.

If you are building a substantial case around any reading, you are strongly recommended to go back to the original source and to check your argument against the full text. These will be available in the libraries of most colleges and universities with teacher education provision. You should then cite the full text only, with the specific page numbers of any material that you quote.

All the citations in the readings from this book have been collected into a single, integrated bibliography at the end of the book and can be followed up from that source (see p. 377).

# PART 1

# Becoming a reflective teacher

# CHAPTER 1
# Reflective teaching

The five readings in this chapter illustrate key ideas about the meaning of reflective practice and its relationship with teacher professionalism.

First, we have excerpts from the highly influential work of Dewey (1.1), Schön (1.2) and the Berlaks (1.3). For them, teaching is a highly complex activity calling for thoughtful action and the development of professional judgement to resolve endemic dilemmas.

Osborn and her colleagues (1.4) demonstate the use of professional judgement in their discussion of how teachers engage in 'creative mediation' when responding to centralized policy initiatives.

Finally, Tabachnick and Zeichner (1.5) review the concept of 'reflective teaching' itself, and identify four specific approaches to it.

The parallel chapter of *Reflective Teaching* emphasizes the importance of *processes* of reflection in the development of successive *states* of practical competence. The chapter also clarifies the 'meaning of reflective teaching' by identifying seven key characteristics – including the use of evaluative evidence and learning with colleagues. There are suggestions for further reading both there and on *RTweb*.

# Thinking and reflective experience

## John Dewey

The writings of John Dewey have been an enormous influence on educational thinking. Indeed, his distinction of 'routinized' and 'reflective' teaching is fundamental to the conception of professional development through reflection. In the two selections below, Dewey considers the relationship between reflective thinking and the sort of challenges which people face through experience.

Do you feel that you are sufficiently openminded to be really 'reflective'?

Edited from: Dewey, J. (1933) *How We Think: A Restatement of the Relation of Reflective Thinking to the Educative Process.* Chicago: Henry Regnery, 15–16, and Dewey, J. (1916) *Democracy and Education.* New York: Free Press, 176–77

The origin of thinking is some perplexity, confusion, or doubt. Thinking is not a case of spontaneous combustion; it does not occur just on 'general principles'. There is something that occasions and evokes it. General appeals to a child (or to a grown-up) to think, irrespective of the existence in his own experience of some difficulty that troubles him and disturbs his equilibrium, are as futile as advice to lift himself by his boot-straps.

Given a difficulty, the next step is suggestion of some way out – the formation of some tentative plan or project, the entertaining of some theory that will account for the peculiarities in question, the consideration of some solution for the problem. The data at hand cannot supply the solution; they can only suggest it. What, then, are the sources of the suggestion? Clearly, past experience and a fund of relevant knowledge at one's command. If the person has had some acquaintance with similar situations, if he has dealt with material of the same sort before, suggestions more or less apt and helpful will arise. But unless there has been some analogous experience, confusion remains mere confusion. Even when a child (or grown-up) has a problem, it is wholly futile to urge him to 'think' when he has no prior experiences that involve some of the same conditions.

There may, however, be a state of perplexity and also previous experience out of which suggestions emerge, and yet thinking need not be reflective. For the person may not be sufficiently critical about the ideas that occur to him. He may jump at a conclusion without weighing the grounds on which it rests; he may forego or unduly shorten the act of hinting, inquiring; he may take the first 'answer,' or solution, that comes to him because of mental sloth, torpor, impatience to get something settled.

One can think reflectively only when one is willing to endure suspense and to undergo the trouble of searching. To many persons both suspense of judgement and intellectual search are disagreeable; they want to get them ended as soon as possible. They cultivate an over-positive and dogmatic habit of mind, or feel perhaps that a condition of doubt will be regarded as evidence of mental inferiority. It is at the point where examination and test enter into investigation that the difference between reflective thought and bad thinking comes in.

To be genuinely thoughtful, we must be willing to sustain and protract that state of doubt which is the stimulus to thorough inquiry.

The general features of a reflective experience are:

● perplexity, confusion, doubt, due to the fact that one is implicated in an incomplete situation whose full character is not yet determined;

- a conjectural anticipation – a tentative interpretation of the given elements, attributing to them a tendency to effect certain consequences;

- a careful survey (examination, inspection, exploration, analysis) of all attainable consideration which will define and clarify the problem in hand;

- a consequent elaboration of the tentative hypothesis to make it more precise and more consistent, because squaring with a wider range of facts;

- taking one stand upon the projected hypothesis as a plan of action which is applied to the existing state of affairs; doing something overtly to bring about the anticipated result, and thereby testing the hypothesis.

It is the extent and accuracy of steps three and four which mark off a distinctive reflective experience from one on the trial and error plane. They make thinking itself into an experience. Nevertheless, we never get wholly beyond the trial and error situation. Our most elaborate and rationally consistent thought has to be tried in the world and thereby tried out. And since it can never take into account all the connections, it can never cover with perfect accuracy all the consequences. Yet a thoughtful survey of conditions is so careful, and the guessing at results so controlled, that we have a right to mark off the reflective experience from the grosser trial and error forms of action.

## READING 1.2

# Reflection-in-action

## Donald Schön

Donald Schön's analysis of reflective practice has influenced training, development and conceptions in many professions. His key insight is that there are forms of professional knowledge which, though often tacitly held, are essential for the exercise of judgement as the complexities and dilemmas of professional life are confronted. Such knowledge is *in* professional action, and may be developed by reflection-in-action.

Edited from: Schön, D. A. (1983) *The Reflective Practitioner: How Professionals Think in Action*. London: Temple Smith, 50–68

When we go about the spontaneous, intuitive performance of the actions of everyday life, we show ourselves to be knowledgeable in a special way. Often we cannot say what it is that we know. When we try to describe it we find ourselves at a loss, or we produce descriptions that are obviously inappropriate. Our knowing is ordinarily tacit, implicit in our patterns of action and in our feel for the stuff with which we are dealing. It seems right to say that our knowing is *in* our action.

Similarly, the workaday life of the professional depends on tacit knowing-in-action. Every competent practitioner makes innumerable judgements of quality for which he cannot state adequate criteria, and he displays skills for which he cannot state the rules and procedures. Even when he makes conscious use of research-based theories and techniques, he is dependent on tacit recognitions, judgements, and skilful performances.

On the other hand, both ordinary people and professional practitioners often think about what they are doing, sometimes even while doing it. Stimulated by surprise, they turn thought back on action and on the knowing which is implicit in action. They may ask themselves, for example, 'What features do I notice when I recognize this thing? What are the criteria by which I make this judgement? What procedures am I enacting when I perform this skill? How am I framing the problem that I am trying to solve?' Usually reflection on knowing-in-action goes together with reflection on the stuff at hand. There is some puzzling, or troubling, or interesting phenomenon with which the individual is trying to deal. As he tries to make sense of it, he also reflects on the understandings which have been implicit in his action, understandings which he surfaces, criticizes, restructures and embodies in further action.

It is this entire process of reflection-in-action which is central to the 'art' by which practitioners sometimes deal well with situations of uncertainty, instability, uniqueness and value conflict.

## Knowing-in-action

There is nothing strange about the idea that a kind of knowing is inherent in intelligent action. Common sense admits the category of know-how, and it does not stretch common sense very much to say that the know-how is *in* the action.

There are actions, recognitions, and judgements which we know how to carry out spontaneously; we do not have to think about them prior to or during their performance. We are often unaware of having learned to do these things; we simply find ourselves doing them. In some cases, we were once aware of the understandings which were subsequently internalized in our feeling for the stuff of action. In other cases, we may usually be unable to describe the knowing which our action reveals. It is in this sense that I speak of knowing-in-action, the characteristic mode of ordinary practical knowledge.

## Reflecting-in-action

If common sense recognizes knowing-in-action, it also recognizes that we sometimes think about what we are doing. Phrases like 'thinking on your feet,' 'keeping your wits about you,' and 'learning by doing' suggest not only that we can think about doing but that we can think about doing something while doing it. Some of the most interesting examples of this process occur in the midst of a performance.

Much reflection-in-action hinges on the experience of surprise. When intuitive, spontaneous performance yields nothing more than the results expected for it, then we tend not to think about it. But when intuitive performance leads to surprises, pleasing and promising or unwanted, we may respond by reflecting-in-action. In such processes, reflection tends to focus interactively on the outcomes of action, the action itself, and the intuitive knowing implicit in the action.

A professional practitioner is a specialist who encounters certain types of situations again and again. As a practitioner experiences many variations of a small number of types of cases, he is able to 'practise' his practice. He develops a repertoire of expectations, images and techniques. He learns what to look for and how to respond to what he finds. As long as his practice is stable, in the sense that it brings him the same types of cases, he becomes less and less subject to surprise. His knowing-in-practice tends to become increasingly tacit, spontaneous and automatic, thereby conferring upon him and his clients the benefits of specialization.

As a practice becomes more repetitive and routine, and as knowing-in-practice becomes increasingly tacit and spontaneous, the practitioner may miss important opportunities to think about what he is doing. He may find that he is drawn into patterns of error which he cannot correct. And if he learns, as often happens, to be selectively inattentive to phenomena that do not fit the categories of his knowing-in-action, then he may suffer from boredom or 'burnout' and afflict his clients with the consequences of his narrowness and rigidity. When this happens, the practitioner has 'over-learned' what he knows.

A practitioner's reflection can serve as a corrective to over-learning. Through reflection, he can surface and criticize the tacit understandings that have grown up around the repetitive experiences of a specialized practice, and can make new sense of the situations of uncertainty or uniqueness which he may allow himself to experience.

Practitioners do reflect *on* their knowing-in-practice. Sometimes, in the relative tranquillity of a postmortem, they think back on a project they have undertaken, a situation they have lived through, and they explore the understandings they have brought to their handling of the case. They may do this in a mood of idle speculation, or in a deliberate effort to prepare themselves for future cases. But they may also reflect on practice while they are in the midst of it. Here they reflect-in-action.

When a practitioner reflects in and on his practice, the possible objects of his reflection are as varied as the kinds of phenomena before him and the systems of knowing-in-practice which he brings to them. He may reflect on the tacit norms and appreciations which underlie a judgement, or on the strategies and theories implicit in a pattern of behaviour. He may reflect on the feeling for a situation which has led him to adopt a particular course of action, on the way in which he has framed the problem he is trying to solve, or on the role he has constructed for himself within a larger institutional context.

Reflection-in-action, in these several modes, is central to the art through which practitioners sometimes cope with the troublesome 'divergent' situations of practice. When the phenomenon at hand eludes the ordinary categories of knowledge-in-practice, presenting itself as unique or unstable, the practitioner may surface and criticize his initial understanding of the phenomenon, construct a new description of it, and test the new description by an on-the-spot experiment. Sometimes he arrives at a new theory of the phenomenon by articulating a feeling he has about it.

When he is confronted with demands that seem incompatible or inconsistent, he may respond by reflecting on the appreciations which he and others have brought to the situation. Conscious of a dilemma, he may attribute it to the way in which he has set his problem, or even to the way in which he has framed his role. He may then find a way of integrating, or choosing among, the values at stake in the situation.

When someone reflects-in-action, he becomes a researcher in the practice context. He does not separate thinking from doing. Because his experimenting is a kind of action, implementation is built into his inquiry. Thus reflection-in-action can proceed, even in situations of uncertainty or uniqueness.

Although reflection-in-action is an extraordinary process, it is not a rare event. Indeed, for reflective practitioners it is the core of practice.

📖 READING 1.3

# Dilemmas of schooling

## Ann Berlak and Harold Berlak

Reflection is a fundamental necessity for professional teachers because there are no simple prescriptions concerning what 'best' educational practice might be. That is what makes the job both so interesting and challenging. A particularly useful way of conceptualizing the reality of these daily struggles is through the concept of 'dilemmas'. Justifiably, Ann and Harold Berlak's book on this topic has become a classic and this reading illustrates the ways in which they link the identification of dilemmas to the need for reflective teaching.

What are the main dilemmas that you face in your work?

Edited from: Berlak, A. and Berlak, H. (1981) *Dilemmas of Schooling*. London: Methuen, 125–37, 237

Dilemmas represent contradictions that reside in the situation, in the individual, and in the larger society – as they are played out in one form of institutional life, schooling. Dilemmas focus on the flux and the reflexivity of the social process that are encapsulated in daily encounters of teachers with children in the social setting of the schools.

We offer an illustration to show how dilemmas may be used to represent schooling processes that are in constant flux, and to illuminate the relationship of past, present and future. We begin with a summary of observations recorded one day in March at Heathbrook Primary School.

'We ought to chain it to your desk so you don't lose it again', Mr Scott says to Susan as he hands her a lined composition book to replace the one she lost. Susan's head droops; tears look imminent. Another child, whose eyes catch Susan's, responds with a grin. Susan twists her half-brooding mouth into a half smile and she returns to her chair, new composition book in hand. Several children's heads turn toward the doorway. The Head enters carrying 'work diaries', lined composition books wherein each child every Friday morning lists the learning tasks completed during the week. He says a few quiet words to Mr Scott as he hands him the stack of books, looks quickly about the classroom which has become noticeably more silent upon his arrival, and departs. Mr Scott from his vantage point in the middle of the room scans the room, his eyes passing over individuals, pairs and trios, some of whom appear to be working diligently while others every now and again become engaged in intense conversation. His eyes fall on Steven and Bruce moments longer than the rest. These boys, who yesterday had been seated on opposite sides of the room, are today seated together, intently examining one of their football cards, engrossed in what appears from a distance to be a particularly vigorous and extended exchange of ideas, their mathematics work as presented on a set of cards cast aside, temporarily forgotten. Mr Scott leaves his place at the centre of the room, approaches Mary, and responding to her request, reads a portion of the story she is writing.

Later, in the teacher's room, Mr Bolton, Mr Scott and the two of us wait for tea water to boil. Mr Bolton tells us of a television programme discussion of the decline of mathematics standards in the schools and its effects on students' qualifications for university entrance. Mr Scott nods assent and says, 'Yes, there is probably something to that'.

Mr Scott this morning walks past Steven rather than telling him to get back to work. One could view this as a non-event since Mr Scott did not do anything to Steven. However, this 'non-event' stands out for several reasons – because he treats Steven somewhat differently from the others and differently than he did yesterday. It also stands out because Steven isn't doing his maths, and Mr Scott, in word and deed, considers maths an especially important part of the work of school. How can we make sense of this non-event? Had we not spent time in his class nor had some access to Mr Scott's and Mr Bolton's views, we might not have noted that Mr Scott looked at Steven but said nothing, or we may have passed it off as something of which he was not aware. We had no way of knowing by observation alone whether, for example, his non-behaviour was studied indifference or benign or even malign neglect. But Mr Scott has also told us about Steven's 'creativity', about the misery of the football fanatics when they were separated from one another, about the press he feels to get the 'fourth years' to progress, we discern his response to Steven as part of a pattern. This pattern includes both his bypassing of Steven and his later confrontation of him.

The act is the fundamental conception on which the dilemma language rests. It includes the observable instances of Mr Scott's behaviour, his visions of the future images from the past, and the circumstances of the present situation (some of which he is aware). To view Mr Scott's schooling behaviour in terms of the dilemma language is to see it not as a set of disconnected, contradictory, discrete, situational behaviours, but as a complex pattern of behaviours that are joined together through his consciousness. We have some limited access to his consciousness as he talks to us about what we see him do in his classroom and through our observations of the context in which his behaviours are embedded. The act portrays Mr Scott not only as a mindless reactor to inside or outside forces, social, physical and psychological, but as a person who is and may become critical, in Dewey's and Mead's terms, increasingly able to engage in reflective action. It appears to us and apparently to Mr Scott as well, that he at times makes choices, more or less consciously, more or less thoughtfully, from among the alternatives as he sees them. This sense of choice is suggested by 'I have yet to come to terms with myself', and as he shares a few of his continuing internal conversations about whether Steven and children generally should be pushed to do mathematics.

As Mr Scott talks to us and as we watch him teach, it becomes apparent that he is responding with some degree of awareness to a wide range of contradictory social experiences and social forces, past and contemporary, both in his classroom, his school and beyond in the wider community. He has internalized these contradictions and they are now 'within' him, a part of his generalized other. We infer these contradictions by observing his behaviour and listening to what he says about it – 'something inside you that you've developed over the years which says children should do this' and 'I didn't want them to be miserable' – and from his frequent admissions to us in conversation that he accepts of his own accord the Head's views on standards in mathematics, and also agrees with him that 'children need a haven'.

We represent these contradictions as dilemmas that are 'in' Mr Scott, in his personal and social history, and 'in' the present circumstances (and are also fundamental contradictions in the culture and society). These contradictions and the 'internal' or 'mental' weighing of these forces that sometimes occurs are joined in the moment he looks at Steven, then past him, and focuses his attention on Mary.

The dilemmas are a language of acts, a means of representing the diverse and apparently contradictory patterns of schooling. Dilemmas do not represent static ideas waiting at bay in the mind, but an unceasing interaction of internal and external forces, a world of continuous transformations. Because they are capable of becoming aware of these internal and external forces that bear on their own *de facto* solutions, persons are capable of altering their own behavioural patterns and/or acting with others in efforts to alter the circumstances in which they act.

Mr Scott's past and present experiences are 'in' his patterns of resolution; he is not only a pawn to these experiences but also an originator of action. Since Steven, like Mr Scott, takes meaning from experiences and may reflect upon them, then Mr Scott's patterns of resolutions may be seen as both transmitting and transforming the society. The problem of the relationship between Mr Scott's past and present experience, his patterns of resolution, and the meanings Steven takes from them, is a representation of the problem of the relationship of past to present to future in the social process and is, thus, one way to formulate the question of the role that schooling plays in social transmission and transformation. By recognizing patterns of resolution, including dominant and more exceptional modes, and viewing teachers' behaviour as both determined and free, the dilemma language enables one to consider the relationship of school to society.

The purpose of inquiry, for teachers and non-teachers, is to enable them to engage in reflective action. Engaging in this process requires that each of the participants render as problematic what they have been taking for granted about what is happening in classrooms, the origins of the schooling activities and their consequences upon children and the society both in the immediate and longer-range future. Using the dilemma language to structure critical inquiry involves an examination, from the widest possible range of perspectives, or present patterns of resolution, alternative possibilities, the consequences of present and alternative patterns, the origins of present patterns and of proposals for alternatives. A critical search for alternatives is not complete if it does not include development of skills and knowledge needed by teachers to alter their schooling patterns. The latter we call craft knowledge.

 **READING 1.4**

# Creative mediation and professional judgement

Marilyn Osborn, Elizabeth McNess and Patricia Broadfoot

This reading is drawn from one of the final reports from the PACE project – an independent analysis of the impact of the introduction of the National Curriculum and assessment on primary teachers and pupils. The study documented many teacher responses to new challenges, including simple compliance, resistance and even retirement, but one of the most constructive was 'creative mediation'. This approach is what might be expected from confident, reflective professionals.

Edited from: Osborn, M., McNess, E. and Broadfoot, P., with Pollard A., and Triggs, P. (2000) *What Teachers Do: Changing Policy and Practice in Primary Education*. London, New York: Continuum, 80–3

A central factor in determining teachers' ability to adopt a creative response to the imposed reforms was their level of professional confidence. As Helsby (1999) argues:

> Teachers who are professionally confident have a strong belief not only in their capacity but also in their authority to make important decisions about the conduct of their work . . . In order to be able to do this, the teacher needs to feel 'in control' of the work situation. Thus professional confidence also implies that the teacher is not overwhelmed by excessive work demands that can never be properly met. The confident teacher has a sense of being able to manage the tasks in hand rather than being driven by them. Instead of crisis management, corner-cutting and ill-considered coping strategies, they are able to reflect upon, and make conscious choices between, alternative courses of action and can feel that they are doing 'a good job'. (p. 173)

The key question here is to be able to identify and foster those factors which contribute to a teacher's level of professional confidence. We have shown previously that teachers' personal biographies, their previous experiences and the values they have developed all influence their level of professional confidence (Osborn, 1996a; Osborn, 1996b). In our report of phase two of the PACE project we drew upon the examples of Sara and Elizabeth, two Key Stage 1 teachers of roughly the same age and level of teaching experience who worked in the same school. A comparison of these two teachers over the first few years of the reforms from 1990 to 1994, showed how personal biography and career trajectories can affect the level of professional confidence and a continued sense of satisfaction with the teaching role.

Both Sara Wilson and Elizabeth West were highly experienced teachers who had been working in the same infant school in the outskirts of a large southern city for well over ten years. Sara had been a teacher for 22 years and Elizabeth for 26 years. In 1990 both were feeling overloaded, stressed and anxious about the effect of the National Curriculum on the children in their class. They had considerable fears about how primary education would develop in the future and about the effect of national assessment on the quality of teaching and learning in their school. During the course of the study, Sara, who was responsible for a Year 2 class, had become Deputy Head. Elizabeth, who taught a mixed Year 1 and Year 2 class, had a point of responsibility for special needs. Strikingly, in spite of many similarities in terms of their experience in teaching, their commitment to the children, and the same school context, the changes impacted quite differently upon them during the course of the four years.

By the end of the four years, Sara felt she had emerged with a new sense of focus and clarity about her role and her practice. She saw the gains and rewards from teaching post-National Curriculum as clearly outweighing the losses, and was particularly confident that she had acquired improved skills in assessment. As she described it:

> I'm more focused now when I plan an activity.

Sara felt that a key factor in helping her to adapt to change was the support she derived from being in a school with a strong, stable staff, and from her own temperament which she defined as calm and practical, enabling her to 'get hold of the changes and do them in the least damaging way, keeping hold of children's happiness and enthusiasm'. However, perhaps the key point in Sara's response to the changes, and the one which most differentiated her from Elizabeth, was the emphasis she placed on the importance of taking control of the changes, and finding ways of making them part of her thinking rather than simply seeing them as external targets which had to be met. She described this in the following way:

> I think that what I hope to do is to internalise myself as a teacher, internalise all this detail and to then be able to use it in good infant practice, etc. etc.

This striving after internalization, taking control, and integration of new demands into what she defined as good infant practice was a hallmark of teachers whom we have described as 'creative mediators', those who feel able to take active control of educational changes and to respond to them in a creative, but possibly selective way.

Sara's emergence as a confident, post-ERA professional, who had successfully integrated the new requirements into her own identity as a teacher, contrasted with the unhappiness and sense of loss expressed by Elizabeth four years into the reforms. Although she also saw gains from teachers having a clearer idea and more awareness of what they were aiming for in their work with children, for her the losses outweighed the gains. She did not feel that she had been able to hold onto the creativity she had before.

> I've tightened up but also narrowed down. We are really missing the fun of the extra bits . . . As someone said in one of our staff meetings, it's like walking through a wood and keeping to a pathway, not seeing the interesting things on either side . . . For me the National Curriculum has narrowed my outlook as much as I have tried for it not to. There is still so much to get through and I still feel in a straitjacket. I do smashing work with the children and then I find it doesn't cover the Attainment Targets, so I realise that I still have all that to do . . . It takes a lot of enjoyment from me. For me, teaching has always been a creative outlet. Now I'm constrained, I've lost a lot of creativity.

Her own identity as a teacher, her confidence, and her ability to be creative were perceived by her to be under threat. A key difference between Elizabeth and Sara seemed to be in their ability to take control and make choices about how to implement the changes. Elizabeth was, by her own description, a perfectionist. She felt that she must conscientiously cover every attainment target with every child no matter what the cost. Sara, on the other hand, saw herself as able to say 'no' to new demands. She was able to avoid the over-conscientiousness which has been a characteristic of many committed primary teachers (Campbell *et al.*, 1991).

Another key difference was in the new roles taken on by both teachers in the course of the study. Sara had been able to move onto a new role as deputy head which arguably gave her a broader view of the reforms, new challenges, and new motivations. Rather than feeling de-skilled, she had been able to make the new demands build upon her strengths. Huberman (1993) argued that a key factor in the professional satisfaction of teachers was a feeling of 'upward mobility and social promotion'. This characterized the career trajectories of many teachers in his sample of middle and high-school teachers who had remained the most energetic and committed throughout their careers.

Another factor for these teachers' continued satisfaction was the continuation of an enjoyable and good relationship with pupils. Whereas Sara had certainly gained a new role which involved 'upward mobility and social promotion', Elizabeth had lost her key 'satisfier', her relationship with the children, which she perceived to be increasingly under threat. Her post of responsibility for special needs children was particularly significant here and may have exacerbated this sense of loss. Of the Key Stage 1 teachers in the 1994 PACE sample, 44 per cent saw the National Curriculum as particularly disadvantaging children with special needs. It was clear from Elizabeth's responses that she shared this view. In primary teaching, there is a close link between a teacher's self or sense of identity as part of the professional role and the self as a person (Pollard, 1985; Nias, 1989; Cortazzi, 1991). In Elizabeth's case it appears that the changes threatened not only her professional identity, but also her sense of 'self' as a person, since for her it was the emotional response of the 'personal self' reinforced by her relationships which made teaching worthwhile.

Both these teachers had been working under many constraints, not the least of which were large classes. The strategies which they evolved to cope with the constraints imposed by multiple change were influenced by their level of professional confidence which, in turn appeared to be influenced by their personal biographies and career trajectories and the level of satisfaction they continued to derive from their work.

Another key factor in the development of professional confidence, even within the constraints imposed by multiple change, is the context and culture within which a teacher works. Our analysis suggested that the socio-economic catchment area of the school may lead to teachers experiencing very different pressures and consequently adopting different strategies for change. Research also suggests that the ability to adopt a response of 'creative mediation' to the National Curriculum is heavily influenced by the presence of a supportive school climate, in particular where a collaborative culture flourishes which gives teachers the confidence to assert their own interpretations upon situations (Helsby and McCulloch, 1997). In the case study drawn upon above, Sara commented upon the importance of the supportive environment provided by the head and the school in which teachers were encouraged to make their own decisions about how they selectively implemented change. Most of the teachers we identified as 'creative mediators' worked within a strong, collaborative school culture where they were given confidence that they could benefit from the structure and guidelines of the National Curriculum without letting it drive them or destroy what they knew to be good about their practice.

We have thus identified some areas where teachers can be seen to have mediated policy through professional practice in ways which may amount to policy creation. At a more detailed level, we can identify four strategies of creative mediation – protective, innovative, collaborative and conspiratorial – by which teachers can be seen to have formulated classroom policy by acting in common, although not necessarily collective, ways.

More recent evidence suggests that even with the introduction of the national literacy and numeracy strategies on schools, many schools and the individual teachers within them are seizing the potential for a margin of manoeuvre between such centralized policies and their implementation. Thus some teachers are finding creative ways of working within the guidelines imposed by these strategies and gaining a new professional discourse (Woods and Jeffrey, 1997) as a result. The evidence suggests that creative mediation by teachers is an important strategy which may have system-wide effects on policy and which will continue as long as there are teachers who feel sufficiently confident to adapt and develop practices that accord with their values and working situations.

Professional confidence may depend upon many variables at both institutional and individual level, including personal biographies and career trajectories, the gaining of an overview through moving to a new level of responsibility and a consequent sense of being re-valued and re-skilled. School context remains important and, perhaps most significant of all, is the existence of a supportive and collaborative school climate and culture.

 **READING 1.5**

# Reflections on reflective teaching

## Robert Tabachnick and Kenneth Zeichner

Is 'reflection' just a catch-all idea, lacking real coherence? This reading reviews four different traditions of reflective teaching which have been identified in North America (the academic, the social efficiency, the developmental and the social reconstructionist), echoes of which can certainly be found elsewhere. Indeed, the influence of each tradition can be seen in the selection of readings for this book.

Do you feel that these emphases are opposed or complementary?

Edited from: Tabachnick, R. and Zeichner, K. (eds) (1991) *Issues and Practices in Inquiry-Oriented Teacher Education.* London: Falmer Press, 1–9

In the last decade, concurrent with the growth of research on teacher thinking and with the increased respect for teachers' practical theories (Clark, 1988), the 'reflective practitioner' has emerged as the new Zeitgeist. There is not a single teacher educator who would say that he or she is not concerned about preparing teachers who are reflective. The criteria that have become attached to reflective practice are so diverse, however, that important differences between specific practices are masked by the use of the common rhetoric.

On the one hand, the recent work of teacher educators such as Cruickshank (1987), who has drawn upon Dewey [see Reading 1.1] for inspiration, gives us some guidance. The distinction that is often made between reflective and routine practice is not trivial and enables us to make some important qualitative distinctions among different teachers and teaching practices. Similarly, the enormously popular work of Schön [see Reading 1.2] which has challenged the dominant technical rationality in professional education and argued for more attention to promoting artistry in teaching by encouraging 'reflection in action' and 'reflection on action' among teachers, also directs our attention to the preparation of particular kinds and not others. However, these generic approaches to reflective teaching lose their heuristic value after a certain point and begin to hide more than they reveal.

After we have agreed with Cruickshank and Schön, for example, that thoughtful teachers who reflect about their practice (on and in action) are more desirable than thoughtless teachers, who are ruled primarily by tradition, authority and circumstance, there are still many unanswered questions. Neither Cruickshank nor Schön have much to say, for example, about what it is that teachers ought to be reflecting about, the kinds of criteria that should come into play during the process of reflection (e.g. which help distinguish acceptable from unacceptable educational practice) or about the degree to which teachers' deliberations should incorporate a critique of the institutional contexts in which they work. In some extreme cases, the impression is given that as long as teachers reflect about something, in some manner, whatever they decide to do is all right since they have reflected about it.

One way in which we can think about differences among proposals for reflective teaching is in light of different traditions of practice in teacher education. Zeichner and Liston (1990) have identified four varieties of reflective teaching practice based on their analysis of traditions of reform in twentieth-century US teacher education:

> an academic version that stresses reflection upon subject matter and the representation and translation of subject matter knowledge to promote student understanding (Shulman, 1987) [see Reading 8.6];

> a social efficiency version that emphasizes the thoughtful application of particular teaching strategies that have been suggested by research on teaching (Ross and Kyle, 1987) [see Chapters 10, 11, 12 and 13 for examples];

> a developmentalist version that prioritizes teaching that is sensitive to students' interests, thinking and patterns of developmental growth (Duckworth, 1987) [see Reading 8.4]; and

> a social reconstructionist version that stresses reflection about the social and political context of schooling and the assessment of classroom actions for their ability to contribute toward greater equity, social justice and humane conditions in schooling and society (Beyer, 1988; Maher and Rathbone, 1986) [see Readings 4.1 and 18.2].

In each of these views of reflective teaching practice, certain priorities are established about schooling and society that emerge out of particular historical traditions and educational and social philosophies.

None of these traditions is sufficient by itself for providing a moral basis for teaching and teacher education. Good teaching and teacher education need to attend to all of the elements that are brought into focus by the various traditions: the representation of subject matter, student thinking and understanding, teaching strategies suggested by research conducted by university academics and classroom teachers, and the social contexts of teaching. These elements do not take the same form, however, or receive the same emphasis within each tradition.

## The academic tradition of reflective teaching

The academic tradition has historically emphasized the role of the liberal arts and disciplinary knowledge in teacher preparation and other clinical experiences (e.g.: Koerner, 1963; Damerell, 1985). This orientation to teacher education emphasizes the teacher's role as a scholar and subject matter specialist and has taken different forms throughout the twentieth century. In recent years, Lee Shulman (1987) and Margaret Buchmann (1984) among others, have advocated views of reflective teaching that emphasize the teacher's deliberations about subject matter and its transformation to pupils to promote understanding.

This group has also proposed a model of pedagogical reasoning and action that identifies six aspects of the teaching act: comprehension, transformation, instruction, evaluation, reflection and new comprehension. One key aspect of their model of pedagogical reasoning (under the transformation process) is representation. According to Shulman (1987) [see Reading 8.6]:

representation involves thinking through the key ideas in the text or lesson and identifying the alternative ways of representing them to students. What analogies, metaphors, examples, demonstrations, simulations, and the like can help to build a bridge between the teacher's comprehension and that desired for the students? Multiple forms of representation are desirable. (p. 328)

This model of pedagogical reasoning and action is a good example of a contemporary view of reflective teaching that prioritizes reflection about the content to be taught and how it is to be taught.

## The social efficiency tradition of reflective teaching

The social efficiency tradition has historically emphasized a faith in the scientific study of teaching to provide the basis for building a teacher education curriculum. According to advocates of this view, research on teaching has provided us with a 'knowledge base' that can form the foundation for the curriculum of teacher education programmes (Berliner, 1984). Feiman-Nemser (1990) has identified two different ways in which contemporary teacher educators have interpreted the social efficiency perspective. First, she describes a technological version in which the intent is to teach prospective teachers the skills and competencies that research has shown to be associated with desirable pupil outcomes.

A second and broader interpretation of the social efficiency tradition in US teacher education is one where the findings of research on teaching are used by teachers as 'principles of procedure' within a wider process of decision making and problem solving. According to the advocates of this deliberative orientation to the use of research on teaching, the crucial task for teacher educators is to foster teachers' capabilities to exercise judgement about the use of various teaching skills suggested by research.

The emphasis is clearly on the intelligent use of 'generic' teaching skills and strategies that have been suggested by research.

## The developmentalist tradition of reflective teaching

The distinguishing characteristic of the developmentalist tradition is the assumption that the natural development of the learner provides the basis for determining what should be taught to students and how it should be taught. Historically, this natural order of child development was to be determined by research involving the careful observation and description of students' behaviour at various stages of development.

According to Perrone (1989), three central metaphors have been associated with the progressive/developmentalist tradition: teacher as naturalist, teacher as researcher and teacher as artist. The teacher as naturalist dimension has stressed the importance of skill in the observation of children's behaviour and in building a curriculum and classroom environment consistent with patterns of child development and children's interests. Classroom practice is to be grounded in close observation and study of children in the classroom either directly by the teacher, or from reflection on a literature based on such study. The teacher as researcher element of this tradition has emphasized the need to foster the teacher's experimental attitude towards practice and to help them initiate and sustain ongoing inquiries in their own classrooms about the learning of specific children to inform their practice. Finally, the teacher as artist element has emphasized the link between creative and fully functioning persons in touch with their own learning and exciting and stimulating classrooms.

This developmentalist conception of reflective teaching has become increasingly popular in recent years with the growing influence of cognitive psychology in education. The emphasis is clearly on reflecting about students.

## The social reconstructionist tradition of reflective teaching

In the fourth tradition of social reconstructionism, schooling and teacher education are both viewed as crucial elements in the movement toward a more just and humane society. According to Valli (1992), proponents of this approach argue that:

> schools as social institutions, help reproduce a society based on unjust class, race, and gender relations and that teachers have a moral obligation to reflect on and change their own practices and school structures when these perpetuate such arrangements. (p. 46)

In a social reconstructionist conception of reflective teaching, the teacher's attention is focused both inwardly at their own practice (and the collective practices of a group of colleagues) and outwardly at the social conditions in which these practices are situated (Kemmis, 1985). How teachers' actions maintain and/or disrupt the status quo in schooling and society is of central concern.

A second characteristic of a social reconstructionist conception of reflective teaching is its democratic and emancipatory impulse and the focus of the teacher's deliberations upon substantive issues that raise instances of inequality and injustice within schooling and society for close scrutiny. Recognizing the fundamentally political character of all schooling, the teacher's reflections centre upon such issues as the gendered nature of schooling and of teachers' work, the relationships between race and social class on the one hand and access to school knowledge and school achievement on the other, and the influence of external interests on the process of curriculum production. These and other similar issues are addressed in concrete form as they arise within the context of the teacher's classroom and school.

The third distinguishing characteristic of a social reconstructionist conception of reflective teaching is its commitment to reflection as a communal activity. Social reconstructionist-oriented teacher educators seek to create 'communities of learning' where teachers can support and sustain each other's growth. This commitment to collaborative modes of learning indicates a dual commitment by teacher educators to an ethic where justice and equity on the one hand, and care and compassion on the other, are valued. This commitment is also thought to be of strategic value in the transformation of unjust and inhuman institutional and social structures. Specifically, it is felt that the empowerment of individual teachers as individuals is inadequate, and that the potential for institutional and social change is greater, if teachers see their individual situations as linked to those of their colleagues.

These four traditions of reflective teaching can be used to interpret various aspects of proposals for teacher education reform and descriptions of existing practices.

## CHAPTER 2

# Learning through mentoring in initial training

Sampson and Yeomans (2.1) begin this chapter by offering an overview of the roles of mentors, particularly regarding planning, support and professional guidance.

Reading 2.2 provides a more analytical account of what is going on. In it, Edwards and Collison suggest that trainees' work in school can be seen as a process of induction into the 'community of practice', with the mentor as their guide. We then have a reading from Maynard (2.3) looking at student-teachers' school-based learning in more detail and helpfully documenting common issues that arise.

Finally, Calderhead (2.4) contrasts the moral, personal and reflective dimensions of teaching with simple approaches to competence. Learning to become a teacher is actually quite a complicated process of induction into professional culture, personal adaption and skill development.

The readings in this chapter can be augmented with those in Chapter 16, on supporting the needs of newly qualified teachers.

The parallel chapter of *Reflective Teaching* starts with further analysis of the complementary roles of the student trainee, mentor and (as appropriate) tutor, and the key issues that have to be faced in school-based learning. Drawing on research by Maynard and Furlong, the major part of the chapter documents typical stages of student learning and suggests most appropriate forms of mentoring for each stage. There is a useful set of 'Key Readings'. Additional 'Notes for Further Reading' can be found on *RTweb*.

## READING 2.1

# Analysing the role of mentors

## John Sampson and Robin Yeomans

This is an insightful reading on the multiple aspects of a school-based mentor's role and it draws on some of the authors' research on relationships in initial teacher education. Sampson and Yeomans identify three main dimensions of the mentor role: structural, supportive and professional. They suggest that effective mentors prioritize the elements of their role to meet changing student needs as a period of school experience develops.

How does their analysis relate to your experience as a mentor or as a student?

Edited from: Yeomans, R. and Sampson, J. (eds) (1994) *Mentorship in the Primary School*. London: Falmer Press, 64–75

The role of the mentor has three dimensions. The structural dimension involves acting to seek to ensure that conditions exist in the school which will enable students to perform as effectively as is possible, Given the limitations of their current stage of development. The elements which we have identified within the structural dimension are: 'planner', 'organizer', 'negotiator' and 'inductor'.

The supportive dimension of mentoring is concerned with students as people, and with making them feel comfortable in or minimizing the stress of situations they encounter in the school. We suggest that its elements are 'host', 'friend' and 'counsellor'.

Finally, the professional dimension relates to all those activities which are concerned with the students' development as potential teachers. Its elements are 'trainer', 'educator' and 'assessor'.

## The structural dimension

Mentors had a key role in preparing the way for students in the school and in the school-based part of their courses. Mentors created the conditions which would enable students to perform as well as they were able. In other words, within their structural role dimension, they were enablers, establishing and modifying social and organizational structures.

*Planner* Particularly when the students first came to the school but also later as their and course demands change, it was the mentor who planned the students' programme so that they were deployed in the most mutually beneficial way. This is not to suggest that mentors planned the last detail of the students' experience. There were opportunities for students to initiate and to influence the detailed structure of their school experience. This happened several times. But, whatever the student initiated, mentors played a part in the necessary organization.

*Organizer* If planning dealt with intentions, then organization was concerned with the necessary conditions for favourable outcomes. However rigorous and ambitious the plans agreed, between students and mentor, effective implementation was more likely if mentors were able to organize conditions conducive to success. Mentors' organizational contribution was concerned with every facet of the student's life in the school. But the emphasis was on student's classroom practice, including the organization of curriculum tasks that related to the college element of the courses.

Mentors needed a clear view of the way ahead if they were to organize the student's day-to-day programme in the school. Typically the structure and detail of the students' teaching commitment was planned by the mentor and students, within the guidelines produced by the college.

*Negotiator* Mentors' ability to create optimum learning conditions for students also required that they negotiate with colleagues on behalf of the students. Mentors' status and credibility within the school were important here. Being deputy head made negotiation easier for some, since making organizational requests to colleagues was an existing part of mentors' deputy head role. Similarly, deputy head mentors could use their close professional relationship with their head to the students' benefit. Non-deputy head mentors relied more on their personal credibility and existing relationships with colleagues.

Mentors had four main negotiating concerns. First, they needed to negotiate time for themselves and students to meet without the distraction of a class. This meant persuading heads or colleagues who had a student to take the mentor's class. Second, they sought opportunities for students to gain access to other classes, in order to observe colleagues at work, interrogate them about classroom practice, or have some teaching time with a different age group. Third, students might find out more about a particular curriculum area by talking to the curriculum co-ordinator. Fourth, since there was normally more than one student in a school, effective supervision of students required mentors to negotiate with host class teachers an unambiguous division or responsibilities for observing, reporting on, and debriefing any student not teaching the mentor's class. Clearly there are implications for mentors' relationships with colleagues, their status in the schools and their own interpersonal skills.

Mentors also needed to negotiate with link tutors a shared perspective of the nature of effective teaching. Without such a common view, conflicting messages were likely. This tended to be a continuing relationship of school and mentor with the college and a specific tutor.

*Inductor* Mentors all took conscious steps to give the students insights into the ways of behaving within their classroom and within the school. They inducted them into the schools' systems, in terms of agreed procedures. But they also talked students through some of the informal habits which were part of the shared understandings, which had evolved within the schools. Though important to the smooth running of schools and classrooms, these were often unacknowledged, seldom written down, and so could offer particular difficulties to unwary students. With such insights, the students could more rapidly learn to 'fit in', feel 'teacher-like' themselves, and convince the children and other staff by their authentic teacher behaviour.

## The supportive dimension

The supportive dimension of mentoring is closely linked to the nature of the relationship created between mentor and student. A mutually open and trusting relationship was both the means to, and the outcome of, effective support. Mentors recognized that student's time in school could be stressful in several ways. First, they were outsiders, experiencing an unknown staff culture, whose rules and norms they needed to assimilate if they were to learn or behave authentically. Second, authentic teacher behaviour in the eyes of the pupils was itself an important condition of successful performance of the role of teacher, students could not take for granted pupils' sympathetic understanding. Third, students knew that however supportive they found the school context, their performance was under close scrutiny. Success and failure had a precise meaning and, in the assessed phases, carried career implications. In other words, school experience had many of the characteristics of a 'life' event.

Thus, the supportive dimension of mentors' role engaged them in minimizing possible stress for students, and ensuring that, when stressful situations were encountered, they enhanced students' self-awareness and became learning experiences.

*Host* Mentors initially acted as a host when they welcomed students on behalf of the whole school. It was then that the mentor and student began to form a relationship, that students were introduced to school rules and procedures. These early moments were important and recognized as such by students in particular. They appreciated the efforts that were made to welcome them.

*Friend* Some mentors were particularly adept at handling role conflict, and so managed to incorporate the extremes of assessor and friend within their role. Friendship could be a consequence of always being a source of positive comment.

*Counsellor* The counselling element in the mentors' role had two sides. Mentors needed to help students cope with judgements on their teaching. The help was particularly needed when negative classroom experiences had undermined students' self-belief, or when circumstances required that they consider their long-term professional future. In an extreme case, a mentor might help a student deal with the consequences of short-term or long-term failure. For student and mentor alike, counselling phases might generate ambivalent feelings. The mentor who was the judge of success and failure also carried the responsibility of reconciling a student to the judgement and building from it. The primary purpose of the mentoring role was to help students towards becoming effective teachers.

## The professional dimension

*Trainer* Mentors acted as trainers when they took steps which enabled students to respond more effectively to current teaching needs. Of course, they hoped that if students successfully incorporated mentors' suggestions into their teaching, the students' long-term professional practice would also be modified. However, any such change tended to be derived from observing mentors at work or listening to advice, explanations or descriptions which reflected the mentors' own strategies for specific situations. In short, the emphasis in training was on successful implementation of the mentors' solutions.

Training was a necessary part of students' development. However, there was a temptation to extend training inappropriately. As experts, mentors drew on extensive experience, could identify underlying problems and suggest relevant strategies. As novices, students tended to recognize mentors' expertise, having observed their classroom practice, perhaps noted their status and credibility in the school, and knew that the college confirmed their mentor status. Consequently students might expect to be told how to deal with their class, particularly if it was also the mentors' own. Mentors' legitimate concern for the needs of their class might also lead to a narrow interpretation of the mentor role. Strategies which a mentor used successfully with that group of children were safer for mentor, student and class than encouraging a student to experiment. Thoughtful commitment to students' development was needed for mentors to recognize that only applying short-term solutions carried long-term dangers for students. They might become unthinking and unquestioning adherents to all the mentor said and did, unquestioning followers of one model who found it difficult to meet new circumstances.

*Educator* To behave as educator was to be a mentor who enabled students to become autonomous, self-referential, teachers, capable of objectively analysing their own and others' professional practice.

Mentors were well-placed to be students' dialogical partners. If as trainers they were largely engaged in helping students construct practice, as educators their concern shifted to helping students deconstruct teaching sessions so that they began to reconstruct their version of effective practice and ultimately to amend their professional schemata. In other words, reconstruction was concerned with students' long-term development rather than merely with the here and now. The intention was that students would develop their own, personal, flexible model of professional practice. This would enable them to adapt their teaching model to new circumstances. It was the mentors' skill in moving students towards independence characterized by self-generated reconstruction that was the essence of effective educative mentoring.

*Assessor* There were advantages in having the mentor as assessor. They knew the school, the class and the children far better than any visiting tutor could. They were also likely to have an established relationship the with other teachers that students worked with, and so were better able to access other perspectives on students' school performance. Mentors were able to discuss with students their performance more frequently than could a visiting tutor. Of course, mentors lacked an overview of a range of students in a variety of settings, and so the final confirmatory pass/fail decision rested with the college. In practice, the arrangement created few difficulties, since there was regular contact and discussion between mentor and link tutor.

There were tensions for mentors in being the assessors. First, when they reported to students on their progress face to face, mentors stated openly what might only have been tacit in other circumstances. Second, they managed the subtleties of reporting assessment, particularly at the interim report stage, so as to provide both warning or praise and stimulus for the student. There was skill in not making the report so positive or so critical that it was a disincentive to renewed effort and so limited further progress. Third, such written confrontations of students with their strengths and weaknesses could be personally threatening to mentors and students alike. Fourth, there was the responsibility of deciding whether the student should pass or fail. The role of a link tutor has some bearing here. Mentors did signal some students as possible failures, link tutors agreed and the judgement was confirmed by external examiners. So although a failure decision was difficult, it was not shirked.

## Conclusion

The complexities of mentorship can best be understood if it is seen as a single role. The role has structural, supportive and professional dimensions, each of which contains specific elements which reflect different modes of mentor behaviour. These are planner, organizer, negotiator and inductor (structural elements); host, friend and counsellor (supportive elements); trainer, educator and assessor (professional elements). Elements of the role are performed at different times in response to predicted needs and particular phases of school experience. But needs can also change from moment to moment. The emphasis within the role also varies with different mentors, so that not all mentors exploit all elements of the role to the same extent.

## 📖 READING 2.2

# Learning through induction into a community of practice

Anne Edwards and Jill Collison

> Mentoring of trainees might simply be seen as explaining school procedures and providing technical advice in the classroom. However, research by Edwards and Collison demonstrated that the gradual process of becoming a professional is based on more subtle engagements with the cultures of schools and their communities. To explain this, they draw on the work of Jean Lave, and her idea that we find 'communities of practice' and shared understanding in many fields of life – including teaching. What then, are the implications for student teachers, and for mentors in schools?
>
> Edited from: Edwards, A. and Collison, J. (1996) *Mentoring and Developing Practice in Primary Schools: Supporting Student-teacher Learning in Schools.* Buckingham: Open University Press, 3, 7, 24–5, 156–7

What is the most important part of the work of teachers in primary schools? If you are a teacher, whether you are mainly a class teacher or mainly a manager, the continued well-being of the children in your school is likely to be central to your answer. For many of the children, caring for their well-being will be a matter of making sure they are doing as well as they might as they are helped through the curriculum. For some children, teachers' concerns will be primarily about their emotional or physical development. Indeed, for the majority of children, teachers will be concerning themselves with the delicate interplay between all three elements of the progress of young children at school. On top of that complexity, if you are a class teacher, you will have to create a climate and rhythm of activity in your classroom that ensures that the various needs of children are met and that your time is used well. Primary teaching is a complex activity and not easily done.

Into the finely balanced system that is the well-run primary classroom comes a new figure. A student teacher arrives and is eager to teach in the classroom. Another set of needs have now to be met. But this newcomer is harder to assimilate into the well-established systems than a new child would be. In addition, the paperwork that explains what students now have to do makes it clear that class teachers are not just people who are generously providing the opportunity for students to try out ideas in their teaching spaces. Rather, they are mentors.

Mentoring is a feature of training in many organizations. It is used primarily to induct newcomers into the expectations and procedures that operate in a specific workplace. It is therefore often an important element in the induction of a new recruit into the way that a particular organization operates. While this aspect of mentoring may be relevant in part to the mentoring of newly qualified teachers, mentoring in initial teacher training is much more than that. Frequently, mentors have to take responsibility for teaching student teachers key aspects of their professional training curriculum and recognize that they are preparing students to work eventually in other schools. Mentoring in initial teacher training is consequently an active process which makes considerable demands on teacher-mentors as it has to lead to students being able to understand quite broad principles of teaching and learning.

To that end, mentoring will, for example, involve mentors in contriving situations in which a teacherly form of mentoring can take place. These contexts will include mentoring conversations between mentors and student, mentoring while teaching, and school-based seminars. These situations will not always occur naturally and students may not always be eager to be seen as learners who require the teacherly help of mentors. Mentoring as a consequence involves careful management of the contexts of student teacher learning.

The work of Jean Lave and her associates in the United States is particularly helpful as we begin to see how this gentle induction into skilful teaching might be achieved (Lave and Wenger, 1991). Lave and Wenger, in common with many of the UK perspectives on teacher training, take the idea of apprenticeship as a starting point for their examination of how skilful practice is achieved. But they believe that although apprenticeship is place to begin, when you are looking at learning how to operate in a complex situation, simple comparisons with 'sitting-by-Nelly' models of apprenticeship collapse.

At the centre of Lave's work is the idea of learning as increasing participation in the communities of practice in which knowledge is located and created. Communities of practice have value systems, give common meanings to particular forms of behaviour, have a shared history, are shaped by those who operate within them and in turn shape their participants and their understandings.

Full participation in a community of practice implies the ability to read the subtle demands of the community and to contribute to the dynamics that are operating in it in order to play a part in its continuous development. It also means being able to use the language of that community in ways that have meaning for the participants within it. Using language does not mean simply learning and applying established meanings, although that is part of the process, also generating and testing of interpretations in the community of practice.

Being a class teacher is to play a major role as a full participant in the community of teacher practice that operates in a school. There may be times, however, when individual teachers are not operating as full participants in elements of the community of practice of a school. For example, some may move more slowly than others towards the integration of new technologies into their classroom practices. They may start by offering technology-based tasks to pupils as limited activities and only cautiously bring them into the centre of their planning.

In this case we would be witnessing what Lave and Wenger describe as peripheral participation. It is, they argue, not a teaching technique but a way of looking at learning. Peripheral participation can be seen as an important stage in the induction of learners into confident and competent practice. Gradually, learners move towards full participation. Once able to participate fully in that element of the community of practice, participants are in the position, through their actions and evaluations, to contribute to the development of under-standings held by others in the community. Central to their view of a community of practice and the development of knowledge within it, is an acceptance that all members are learners who participate through their learning in the development of practices and the ways that are understood within the community.

Learning is not something that students do in isolation as a result of being given access to sites for trial and error attempts at mastery. Rather, learners are positioned within a set of social processes which constitute what is to be learned and the mastery of which represents learning. Learning to be a teacher consequently needs to be placed in wider understandings of policy, school improvement and staff development.

## READING 2.3

# Students' school-based learning

Trisha Maynard

This reading is likely to be of particular interest to both mentors and trainees working together in school. Whilst it clearly builds on the idea of student induction into the community of practice of teachers in the school (as suggested by Edwards and Collison, Reading 2.2), the reading also points out various difficulties. The process of induction is shown to be highly complex, with the gradual adjustment of aspirations and trialling of ideas and understanding as well as of more overt skills. Nobody said that learning to be a teacher is easy, or that the role of the mentor is simple either!

Does this reading help you in reflecting on your own professional learning?

Edited from: Maynard, T. (2001) 'The student teacher and the school community of practice: a consideration of "learning as participation" ', *Cambridge Journal of Education*, **31** (1) 44–9

My research with John Furlong showed that students at the beginning of their first block school placement may hold a clear, if idealistic, image of the sort of teacher they wanted to be, and of the kind of relationship that they wanted to develop with their pupils (Furlong and Maynard, 1975). For example, students often maintained that they wanted to be seen by pupils as 'warm', 'caring', 'enthusiastic' and 'popular' teachers. Underlying these ideals there was often a view that teaching was 'easy' and essentially about establishing close, personal relationships with pupils.

Unsurprisingly, these teacher ideals did not stand up in the face of the realities of the first weeks of their teaching placement. Students became aware that in order to teach, to 'survive' as a person and as a teacher, they had to establish and maintain control and this necessitated asserting their authority and retaining a distance from the children. The challenge students faced was thus fundamental and urgent: how to reconcile their own, often deep-rooted expectations and aspirations with the immediate professional demands made upon them. How could students maintain their self-image in the face of having to control and teach the children?

Students' difficulties at this time seemed to be exacerbated by the public nature of their learning, which increased students' self-awareness and self-consciousness. Fuhrer (1993) suggests that impression management is an important goal for newcomers in a community of practice: it is not simply that newcomers want quickly to gain useful knowledge and skill but that they also want to avoid or lessen negative impressions and to promote positive impressions. Fuhrer states that as part of this process newcomers tend to note the behaviour of 'significant others' and seek to minimize the discrepancies between their own performance and what they see as the performance ideal. Certainly, the students in this study maintained that if they were to survive then they had at least to appear competent and confident: they had to be 'seen' as a teacher. Thus survival meant that students had to convince others, particularly the children, that they already knew what, as yet, they did not know. It was unsurprising, therefore, that the students commented on the importance of 'fitting in' with the class teacher's 'style': as one student explained 'so the children won't see the join'.

As personal survival gave way to a concern with professional survival, for example a concern to impress those concerned with their assessment, it was noted that students tended to make use of their class teachers' suggestions for the content of their teaching. As one student commented:

I use the teacher's ideas – there's no time to think of your own and you know their ideas are going to work.

Appropriating the 'behaviour' of their class teacher was a useful strategy. It enabled the students to obtain some measure of class control, to disguise their own lack of knowledge and understanding and also to gain the support of, and possibly to impress, the class teacher and the pupils. I am not suggesting, however, that modelling themselves on the teachers was a simple process. As Schön (1987, p. 108) points out, imitation is not passive in that it requires 'selective construction': students had to identify exactly what it was in the performance that it was essential for them to imitate. Moreover, 'fitting in' with the class teacher was a source of conflict for many students. While students stated that they wanted their own personality to come out, students also maintained that if they did not emulate the teacher's style the children would not respond to them.

Making use of the class teacher's suggestions for pupil activities also resulted in difficulties for many students. Content and pedagogy are inextricably linked in teachers' practice (see for example Putnam, 1987; Doyle, 1990; Brown and McIntyre, 1993) and activities will reflect the person as well as the teacher. As one student explained:

An idea or method of doing something is all very well but if you're not the kind of person to do it that way then it's not going to work. The teacher could think of something brilliant that's going to dazzle them but if you don't feel comfortable then it's not going to work.

Whatever the difficulties, 'fitting in' with the class teacher and making use of the teacher's suggestions for pupil activities appeared to be a deliberate, i.e. a conscious, survival strategy. This did not appear to be the case, however, with the appropriation of discourse: of ways of talking as a teacher and about their practice. On one level, appropriating the discourse of teachers referred simply to using certain phrases: 'teacher talk'. For example, several early-years students began to refer to themselves in the third person 'Does Mrs Jones look happy?' or to ask the children to 'sit nicely'. As one student indicated, 'teacher talk' was not something she had been aware of appropriating:

I was saying something and then I heard the teacher next door and realised where I had got it from.

But the appropriation of teachers' discourse extended beyond 'teacher talk'. It was noted that, in their conversations with class teachers, students began to use terms such as 'motivation', 'scaffolding' and 'investigation'. However, it became apparent that initially the students did not share the rich and complex meanings that their teachers ascribed to these terms. This was particularly the case with teachers' and students' interpretation of 'active learning'.

## Teacher and student views of 'active learning'

When teachers referred to the importance of active learning they seemed to be implying that children needed to 'engage' with curriculum content. The activity therefore had to be linked to the children's present understandings and be seen by the children as purposeful. Teachers also maintained that in their learning children needed to 'use' and transform new ideas. That is, children need to be given a certain amount of knowledge or information but then need 'to react back'. One teacher explained:

At some level children need to reinterpret, whether it's drawing or talking about it or thinking internally. In order for anybody to learn, something comes in and connects to something and by coming out again in some form, writing, modelling, drawing, talking, you are reaffirming (learning) to your brain.

Learning was therefore seen as an active and interactive process. Teachers commented that they constantly altered their approach or ways of working in response to the children's reactions in order to ensure understanding. As a teacher explained:

I must be picking up signals, asking or challenging the children to think somewhere else. When you're picking up those signs you must react to them. It comes back to knowing where their understanding is and the next bit they can go to and that interface is where the learning takes place. It's not linear . . . you have to keep sensing where the gaps are and how far the jumps can be.

Students interpreted 'active learning' in a number of different ways. For many students the term 'active learning' initially appeared to mean simply 'doing practical work'. This was important because 'after you've been telling them, the children get bored and you have to let them get on with it'. Active learning was thus often understood solely as being physically active. Children were believed to be actively learning as long as they were, for example, 'busy cutting and gluing'. Other students saw active learning as 'finding out', specifically 'looking things up in books'. At the other extreme were students who maintained that the teacher should not intervene at all. This was linked to the view that active learning was 'natural', particularly for younger children. One student explained: 'Children aren't designed to sit in rows and listen to someone spouting off facts to them'. Another student commented that it was important to 'let them come to their own conclusions before stepping in'. This student maintained:

You leave them with the task for five minutes to do themselves and then come back and see. And if they're not going anywhere you give them little bits of help along the way.

## The development of pseudoconcepts

Students' initial understandings could thus be likened to what Vygotsky (1962) termed 'pseudoconcepts'. Sara Meadows explains that pseudoconcepts are:

apparently rule governed and often labelled exactly as true concepts would be, but not properly formed, not properly understood and problematic in various ways, not least that they are talked about and used parrot-fashion. (Meadows, 1993, p. 107)

Meadows states that according to Vygotsky 'pseudoconcepts' have their developmental place because children who use them, even though they do not understand them, will evoke a positive response from adults. This is because adults see the child behaving as they themselves do and assume that the child's understanding is as advanced as his or her behaviour. Meadows comments that:

Because children need to function and communicate adequately, they seek to understand and talk as adults do, taking on ready-made meanings without necessarily understanding their conceptual basis. (Meadows, 1993, p. 107)

Thus the adult and child may think alike and talk alike but have different underlying concepts and conceptual reasoning. Similarly, Wertsch and Stone claim that it is possible for children to produce what appears to be 'appropriate' conversation before they are able to recognize 'all aspects of its significance as understood by more experienced members of the culture'. In other words:

Children can say more than they realize and it is through coming to understand what is meant by what is said that their cognitive skills develop. (Wertsch and Stone, 1985, p. 167)

The formation of pseudoconcepts was thus significant in that it enabled students to function and communicate adequately within the school 'community of practice'. It was also a useful strategy in dealing with embarrassment and social anxiety: the use of what was seen as appropriate discourse may have promoted a positive impression and thus supported students' acceptance by and as class teachers. Moreover, through actively using this discourse students were able gradually to negotiate richer and more appropriate understandings of their practice.

It is important to emphasize that in appropriating this discourse the students did not claim a commitment to a child-centred approach while their teaching remained 'traditional', gaining approval from the class teacher did not seem to be the students' main concern. Rather, students appeared gradually, and to a limited extent, to develop what were seen as more appropriate ways of teaching without a conscious awareness of doing so. One student, for example, who was congratulated by her teacher on a 'much improved science lesson' later asked me (as her tutor):

> Can you tell me what it is I'm doing now that I wasn't doing before? My teacher says I'm getting better, and I can tell by the children's reactions that my activities are getting better. But I don't know how or why.

As I have indicated above, the negotiation of appropriate understandings about 'good' teaching was gradual and limited. At a later stage in students' school placement, then, when they appeared to have 'hit the plateau' (Maynard and Furlong, 1993, Furlong and Maynard, 1995), student teachers were more directly and forcefully challenged to re-evaluate their planning and reflect on the broader implications of the activities they devised. For many students, at a time when teaching had begun to look manageable, this 'push' was painful and met with varying degrees of resistance. Two points should be noted here. First, the role of challenging students was generally undertaken by tutors; most teachers commented that they 'felt happier taking a more supportive stance'. Even so, it was the teachers who worked with the students on a day-to-day basis. Thus while tutors may have ensured students appreciated the problems with their practice, it was usually the teachers who provided the solutions. Second, while in their interactions with students there were differences of approach and emphasis, for example teachers tended to focus on general and tutors on subject-specific aspects of children's learning, the data appeared to show many commonalities in teachers' and tutors' underlying views of 'good' practice.

By the end of the placement, most students did begin to teach in ways that reflected more culturally appropriate understandings about teaching and learning. How far these students were, in Lacey's (1977) terms, adopting a strategy of 'strategic compliance' and how far they had actually gone through a process of 'internalized adjustment' was unclear. Students often maintained, however, that at this point they began to feel they were 'really progressing as a teacher'. They also commented that they had received approval and encouragement not only from the teacher and tutor but also from the pupils. As one student explained:

> I could see it in the children's faces . . . I must have been doing something right.

# Competence and the complexities of teaching

## James Calderhead

> In this reading, James Calderhead identifies five distinct areas of research on teaching and learning to teach and provides a concise overview of the main issues which have been considered. He summarizes this by highlighting the complexity of teachers' work and warning against partial and oversimplified conceptions.
>
> Edited from: Calderhead, J. (1994) 'Can the complexities of teaching be accounted for in terms of competences? Contrasting views of professional practice from research and policy', mimeo produced for an ESRC symposium on teacher competence, 1–2

Within recent policy on teaching and teacher education, there has been a popular trend to consider issues of quality in teaching in terms of competences that can be pre-specified and continuously assessed. In particular, the competences that have received most attention have related to subject matter knowledge and classroom management skills, a view which might be simplistically matched to the different responsibilities of higher education institutions and schools as closer working partnerships are formed in initial training. Such a view of teaching, however, is in sharp contrast to the complexity of teachers' work highlighted by empirical research on teaching over the past decade.

Research on teaching and learning to teach falls into several distinct areas, each exploring different aspects of the processes of professional development among teachers, and each highlighting some of the influential factors involved.

## Socialization into the professional culture

The material and ideological context in which teachers work has been found to be one of the major influences upon the ways in which teachers carry out their work. New teachers are greatly influenced by traditions, taken-for-granted practices and implicit beliefs within the school, and a powerful 'wash out effect' has been identified (see Zeichner and Gore, 1990). Socialization studies on professional development have succeeded in highlighting some of the complex interactions that occur between an individual's values, beliefs and practices and those of the school, and also the importance of the individual's capacity to negotiate and manoeuvre within a social system where there may well be several competing professional cultures. This raises issues concerning how student teachers might be appropriately prepared to work as members of teams or as individuals within institutions.

## The development of knowledge and skills

This is perhaps the most often cited perspective on learning to teach which emphasizes the knowledge and skills that contribute to classroom practice. Studies comparing experienced and novice teachers have demonstrated how experienced teachers often has a much more sophisticated understanding of their practice. The experienced teacher appears to have access to a wide range of knowledge that can be readily accessed when dealing with classroom situations and which can help in interpreting and responding to them. Recent research on teachers' subject matter knowledge also indicates that teachers, for the purposes of teaching, relearn their subject and also develop a new body of knowledge concerning the teaching of the subject – Shulman's 'pedagogical content knowledge' [see Reading 8.6]. Studies of novice and experienced teachers suggest that there is an enormous diversity of knowledge that the experienced teacher possesses, and that acquiring appropriate professional knowledge is often a difficult and extremely time-consuming process for the novice.

## The moral dimension of teaching

Teaching as well as being a practical and intellectual activity is also a moral endeavour. Teaching involves caring for young people, considering the interests of children, preparing children to be part of a future society, and influencing the way in which they relate to each other and live. The ethic of caring has been claimed to be a central facet of teaching, often valued by teachers, parents and children, but frequently unacknowledged in discussions of professional development. Teaching in schools inevitably presents several moral dilemmas in the form of decisions about how to allocate time in the classroom, how to cater for individual needs, and how to maintain principles such as 'equality of opportunity'. How are teachers to be prepared for this?

## The personal dimension of teaching

Several different aspects of the personal dimension have been emphasized in the research literature. First of all, teachers bring their own past experiences to bear on their interpretation of the teacher's task. Individual past experiences of school, of work, or parenting have been found to provide teachers with metaphoric ways of thinking about teaching that shape their professional reasoning and practice. Second, teachers' personalities are themselves an important aspect of teachers' work. In order to establish working relationships with children, to command their attention and respect and to ensure the smooth running of their classes, teachers' personalities are intrinsically involved. Part of the professional development of the novice teacher requires teachers to become aware of their personal qualities and how other people respond to them, so that they can take greater control in their interactions with others. Third, evidence from research on teachers' life cycles suggests that people pass through different phases in their lives in which they adopt different perspectives on life and work, and experience different needs in terms of inservice support [e.g.: see Nias, Reading 5.1].

## The reflective dimension of teaching

Notions of reflection have become extremely popular in recent discussions of teacher education. What reflection actually amounts to, however, is considerably less clear. Several notions of reflection are identifiable in the literature – reflection-in-action, reflection-on-action, deliberative reflection, etc. Attempts to generate greater levels of reflection among student teachers have taken many forms – reflective journals, action research, the use of theory and research evidence as analytical frameworks, etc. Creating a course that helps students to become more analytical about their practice and to take greater charge of their own professional development is a task with a number of inherent difficulties. For instance, how do the teacher educators reconcile their traditional role as gatekeeper to the profession with that of mentor and facilitator of reflection? How is reflection fostered when in schools a much higher priority is given to immediate, spontaneous action rather than analysis and reflection? Efforts in this area, however, have stimulated enquiry into identifying the cognitive, affective and behavioural aspects of reflection: what are the skills, attitudes and conditions that promote reflection and enable greater levels of learning from experience to be achieved?

Research on teaching and teachers' professional development points towards the complexity of teachers' work. Each of the dimensions discussed above identifies an important set of variables and provides a partial picture of the whole professional development process. Learning to teach involves the development of technical skills, as well as an appreciation of moral issues involved in education, an ability to negotiate and develop one's practice within the culture of the school, and an ability to reflect and evaluate both in and on one's actions.

Such a view of teaching is in sharp contrast to that promulgated in the narrow language of 'competences' and 'subject matter knowledge'.

## CHAPTER 3

# Developing an evidence-informed classroom

There are four readings in this chapter, mainly focused on the rationale for teachers investigating classroom practice and using evidence to inform their professional judgements.

Stenhouse (3.1) provides a classic statement on how teachers can research their own practice – the concept of the 'teacher as researcher'. The reading from Pring (3.2) further explores the key characteristics of action research, including its parallels with and differences from conventional research. In Reading 3.3, the Teacher Training Agency makes the case for evidence-based teaching as a form of professional development and as a key means of improving standards. Finally, Bassey (3.4) offers a useful clarification of three approaches to educational research which are often found in the literature.

The parallel chapter of *Reflective Teaching* complements these readings very extensively. The chapter begins by setting out the rationale for the use of evidence, of all types, to improve performance. Key issues for planning classroom enquiry are then discussed, and 25 techniques for collecting data on classroom practice are reviewed. Finally, a section on 'learning from other research' extends Bassey's (3.4) analysis on the varieties of available research and offers a simple explanation of them. 'Key Readings' are provided, but the 'Notes for Further Reading' on *RTweb* are much more extensive and include more books offering practical advice on techniques for enquiry.

## 📖 READING 3.1

# The teacher as researcher

Lawrence Stenhouse

Lawrence Stenhouse led the Humanities Project during the late 1960s – curriculum development work that revolutionized thinking about professional development. One of his central concerns was to encourage teachers as 'researchers' of their own practice, thereby extending their professionalism. There is a strong link between the argument of this reading and Dewey's conception of 'reflection' (Reading 1.1).

Edited from: Stenhouse, L. (1975) *An Introduction to Curriculum Research and Development*. London: Heinemann, 143–57

All well-founded curriculum research and development, whether the work of an individual teacher, of a school, of a group working in a teachers' centre or of a group working within the coordinating framework of a national project, is based on the study of classrooms. It thus rests on the work of teachers.

It is not enough that teachers' work should be studied: they need to study it themselves. My theme is the role of the teacher as a researcher in his [sic] own teaching situation. What does this conception of curriculum development imply for him?

The critical characteristics of that extended professionalism which is essential for well-founded curriculum research and development seem to me to be:

The commitment to systematic questioning of one's own teaching as a basis for development;

The commitment and the skills to study one's own teaching;

The concern to question and to test theory in practice.

To these may be added as highly desirable, though perhaps not essential, a readiness to allow other teachers to observe one's work directly or through recordings – and to discuss it with them on an open and honest basis. In short, the outstanding characteristics of the extended professional is a capacity for autonomous professional self-development through systematic self-study, through the study of the work of other teachers and through the testing of ideas by classroom research procedures.

It is important to make the point that the teacher in this situation is concerned to understand better his own classroom. Consequently, he is not faced with the problems of generalizing beyond his experience. In his context, theory is simply a systematic structuring of his understanding of his work.

Concepts which are carefully related to one another are needed both to capture and to express that understanding. The adequacy of such concepts should be treated as provisional. The utility and appropriateness of the theoretical framework of concepts should be testable; and the theory should be rich enough to throw up new and profitable questions.

Each classroom should not be an island. Teachers working in such a tradition need to communicate with one another. They should report their work. Thus a common vocabulary of concepts and a syntax of theory need to be developed. Where that language proves inadequate, teachers would need to propose new concepts and new theory.

The first level of generalization is thus the development of a general theoretical language. In this, professional research workers should be able to help.

If teachers report their own work in such a tradition, case studies will accumulate, just as they do in medicine. Professional research workers will have to master this material and scrutinize it for general trends. It is out of this synthetic task that general propositional theory can be developed.

 **READING 3.2**

# Action research and the development of practice
Richard Pring

> Richard Pring, a leading educational philosopher, builds on the Stenhouse tradition (see Reading 3.1) to take stock of some key characteristics of 'action research'. The reading makes useful comparisons with the characteristics of conventional academic research. Although there are important differences in objectives, there are also many similarities in the issues that must be faced in any classroom enquiry. Pring emphasizes the need for openness, the importance of dialogue with colleagues and of critical reflection on practice. Action research may thus involve scrutiny of values, including those which might be embedded in centrally prescribed curricula, pedagogies or forms of assessment.
>
> Edited from: Pring, R. (2000) *Philosophy of Educational Research*, London: Continuum, 130–34

Respect for educational practitioners has given rise to the development of 'action research'. This may be contrasted with conventional research. The goal of research is normally that of producing new knowledge. There will, of course, be many different motives for producing such knowledge. But what makes it research is the systematic search for conclusions about 'what is the case' on the basis of relevant evidence. Such conclusions might, indeed, be tentative, and always open to further development and refinement. But the purpose remains that of getting ever 'nearer the truth'. Hence, it makes sense to see the outcomes of research to be a series of propositions that are held to be true.

By contrast, the research called 'action research' aims not to produce new knowledge but to improve practice – namely, in this case, the 'educational practice' in which teachers are engaged. The conclusion is not a set of propositions but a practice or a set of transactions or activities that are not true or false but better or worse. By contrast with the conclusion of research, as that is normally conceived, action research focuses on the particular. Although thereby not justifying generalization, no one situation is unique in every respect and therefore the action research in one classroom or school can illuminate or be suggestive of practice elsewhere. There can be, among networks of teachers, the development of a body of professional knowledge of 'what works' or of how values might be translated into practice – or come to be transformed by practice. But there is a sense in which such professional knowledge has constantly to be tested out, reflected upon, adapted to new situations.

Research, as that is normally understood, requires a 'research forum' – a group of people with whom the conclusions can be tested out and examined critically. Without such openness to criticism, one might have missed the evidence or the counter argument which casts doubt on the conclusions drawn. Hence, the importance of dissemination through publications and seminars. To think otherwise is to assume a certitude which cannot be justified. Progress in knowledge arises through replication of the research activity, through criticism, through the active attempt to find evidence against one's conclusions.

Similarly, the growth of professional knowledge requires the sympathetic but critical community through which one can test out ideas, question the values which underpin the shared practice, seek solutions to problems, invite observation of one's practice, suggest alternative perspectives and interpretation of the data.

This is an important matter to emphasize. The temptation very often is to seek to justify and to verify, rather than to criticize or to falsify one's belief, and to protect oneself by not sharing one's conclusions or the way in which one reached them. Therefore, the criticisms of a lot of educational research by Tooley and Darby (1998), namely, that the methods of selecting or gathering evidence are often not sufficiently clear as to permit criticism, were perfectly valid. Research conclusions are drawn in the light of evidence, and, for them to be accepted by others, there needs to be openness to the way in which evidence is obtained.

Similarly with action research: the active reflection upon practice with a view to its improvement needs to be a public activity. By 'public' I mean that the research is conducted in such a way that others can scrutinize and, if necessary, question the practice of which it is part. Others become part of the reflective process – the identification and definition of the problem, the values that are implicit within the practice, the way of implementing and gathering evidence about the practice, the interpretation of the evidence. And yet teacher research, in the form of action research, is so often encouraged and carried out as a lonely, isolated activity. Those who are concerned with the promotion of action research – with the development in teachers of well-tested professional knowledge – must equally be concerned to develop the professional networks and communities in which it can be fostered.

There is a danger that such research might be supported and funded with a view to knowing the most effective ways of attaining particular goals – goals or targets set by government or others external to the transaction which takes place between teacher and learner. The teacher researches the most efficient means of reaching a particular educational objective (laid out, for instance, in the National Curriculum or a skills-focused vocational training). But this is not what one would have in mind in talking about research as part of professional judgement or action research as a response to a practical issue or problem. The reflective teacher comes to the problem with a set of values. The problem situation is one which raises issues as much about those values as it does about adopting an appropriate means to a given end. Thus, what makes this an educational practice is the set of values which it embodies – the intrinsic worth of the activities themselves, the personal qualities which are enhanced, the appropriate way of proceeding (given the values that one has and given the nature of the activity).

One comes to science teaching, for example, with views about the appropriate way of doing science – evidence-based enquiry, openness to contrary evidence, clarity of procedures and conclusions. The practice of teaching embodies certain values – the importance of that which is to be learned, the respect for the learner (how he or she thinks), the respect for evidence and the acknowledgement of contrary viewpoints. Therefore, when teacher researchers are putting into practice a particular strategy or are implementing a curriculum proposal, then they are testing out the values as much as the efficaciousness of the strategy or proposal. Are the values the researchers believe in being implemented in the practice? If not, does this lead to shifts in the values espoused or in the practice itself? Action research, in examining the implementation of a curriculum proposal, involves, therefore, a critique of the values which are intrinsic to the practice. Such a critique will reflect the values which the teacher brings to the practice, and those values will in turn be refined through critical reflection upon their implementation in practice. Action research captures this ever-shifting conception of practice through the attempt to put into practice certain procedures which one believes are educational.

However, such constant putting into practice, reflecting on that practice, refining of beliefs and values in the light of that reflection, subjecting the embodied ideas to criticism, cannot confine itself to the act of teaching itself. It cannot but embrace the context of teaching – the physical conditions in which learning is expected to take place, the expectations of those who determine the general shape of the curriculum, the resources available for the teachers to draw upon, the constraints upon the teacher's creative response to the issues, the scheme of assessment. It is difficult to see how the clash between the 'official curriculum' and the 'teacher researcher' can be avoided when the latter is constantly testing out the values of the teaching strategies. One can see, therefore, why the encouragement of teacher research is so often defined within official documents in a rather narrow sense.

Action research, therefore, is proposed as a form of research in which teachers review their practice in the light of evidence and of critical judgement of others. In so doing, they inevitably examine what happens to the values they hold, and which they regard as intrinsic to the transaction they are engaged in. Such critical appraisal of practice takes in three different factors which impinge upon practice, and shape the activities within it – the perceptions and values of the different participants, the 'official expectations and values' embodied within the curriculum, and the physical conditions and resources. To do this, various methods for gathering data will be selected – examination results, classroom observation, talking with the pupils. And the interpretation of what is 'working' will constantly be revised in the light of such data. But, of course, others too might, in the light of the data, suggest other possible interpretations. Thus, the dialogue continues. There is no end to this systematic reflection with a view to improving practice.

 **READING 3.3**

# Improving standards through evidence-based teaching

## Teacher Training Agency

> In England, the Teacher Training Agency led an important initiative in recent years to encourage classroom teachers to engage in classroom research. They offered a number of support schemes and excellent promotion of the value of classroom enquiry in raising standards and finding evidence for 'what works'. Some argue that their approach was instrumental, but it did have a significant and constructive impact. In particular, it offered official support for classroom enquiry as a form of continuing professional development and indicated how this can be both informed by other types of evidence and linked to school improvement. Such work is now promoted by the General Teaching Councils.
>
> How far are you down the road towards 'evidence-based teaching'?
>
> Edited from: Teacher Training Agency (2000) *Improving Standards Through Evidence-based Teaching*. London: TTA, 1–3

The Teacher Training Agency (TTA) is developing a network of teachers to investigate practical ways of using research evidence in the classroom in order to improve standards.

Teachers who use research and evidence effectively in order to improve their practice and raise attainment:

● know how to find and interpret existing, high-quality evidence from a range of sources, such as research reports, other schools' experience, OFSTED inspection and performance data as a tool for raising standards;

- see professional development, which includes elements of research, as a means of improving classroom practice and raising standards, rather than as an end in itself;

- see pedagogy as integral to learning;

- interpret external evidence confidently, in relation to pupil or subject needs, rather than viewing it as a threat;

- accept that systematic enquiry into specific elements of teaching is a hard but crucial component of continuing professional development – and a key to raising the esteem in which the profession is held;

- should be seen as equal partners with academic researchers in the process of producing evidence about teaching and using it to raise standards.

Every teacher wants and needs up-to-date knowledge about teaching and learning. This is why the TTA promotes teaching as a research and evidence-based profession. It recognizes the challenges that teachers face:

- classrooms are complex work settings. Effective teachers much internalize knowledge and skills so that they can deploy them quickly and flexibly;

- taking messages from new evidence from research, from OFSTED and from target-setting data into account is complex. It means making routine and often implicit practices, explicit so that they can be evaluated and developed in the light of new information. It also means teachers interpreting the implications of research findings and evidence for their own specific context;

- finally, research itself needs to focus upon what teachers need to know, understand and do to improve classroom practice and raise standards.

There is particular concern about linking theory and practice. Effective teachers welcome theories or explanations which help them to judge the match between specific teaching strategies and particular contexts. But they also want practical entry points to theories so that they can test the effectiveness of ideas in their own classroom settings.

One of the most effective ways of persuading teachers that paying attention to external research and evidence is worth the effort is by convincing them that their pupils will learn more. For example, teacher researchers report that their colleagues become enthusiastic about using research evidence to tackle problems when it is clearly linked to pupil-learning gain. Without such links they are reluctant to start 'unlearning' previous approaches and ideas or experiment with new ones to the point where they too have been internalized. This can be an uncomfortable business. Updating routine knowledge and skills can seem to make things worse before they get better. Teachers rightly look for assurances that they and their pupils will gain more than they lose from the process.

The TTA's promotion of research and evidence-based practice is designed to help teachers respond to external evidence systematically, confidently and objectively in the light of the potential benefits and costs to their own subjects and pupils.

Research and evidence-based practice requires sophisticated professional skills to:

- identify teaching and learning problems;

- weigh up research and evidence objectively;

- make the links with classroom practice;

- evaluate ways of putting new knowledge and skills to work.

These activities are important components for all teachers in supporting their colleagues and developing their own practice. Beyond this a small number of teachers will want to become more directly involved in undertaking research. They will be interested not only in finding and interpreting evidence but also in creating it for the use of others. Such teachers have a particular role to play in exciting the interest of their colleagues in research and evidence that can, directly or indirectly, improve practice and raise standards.

READING 3.4

# Three paradigms of educational research

## Michael Bassey

Michael Bassey has the ability to take complex ideas and express them with exceptional directness and clarity. In the reading below, he provides this service to explain the three 'paradigms' from which many educational enquiries are derived: positivist, interpretive and action research. Many of the other readings in this book could be categorized in these terms. For instance, Reading 6.5 derives from a large-scale quantitative study, 5.5 reflects an interpretive approach and 13.8 rests on an action research perspective (see also *Reflective Teaching*, Chapter 3, section 4).

Edited from: Bassey, M. (1990) 'Creating education through research', *Research Intelligence*, autumn, 40–4

A research paradigm is a network of coherent ideas about the nature of the world and of the functions of researchers which, adhered to by a group of researchers, conditions the patterns of their thinking and underpins their research actions. Sometimes the network of a paradigm is so strong in the minds of its practitioners that they may deny the validity of other paradigms.

The present attempt at description distinguishes between the positivist research paradigm, the interpretive research paradigm and the action research paradigm.

## The positive research paradigm

To the positivist there is a reality 'out there' in the world that exists irrespective of people. This reality is discovered by people using their senses and observing. Discoveries about the reality of the world can be expressed as factual statements – statements about things, about events, and about relationships between them. To the positivist the world is rational, it makes sense, and, given sufficient time and effort, it should be possible for it to be understood through patient research. The researcher can then explain the reality he/she has discovered to others, because language is an agreed symbolic system for describing reality.

Positivist researchers do not expect that they themselves are significant variables in their research; thus in testing a hypothesis, they expect other researchers to come to the same conclusion that they find. Because of this, the positivists' preferred method of writing reports is to avoid the personal pronouns 'I' or 'me'.

To the positivist (as with the interpretive researcher) the purpose of research is to describe and understand the phenomena of the world and to share this understanding with others. Understanding enables one to explain how particular events occur and to predict what will be the outcome of future events.

Positivists usually seek to express their understandings in the form of generalizations, i.e. general statements. The data collected by positivists tends to be numerical and suitable for statistical analysis; hence their methodology is often described as quantitative.

The word 'positivist' is not always recognized by those who work within this paradigm and sometimes is used pejoratively by those engaged in alternative paradigms. In return it is sometimes the case that the positivist researchers reject the idea than an enquiry into a singularity – such as interpretive researchers and action researchers may engage in – can be deemed to be useful research.

Researchers in the sciences, particularly chemistry and physics, are archetype positivists, but this paradigm is also important in education.

## The interpretive research paradigm

The interpretive researcher cannot accept the idea of there being a reality 'out there' which exists irrespective of people, for reality is a construct of the human mind. People perceive and so construe the world in ways which are often similar but not necessarily the same. So there can be different interpretations of what is real. Concepts of reality can vary from one person to another. Instead of reality being 'out there', it is the observers who are 'out there'. They are part of the world which they are observing and so, by observing, may change what they are trying to observe. The interpretive researcher sees language as a more-or-less agreed symbolic system, in which different people may have some differences in their meanings; in consequence, the sharing of accounts of what has been observed is always to some extent problematic. Because of differences in perception, in interpretation and in language it is not surprising that people have different views on what is real.

Interpretive researchers reject the positivists' view that the social world can be understood in terms of casual relationships expressed in universal generalizations. To them, human actions are based on social meanings, such as beliefs and intentions. People living together interpret the meanings of each other, and these meanings change through social intercourse.

Interpretive researchers recognize that by asking questions or by observing they may change the situation which they are studying. They recognize themselves as potential variables in the enquiry and so, in writing reports, may use personal pronouns.

To the interpretive researcher, the purpose of research is to describe and interpret the phenomena of the world in attempts to get shared meaning with others. Interpretation is a search for deep perspectives on particular events and for theoretical insights. It may offer possibilities, but no certainties, as to what may be the outcome of future events. The word 'hermeneutics' is sometimes used to describe work in this paradigm. It means the art of interpretation.

Interpretive researchers inevitably study singularities, but they differ in their views on the extent to which the collated evidence from many singularities can be expressed in the form of generalizations.

The data collected by interpretive researchers is usually verbal – fieldwork notes and transcripts of conversation. Sometimes this can be analysed numerically but more usually it is not open to the quantitative statistical analysis used by positivists. Hence it is described as qualitative.

Historians and anthropologists are the archetypal interpretive researchers. Historians try to interpret the past in relation to the understandings of today; anthropologists try to interpret other cultures in relation to the understandings of their own society.

Ethnography is an important branch of the interpretive paradigm, concerned with participant observation – where the observer is not 'a fly on the wall', but becomes a participant in the activity which she/he is studying. Phenomenology and ethnomethodology are alternative terms for the interpretive paradigm.

## The action research paradigm

The positivist paradigm and the interpretive paradigm both involve the idea of observers trying to describe the phenomena of their surroundings. The action research paradigm is about actors trying to improve the phenomena of their surroundings. That isn't the way that most action researchers choose to express their purposes, but it puts their paradigm into the context of the other two paradigms.

Action research in education has blossomed in the last ten years. Inevitably different people define it in different ways, but the universally agreed characteristic, is that it is research designed to improve action. Sometimes this is expressed as 'to enhance the quality of action'. Theory is created not as an end to itself, but in order to advance practice. The topics of enquiry, methods of data collection, analytical techniques, and styles of presenting findings reflect the pragmatic needs of teachers, the intended audience may be no one other than the teacher researcher him/herself, but is more likely to be fellow teachers engaged in similar teaching. The researcher in this kind of enquiry may find little in the education literature to guide his/her enquiries and may need to invent procedures grounded in classroom practice in order to pursue the research.

The intention to improve practice often results in action research being cyclical, because striving for improvement is seen by many practitioners (teachers, social workers, managers, etc.) as an ongoing professional commitment.

Because action research entails an intention to change action involving people, it is seen by those who practise it to demand not only a strong ethic of respect for persons, but also demand democratic involvement of the people on whom it impinges. Thus, negotiation about the ownership of data and about the uses that the researcher may put it to, are deemed important.

Action research in education is grounded in school and classroom practice, and does not have an established theoretical background which can provide a framework for testing the validity of new findings. In its place action researchers have recognized the importance of criticism as a means of testing whether findings represent what they purport to represent. Action researchers aim to leave themselves open to criticism – meaning that they reckon to make the raw data of their enquiries available for criticism. The concept of the 'critical friend' has been developed by action researchers, meaning someone who responds to the invitation to invest some time and effort into critically examining one's action research findings, and who agrees to work within the ethical framework of the enquiry – which defines matters such as the ownership of data.

# PART 2

# Being a reflective teacher

# CHAPTER 4

# Social context. What are our circumstances?

The five readings in this chapter indicate some of the ways in which the actions of individuals and groups reflect their circumstances but also contribute to the future of society.

The classic reading by Mills (4.1) focuses on the relationship between individuals and society. It accounts for social change through the continuous interaction of biography and history. This analysis underpins a reflective and questioning attitude towards existing taken-for-granted structures, policies and assumptions; they are seen as products of previous actions and circumstances rather than as being inevitable.

Modern diversity of social context and action can be seen from cross-cultural studies, and Thomas (4.2) highlights some of the national variations in primary education which result from the different histories, cultures and policy-making processes within Europe. Such diversity is also apparent in historical analysis. Focusing on teachers, Webb and Vulliamy (4.3) demonstrate how the professional challenge has grown in recent years from both pressure for academic performance and from the particular needs of socially disadvantaged pupils. Regarding children's overall predicament, Pollard and Triggs (4.4) provide a longer-term historical review, analyse their current circumstances and raise questions about the appropriateness of policy. Considering home–school relations, Reay (4.5) focuses on mothers, and demonstrates both the significance of emotional support for children and social class factors in its provision.

The parallel chapter of *Reflective Teaching* engages with many additional issues. The 'social context' of education is analysed in terms of the concepts of ideology, culture, resources and accountability, as these influence schools in each country within the UK. Teachers, pupils and families are then considered, both as individuals and as groups, with particular attention on how they act within their circumstances. There are suggestions for 'Key Readings', and further advice is available on *RTweb*. The social context within which teachers and pupils work is, after all, an extremely important topic with a great many potential avenues for exploration in sociology, economics, history, politics, cultural studies, anthropology, comparative education, etc. The available literature is very extensive indeed.

Whilst the selections in this chapter are heavily constrained by space, see also the readings in Chapter 18 of this book. For example, there are echoes of Mills's views in the reading by Freire (18.2) and of the discussion of policy impact in Readings 18.4 and 18.5.

## READING 4.1

# The sociological imagination

## C. Wright Mills

> This reading comes from a classic sociological text. Wright Mills focused on the interaction between individuals and society, and thus on the intersection of biography and history. Teachers have particular responsibilities because, though acting in particular historical contexts, we shape the biographies of many children and thus help to create the future. Mills poses several questions which can be used to think about our society and the role of education in it.
>
> How do you think what you do today may influence what others may do in the future?
>
> Edited from: Mills, C. W. (1959) *The Sociological Imagination*. New York: Oxford University Press, 111–13

The sociological imagination enables its possessor to understand the larger historical scene in terms of its meaning for the inner life and the external career of a variety of individuals. It enables him [sic] to take into account how individuals, in the welter of their daily experience, often become falsely conscious of their social positions. Within that welter, the framework of modern society is sought, and within that framework the psychologies of a variety of men and women are formulated. By such means the personal uneasiness of individuals is focused upon explicit troubles and the indifference of publics is transformed into involvement with public studies.

The first fruit of this imagination – and the first lessons of the social science that embodies it – is the idea that the individual can understand his own experience and gauge his own fate only by locating himself within his period, that he can know his own changes in life only by becoming aware of those of all individuals in his circumstances. In many ways it is a terrible lesson; in many ways a magnificent one. We do not know the limits of man's capacities for supreme effort or willing degradation, for agony or glee, for pleasurable brutality or the sweetness of reason. But in our time we have come to know that the limits of 'human nature' are frighteningly broad. We have come to know that every individual lives, from one generation to the next, in some society; that he lives out a biography, and that he lives it out within some historical sequence. By the fact of his living he contributes, however minutely, to the shaping of this society and to the course of its history, even as he is made by society and by its historical push and shove.

The sociological imagination enables us to grasp history and biography and the relations between the two within society. That is its task and its promise. To recognize this task and this promise is the mark of the classic social analyst. And it is the signal of what is best in contemporary studies of man and society.

No social study that does not come back to the problems of biography, of history, and of their intersections within a society, has completed its intellectual journey. Whatever the specific problems of the classic social analysts, however limited or however broad the features of social reality they have examined, those who have been imaginatively aware of the promise of their work have consistently asked three sorts of questions:

What is the structure of this particular society as a whole? What are its essential components, and how are they related to one another? Within it, what is the meaning of any particular feature for its continuance and for its change?

Where does this society stand in human history? What are the mechanics by which it is changing? What is its place within and its meaning for the development of humanity as a whole? How does any particular feature we are examining affect, and how is it affected by, the historical period in which it moves? And this period – what are its essential features? How does it differ from other periods? What are its characteristic ways of history-making?

What varieties of men and women now prevail in this society and in this period? And what varieties are coming to prevail? In what ways are they selected and formed, liberated and repressed, made sensitive and blunted? What kinds of 'human nature' are revealed in the conduct and character we observe in this society in this period? And what is the meaning for 'human nature' of each and every feature of the society we are examining?

## READING 4.2

# European variations in primary education

## Norman Thomas

Policy-making processes in different countries reflect the particular circumstances, traditions and balance of social forces that obtain. As Norman Thomas shows, the result across Europe is considerable diversity even at the most general level of aims for primary education. The reading is also important for reminding us that 'the way we do it here' is not the only way in which it can be done. The case for comparative studies is a strong one.

Edited from: Thomas, N. (1989) 'The aims of primary education in member states of the Council of Europe', in Galton, M. and Blyth, A. (eds) *Handbook of Primary Education in Europe*. London: David Fulton, 19–23

Across Europe there is considerable variation regarding the stress on development of pupils to the full, and on accepting priorities and constraints characteristic of the society that provides education. The issue is illuminated in many of the reports from member states. That from Iceland quotes an Act of Parliament on the needs for cooperation between home and school and for preparation for life in a modern democratic state. The Act requires that schools should 'endeavour to widen the children's horizon and develop their understanding of their environment, social conditions, the characteristics and history of Icelandic society and the obligations of the individual to society'. The periods of history to be covered in French primary schools have an understandably French bias. The Norwegian Basic School Act of 1969, as amended in 1975, requires the basic schools 'to help give the pupils a Christian and moral upbringing'. The Swedish curriculum 'reflects the view of the democracy on society and man, the implication being that human beings are active and creative and that they both can and must assume responsibility and seek knowledge in order to co-operate with others . . .'. The official aims of primary education in Turkey require schools to 'enable every Turkish child to acquire all the necessary basic knowledge, skills and habits required for effective citizenship and to raise him in a manner commensurate with national ethical concepts'. Children need to know that they must obey the rules of society as well as use them; contribute to social well-being as well as draw from it.

There are complications. No society is static, though some – world-wide – are more stable than others. It is not sufficient simply to act in accord with today's social practices and ambitions: everyone who can should assist in improving the general lot, socially and materially. As seen by the current providers – and there is no intention here to imply that any other stance could reasonably be expected at government level – the changes should be within limits that are acceptable to current society. In the words of the Icelandic Act: 'the school must foster independent thought and co-operative attitudes'.

The stimuli for change stem from different sources.

## The acceptance and promotion of modern scientific and technological developments

It is no accident that the National Curriculum introduced in England and Wales in 1989 includes science as well as English and mathematics among its core subjects, and technology among its foundation subjects for primary schools. It is unlikely that science would have been given the same priority or technology have appeared at all for the primary stage even as recently as twenty years ago. Portugal also requires schools to keep pupils abreast of new scientific knowledge. The Netherlands Primary Education Act requires that science including biology, is taught in primary schools, and the arrival of micro-computers in Netherlands' primary schools was heralded. In Malta, 'it is a fact that innovation was prompted by radical changes in contemporary society and the challenge children have to cope with owing to new discoveries in science and technology'.

## Changes in the cultural, racial and religious make-up of the community

The populations of many countries of Western Europe have, in recent years become far more mixed in culture, race and religion than they were. They contain a substantial number of families who speak languages and, to a marked degree, retain life-habits they brought with them from afar. Some children may speak little or none of the national language of the country when they first enter school. Those children may be concentrated in districts where they form a large part of the school population: almost 100 per cent in a small proportion of schools. In the city of Luxembourg, 55 per cent of school children are foreigners.

The main issues referred to in the aims of primary education in countries experiencing these changes relate, on the one hand, to the indigenous population and, on the other, to the ethnic minority groups. The minimum aim with regard to the indigenous population is, usually, that its members should exercise tolerance towards and understanding of the newcomers. They were, after all, permitted and even encouraged to enter the country to fill gaps in the existing workforce. Better still, the indigenous population should welcome the presence of the minority ethnic groups because of the skills and cultures they bring, not only in music, art and food, but also in richness of language. The presumption is that tolerance will grow as knowledge grows and contact between groups increases. For the minority groups the issues are often sharper. Maintenance of one's religion, culture and language contributes to one's sense of identity. However, individuals do not have a full range of opportunities open to them, in either education or employment unless they can speak and write the national language in its standard form. Generally speaking, provision is made, although there can be difficulties for children who enter the education system late. In Luxembourg, as in a number of other countries, special classes in the local language are set up for new entrants. In the United Kingdom, teachers may be specially funded and employed to assist children who have little or no English. In the Federal Republic of Germany, Turkish supplementary teachers are employed both to help children with their own language and to assist them when German is the language of instruction.

## Political change

Where there have been marked changes in the political beliefs underpinning the government of a country, they are reflected in the strength of expression in some educational aims. In

Spain and Portugal, recently emerged from authoritarian and nationalistic regimes, there is more than ordinary stress on children as citizens of the world and on the freedom of individuals and their rights, including the right to participate in decisions about their own lives as soon as they are ready.

Some differences within a country are regarded as necessary to the national character and supported through the school system. Notably, they include the preservation and development of indigenous languages spoken by a minority of the population. In some countries there is a strong delegation of authority to local levels so that differences among them can be reflected, such as provision for the Sami population of Norway. The *Foldeskoler* in Denmark are encouraged to relate their curricula to local circumstances. In The Netherlands, Denmark and Norway, schools may be established that operate according to the preferred pedagogies of the founding group and be supported financially by the government. For example, a group may establish a school based on principles advocated by one or other of the educational pioneers such as Dalton, Montessori, Peter Peterson or Rudolf Steiner. Indeed, the same variety may be achieved within the different *Länder* in the Federal Republic of Germany. In the United Kingdom, it was the case that schools' curricula were settled locally, almost completely by the wishes of the head and teachers of the school, but that is no longer so since the National Curriculum was introduced in 1989.

Many countries have some schools that are sustained by fees charged to parents, or from charitable or other private funds, including voluntary contributions via the church, mosque or synagogue. Schools serving particular religious foundations may also be grant-aided by a state.

Parents make contact with, influence and may take part in the conduct of a school, and in doing so, express opinions, offer advice and possibly take part in the appointment of staff. The precise mechanisms vary such as the combined parent/teacher group that makes up the French school board, and more informal discussions between parents and teachers. In countries such as Turkey, issues may be discussed by the elementary education councils established in villages.

The ethos and pedagogy of a school are frequently finely tuned to the needs of the community it serves, but schools must offer an education acceptable to the nation to which they belong. Schools, including primary schools, are tools of the community. Even those financed independently of the state are permitted to exist only in so far as what they do is tolerated by the nation as a whole. The point is clearly made in the Italian paper: 'all; schools, state-controlled or otherwise, public or private, must comply with the national legislation decrees and regulations'.

Schools' conformity to national requirements may be achieved through the establishment of national criteria and inspection. Various systems of inspection operate and, with differences of balance from one country to another, they report (a) on the conduct of individual schools and (b) on the quality of the educational system as a whole.

## READING 4.3

# Primary teaching and 'social work'

## Rosemary Webb and Graham Vulliamy

There have been many studies of teachers' work in recent years, for morale has often not been good. This reading is specific, however, and highlights the plight of a significant number of teachers who find themselves supporting children and their families in terms of their social, as well as educational, needs. The issue is acute where economic disadvantages and social exclusion produce family stress. Schools tend to be the most localized and accessible source of welfare provision and their caring ethos often offers a sympathetic reception. What however, is the educational, professional and personal cost to teachers? In terms of Mills's analysis (Reading 4.1), one might ask how teacher 'biography' is affected by the circumstances (the 'history') of their work? But how too does their commitment change and improve the situation, thus creating a different history and biography for the children and families that they serve?

Do you have experience of fulfilling a 'social work' role on behalf of children in your class?

Edited from: Webb, R. and Vulliamy, G. (2002) 'The social work dimension of the primary teacher's role', *Research Papers in Education*, **17** (2)

The former Secretary of State for Education in England, David Blunkett, recently declared: 'We don't expect teachers to be social workers. We expect teachers to teach' (Chaudhary, 1998). Few teachers would disagree in principle with this view as they are not trained to do social work. However, the Social Work in Primary Schools (SWIPS) project, involving qualitative research in fifteen schools and a national survey, revealed that the reality of school life was very different. As Cunningham (1999) pointed out, 'as we see out the twentieth century, a characteristic feature of teachers' experience is the yawning gap between official constructions of their role on the one hand and their lived experience on the other' (p. 1). The vital social work dimension to the role of primary school headteachers and class teachers is an increasingly important element of this credibility gap that needs to be acknowledged.

Over the last two decades, whilst the provision of social work support for primary schools has been diminishing, there has been a growth in social exclusion and inequality, particularly as a result of Conservative policies on education, housing, health and unemployment (Walker and Walker, 1997). The Poverty and Social Exclusion Survey of Britain (Gordon *et al.*, 2000) reports that between 1983 and 1990, the number of households living in poverty increased dramatically – from 14 per cent to 21 per cent of the population. Poverty continued to spread during the 1990s and by the end of 1999 approximately 14.5 million people (26 per cent) were living in poverty. The implications for children, in addition to living in poor housing conditions, are that 'a third of British children go without at least one of the things they need, like three meals a day, toys, out of school activities or adequate clothing' (p. 68). The disadvantages and stress experienced by families faced with poverty and the unemployment, lack of essential services and lack of personal support which characterizes areas of deprivation generate social and emotional needs. Our research conducted for ATL (Webb and Vulliamy, 1996) suggested that families are looking increasingly to primary schools for empathy and help to meet those needs.

The New Labour government made social exclusion a policy priority and, following the 1997 General Election, set up the Social Exclusion Unit (SEU) within the Cabinet office to take this work forward. Central to the government's Inclusion Agenda is an acknowledgement that social exclusion has multiple causes and requires strategies that bring together agencies which all too often work in isolation in order to achieve 'joined-up solutions' to social problems.

Primary teachers are generally acknowledged for a range of historical, gendered and altruistic reasons to provide 'a culture of care' in primary schools (Acker, 1999; Nias, 1999). However, as commentators on primary education, such as Hayes (2001), have observed, the government's use of pupils' academic performance as the main criterion to judge effectiveness devalues caring and encourages a move away from a nurturing paradigm for teaching. The government's bid to drive up standards, especially the national literacy and numeracy targets, and school inspections, are pressuring primary teachers to concentrate exclusively on the quality and outcomes of their teaching. A few educationalists welcome this because they argue that poor teaching methods and ineffective schools are more to blame for educational failure than social disadvantage (Woodhead, 1998). As Smith and Noble (1995) argue, the importance of the relationship between social disadvantage and educational achievement has been 'almost a taboo subject in public policy debate in recent years' (p. 133). However, many studies have revealed the adverse effects of social disadvantage on children's behaviour (Chazan, 2000), educational achievement (Smith and Noble, 1995) and life chances (Cullingford, 1999). Consequently, in addition to being an ideological concern for many primary teachers, caring is viewed as a prerequisite for creating conditions in which children are predisposed to learn and attainment targets may be met. Thus the 'potential conflicts' of role identified by Cyster *et al.* (1979) appear to have become exacerbated by the education policy of the current government because of the pressures on, and requirements from, schools to meet both the government's Standards agenda and its Inclusion Agenda. Also, as we have argued elsewhere (Vulliamy and Webb, 2000), the measures implemented by schools to raise attainment to meet targets set by the Standards Agenda in the context of a market economy are having very detrimental effects on precisely those vulnerable pupils targeted by the Inclusion Agenda.

SWIPS case-study data were collected during 1998–9 through document analysis, interviews and observation in fifteen schools in the primary phase across five LEAs in the North-East of England. While the locations of the sample schools varied (including a former mining village, seaside resort, industrial town and cathedral city), nine of the schools were in areas of economic and social deprivation including seven that were situated on large estates of predominantly council-owned homes. Residents living on such estates faced multiple disadvantages that can lead to their being trapped into poverty with all its attendant problems. As a consequence, family and community life were subject to intense pressure, with some families becoming caught in a downward spiral of decline and despair. This had a profound effect on the amount and nature of social work carried out by headteachers and other staff.

Teachers in the sample schools in disadvantaged areas enthusiastically expressed their commitment to the children and families served by the school:

> Unemployment is very bad and a small number of parents have alcohol problems, drug problems and mental health problems as well as all the financial and social problems. However, we have a lot of families who despite the adversity are doing really well. But all of this makes our job a daily grind and you do feel you're spitting in the wind sometimes. I wouldn't change it mind. I mean I love being here. I love the families and I think that it's very rewarding working in areas like this. (Headteacher, Primary School K)

The genuineness of this commitment appeared evidenced by the length of time many of them had worked there and/or in similar types of schools elsewhere and the range of activities for parents and children in which they were involved outside of school hours. Nias (1999) and Cunningham and Gardner (2000) also found a strong feeling of responsibility for children in difficult circumstances to be central to some teachers' accounts of their lives and careers. However, teaching in schools in areas of social and economic deprivation was viewed as experientially different and additionally demanding from working in schools in mixed or middle-class areas. The teachers interviewed were critical of OFSTED inspectors for taking insufficient notice of the school's contextual data and of national policymakers for seeming only to acknowledge that such difficulties existed in inner cities. It was also increasingly difficult to reconcile the wider community role of the schools with the need to raise standards. For example, the headteacher of Primary School H explained how the school had ceased running its Citizenship award – whereby junior pupils took ten modules covering topics such as healthy eating, drug awareness, child care and decision making – in order to concentrate on literacy initiatives. A few teachers also felt that their work and concerns were insufficiently understood by teaching colleagues lacking their experience.

While schools in areas of social deprivation and high unemployment were much more frequently called upon to assist parents with social problems, these are experienced to some degree by all schools. As the headteacher of one primary school in an attractive and affluent residential area on the edge of town pointed out: 'If you look at the area, you see a lot of our parents have very high powered jobs and all that goes with it, they live in beautiful houses, but it is what we don't see that is the problem'. She then recounted three ongoing situations – a husband's disappearance accompanied by a suicide note, the death of a partner and a husband leaving the family for a woman with whom he had been working – which had caused three distraught mothers to come into school for sympathetic counselling and support for their children.

The SWIPS project demonstrated the range and extent of social work tackled by teachers. While these demands were most acute in the sample schools in areas of greatest deprivation, an important implication of our findings for government policy is that such demands were a feature of all schools. The mounting pressure on teachers created by the government's Standards Agenda is paralleled by the growing social work dimension of their role, thus creating increasingly unrealistic and unmanageable workloads. Teachers have only so much time and energy and as Nias (1997) bluntly states: 'No-one's interests are served when the path to school improvement is paved with the ashes of burnt out teachers' (p. 21). She finds '"care" construed as altruism and self-sacrifice, as a convenient way of exploiting teachers, especially those who are women; and also of conning them into taking on, unpaid, work which would be better done by other trained professionals such as counsellors and social workers' (p. 21). It is therefore important that primary schools' growing social work responsibilities are acknowledged by policy makers and resourced adequately.

## READING 4.4

# Childhood and education

Andrew Pollard and Pat Triggs

Throughout history, the ways in which childhood has been conceptualized has varied in relation to social and economic circumstances. Building on Mills's argument (Reading 4.1), the opportunities and constraints that children experience in the present have to be understood in the context of both historic and contemporary structures and interests. The significance of this, of course, is to suggest that modern education policies (including the National Curriculum, assessment, school inspection, teacher training, etc.) reflect the socio-economic circumstances and cultural interpretations of 'childhood' of our own time and place. A brief history of the last 200 years of 'childhood' in England illustrates the point and poses a question: Are our education policies really appropriate for the future we aspire to?

Edited from: Pollard, A. and Triggs, P., with Broadfoot, P., McNess, E. and Osborn, M. (2000) *What Pupils Say: Changing Policy and Practice in Primary Education*. London, New York: Continuum, 306–16

We begin by briefly reviewing and contrasting three periods in English history as they affected the mass of working people – first the nineteenth-century transition from agricultural to industrial society; second, the gradual growth of social welfare provision in the late nineteenth and early twentieth century; and finally, recent decades of radical change in education policy. For each of these periods, it is possible to identify the prominence of particular assumptions about childhood.

## Childhood in the nineteenth century

At the start of the Industrial Revolution, most of the population of England lived in rural locations. Almost 90 per cent of men worked in agriculture and family life for the majority of working people was focused on the farm, small-holding or village. Family networks were often large and mobility was low, so that most young children grew up within a relatively stable web of extended-family relationships. There were high levels of fertility and infant mortality, and women spent large proportions of their adult lives in childbirth, childcare and in agricultural and domestic work. Life could be extremely hard, and children of working families were expected to become relatively independent and make a contribution from a young age. They were inducted to labour in the fields, to assume childcare duties to help with other practical family needs as deemed appropriate to their gender. In most communities there was very little organized provision for health or education. In consequence, serious illnesses or accidents were often disabling or fatal and most of the population was illiterate. However, the church was much respected as the moral cornerstone of the rural community, and children were inducted into its beliefs and seasonal rituals from a young age. Roads were poor; travel depended on walking or riding; and there were few means of information and communication available to working people about the world beyond their communities. Although broadsheets gradually became available in market towns, news was still largely conveyed by word of mouth among the mass of the rural poor, as a complement to the stories and songs of the oral tradition.

Thus both boys and girls were expected to work and to contribute to satisfying the needs of family and community. There was very little sentimentalization of childhood as an age of innocence, rather, the church emphasized the fall from grace, the deficiencies of humankind and need for discipline in work, family and religious devotion. The Industrial Revolution began a gradual process of urban migration but children's labour in the countryside remained very significant right up to the middle of the twentieth century.

The Industrial Revolution saw a gradual growth in the population of new towns and cities, and a decrease in the rural population as families migrated to find work. In the urban setting, children continued to make an economic contribution from a relatively young age, and were a significant element in the workforce of textile mills, coal mines and other industrial settings. It is well known that their labour was considerably abused, for production technologies and working conditions were extremely demanding and safety was often compromised. High levels of fertility and mortality were sustained, particularly among the poor, and the average family size was still over six children in the 1860s.

However, the expanding urbanization and industrialization gradually brought the development of a social and economic infrastructure. Roads, canals, railways and postal communications were improved immeasurably so that different towns and regions began to be interconnected economically, socially, culturally and politically. New manufacturing and other technologies produced considerable increases in productivity, making the reliance on child labour less necessary. Religious and charitable bodies began the provision of schools and hospitals, until these roles were taken up by the state. Slowly, the previously dominant vision of children as deficient or flawed, requiring the discipline of family, work or schooling, began to be challenged by a new conception of children as capable of moral and intellectual growth, but as corrupted by the social and economic pressures of the time.

## Childhood and the development of social welfare

In the last decades of the nineteenth century and early decades of the twentieth, there were profound changes in the ways in which children were perceived. In the first place, the development of new public health and education provision began to be thought of in terms of human resource and social control. Thus, more skilful and reliable workers were required by the rapidly growing domestic economy and to exploit the opportunities offered by imperial expansion around the world. Standards in the 'basics' had to be raised, and the system of payment by educational results ensured that costs of elementary schooling were kept under control. In addition, particularly following the extension of the franchise in 1867, it was considered essential to ensure the provision of an appropriately 'civilizing' education. The new scientific understandings of medicine, child development, education and social welfare provided an additional impetus in the identification of children's distinct needs as a social group. Indeed, the major influence of the modernist social project can be seen as beginning at this time with the gradual institutionalization of provision for children and the progressive establishment of new, specialist, child-focused professions.

Through such processes, the status of children was transformed. Rather than being seen from a relatively young age as resources whose virtue and well-being would, by fortunate coincidence, be enhanced by agricultural or industrial work, the newly identified social and personal needs of children were now to be met by the new institutions and professionals of the education, health and welfare services. Compulsory schooling replaced wage-earning work as the accepted occupation of children from the ages of five to twelve or thirteen and, indeed, such 'pupils' were to be separated off, and protected from, the harsher realities of the adult world until they had matured and become educationally prepared to enter it. Thus, whilst exploitation of children's labour had been culturally acceptable in both agricultural and early industrial societies, a new, sentimentalized ideal of the 'natural' and 'dependent' child emerged. This conception was particularly promoted through the development of a middle, or petty bourgeois class, the rise in significance of the nuclear family, increases in living standards and a steady fall in the birth rate. In such circumstances, far from being seen as an economic asset, children gradually came to be seen more in terms of their emotional and affective value. Feminist historians have linked this transformation to similar processes which affected women at the same time. Thus Firestone argues that:

The rise of the modern nuclear family . . . reinforced the development of an ideology of childhood, with its special indigenous life style, language, dress, mannerisms, etc. And with the increase and exaggeration of children's dependence, women's bondage to motherhood was also extended to its limits. Women and children were in the same lousy boat. (Firestone, 1979, p. 39)

This 'lousy ideological boat' carried women and children on the same basic course for most of the twentieth century. Education, health and welfare systems developed to support them, and the ideal of motherhood and conception of childhood as an age of dependence and innocence grew. Perhaps this conjunction of ideas reached its apotheosis in the post-war 1950s, when women were encouraged to return to the home after the Second World War. By then, labour-saving domestic equipment had become more affordable and mothers were thus able to invest more time in childcare and the family. There were strong norms and expectations around this. For instance, Bowlby's book, *Maternal Care and Mental Health* (1951), helped to establish the idea of 'maternal deprivation' as a explanation for poor social adjustment and educational progress. Most children were born within marriage and divorce was unusual, carrying considerable social stigma. The ideal, projected now by advertising, the growing mass media and even the introductory reading books used in school, was the nuclear family – Mummy at home, Daddy out at work, a girl, a boy and the family pet. Welfare state provision for health, education, housing, social services, etc. grew rapidly, and there were thus increasing numbers of professional groups with an interest in the upbringing of children, as well as a steadily rising quality of life for adults. The Plowden Report (CACE, 1967), with its advocacy of a child-centred curriculum, responsiveness to children's interests and flexible use of time through the 'integrated day', can be seen in this context. It reflected a faith in children's creativity and innate goodness, which was to be drawn out by the skilful teacher through the provision of activity and direct experience. Partnerships with parents were seen as a considerable help in providing holistic support to the 'whole child'.

## Modern English childhoods

In the last decades of the twentieth century, new patterns emerged as women challenged the domestic roles into which they had been positioned and then entered the paid work-force in large numbers. Overall fertility continued to fall, and the age at which women became mothers rose. The affluence of families with two wage-earners increased steadily, and new communication technologies and media brought easy access to the diversity of global cultures. There was sustained economic growth, and new patterns of lifestyle consumption on clothes, cars, leisure, international travel, etc. Thus, for those in work, it seemed possible that long hours, combined with new advances in science, communications and technology, would yield consistently rising living standards and thus underpin the diverse adult consumption patterns of the modern (and post-modern) world.

Importantly, however, Halsey and Young (1997) have questioned whether these 'gains for adults are at the expense of the interests of children'. In particular, they drew attention to the fallacy, assiduously promoted by Margaret Thatcher, that such individual freedom of choice is also a collective good. Such individualism has serious implications for children, for, as Halsey and Young put it:

Children thereby become commodities . . . just like cars or videos or holidays, which adults can choose to have in preference to other consumables. And if they do, that is their choice and responsibility. Contraceptive control of our bodies enhances that illusion, so who needs a family or a community or, for that matter, a government other than to prevent ruin of the market for these good things by thieves and frauds? Surely technology has conquered nature and we can safely allow individuals to choose a consuming style, limited only by their willingness to work for money. Everybody is then free to buy the good life of their own definition. Marriage becomes a mere contract. (p. 791)

Indeed, in the midst of this affluence and apparent progress, the traditional nuclear family began to show signs of considerable stress. The best-known indicator is the divorce rate, which showed a significant increase. Thus by the 1990s, 40 per cent of new marriages were expected to break down and there was little associated stigma. Co-habitation prior to marriage had become commonplace, and one-third of children were born to couples who were not married. At the millennium, the proportion of children in one-parent families was almost 15 per cent – over one and a half million individuals. Thus overall, the traditional nuclear family, though still idealized, became by no means the dominant manifestation of 'the family'.

Some children were rendered particularly vulnerable by these social changes in family forms. Indeed, one-parent and workless families were especially likely to suffer from low incomes. Thus, despite the general rise in incomes for those in work, income inequality rose throughout the 1980s and early 1990s. By 1996/7 over half of one-parent households received less than half of average income – the official definition of 'poverty'. In total, 4.3 million British children, one-third of the total, lived in households suffering from such poverty (Gregg, Harkness and Machlin, 1999), and these households were increasingly concentrated in large cities and areas of public housing. In 1968, the comparable figure was much less, at 1.4 million. At the start of the new century, avoidance of child poverty is strongly associated with the capacity of an adult to sustain work, and this is more significant than the number of parents in a household. Ironically, however, high hours worked by single parents reduces the available time to spend with their children.

Some major aspects of these structural changes over the past 200 years, and their implications for children, are highlighted below:

The proportion of children in the population has dramatically decreased. There are now far fewer young people but many more of the retired and elderly. For instance, the number of households with children within them has decreased from around 90 per cent in 1900 to under one-third today. Children thus have fewer direct advocates, and there is a much smaller proportion of the adult population with an immediate, daily interest in children's concerns.

Women now spend a much smaller proportion of their lives in childbirth and child-rearing, and are able to seek personal and economic fulfilment in new ways. Over 90 per cent of women now work outside the home during their working years. The ideology of the maternal home-maker has been challenged, and many women aspire to combine work, family and personal satisfaction. Children are a part of this, but not the only element.

Family size and form have changed enormously. Large, stable extended families gradually gave way to the smaller nuclear family, and this is now becoming fractured into a new diversity of household forms. Men have become less significant economically, and the underlying balance of power within families has thus altered.

The economic contribution of children has significantly decreased. Children's agricultural work was valued and their labour was used (and exploited) in the Industrial Revolution, but compulsory education now prevents most children engaging in anything other than relatively marginal economic activity. Children are both more dependent on adults and, with the school leaving age at 16 and many young people remaining in colleges or universities until much later, they are more dependent for much longer. Children have therefore become a significant expense, rather than an economic asset during childhood.

Legal, institutional and professional provision for the welfare of children has increased enormously, particularly in education, medicine and social welfare. However, this has also created large numbers of people and organizations who have vested interests in defining 'childhood' and children's needs in ways that enable them to further their objectives. Teachers are one such group.

Open, rural and communal environments in which children had considerable autonomy in their movements have been replaced by urban settings in which security and risk have become significant considerations for parents or carers. Modern play spaces now tend to be designated and controlled, whilst family life is becoming increasingly privatized. Simple toys and games have been superseded by a multiplicity of complex, mass-produced and gendered designs emphasising excitement and innovation, whilst the continued development of multi-channel television, video and computer games furthers an individualistic, consumerist and privatizing trend.

The conservative agricultural society of the eighteenth century, with its entrenched religious values and social hierarchy, has been replaced through the development of secular science, and its capitalist application to industrial development. However, whilst its more divisive consequences have been ameliorated by the development of social democratic welfare provision, it can still produce extremes of inequality. Present society is more diverse, secular, mobile and individualistic than the past. It is more meritocratic; but can be just as cruel in terms of the distribution of wealth and life-chances.

Old patterns of communal recreation, reflecting seasonal rhythms, cultural histories and relatively stable social structures, have been replaced by an incredible diversity of global, commercialized mass media. Thus, rather than inhabiting an ascribed social status and identity, it is now possible to experiment with lifestyles and entertain the notion of 'multiple selves'. Young people are particularly exposed and disposed to such experimentation as they strive to establish themselves in the adult world.

The sphere of meaningful economic activity has moved from the locality to a global level. With the development of huge multi-national companies, global production and marketing strategies mean that there is now a considerable degree of economic interdependence. However, on the labour supply side international competition is extremely fierce. In this context, the children of each country are seen as a vital national resource for the future – and the UK is a particular case in point.

So, if these are some to the major structural changes affecting family forms and children, how have they impacted on education policy?

## Structural change and education policy

In the specific case of the 1990s, it is possible to identify three main sources of the education controls which have affected children and young people. We might term them: the indirect; the responsive; and the futuristic.

First, children were indirectly affected by the struggle between teachers and successive governments of the 1980s and 1990s. As we documented in the first PACE book (Pollard *et al.*, 1994), this essentially began as a battle between the government and the teaching profession, with parents being enlisted on the government's side through membership of governing bodies, promotion of a 'Parents' Charter', and encouragement to think of themselves as 'consumers'. Pupils were not consulted as consumers. Indeed, throughout the entire period, very little regard was paid to their perspectives at all. In part, this may have been a deliberate reaction against 'child-centred' ideas of the Plowden era – about which a discourse of derision was regularly mounted. More significantly, however, pupil perspectives were simply not considered to be an issue of concern. This appears to have reflected the confident assumption amongst politicians that it was adults' responsibility to determine the curriculum, and children's job to receive and respond to it. The real problem was to curtail the power of teachers, LEAs and educationists, and to restructure their work, rather than worrying about pupils. Policy was thus essentially based on a delivery model of learning, with children cast in relatively passive positions.

However, as Pollard and Triggs (2000) demonstrated, the introduction of the National Curriculum and assessment procedures did have significant controlling effects on children, and these, of course, continued following the 1997 election of a Labour government. Blair's cry of 'education, education, education' brought a greater focus on literacy, numeracy, citizenship and ICT, but the emphasis on assessment and inspection remained and the new discipline of school 'target setting' intensified. We are not suggesting that 'constraining pupils' was an explicit aim of either Conservative or Labour education policy – but it seems apparent that it was a major consequence of their efforts to control teachers and ratchet up standards of pupil attainment.

The second, more responsive motivation for public policy has been awareness of family and community breakdown, and the role of the state in providing practical support and even moral guidance. In particular, as we described earlier, structural changes during the last decades of the twentieth century have seen the emergence of new patterns of family life, marriage and divorce, lifestyles, work participation, leisure, mass communication, and global economic competition. The world became a fast-moving, highly complex and diverse place. Certainly, this environment enabled many people to flourish. However, there were problems too, for economic growth was bought by successive Conservative governments of the 1980s and 1990s at the price of increasing social differentiation. In particular, there was a considerable difference in the experience of those in paid employment and those out of it.

Successive Conservative governments offered moral exhortation and stiffer sentencing, whilst emphasizing individual freedoms and market mechanisms, and denying the significance of social circumstances. More recently, New Labour governments are directly addressing patterns of social exclusion. Policies such as the 'New Deal' and the introduction of 'Education Action Zones' were designed to tackle youth unemployment and regenerate run-down communities. Similarly, additional resources were routed back to families through policies such as increased child benefit and pre-school provision. However, both the policies of condemnation and of amelioration have consequences that are firmly structuring of children's experiences. Campbell (1999) has expressed the role of schools:

> As modern society fractures morally, the state will need to reinforce the social and moral functions of schooling, primarily because it remains the only common site for moral socialisation, as respect for family, church, the law and other socialisation agencies weakens. The role of primary teachers has become even more diffuse. In addition to teaching the curriculum, they are expected to be secretaries, social workers, community liaison officers, paramedics, priests, teacher trainers, expert spotters of drug abuse, advisers on safe sex and unsafe drugs. (p. 25)

Schooling, in other words, is positioned on the front line in respect of combating social fragmentation – not because it has sought this responsibility, but because it is one of very few public institutions that is nationally available to fulfil the necessary role. For many pupils, then, schooling has been and is likely to continue to be seen as an institution of social control – whether at the level of 'healthy eating', challenging vandalism, checking up on homework, or policing a local 'curfew'.

The third, futuristic way in which children are defined reflects adult preparations for the emergent economic, technological and social challenges of the twenty-first century. As Gordon Brown put it in his budget speech of March 1999: 'children are 20 per cent of the British people, but 100 per cent of Britain's future'. New Labour has adopted immediate targets to increase the skill, knowledge and capability of school pupils to meet the needs of industry. With Curriculum 2000, it has also re-emphasized inclusivity and introduced a new emphasis on citizenship. On a longer, twenty-year, time-scale, the government has also targeted the eradication of child poverty in the UK. However, their insistent emphasis is on the development of higher educational standards to provide a better supply of technologically skilled labour to enhance Britain's international competitiveness. There is a tension here in New Labour thinking between the basic skills agenda and the discourse of the 'flexible life-long learner'.

How does modern English society wish to bring up its children? Is it satisfactory to process them through an increasingly constrained education system focused on 'the basics', whilst also generating massive expectations that they should become 'flexible, creative learners'? The best hope for the success of this conflation of objectives at present may lie with teachers, for their creative mediation of government policy does go some way to weaken the damaging effects of overstructuring. However, if we really believe that our future lies in the quality of the thinking, learning and capability of our children – then it is essential that we develop our education and family support systems to tap fundamental learning processes as physical, cognitive and affective development and socio-environmental experiences interact together. In particular, rather than ignoring, misunderstanding or undermining the spark of independent creativity in children, it is precisely what we need to foster for the future.

The real challenge, then, is not whether we can ratchet up each and every measurement of performance in the basics, but how we can create policies and practices that enable a virtuous cycle to develop between standards, imagination, capability, flexibility and self-confidence. We must combine knowledge, skill, creativity and commitment to learning. Only then will we have an education system that is really providing what our citizens deserve and need for the twenty-first century.

## READING 4.5

# Family capital, schooling and social class

## Diane Reay

This reading provides a case-study example of social differences in modern society. It highlights inequalities in the resources available to middle and working-class families and draws particular attention to the significance of mothers in providing emotional support to children at school. Diane Reay's use of the concept of 'emotional capital' draws on the economic analogy popularized by Bourdieu. Beyond class differences in economic resources, he drew attention to the status and advantages brought by middle-class possession of 'cultural capital'. Others have suggested similar networks of influence and patronage offer 'social capital', and now Reay suggests that differences in the capacity of mothers to offer emotional support could be crucial. Given what we know about the personal challenges to children that schooling presents, this is an important argument.

Edited from: Reay, D. (2000) 'A useful extension of Bourdieu's conceptual framework? Emotional capital as a way of understanding mothers' involvement in their children's education' *The Sociological Review*, 48 (4), 568–85

One of the most surprising findings from my research study of home–school relationships was the recurrence of intense emotions, both positive and negative, permeating mothers' accounts of their children's schooling. I have used the concept of 'emotional capital' to better understand the welter of emotions that mothers both expressed and talked about in relation to their children's schooling.

Emotional involvement did not differ greatly by social class. However, working-class women found it more difficult to supply their children with resources of emotional capital than their middle-class counterparts because they were frequently hampered by poverty, insufficient educational knowledge and lack of confidence. We find the same dynamic relationship between the different forms of capital that Allatt writes about in relation to privileged families, but this time operating in a depreciating spiral rather than the one that

Allatt describes in which the different forms of capital augment each other (Allatt, 1993). Working-class women were often caught up in a spiral in which low levels of dominant cultural capital, economic capital and social capital all made it relatively difficult to provide their children with the benefits of emotional capital. Class differences also played a part in determining whether mothers could divert their emotional involvement into generating academic profits for their children. Working-class women often lacked the right conditions for provoking either emotional or cultural capital. Contrast:

> When I get in I get them both something to eat, then do whatever needs to be done in the house and that includes getting their clothes ready for school so by the time everything is done I find I never have a minute to sit down until half eight or nine. Then she'll come and sit with me and read and that's every night. (Lisa, white working-class lone mother)

with:

> I try and make sure that at least twice a week I take my children out to tea somewhere relaxed and leisurely where we can all chat about our day. I've always worked on the principle of taking my children somewhere nice for tea, for socialising since they were little, that's always been the way I have made space for them to tell me about what's happening to them. (Linsey, white middle-class married mother)

Lisa, dealing with the pressure of domestic chores after a day's paid work, finds it extremely difficult to focus exclusively on her children's educational needs in the way that Linsey does. This is not an issue of 'good mothering' but of resources. Linsey can afford both a cleaner and an au pair. She talks of being able to concentrate on her children's schooling in a 'relaxed and leisurely' way in contrast to Lisa, on an income of under £15,000 per annum, who describes a frenetic juggling of competing, equally pressing demands.

However, that is not the same as saying working-class mothers did not provide emotional capital through their involvement in schooling, rather it did not go hand in hand with cultural capital to anything like the extent middle-class women's did. Lisa, talking about Lucy's reluctance to go swimming, combined powerful feelings of empathy with an incisiveness about what was in Lucy's best interest:

> She had never come up against anything she didn't want to do at school before. I didn't want her as soon as she came up against something she didn't want to do to think she could opt out. I wanted her to develop strategies to deal with it, you know. I mean I did feel for her and so I ended up phoning up the school a few times and went along with Lucy saying she felt unwell, but then I said to her 'You can't keep avoiding it'. Then I went to talk to her teacher first to say, you know, 'this is going to be very hard for Lucy, can you keep a special eye on her'. Then her teacher and I spoke to Lucy together and I said 'You mustn't give in without trying'. She took a lot of helping through the first few weeks she went but it got better. She's passed her first two grades. I've had them framed (pointing to where they hung on the wall), you know, to show her efforts are appreciated because it was hard for her. (Lisa, white working-class lone mother)

This is just one of many examples of working-class women's sensitivity, emotional support and encouragement all combining to enhance their children's emotional capital. Yet, it was far more difficult for the working-class mothers, often dealing with a personal history of academic failure, to generate the same levels of academic confidence and enthusiasm among their children as their middle-class counterparts. History is key here and I suggest that, in common with other forms of capital, there are generational aspects of emotional capital in that reserves are built up in families over time. While working-class Dawn talks in terms of a mother working long hours in the labour market who 'was never there for her and so I found primary school terrifying', middle-class Linsey talks of a mother who always encouraged and helped her with her school work; 'she was always certain all her daughters could do anything they set their minds to'.

Much of the data demonstrate the costs to mothers of their emotional involvement in their children's schooling. They are using up a lot of time and emotional energy in their support which, as I have demonstrated above, sometimes brings them into conflict rather than harmony with their children. They are often unsupported in this emotional work by male partners (David, 1993; Reay, 1998). Involvement in children's schooling generated intense class anxiety, in particular, for some of the middle-class mothers who expressed fears that credential inflation and increased marketization within education was making it more difficult than in the past for children from middle-class background to attain appropriate jobs (Jordan *et al.*, 1994; Brown, 1995).

Within contemporary educational markets, class continues to infuse attitudes and actions. There are potent signs of 'the unremitting emotional distress generated by the doubts and insecurities of living class that working-class women endure on a daily basis' (Skeggs, 1997, p. 167). I suggest that the concept of emotional capital is useful for unravelling some of the confusing class and gender processes embedded in parental involvement in education.

The concept problematizes prevailing values which uncomplicatedly identify academic success as uniformly positive. It also uncovers a contemporary conundrum in which both middle-class mothers in their pursuit of educational advantage for their children at the cost of their emotional well-being and working-class mothers constrained in ways which mitigate against the acquisition of both emotional and cultural capital are at risk of disadvantaging their children, albeit in differing ways. I suggest that the relationships between educational success, emotional capital and emotional well-being, and the extent of overlap and different between them, could provide new ways of understanding how a range of disadvantages which cross class barriers are being manufactured in the contemporary educational marketplace.

# CHAPTER 5

# Values and identity.
# Who are we?

The seven readings in this chapter assert the significance of values, perspectives and identities of both teachers and pupils. Whilst these are explicitly personal, significant cultural influences are also apparent.

On teachers, Nias (5.1) begins with an important reading on how teaching relates to personal satisfaction and identity. Cortazzi (5.2) reviews some prominent dimensions of teacher thinking which tend to evolve through classroom experience. Woods (5.3) insists that 'creative teachers' work to defend a commitment to their personal values.

On pupils, Davies (5.4) argues that children and adults see the world in very different ways, largely because of the differences in their experiences and power to influence events. Pollard and Filer (5.5) review their work on teacher–pupil relationships and the classroom-coping strategies of 'goodies', 'jokers' and 'gangs' and suggest how children develop 'learner identities' as a product of school, playground and home experiences. In Reading 5.6, Jackson and Warin focus on gender identity and show that it is particularly significant when children feel vulnerable, such as at times of school transfer. Finally, at the individual level, Maylor (5.7) provides an autobiographical illustration of the influence of personal circumstances on educational experience.

The parallel chapter of *Reflective Teaching* is also in two major parts. 'Knowing ourselves as teachers' suggests ways of thinking about personal values and the ways in which they influence teaching. The second part is on 'knowing children as pupils'. This reviews the educational literature on pupil cultures and offers activites for investigating young children's perspectives and experiences of schooling. The chapter concludes with suggestions for 'Key Readings'. Further ideas can be found on *RTweb* in the 'Notes for Further Reading' that are associated with this chapter.

## 📖 READING 5.1

# Feeling like a teacher

Jennifer Nias

The book from which this extract has been edited, *Primary Teachers Talking*, is an insightful and sensitive representation of teachers' feelings in respect of their work. Jennifer Nias interviewed 50 teachers over a period of ten years as their careers and lives developed. The result is a unique account of the pleasures and pain of 'becoming a teacher', with the gradual integration of the role with identity and self. The analysis suggests reasons why primary school teachers have such a strong commitment to their pupils, and why the job is inherently challenging.

How do you feel about yourself and your career?

Edited from: Nias, J. (1989) *Primary Teachers Talking: A Study of Teaching as Work*. London: Routledge, 181–97

It is possible to teach for years, successfully and with the affirmation of one's head teacher and colleagues, without incorporating 'teacher' into one's self-image. As several of my interviewees said in their first decade of work, 'I teach, but I do not feel like a teacher'. However, by their second decade most of those whom I interviewed had incorporated their professional identity into their self-image (i.e. they 'felt like teachers'). Clearly, in any attempt to understand the nature of teaching as work, it is important to include the affective reality of experienced, committed teachers. Accordingly, this chapter is built around an analysis of conversations with 50 people in mid-career of whom I asked, 'Do you feel like a teacher?', and explained why I wanted to know. If they said they did, I then requested an explanation. In addition, I have used comments they made when they were talking more generally about their work.

What emerges from this analysis is the contradictory nature of the feelings associated with teaching. Various reasons can be given for this. The outcome of all of them, for the successful teacher, is mastery over a complex and difficult skill – the theme of 'balance' – and this, it can be argued, accounts for the sense of fit between identity and work which, at its best, characterizes 'feeling like a teacher'.

## 'Being yourself'

Most of the teachers believed that to adopt the identity of 'teacher' was simply to 'be yourself' in the classroom. They expressed this idea in three similar but slightly different ways. Some stressed a sense of fit between self and occupation (e.g. 'I feel as if I've found my niche'; 'However annoyed I may be at the end of a day in school . . . I still feel I'm in the right job for me'). Others saw little distinction between their 'selves' at work and outside it; as one said, 'What's happening to you as a person can't be separated from what's happening to you as a teacher'.

## 'Being whole'

Many teachers linked the notions of 'being yourself' and 'being whole'. Some achieved 'wholeness' by blurring the boundaries between their personal and professional lives. One woman said:

I tend to bring a lot of my personal life into school with the children. They know a lot about what I'm doing all the time so in that way teaching is never separate from my personal life. They know all about my cat, everything that happened to me the previous evening, they know that I sail, they know that I paint, they know what my house is like, so they're not separate lives at all.

The desire to create 'wholeness' also showed itself in attempts to soften the barriers of role, age and status and to prevent the erection of new ones (particularly those of curriculum or timetabling). Several teachers attacked what they described as 'fragmentation' or 'splitting' of their pupils' learning experiences. Many talked enthusiastically and, in the case of some head teachers, nostalgically, about their involvement with children in extra-curricular activities, clubs, on field trips and school journeys, and in residential study centres.

The urge to work in an environment characterized by unity, not division, extended to staff relationships as well. In the words of one head teacher, 'The school was a part of me, the staff were a part of me . . . I couldn't separate myself from them'.

## 'Establishing relationships with children'

Embedded in the notions of belonging, and of education as an extension of family life, is a belief that to teach one must 'establish a relationship with pupils'. For instance:

I've met kids that I taught when I first went there who are now working . . . They don't just say, 'Aren't you Mr Jones?', they say, 'Alright Sir?' and that's the difference. It's not a question of education, it's a question of relationships.

Teachers described their work in terms such as 'getting co-operation from my children', 'it's a joint effort between you and them', 'what a teacher is to any individual child could be something totally different, it's a function of the two personalities involved'.

Although they knew it existed, my interviewees found it hard to describe what they meant by their 'relationship' with children. Occasionally it was seen as playing a parental role, sometimes as relating to peers – e.g. 'It can be as close as another friend', 'Some of those children I'd really like to keep as friends'. Very frequently it contains a marked element of humour, often based on shared understandings (Walker and Adelman, 1976; Woods, 1979). Many teachers appear to gauge the state of their relationship with a class by the extent to which 'we can all have a laugh together', 'I can be myself, laugh and joke', or, 'we can share a joke and then get down to work again'. However, to many teachers the relationship is more than being either a parent or a friend. Several people described teaching as 'communication with another human being' or 'learning to communicate with other people'. A woman reflected:

I've come to realize that if you really want to educate children you've got to share yourself with them, as a person. They've got to know about you, your interests, your life out of school, the sort of person you are. But most of all it means being open to them as a person, and that makes you vulnerable. Yes, being a teacher is being ready to be vulnerable.

## Control

To the person who undertakes to build this relationship, it has three main characteristics: control, responsibility and concern. Virtually every teacher responded to my request to explain what it was to 'feel like a teacher' by saying that it was to be in control (e.g. 'It's doing things you're in control of to a large extent'; 'It's being in control of what goes on in the classroom'; 'To start with, it's your will against theirs'.

Whether or not they enjoyed the exercise of control, interviewees all accepted that, as a teacher, 'You have to exercise authority. Treating children like human beings and yet maintaining discipline is a constant challenge'. Indeed, being willing to exercise authority was widely seen as the one necessary condition for 'feeling like a teacher'. Two teachers suggested:

> A teacher's relationship with children is quite distinctive. However much you care and however much you share with them, you assume an air of authority. I didn't have any authority for a couple of years, partly because I didn't really have any conviction that I was doing anything right.

> There is no way round it. If you want to be a teacher you have to find a way of establishing your control because it's a sort of barrier you have to get through. If you want to do the job you have to do that because it is part of being a teacher. You cannot do the rest of the job, which I wanted to do, without getting over the first barrier.

Closely related to feeling in control was the sense of being well organized and purposeful – 'having specific ends in view, not muddling through, knowing what you're about', 'knowing what you want from and for children', 'being organized, so that in any teaching situation you have a sense of direction'.

## Responsibility and concern

Assuming responsibility for children was also seen to be linked with feeling in control. People believed that, as teachers, they must 'accept the children's dependence on you', 'feel a great responsibility for every child in my care', 'accept that you will influence them by what you are, whether you want to or not'. One man claimed:

> It means that you have got to accept them for what they are, and if an 8-year-old says 'I love you, Mr Smith' she means it, and you can't play with that, you cannot dismiss it, you cannot turn round to her and say, 'I love you as well, Sarah' if you don't mean it. And I think that's what feeling like a teacher is: when you realize what an awesome responsibility you bear. If teachers realized just what influence they have on children, I think then they'd realize what being a teacher was.

Related to both control and responsibility, but less detached than either, is affection. Many teachers emphasized the caring aspects of their role, using such terms as 'being prepared to put their interests first', 'doing your best for all the children in your class'. Five, four of them men, put it more strongly than this. One said:

> There are one or two children that I love very dearly. There have been one or two children in the past twelve years I have loved totally . . . only one or two. The difference that having my own son has made to my relationships at school has not been that strong. I still have one or two children I'm really fond of, not as pupils, but as people.

In whatever way these teachers expressed the essential characteristics of their relationship with children, they became, in the words of one man, 'more intuitive, relaxed and spontaneous' as they came to 'feel like teachers'. Individuals repeatedly spoke of being more relaxed in the classroom and the staffroom, of feeling more able to be 'adaptive and flexible', of 'being less of a worrier', 'more laid back', and above all more self-confident. As one person crisply responded, 'Feeling confident in what you do, that's what it all hinges on'.

At this point the circular nature of what they were saying becomes apparent: to 'feel like a teacher' is to feel you can be yourself in the classroom; to be yourself is to feel whole, to act naturally; to act naturally is to enter into a relationship with children, a relationship in which control makes possible the exercise of responsibility and the expression of concern; together, these states enable you to 'be yourself' in the classroom and therefore to 'feel like a teacher'.

## Living with tension, dilemma and contradiction

Yes this sense of 'wholeness' and fit between self and occupation is dearly bought. There is little consistency in the lived experience of primary teaching. To 'be' a teacher is to be relaxed and in control yet tired and under stress, to feel whole while being pulled apart, to be in love with one's work but daily to talk of leaving it.

There are three interrelated sets of reasons for this contradictory state of affairs: socio-historical, psychological and philosophical. Sociologically, the teacher's role is ambiguous and ill-defined, hedged about with uncertainty, inconsistency and tension. Primary teachers occupy many roles, some (e.g. instructor, parent, judge, friend) perpetually at war with one another (Blyth, 1967; Woods, 1987a). The essentially conflictual nature of the job is emphasized by teachers' inescapable obligation to control children. The American sociologist, Waller, has made a powerful case for the view that 'the teacher–pupil relationship is a form of institutionalized dominance and subordination . . . Teacher and pupil confront each other with attitudes from which the underlying hostility can never be removed' (Waller, 1961: p. 195). The need for teachers to exercise power stems from the fact that adult groups (of whom in school the teacher is representative) and the formal curriculum, which offers children 'desiccated bits of adult life' (*ibid.*) confront pupils who are 'interested in life in their own world' and 'striving to realize themselves in their own way' (*ibid.*).

Education cannot escape from being a process in which the older generation (represented by teachers) force-feeds the younger. In the clash of interests which follows, teachers have to use every resource they can muster to curb and harness children's energies, to render the 'desiccated bits of adult life' palatable to classes full of the richness of their own experience. Add to that the fact that in England this process of compulsory socialization is invested in teachers who, with negligible adult help and relatively few resources, daily face large numbers of physically active children, and it is inevitable that control becomes for them a central issue in school and classroom life.

Leiberman and Miller put it this way:

> Once inside the classroom, a teacher knows that all control is tenuous. It depends on a negotiated agreement between students and the teacher. If that agreement is violated, a teacher will subordinate all teaching activities to one primary goal: to regain and maintain control . . . when one loses control, one loses everything. (Leiberman and Miller, 1984, p. 14)

Since the exercise of dominance by one person over others can never be without strain, stress is therefore built into the teacher's job.

Furthermore, the teacher's work is riddled with uncertainties. The goals of their schools and the values which underpin these are conflicting and, in an attempt to reduce the impact of this conflict, have often become imprecise, ambiguous and unattainable. The resulting vagueness masks a number of dilemmas which teachers' daily practice expresses, even if they do not themselves voice them (Berlak and Berlak, 1981) [see Reading 1.3]. These authors vividly portray dilemmas-in-action in English primary classrooms, showing how teachers resolve, on a minute-by-minute basis, conflicting expectations about, for instance, their role, the curriculum, their teaching methods and response to pupils' work. For example: how can the needs of individuals be reconciled with those of the whole class group? Should the teacher or the pupil control the content and pace of learning and determine the standards by which it is judged? By what criteria should particular elements be included in or excluded from the curriculum?

Vagueness on goals (and therefore responsibilities) is coupled with the absence of clear or valid criteria by which teachers may be judged. This ambiguity itself rests on insecure foundations, since little is known with certainty about the connection between teaching and learning. Nor is there any consensus about the knowledge base of teaching as a profession and therefore about what teachers should know.

Further, the many roles which teachers already occupy are currently expanding. In the past two decades these roles have grown to include work (of many sorts) with parents, governors, outside agencies, support services and colleagues. In the 1990s, these demands are likely to be augmented by the need for teachers to assume greater responsibilities for school-based in-service education, and national assessment, and for head teachers of larger schools to talk on, with their governors, the running of their school's finances and physical plant – and all this on top of English teachers' documented tendency to assume a very wide range of moral responsibilities for their pupils (Osborn, 1986).

Psychologically, the job itself is not only 'incredibly, unexpectedly demanding' (Fuller and Bown, 1975, p. 48) but also shifting and elusive. It rests upon relationships with pupils whose attendance may be erratic, even arbitrary. The time of day, the weather, children's moods, staff illnesses, break-ins, visitors from medical and other support services, and a myriad of other minor alterations in the teachers' context and programme mean that they experience continuous and endemic change, in circumstances already characterized by uncertainty and unpredictability (Nias *et al.*, 1989) [see Reading 11.1]. The classroom is never the same place from one day to the next, often it can alter radically from one moment to another. Yet teachers are expected to maintain throughout an aura of 'professional pleasantness' (King, 1978) and to 'correct for the capriciousness of students with the steadiness, resolve and sangfroid of one who governs' (Lortie, 1975, p. 156).

## Living with paradox

Primary school teachers in England appear to have a conception of teaching which imposes upon them the need continually to live and work with paradox. The very nature of teaching, as they experience it, is contradictory. Teachers must nurture the whole while attending to the parts, liberate their pupils to grow in some directions by checking growth in others, foster and encourage progress by controlling it, and show love and interest by curbing and chastising. Indeed, there is some evidence that these teachers were themselves aware of the paradoxical nature of their task. In particular, they see themselves facing three quandaries, each of them relating in some way to their perception of themselves.

First, they could not become the sort of teachers they wanted to be without also accepting the need to behave in ways they found disagreeable. One talked of 'learning that you've got to establish yourself and your authority first – let them dislike you so they can like you later'. Another said, 'I have learnt that you must dominate the children in order to free them . . . I quite accept that now, it's just the pain of doing it'.

Second, they could encounter children as individuals and care for them only if they were also aware of and valued themselves. One of them put it this way:

> I don't think anyone could teach young children unless they're both egocentric and selfless. You've got to be very sure of who you are yourself and yet quite prepared to forget who you are, not forget it, but put who you are second to who the kids are.

Similarly, they could meet the children's personal calls upon them only if they had something left to give (i.e. if they safeguarded opportunities out of school to replenish the 'selves' who went to work).

Third, they could not be fulfilled by their work unless they allowed themselves to be depleted by its demands. I asked several people, 'Why do you let the school take so much of you?'. The typical reply was: 'I enjoy giving it'.

My claim is, therefore, that to adopt the identity of an English primary school teacher is to accept the paradoxical nature of the task and inexorably to live with tension. Those who claim that they can be themselves in and through their work – i.e. that they can 'feel like teachers' – are signalling that they have learned to live not just with stress but with paradox.

Primary teaching is, then, an occupation which requires the ability to live with, and handle constructively, a multitude of dilemmas, tensions, contradictions, uncertainties and paradoxes.

## READING 5.2

# Polarities in teachers' thinking

## Martin Cortazzi

Martin Cortazzi collected and studied teachers' narrative accounts of classroom experiences. As a result, he was able to identify what he called 'polarities' in teachers' thinking, and these are summarized in this reading. The suggestion is that these paired ideas are drawn on by teachers to make sense of classroom and school situations and to provide a basis for future action. They have something in common with the notion of dilemmas (see Reading 1.3) and, in common with many other papers in this collection, they underline the significance of teacher judgement.

Edited from: Cortazzi, M. (1990) *Primary Teaching: How It Is*. London: David Fulton, 126–35

Underlying teacher narratives are some abstract binary oppositions. These oppositions are presented here as polarities between which teachers operate on a continuum, oscillating between the tensions of two poles according to the demands of the situation, never able to adhere completely to only one of them. The polarities are important as pairs, rather than as discrete categories. It is assumed that both poles are consciously accepted by teachers as necessary. The importance of these theoretical constructs lies in the relationship between the elements. The constructs are proposed as cultural models since they have been derived from the narratives of large numbers of teachers interviewed independently.

## Individual < - - - > Class

'You want to make sure every child is being taught at his or her own level. It is difficult.'

'I feel under tremendous pressure with thirty-eight children.'

This polar opposition summarizes the problem of the class teacher working with a large number of children within a tradition of education which emphasizes individuals rather than groups. Teachers believe that it is necessary to focus at different times either on individuals or on the class as a whole. Some individuals always stand out in teachers' perceptions: for academic ability, problems or character. While trying to follow the primary education dictum to 'meet the needs of the individual', it is the extremes from the total whose needs the teacher apparently gives greater attention. Because of the demands of the whole class he or she cannot meet every need of every child.

## Parent < - - - > Teacher

'You get those who cooperate with you, and those for whom the school is a battle.'

This polarity captures the potential conflict between teachers and parents. Teachers see great importance in eliciting cooperation and support from parents to benefit pupils. They also affirm their need to know pupils' background, which is partly obtained from parents.

When pupils have behavioural, social or emotional problems, teachers tend to use a social pathology model to interpret the sources of these problems as being in the home, rather than in school. With awkward parents, teachers move away from the need to know the home (the parent end), and focus parents' attention on the teacher's concerns for the whole class (the teacher end). Explaining the teacher's situation overcomes parental misunderstandings.

## Flexibility < - - - > Planning

'We're reasonably planned, but flexible, too.'

'Every day something happens, like someone wets themselves, somebody is sick, somebody is unhappy about something that happened at playtime . . . and you cannot get through what you planned to do.'

The need for planning, organization, structure and system was recognized, but was offset by the frequent need to be flexible or to 'play it by ear.' Teachers said they could neither rigidly stick to plans, nor continually 'play it by ear' without planning. Both poles were necessary. Planning was generally for the whole class or for groups, rarely for individuals. Being flexible meant responding to individual children's interests and excitement when something unexpectedly 'cropped up'. This was then used with the whole class. Some long-term plans originated through being flexible to children's interests. In these cases the class apparently followed the individual. There is a constant movement between these poles, with the teacher's focus continually changing.

## Breakthrough < - - - > Incremental learning

'Although you think that it's sudden, a miracle, it's not really, it's just that you've been plodding on and on, going over the same thing every day.'

'Yes it has clicked, but I don't think personally that it's instantaneous.'

Children's breakthroughs are reported as being sudden 'clicks' after a period of little progress. This can be contrasted with slower continuous incremental learning. As the teachers perceived learning, some takes place suddenly and is noticed as such (a breakthrough), other learning is a slow accumulation and is noticed gradually (incremental learning). Other points on the scale are where the learning is gradual but is noticed suddenly (a breakthrough, according to some teachers) or where sudden learning is noticed gradually.

## Disaster < - - - > Stability

'Teachers are so resourceful that they overcome disasters. That's experience, isn't it?'

'You always think you can do something better. In retrospect you think you haven't done it well enough, but you have to be satisfied with a compromise anyway because there are so many pressures. You have to reconcile these things. It's not a rejection of the perfect, nor an acceptance of the substandard, but it's . . . well, bearing in mind the other pressures.'

Many disasters were reported as unanticipated interruptions to stability. Disasters are of various types, on a scale from mild events or accidents (like falling off a chair) to severely disturbing incidents (e.g. concussion or child suicide). The teacher's response must be to restore stability. The majority of disasters in narratives occurred with individual children, potentially disrupting the stability of the whole class.

## Laughter < - - - > Seriousness

'It's the laughing and joking you can have . . . you can sort of think to yourself, "Yes, that was a good day. We had a good laugh in that lesson, but they still did some work".'

This opposition is between the assumed serious tone of most classroom time and the smiles or laughter which arise from the incongruity of children's sayings and doings. The humour is unexpected and nearly always associated with an individual child. After laughter the teacher must restore seriousness and order. Humour turns out to be a key element in the teacher's job satisfaction, supporting the notion that both poles here are necessary.

## Unpredictability < - - - > Routine

'The variability, that's always made teaching to me, because of the unexpected things that happen.'

'That's what makes teaching: the variability, the unexpected things that happen.'

Planned, serious, 'normal' classroom work is the routine, aimed at incremental learning. The opposite to this is the pole of the unpredictable, the unexpected and the variety. There are few narratives about routine teaching, perhaps because what is routine is basically less newsworthy. There are, however, literally hundreds of unpredictable elements in most 'breakthrough', 'disaster', 'awkward parent' and 'humorous' narratives. Teachers commented that such variety made teaching interesting and enjoyable.

## Enjoyment < - - - > Grind

'It's a very satisfying life, but it's hard work.'

'I moan like hell, but I enjoy it.'

This opposition puts the hard-work aspect of teaching against enjoyment. Many teachers mentioned that teaching was inevitably often a 'grind', 'slog' or 'struggle'. It was 'hard work' and 'extremely busy'. This pressure can be endured if there is also enjoyment. 'Breakthrough of planning' and 'humorous' narratives frequently include evaluations where enjoyment is a prime element, often linked with being 'thrilled', 'amazed' and 'interested'. This enjoyment was often shared with children. Sometimes the teacher's pleasure was derived from children's enjoyment. The enjoyment pole emerges very clearly from narratives. In the staffroom this sharing of fun in anecdotes may be an important element of camaraderie among teachers. However, it must be balanced with the conventional complaining about the grind, which is also an element of camaraderie.

## Social < - - - > Cognitive

'It's very much a social job that we do, as well as a teaching job.'

'I see my role in helping them learn.'

This opposition expresses the important polarity between social relationships, feelings, attitudes and the like on the one hand, and learning, remembering, understanding concepts and developing cognitive skills on the other. Both are obviously necessary and important in education. It might be expected that both would feature heavily in teachers' narratives about, for example, children, learning, planning or parents. In fact, there is scant mention of the cognitive end of this binary opposition in the narratives. Usually the social pole is given greater emphasis.

There are a few references to children's 'progress', without further specification, except in the case of reading, where reading ages are mentioned. Terms such as concept, understanding, generalization or insight simply do not occur in the data. In contrast, the social pole is continually mentioned: teachers specifically and repeatedly stress children's 'interest', 'involvement', 'enjoyment' and 'excitement'. More generally, they continually refer to relationships in the classroom and to the social situations in children's homes, sometimes with great detail. Parallel cognitive situations are never referred to.

The tension between the poles is most evident in the 'breakthrough' narratives, where cognitive learning is described, but the teachers' reactions are broadly social or emotional. They are 'thrilled', 'excited', 'surprised', 'delighted', but they do not specify exactly what children learned, or how, or how it might or should develop and why it was important or worthwhile.

## General < - - - > Technical

'Is the word "autonomy"? I've forgotten big words since I've been in this job.'

This polarity refers to the teachers' use of language, expressed on a continuum drawing on professional technical terms from disciplines relevant to education, as opposed to general everyday terms used to discuss education.

Teachers' narratives overwhelmingly avoid technical or more academic terms. It may well be that the teachers were perfectly capable of using technical language but that there are cultural inhibitions against using technical terms in the staffroom or that narrative does not require it. On the other hand, the topics would seem to require at least some technical reference: in children's learning and lesson planning, for example.

The teachers' use of metaphor is an interesting case of using general terms in contexts which would otherwise be expected to be technical. The teachers' metaphors are so frequent in use, yet so limited in range, that they appear to constitute a folk terminology for learning. The metaphors seem to aid verbalization about the unknown or the inexplicable, yet they may inhibit deeper reflection or professional development. To say 'it clicked', or 'light dawned' or 'she really came on in leaps and bounds' is meaningful as metaphorical description, but without further analysis does seem limited as a professional way of focusing on one of the central issues of education – children's learning.

As cultural descriptions, the metaphors provide a perspective in their own right. They could be used for conceptual or theoretical development, as metaphors are used in scientific research, but teachers do not seem to do this. In this polarity, the social and cultural pressures of the occupation seem to cause teachers to favour the general pole.

READING 5.3

# The self-determination of creative teachers

Peter Woods

This reading derives from research with teachers who maintained a highly creative approach to teaching over the period of the introduction of the National Curriculum, when many teachers were extremely stressed. We are introduced to teachers from Ensel and Coombes Primary Schools, Susan, Dave and Sue, and to the ways in which their 'self' was defended and realized through their work. In a sense this reading can be seen as an account of teachers' resistance to central direction when it was felt to be inappropriate. See also Reading 1.4 on 'creative mediation'.

Edited from: Woods, P. (1995) *Creative Teachers in Primary Schools.* Buckingham: Open University Press, 157–78

The teachers I studied have many things in common. They all have strong vocational and professional commitment to teaching. For them, teaching is the activity and the arena in which they become whole, achieve their ultimate ambitions, become the persons they wish to be. They are dedicated professionals who have given their lives and their selves to their job.

All teachers have certain primary interests. Pollard (1985), in examining how considerations of self bears on teachers' actions, identified certain interests associated with maintaining a sense of self in the classroom: maximizing enjoyment; controlling the workload; maintaining one's health and avoiding stress; retaining autonomy; maintaining one's self-image. All of these are important for our teachers, but the last is particularly so as the others are integral to it. From their perceptions of self arise their philosophies of teaching and their values.

Neither self nor creativity, however, is constant. Both are social products and are influenced by social circumstances. Berger (1963, p. 106) affirms that, 'the self is no longer a solid, given entity that moves from one situation to another. It is rather a process, continuously created and re-created in each social situation that one enters'. It is therefore in continual need of defence, maintenance and promotion. Some occasions and periods may be more favourable to promotion. Others may bring teachers' preferred perceptions of self under attack. Inasmuch as their work has become intensified, creative teachers would appear to be going through one of the latter periods.

To the extent that teachers' work is becoming intensified, so their selves are in danger of a degree of debasement – less autonomy, less choice, less freedom, less reflection, less individuality, less voice and ultimately perhaps, less commitment, and/or a change to a more instrumental form.

White (1993), lists self-determination as a core value in a liberal democratic society. Prominent aspects of this are defence, reinforcement, realization and renewal of the self. I shall examine examples of each.

## Self-defence

Nias's teachers (1989 [see Reading 5.1]), though undergoing continual professional development, were always at pains to protect their substantial selves from uncomplimentary change. She notes that the most effective form of self-protection was the reference group:

> Regular contact with other people who shared their beliefs about the social and moral purposes of education and about how children learnt, not only reinforced their view of

themselves but also enabled them to filter and even distort messages reaching them from other sources. (pp. 204–5)

We have seen how, in resistance at Ensel School, perceived assaults on the self threw people even closer together. But the self in these circumstances frequently has a resilience of its own, which contributes to the strength of the whole-school perspective. I identified the following factors.

## Individual biography

Teachers' theories are grounded in their own lives. The nature and significance of the perspective might not be realized at the time. It may be little more than vaguely but acutely felt experience, not articulated, but sedimented in the self in embryo. The influence of childhood years are formative. The following examples from Ensel School show other ways in which teacher beliefs have strong roots deep in their past. Some Ensel teachers claim that their practices are in large measure a reaction to their own earlier personal experiences. For instance, Susan as a child went to a 'very, very formal school', where you

> had to memorize and spew out information in examinations. You sit at a desk, listen, teacher imparts knowledge, you take it on board, do a spelling test, a maths test . . . and you don't really have much of a stake in your own learning.

Susan described her first teaching post as a:

> very difficult situation but with very, very, positive, constructive, supportive staff. Had it not been quite like that, I would have thought, 'Oh no, this progressive way of working doesn't work'. But I was supported, and it was a very good, positive model to start working, because it put into action a lot of things I'd been told at college.

Following that, she moved to an all-white, middle-class school where teachers practised more traditional methods:

> I couldn't really cope with that . . . There was no centrality and no basic philosophy . . . I was fighting and saying 'I don't believe in rote learning, they don't understand what they're doing. I'm going to teach differently', and they were saying, 'No, it's always been done like this' and 'we demand that you give my child spelling lists', and the head was supporting them. I thought, 'I can't work somewhere that doesn't really believe what I believe', and then I came here. So apart from that one year I've been very lucky.

Ensel teachers' initial training and educational studies introduced them to a range of their theory and practice that confirmed their intuition and cast new light on some of their own experiences. Training illuminated and legitimated their partially formed but keenly felt views, by introducing them to theory, literature and research; illustrating their application to practice; and giving realistic assessments of how they might become modified over time.

Their own professional experience as teachers validates the perspective. The particular circumstances of Ensel School, with its large proportion of children who speak English as a second language, stress the relevance of the perspective. There is a strong emphasis on issues of equality, social justice and multiculturalism. Access to the National Curriculum is a current major concern, with a strong focus of attention on language. Having 'assimilated cultural awareness', as Dave expressed it, teachers then proceed through trial and error. They refine approaches that work, modify those that do not, and reflect on circumstances that affect them. They build up a stock of experience, an accumulating resource with which to help meet new situations.

Collaboration through working and discussing with like-minded colleagues consolidates, defends and fortifies the perspective. It is difficult for creative teachers to survive on their own. Together, they are a potent force. Penny, who was at the time acting as mentor for Vanessa, said:

> It's lovely with Vanessa, because she shares the philosophy 100 per cent, and it's very easy for us to see the value in what each is doing. If I look in her classroom I can see all the good things that are going on.

By contrast, as Susan noted, 'If you've got rifts in the staffroom about various philosophies, then I think you've got problems'. She believes strongly in the idea of 'a team all working together to achieve the same ends'.

The whole-school perspective, especially where also supported by governors and parents, as at Ensel, is both a knowledge and a power base. It expands the range of thought and experience, offers therapy in times of difficulty, and resolve and determination when challenged. The perspective is not just a matter of cognition, but is part of the self infused with aesthetics and emotions.

Constraints delimit the perspective, bringing it to earth and gearing it to practicalities. Things like class size, lack of material resources, and the heavy demands of the National Curriculum can impede the prosecution of strategies indicated by theories emphasizing individualism, space and creativity. However, all teaching is constrained to some extent, and a modicum can lead to more creativity. The ideals guiding the perspective are principles to inform one's approach rather than ends to be met. The creative teacher is always trying to find ways to apply her principles, and to manage the constraints, which might involve outflanking them or using them to advantage.

## Self-reinforcement

Collaboration has been represented here as operating in self-defence. But it also operates in a more expansive sense.

The use of critical others illustrates a way in which the self can be reinforced. Critical others can help teachers recover their creativity, bring a long-standing ideal project to fruition, develop new interests, fain new insights into their selves through challenging basic assumptions, help cultivate charisma. Currently, there is a demand for more specialist teaching in primary schools (Alexander, 1992), and for greater flexibility in the teacher role (Campbell, 1993; Brighouse, 1994). Flexibility, however, is not a prominent attribute of extreme rational–legal systems. Critical others add to teachers' specialist knowledge, while still leaving the teacher in control as 'orchestrator' (Woods, 1990). They help them to be 'extended professionals' in Hoyle's (1980) sense of being interested in theory, involved in non-teaching professional activities, and reading professional literature. They help swing the always precarious balance between the preferred, principled mode of teaching, and pragmatic action forced by circumstantial dilemmas.

## Self-realization

Whereas self-defence is aligned against perceived threat, and self-reinforcement strengthens existing tendencies, self-realization is about coming to fruition. Perhaps the best example is in 'appropriation' at Coombes. At the centre of the Coombes achievement is the charismatic again, the head, who had the vision, faith, values and beliefs to launch the project, the resolve and patience to sustain and develop it, and the personal skills and judgement in surrounding herself with and inspiring like-minded people to contribute to the enterprise. At Coombes, there was a strong sense of purpose. At heart, there was a clear conviction about the central importance of environmental issues, a love of and deep respect for nature, a concern for the future of the planet. I asked Sue Humphries how she managed so often to get her own way with exterior bureaucratic forces, and she replied: 'Well, I think having a reputation as an eccentric helps'. Part of this 'eccentricity', perhaps, is Sue's ability to challenge the 'givens' of school, which Sarason (1982) feels is one of the most important factors in inducing change. Some of these 'givens' are the inside classroom as the main context of teaching and learning, the sharp division between inside and outside school, the playground as a plain hard surface, the National Curriculum, and assessment. At Coombes, Sue retains her independent vision. Certain aspects of the National Curriculum are welcome, others are an irritant, but, by and large, it is subsumed within their grand design. Sue makes capital in other ways. To run and develop such a project requires funds and services from others:

> We need money for repairs. For example, a pond cracked in last year's drought and will cost about £600 to put right . . . We also need money for ephemeral things, like feeding sheep, paying vets' bills, giving expenses to people like hot air balloonists . . . You can't actually see what they've left you with. They are the intangibles, but they are the things that give a quality and a certain edge to this kind of education, if it's what you believe in.

It also means entrepreneurial skills, powers of persuasion and considerable determination. To get opera singers, under-belly horse riders, internationally acclaimed writers, helicopter pilots, parachutists, etc., to the school, Sue feels rests on:

> the way you present the case, the tone of the approach, and the doggedness of the approach . . . and, of course, the way a group decides how it spends its money.

A colleague reported that 'when a small circus visited the area, Sue was absolutely determined we were going to get this camel into the playground . . . and she did it'. Why was it so important?

> It was to do with the Epiphany and the journey of the wise men, and it was really something that just put that special memory into all the talk that had gone on . . . Children are talked at by teachers for hundreds of hours, and so much of it must sail directly over them.

In many ways, Coombes is an expression of Sue's self.

## Self-renewal

Self-realization is never complete, but needs what Sue calls 'self-renewal'. Just as the self has a long history with deep biographical roots, so it has a constant dynamic which drives it on.

> The fact that we are deeply immersed in the work and energized by it is going to be the most significant thing, because if you're not, you become terribly tense and stressed. You avoid that with the constant novelty. (She mentioned things that were happening next term for the first time around the theme of 'the performing arts': an early harp recital, a brass quintet, street buskers . . .) Most teachers want to go back to teaching because they actually want to finish off their own education. This is a calling for us, but actually it's from needs which were never met when we were at school. You have this great hunger to continue to learn. If the teachers don't get satisfied, the children don't get the buzz out of it.

New themes, or new ways of approaching the same themes, was a deliberate policy. They believed in:

> first-class experiences for adults and children, so that they can resonate with those experiences and be energized next day.

A concert, for example, provided valuable reflective time . . . a chance to reorganize their thinking, to be refreshed, and up-and-running the next day.

It might take you away from a task, but 'you get back to it with renewed vigour'. Sue 'believed passionately in the ability of certain experiences to regenerate everyone', 'reflective nuggets' she called them, which were:

even more important now than formerly because of the mechanistic approaches induced by current developments.

Self-renewal was a major factor behind Peter's retirement. With his experiences of marginality, he needed disalientating experiences from time to time to retain realistic sight of his preferred side of the margins, and to reaffirm his perception of the substantial self. Even more than this, however, he felt that that self had not yet been fully realized, and still had great potential. Peter was fully committed to the integrity of the self. However, the strategies that he had developed over the years to protect that integrity were no longer sufficient. Retirement was a catalyst not only to save the self, but also to provide it with a springboard to new endeavour.

> I hope my retirement is not perceived as someone abandoning ship. Rather, it's transferring from one ship to another ship that's going rather more in the direction that I want to go.

Retirement for Peter, therefore, is a strategy to save and to promote the self. In those terms it is less radical than it may appear, since it is an act entirely consistent with his holistic philosophy. It is expansive and forward-looking, rather than traumatic and retreatist. In terms of self, Peter is making an empowered exit. For some, retirement might mean 'putting their feet up, having a rest, taking life easy'. But for Peter, retirement offered reinvigoration and rebirth through 'restoration', 'continuity' and an 'end of marginality'.

In England and Wales, 5549 teachers under the age of 60 retired on grounds of ill health in 1993–4, compared with 2551 in 1987–8, the year before the National Curriculum was introduced (Macleod and Meikle, 1994).

Self-determination takes its toll and has its limits. The self's defences can be penetrated. It can be weakened as well as reinforced, ruined as well as renewed. I am reluctant, however, to let intensification have the final work. Clearly it cannot be discounted. But my message is still an optimistic one, in terms of the principles for which these teachers stand, the degree for manoeuvre that is there between policy-making and implementation, teachers' undoubted successes, and the strength of their resolve. The future depends to a large extent, however, on a new generation of teachers, trained in the National Curriculum, but remembering the principles that others have fought for, and no less creative and self-determined.

## READING 5.4

# The worlds of children and adults

Bronwyn Davies

> Adults will need to draw on their commitment to open-mindedness when studying this reading, for Bronwyn Davies sets out the reasons why the perceptions of children may vary significantly from those of adults. The structural position of teachers and pupils is fundamentally different, and empathy and understanding is needed for adults to understand 'the culture of childhood'.
>
> To what extent do you really understand the way classroom and school life feels to young children?
>
> Edited from: Davies, B, (1982) *Life in the Classroom and Playground*. London: Routledge, 28–33

Adults structure the world in ways that appear external and inevitable to children, though children bring their own interpretations to bear upon these structures, and thus have a different view of them than adults do. Examples of such external and inevitable structures are: language and social skills necessary for getting about as a socially competent person. Additional structures which may not have the same degree of inevitability but which bind children to the adults' conceptual framework are schools and school attendance and the curriculum and basic skills, such as reading and writing useful for future occupation.

These are the 'givens' in the children's world which appear to be inevitable. Words have specific meanings, school is compulsory, social interaction is disrupted if you don't follow certain basic rules, and finally, teachers tell you certain things and then test you on them. These are the 'facts', external facts that must be incorporated into the world of children and which give them partial membership in the adults' world.

Yet despite the power of adults to define reality, children do develop their own manner of construing the world.

There are several fairly powerful reasons both from the adults' and from the children's perspective for the development of a separate world.

Adults have their own private life and expect children not to intrude on this. As a result, children spend more time with their peers who, because of their similar placement in the social world, are more likely to perceive similar problems. That is, problems that arise out of the nature of the institutions of family and school and their positions or roles within those institutions. And like-situated people will help formulate workable solutions, based on similar perspectives, perspectives that may well be incommensurate with parents' and teachers' perspectives. Further, adults may provide 'solutions' that are unworkable for children because the children do not have certain powers or the necessary skills to carry out adult solutions. Alternatively, adults provide solutions which require the child to act in ways that conflict with what he and his peers define as acceptable behaviour.

A further, and perhaps more compelling reason for the development of a separate culture is that the balance of power between children, particularly of the same age and size, is more handleable. Here the adult rules of unquestioned deference, politeness, respect for elders, can be dropped and a basis for relating in terms of equality worked out – or power differentials won through fighting or prowess clearly demonstrated, the rules being closer to what they can manage for themselves without adult interference. Moreover, since the rules are established through experience, they have greater immediacy and convincingness as rules to be followed. Resorting to adult authority can rob the children of their own power to make decisions and to control the situation.

The adults' perception of reality which they, as adults, assume to be superior does not always appear so to children. Because of the taken-for-granted knowledge which informs adults' world, they do not or cannot spell out to children why they think as they do. When children ask adults questions, the adults may produce what for them are hard-won solutions to earlier problems, and yet are, for the children, meaningless riddles because even where the adults are aware of the links they have made, the children can't trace the steps from the first viewing of the problem to the ultimate solution. And adults may not even answer children's questions at all. Children's questions can be irritating, embarrassing and awkward, and they may on occasion appear to be futile and pointless. Adults sometimes find the perspective from which children's questions arise quite beyond them.

And yes, if children behave like mini-adults, or converse in an adult manner (as Aries, 1962, has shown children of the past were wont to do), they are seen as inappropriate, even immoral. This ambivalence towards children – wanting them to be like adults and wanting them to be like children is an interestingly inconsistent feature of adults' attitudes towards children.

Children, to be acceptable, must act like children. Yet the credibility that adults are prepared to give to the associated world-view that goes with acting like or being a child is somewhat lacking. Children's views which differ markedly from adult views may be seen simply as a result of incomplete socialization or even failed socialization, rather than the legitimate products of another culture – the culture of childhood.

There is a further barrier that exists between the child's and the adult's reality which stems from the fact that the roles each are required to play within the school system lead to differing perceptions of what is relevant or meaningful.

For teachers, responsibility for discipline and for teaching create the central tasks relating to their role. What the teachers perceive in their day-to-day carrying out of their roles will be closely related to these central tasks. Though teachers may wish that children would take on these tasks as their own, they cannot escape from the fact that school is an adult-imposed institution and the curriculum and many of the requirements made of children in school are adult imposed. From the children's perspective, the aspects of their environment that they may feel they have some say in will more likely be how to avoid trouble with teachers, how to make and keep friends, and how to survive in the system.

These are the topics of conversation often touched on by the children. In looking at children's account of school it is clear that they have little interest in tasks related to the teacher's role. Those aspects of their lives that the children can most easily give accounts of are ones which they feel are related to their tasks rather than teacher-initiated tasks. For example, when I first started talking to the children I perceived the oft-used phrase 'I don't know' as an easy way out of not answering my questions, or as evasion. I began to realize, however, that 'I don't know' just as often signalled 'I don't know and I don't think I could or should know, since that is to do with the adult world.'

In other words, children develop the capacity to see clearly from their own position within the social structure, and do not worry unduly about what it looks like to the adults. It is enough to learn to play successfully the role of child without having to know more about adults than is necessary to interact with them. Yet the adults perceive their task, in socializing the children, as helping them to see the world correctly, i.e., as adults do, and as teaching them to become adults. Children are caught in a world where they must balance on the one hand the convincing world of adults. In this latter world of the adults, moreover, there is no real recognition of the former world as experienced and developed by the children. Adults provide structures which children are dependent on and legitimate these very structures in the process of socializing their children. Yet adults do not want children to share this adult world or to be adults But even without the rights enjoyed by adults, and despite the expectations placed on them as members of the institution of childhood, children busily get on with the business of constructing their own reality with each other, as well as making sense of and developing strategies to cope with the adult world as and when it impinges on their world. This reality and its related strategies I refer to as the culture of childhood.

📖 READING 5.5

# The social world of primary school learning

Andrew Pollard and Ann Filer

This reading summarizes a series of studies of social influences on children's learning in primary schools. In particular, it highlights key issues from *The Social World of the Primary School* (Pollard, 1985) and *The Social World of Children's Learning* (Pollard with Filer, 1996). Andrew Pollard and Ann Filer were particularly concerned to try to identify patterns in the ways in which children interpret and then respond to classroom, playground and family contexts. Their first attempts to do this used the concept of 'coping strategy'. Their analysis then evolved to focus on the development of each child's 'identity' as a learner, and on the ways in which this is progressively shaped by life experiences.

Edited from: Pollard, A. and Filer, A. (1999) *The Social World of Pupil Career: Strategic Biographies Through Primary School*. London, New York: Cassell, 10–19

Development of the concept of coping strategy can be traced through Woods (1977), Hargreaves (1978), Pollard (1982) and Filer (1993). It is the central concept in what has been an explicit attempt by qualitative sociologists to analyse the relationships between society and individuals, history and biography (see also Mills 1959, [Reading 4.1]).

The analysis recognizes the extent of structural, material and ideological constraint in society. In the case of education, this highlights the subservient position of schools and teachers within state policy frameworks, the limited resources made available, and the existence of particular conceptions and concerns about education which dominate the mind-set of much of the public and media. Children are also constrained, by legal restraints on their rights, dependence on parents or carers, media pressures, and by the existence of particular conceptions of what 'childhood' should be like and of how 'child' or 'pupil' roles should be fulfilled [see Reading 4.4]. Such pressures and constraints penetrate, and are mediated, through multiple levels of educational provision, until they have their effect in classroom contexts. We thus have particular curricula requirements, recommended pedagogies, prescribed forms of assessments, delineated resource frameworks, and management and accountability systems to which both teachers and pupils must respond. We can answer the question: 'What has to be "coped with"?'.

However, such an analysis cannot tell us what 'coping' will actually mean to any individual. To understand this, we need to know much more about the unique character of each person. In particular, we need to understand the subjective interpretations that each individual makes of the contexts in which they find themselves. The key factor here is that of 'self'. How does each person think about themselves? What is their sense of identity? How do they present themselves to others? Who, in the context of their social group, do they think they are? Study of the perspectives and self of individual pupils and teachers enable us to learn about their uniqueness, and about the ways in which they interpret their experiences. We can then address the question: 'What does coping mean for any particular individual?'.

*The Social World of the Primary School* (Pollard, 1985) began with just such an analysis of teacher and pupil perspectives. The data derived from interviews and participant observation with teachers and pupils in three primary schools. It was collected whilst Andrew Pollard was a practising teacher and, in one school, with the direct assistance of pupils themselves.

Regarding teachers, a major disjunction was identified between the 'educationist context' and the 'teacher context'. Whilst the former offered prescriptions on how teachers 'should' teach in line with educational theorizing and policy prescription, the latter spoke from the realities of classroom life. Thus, teachers' emphasized classroom management and the need to maintain discipline, together with the challenge of providing a stimulating and worthwhile curriculum. However, teachers also talked about how they coped with classroom life in much more personal ways. Starting from their own sense of 'self', they were concerned with retaining their dignity, with workload, health and stress issues, and with job satisfaction obtained through enjoyment of their work with children and the exercise of autonomous professional judgement in their classrooms.

Regarding pupils, a tension was identified between expectations of friends and peer culture, as developed in the informal contexts of the playground and beyond, and more formal requirements of teachers as a reflection of the school context. Normative prescriptions, both tacit and overt, delineated how pupils 'should' behave in school. Indeed, the teachers had clear ideas on the characteristics of their 'ideal pupil', to which some children were able to respond. On the other hand, the security and enjoyment of peer-group membership was very important for most children, reflecting shared experiences and a similar structural position of relative powerlessness in school. Underlying all this, more personal pupil concerns were detected, many of which were connected to the relative vulnerability of pupils in the evaluative setting of the school. Thus we have concerns with maintaining dignity and self-image, particularly when being 'told off', with workload and avoiding stress, and, as with teachers, with deriving enjoyment and self-fulfilment from classroom life.

In *The Social World of the Primary School* it was suggested that the personal concerns of teachers and pupils could be seen as 'primary interests-at-hand' in classroom life. This means that they would be seen as being fundamental to each individual's attempt to cope, and in this respect it is interesting to note a degree of overlap in the primary interests of teachers and pupils. However, to actually succeed in coping – to 'survive' – teachers and pupils must also address the particular context and structural position in which they find themselves, as indeed they do when interviewed. Teacher concerns with 'order' and 'instruction' and pupil concerns with 'peer-group membership' and 'learning' were identified, and these were defined as 'enabling interests-at-hand'. What was suggested, then, was that both teachers and pupils, as people, have a fundamental and primary concern with maintaining and defending their sense of 'self', but that they have to try to do that in different ways. Teachers work to cope personally by maintaining order and by teaching effectively, whilst pupils cope by trying to achieve an appropriate balance between maintaining their peer-group status and satisfying school goals though learning.

Figure 5.5.1 sets out the key elements of this analysis.

Of course, a vital, additional element of this story is the fact that teachers and pupils have to cope with each other in classrooms. The fact is that both parties do have sufficient power to threaten the interests of the other. For teachers, this power is ascribed and backed by their socially sanctioned role. They can thus draw on support from other adults in school, at home and beyond, and the expectation is that they will initiate, lead and evaluate most classroom activities. Pupils largely accept this teacher authority and, on an individual basis, each may feel personally vulnerable. However, each class of pupils also has a considerable amount of power over their teacher, for collectively they can threaten classroom order and instruction and challenge the teacher's self-confidence. Further, as Waller (1932) demonstrated, there is latent conflict in all classrooms, since the basic yardstick of teacher success is to achieve some change in pupils' thinking to which they may, or may not, be receptive. The reality however, is that life in primary school classrooms is very rarely conflictual. How is this achieved?

*The Social World of the Primary School* analysed teacher–pupil relationships as a process of negotiation through which tacit understanding and rules are evolved [see also Reading 6.4]. A 'process of establishment' (Ball, 1980) at the start of each school year is a particularly active period during which teachers normally take the initiative. Pupils get to know their teacher's expectations but will also test his or her skill and resolve. Because both

|  | Teachers | Pupils |
|---|---|---|
| **Primary interests-at-hand** | SELF<br>• self-image<br>• workload<br>• health and stress<br>• enjoyment<br>• autonomy | SELF<br>• maintenance of self-image<br>• retention of dignity<br>• control of stress<br>• enjoyment |
| **Enabling interests-at-hand** | Order<br>Instruction | Peer-group membership<br>Learning |

**Figure 5.5.1** Primary and enabling interests of teachers and children (from Pollard 1985, pp. 35 and 82)

teachers and pupils have sufficient power to threaten the interests of the other, there are genuine negotiations over issues such as noise levels, movement, behaviour, quality and quantity of work and routine procedures. Gradually the class becomes more 'settled' as understandings, conventions and taken-for-granted rules become established. Such a 'working consensus' reflects mutual acceptance by the teacher and pupils. Whilst each could disturb the life of the other, negotiation produces sufficient understanding to enable them to 'get along together' in reasonably amicable ways. A type of moral order in the classroom is established.

However, not all pupils will interpret classroom rules and understandings in the same ways, nor do all pupils face similar circumstances in their lives. In *The Social World of the Primary School* three types of pupil friendship group were identified from detailed study of one year-group of eleven-year-olds. 'Goodies' were relatively conformist but did not attain particularly highly. A significant proportion were girls' groups, but by no means all. Regarded as 'quiet but dull', they were not popular with their other peers and were sometimes overlooked by teachers. 'Gangs', on the other hand were quite prepared to be disruptive, particularly if they became bored or felt that they had been 'picked on'. They were generally less successful academically than most of the pupils but revelled in their reputations as 'rough and tough'. More, but not all, of the gang groups were made up of boys and they tended to be from lower social-class family backgrounds. The most successful type of group were termed 'Jokers'. Although of both sexes, Jokers often came from more middle-class families. These children were able to perform well academically and were also popular with their peers. They were active in sport and school events and took a disproportionate share of school responsibilities. Apart from their capabilities, they were distinguished by the close relationships which they established with their teachers and by their social awareness and skill. They could thus 'read' an evolving classroom situation, and 'have a laugh' with their teacher whilst also being alert to signals which might indicate a change of mood. For many teachers, these were seen as 'ideal' pupils.

Figure 5.5.2 represents the differences between these three types of group in terms of their response to classroom rules. It is suggested that the central role in the negotiation of the working consensus is played by members of Joker groups, who use their skills, reputation and relationship to work with the teacher whilst also having a little mischief or light relief along the way. Teachers tend to indulge this within reason, for it also provides them with some amusement, diversion and enjoyment whilst not threatening their primary interests. Goodies then conform to the teacher expectations, and may even remain nervous about 'doing something wrong'. Gang members, on the other hand, may not feel constrained by the

| | Actions within the understandings of the working consensus | | Unilateral actions |
|---|---|---|---|
| | Conformity | Routine deviance | Rule-framed disorder |
| Goodies | >>>>>>>> | | |
| Jokers | >>>>>>>>>>>>>>>>>>>>>>>>>>>>>> | | |
| Gangs | >>>>>>>>>>>>>>>>>>>>>>>>>>>>>>>>>>>>>>>>>>>>>>>>>> | | |

**Figure 5.5.2**  Parameters of child behaviour (from Pollard 1979, p. 90)

working consensus. If they feel aggrieved by something that the teacher has done, they may act unilaterally and challenge the teacher in disorderly ways. In so doing, their actions will be framed by the different set of rules which have been negotiated within the peer group.

*The Social World of the Primary School* thus provided a sociological analysis of teacher and pupil perspectives, of classroom relationships and of coping strategies. However, it did not directly face the question of children's learning itself, or of how children develop their perspectives and identities as learners over time.

## Social relationships, learning and development

*The Social World of Children's Learning* (Pollard with Filer, 1996) is based on a detailed longitudinal ethnography in one primary school tracking pupils from the age of 4 and through their schooling. They were followed to age 16 when they took their GCSEs.

The book was intended to make a contribution to a 'sociology of learning' (Pollard, 1990) and it explicitly attempted to link symbolic interactionist sociology with social constructivist psychology. Social constructivism derives from the work of Vygotsky (1962, 1978, [Reading 7.3]) who suggested how language, conceptual tools and meanings are culturally embedded, and how social processes can extend or constrain the learner. From this perspective, the traditional concerns of psychology, such as 'ability', motivation, cognition, memory and attainment, are seen as providing only a partial account of influences on learning. Thus Bruner (1990, [Reading 7.8]) for instance, argues for a 'cultural psychology' which would unite social and psychological factors in an integrated and holistic analysis.

*The Social World of Children's Learning* was intended to provide an analysis of social influences on the learning of young children as they developed from year to year. We focused particularly on three clusters of influence: on the homes, parents and siblings; on the school playground and peer relations; and on the classrooms and interaction with each child's successive teachers. The book provided very detailed case-studies of these influences on the learning of five children over the three years of Key Stage 1 (ages 4/5, 5/6 and 6/7).

In terms of its research design, the longitudinal ethnography represents three crucial forms of development beyond that of *The Social World of the Primary School*. First, the focus is on individual children; second, they are studied longitudinally; and third, each of the most significant social contexts in their lives are included in the study. The result is an extremely holistic set of case-study accounts of young people growing up in their families and community. Using narrative approaches, biographical stories of development and change were constructed. Five deceptively simple questions were posed, and these are represented in Figure 5.5.3.

The first question, 'When and where is learning taking place?', asserts the significance of the socio-historical context. This requires that attention is paid to the social, cultural,

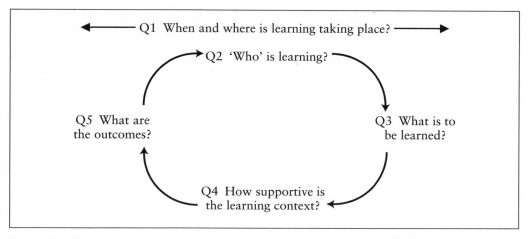

**Figure 5.5.3** A simple model of learning, identity and social setting (from Pollard with Filer 1996, p. 14)

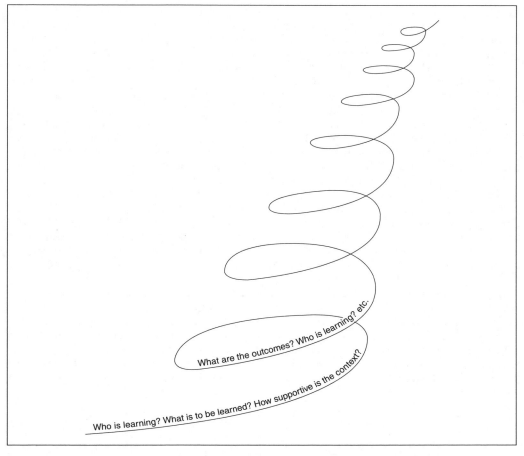

**Figure 5.5.4** The spiral of learning and identity (Pollard with Filer 1996, p. 284)

economic and political circumstances of the country, region, city, community, families and school in relation to the period of the study (see, for instance, Chapter 4 of *Reflective Teaching* and in this book).

'Who is learning?', which is a reference to the key issue of identity – of 'self'. In *The Social World of Children's Learning* each child's sense of self is seen primarily as a product of their relationships with significant others. However, the influence of biological endowment and social circumstances are also considerable. Thus interpersonal factors in the development of identity are conditioned by both intellectual and physical potential and by the opportunities or constraints afforded by the material, cultural and linguistic resources available to each family.

The third question, 'What has to be learned?', draws attention to the form and content of new learning challenges and to the learning stance and strategies which each child adopts. New learning challenges arrive in the form of experiences and relationships as well as in the form of curricular tasks. In each case, the content of the particular learning challenge will affect each child's motivation and self-confidence. In turn, this may affect the range of strategic resources on which they draw.

'How supportive is the learning context?' takes us back to questions about the quality of classroom relationships and the working consensus. Put another way, 'How is power used, and how does this affect children's willingness to take risks as they engage in learning?'. This issue is as apposite in homes as it is in schools. It is complemented by a further set of questions about adult provision: 'What is the quality of assistance in learning?', 'Is instruction well matched to the child's cognitive and motivational needs?' 'Does the adult have appropriate knowledge and skill to offer the child?'. The analysis of case-study children in *The Social World of Children's Learning* shows that children learn most in an atmosphere in which they feel secure and when they are offered appropriate instruction by more knowledgeable others.

Question five, 'What are the outcomes?', draws attention both to formal and informal outcomes. In formal terms, the learner achieves a new capability, attainment or standard, and may even be tested and certificated for it. In terms of identity formation, however, the informal processes which then occur as friends, family and teachers affirm, mediate and interpret those achievements are perhaps even more significant. The consequence is that social status and self-esteem are both affected and their influence rolls round to contribute once more to the question, "Who' is learning?". Interestingly, such overall processes can also be seen as socially embedded forms of assessment [see Reading 14.7].

The cyclical process which has been described above is dynamic and continuous, as is demonstrated through the narratives of our own lives and those of our children and pupils. We see it as a fundamental process which continues through life, with key questions and factors being played out through successive episodes and phases of experience. And so we become what we are, as we interpret past experiences and respond to new ones, and develop further again. As Rowan Williams (cited in Maitland, 1991) put it: 'the self is, one might say, what the past is doing now'.

Figure 5.5.4 represents this spiral continuing through life, with positive, progressive imagery. Analytically, this is accurate, for the process will continue as individuals construct their 'strategic biographies'. However, as we all know, the outcomes of life experience vary considerably for different individuals, and sociologists attempt to trace patterns for richer and poorer, male and female, white and black, old and young, healthy and less-healthy, etc. Schooling, of course, is an important early influence on such trajectories. (See Reading 7.11 for an application of this model to recent developments in primary education policy and experience.)

READING 5.6

# The importance of gender identity during school transfer

Carolyn Jackson and Joanna Warin

This reading highlights the ways in which children seek the reassurance of culturally approved gender identities at times when their sense of 'self' may feel threatened. Jackson and Warin draw particular attention to periods of school transfer, and draw on their studies of first entry to school and of primary–secondary transfer.

Can you think of examples of this phenomenon? What implications might it have for how transfers and transitions are managed?

Edited from: Jackson, C. and Warin, J. (2000) 'The importance of gender as an aspect of identity at key transition points in compulsory education', *British Educational Research Journal*, **26** (3), 375–88

Why is gender a particularly significant aspect of identity during the phases of life when a person is undergoing a major change from one set of circumstances to another? We explore the commonalties of such changes or transition points through a focus on gender which, we suggest, acts as a very basic principle of cultural categorization. This suggestion rests on two premises. First, knowledge of gender group membership is a highly accessible aspect of sociocultural information. We are not wanting to claim that such knowledge is the only categorization principle since ethnicity and class, for example, are also likely to operate as key concepts within the organization of identity. Nevertheless, awareness of one's own gender, and the gender of others, is knowledge that is laid down early on in life and which then proceeds to be a salient aspect of the sociocultural world. Second, during phases of disequilibrium such as a person's entry to an unfamiliar social context, there is a dependence on the more entrenched aspects of self-concept, that is, those that have been tried and tested over time. Putting these ideas together, it seems highly plausible that gender operates as a key organizational feature of identity during transitional phases.

We illustrate the importance of gender during times of transition by focusing upon two studies, each conducted at a different transition point of the school career. Locating her study within the first years of formal schooling, Warin (1998) undertook a series of longitudinal case studies aiming to describe the role of gender awareness during the first transition. A sample of ten children was involved in the research, which spanned a period of several months before their induction into reception class until the end of their second year of school. Jackson's study (1997) focused on the transition from primary to secondary schooling in one inner-city comprehensive school. The school is a mixed-sex comprehensive located in the south-west of England.

Why are transitions significant with respect to identity? Transitional points are particularly rich sites for exploring changes in a person's construction of self. Entry into a new social context entails a reappraisal of self-beliefs and may act as a catalyst for significant changes.

Transitional phases require a person to 'cope'. The idea of 'coping' is a particularly appropriate way of conceptualizing the operation of the sense of self since it incorporates both cognitive and affective dimensions. The term 'coping' conveys the person confronting the threats, anxieties, challenges and excitements of unfamiliar environments. It also conveys the person schematizing and managing a new range of experience and relating new experiences to old ones. The idea of the construction of self as the method by which a person copes is a way of marrying up both the cognitive and affective imperatives facing the child in relation to her/his environment. How then does a person cope during transitions? One obvious and accessible principle to select, manage and organize the volume of stimuli is to categorize it on the basis of what is 'like me' and what is 'unlike me', in other words to make social comparisons.

A very brief description of the conduct of a child from Warin's (1998) range of reception case studies will serve to illustrate how an awareness of gender guided the child's early social comparisons and construction of self. The example derives from Sophia's first three months at school. During this time, Sophia developed an identity as a hardworking schoolgirl. From her first few days at school she developed a friendship with two other girls and together, as a threesome, they sought and gained approval from their admired, female teacher. They gained her approval by engaging conscientiously and enthusiastically in pre-reading and writing activities in which there was a subtle blend of cooperation and competition between the three of them. Sophia demonstrated awareness of the classroom rules and conformed to both the explicit and implicit aspects of classroom expectations. She developed successful relationships with female peers and she developed a good rapport with her female class teacher. She put particular effort into the more 'academic' of the classroom activities on offer. These three aspects of her behaviour reinforced and compounded each other, providing continuity in her awareness of self and others. Consequently, she very quickly established a secure and consistent position in the class in relation to peers, school staff and the curriculum. It is possible to view this behaviour through the lenses of gender. It seems highly plausible that a gendered sense of self was guiding Sophia in much of this behaviour. This claim can be illustrated by considering one particular aspect of this group of associated behaviours, namely, her approach to peers during the first few days in her reception class.

> Video-recordings of Sophia during the first four days provide evidence of a child who is aware of opportunities for social interaction and who is developing strategies for making contact with her peers. She looks about her, her gaze follows certain individuals, she moves closer to them, moves her chair up, or stands next to them, and she imitates their behaviour. However, these strategies are directed exclusively towards her female class-mates. The following account, derived from a video-recording, describes her first verbal interaction with a classmate, Jennifer.

> Sophia and Jennifer are sitting side by side. They are both drinking their milk and each is eating a piece of fruit. They both look relaxed and content, and although they are not looking at each other, and have not exchanged words, they are both aware of each other's presence since they both seem to be making small sideways glances. Sophia moves her chair closer to Jennifer. There is a loud and competitive conversation at the next table between two boys concerning their Dads: 'my Dad could batter yours', says one; 'Well my Dad could batter yours', says the other. Jennifer looks at Sophia, leans towards her in a conspiratorial manner and says, 'My Dad could batter all of them', whereupon they both giggle, using matching gestures with hands to their mouths. Sophia moves her chair nearer still. Then her attention is caught by some activity outside the window. She stands up and watches the Juniors who are going into the playground. 'My sister's out there', she says. She sits down again. 'My sister's in Mrs Brown's.' They trade their knowledge about the school since both have older sisters. 'Mrs White?' asks Jennifer and Sophia repeats 'Mrs Brown'. Both girls happen to have identical hairstyles on this particular day. Jennifer leans over and frees Sophia's pony tail since it is trapped against her back, against the chair seat. She stretches it out, looking at the length of it. Then Sophia reaches for Jennifer's pony tail and does exactly the same. At that moment their tête-à-tête is interrupted by the school bell.

This interaction can be interpreted in the light of Martin and Halverson's (1981) exposition of the role of gender awareness mediating a process of rudimentary social comparisons, selecting the self-relevant features of the environment and filtering out those aspects that are not self-relevant. Sophia sat next to another girl, self-relevant, who had a particular hairstyle, self-relevant, and an older sister, self-relevant.

The transfer from primary to secondary school is undoubtedly a difficult time for many pupils. Many of the anxieties apparent at the point of starting formal education are replicated at this stage of the school career. Structural and organizational differences between the two school settings provide pupils with the most apparent changes. The sheer size of the secondary school relative to the primary school renders most pupils feeling rather lost. Interviews with Year 7 pupils about the main differences between primary school and secondary school inevitably prompt the response that secondary school is 'so big that I keep getting lost all the time'. In addition to the increase in size, organizational differences loom large. Eccles *et al.* (1984) point out that in contrast to primary schools, secondary schools usually group classes by ability, and whole-class teaching by subject-specialist teachers is common. The general ethos of the secondary school is more competitive than that of the primary school, and there is a focus upon ability rather than effort at the secondary level. This list is by no means exhaustive, but offers merely a taster of the variety of changes that occur over the primary to secondary transfer. Furthermore, this move from an environment that is familiar and therefore relatively 'safe' into an environment that is unfamiliar and so less 'safe' is recognized to prompt a number of negative consequences. For example, evidence suggests declines in self-esteem following the transfer from primary to secondary school (Wigfield *et al.* 1991); Harter *et al.* (1992) revealed an increase in school-related anxiety post-transfer; and pupils demonstrate a decline in adaptive forms of motivation following the transition (Galloway *et al.*, 1998).

How, then, does this transfer process impact upon identity? In research undertaken by Jackson (1997) both the girls and the boys interviewed during the course of the study indicated gendered social comparison patterns – both groups indicated a tendency to compare with same-sex others.

However, despite this tendency common to the majority of both boys and girls to express a preference to compare with same-sex others, evidence suggests that girls and boys respond in gender-specific ways. First, there is a gender difference in the ways that pupils respond to the transfer – girls shifted their social comparison patterns far more than the boys did. Second, there is a gender dimension to the ways that girls respond to the transfer – more girls expressed a preference to compare with girls rather than with boys after the transfer than was the case before the transfer. Many boys respond by increasing their levels of competition, status-seeking and issuing put-downs and challenges. Many girls respond to their new environment and to the increasingly threatening behaviour of boys by retreating into girls-only groups, and by avoiding contact and social comparisons with the boys. Thus, for both groups gender is central to 'protecting their selves'. For the boys this involves avoiding overt comparisons with the girls, and hence avoiding the embarrassment and teasing that ensues from such comparisons.

A central notion of our analysis is that people rely on a sense of gender to cope with the unfamiliar. Whilst anecdotal evidence suggests that this reliance on gender occurs in a wide range of settings, the focus in this piece has been upon two major educational transitions, namely, the start of formal education and the transfer from primary to secondary school. We have argued that at times of transition the self-system avoids cognitive overload of relying upon basic categorizing systems, one of which is gender.

The conclusions presented here pose a dilemma for both teachers and educational policy-makers. Teachers want to support the socio-emotional processes that will help the child to develop a secure sense of self, and they acknowledge the centrality of gender within this process. However, many teachers increasingly want to promote more gender-flexible ways of being. The solution is perhaps for teachers and policy-makers to steer a delicate course, balancing a sensitivity to the young person's development of a gendered self whilst attempting to extend perceptions of what it means to be male or female. Davies (1987) suggests such an approach:

Children much be encouraged to find ways of signalling their maleness and femaleness without limiting or constricting their potential. Most children will need a great deal of support and reassurance in this extension of themselves into liberated forms of activity. (pp. 56–7)

## READING 5.7

# Identity, migration and education

Uvanney Maylor

This is a short reading which is intended to signal the very important topics of how biography and structural position affect pupil experiences. Uvanney Maylor reflects on the upbringing she received from her father, who had come to the UK from Jamaica, and she provides an account of her own experiences and feelings as a black child in predominantly white schools. The important point is that all children are affected by the circumstances of, and relationships within, their family. Some are likely to be advantaged and others disadvantaged in a society in which inequalities are endemic. However, teachers have the responsibility to maximize the quality of life and fulfilment of potential of each and every child.

Edited from: Maylor, U. (1995) 'Identity, migration and education', in Blair, M. and Holland, J. (eds) *Identity and Diversity*. Clevedon: Multilingual Matters, 39–49

The autobiography outlined below is my version of events. A mere fraction of my whole life, it is what I could safely allow the public to know without knowing all of me. It is part of the journey I took to becoming an 'educated self'.

My mother died when I was three years old. Since that day my father has been mother and father to me. He seemed to me to be at once all knowing and frightening. In one breath he could shout loudly in anger and in another he would quietly reveal the wealth of historical data he had acquired as a child and as an adult. He expected obedience at all times, and adhered to the philosophy of 'spare the rod and spoil the child'. But although some might consider this a violent philosophy, I never thought of my father as a violent man.

He seemed to me to be kind, generous and thoughtful. Materially, I wanted for nothing, but I did crave a more open demonstration of the love he had for me. I suppose the love that might have been there for me died when my mother passed away. I had never considered my father unloving until I was about ten years old when I began to notice that he did not return my kiss as he left for work. I was always the demonstrative one – I liked to be loved.

Father was 'a man's man', an authoritarian. In his relations with women and children he considered himself always to be right, never wrong. This was a particularly difficult trait of his personality. It did not matter how plausible your explanation was, if it did not coincide with his it was automatically deemed wrong.

It is difficult to assess whether my father's assumed power would have gone unchallenged had my mother lived. However, such dominance needs to be understood in the light not only of a patriarchal culture, but the social context in which my father found himself after my mother's death. On reflection, I associate his need to be respected, to be obeyed, to have status, with his status in Britain. When he arrived in Britain, the difficulties in settling in a foreign land were compounded by the denial and rejection of his skills as a tailor, of him as a man. He was vilified because of the colour of his skin. Coming from a country where his family name commanded respect, father found his treatment difficult to comprehend.

Father was a proud man, who had assumed that his British passport afforded him the rights that fellow citizens took for granted. He found it difficult to acknowledge the alien and lowly status accorded to him. With these denials it is possible to understand why father proceeded on the track that he did. He sought to regain his pride through the achievements of his children, and with my brother and sister still in Jamaica, I bore the brunt of his ambitions. Father's belief in Britain as a meritocratic society created several problems for me.

Father believed implicitly in the power of education. He lived by such maxims as: 'if at first you don't succeed, try and try again'; 'never let them use your colour as an excuse not to employ you, let it be for lack of qualification'. Dad's obsession with education was both the source of my subordination at home and the key to my freedom.

He believed that with education came a good job, a decent income, decent housing, better economic and social opportunities and more importantly the ability to choose.

Unfortunately, father did not realize that the very education system in which he placed so much faith, was built upon and perpetuated the social divisions of class and 'race' now responsible for his diminished self-image. Like Martin Luther King, father had a dream, but it was a dream of social mobility. A dream thwarted in a world where skin colour persisted as a marker of exclusion. A fact which father would not acknowledge.

From the age of 7, life at school was a constant struggle. At that point in time I became more aware of my racial identity. As one of a small minority of black pupils, I was subjected to continuous racial abuse. I wore my hair in plaits to school – it was both convenient and made my hair easier to manage. The partings in my hair led the children to invent the nickname of 'square head'. I longed for the day when I could wear my hair in one as the other girls did. I was 'affectionately' known as 'blackie'/'darkie'. At secondary school 'square head' was replaced by 'monkey'. The contrast between my dark skin and white teeth provided a source of derision for one of my teachers: 'if we turn the lights out we will be able to see Uvanney's teeth'.

It was not the name calling which bothered me so much – it was the malicious intent that I found painful. These were children with whom I shared 35 hours of the week. I considered them to be my friends. Behind their surface smiles seemed to lurk a mountain of hostility. Who taught them to hate me? And why did racial forms of abuse hurt me so much more than any other forms? Although I did not understand it at the time, I realize now that this kind of abuse did not make me feel less of a person, less human, but I must have known at some level that they also referred to my father, my friends and all the other black people in the world.

## CHAPTER 6

# Relationships. How are we getting on together?

The seven readings in this chapter address various aspects of the 'classroom climate' – an important factor in creating positive conditions for learning.

The first two readings are classics. Withall and Lewis (6.1) describes the research that demonstrated the importance of leadership style on interpersonal relationships. On the other hand, from the pupil perspective, the experience of schooling is described by Jackson (6.2) in terms of 'crowds, praise and power'.

This is followed by three articles directly on teacher–pupil relationships. Whilst Woods (6.3) emphasizes the 'art' of teaching, Pollard (6.4) analyses the negotiation of classroom rules. These papers are complementary in analysing major processes in the formation of classroom relationships and their significance. The key concept, that of 'the working consensus', is reinforced by extensive observational research by Galton and his colleagues (6.5). In particular, they show how teacher style and pupil responses tend to vary together.

Finally, the chapter focuses on teacher expectations and their consequences. Evidence of their impact, both positive and negative, are reviewed by Gipps and MacGilchrist (6.6). Lawrence, in Reading 6.7, offers a very clear account of the important issue of self-esteem. This may be enhanced or diminished by a great many influences, but teacher actions are among the most significant.

The parallel chapter of *Reflective Teaching* addresses similar issues and provides practical classroom activities for investigating them further. There are sections on interpersonal relationships, on negotiating classroom rules and on enhancing classroom climate through the development of children's self-esteem and incorporative strategies such as 'circle time'. There are suggestions for 'Key Reading' and *RTweb* also offers further ideas.

📖 READING 6.1

# Leadership and the socio-emotional climate in classrooms

John Withall and W. W. Lewis

This reading is a short description of a very influential, early research study which shows how an adult's leadership style can affect the behaviour of a group. It has clear implications for teachers and suggests that a 'democratic' approach to classroom relationships can produce a positive climate for learning and behaviour.

How would you characterize your own leadership style in the classroom?

Edited from: Withall, J., and Lewis, W. W. (1963) 'Social/emotional climate in the classroom', in Gage, N. L. (ed.) *Handbook of Research on Teaching*. American Educational Research Association, 696–7

The early work on the effect of social climate and of leadership roles on group life and productivity is best represented by Lippitt's Iowa investigation (Lewin, Lippitt and White, 1939). He organized four clubs of five boys each. The boys were eleven years old and drawn from public state (i.e. maintained) school populations. Each club met for six weeks under a leader who implemented a specified style of leadership. Thus, in a consecutive eighteen-week period the four clubs each had three different leaders who employed either a democratic, autocratic, or laisser-faire leadership style. The leadership styles were rotated among the several leaders so that personality might be partially ruled out as a biasing factor. Two clubs met concurrently in adjoining rooms and were headed by leaders implementing two different leadership methodologies according to stated criteria. Two sets of observers recorded: quantitative running accounts of social interaction between the five boys and the leader; a continuous stenographic record of the conversation of the six persons in each club; activity subgroupings and activity goals of each; a running account of psychologically interesting interactions in each group; and an account of interclub contacts. The mean percentage of agreement between two investigators categorizing the verbal behaviour was 80 per cent. Other data included interview material secured from each club member; interview data from the parents of the boys at the end of the experiment; ratings by parents of a boy's cooperativeness, hobbies, and developmental history; information on the boy filled out by his room teacher; and, finally, the results of a Rorschach test given to each child. Analyses were made of the verbal behaviour of the six individuals in each club. Their social behaviour was analysed in terms of: 'ascendant', 'fact-minded', 'submissive' and 'ignoring' categories.

Lippitt's major conclusions were:

- that different styles of leader behaviour produce differing social climates and differing group and individual behaviours;

- that conversation categories differentiated leader–behaviour techniques more adequately than did social behaviour categories;

- that different leaders playing the same kind of leadership roles displayed very similar patterns of behaviour and that group members reacted to the same kind of leadership style in strikingly similar and consistent fashion;

- that group members in a democratic social climate were more friendly to each other, showed more group-mindedness, were more work-minded, showed greater initiative, and had a higher level of frustration tolerance than members in the other groups;

● that leader–behaviour categories represent the important parameters to which the children reacted.

The significance of Lippitt's work lies in the fact that it is the earliest, major, successful attempt to observe and control objectively the climate variable in group life. His clear demonstration of the influence of the leader on group life and productivity had strong implications for teachers and education.

<hr>

### READING 6.2

# Life in classrooms

## Philip Jackson

> This a short extract from Philip Jackson's classic book which revolutionized ways of thinking about classrooms by highlighting the experience of pupils. He sets out the nature of school attendance and of the school context: schooling is compulsory; a pupil is one in the classroom crowd; is subject to praise or sanction; and is constrained by the power of the teacher. There are echoes here of Reading 5.4, in which Davies analyses 'the worlds of children and adults'.
>
> Crowds, praise and power are inevitable elements of children's school experiences, and they gradually learn to adapt and cope with them. The most rapid adaption is needed at school entry but the issues never entirely go away. Can you identify children in your class who adapt particularly well, and others who have difficulties? How does this issue of social adaption affect their learning?
>
> Edited from: Jackson, P. W. (1968) *Life in Classrooms*. New York: Teachers College Press, 4–11

School is a place where tests are failed and passed, where amusing things happen, where new insights are stumbled upon, and skills acquired. But it is also a place in which people sit, and listen, and wait, and raise their hands, and pass out paper, and stand in line, and sharpen pencils. School is where we encounter both friends and foes, where imagination is unleashed and misunderstanding brought to ground. But it is also a place in which yawns are stifled and initials scratched on desktops, where milk money is collected and lines are formed. Both aspects of school life, the celebrated and the unnoticed, are familiar to all of us, but the latter, if only because of its characteristic neglect, seems to deserve more attention than it has received to date from those who are interested in education.

In order to appreciate the significance of trivial classroom events it is necessary to consider the frequency of their occurrence, the standardization of the school environment, and the compulsory quality of daily attendance. We must recognize, in other words, that children are in school for a long time, that the settings in which they perform are highly uniform, and that they are there whether they want to be or not. Each of these three facts, although seemingly obvious, deserves some elaboration, for each contributes to our understanding of how students feel about and cope with their school experience.

The magnitude of 7000 hours spread over six or seven years of a child's life is difficult to comprehend. Aside from sleeping, and perhaps playing, there is no other activity that occupies as much of the child's time as that involved in attending school. Apart from the bedroom there is no single enclosure in which he spends a longer time than he does in the classroom. From the age of six onward he is a more familiar sight to his teacher than to his father, and possibly even to his mother.

Thus, when our young student enters school in the morning he is entering an environment with which he has become exceptionally familiar through prolonged exposure. Moreover, it is a fairly stable environment – one in which the physical objects, social relations, and major activities remain much the same from day to day, week to week, and even, in certain respects, from year to year. Life there resembles life in other contexts in some ways, but not all. There is, in other words, a uniqueness to the student's world. School, like church and home, is some place special. Look where you may, you will not find another place quite like it.

There is an important fact about a student's life that teachers and parents often prefer not to talk about, at least not in front of students. This is the fact that young people have to be in school, whether they want to be or not. The school child, like the incarcerated adult, is, in a sense, a prisoner. He too must come to grips with the inevitability of his experience. He too must develop strategies for dealing with the conflict that frequently arises between his natural desires and interests on the one hand and institutional expectations on the other.

In sum, classrooms are special places. The things that make schools different from other places are not only the paraphernalia of learning and teaching and the educational content of the dialogues that take place there. There are other features, much less obvious though equally omnipresent, that help to make up 'the facts of life', as it were, to which students must adapt.

They may be introduced by the key words: crowds, praise and power.

Learning to live in a classroom involves, among other things, learning to live in a crowd. Most of the things that are done in school are done with others, or at least in the presence of others, and this fact has profound implications for determining the quality of a student's life.

Of equal importance is the fact that schools are basically evaluative settings. The very young student may be temporarily fooled by tests that are presented as games, but it doesn't take long before he begins to see through the subterfuge and comes to realize that school, after all, is a serious business. It is not only what you do there but what others think of what you do that is important. Adaptation to school life requires the student to become used to living under the constant condition of having his words and deeds evaluated by others.

School is also a place in which the division between the weak and the powerful is clearly drawn. This may sound like a harsh way to describe the separation between teachers and students, but it serves to emphasize a fact that is often overlooked, or touched upon gingerly at best. Teachers are indeed more powerful than students, in the sense of having greater responsibility for giving shape to classroom events, and this sharp difference in authority is another feature of school life with which students must learn how to deal.

In three major ways then – as members of crowds, as potential recipients of praise or reproof, and as pawns of institutional authorities – students are confronted with aspects of reality that at least during their childhood years are relatively confined to the hours spent in classrooms. It is likely during this time that adaptive strategies having relevance for other contexts and other life periods are developed.

## READING 6.3

# Teachers and classroom relationships

## Peter Woods

> In this interesting reading, Peter Woods grapples with the issue of how teachers derive fulfilment from their work. He relates this to the 'art' of managing classroom relationships to minimize conflictual aspects of the teacher role. He identifies the skills which contribute towards the 'productive blend' of rapport and control which is often found in primary school classroom as teachers resolve the dilemmas that must be faced.
>
> Edited from: Woods, P. (1987) 'Managing the primary teachers' role', in Delamont, S. (ed.) *The Primary School Teacher*. London: Falmer Press, 120–43

Why do teachers carry on teaching? Material rewards are not great, unlike the risk of stress, so there must be other factors. Prominent among these, according to Pollard (1985) is 'enjoyment' deriving from the pleasure of working with children, but curiously this has been largely left out of account in consideration of the teacher role – probably as a legacy of the tendency to see the world largely through official interpretations.

There are at least three interrelated reasons why this is so. The first is to do with stage of pupil development. In the one, they are still undergoing primary socialization (Berger and Luckmann, 1967) which takes place under circumstances that are highly charged emotionally. Indeed, there is good reason to believe that 'without such emotional attachment to the significant others the learning process would be difficult if not impossible. The child identifies with the significant others in a variety of emotional ways . . .' (p. 151). These feelings are to some extent reciprocated. As Jackson (1977) argues, 'Like parents, teachers develop possessive feelings about their students, who become a source of worry, annoyance and pride'.

A second reason is to do with the organization and ethos of schools. Primary schools are much smaller than secondary, more locally centred, community related, 'warm and caring', family orientated. Teachers and pupils all come to know each other very well as individuals. As one teacher told me 'I think it important that you know the kids and you all grow up together'. There can be, then, also, a strong degree of group cohesiveness in primary schools where 'affective ties bind members to the community and gratification stems from involvement with all the members of the group' (Kanter, 1974).

A third reason is to do with teaching approaches. While so-called 'pupil-centred' approaches are by no means exclusive to primary schools, there has been a heavy emphasis on these within them especially since the Plowden Report (CACE, 1967) [Reading 8.3], to a degree which secondary schools, given their commitments to external public examinations have not, as yet, been able to match.

These factors – the need to provide for primary socialization, the organization of primary schooling and teacher approach – have implications for the teacher role. Inasmuch as the teacher–pupil relationship involves a certain degree of intimacy and emotional attachment, mutual interest and help, equality and steadfastness, it is one of friendship. The notion of 'teacher as friend', however, would appear alien to some approaches, except, perhaps, as a teaching strategy. The reciprocality here involves friendliness in exchange for good order and work on a sliding proportional scale – rather than friendship for friendship's sake. The principles involved here seem to require more affective neutrality and social distance. Even here, however, the requirements of 'teachers as parent' call for some affective relationship.

92

More importantly, in my experience many teachers who would subscribe to certain principles of teacher-directed learning (involving teacher ownership of knowledge and transmission forms of pedagogy) would also subscribe to forming strong, friendly, relationships with their pupils informally, which cannot help but overrun into the formal area. Few teachers, in consequence, if any, are able to regard their clients as just 'cases', as doctors and lawyers might do. In a sense, friendship cuts across 'teacher as teacher', that is, the need to instruct and to control, and becomes a potential source of role conflict and strain for both sorts of teacher.

The potential conflict can be heightened by the pressures operating on teachers to be (a) 'teacherly' – the emphasis on measurable objectives, evaluation, results – from parents, inspectors, central government; also by the lack of resources to mount a learner-centred approach entirely adequately (the system is very much geared to transmission modes); (b) 'friendly' – their own need for enjoyment and pleasure in the company of their pupils, as already noted. Pollard (1985), in fact, rates this kind of enjoyment as one of teachers' primary interests, whilst 'instruction' and 'control' are only enabling interests – a means to enjoyment and a satisfactory self-image. Pollard points to teachers' liking for humour and jokes which 'seemed to provide opportunities for the relaxation of roles, and clearly teachers enjoyed relating closely with the children on these occasions, provided of course that they controlled the humour rather than becoming its butt' (p. 24). This neatly points the contrast between different teachers – for some, the humour is part of the role, an essential element in the way they conceptualize it. For others, it is 'time out', to be indulged in 'back regions' (Goffman, 1961). For both, however, it has a key importance. Here again, overindulgence in friendliness can mean that it is difficult to break free when the situation demands one to be teacherly. This in turn can undermine the basis of the friendship, for this has to include a mutual respect. The relationship thus fails in all respects.

If the role strain is unresolved, it may promote stress, which the teacher will seek to relieve in one or more ways – for example cultivating split personalities (Lacey, 1976), compromising their ideal classroom organization (Gracey, 1972), modifying their attitudes (Morrison and McIntyre, 1969), revising their commitment (Sikes et al., 1985). If, however, the role strain is resolved, it can lead to effective and enjoyable teaching for all concerned.

I have argued that the primary school teacher role is intrinsically conflictual. The need for strong affective relationships between pupil and teacher (whether progressive, traditional or whatever) is demanded by the teachers' parental role, by their own interests among which enjoyment figures large (and much of which is derived from their relationships with pupils), by pupil needs. And so teacher–pupil friendships are formed.

However, it is difficult for teachers to escape altogether some old-fashioned instruction and control, whatever their ideals and beliefs. There are pressures operating on them from central and local government, from school and parents, from pupils, from themselves, to meet objectives and achieve results. With adequate resources, these might be achieved through purer pupil-directedness. Where they are inadequate, the 'purity' will go down on a proportionate scale. At one extreme, we may find the 'survival' syndrome where teacher strategies are focused on survival rather than pedagogy (Woods, 1979). More often, one might expect to find a productive blend.

The skills that go into its manufacture are fashioned, I would argue, from three main resource areas:

- Personal abilities, beliefs, attitudes, commitment. Teachers will not strike a happy combination if, for example, they do not like children, or if they are too 'wet' to shout at them occasionally, or if they do not like teaching; conversely, those that have a certain flair or charisma have a head start.

- Training and education. This undoubtedly adds something to a teacher's 'omniscience' – subject knowledge and the craft of pedagogy.

- Teaching experience. This is the day-by-day experimentation over the years, that reveals what works and what does not, the progressive compilation and refinement of techniques and strategies, smoothing off unnecessarily abrasive edges, tightening up on indulgent or slack approaches and activities, knowing one's abilities as diplomat, negotiator, socializer, increasing knowledge of pupils and themselves and their interrelationships in the classroom . . . and so on.

Success in all these areas as manifested in a 'good teacher teaching well' almost defies analysis and comes back to a conception of teaching as an art. It involves combining roles, solving dilemmas, and inventing patterns of events and relationships, that, seen in their entirety, have a certain beauty. Herein lie the greater rewards of teaching – for both teachers and pupils.

 **READING 6.4**

# Teachers, pupils and the working consensus

Andrew Pollard

This reading provides a sociological analysis of how teacher–pupil relationships are formed. At the start of each new year it is suggested that a 'process of establishment' takes place, through which understandings and tacit rules about classroom life are negotiated. This 'working consensus' reflects the needs and coping strategies of both pupils and teacher as they strive to fulfil their classroom roles. Given the power of each to threaten the interests of the other, the working consensus represents a type of moral agreement about 'how we will get on together'. It thus frames future action and relationships.

This argument is closely related to readings on teacher thinking (e.g. 5.1 and 5.2) and on pupils' classroom interests (5.5). Many of the issues which it raises are also taken up in the readings in Chapter 11.

Do you feel that you have successfully negotiated and maintained a working consensus with your class?

Edited from: Pollard, A. (1985) *The Social World of the Primary School*. London: Cassell, 158–71

The interests of teachers and children are different in many ways and yet, in a sense, teachers and children face an identical and fundamental problem: they both have to 'cope' if they are to accomplish their daily classroom lives satisfactorily. I contend that this is possible only with some degree of accommodation of each other's interests. This is the essence of the interaction concept of working consensus, which encapsulates the idea of teacher and children mutually negotiating interdependent ways of coping in classrooms. This working consensus is created through a process of establishment (Ball, 1980) at the start of the school year. For instance, one experienced teacher at Moorside commented:

I always start off the year carefully, trying to be well organized and fairly strict so that the children get into a routine, and then we get to know each other gradually. Usually by the summer term I can relax the routine, do more interesting topics, have a few more jokes and discussions. By then everyone knows what sort of things are allowed, and I know the children well enough to do that kind of thing without them trying things on.

In this 'getting to know each other' period the teacher usually attempts to set up routines, procedures and standards which are offered as 'the way to do things'. This attempt to impose routines is not surprising, since the most salient threat to a teacher's interests is that of the large numbers of children, and routines will to some extent absorb some of the pressure. Meanwhile, the teacher watches the children, interpreting their actions from the point of view of his or her perspective and evaluating the effect of them on his or her interests.

The teacher often holds the initial advantage and may think that everything is going well. However, from the point of view of the children, the salient threat to their interests is that of teacher power, the particular use of which is initially unknown. Thus the children have good reason to watch and evaluate, gradually accumulating a stock of knowledge and experience of the teacher and of situations, most of which is defensively organized around the threat of teacher power. For instance, one boy said:

Last year was great; Mrs Biggs, she was very strict to start with, but then she used to sit at her desk and mark books a lot, so we could talk and send notes. I used to play noughts and crosses with Nigel and draw pictures. If she got up we'd just slide the papers under our books. When she was explaining things to people – that was good, but we had to hand our work in or if we didn't we'd get lines, and it had to be reasonable or we'd get into bother. It wasn't too bad really.

Gradually, as incidents occur and as sparring goes on, classes are seen to settle down and children feel they have got to know their teacher better.

This more settled accord is often described by teachers and other educationists as a 'good relationship'. It is rightly regarded as being extremely important and a teacher may well be judged by colleagues partly by his or her ability to foster such a relationship with pupils. However, the concept of a good relationship has always been a rather vague one, only accessible in some accounts to those with particular levels of sensitivity and intuition.

In fact it is possible to be more analytical. In my view the process of establishment normally and naturally leads to a stabilization of relationships because of mutuality of the coping needs of the teacher and pupils. What emerges is essentially a negotiated system of behavioural understandings for the various types of situations which routinely occur in the classroom. Through interaction, incidents and events, a type of case law of intersubjectively understood rule systems, expectations and understandings emerges and begins to become an assumed, taken-for-granted reality that socially frames each situation. These socially understood, but tacit, conventions and rules constrain the behaviour of the children to varying degrees, depending on the quality and definition of the working consensus, but it is not unusual to find classes in some primary schools which a teacher can confidently leave for a time in the secure expectation that productive activities will continue just as they would have done had the teacher been present.

It is significant that these rules and understandings constrain not only the children, but also the teacher. This point follows from the fact that the rules are interactively constructed through negotiating processes to which teachers are party. Thus, from the child perspective, teachers can be seen as morally bound, and indeed the working consensus can be seen as providing a type of moral order in the classroom.

If the teacher breaks the understood rules then the action is considered unfair. Children commented:

Well, I just dropped this marble in class and usually she just tells us off, but she took it and wouldn't give it back. It wasn't hers to take just because I dropped it.

I answered the register in a funny voice and he went right mad. Yesterday he was cracking jokes himself. He's probably had a row with his wife.

These examples are instances of the most common teacher infringement of the working consensus – that of reaction to a routine deviant act which is seen as being too harsh. Such a reaction tends to produce bad feeling and often provokes more deviance.

It is thus the case that if the working consensus and the good relationship are to be maintained, both teacher and pupil strategies are partially circumscribed by them.

Of course it has to be recognized that a teacher's absolute power resources are greater than those of pupils. However, it can be argued that to an extent the working consensus incorporates and accepts differentiated status and behaviours, that it takes into account material realities and differences in socially sanctioned authority, differences in knowledge and differences in experience, and that these become accommodated into the relationships and understandings which are established between teachers and children.

The working consensus is thus an interactive product; indeed it can be seen as a collective, interdependent adaptation by the teacher and children to survival problems which are, in different ways, imposed on them both. [See also Reading 5.5]

As we have seen, a crucial feature of classroom life which derives directly from the working consensus is the system of intersubjectively understood rules. These are tacit and taken-for-granted conventions which are created through the dynamics of interaction and through negotiation. They develop through incident and case law as the teacher and children come to understand each other and to define the parameters of acceptable behaviour in particular situations. The result is that such tacit understandings influence and 'frame' the actions of both teacher and pupils.

Two further points have to be made. In the first place such rules are not static; they change depending on the situation, which can be analysed in terms of the time, place, activity and people involved. In the second place they vary in strength. On some occasions the rule frame may be high and the expected behaviour is very clearly defined, while on other occasions, when the rule frame is weak, action is less circumscribed.

The concepts of working consensus and rule frame provide a means of analysing the social context within classrooms. They relate to self, and are the product of processes of classroom interaction in which the coping necessities and interests of each party play a major part.

The working consensus – the 'good relationship' – represents a mutual agreement to respect the dignity and fundamental interests of the other party. As such it is produced by creative and interactive responses to the structural position which teachers and pupils face in their classrooms. The additional point, though, is that these responses themselves create a micro social structure and context – analysable in terms of rule frame – to which individuals also have to relate as they act.

READING 6.5

# Establishing a working consensus: teaching styles and pupil types

Maurice Galton, Linda Hargreaves, Chris Comber and Debbie Wall with Anthony Pell

This reading builds on an influential observational study of primary classrooms in the late 1970s (ORACLE), which was then replicated in the 1990s. The selection reinforces Reading 6.4, by demonstrating how teacher and pupil classroom strategies mesh together interactively. The patterns of our actions as teachers are thus closely related to pupil behaviour – which, of course, emphasizes our responsibility for creating a positive learning context in our classrooms. To describe common teaching styles Galton and his colleagues use the terms 'class enquirers', 'group instructors', 'individual monitors' and 'style changers'. Associated pupil responses were those of 'solitary workers', 'intermittent workers', 'easy riders' and 'attention seekers'. Galton *et al.* use their comparative findings to question some unintended consequences of the introduction of the National Curriculum.

How does your teaching style affect pupil behaviour, and how does this relate to your values and objectives?

Edited from: Galton, M., Hargreaves, L., Comber, C., Wall, D. and Pell, A. (1999) *Inside the Primary Classroom: 20 Years On*. London: Routledge, 128–32

One of the key findings in the first ORACLE study was the existence of a set of relationships between the different teaching styles and the various pupil types (Galton *et al.*, 1980, p. 148). These relationships appeared to be remarkably stable from year to year, such that when pupils moved to a new teacher who made greatest use of a different style, they tended to adopt the characteristics of the pupil types associated with that style. Such patterns are a manifestation of what Pollard (1985) described as the 'working consensus', a state or equilibrium in which certain teacher behaviours produce certain pupil reactions, while at the same time other pupil behaviours appear to condition the teacher's actions. For example, pupil attention seeking was almost non-existent in classes of the group instructors, which perhaps explains why, in the 1990s, it has largely disappeared, because of the extent to which direct instruction now accounts for a large part of the primary diet. On the other hand, nearly half of the 1976 children (46 per cent) in the classes of teachers categorized as individual monitors were intermittent workers. Nearly two-thirds (64.5 per cent) of children who were taught by the class enquirers were solitary workers. The highest number of attention seekers were found among teachers who were style changers. Figure 6.5.1 shows the distribution of pupil types by teaching style for the 1996 sample.

The first point to strike one is that, across all four teaching styles, there was a sizeable proportion of easy riders. This is best seen pictorially in the pie charts. The smallest proportion can be found when the individual monitoring style was being used (29.6 per cent). With this style, however, the number of pupils involved in some form of task avoidance was reinforced by the presence of others engaged in intermittent working (40.8 per cent). This latter figure is very close to that recorded under the same style twenty years previously. However, the highest proportion of easy riders were in classes taken by class enquirers (39.6 per cent) and the group supervisors (39.1), some 3 per cent greater than during the use of the direct instruction approach by the class and group instructors. Furthermore, the number of intermittent workers

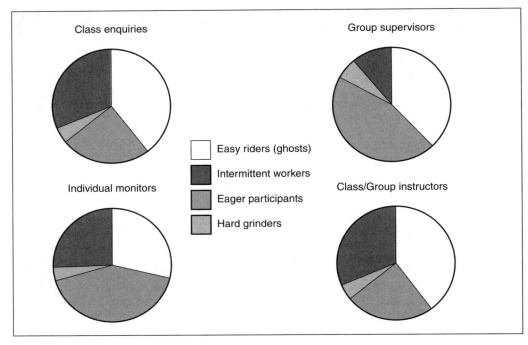

**Figure 6.5.1**  Distribution of pupil types across teaching styles (1996)

also increased dramatically when the class enquiry style was used (25.3 per cent compared to 9.2 per cent twenty years ago). The group supervisor style also appeared to afford plenty of opportunities for intermittent working as the teacher moved from table to table making suggestions about how pupils could proceed with their tasks. Group supervisors also had the lowest number of hard grinders (10.9 per cent).

These patterns make sense if it is remembered that the teaching styles of the 1990s are not as distinct as those of the 1970s. What appears to be happening, therefore, is that some pupils in these classes (given that they spend nearly half of their day on whole-class activities, many of which involve sitting in a confined space, listening to the teacher) regard an instruction to work on one's own, or with a group of pupils, as welcome relief. At such times, more opportunities to relax and enjoy a joke are being taken than was the case in 1976. At the same time, despite the proportionate increase in off-task behaviour, more work was done by pupils, because the overall levels of engagement in the 1990s are now much higher that was the case in the 1970s.

The findings presented here tell a story that reinforces other findings. The decision taken a decade ago, to leave the design of the primary phase of the National Curriculum to subject panels dominated by experts whose teaching experience was mostly gained in secondary schools has produced a curriculum dominated by subject content. As a result, much of the teaching at Key Stage 2 appears to be similar to that which operates in the bottom half of the secondary school. As Hargreaves (1982) and others have argued, a feature of this secondary approach is that it regularly produces a sizeable number of disaffected pupils, particularly in the year immediately after transfer from primary school. In extreme form, this can result not only in an increase in the number of serious incidents of misbehaviour but also in a hiatus in pupil progress, so that some children do less well on tests of attainment at the end of the first year after transfer than they did at the end of their last year in the primary school. Our 1996 data might suggest that the first signs of this disaffection are now being practised by a sizeable number of primary pupils. SAT results demonstrate that pupils still perform reasonably well in examinations despite these manifestations of disaffection, in much the same way that secondary school pupils would appear to overcome the first-year hiatus in progress, since GCSE examination standards have continually risen. Nevertheless, the present findings suggest that, for many pupils (particularly at Key Stage 2), school is no longer as enjoyable as it was before the National Curriculum.

 READING 6.6

# Teacher expectations and pupil achievement

Caroline Gipps and Barbara MacGilchrist

In this excellent review, Gipps and MacGilchrist summarize key evidence on the significance of teachers maintaining high expectations and pupil performance. There seems to be little doubt that this is a crucial factor in effective teaching, as children's self-confidence flourishes from the affirmation and encouragement of their teachers. Again, as in the previous readings, teacher and pupil behaviour are seen to be inextricably linked. Interestingly, however, research studies of classroom practice often document relatively low levels of explicit encouragement, praise and communication of expectations.

Can you support the performance of your children by explicitly conveying your confidence in them? How will they respond?

Edited from: Gipps, C. and MacGilchrist, B. (1999) 'Primary school learners', in Mortimore, P. (ed.) *Understanding Pedagogy and its Impact on Learning*. London: Paul Chapman Publishing, 52–5

One of the hallmarks of effective teachers is their belief that all children can achieve. This belief manifests itself in a variety of ways in the classroom, the most common being through the high expectations teachers set for the children they are teaching. When drawing attention to some of the knowledge and skills teachers need to have in order to bring about effective learning, Mortimore (1993) identified the essential need for teachers to have psychological and sociological knowledge: 'Psychological knowledge so that they can understand how young minds operate and how young people cope with different cultural patterns and family traditions. Sociological knowledge of the way factors such as race, gender, class or religion operate to help or hinder successful teaching' (p. 296).

The research literature that has focused on the relationship between disadvantage and achievement and the extent to which schools can enhance the achievement of pupils whatever their background provides important sociological knowledge for teachers. Two common themes emerge from the literature. The first is that socio-economic inequality is a powerful determinant of differences in cognitive and educational attainment (Mortimore and Mortimore, 1986). Longitudinal studies support this finding (Douglas, 1964; Davie *et al.*, 1972). Social class, along with ethnic background, gender and disability, has been found to have a substantial influence on the life chances of young people (ILEA, 1983). The other common theme is that schools can and do make a difference, but that some schools are much more effective than others at counteracting the potentially damaging effects of disadvantage (Edmunds, 1979; Rutter *et al.*, 1979; Reynolds, 1982; Mortimore *et al.*, 1988; Smith and Tomlinson, 1989; Sammons *et al.*, 1995).

There have been numerous studies to identify the characteristics of highly successful schools (Sammons *et al.*, 1995). Whilst researchers are rightly cautious about identifying causal relationships, the review of the effectiveness literature by Sammons *et al.* (1995) has revealed a set of common features that can be found in effective schools. The majority of these concern the quality and nature of teaching and learning in classrooms along with the overall learning ethos of the school. Some draw attention in particular to the relationship between teachers' beliefs and attitudes and pupils' progress and achievement.

The idea of a self-fulfilling prophecy was first introduced by Merton (1968), and the well-known study by Rosenthal and Jacobson (1968) demonstrated how this concept can operate in the classroom. They showed that it was possible to influence teachers' expectations of certain pupils even though the information they had been given about those pupils was untrue. In their review of the literature, Brophy and Good (1974) and Pilling and Pringle (1978) identify the power of teacher expectation in relation to pupils' learning.

In two studies of primary age pupils (Mortimore *et al.*, 1988; Tizard *et al.*, 1988), the importance of teacher expectations emerged. Tizard and colleagues focused on children aged 4 to 7 in 33 inner London infant schools. The purpose of the research was to examine factors in the home and in the school that appeared to affect attainment and progress during the infant school years. Particular attention was paid to the different levels of attainment of boys and girls, and of white British children and black British children of Afro-Caribbean origin. The team found that there was a link between disadvantage and pupil progress and attainment. The literacy and numeracy knowledge and skills that children had acquired before they started school were found to be a strong predictor of attainment at age 7.

The study was able to identify those school factors that appear to exert a greater influence on progress than home background. The two most significant factors were the range of literacy and numeracy taught to the children and teachers' expectations. Whilst each of these factors was independently associated with progress, the team found that the school and class within it that the child attended proved to be an overriding factor in terms of the amount of progress made. A relationship was found between teacher expectations and the range of curriculum activities provided for children, especially in the areas of literacy and numeracy. The team reported that, 'of the school-based measures we looked at, we found that teachers' expectations of children's curriculum coverage showed the strongest and most consistent association with school progress' (*op. cit.*, p. 139). Where teachers had low expectations of children they provided a narrower curriculum offering.

The junior School Project (Mortimore *et al.*, 1988) was a longitudinal study of a cohort of seven-year-old pupils in 50 London schools. The project drew together different aspects of disadvantage. Using sophisticated research techniques, the team was able to account for what were called pupil and school 'givens'; for example, they were able to take account of pupil factors such as home language, family circumstances, age and sex, and school factors such as size and the stability of staffing. This enabled the team to focus on those factors over which the school had control, such as teaching methods, record keeping and curriculum leadership. They were able to examine which of these factors appear to have a positive impact on pupils' progress and achievement.

The research revealed significant differences in children's educational outcomes during the junior years. Age, social class, sex and race were each found to have an impact on cognitive achievement levels at age 7 and 11. For example, at age 7 those children whose parents worked in non-manual jobs were nearly ten months further ahead in reading than pupils from unskilled manual homes. By the end of the third year the gap had widened. It was also found that with non-cognitive outcomes, such as behaviour and self-concept, there were differences according to age, social class, sex and race. Overall, however, it was found that it was the social-class dimension that accounted for the main differences between groups of pupils.

It was the focus on progress that the pupils made over the four years of the study that demonstrated that some schools (and the teachers within them) were far more effective than others. With reading, for example, the average child in the most effective school increased his or her score on a ten-point reading test by 25 points more than the average child attending the least effective school. The team found that schools which did better on one measure of academic progress tended to do better on others, and that effective schools tended to be effective for all pupils regardless of social class, ethnic group, sex or age.

High teacher expectations were a common characteristic of these schools. The team looked at ways in which expectations were transmitted in the classroom. They found, for example, that teachers had lower expectations of pupils from socio-economically disadvantaged backgrounds. Denbo's (1988) analysis of the research literature over a twenty-year period supports the importance of teacher expectation. Denbo found that many studies demonstrated that both low and high teacher expectation greatly affected student performance. It has been demonstrated that if appropriate teaching styles and teaching expectations are used (OFSTED, 1993a) then pupils can become positive about learning and improve their levels of achievement.

If the learner is seen as an active partner in the learning process, then his/her motivational and emotional state becomes more relevant. One of the school outcomes studied by Mortimore *et al.* was the attitude of students towards themselves as learners. The team designed a measure of self-concept which revealed clear school differences. Some schools produced pupils who felt positive about themselves as learners regardless of their actual ability. Others produced pupils who were negative about themselves even though, according to their progress, they were performing well. Kuykendall (1989) argues that low teacher expectations have been shown to reduce the motivation of students to learn, and that 'perhaps the most damaging consequence of low teacher expectations is the erosion of academic self-image in students' (p. 18). Mortimore (1993) supports this view: 'for a pupil who is regularly taught by a teacher with low expectations, the experience can be demoralizing and too often leads to serious underachievement' (p. 295). Not unrelated to this, he draws attention to the need for teachers to provide good role models for pupils.

It is interesting that these findings mirror, in many respects, some of the recent studies about the brain and learning. Drawing on the work of LeDoux (1996), Goleman (1996) argues that emotions play a key role in cognitive development. He takes the view that emotional intelligence, as he calls it, is a vital capacity for learning. It involves, for example, motivation, the ability to persist and stay on task, control of impulse, regulation of mood and the capacity for keeping distress from swamping the ability to think. Not unrelatedly, Smith (1998) comments that many learners in the classroom avoid taking risks and prefer to stay in 'the comfort zone'. He reminds us that young learners will happily 'copy out in rough, copy it out in neat, draw a coloured border around it, highlight the key words in primary colour, draw you a picture' but that this 'rote, repetitive comfort zone activity is not where real learning takes place' (p. 43). He describes how studies of the brain indicate that 'the optimal conditions for learning include a positive, personal learning attitude where challenge is high and anxiety and self-doubt is low' (p. 41). In her review of the literature on effective primary teaching, Gipps (1992) identified some important factors that mark out effective primary teaching. Amongst these is 'the importance of a good positive atmosphere in the classroom with plenty of encouragement and praise, high levels of expectations of all children and high levels of work-related talk and discussion' (p. 19). She came to the conclusion that, over and above what theories inform us about good teaching, theorists tell us that children are capable of more than we expect.

So, it seems clear that teachers do have beliefs about how children learn and that they need a teaching strategy able to negotiate a path among the rocks and hard places of context, content, child and learning. This resonates with the complexity of real classrooms. Furthermore, those teachers who see children as thinkers, and therefore capable of achieving more and more, are the ones who can enable children to view themselves as able to learn. This is a virtuous circle which needs to be encouraged.

READING 6.7

# What is self-esteem?

## Denis Lawrence

> Denis Lawrence provides a wonderfully clear account of the collection of ideas associated with self-esteem. Distinguishing between self-concept, self-image and the sense of ideal self, he describes self-esteem in terms of an individual's evaluation of his/her personal worth. Such self-conceptions initially derive from family relationships but during the school years these are augmented by the impressions offered by teachers and peers.
>
> Self-esteem is a vital issue in respect of the formation of identity and self-confidence (see Reading 5.7 for an example of this). However, it also has a direct effect on the ways in which pupils approach learning challenges. Clearly, teacher expectations are a particularly significant influence on the ways in which pupils see themselves, and these are the subject of Reading 6.6.
>
> How could you build up the self-esteem of your pupils?
>
> Edited from: Lawrence, D. (1987) *Enhancing Self-Esteem in the Classroom*. London: Paul Chapman Publishing, 1–9

What is self-esteem? We all have our own idea of what we mean by the term, but in any discussion of self-esteem amongst a group of teachers there are likely to be several different definitions. The chances are that amongst these definitions the words self-concept, self-image and ideal self will appear.

## Self-concept

First, the term self-concept is best defined as the sum total of an individual's mental and physical characteristics and his/her evaluation of them. As such it has three aspects: the cognitive (thinking); the affective (feeling) and the behaviourial (action). In practice, and from the teacher's point of view, it is useful to consider this self-concept as developing in three areas – self-image, ideal self and self-esteem.

The self-concept is the individual's awareness of his/her own self. It is an awareness of one's own identity. The complexity of the nature of the 'self' has occupied the thinking of philosophers for centuries and was not considered to be a proper topic for psychology until James (1890) resurrected the concept from the realms of philosophy. As with the philosophers of his day, James wrestled with the objective and subjective nature of the 'self' – the 'me' and the 'I' – and eventually concluded that it was perfectly reasonable for the psychologist to study the 'self' as an objective phenomenon. He envisaged the infant developing from 'one big blooming buzzing confusion' to the eventual adult state of self-consciousness. The process of development throughout life can be considered, therefore, as a process of becoming more and more aware of one's own characteristics and consequent feelings about them. We see the self-concept as an umbrella term because subsumed beneath the 'self' there are three aspects: self-image (what the person is); ideal self (what the person would like to be); and self-esteem (what the person feels about the discrepancy between what he/she is and what he/she would like to be).

Each of the three aspects of self-concept will be considered in turn. Underpinning this theoretical account of the development of self-concept will be the notion that it is the child's interpretation of the life experience which determines self-esteem levels. This is known as the phenomenological approach and owes its origin mainly to the work of Rogers (1951). It attempts to understand a person through empathy with that person and is based on the premise that it is not the events which determine emotions but rather the person's interpretation of the events. To be able to understand the other person requires therefore an ability to empathize.

## Self-image

Self-image is the individual's awareness of his/her mental and physical characteristics. It begins in the family with parents giving the child an image of him/herself of being loved or not loved, of being clever or stupid, and so forth, by their non-verbal as well as verbal communication. This process becomes less passive as the child him/herself begins to initiate further personal characteristics. The advent of school brings other experiences for the first time and soon the child is learning that he/she is popular or not popular with other children. He/she learns that school work is easily accomplished or otherwise. A host of mental and physical characteristics are learned according to how rich and varied school life becomes. In fact one could say that the more experiences one has, the richer is the self-image.

The earliest impressions of self-image are mainly concepts of body image. The child soon learns that he/she is separate from the surrounding environment. This is sometimes seen amusingly in the young baby who bites its foot only to discover with pain that the foot belongs to itself. Development throughout infancy is largely a process of this further awareness of body as the senses develop. The image becomes more precise and accurate with increasing maturity so that by adolescence the individual is normally fully aware not only of body shape and size but also of his/her attractiveness in relation to peers. Sex-role identity also begins at an early age, probably at birth, as parents and others begin their stereotyping and classifying of the child into one sex or the other.

With cognitive development, more refined physical and mental skills become possible, including reading and sporting pursuits. These are usually predominant in most schools so that the child soon forms an awareness of his/her capabilities in these areas.

This process of development of the self-image has been referred to as the 'looking-glass theory of self' (Cooley, 1902) as most certainly the individual is forming his/her self-image as he/she receives feedback from others. However, the process is not wholly a matter of 'bouncing *off* the environment' but also one of 'reflecting *on* the environment' as cognitive abilities make it possible for individuals to reflect on their experiences and interpret them.

## Ideal self

Side by side with the development of self-image, the child is learning that there are ideal characteristics he/she should possess – that there are ideal standards of behaviour and also particular skills which are valued. For example, adults place value on being clean and tidy, and 'being clever' is important. As with self-image, the process begins in the family and continues on entry to school. The child is becoming aware of the mores of the society. Peer comparisons are particularly powerful at adolescence. The influence of the media also becomes a significant factor at this time with various advertising and show-business personalities providing models of aspiration.

## So, what is self-esteem?

Self-esteem is the individual's evaluation of the discrepancy between self-image and ideal self. It is an affective process and is a measure of the extent to which the individual cares about this discrepancy. From the discussion on the development of self-image and ideal self, it can be appreciated that the discrepancy between the two is inevitable and so can be regarded as a normal phenomenon.

Indeed, there is evidence from clinical work that without this discrepancy – without levels of aspiration – individuals can become apathetic and poorly adjusted. For the person to be striving is therefore a normal state.

What is not so normal is that the individual should worry and become distressed over the discrepancy. Clearly, this is going to depend in early childhood on how the significant people in the child's life react to him/her. For instance, if the parent is overanxious about the child's development this will soon be communicated and the child, too, will also become overanxious about it. He/she begins first by trying to fulfil the parental expectations but, if he/she is not able to meet them, he/she begins to feel guilty.

The subject of reading is probably the most important skill a child will learn in the primary school and normally will come into contact with reading every day of school life. It is not surprising therefore, that the child who fails in reading over a lengthy period should be seen to have developed low self-esteem, the end product of feeling guilt about his/her failure. The child then lacks confidence in him/herself.

It can be appreciated from the foregoing description of the development of self-concept that teachers are in a very strong position to be able to influence self-esteem.

In summary, it is not failure to achieve which produces low self-esteem, it is the way the significant people in the child's life react to the failure. Indeed, it could be argued that failure is an inevitable part of life. There is always someone cleverer or more skilful than ourselves. This must be accepted if we are to help children develop happily without straining always to be on top. Eventually, of course, children become aware of their own level of achievement and realize that they are not performing as well as others around them. Then they can develop low self-esteem irrespective of the opinion of others; they have set their own standards. It is probably true to say, however, that the primary schoolchild is still likely to be 'internalizing' his/her ideal self from the significant people around him/her.

Self-esteem as defined so far refers to a 'global self-esteem' – an individual's overall feeling of self-worth. This is relatively stable and consistent over time. In addition to this overall, or global, self-esteem we can have feelings of worth or unworthiness in specific situations. Accordingly we may feel inadequate (low self-esteem) with regard to mathematics or tennis playing. However, they do not affect our overall feeling of self-worth as we can escape their influences by avoiding those situations. If, of course, we cannot avoid them and regularly participate in these activities which make us feel inadequate they may eventually affect our overall self-esteem. Also if we continue to fail in areas which are valued by the significant people in our lives then our overall self-esteem is affected. It is worth reflecting on how children cannot escape school subjects which is why failure in school so easily generalizes to the global self-esteem.

In summary, self-esteem develops as a result of interpersonal relationships within the family which gradually give precedence to school influences and to the influences of the larger society in which the individual chooses to live and to work. These extraneous influences lose their potency to the extent to which the individual becomes self-determinate. For the student of school age, however, self-esteem continues to be affected mainly by the significant people in the life of the student, usually parents, teachers and peers.

## CHAPTER 7

# Learning. How can we understand children's development?

There are eleven readings in this important chapter on the psychology of children's learning.

The first group of readings derive from key exponents of three major theoretical approaches to learning. Behaviourism is represented by the reading from Skinner (7.1) whilst the reading from Piaget (7.2) reviews major elements of his constructivist psychology. Modern theories of social cognition have a common root in the work of Vygotsky, and his work is represented by a classic account on the 'zone of proximal development' (7.3). For a further extension of these ideas in relation to instruction, see Reading 13.2 by Tharp and Gallimore). In Reading 7.4, Parker-Rees builds on Vygotsky's constructivist insights to highlight the significance of 'playfulness' in exploring new meanings and building a confident, mastery orientation to learning.

Turning to a group of experts on intellectual capacity and motivation, Reading 7.5 offers Gardner's theory of multiple intelligence, stimulating the educational ambition to connect with the diversity of abilities – not something that modern education is good at. For Dweck (7.6), a mastery orientation is connected to each child's view of his or her own intelligence, as fixed or malleable, and she worries at the propensity of schooling to undermine confidence. Claxton (7.7) focuses on the need for, and development of, 'resilience'. This disposition is seen as a crucial foundation for lifelong learning and, he argues, should be a major goal of schools.

The readings by Bruner (7.8) and Mercer (7.9) focus on 'socio-cultural psychology', emphasizing the cultural contexts within which knowledge is appropriated and understanding is developed. This approach is used by Hughes et al. (7.10) as part of an explanation of the difficulties that pupils find in transfering and applying school knowledge. Finally, Pollard and Triggs (7.11) review some major social and educational influences on children as they develop their identities and confidence as learners though their school years. This reading draws on studies of the impact of recent education policies in England, and raises some serious issues about possible unintended consequences of the drive for performance.

The parallel chapter of *Reflective Teaching* reviews a similar range of issues and considers them in relation to classroom work. The chapter begins with a discussion of behaviourist, constructivist, social constructivist and socio-cultural models of learning. The second part of the chapter addresses a wide range of factors affecting how children learn. These include, health and physical development, the brain, 'intelligence', culture, personality and learning style, motivation and meta-cognition (the capability to reflect on one's own learning). The significance of these factors is summarised by drawing on American research. Finally, there is a section on the challenge of applying school learning.

There are also suggestions for *Key Readings* and, of course, many other ideas for more detailed study can be accessed from *RTweb*. Just see the *Notes for Further Reading* in relation to this chapter.

## READING 7.1

# The science of learning and the art of teaching

Burrhus Skinner

B. F. Skinner made a very important contribution to 'behaviourist' psychology, an approach based on study of the ways in which animal behaviour is shaped and conditioned by stimuli. In this reading, Skinner applies his ideas to the learning of pupils in schools. Taking the case of learning arithmetic, he highlights the production of correct 'responses' from children and considers the forms of 'reinforcement' that are routinely used in classrooms. He regards these as hopelessly inadequate.

The behaviourist approach is applied to discipline issues in Reading 11.7.

What do you see as the implications of behaviourism for the role of the teacher?

Edited from: Skinner, B. F. (1954) 'The science of learning and the art of teaching', *Harvard Educational Review*, 24, 86–97.

Some promising advances have been made in the field of learning. Special techniques have been designed to arrange what are called 'contingencies of reinforcement' – the relations which prevail between behaviour on the one hand, the consequences of that behaviour on the other – with the result that a much more effective control of behaviour has been achieved. It has long been argued that an organism learns mainly by producing changes in its environment, but it is only recently that these changes have been carefully manipulated.

Recent improvements in the conditions which control behaviour in the field of learning are of two principal sorts. The law of effect has been taken seriously; we have made sure that effects do occur and that they occur under conditions which are optimal for producing the changes called learning. Once we have arranged the particular type of consequence called a reinforcement, our techniques permit us to shape up the behaviour of an organism almost at will. It has become a routine exercise to demonstrate this in classes in elementary psychology by conditioning such an organism as a pigeon. Simply by presenting food to a hungry pigeon at the right time, it is possible to shape up three or four well-defined responses in a single demonstration period – such responses as turning around, pacing the floor in the pattern of a figure of eight, standing still in a corner of the demonstration apparatus, stretching the neck or stamping the foot. Extremely complex performances may be reached through successive stages in the shaping process, the contingencies of reinforcement being changed progressively in the direction of the required behaviour. The results are often quite dramatic. In such a demonstration one can see learning take place. A significant change in behaviour is often obvious as the result of a single reinforcement.

A second important advance in technique permits us to maintain behaviour in given states of strength for long periods of time. Reinforcements continue to be important, of course, long after an organism has learned how to do something, long after it has acquired behaviour. They are necessary to maintain the behaviour in strength of special interest is the effect of various schedules of intermittent reinforcement. We have learned how to maintain any given level of activity for daily periods limited only by the physical exhaustion of the organism and from day to day without substantial change throughout its life. Many of these effects would be traditionally assigned to the field of motivation, although the principal operation is simply the arrangement of contingencies of reinforcement.

These new methods of shaping behaviour and of maintaining it in strength are a great improvement over the traditional practices of professional animal trainers, and it is not surprising that our laboratory results are already being applied to the production of performing animals for commercial purposes.

From this exciting prospect of an advancing science of learning, it is a great shock to turn to that branch of technology which is most directly concerned with the learning process – education. Let us consider, for example, the teaching of arithmetic in the lower grades. The school is concerned with imparting to the child a large number of responses of a special sort. The responses are all verbal. They consist of speaking and writing certain words, figures and signs which, to put it roughly, refer to numbers and to arithmetic operations. The first task is to shape up these responses – to get the child to pronounce and to write responses correctly, but the principal task is to bring this behaviour under many sorts of stimulus control. This is what happens when the child learns to count, to recite tables, to count while ticking off the items in an assemblage of objects, to respond to spoken or written numbers by saying 'odd', 'even', 'prime' and so on. Over and above this elaborate repertoire of numerical behaviour, most of which is often dismissed as the product of rote learning, the teaching of arithmetic looks forward to those complex serial arrangements of responses involved in original mathematical thinking. The child must acquire responses of transposing, clearing fractions and so on, which modify the order or pattern of the original material so that the response called a solution is eventually made possible.

Now, how is the extremely complicated verbal repertoire set up? In the first place, what reinforcements are used? Fifty years ago the answer would have been clear. At that time educational control was still frankly aversive. The child read numbers, copied numbers, memorized tables and performed operations upon numbers to escape the threat of the birch rod or cane. Some positive reinforcements were perhaps eventually derived from the increased efficiency of the child in the field of arithmetic and in rare cases some automatic reinforcement may have resulted from the sheer manipulation of the medium – from the solution of problems or the discovery of the intricacies of the number system. But for the immediate purposes of education the child acted to avoid or escape punishment. It was part of the reform movement known as progressive education to make the positive consequences more immediately effective, but anyone who visits the lower grades of the average school today will observe that a change has been made, not from aversive to positive control, but from one form of aversive stimulation to another. The child at his desk, filling in his workbook, is behaving primarily to escape from the threat of a series of minor aversive events – the teacher's displeasure, the criticism or ridicule of his classmates, an ignominious showing in a competition, low marks, a trip to the office 'to be talked to' by the principal, or a word to the parent who may still resort to the birch rod. In this welter of aversive consequences, getting the right answer is in itself an insignificant event, any effect of which is lost amid the anxieties, the boredom and the aggressions which are the inevitable by-products of aversive control.

Second, we have to ask how the contingencies of reinforcement are arranged. When is a numerical operation reinforced as 'right'? Eventually, of course, the pupil may be able to check his own answers and achieve some sort of automatic reinforcement, but in the early stages the reinforcement of being right is usually accorded by the teacher. The contingencies she provides are far from optimal. It can easily be demonstrated that, unless explicit mediating behaviour has been set up, the lapse of only a few seconds between response and reinforcement destroys most of the effect. In a typical classroom, nevertheless, long periods of time customarily elapse. The teacher may walk up and down the aisle, for example, while the class is working on a sheet of problems, pausing here and there to say right or wrong. Many seconds or minutes intervene between the child's response and the teacher's reinforcement. In many cases – for example, when papers are taken home to be corrected – as much as 24 hours may intervene. It is surprising that this system has any effect whatsoever.

A third notable shortcoming is the lack of a skilful programme which moves forward through a series of progressive approximations to the final complex behaviour desired. A long series of contingencies is necessary to bring the organism into the possession of mathematical behaviour most efficiently. But the teacher is seldom able to reinforce at each step in such a series because she cannot deal with the pupil's responses one at a time. It is usually necessary to reinforce the behaviour in blocks of responses – as in correcting a work sheet or page from a workbook. The responses within such a block must not be interrelated. The answer to one problem must not depend upon the answer to another. The number of stages through which one may progressively approach a complex pattern of behaviour is therefore small, and the task so much the more difficult. Even the most modern workbook in beginning arithmetic is far from exemplifying an efficient programme for shaping up mathematical behaviour.

Perhaps the most serious criticism of the current classroom is the relative infrequency of reinforcement. Since the pupil is usually dependent upon the teacher for being right, and since many pupils are usually dependent upon the same teacher, the total number of contingencies which may be arranged during, say, the first four years, is of the order of only a few thousand. But a very rough estimate suggests that efficient mathematical behaviour at this level requires something of the order of 25,000 contingencies. We may suppose that even in the brighter student a given contingency must be arranged several times to place the behaviour well in hand. The responses to be set up are not simply the various items in tables of addition, subtraction, multiplication and division; we have also to consider the alternative forms in which each item may be stated. To the learning of such material we should add hundreds of responses concerned with factoring, identifying primes, memorizing series, using shortcut techniques for calculation, constructing and using geometric representations or number forms and so on. Over and above all this, the whole mathematical repertoire must be brought under the control of concrete problems of considerable variety. Perhaps 50,000 contingencies is a more conservative estimate. In this frame of reference the daily assignment in arithmetic seems pitifully meagre.

The result of this is, of course, well known. Even our best schools are under criticism for the inefficiency in the teaching of drill subjects such as arithmetic. The condition in the average school is a matter of widespread national concern. Modern children simply do not learn arithmetic quickly or well. Nor is the result simply incompetence. The very subjects in which modern techniques are weakest are those in which failure is most conspicuous, and in the wake of an ever-growing incompetence come the anxieties, uncertainties and aggressions which in their turn present other problems to the school. Most pupils soon claim the asylum of not being 'ready' for arithmetic at a given level or, eventually, of not having a mathematical mind. Such explanations are readily seized upon by defensive teachers and parents. Few pupils ever reach the stage at which automatic reinforcements follow as the natural consequences of mathematical behaviour. On the contrary, the figures and symbols of mathematics have become standard emotional stimuli. The glimpse of a column of figures, not to say an algebraic symbol or an integral sign, is likely to set off – not mathematical behaviour – but a reaction of anxiety, guilt or fear.

The teacher is usually no happier about this than the pupil. Denied the opportunity to control via the birch rod, quite at sea as to the mode of operation of the few techniques at her disposal, she spends as little time as possible on drill subjects and eagerly subscribes to philosophies of education which emphasize material of greater inherent interest.

There would be no point in urging these objections if improvement were impossible. But the advances which have recently been made in our control of the learning process suggest a thorough revision of classroom practices and, fortunately, they tell us how the revision can be brought about. This is not, of course, the first time that the results of an experimental science have been brought to bear upon the practical problems of education. The modern classroom does not, however, offer much evidence that research in the field of learning has been respected or used. This condition is no doubt partly due to the limitations of earlier research, but it has been encouraged by a too hasty conclusion that the laboratory study of learning is inherently limited because it cannot take into account the realities of the classroom. In the light of our increasing knowledge of the learning process we should, instead, insist upon dealing with those realities and forcing a substantial change in them. Education is perhaps the most important branch of scientific technology. It deeply affects the lives of all of us. We can no longer allow the exigencies of a practical situation to suppress the tremendous improvements which are within reach. The practical situation must be changed.

There are certain questions which have to be answered in turning to the study of any new organism. What behaviour is to be set up? What reinforcers are at hand? What responses are available in embarking upon a programme of progressive approximation which will lead to the final form of behaviour? How can reinforcements be most efficiently scheduled to maintain the behaviour in strength? These questions are all relevant in considering the problem of the child in the lower grades.

 **READING 7.2**

# The genetic approach to the psychology of thought

Jean Piaget

---

The present reading provides a concise overview of Piaget's constructivist psychology, but is necessarily packed with ideas. The distinction between formal knowledge and the dynamic of transformations is important, with the latter seen as providing the mechanism for the development of thought. Successive 'stages' of types of thinking are reviewed and are related to maturation, direct experience and social interaction. Finally, attention is drawn to the ways in which children 'assimilate' new experiences and 'accommodate' to their environment, to produce new levels of 'equilibration' at successive stages of learning.

Interpretations of Piaget's work have been of enormous influence on the thinking of primary school teachers. Indeed, it was specifically used as a rationale for the policy recommendations contained in the Plowden Report (Reading 8.3), which emphasized the importance of providing a rich, experiential learning environment which would be appropriate for the 'stage' of each child.

What importance do you attach to concepts such as 'stages of development', 'readiness' and 'learning from experience'?

Edited from: Piaget, J. (1961) 'A genetic approach to the psychology of thought', *British Journal of Educational Psychology* 52, 151–61

---

Taking into consideration all that is known about the act of thinking, one can distinguish two principal aspects:

● The formal viewpoint, which deals with the configuration of the state of things to know,

● The dynamic aspect, which deals with transformations

The study of the development of thought shows that the dynamic aspect is at the same time more difficult to attain and more important, because only transformations make us understand the state of things. For instance: when a child of 4 to 6 years transfers a liquid from a large and low glass into a narrow and higher glass, he believes in general that the quantity of the liquid has increased, because he is limited to comparing the initial state (low level) to the final state (high level) without concerning himself with the transformation. Towards 7 or 8 years of age, on the other hand, a child discovers the preservation of the liquid, because he will think in terms of transformation. He will say that nothing has been taken away and nothing added, and, if the level of the liquid rises, this is due to a loss of width, etc.

The formal aspect of thought makes way, therefore, more and more in the course of the development to its dynamic aspect, until such time when only transformation gives an understanding of things. To think means, above all, to understand; and to understand means to arrive at the transformations, which furnish the reason for the state of things. All development of thought is resumed in the following manner: a construction of operations which stem from actions and a gradual subordination of formal aspects into dynamic aspects.

The operation, properly speaking, which constitutes the terminal point of this evolution is, therefore, to be conceived as an internalized action bound to other operations, which form with it a structured whole.

So defined, the dynamics intervene in the construction of all thought processes; in the structure of forms and classifications, of relations and serialization of correspondences, of numbers, of space and time, of the causality, etc.

Any action of thought consists of combining thought operations and integrating the objects to be understood into systems of dynamic transformation. The psychological criterion of this is the appearance of the notion of conservation or 'invariants of groups'. Before speech, at the purely sensory-motor stage of a child from 0–18 months, it is possible to observe actions which show evidence of such tendencies. For instance: from 4–5 to 18 months, the baby constructs his first invariant, which is the schema of the permanent object (to recover an object which escaped from the field of perception).

When, with the beginning of the symbolic function (language, symbolic play, imagery, etc.), the representation through thought becomes possible, it is at first a question of reconstructing in thought what the action is already able to realize. The actions actually do not become transformed immediately into operations, and one has to wait until about 7–8 years for the child to reach a functioning level. During this preoperative period the child, therefore, only arrives at incomplete structures characterized by a lack of logic.

At about 7–8 years the child arrives at his first complete dynamic structures (classes, relations and numbers), which, however, still remain concrete – in other words, only at the time of a handling of objects (material manipulation or, when possible, directly imagined). It is not before the age of 11–12 years or more that operations can be applied to pure hypotheses.

The fundamental genetic problem of the psychology of thought is hence to explain the formation of these dynamic structures. Practically, one would have to rely on three principal factors in order to explain the facts of development: maturation, physical experience and social interaction. But in this particular case none of these three suffice to furnish us with the desired explanations – not even the three together.

## Maturation

First of all, these dynamic structures form very gradually. But progressive construction does not seem to depend on maturation, because the achievements hardly correspond to a particular age. Only the order of succession is constant. However, one witnesses innumerable accelerations or retardations for reasons of education (cultural) or acquired experience.

## Physical experience

Experiencing of objects plays, naturally, a very important role in the establishment of dynamic structures, because the operations originate from actions and the actions bear upon the object. This role manifests itself right from the beginning of sensory-motor explorations, preceding language, and it affirms itself continually in the course of manipulations and activities which are appropriate to the antecedent stages. Necessary as the role of experience may be, it does not sufficiently describe the construction of the dynamic structures – and this for the following three reasons.

First, there exist ideas which cannot possibly be derived from the child's experience – for instance, when one changes the shape of a small ball of clay. The child will declare, at 7–8 years, that the quantity of the matter is conserved. It does so before discovering the conservation of weight (9–10 years) and that of volume (10–11 years). What is the quantity of a matter independently of its weight and its volume? This abstract notion is neither possible to be perceived nor measurable. It is, therefore, the product of a dynamic deduction and not part of an experience.

Second, the various investigations into the learning of logical structure, which we were able to make at our International Centre of Genetic Epistemology, lead to a unanimous result: one does not 'learn' a logical structure as one learns to discover any physical law.

Third, there exist two types of experiences: physical experiences that show the objects as they are, and the knowledge of them leads to the abstraction directly from the object; and logicomathematical experience, which does not stem from the same type of learning as that of the physical experience, however, but rather from an equilibration of the scheme of actions, as we will see.

## Social interaction

The educative and social transmission (linguistic, etc.) plays, naturally, an evident role in the formation of dynamic structures, but this factor does not suffice either to explain entirely its development.

Additionally, there is a general progression of equilibration. This factor intervenes, as is to be expected, in the interaction of the preceding factors. Indeed, if the development depends, on one hand, on internal factors (maturation), and on the other hand on external factors (physical or social), it is self-evident that these internal and external factors equilibrate each other. The question is then to know if we are dealing here only with momentary compromises (unstable equilibrium) or if, on the contrary, this equilibrium becomes more and more stable. This shows that all exchange (mental as well as biological) between the organism and the environment (physical and social) is composed of two poles: (a) of the assimilation of the given external to the previous internal structures, and (b) of the accommodation of these structures to the given ones. The equilibrium between the assimilation and the accommodation is proportionately more stable than the assimilative structures which are better differentiated and coordinated.

To apply these notions to children's reasoning we see that every new problem provokes a disequilibrium (recognizable through types of dominant errors) the solution of which consists in a re-equilibration, which brings about a new original synthesis of two systems, up to the point of independence.

# Mind in society and the ZPD

## Lev Vygotsky

> Vygotsky's social constructivist psychology, though stemming from the 1930s, underpins much modern thinking about teaching and learning. In particular, the importance of instruction is emphasized. However, this is combined with recognition of the influence of social interaction and the cultural context within which understanding is developed. Vygotsky's most influential concept is that of the 'zone of proximal development' (ZPD) which highlights the potential for future learning which can be realized with appropriate support.
>
> The influence of Vygotsky's work will be particularly apparent in Readings 7.8, 7.9, 7.11, 13.2 but it is also present in many other readings, particularly in Chapters 11 and 12.
>
> Thinking of a particular area of learning and a child you know, can you identify an 'actual developmental level' and a 'zone of proximal development' through which you could provide guidance and support?
>
> Edited from: Vygotsky, L. S. (1978) *Mind in Society: The Development of Higher Psychological Processes.* Cambridge, MA: Harvard University Press, 84–90

That children's learning begins long before they attend school is the starting point of this discussion. Any learning a child encounters in school always has a previous history. For example, children begin to study arithmetic in school, but long beforehand they have had some experience with quantity – they have had to deal with operations of division, addition, subtraction and determination of size. Consequently, children have their own pre-school arithmetic which only myopic scientists could ignore.

It goes without saying that learning as it occurs in the pre-school years differs markedly from school learning, which is concerned with the assimilation of the fundamentals of scientific knowledge. But even when, in the period of her first questions, a child assimilates the names of objects in her environment, she is learning. Indeed, can it be doubted that children learn speech from adults; or that, through asking questions and giving answers, children acquire a variety of information; or that through imitating adults and through being instructed about how to act, children develop an entire repository of skills? Learning and development are interrelated from the child's very first day of life.

In order to elaborate the dimensions of school learning, we will describe a new and exceptionally important concept without which the issue cannot be resolved: the zone of proximal development.

A well-known and empirically established fact is that learning should be matched in some manner with the child's developmental level. For example, it has been established that the teaching of reading, writing and arithmetic should be initiated at a specific age level. Only recently, however, has attention been directed to the fact that we cannot limit ourselves merely to determining developmental levels if we wish to discover the actual relations of the developmental process to learning capabilities. We must determine at least two developmental levels.

The first level can be called the actual developmental level, that is, the level of development of a child's mental functions that has been established as a result of certain already *completed* developmental cycles. When we determine a child's mental age by using tests, we are almost always dealing with the actual developmental level. In studies of children's mental development it is generally assumed that only those things that children can do on their own are indicative of mental abilities. We give children a battery of tests or a variety of tasks of varying degrees of difficulty, and we judge the extent of their mental development on the basis of how they solve them and at what level of difficulty. On the other hand, if we offer leading questions or show how the problem is to be solved and the child then solves it, or if the teacher initiates the solution and the child completes it or solves it in collaboration with other children – in short, if the child barely misses an independent solution of the problem – the solution is not regarded as indicative of his mental development. This 'truth' was familiar and reinforced by common sense. Over a decade, even the profoundest thinkers never questioned the assumption; they never entertained the notion that what children can do with the assistance of others might be in some sense even more indicative of their mental development than what they can do alone.

The zone of proximal development is the distance between the actual developmental level as determined by independent problem solving and the level of potential development as determined through problem solving under adult guidance or in collaboration with more capable peers.

If we naively ask what the actual developmental level is, or, to put it more simply, what more independent problem solving reveals, the most common answer would be that a child's actual developmental level defines functions that have already matured, that is, the end products of development. If a child can do such-and-such independently, it means that the functions for such-and-such have matured in her. What, then, is defined by the zone of proximal development, as determined through problems that children cannot solve independently but only with assistance? The zone of proximal development defines those functions that have not yet matured but are in the process of maturation, functions that will mature tomorrow but are currently in an embryonic state. These functions could be termed the 'buds' or 'flowers' of development rather than the 'fruits' of development. The actual developmental level characterizes mental development retrospectively, while the zone of proximal development characterizes mental development prospectively.

The zone of proximal development furnishes psychologists and educators with a tool through which the internal course of development can be understood. By using this method we can take account of not only the cycles and maturation processes that have already been completed but also those processes that are currently in a state of formation, that are just beginning to mature and develop. Thus, the zone of proximal development permits us to delineate the child's immediate future and his dynamic developmental state, allowing not only for what already has been achieved developmentally but also for what is in the course of maturing. The state of a child's mental development can be determined only by clarifying its two levels: the actual developmental level and the zone of proximal development.

A full understanding of the concept of the zone of proximal development must result in re-evaluation of the role of imitation in learning. Indeed, human learning presupposes a specific social nature and a process by which children grow into the intellectual life of those around them.

Children can imitate a variety of actions that go well beyond the limits of their own capabilities. Using imitation, children are capable of doing much more in collective activity or under the guidance of adults. This fact, which seems to be of little significance in itself, is of fundamental importance in that it demands a radical alteration of the entire doctrine concerning the relation between learning and development in children.

Learning which is oriented towards developmental levels that have already been reached is ineffective from the viewpoint of a child's overall development. It does not aim for a new stage of the developmental process but rather lags behind this process. Thus, the notion of a zone of proximal development enables us to propound a new formula, namely that the only 'good learning' is that which is in advance of development.

The acquisition of language can provide a paradigm for the entire problem of the relation between learning and development. Language arises initially as a means of communication between the child and the people in his environment. Only subsequently, upon conversion to internal speech, does it come to organize the child's thought, that is, become an internal mental function.

We propose that an essential feature of learning is that it creates the zone of proximal development; that is, learning awakens a variety of internal developmental processes that are able to operate only when the child is interacting with people in his environment and in cooperation with his peers. Once these processes are internalized, they become part of the child's independent developmental achievement.

From this point of view, learning is not development; however, properly organized learning results in mental development and sets in motion a variety of developmental processes that would be impossible apart from learning. Thus, learning is a necessary and universal aspect of the process of developing culturally organized, specifically human, psychological functions.

## READING 7.4

# Playful learning

## Rod Parker-Rees

Rod Parker-Rees uses his insights as an early-years educator to make some powerful points about the significance of playfulness in learning. In particular, he locates play within a Vygotskian framework, demonstrating how it enables interaction between social and personal meanings. Play with sand, water, dough, etc., is thus matched by playfulness with words, concepts, roles and identities. It can be a way of experimentally transforming ourselves, transcending problems, imagining possibilities and of learning throughout life.

Do children have appropriate opportunities for play, in a form appropriate to their age, within your classroom? And what about yourself? Beyond 'what is', can you imagine 'what might be'?

Edited from: Parker-Rees, R. (1999) 'Protecting playfulness', in Abbott, L. and Moylett, H. (eds) *Early Education Transformed: New Millennium Series*. London, New York: Falmer Press, 64–6

The Piagetian model of the child as 'little scientist' smoothing the tangle of everyday experience into increasingly tidy, cool and formal concepts is itself only one of many possible ways of mapping the complexity of cognitive development. Vygotsky insisted that this 'natural line' of development was accompanied by a 'cultural line' (Wertsch, 1991, p. 25) because we construct our ways of interpreting experience within a cultural environment which is deeply rutted by the social process of communication. The flow of our perceptions is channelled into shared forms as we tune our interpretations and adopt common ways of organizing what we know.

Communication both generates and depends upon common ways of simplifying and making sense of experience; words mean what people mean when they use them. But communication also depends on a certain amount of play in the cultural machine; word meanings are far from fixed or static. Our personal sense-making can never correspond exactly with another person's because, although we may share a broad system of simple definitions, the colour, richness and warmth of the meanings and connotations which we attach to these is rooted in our own, unique, subterranean tangle of experience. This inevitable looseness of meaning is what makes conversation both interesting and emotionally rewarding; it is 'just what is needed to allow change to happen when people with different analyses interact' (Newman *et al.*, in Bliss *et al.*, 1996, p. 62).

Children play with sand, water, dough and construction kits, forming and transforming materials and exploring their possibilities, but they can also transform the more abstract, cultural properties of objects, playing with what things are meant to mean. When a child uses a leaf to represent a plate in her play she can observe similarities and differences between her direct perception of the leaf and remembered information about plates, becoming more aware of physical properties such as flatness, smoothness, hardness and rigidity. She may also, if only implicitly, inform her understanding of the metaphorical, transformational nature of representation.

Playful transformation of experience depends on, and gives access to, the '100 languages of children' (Edwards *et al.*, 1993), the patterned forms of representation which make communication possible. Adults are responsible for 'making and protecting the child's space' but also for 'introducing into it appropriate structural elements which derive from the surrounding culture' (Hodgkin, 1985, p. 26), 'open materials leave the most room for children to create their own ideas in play' (Jones and Reynolds, 1992, p. 20). Jones and Reynolds emphasize the importance of a plentiful supply of 'loose parts' which can be combined and recombined in different ways (ibid., p. 23) and this is precisely what the languages of representation provide (Parker-Rees, 1997). Children who have been encouraged to use these languages in playful ways, as construction kits which can be deconstructed, transformed and reassembled, may feel more confident about choosing how to make sense of problem situations by remembering possible ways of responding:

> Transfer seems to involve grasping the structural features of a task, comparing these with analogous tasks, and taking the risk of 'going beyond the information given' and applying the old skills to the new situation where they may possibly be useful. (Meadows, 1996, p. 93)

This sort of risk taking requires both confidence and flexibility; the mastery orientation which children are more likely to develop if they have opportunities to practise and represent decision making in play situations (Sylva, 1992). Children can also be encouraged to transform artefacts and situations in their imaginations: how else might things be done? What else could be used? What else might have caused this? Playing with 'what might be' helps children to escape from the shackles of 'what is' but it also deepens their understanding of why things are the way they are (Parker-Rees, 1997). By holding open a space within which we are protected from the stresses and pressures of 'everyday life', playful activities can allow us to wander between the well-trodden paths which we must use when we are hurried. The looser, more complicated and more interconnected knowledge which results from this sort of wandering (or wondering) prepares us to cope more creatively when we find our path blocked: instead of giving up, we are able to strike out in a different direction, using both our implicit knowledge of the terrain and our explicit mental map of established tracks to remember another route (Claxton, 1997).

📖 **READING 7.5**

# The idea of multiple intelligences

## Howard Gardner

> The concept of intelligence is a powerful one and is usually taken to denote a generalized intellectual capability. Howard Gardner has synthesized the thinking of many modern psychologists, neurobiologists and others to challenge the dominant view of 'intelligence' in favour of a conception of multiple forms of competence and intellectual capacity. The seven intelligences which he suggests represent an interesting proposition which might be contested, though this does not detract from his major point of critique.
>
> This type of argument has considerable implications for teachers. In particular, it affirms the importance of seeking pupil capabilities across a wide range, rather than becoming locked into an evaluative mind-set which is locked into narrow curriculum capabilities (see for instance, Reading 11.3 on 'learning to be stupid').
>
> Thinking about a class of children you know, do some have forms of intelligence and capability which it is hard for them to realize at school? Are some forms of intelligence valued more highly than others?
>
> Edited from: Gardner, H. (1985) *Frames of Mind: The Theory of Multiple Intelligences*. London: Paladin Books, 3–4, 59–70, 277–387

A young girl spends an hour with an examiner. She is asked a number of questions that probe her store of information. ('Who discovered America?' 'What does the stomach do?'), her vocabulary ('What does "nonsense" mean?' 'What does "belfry" mean?'), her arithmetic skills ('At eight cents each, how much will three candy bars cost?'), her ability to remember a series of numbers (5, 1, 7, 4, 2, 3, 8), her capacity to grasp the similarity between two elements (elbow and knee, mountain and lake). She may also be asked to carry out certain other tasks – for example, solving a maze or arranging a group of pictures in such a way that they relate a complete story. Some time afterward, the examiner scores the responses and comes up with a single number – the girl's intelligence quotient, or IQ. This number (which the little girl may actually be told) is likely to exert appreciable effect upon her future, influencing the way in which her teachers think of her and determining her eligibility for certain privileges. The importance attached to the number is not entirely inappropriate: after all, the score on an intelligence test does predict one's ability to handle school subjects, though it foretells little of success in later life.

The preceding scenario is repeated thousands of times every day, all over the world, and, typically, a good deal of significance is attached to the single score. Of course, different versions of the test are used for various ages and in diverse cultural settings. At times, the test is administered with paper and pencil rather than as an interchange with an examiner. But the broad outlines – an hour's worth of questions yielding one round number – are pretty much the way of intelligence testing the world around.

Many observers are not happy with this state of affairs. There must be more to intelligence than short answers to short questions – answers that predict academic success – and yet, in the absence of a better way of thinking about intelligence, and of better ways to assess an individual's capabilities, this scenario is destined to be repeated universally for the foreseeable future.

But what if one were to let one's imagination wander freely, to consider the wider range of performances that are in fact valued throughout the world? Consider, for example, the twelve-year-old male Puluwat in the Caroline Islands, who has been selected by his elders to learn how to become a master sailor. Under the tutelage of master navigators, he will learn to combine knowledge of sailing, stars, and geography so as to find his way around hundreds of islands. Consider the fifteen-year-old Iranian youth who has committed to heart the entire Koran and mastered the Arabic language. Now he is being sent to a holy city, to work closely for the next several years with an ayatollah, who will prepare him to be a teacher and religious leader. Or, consider the fourteen-year-old adolescent in Paris, who has learned how to programme a computer and is beginning to compose works of music with the aid of a synthesizer.

A moment's reflection reveals that each of these individuals is attaining a high level of competence in a challenging field and should, by any reasonable definition of the term, be viewed as exhibiting intelligent behaviour. Yet it should be equally clear that current methods of assessing the intellect are not sufficiently well honed to allow assessment of an individual's potentials or achievements in navigating by the stars, mastering a foreign tongue, or composing with a computer. The problem lies less in the technology of testing than in the ways in which we customarily think about the intellect and in our ingrained views of intelligence. Only if we expand and reformulate our view of what counts as human intellect will we be able to devise more appropriate ways of assessing it and more effective ways of educating it.

My review of studies of intelligence and cognition has suggested the existence of a number of different intellectual strengths, or competences, each of which may have its own developmental history. Recent work in neurobiology has suggested the presence of areas in the brain that correspond to certain forms of cognition, and these same studies imply a neural organization that proves hospitable to the notion of different modes of information processing.

But science can never proceed completely inductively. We might conduct every conceivable psychological test and experiment, or ferret out all the neuro-anatomical wiring that we desired, and still not have identified the sought-after human intelligences.

And so it becomes necessary to say that there is not, and there can never be, a single irrefutable and universally accepted list of human intelligences. There will never be a master list of three, seven, or three hundred intelligences which can be endorsed by all investigators.

This risk of reification is grave in a work of exposition, especially in one that attempts to introduce novel scientific concepts such as 'multiple intelligence'. I, and sympathetic readers, will be likely to think – and to fall into the habit of saying – that we here behold the 'linguistic intelligence,' the 'interpersonal intelligence,' or the 'spatial intelligence' at work, and that's that. But it's not. These intelligences are fictions – at most, useful fictions – for discussing processes and abilities that (like all of life) are continuous with one another; Nature brooks no sharp discontinuities. It is permissible to lapse into the sin of reifying so long as we remain aware that this is what we are doing. Specific intelligences exist not as physically verifiable entities but only as potentially useful scientific constructs.

We might perhaps conceptualize our family of seven intelligences in broad strokes in the following way. The 'object-related' forms of intelligence – spatial, logical–mathematical, bodily–kinaesthetic – are subject to one kind of control: that actually exerted by the structure and the functions of the particular objects with which individuals come into contact. Were our physical universe structured differently, these intelligences would presumably assume different forms. Our 'object-free' forms of intelligence – language and music – are not fashioned or channelled by the physical world but, instead, reflect the structures of particular languages and music. They may also reflect features of the auditory and oral systems, though (as we have seen) language and music may each develop, at least to some extent, in the absence of these sensory modalities. Finally the personal forms of intelligence reflect a set of powerful and competing constraints: the existence of one's own person; the existence of other persons; the culture's presentations and interpretations of selves. There will be universal features of any sense of person or self, but also considerable cultural nuances, reflecting a host of historical and individuating factors.

Intelligences should not be assessed in the same ways at different ages. The methods used with an infant or a pre-schooler ought to be tailored to the particular ways of knowing that typify these individuals and may be different from those employed with older individuals. My own belief is that one could assess an individual's intellectual potentials quite early in life, perhaps even in infancy.

Involvement with inherently engrossing materials provides an ideal opportunity to observe intelligences at work and to monitor their advances over a finite period of time. If one could watch a child as he learns to build various constructions out of blocks, one would receive insight into his skills in the areas of spatial and kinaesthetic intelligence: similarly, the child's capacities to relate a set of stories would reveal facets of his linguistic promise, even as his capacity to operate a simple machine would illuminate kinaesthetic and logical–mathematical skills. Such involvements in rich and provocative environments are also most likely to elicit 'markers' – those signs of early giftedness that are readily noticed by adults expert in a particular intellectual domain. The future musician may be marked by perfect pitch; the child gifted in personal matters, by his intuitions about the motives of others; the budding scientist, by his ability to pose provocative questions and then follow them up with appropriate ones.

Naturally, the specific experiences favoured for the assessment of intellectual potential will differ, given the age, the sophistication and the cultural background of the individual. Thus, when monitoring the spatial realm, one might hide an object from the one-year-old, pose a jigsaw puzzle to the six-year-old, or provide the pre-adolescent with a Rubik's cube. Analogously, in the musical realm, one might vary a lullaby for the two-year-old, provide the eight-year-old with a computer on which he can compose simple melodies, or analyse a fugue with an adolescent. In any case, the general idea of finding intriguing puzzles and allowing children to 'take off' with them seems to offer a far more valid way of assessing profiles of individuals than the current favourites worldwide: standard measures designed to be given within a half-hour with the aid of paper and pencil.

## READING 7.6

# Motivational processes affecting learning

## Carol Dweck

Pupils' motivation and approaches in new learning situations is obviously crucial to outcomes and this has been the focus of Carol Dweck's research for many years. In this reading, she shows how children's view of intelligence (as fixed or something that can be developed) may lead them to adopt relatively pragmatic performance goals or more developmental learning goals. These are associated with different beliefs in themselves (helpless or mastery orientated), different forms of classroom behaviour and different learning outcomes.

This analysis has important links with Lawrence's reading on self-esteem (6.7), with views of intelligence/s (Reading 7.5) and with ideas on pupil self-regulation of learning (Reading 13.2) and self-assessment (Reading 14.5).

How can we help children to really believe in themselves and their potential?

Edited from: Dweck, C. S., (1986) 'Motivational processes affecting learning', *American Psychologist*, October, 1040–6

It has long been known that factors other than ability influence whether children seek or avoid challenges, whether they persist or withdraw in the face of difficulty and whether they use and develop their skills effectively. However, the components and bases of adaptive motivational patterns have been poorly understood. As a result, common-sense analyses have been limited and have not provided a basis for effective practices. Indeed, many 'common-sense' beliefs have been called into question or seriously qualified by recent research – for example, the belief that large amounts of praise and success will establish, maintain, or reinstate adaptive patterns, or that 'brighter' children have more adaptive patterns and thus are more likely to choose personally challenging tasks or to persist in the face of difficulty.

In the past ten to fifteen years a dramatic change has taken place in the study of motivation. This change has resulted in a coherent, replicable, and educationally relevant body of findings – and in a clearer understanding of motivational phenomena. During this time, the emphasis has shifted to a social – cognitive approach – away from external contingencies, on the one hand, and global, internal states on the other. It has shifted to an emphasis on cognitive mediators, that is, to how children construe the situation, interpret events in the situation, and process information about the situation. Although external contingencies and internal affective states are by no means ignored, they are seen as part of a process whose workings are best penetrated by focusing on organizing cognitive variables.

Specifically, the social–cognitive approach has allowed us to (a) characterize adaptive and maladaptive patterns, (b) explain them in terms of specific underlying processes, and thus (c) begin to provide a rigorous conceptual and empirical basis for intervention and practice.

The study of motivation deals with the causes of goal-oriented activity. Achievement motivation involves a particular class of goals – those involving competence – and these goals appear to fall into two classes: (a) 'learning goals', in which individuals seek to increase their competence, to understand or master something new, and (b) 'performance goals', in which individuals seek to gain favourable judgements of their competence.

Adaptive motivational patterns are those that promote the establishment, maintenance, and attainment of personally challenging and personally valued achievement goals. Maladaptive patterns, then, are associated with a failure to establish reasonable, valued goals, to maintain effective striving toward those goals, or, ultimately, to attain valued goals that are potentially within one's reach.

Research has clearly documented adaptive and maladaptive patterns of achievement behaviour. The adaptive ('mastery-oriented') pattern is characterized by challenge seeking and high, effective persistence in the face of obstacles. Children displaying this pattern appear to enjoy exerting effort in the pursuit of task mastery. In contrast, the maladaptive ('helpless') pattern is characterized by challenge avoidance and low persistence in the face of difficulty. Children displaying this pattern tend to evidence negative affect (such as anxiety) and negative self-cognitions when they confront obstacles.

Although children displaying the different patterns do not differ in intellectual ability, these patterns can have profound effects on cognitive performance. In experiments conducted in both laboratory and classroom settings, it has been shown that children with the maladaptive pattern are seriously hampered in the acquisition and display of cognitive skills when they meet obstacles. Children with the adaptive pattern, by contrast, seem undaunted or even seem to have their performance facilitated by the increased challenge.

If not ability, then what are the bases of these patterns? Most recently, research has suggested that children's goals in achievement situations differentially foster the two patterns. That is, achievement situations afford a choice of goals, and the one the child preferentially adopts predicts the achievement pattern that child will display.

Figure 7.6.1 summarizes the conceptualization that is emerging from the research. Basically, children's theories of intelligence appear to orient them towards different goals: children who believe intelligence is a fixed trait tend to orient towards gaining favourable judgements of that trait (performance goals), whereas children who believe intelligence is a malleable quality

| Theory of intelligence | Goal orientation | Confidence in present ability | Behaviour pattern |
|---|---|---|---|
| **Entity theory** (Intelligence is fixed) | → **Performance goal** (Goal is to gain positive judgements/ avoid negative judgements of competence) | **If high** → <br><br> **but** <br><br> **If low** → | **Mastery orientated** Seek challenge High persistence <br><br> **Helpless** Avoid challenge Low persistence |
| **Incremental theory** (Intelligence is malleable) | → **Learning goal** (Goal is to increase competence) | **If high** → <br> **or** <br> **low** | **Mastery orientated** Seek challenge (that fosters learning) High persistence |

**Figure 7.6.1**  Achievement goals and achievement behaviour

tend to orient towards developing that quality (learning goal). The goals then appear to set up the different behaviour patterns.

Much current educational practice aims at creating high-confidence performers and attempts to do so by programming frequent success and praise. How did this situation arise? I propose that misreadings of two popular phenomena may have merged to produce this approach. First was the belief in 'positive reinforcement' as the way to promote desirable behaviour. Yet a deeper understanding of the principles of reinforcement would not lead one to expect that frequent praise for short, easy tasks would create a desire for long, challenging ones or promote persistence in the face of failure.

Second was a growing awareness of teacher expectancy effects. As is well known, the teacher expectancy effect refers to the phenomenon whereby teachers' impressions about students' ability actually affect students' performance, such that the students' performance falls more in line with the teachers' expectancies (Rosenthal and Jacobson, 1968). The research on this 'self-fulfilling prophecy' raised serious concerns that teachers were hampering the intellectual achievement of children they labelled as having low ability. One remedy was thought to lie in making low-ability children feel like high-ability children by means of a high success rate.

The motivational research is clear in indicating that continued success on personally easy tasks is ineffective in producing stable confidence, challenge seeking and persistence (Dweck, 1975). Indeed, such procedures have sometimes been found to backfire by producing lower confidence in ability. Rather, the procedures that bring about more adaptive motivational patterns are the ones that incorporate challenge, and even failure, within a learning-oriented context and that explicitly address underlying motivational mediators. For example, retraining children's attributions for failure (teaching them to attribute their failures to effort or strategy instead of ability) has been shown to produce sizeable changes in persistence in the face of failure, changes that persist over time and generalize across tasks (Andrews and Bebus, 1978).

Motivational processes have been shown to affect (a) how well children can deploy their existing skills and knowledge, (b) how well they acquire new skills and knowledge, and (c) how well they transfer these new skills and knowledge to novel situations. This approach does not deny individual differences in present skills and knowledge or in 'native' ability or aptitude. It does suggest, however, that the use and growth of that ability can be appreciably influenced by motivational factors.

📖 READING 7.7

# Learning and the development of 'resilience'

## Guy Claxton

Guy Claxton has constructed an analysis of how young learners need to develop positive learning dispositions to support lifelong learning. He identifies his 'three Rs' – resilience, resourcefulness and reflection – as being crucial. This reading is focused on the first of these. Resilience is closely associated with having the self-confidence to face problems and the resolve to overcome them. It articulates well with Dweck's concept of 'mastery' (Reading 7.6).

How, through our classroom practices, could we support the development of resilience in our pupils?

Edited from: Claxton, G. (1999) *Wise Up: The Challenge of Lifelong Learning.* Stoke on Trent: Network Press, 331–3

As the world moves into the age of uncertainty, nations, communities and individuals need all the learning power they can get. Our institutions of business and education, even our styles of parenting, have to change so that the development and the expression of learning power become real possibilities. But this will not happen if they remain founded on a narrow conceptualization of learning: one which focuses on content over process, comprehension over competence, 'ability' over engagement, teaching over self-discovery. Many of the current attempts to create a learning society are hamstrung by a tacit acceptance of this outmoded viewpoint, however watered down or jazzed up it may be. The new science of learning tells us that everyone has the capacity to become a better learner, and that there are conditions under which learning power develops. It is offering us a richer way of thinking about learning, one which includes feeling and imagination, intuition and experience, external tools and the cultural milieu, as well as the effort to understand. If this picture can supplant the deeply entrenched habits of mind that underpin our conventional approaches to learning, the development of learning power, and the creation of a true learning society might become realities. In this reading, let me summarize the lessons that the new science of the learning mind has taught us.

Learning is impossible without resilience: the ability to tolerate a degree of strangeness. Without the willingness to stay engaged with things that are not currently within our sphere of confident comprehension and control, we tend to revert prematurely into a defensive mode: a way of operating that maintains our security but does not increase our mastery. We have seen that the decision whether, when and how to engage depends on a largely tacit cost–benefit analysis of the situation that is influenced strongly by our subjective evaluations of the risks, rewards and available resources. These evaluations derive from our beliefs and values, our personal theories, which may be accurate or inaccurate. Inaccurate beliefs can lead us to over- or underestimate apparent threats and to misrepresent to ourselves what learning involves.

So when you find people declining an invitation to learn, it is not because they are, in some crude sense, lazy or unmotivated: it is because, for them, at that moment, the odds stack up differently from the way in which their parents or tutors or managers would prefer. Defensiveness, seen from the inside, is always rational. If the stick and the carrot don't do the trick, it may be wiser to try to get a clearer sense of what the learner's interior world looks like. Often you will find that somewhere, somehow, the brakes have got jammed. Sensitivity to the learner's own dynamics is always smart.

Some of these beliefs refer to the nature of knowledge and of learning itself. For example, if we have picked up the ideas that knowledge is (or ought to be) clear and unequivocal, or that learning is (or ought to be) quick and smooth, we withdraw from learning when it gets hard and confusing, or when we meet essential ambiguity. Some belies refer to hypothetical psychological qualities such as 'ability'. The idea that achievement reflects a fixed personal reservoir of general-purpose 'intelligence' is pernicious, leading people to interpret difficulty as a sign of stupidity, to feel ashamed, and therefore to switch into self-protection by hiding, creating diversions or not trying. Some beliefs determine how much we generally see the world as potentially comprehensible and controllable ('self-efficacy', we called it). High self-efficacy creates persistence and resilience; low breeds a brittle and impatient attitude. Some beliefs forge a connection between self-worth on the one hand and success, clarity and emotional control on the other, making failure, confusion and anxiety or frustration induce a feeling of shame. All these beliefs can affect anyone, but there are a host of others that specifically undermine or disable the learning of certain groups of people, or which apply particularly to certain types of material. For example, girls and boys have been revealed as developing different views of themselves as learners of mathematics.

These beliefs are rarely spelled out, but are transmitted implicitly and insidiously through the kinds of culture that are embodied in the settings that learners inhabit, such as family, school or workplace. Learning messages are carried by a variety of media. The habits and rituals of the culture enable certain kinds of learning and disable others.

The implications of these conclusions for the kinds of learning cultures we create are self-evident. Parents, teachers and managers have to be vigilant, reflective and honest about the values and beliefs which inform the ways they speak, model and organize the settings over which they have control. Inadvertently create the wrong climate and the development and expression of learning power are blocked. Experience in childhood, at home and at school, is particularly important because these early belief systems, whether functional or dysfunctional, can be carried through into people's learning lives as adults.

📖 READING 7.8

# Cultural psychology

## Jerome Bruner

Jerome Bruner is one of the most distinguished cognitive psychologists of the post-war years and in this reading he looks back at the critique of behaviourism (see Reading 7.1) in which he was so influential. Following Vygotsky (see Reading 7.3), he argues that understanding the thinking of any individual must take account of the symbolic systems in use, and these are embedded in the social and cultural context in which action takes place. Psychology has therefore become interdisciplinary in outlook and a new 'cultural psychology' is developing.

Bruner's argument is further developed in Reading 7.9.

The implication for teachers of Bruner's work is that we cannot fully understand pupil learning without engaging with the cultural influences which influence language, concepts and thinking. We need to understand the social context which structures the identity and capability of each child, and then work constructively within it. How might this be done?

The present reading also provides a good example of the juxtaposition of educational paradigms (see Bassey's distinctions in Reading 3.4).

Edited from: Bruner, J. (1990) *Acts of Meaning*. Cambridge, MA, Harvard University Press, 1–32

I want to begin with the cognitive revolution as my point of departure. That revolution was intended to bring 'mind' back into the human sciences after a long cold winter of objectivism.

Let me tell you first what I and my friends thought the revolution was about back there in the late 1950s. It was, we thought, an all-out effort to establish meaning as the central concept of psychology – not stimuli and responses, not overtly observable behaviour, not biological drives and their transformation, but meaning. It was not a revolution against behaviourism with the aim of transforming behaviourism into a better way of pursuing psychology by adding a little mentalism to it [see Reading 7.1]. It was an altogether more profound revolution than that. Its aim was to discover and to describe formally the meanings that human beings created out of their encounters with the world, and then to propose hypotheses about what meaning-making processes were implicated. It focused upon the symbolic activities that human beings employed in constructing and in making sense not only of the world, but of themselves. Its aim was to prompt psychology to join forces with its sister interpretive disciplines in the humanities and in the social sciences. Indeed, beneath the surface of the more computationally oriented cognitive science, this is precisely what has been happening – first slowly and now with increasing momentum. And so today one finds flourishing centres of cultural psychology, cognitive and interpretive anthropology, cognitive linguistics, and above all, a thriving worldwide enterprise that occupies itself as never before since Kant with the philosophy of mind and of language.

We were not out to 'reform' behaviourism, but to replace it.

Begin with the concept of culture itself – particularly its constitutive role. What was obvious from the start was perhaps too obvious to be fully appreciated, at least by us psychologists who by habit and by tradition think in rather individualistic terms. The symbolic systems that individuals used in constructing meaning were systems that were already in place, already 'there', deeply entrenched in culture and language. They constituted a very special kind of communal tool kit whose tools, once used, made the user a reflection of the community. We psychologists concentrated on how individuals 'acquired' these systems, how they made them their own, much as we would ask how organisms in general acquired skilled adaptations to the natural environment. We even became interested (again in an individualistic way) in man's specific innate readiness for language. But with a few exceptions, notably Vygotsky, we did not pursue the impact of language use on the nature of man as a species. We were slow to grasp fully what the emergence of culture meant for human adaptation and for human functioning. It was not just the increased size and power of the human brain, not just bipedalism and its freeing of the hands. These were merely morphological steps in evolution that would not have mattered save for the concurrent emergence of shared symbolic systems, of traditionalized ways of living and working together – in short, of human culture.

The divide in human evolution was crossed when culture became the major factor in giving form to the minds of those living under its sway. A product of history rather than of nature, culture now became the world to which we had to adapt and the tool kit for doing so. Once the divide was crossed, it was no longer a question of a 'natural' mind simply acquiring language as an additive. Nor was it a question of a culture tuning or modulating biological needs. As Clifford Geertz puts it, without the constituting role of culture we are 'unworkable monstrosities . . . incomplete or unfinished animals who complete or finish ourselves through culture' (Geertz, 1973).

A culturally oriented psychology neither dismisses what people say about their mental states, nor treats their statements only as if they were predictive indices of overt behaviour. What it takes as central, rather, is that the relationship between action and saying (or experiencing) is, in the ordinary conduct of life, interpretable. It takes the position that there is a publicly interpretable congruence between saying, doing, and the circumstances in which the saying and doing occur. That is to say, there are agreed-upon canonical relationships between the meaning of what we say and what we do in given circumstances, and such relationships govern how we conduct our lives with one another. There are procedures of negotiation, moreover, for getting back on the track when these canonical relations are violated. This is what makes interpretation and meaning central to a cultural psychology – or to any psychology or mental science, for that matter.

A cultural psychology, almost by definition, will not be preoccupied with 'behaviour' but with 'action,' its intentionally based counterpart, and more specifically, with situated action – action situated in a cultural setting, and in the mutually interacting intentional states of the participants.

Intellectuals in a democratic society constitute a community of cultural critics. Psychologists, alas, have rarely seen themselves that way, largely because they are so caught up in the self-image generated by positivist science. Psychology, on this view, deals only in objective truths and eschews cultural criticism. But even scientific psychology will fare better when it recognizes that its truths, like all truths about the human condition, are relative to the point of view that it takes toward that condition. And it will achieve a more effective stance towards the culture at large when it comes to recognize that the folk psychology of ordinary people is not just a set of self-assuaging illusions, but the culture's beliefs and working hypotheses about what makes it possible and fulfilling for people to live together, even with great personal sacrifice. It is where psychology starts and wherein it is inseparable from anthropology and the other cultural sciences.

READING 7.9

# Culture, context and the appropriation of knowledge

Neil Mercer

> Neil Mercer provides an extension and illustration of the application of Bruner's argument for 'cultural psychology' (Reading 7.8). He relates this to the Piagetian approach (Reading 7.2) which it has largely superseded. His discussion of 'appropriation' is of particular interest. The account of Mercer's nine-month-old baby shows her adopting 'brrm-brrming' and a culturally based form of play with a toy car which she learned directly from an older child at day nursery. On the other hand, Mercer also cites examples of teachers appropriating pupil concepts and using them as part of their attempt to extend pupil understanding.
>
> Mercer also draws attention to the wider social and historical context and points out that 'what counts as knowledge is quite culturally specific'. Considering England, what counted as knowledge in the mid-ninteenth century is very different from that implied in the 1960s (see Reading 4.4 for a parallel historical analysis). At any point in time, this variation will also be found across countries, as suggested by Reading 14.2.
>
> Can you identify instances of pupils appropriating concepts and ways of thinking from the culture around them?
>
> Edited from: Light, P. and Butterworth, G. (eds) (1992) *Context and Cognition: Ways of Learning and Knowing.* Hemel Hempstead: Harvester Wheatsheaf, 28–44

The 1980s was an interesting, if unsettled, period for the study of children's cognition and learning. On the theoretical level, there was a growing unease with theoretical perspectives which focused on individual development to the extent that social and interactional factors in learning and development were marginalized or even ignored. Despite widespread dissatisfaction with the theory and methods of earlier research on the educational attainment of children from different cultural groups (e.g. Jensen, 1967; Bernstein, 1971), more recent research on social experience and children's educational progress (e.g. Tizard and Hughes, 1984; Wells, 1985) made it clear that 'culture' could not be ignored. In particular, it seemed that more attention needed to be paid to the relationship between children's experiences within the cultural environments of home and school, and to the form and content of communication between parents and children and between teachers and children.

But culture and communication were themes that were not clearly or centrally represented within the Piagetian theory which dominated developmental psychology and which had most influence on educational theory and practice [see Reading 7.2]. And so the adequacy of Piagetian theory was questioned (e.g. Walkerdine, 1984; Edwards and Mercer, 1987) and some radical revisions of the Piagetian account of cognitive development were proposed.

Moreover, from the mid-1970s through the 1980s misgivings grew among researchers about how experimental methods had been used to study cognitive development. One important influence was Margaret Donaldson's work (Donaldson, 1978), which showed how strongly experimental results could be influenced by contextual cues carried implicitly within an experimental design or setting. Naturalistic, observational methods thus became rather more popular and experimental methods were devised which were more sensitive to situational factors. It also seemed that Vygotsky's work (e.g. Vygotsky, 1978, [see Reading 7.3]), with its recognition of cultural and linguistic factors on cognitive development and learning, might offer a better basis for such observational and experimental research than did Piaget's.

Culture and context thus became necessary and important concepts for the field of cognitive development and learning.

Anthropology, of course, is the discipline with first claims on culture. The eminent anthropologist Geertz (1968, p. 641) offered the following definition: 'an historically transmitted pattern of meaning embodied in symbols, a system of inherited conceptions expressed in symbolic form by means of which men [sic] communicate, perpetuate and develop their knowledge about and attitudes towards life'. Geertz's definition seems to me to be compatible with the notion of culture employed by Vygotsky (e.g. 1978, 1981). As Scribner (1985, p. 123) points out: 'We find Vygotsky introducing the term 'cultural development' in his discussion of the origins of higher psychological functions and in some contexts using it interchangeably with 'historical development'.' For Vygotsky, the concept of culture offers a way of linking the history of a social group, the communicative activity of its members and the cognitive development of its children.

The culturally based quality of most learning is represented in the concept of 'appropriation', introduced by Vygotsky's colleague Leont'ev (1981) but taken up and developed by Newman, Griffin and Cole (1989). According to Newman *et al.*, it was proposed by Leont'ev as a socio-cultural alternative to Piaget's biological metaphor of 'assimilation'. In saying that children appropriate understanding through cultural contact, the point is being made that 'the objects in a child's world have a social history and functions that are not discovered through the child's unaided explorations' (Newman *et al.*, 1989, p. 62). This is more than a complicated way of saying that children do not need to reinvent the wheel. At the simplest level, it is arguing that because humans are essentially cultural beings, even children's initial encounters with objects may be cultural experiences, and so their initial understandings may be culturally defined. In this sense, appropriation is concerned with what children may take from encounters with objects in cultural context.

Here is an example from my experience. My daughter Anna, when about nine months old, was offered a toy car to play with by her older brother. Although this was the first time she had seen one at home, she immediately began pushing it along the floor, going 'brrm, brrm' as she did so. The explanation for this surprising but conventional response lay in her regular attendance at day nursery. Although not given the opportunity there to handle a car, she had been able to observe an older child playing with one. On being given the car to play with, Anna did not need to 'discover' its nature purely through sensori-motor contact to make use of it as a toy. She recognized it as a tool for 'brrm-brrming', because she had appropriated from the older child the culturally based conception and function of the toy. Right from the start, it was a culturally defined object, and not simply a bit of material reality which she had to act on to discover its properties and functions.

The concept of appropriation also incorporates the socio-dynamics of the development of understanding in another, more complex, way, because within the educational process appropriation may be reciprocal. Thus Newman *et al.*, use appropriation to explain the pedagogic function of a particular kind of discourse event whereby one person takes up another person's remark and offers it back, modified, into the discourse. They show how teachers do this with children's utterances and actions, thereby offering children a recontextualized version of their own activities which implicitly carries with it new cultural meanings. Teachers often paraphrase what children say, and present it back to them in a form which is considered by the teacher to be more compatible with the current stream of educational discourse. Teachers also reconstructively recap what has been done by the children in class, so as to represent events in ways which fit their pedagogic framework. By strategically appropriating children's words and actions, teachers may help children relate children's thoughts and actions in particular situations to the parameters of educational knowledge.

The acquisition of knowledge should not be theoretically isolated from the processes by which knowledge is offered, shared, reconstructed and evaluated. As Vygotsky suggested, the concept of culture helps us understand learning as a socio-historical and interpersonal process, not just as a matter of individual change or development. This has particular significance for the study of learning in school, where what counts as knowledge is often quite culturally specific. Culture represents the historical source of important influences on what is learned, how it is learned, and the significance that is attached to any learning that takes place. We likewise need a satisfactory definition of context to deal with learning as a communicative, cumulative, constructive process, one which takes place in situations where past learning is embodied in present learning activity, and in which participants draw selectively on any information which is available to make sense of what they are doing. Only by taking account of these situated qualities of learning can we properly begin to describe how people learn.

## READING 7.10

# Applying school learning

Martin Hughes, Charles Desforges and Christine Mitchell, with Clive Carré

One of the biggest problems with school learning is that it is artificial. Children may well be able to 'do' all sorts of things in the school situation, but they often find it extremely hard to apply this knowledge or skill in the other 'real world' contexts. Often, the relevance of what they know is not understood. A key issue for all educators, therefore, is how knowledge can be more effectively applied. To be effective, knowledge must be transformed from 'something we have to do', and converted into 'something that is useful to me'. The reading by Hughes and his colleagues illustrates this challenge in the case of mathematics.

Edited from: Hughes, M., Desforges, C. and Mitchell, C., with Carré, C. *Numeracy and Beyond: Applying Mathematics in the Primary School.* Buckingham: Open University Press (2000), 6–9, 108–9

We learn mathematics in school with a view to going beyond classroom exercises and to using mathematical knowledge and skill in all relevant aspects of our professional and domestic lives. Here, unfortunately, and in sharp contrast to reading, we find learners are not at all fluent in application. People seem to be readily defeated when they meet situations that vary, sometimes by very little, from those they meet in their classroom exercises.

Examples of failure to use basic mathematical competences are legion. In one national mathematics survey, for example, it was found that 80 per cent of twelve-year-olds could quickly and correctly divide 225 by 15. However, only 40 per cent of the same sample could solve the problem 'if a gardener had 225 bulbs to place equally in 15 flower beds, how many would be put in each bed?' Most of the failing pupils did not know which mathematical procedure to use, although they were capable of conducting the routine once the appropriate process was named.

Another well-known example comes from a survey of mathematical understanding carried out in the USA in the 1980s (National Assessment of Educational Progress 1983). As part of this survey, thirteen-year-old students were told that an army bus holds 36 soldiers and asked how many buses would be needed to transport 1128 soldiers to their training site. Most of the students knew that they needed to carry out a division calculation, and many successfully divided 1128 by 36 to produce an answer of 31.33. However, nearly a third of the students proceeded to write 31.33 as the answer to the problem, thus ignoring the need for a whole number of buses. Nearly a quarter of the students made a different kind of mistake and ignored the remainder altogether, thus leaving twelve soldiers with no transport.

Clearly, people often show a very limited capacity to use or apply mathematics. It might be felt that the matter could be dismissed by arguing that the people who fail simply have a rather weak grasp of the basic skills in mathematics. But this is not the case. This was evident in a study of some Swedish twelve and thirteen-year-olds who were accomplished at basic mathematics (Säljö and Wyndhamn, 1990). In this study the pupils were asked to find the cost of posting a letter. They were given the letter (which weighed 120 grams), some scales and a simple post office chart showing rates of postage. For example, letters up to 100 grams would cost 4 kronor, while letters up to 250 grams would cost 7.5 kronor. This is in fact a very simple problem, requiring only that the letter be weighed and the appropriate rate read off from the chart. However, many of the pupils failed to find the correct cost of postage and most of those who succeeded did so after a great deal of trouble. The higher the mathematical attainment of the pupils, the more roundabout were their problem-solving procedures. These pupils, it seemed, had considerable difficulty in knowing which aspect of their classroom knowledge to apply to this 'real world' problem. Even these accomplished youngsters showed severe limitations in their capacity to use or apply their mathematical knowledge and skills from one setting to another.

A further illustration of the problem of application comes from a study of Brazilian children's mathematical competencies described by Nunes *et al.* (1993). The children in question were street traders in a large Brazilian city. Street trading is an economic necessity for large numbers of urban youngsters in Brazil. Children trade in fruit, cigarettes, paper goods, drinks and a wide range of other low-cost goods. Trading involves purchasing goods from a variety of wholesalers, pricing the goods to sell in a variety of units (for example single items or multiple-item packs) and selling the goods, which involves calculating the price of complex purchases and the change due to the customers. An added complication for the children was that Brazil's inflation rate at the time of the study was 250 per cent per annum and, as a consequence, selling not only had to make a straight profit but a profit allowing for the inflated cost of restocking.

Nunes and her colleagues studied several of these children in the working environment of their street stalls. Only one of the children had more than four years of schooling. The children's capabilities were first observed in normal trading transactions, for example:

| Customer/researcher: | How much is one coconut? |
| Trader: | Thirty-five. |
| Customer: | I'd like ten. How much is that? |
| Trader: | (Pause) Three will be one hundred and five; with three more, that will be two hundred and ten. (Pause) I need four more. That is . . . (Pause) three hundred and fifteen . . . I think it is three hundred and fifty. |

(Nunes *et al.*, 1993, pp. 18–19)

In all, 63 problems were set in this way to five traders aged between 9 and 15 years. Overall, the traders had a success rate of 98 per cent. Next, the same children were presented with formal arithmetic tests. For these tests the items were exactly the same as those met on the streets, except that they were reduced to the arithmetic question only. For example, instead of asking, 'What is the cost of ten coconuts at 35 each?', the trader was given pencil and paper and asked 'What is $10 \times 35$?' With these tests the children had a great deal more difficulty. Their success rate fell from 98 per cent in the mental arithmetic of the street to 37 per cent in the formal school test.

On the surface, the Brazilian children and the Swedish children might seem to have the reverse problem to each other. The Brazilian children have trouble transferring their street knowledge to the school test, while the Swedish children have trouble applying their school knowledge to the street problem. However, we could put the problem another way. We could say that both groups of children have trouble in applying mathematical expertise learned in one setting to problems posed in another context.

Whichever way we look at it, the examples serve to illustrate powerfully a well-known problem of mathematics education wherever it is fostered. People seem to have enormous difficulty in using and applying mathematical skills and knowledge from the instructions and formats in which they are learned to novel situations. This poses a major challenge to a key area of schooling, that key aim being to make the lessons of school applicable to the larger world of everyday life.

It should not be assumed that mathematics is the only area of the school curriculum in which there is evidence of pupils' difficulties in using and applying knowledge and skills. The problem is evident in many other areas of the curriculum.

One of our students reported that in a PE lesson she had taught her class the skills of lifting heavy, cumbersome objects safely: back straight, knees bent, load held securely at its base, and so on. The pupils were good at using these skills in the school hall whenever it was necessary to get out or put away PE apparatus, but they never used the skills spontaneously when moving large pieces of classroom furniture.

Another student reported teaching pupils several approaches to ball passing, including loop passes, bounce passes and feinting. Once the pupils returned to the context of a game of netball, however, the usual maelstrom ensued and it was as if the lesson on passing had never existed. There was a complete failure to transfer to a real game skills that had been clearly demonstrated in skill-focused lessons.

As these examples suggest, the problem of application is widely evident and deep seated. It has a long history of perplexing the teaching profession.

How is the problem, of application conceptualized within theories of learning? We can look at application from three contrasting theoretical perspectives: those of associationism, constructivism and situated cognition. From the associationist perspective, learning is regarded as a process of making links, or connections, between small elements of experience. From this point of view, the successful transfer of knowledge to a new situation depends on the amount of similarity between elements of the new situation and associations that have already been acquired. From the associationist perspective, transfer to very different situations is unlikely to occur. In contrast, from the constructivist perspective learning is regarded as a process whereby learners construct from experience increasingly powerful and more general intellectual structures Once acquired, these intellectual structures can then be applied to a range of situations, even if these are very different from those already encountered. From the constructivist point of view, transfer to new situations should not be too problematic. The third theoretical perspective, situated cognition, differs from both associationism and constructivism in arguing that knowledge is essentially situated in the social contexts in which it is acquired or used. From this perspective, the notion that knowledge can be, transferred from one situation to another is incoherent, resting as it does on a faulty assumption about the nature of knowledge. Instead, the situated cognition perspective suggests that teachers should aim to introduce learners to the 'authentic working practices' of particular cultures; in the case, mathematics as it is practised by mathematicians.

As can be seen, there is no obvious consensus between these different perspectives. Each theory makes different predictions about the amount of transfer that might be expected. Each theory also makes different recommendations about what teachers might do. These theories of learning provide interesting perspectives on the problem of application, they do not provide definitive answers. We hope that teachers, curriculum designers and researchers will take up our challenge to keep application high on their respective agendas, and to continue the search for solutions that work both in theory and in practice.

## READING 7.11

# Learning through the years of schooling

Andrew Pollard and Pat Triggs

This reading highlights the relationship between learning and personal development throughout school life and beyond. Drawing on a twelve-year study of children moving through primary and secondary school, it sets out a model of key factors that enable, or constrain, learning (see also Reading 5.5). In particular, it draws attention to the significance of the development of a positive personal identity and confidence in oneself as a learner. Further, taking account of evidence from the PACE (Primary Assessment, Curriculum and Experience) project on the impact of the introduction of the National Curriculum, the reading also raises concerns that the pressures of modern schooling could actually undermine such developments. Indeed, the drive to raise standards, may have the unintended long-term consequence of reducing commitment to lifelong learning. A more balanced approach to policy is recommended.

Are your pupils developing positive learning identities? How does their present self-confidence relate to their previous experience, and to their futures?

Edited from: Pollard, A. and Triggs, P., with Broadfoot, P., McNess, E. and Osborn, M. (2000) *What Pupils Say: Changing Policy and Practice in Primary Education*. London: Continuum, 298–305

The *Identity and Learning Programme* (Filer and Pollard, 2000; Pollard, 1990; Pollard and with Filer, 1996; Pollard and Filer, 1999) is a longitudinal ethnography – a very detailed study of the lives of eighteen children through each year of their compulsory schooling. It began in 1987 and lasted until 2001. Whilst initially drawn from two contrastive primary schools, the children attended ten different secondaries, and the research focused on how they learned and made their way through a succession of new situations and experiences during their schooling. Whilst parents and teachers may hope to provide security and opportunity within the social settings which are created in homes, classrooms and playgrounds, such contexts also often contain challenges and threats which children have to negotiate. As children develop, perfect or struggle with their strategies for coping with such situations, so they learn about other people, about themselves and about life. Of course, the introduction and development of the National Curriculum, with its associated changes in pedagogy and assessment have generated a particular set of challenges.

A major outcome of the ethnographic study has been to develop theoretically informed models of social factors involved in learning. For example, Figure 7.11.1 derives from Pollard with Filer (1996) (see also Figure 5.5.3).

In Figure 7.11.1, the question 'Where and when is learning taking place?' raises socio-historical issues at the levels of country, region, community, school, home, etc. For instance, the context of government and policy-making in England during the 1980s and 1990s was clearly extremely significant to the children studied as part of the PACE project. Regional and LEA differences in economic, political and cultural factors also affected each child's experiences – even if they may not have been aware of such influences. Although these were not a particular focus of the PACE project, our national sampling in four different regions and eight LEAs, and across urban–rural and varied socio-economic settings, made us acutely aware of these significant structural contrasts in circumstances. At the school level, too, our 48 schools revealed major variations in the nature of head-teacher management practices and teacher culture, and consequential contrasts in the school climate as a learning environment (see Osborn *et al.*, 2000). At more detailed levels, the specific contexts within which children

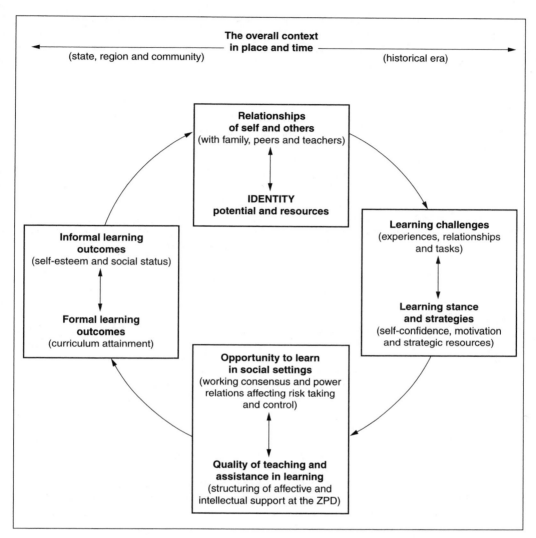

**Figure 7.11.1**   A model of learning, identity and social setting

interact with others – the home, the classroom and the playground – each have unique characteristics with socially constructed rules and expectations guiding behaviour within them (Pollard, 1985). Those of the classroom tend to be more constraining than those found in home or playground, but each is important in structuring children's experiences. Teachers, parents and children live through the particular circumstances of time, place, culture and experience. They thus contribute to the biography and identity of each individual. For instance, the classroom vignette of Jessica and Scott taking their Writing SAT in Kenwood Juniors (see Pollard and Triggs, 2000) provides an example of a specific, high-stakes, classroom episode in which the interplay on the pupils of circumstance, task and identity is extremely clear. Whilst the children struggle, their teacher is shown to be torn between her culturally embedded commitment to individual children whom she knows so well and the new, impersonal and procedural requirements of the national testing system.

To understand children's identities, we must pay particular attention to the 'significant others' in each child's life; to those who interact with them and influence the ways in which they see themselves. Beyond interview and observations such as those conducted by the PACE team, we thus need to understand each child's relationships with parents, siblings, peers and teachers, and the ways in which these relationships may enhance or diminish their self-confidence in themselves as learners and their views of how learning occurs. For instance, are children encouraged to believe that they have a fixed intelligence, or that they can progressively develop from new learning experiences? The case of Neil (Pollard and Triggs, 2000) illustrates how a father's support for maths can contribute to pupil resilience even when a teacher is less supportive. The cases of Laura and Vicky reinforce the importance of parental expectations, but also draw attention to pupils' need to manage their identities in the evaluative context of peer culture. For instance, Laura felt extremely exposed by her parents' and teacher's decision that she should take a maths extension test.

Every child also has both physical and intellectual potential which, over the primary school years, continue the formative and developmental stages which began at birth. The gradual realization of physical and intellectual potential rolls forward to influence self-confidence. Physical and intellectual capability are areas in which psychologists and biologists have made extensive contributions to studies of child development and learning (e.g. Meadows, 1993). Understanding is still developing rapidly, particularly in neurological studies of the brain and mind (Greenfield, 1997).

Identity is also very much influenced by factors such as gender, social class and ethnicity, each of which is associated with particular cultural and material resources and with particular patterns of social expectation which impinge on children through their relationships with others. For instance, the influence of gender is very apparent in the cases reviewed by Pollard and Triggs (2000). Philip reaches towards the male youth identity of 'toughness' to salvage his dignity as he became increasingly exposed by more differentiated pedagogy and categoric assessment. On the other hand, girls such as Alice, though active with friends in private spaces, tended to present themselves more cautiously to teachers and sought to satisfy teacher expectations despite their feelings of unease. Age, status and position, within the family, classroom and playground, are also important for the developing sense of identity of young children because of associated patterns of experience and cultural forms of interpretation.

The model contained in Figure 7.11.1 then focuses on the learning challenges which children face as they grow up. These are very wide-ranging and occur in home, playground and many other settings as well as in the classroom. However, once at primary school, each child has to learn the pupil role – for instance, to cope with classroom rules and conventions, to answer his or her name at registration, to sit cross-legged on the carpet and to listen to the teacher. Then, they must respond to the curricular tasks which they are set. In English primary schools at Key Stage 1 during the early 1990s this included large amounts of work on the core curriculum – perhaps 35 per cent of time spent on English, 15 per cent on maths and 8 per cent on science – and at Key Stage 2 the amount of English fell whilst maths increases, and testing and individual work also grew in significance.

In close association with these issues concerning the content of new learning challenges, we need to consider the perspectives of children about their curriculum and schooling. The issue of motivation when facing a new learning challenge is particularly important. Whilst studies such as those of Rotter, Bandura, Weider, Dweck (Reading 7.6) and Claxton (Reading 7.7) have shown the enormous significance of self-efficacy and learning disposition, implicit theories of capability and qualities of resilience, the *Identity and Learning Programme* has analysed and illustrated in detail how such factors connect to formative social processes of identity construction and to available cultural resources and social expectations throughout school careers. The longitudinal nature of the PACE project, enabled us to mirror this analysis.

Whatever the initial stance of a learner, he or she must then deploy specific strategies in new learning situations. The range of strategies available to individual children will vary, with some being confident to make judgements and vary their approach to tasks, whilst others need guidance and encouragement to move from tried and tested routines. Jessica and Scott, when confronted by their writing SAT (see Pollard and Triggs, 2000) again provide an example of this, with Jessica's persistence and strategic resolve contrasting considerably with Scott's almost fatalistic resignation and dependence on his mascots and any teacher advice he could glean during the test.

Another key set of issues is concerned with the risks and opportunities associated with learning. In particular: how supportive is the specific learning context? On this, one might consider a full range of settings in home, playground, classroom, etc. For instance, in the context of traditional white English middle-class families, social expectations are perhaps at their most structured where set meals occur, such as Sunday lunch; but the same social phenomenon crops up in playgrounds when children confidently assert the rules of games, such as 'tig' or 'What's the time Mr Wolf?'. There are also many times when actions are far less constrained, when family or peer expectation takes a more relaxed form, allowing more scope for individual action and playfulness. The same phenomenon occurs in classroom life. Indeed, Pollard (1985) used the concept of 'rule frame' to describe the nature of the rules-in-play in any particular situation or phase of a teaching session. Rules-in-play derive from the gradual negotiation of understandings about behaviour which routinely takes place between the teacher and pupils. Thus a teacher's introduction to a lesson is usually more tightly framed and controlled than the mid-phase of a session in which children may disperse to engage in various tasks or activities. Such contextual variation is inevitable, but the PACE study suggests that the framing of classroom life has steadily increased during the 1990s. This is an incremental pattern, and the PACE data raise questions concerning its consequences for pupil engagement in learning. We saw, in the cases of Sean, Philip and others that the combination of pedagogic frame, curriculum prescription and categoric assessment had a demotivating effect because the children could not find a means of expressing themselves and affirming their identities within school.

Of course, the nature of negotiation between children and others has always varied in different settings and there is always an element of this which is concerned with the exercise of power. In general, adults have the power to initiate, assert, maintain and change rules, whilst children must comply, adapt, mediate or resist. Most teachers and most parents, for most of the time and in most settings, act sensitively towards young children so that there is an element of negotiation and legitimacy in the social expectations and rules which are applied in particular situations. Sometimes this is not the case, there is less legitimacy and the children may well become unhappy or believe that they have been treated 'unfairly'. Following the introduction of the 1988 Education Reform Act, many teachers reported a concern that, because of curriculum overloading, assessment and other requirements, they were unable to maintain the 'good relationships' with children which they felt to be so important (see Osborn et al., 2000). This teacher concern was not affirmed by the children in our study, indeed, they felt that their relationships with teachers were generally good. However, it is interesting that the criteria that they apply to the curriculum so clearly reflect the priorities of child culture, rather than those of the formal school agenda. School pupils may get on reasonably well with their teachers, but they still occupy the structural position of children and develop associated perspectives.

The question of teacher–pupil relationships is important because, within the relatively individualized and competitive context of English culture (Broadfoot et al., 2000), only a child with a confident learning stance is likely to take chances within a context in which risks and costs of failure are high. In some classrooms, children may thus 'keep their heads down' and the same may be true in some families or playground situations, perhaps where sibling or peer rivalry creates a risk to status or dignity. In focusing on learning processes, we thus need to consider the opportunities and risks which exist for each child to learn within different social settings – the context of power relations and social expectations within which he or she must act and adapt. The PACE findings showed how pupils prioritized their concern to 'avoid embarrassment' and the risks of being 'told off'. Some situations may be low key and feel safe, in which the child can feel secure to 'give it a try'. In the case of others, the stakes may be higher and a child's self-esteem may be vulnerable to social pressure or public critique from siblings, parents, peers or their teacher. As has been well established through media incidents in the last decade, the publication of league tables and high-profile media critiques of teachers and schools in England has a regulative and differentiating effect on the cultural context in which education takes place. PACE findings regarding years five and six suggest that avoidance of risk through instrumentalist conformity may have begun to drive out the playfulness and emotional engagement which is associated with deeper and more creative personal learning (Claxton, 1999; forthcoming; Goleman, 1998).

The quality of the teaching and assistance that a child receives in different settings is also clearly vital to his or her success as a learner, and this has been a priority area for initial and in-service teacher development programmes focusing on subject knowledge and instructional techniques. Social constructivist psychology offers a clear analysis of the importance for learning of the guidance and instruction of more skilled or knowledgeable others (Wood, 1988; Mercer, 1995). Whether support is provided by parents or teachers, siblings or peers, the principle is the same; that children's learning benefits from the 'scaffolding' of their understanding so that it can be extended across the next step in their development. Unfortunately, PACE findings indicate that classroom processes are far more mundane – at least from the pupil perspective. In the first place, we found that children had only vague conceptions of teachers' instructional objectives. Rather than engaging in some synergetic process between teacher and taught to extend existing understanding, most pupils were simply concerned to do what they needed to do to avoid being embarrassed, told off or having to 'do work again'. We found that children felt pressured by classroom time constraints and struggled to develop task engagement. There was little evidence of meta-cognitive, learning-focused awareness by pupils.

However, the ways in which a child's understanding is challenged through teaching are recognised to be of great importance, and Pollard with Filer (1996) suggest that it is necessary to facilitate emotional engagement as well as intellectual challenge. Goleman's work on emotional intelligence (1996) assembles a wide range of evidence on this point. Additionally he argues (1998) that new patterns of life in modern developed societies are threatening emotional stability. Indeed, in the case of modern schooling, both parents and teachers have been found to be worried that children can feel 'overpressured' and we should note the continuing emphasis which is placed on children being 'happy and settled' (Hughes *et al.*, 1994; Osborn *et al.*, 2000, Chapter 4). However, PACE pupil data suggest that children's perception is more practical and prosaic. Accepting their lot, they simply want to find things 'interesting', have a little 'fun' and be treated fairly at school. However, given the opportunity to imagine freely, they seem likely to opt for more physical activity, imaginative play and choice over how they spend time. That, of course, would not necessarily provide experiences from which pupils would satisfy government basic skill targets, but a new priority of creating positive levels of learning disposition, intellectual engagement, and self-awareness as learners might require more learner-aware forms of provision.

'What are the outcomes?' is the final question posed by Figure 7.11.1. The first and most obvious outcome concerns the achievement of intended learning goals. These may range from the official curricular aims which are set by teachers as a result of school or National Curriculum policy, through to the challenges which are presented as part of peer activities in the playground and the new learning experiences which confront each child as he or she grows up within the family at home. Learning thus produces relatively overt yardsticks of attainment, whether the child is learning letter formation in handwriting or about number bonds, how to skip, swim or play a new game, or how to hold their own in family conversation. What then, has been achieved? What is the new level of attainment? What can the child now do and understand? Such questions are of particular importance because, beyond issues of explicit achievement and the new forms of action which become possible, lie associated consequences for the ways in which young learners perceive themselves and are perceived by others. We saw the process and pressures of assessment and noted how pupils perceived assessment in summative terms. This has a direct affect on their self-perception, albeit after mediation by parents, peers and teachers (Filer and Pollard, 2000; Reay and William, 1999).

Social differentiation occurs when children become distinguished, one from another. In school, children may have little control over this – for instance, they may be organized by age-group, 'ability' group or gender. Ability grouping or setting has come to be of particular significance following the introduction of categoric assessment, formal reports, target setting and inspection. Pupil performance has become more high stakes and more overt – a classic form of differentiation. The consequence of this is likely to be a growth in polarization – the cultural response of children who experience differentiation. Thus those who succeed choose to socialize with each other, and those who do less well seek to preserve their dignity by discarding any learning ambitions they may have once held, and join forces with others in the same position. We saw the beginning of this in the case of Philip. The social consequences of such patterns are that there is a progressive divergence in children's sense of identity and capability, and this leads, ultimately, to different life chances and the risk of social exclusion (e.g. Connell *et al.*, 1982; Banks *et al.*, 1992; Gillborn and Youdell, 1999).

Children's self-esteem is likely to rise as achievements are made. Maturational 'achievements', such as having birthdays, losing teeth or just becoming taller, are often marked with particular pleasure by younger pupils as they see themselves 'growing up', but many more attainments are accomplished in the home, playground and classroom as children face new experiences and challenges. The classroom setting is, of course, particularly important because it is the source of official educational judgements, whilst the home setting offers the support, or otherwise, of parents – the crucial 'significant others'. We saw this in the cases of Neil, Laura and other case study children.

Regarding social status, it is arguably relationships within peer groups which are of most significance to children. For many children, peer-group membership is both a source of great enjoyment in play and a source of solidarity in facing the challenges that are presented by adults. In such circumstances, some children lead whilst others follow and high status may well be associated with popularity, style and achievement in facilitating 'good fun'. On the other hand, peer-group cultures can also be exclusive and reject children from membership if they are unable to conform to group norms. We saw how Laura and Vicky, whilst trying to attain highly, had to manage this aspect of their identities. However, if a child's learning and performance regarding peer expectations is deficient, their social status is likely to be low – with a consequent roll-forward effect on their sense of self-esteem and of personal identity and the risk of a negative spiral.

Thus, then, the process is brought full circle and we return to the first question posed by Figure 7.11.1 – to identity, ' "who" is learning?'.

This cyclical conceptualization represents the process of learning in a social context, with the effects of social relationships and learning achievements accumulating over time to contribute to the formation of identity. In the case of young children, as we saw from our case study consideration of Haley, Kevin, Richard and Amanda over their six years of primary schooling, it is particularly necessary to monitor the ways in which patterns of adaption and achievement evolve or stabilize in response to changing social circumstances.

Standing back from this analysis, we might reflect on the fact that human learning has been a continuous process for millions of years. We develop our biological inheritance by interacting with our physical and social environment. Thus, development and experience work together, producing learning and change (Blyth, 1984). Modern educational innovations, such as schooling and planned curricula, represent a socially constructed intervention into this fundamental process.

At the start of a new century, as new literacy and numeracy campaigns become institutionalized together with a renewed emphasis on targeted instruction, homework and assessment, we would do well to really think through the implications of how to maximize pupil motivation and belief in personal learning capacity. Successive phases of the PACE project

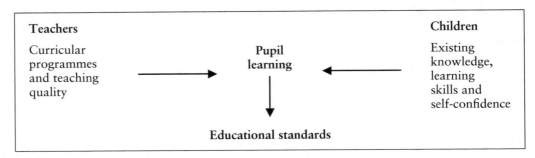

**Figure 7.11.2**  Complementary factors in pupil learning

have shown how pupil motivation and engagement in school is vulnerable to erosion at a time when national requirements are imposed and when teachers' scope for curricular and pedagogic responsiveness to children becomes limited.

The comprehensive findings of PACE on pupil perspectives has been linked to the *Identity and Learning Programme*. Together, they highlight and substantiate the major intervening variables concerned with children's personal self-confidence as learners as they negotiate their pupil careers. It is clear that parents have a significant mediating role in learning, as do relationships with siblings and peers. There is also a continuous need for skilful, sensitive and socially aware management of pupil motivation by teachers. A simple way of expressing key complementary factors in the educational process is shown in Figure 7.11.2.

It is important to note the differences in the nature of these elements. An instructional programme can be organized in sequence and can be specifically targeted to yield measurable outcomes. It is relatively discrete and precise, and is readily amenable to policy prescription, school development plans, teacher training, assessments and the new technologies of 'performativity'. However, the development of the knowledge, learning skills and self-confidence of a learner is built on the entire accumulation of a child's previous experiences. It is subtle and multifaceted, requiring empathy, understanding and judgement from teachers as well as subject knowledge. The child in the classroom is working through a pupil career, is developing physically as well as personally, is engaged in a process of becoming. Whilst this is much less tangible than the 'raising of standards', it is no less important. Indeed, the reality is that these two major set of factors interact together to produce both educational and personal outcomes.

This suggests a need for balance. Sustained attention to curricular instruction should be complemented by provision for the development of pupils' learning skills and self-confidence. An overemphasis on focused, basic instruction risks undermining curriculum engagement and the self-belief of children as learners.

## CHAPTER 8

# Curriculum. How do we develop knowledge and understanding?

A curriculum reflects the values and understanding of those who construct it, and the readings in this chapter illustrate a seemingly endemic tension in the perspectives of both policy-makers and practitioners.

We start, however, with two ground-clearing readings. First, Meyer and Kamens (8.1) suggest that, despite all the debates, there is in fact an international convergence in official statements of national curricula, though there are certainly significant divergences in actual classroom practices (Alexander, 2000). Reading 8.2 introduces Bernstein's two important conceptual tools for analysing classroom currricula – 'classification' and 'frame'. To what extent should the curriculum be integrated, or subject compartmentalized? To what extent should classroom practice be flexibly responsive, or structured and targeted? The answers to these questions change from era to era, and depending on basic assumptions about teaching and learning.

The next five readings illustrate this. We begin with a selection from the Plowden Report (8.3), a classic statement of child-centred principles. This is supported by a modern rationale, by Katz (8.4), for a developmentally appropriate curriculum. We cannot, in other words, ignore the reality of children's physical, social, emotional and cognitive development and the need to engage pupils' interest in the curriculum. On the other hand, Wilson (8.5) asserts the inevitability of 'subjects', argues that children's interests can be engaged through them and offers a philosophical rationale for the subjects of the school curriculum (though not in quite the form currently promoted in England and Wales). Shulman (8.6) analyses three forms of subject knowledge needed by teachers, and argues that each makes an important contribution to effective teaching. Finally, O'Hara and O'Hara offer practical advice on how to fulfil the role of a subject coordinator. Here, then, we have the rationale and implications of a subject-based curriculum.

The tensions between developmental and subject-based approaches to curriculum will endure, for they are endemic to the process of education itself. Reflective teachers need to learn how to manage them, whatever the particular steer from the government of the day. In this context, it is interesting to see how Labour Party policy has changed over time. When the National Curriculum was first implemented, a Labour Party Green Paper (see Reading 8.8) presented criticisms of its 'overloaded' nature and argued that the curriculum should be 'balanced and broadly based' as specified in the Education Reform Act of 1988. How does this statement stand up today?

We conclude this chapter with a reading by Alexander (8.9) who provides an excellent framework for analysing the political, conceptual, pragmatic, empirical and value-led aspects of 'good practice'.

The parallel chapter of *Reflective Teaching* begins by pointing out how an official curriculum may differ considerably from the curriculum as experienced by pupils. Patterns of primary school practice are then considered, with particular reference to the 'basics' and 'other' curriculum subjects and to alternative ways of curriculum organization in subject-based or integrated ways. The second major part of the chapter describes the structure and content of national curricula within the UK, and also highlights their relationship to issues such as values, learning and inclusion. Finally, there is a section on subject knowledge and the curriculum. This includes discussion on developing confidence in subject knowledge and on professional support through subject associations.

There are also suggestions for 'Key Readings' in relation to each of the topics covered. More extensive ideas are offered in the relevant section of *RTweb*.

### READING 8.1

# Accounting for a world curriculum

John Meyer and David Kamens

The American team of researchers reporting here conducted a global survey of official curricular requirements in primary schools. Their core finding is that there are enormous similarities in the subject areas taught and the time given to them, despite the diverse histories, cultures and circumstances of different countries. They speculate about why this should be so.

Do you think we are moving towards a world curriculum? And what influences will follow if the global influence of the United States wanes?

Edited from: Meyer, J. W. and Kamens, D. H. (1992) 'Conclusion: accounting for a world curriculum', in Meyer, J. W., Kamens, D. H. and Benavot, A., with Cha., Y. K. and Wong, S. Y. (eds) *School Knowledge for the Masses: World Models and National Primary Curricular Categories in the Twentieth Century*. London: Falmer Press, 165–75.

The most important finding in our research is the relative homogeneity of the world's primary curricular outlines in the twentieth century. This is true descriptively – in the sense that there is considerably less variation among curricular outlines than reasonable arguments would have predicted. And it is true in an explanatory sense – factors that vary among countries play a smaller role than most theories would have proposed, in affecting variations among curricula. Further, we notice a pronounced tendency for curricular changes in particular countries to parallel each other and to take the form of conformity to world curricular patterns.

It turns out, thus, that through this century one may speak of a relatively clear 'world primary curriculum' operating, at least as an official standard, in almost all countries. A bit more than a third of the student's time is to be spent on language – and mainly on national language(s), not on local or foreign or classical ones. About one-sixth of the time goes to mathematics. A set of other subjects is practically always found (especially since the Second World War), with each subject taking 10 per cent of curricular time, or a bit less – social science, science, arts and physical education. Religious or moral education, and vocational education, are less universally present, and get only 5 per cent of the time. All other possible subjects – and many are found in one or another country at one or another time – take up in total less than a twentieth of the curriculum in the typical case.

The stylized character of the overall outline of the curriculum, or its readability in terms of world norms, is striking. Put simply, curricular categories, and even allocations of time to these categories, conform to the standard world outline.

What then explains the world curriculum and its evolution? It is difficult to address such questions in empirical terms, but some general arguments may be useful.

The nineteenth-century rise of the modern secular mass curriculum seems closely linked to the rise of the model of the national state, with a universalized citizenry closely linked to a national culture (in language and art and, in a sense, physical education) and organized around rationalistic themes of social and natural progress (emphasizing science, mathematics, and social science, in addition to more traditional subjects). Themes left from an older Christendom – classical languages and literatures, and a strong emphasis on religion – were attenuated (though religion remained, especially in those countries where it was tied to a national state).

Two dimensions are built into this educational model – we may be so habituated to them as not to notice how distinct they are. First, there is the nominally arational or irrational side – the construction of what Anderson (1983) calls the 'imagined national community', or what Thomas *et al.* (1987), call the 'ontology of modernity'. Here we have the laborious construction of national languages (often at considerable cost to both local practice and international exchange), of national culture and history. Here we also have the surprising emphasis on tightly linking the identity of the individual child to national society through art and culture and physical education. Second, there is the rationalistic side of this same constructed world – the scientific and social scientific emphasis on the rationality and progressiveness of the national societies being constructed. Both dimensions are strikingly built into the modern curriculum as it develops, and both are now found everywhere: there seem to be no countries left whose curricula lack a strong sense of national identity; and none left whose curricula lack most of the modern rationalities.

Through the subsequent century, this model of the high national state and society seems to have remained relatively constant in the world curriculum – if anything, intensified as it became more universal. The one dramatic change since the First World War, is the shift towards a more integrated social studies subject – which is arguably a reflection of the more and more complete interpenetration of state and society characteristic of the twentieth century.

We may be nearing the end of the high period of the national state as sovereign and autonomous social system in a world society imagined to be anarchic. The citizen status of individuals is being redefined in terms of their human rights in a larger system; there is a worldwide discussion of the limits on national sovereignty, and national societies are seen as in a worldwide natural and social environment requiring greater attention.

Our curricular data may not be detailed enough to capture many of the educational shifts that might follow such changes. But some findings of our analyses could well be reflecting them. There is, for one thing, the expansion in modern foreign language instruction and particularly the emphasis on English as a world medium of communication rather than the simple retention of any language of the colonial period. There is also the expansion of social studies – with the potential vision of human societies anywhere as comparable and comprehensible rather than a narrower vision of national history and geography. There may also be a slight rise in instruction in moral education rather than religion reflective of a more universalistic approach to basic norms.

Aside from arguments explaining substantive changes in the world curriculum, our observations permit clear arguments about the processes involved. The developments we observe over the past century have two clear properties we must note. First, they occur in the centres of world educational communication. The nineteenth-century development of the modern curriculum occurred in the European centres, spreading outward from them in waves of imitation – sometimes coerced through colonial power and authority, sometimes more voluntaristic (DiMaggio and Powell, 1983). Similarly with the mid-twentieth-century changes we observe – they seem to reflect the dominance of the models of the metropolitan powers, and more recently, the hegemonic United States. Perhaps future changes in world curricular customs will reflect a more egalitarian system – for example, through discussions in such forums as UNESCO, which might give more peripheral countries more relative influence. But in the period of our observations, the world centres have been dominant.

Second, the main changes we observe over time in the world curriculum have been structured by the conceptions of the educational professionals and scientists. They are theorized changes, rather than changes that seem simply to reflect raw power. Every one of them – changes in language instruction, the rise of science and expansion of mathematics, the reorganization of social science instruction, the rise of aesthetic and physical education, and so on – is a creature of elaborate educational theorizing, whatever its possible ultimate origins in power or interest.

It is important not to overstate the power of the educational professionals as local interest groups, or as agents of local forces. But it is equally important to see that such groups – operating on their central terrain as agents of great scientific truths in a more universalistic way – embody and represent wider world cultural forces, and gain authority as they do so. Their authority rests on knowledge claims, and in good part such claims tend to have not only a universalistic flavour but a worldwide structural location.

With all this said, it seems obvious that idiosyncratic features of the metropolitan powers (and in particular the United States, since the Second World War) and their professional theorists play a considerable role in the evolution of the world curriculum. It is not simply a matter of the worldwide evolution of the natural principles of the modern nation-state. A rather liberal version of this nation-state has been politically and educationally dominant in our period – clearly the world curriculum would have looked very different with different outcomes of the First and Second World Wars.

This suggests that future changes in the types of countries that are most dominant in world society may also produce changes in curricular emphasis.

READING 8.2

# On the classification and framing of educational knowledge

Basil Bernstein

Basil Bernstein's work on the classification and framing of knowledge has been of enormous importance as a means of analysing the relationship between the wider values of society and schooling practices. He distinguishes between a 'collection' type of curriculum in which subject knowledge is distinct, and an 'integrated' type in which subjects may be merged. The concept of 'classification' describes the strength of boundary between subjects, and the related concept of 'frame' denotes the degree of control experienced by teachers and pupils, given the particular forms of curriculum, pedagogy and assessment within the classroom.

Particular interest groups within the wider society often seek to promote their values though advocacy of particular forms of educational practice (see also Reading 18.4). In the case of curriculum, this is illustrated by the media and policy-maker interest which is often engendered in controversies over topic-based and subject-based curriculum planning (Readings 8.3 and 8.5 are relevant here).

How do you see the links between values, forms of curricular organization and classroom practices?

Edited from: Bernstein, B. (1971) 'On the classification and framing of educational knowledge' in Young, M. F. D. (ed.) *Knowledge and Control: New Directions for the Sociology of Education*. London: Collier-Macmillan, 47–51.

How a society selects, classifies, distributes, transmits and evaluates the educational knowledge it considers to be public, reflects both the distribution of power and the principles of social control.

Educational knowledge is a major regulator of the structure of experience. From this point of view, one can ask, 'How are forms of experience, identity and relation evoked, maintained and changed by the formal transmission of educational knowledge and sensitivities?' Formal educational knowledge can be considered to be realized through three message systems: curriculum, pedagogy and evaluation. Curriculum defines what counts as valid knowledge, pedagogy defines what counts as a valid transmission of knowledge, and evaluation defines what counts as a valid realization of this knowledge on the part of the taught. The term, educational knowledge code, refers to the underlying principles which shape curriculum, pedagogy and evaluation.

I shall distinguish between two broad types of curricula. If contents stand in a closed relation to each other, that is if the contents are clearly bounded and insulated from each other, I shall call such a curriculum a 'collection' type. Here, the learner has to collect a group of favoured contents in order to satisfy some criteria of evaluation. There may of course be some underlying concept to a collection: the gentleman, the educated man, the skilled man, the non-vocational man.

I want to juxtapose against the collection type, a curriculum where the various contents do not go their own separate ways, but where the contents stand in an open relation to each other. I shall call such a curriculum an 'integrated' type.

Now we can have various types of collection, and various degrees and types of integration.

I shall now introduce the concepts, classification and frame, which will be used to analyse the underlying structure of the three message systems, curriculum, pedagogy and evaluation, which are realizations of the educational knowledge code. The basic idea is embodied in the principle used to distinguish the two types of curricula: collection and integrated. Strong insulation between contents pointed to a collection type, whereas reduced insulation pointed to an integrated type. The principle here is the strength of the boundary between contents. This notion of boundary strength underlies the concepts of 'classification' and 'frame'.

Classification, here, does not refer to what is classified, but to the relationships between contents. Classification refers to the nature of the differentiation between contents. Where classification is strong, contents are well insulated from each other by strong boundaries. Where classification is weak, there is reduced insulation between contents, for the boundaries between contents are weak or blurred. Classification thus refers to the degree of boundary maintenance between contents. Classification focuses our attention upon boundary strength as the critical distinguishing feature of the division of labour of educational knowledge. It gives us, as I hope to show, the basic structure of the message system, curriculum.

The concept, frame, is used to determine the structure of the message system, pedagogy. Frame refers to the form of the context in which knowledge is transmitted and received. Frame refers to the specific pedagogical relationship of teacher and taught. In the same way as classification does not refer to contents, so frame does not refer to the contents of the pedagogy. Frame refers to the strength of the boundary between what may be transmitted and what may not be transmitted, in the pedagogical relationship. Where framing is strong, there is a sharp boundary, where framing is weak, a blurred boundary, between what may and may not be transmitted. Frame refers us to the range of options available to teacher and taught in the control of what is transmitted and received in the context of the pedagogical relationship. Strong framing entails reduced options; weak framing entails reduced options; weak framing entails a range of options. Thus frame refers to the degree of control teacher and pupil possess over the selection, organization, pacing and timing of the knowledge transmitted and received in the pedagogical relationship.

From the perspective of this analysis, the basic structure of the curricular message system, is given by variations in the strength of classification, and the basic structure of the pedagogic message system is given by variations in the strength of frames.

Where classification is strong, the boundaries between the different contents are sharply drawn. If this is the case, then it presupposes strong boundary maintainers. Strong classification also creates a strong sense of membership in a particular class and so a specific identity. Strong frames reduce the power of the pupil over what, when and how he receives knowledge, and increases the teacher's power in the pedagogical relationship. However, strong classification reduces the power of the teacher over what he transmits, as he may not overstep the boundary between contents, and strong classification reduces the power of the teacher vis-à-vis the boundary maintainers.

# Aspects of children's learning

Central Advisory Council for England (Plowden Report)

---

This reading from the Plowden Report conveys the tone and emphasis of what has been taken as the most influential statement of 'progressivism' in primary education. The role of play in early learning is clearly set out, together with the conception of 'the child as the agent of his own learning', and the necessity of building a curriculum on children's interests and experiences. Towards the end, the influence of Piaget (see Reading 7.2) is apparent in the discussion of the teacher role. It is interesting to speculate on how this might have been written under a Vygotskian influence (see Readings 7.8 and 13.2).

There has been much debate on Plowden. However, do the ideas ring true to you now? Which seem naive or outdated and which remain significant?

Edited from: Central Advisory Council for Education (England) (1967) *Children and their Primary Schools* (The Plowden Report). London: HMSO, 193–7

---

Play is the central activity in all nursery schools and in many infant schools. This sometimes leads to accusations that children are wasting their time in school: they should be 'working'. But this distinction between work and play is false, possibly throughout life, certainly in the primary school. Its essence lies in past notions of what is done in school hours (work) and what is done out of school (play). We know now that play – in the sense of 'messing about' either with material objects or with other children, and of creating fantasies – is vital to children's learning and therefore vital in school. Adults who criticize teachers for allowing children to play are unaware that play is the principal means of learning in early childhood; it is the way through which children reconcile their inner lives with external reality. In play, children gradually develop concepts of causal relationships, the power to discriminate, to make judgements, to analyse and synthesize, to imagine and to formulate. Children become absorbed in their play and the satisfaction of bringing it to a satisfactory conclusion fixes habits of concentration that can be transferred to other learning.

From infancy, children investigate the material world. Their interest is not wholly scientific but arises from a desire to control or use the things about them. Pleasure in 'being a cause' seems to permeate children's earliest contact with materials. To destroy and construct involves learning the properties of things and in this way children can build up concepts of weight, height, size, volume and texture.

Primitive materials such as sand, water, clay and wood attract young children and evoke concentration and inventiveness. Children are also stimulated by natural or manufactured materials of many shapes, colours and textures. Their imagination seizes on particular facets of objects and leads them to invent as well as to create. All kinds of causal connections are discovered, illustrated and used. Children also use objects as symbols for things, feelings and experiences, for which they may lack words. A small girl may use a piece of material in slightly different ways to make herself into a bride, a queen, or a nurse. When teachers enter into the play activity of children, they can help by watching the connections and relationships which children are making and by introducing, almost incidentally, the words for the concepts and feelings that are being expressed. Some symbolism is unconscious and may be the means by which children come to terms with actions or thoughts which are not acceptable to adults or are too frightening for the children themselves. In play are the roots of drama, expressive movement and art. In this way too children learn to understand other people. The earliest play of this kind probably emerges from play with materials. A child playing with a toy aeroplane can be seen to take the role of both the aeroplane and the pilot apparently simultaneously. All the important people of his world figure in this play: he imitates, he becomes, he symbolizes. He works off aggression or compensates himself for lack of love by 'being' one or other of the people who impinge on his life. By acting as he conceives they do, he tries to understand them. Since children tend to have inflexible roles thrust on them by adults, they need opportunities to explore different roles and to make a freer choice of their own. Early exploration of the actions, motives and feelings of themselves and of others is likely to be an important factor in the ability to form right relationships, which in its turn seems to be a crucial element in mental health. Adults can help children in this form of play, and in their social development, by references to the thoughts, feelings and needs of other people. Through stories told to them, children enter into different ways of behaving and of looking at the world, and play new parts.

Much of children's play is 'cultural' play as opposed to the 'natural' play of animals which mainly practises physical and survival skills. It often needs adult participation so that cultural facts and their significance can be communicated to children. The introduction into the classroom of objects for hospital play provides opportunities for coming to terms with one of the most common fears. Similarly, the arrival of a new baby in the family, the death of someone important to the child, the invention of space rockets or new weapons may all call for the provision of materials for dramatic play which will help children to give expression to their feelings as a preliminary to understanding and controlling them. Sensitivity and observation are called for rather than intervention from the teacher. The knowledge of children gained from 'active' observation is invaluable to teachers. It gives common ground for conversation and exchange of ideas which it is among the most important duties of teachers to initiate and foster.

The child is the agent in his own learning. This was the message of the often quoted comment from the 1931 Report: 'The curriculum is to be thought of in terms of activity and experience rather than of knowledge to be acquired and facts to be stored'. Read in isolation, the passage has sometimes been taken to imply that children could not learn from imaginative experience and that activity and experience did not lead to the acquisition of knowledge. The context makes it plain that the actual implication is almost the opposite of this. It is that activity and experience, both physical and mental, are often the best means of gaining knowledge and acquiring facts. This is more generally recognized today but still needs to be said. We certainly would not wish to undervalue knowledge and facts, but facts are best retained when they are used and understood, when right attitudes to learning are created, when children learn to learn. Instruction in many primary schools continues to bewilder children because it outruns their experience. Even in infant schools, where innovation has gone furthest, time is sometimes wasted in teaching written 'sums' before children are able to understand what they are doing.

The intense interest shown by young children in the world about them, their powers of concentration on whatever is occupying their attention, or serving their immediate purposes, are apparent to both teachers and parents. Skills or reading and writing or the techniques used in art and craft can best be taught when the need for them is evident to children. A child who has no immediate incentive for learning to read is unlikely to succeed because of warnings about the disadvantages of illiteracy in adult life. There is, therefore, good reason for allowing young children to choose within a carefully prepared environment in which choices and interest are supported by their teachers, who will have in mind the potentialities for further learning. Piaget's observations support the belief that children have a natural urge to explore and discover, that they find pleasure in satisfying it and that it is therefore self-perpetuating. When children are learning new patterns of behaviour or new concepts, they tend both to practise them spontaneously and to seek out relevant experience, as can be seen from the way they acquire skills in movement. It takes much longer than teachers have previously realized for children to master through experience new concepts or new levels of complex concepts. When understanding has been achieved, consolidation should follow. At this stage children profit from various types of practice devised by their teachers, and from direct instruction.

Children will, of course vary in the degree of interest that they show and their urge to learn will be strengthened or weakened by the attitudes of parents, teachers and others with whom they identify themselves. Apathy may result when parents show no interest, clamp down on children's curiosity and enterprise, tell them constantly not to touch and do not answer their questions. Children can also learn to be passive from a teacher who allows them little scope in managing their own affairs and in learning. A teacher who relies only on instruction, who forestalls children's questions or who answers them too quickly, instead of asking the further questions which will set children on the way to their own solution, will disincline children to learn. A new teacher with time and patience can usually help children who have learned from their teachers to be too dependent. Those who have been deprived at home need more than that. Their self-confidence can only be restored by affection, stability and order. They must have special attention from adults who can discover, by observing their responses, what experiences awaken interest, and can seize on them to reinforce the desire to learn.

External incentives such as marks and stars, and other rewards and punishments, influence children's learning mainly by evoking or representing parents' or teachers' approval. Although children vary temperamentally in their response to rewards and punishments, positive incentives are generally more effective than punishment, and neither is an damaging as neglect. But the children who most need the incentive of good marks are least likely to gain them, even when, as in many primary schools, they are given for effort rather than for achievement. In any case, one of the main educational tasks of the primary school is to build on and strengthen children's intrinsic interest in learning and lead them to learn for themselves rather than from fear of disapproval or desire for praise.

Learning is a continuous process from birth. The teacher's task is to provide an environment and opportunities which are sufficiently challenging for children and yet not so difficult as to be outside their reach. There has to be the right mixture of the familiar and the novel, the right match to the stage of learning the child has reached. If the material is too familiar or the learning skills too easy, children will become inattentive and bored. If too great maturity is demanded of them, they fall back on half-remembered formulae and become concerned only to give the reply the teacher wants. Children can think and form concepts, so long as they work at their own level, and are not made to feel that they are failures.

Teachers must rely both on their general knowledge of child development and on detailed observation of individual children for matching their demands to children's stages of development. This concept of 'readiness' was first applied to reading. It has sometimes been thought of in too negative a way. Children can be led to want to read, provided that they are sufficiently mature. Learning can be undertaken too late as well as too early. Piaget's work (see Reading 7.2) can help teachers in diagnosing children's readiness in mathematics, and gives some pointers as to how it can be encouraged.

At every stage of learning, children need rich and varied materials and situations, though the pace at which they should be introduced may vary according to the children. If children are limited in materials, they tend to solve problems in isolation and fail to see their relevance to other similar situations. This stands out particularly clearly in young children's learning of mathematics. Similarly, children need to accumulate much experience of human behaviour before they can develop moral concepts. If teachers or parents are inconsistent in their attitudes or contradict by their behaviour what they preach, it becomes difficult for children to develop stable and mature concepts. Verbal explanation, in advance of understanding based on experience, may be an obstacle to learning, and children's knowledge of the right words may conceal from teachers their lack of understanding. Yet it is inevitable that children will pick up words which outstrip their understanding. Discussion with other children and with adults is one of the principal ways in which children check their concepts against those of others and build up an objective view of reality. There is every justification for the conversation which is a characteristic feature of the contemporary primary school. One of the most important responsibilities of teachers is to help children to see order and pattern in experience, and to extend their ideas by analogies and by the provision of suitable vocabulary. Rigid division of the curriculum into subjects tends to interrupt children's trains of thought and of interest and to hinder theme from realizing the common elements in problem solving. These are among the many reasons why some work, at least, should cut across subject divisions at all stages in the primary school.

 **READING 8.4**

# A developmental approach to the curriculum in the early years

Lilian G. Katz

This reading is of particular interest for the way it grounds principles of curriculum planning in what is known about children's development, rather than in the requirements of nationally prescribed subjects. The case for this is particularly strong in work with very young children, but developmental issues remain significant throughout the years of schooling. Those in Key Stage 2 and the teenageers of lower secondary also have particular needs as they develop physically, mentally, socially and emotionally.

To what extent is your teaching of curriculum subjects affected by your pupils' developmental needs? Is it possible to achieve a satisfactory balance?

Edited from: Katz, L. G. (1998) 'A developmental approach to the curriculum in the early years', in Smidt, S. *The Early Years: A Reader*. London, New York: Routledge, 11–16

Everyone responsible for planning a curriculum must address at least the following three questions:

1 What should be learned?
2 When should it be learned?
3 How is it best learned?

Responses to the first question provide the goals of the programme for which pedagogical practices are to be adopted. The second question is the developmental one in that it draws upon what is known about the development of the learner. In other words, child development helps to address the when questions of programme design. The third question turns specifically to matters of appropriate pedagogy itself; it includes consideration of all aspects of implementing a programme by which the programme's goals can be achieved, depending, of course, on what is to be learned, and when it is to be learned. In other words, responses to one of the three questions are inextricably linked to responses to the other two.

Thus what should be learned and how it is best learned depends on when the learning is to occur. Similarly, how something is learned depends upon what it is, as well as upon the developmental characteristics of the learner. For example, virtually all stakeholders in early childhood education would place literacy high on the list of answers to the question, 'What should be learned?' However, they are likely to diverge considerably upon the question of when as well as how it should be learned – the latter considerations being related to each other. Terms such as emergent literacy and preliteracy have recently appeared in the early childhood literature, partly in order to address the confounding of the when and how questions. Even though the three questions are clearly linked, for the sake of discussion, they are taken up separately below.

## What should be learned?

The values and preferences of the parents served by the programme would seem to have first claim among criteria for determining what should be learned. However, parents are rarely a homogeneous or monolithic group with a clear consensus about the goals of their children's education. While the community and parents' preferences contribute to determining the goals, the special expertise of professional educators should be brought to bear on addressing the questions of when and how the goals can be best implemented.

Whatever specific learning goals and objectives are identified by clients and educators, they are all likely to fit into each of four types of learning goals: knowledge, skills, dispositions and feelings.

*Knowledge* During the pre-school period, this can be broadly defined as ideas, concepts, constructions, schemas, facts, information, stories, customs, myths, songs and other such contents of mind that come under the heading of what is to be learned. Three Piagetian categories of knowledge – social, physical and logically mathematical – are often used in discussions of the knowledge goals in early childhood education.

*Skills* These are defined as small, discrete and relatively brief units of behaviour that are easily observed or inferred from behaviour (e.g., skills such as cutting, drawing, counting a group of objects, adding, subtracting, friendship-making, problem-solving skills, and so on).

*Dispositions* These are broadly defined as relatively enduring 'habits of mind', or characteristic ways of responding to experience across types of situations (including persistence at a task, curiosity, generosity, meanness, the disposition to read, to solve problems). Unlike an item of knowledge or a skill, a disposition is not an end state to be mastered once and for all. It is a trend or consistent pattern of behaviour and its possession is established only if its manifestation is observed repeatedly. Thus a person's disposition to be a reader, for example, can only be ascertained if he or she is observed to read spontaneously, frequently and without external coercion.

*Feelings* These are subjective emotional or affective states (e.g. feelings of belonging, or self, esteem, confidence, adequacy and inadequacy, competence and incompetence, and so on). Feelings about or towards significant phenomena may range from being transitory or enduring, intense or weak, or perhaps ambivalent. In early childhood, education attitudes and values can also be included in this category; in education for older children they merit separate categories.

In principle, pedagogical practices are developmentally and educationally appropriate if they address all four categories of learning goals equally and simultaneously. Pedagogical practices are not appropriate if they emphasize the acquisition of knowledge and the mastery of skills without ensuring that the dispositions to use the knowledge and skills so learned are also strengthened. Similarly, if the desired knowledge and skills are mastered in such a way that dislike of them or of the school environment itself develops throughout the learning process, then the pedagogy may be judged inappropriate. Similarly, if a pedagogical approach succeeds in generating feelings of joy, pleasure, amusement or excitement, but fails to bring about the acquisition of desirable knowledge and skills, it cannot be judged appropriate.

Most stakeholders in early childhood education are likely to agree on broad goals in all four categories of learning. For example, most education authorities' curriculum guides list such goals as knowledge and skills related to literacy and numeracy and various items of cultural knowledge, plus such dispositions as the desire to learn, creativity, cooperativeness, and so on; the list of goals related to feelings usually includes 'positive feelings about themselves', or 'self-confidence'.

Once the knowledge, skills, dispositions and feelings to be learned have been agreed upon, the next question is when they should be learned.

## When should it be learned?

Learning in the four categories of learning goals proposed above occurs constantly, whether intentional or incidental. However, a developmental approach to curriculum planning takes into account both dimensions of development: the normative and the dynamic dimensions. These two equally important dimensions of development are defined as follows.

*The normative dimension of development* This addresses the characteristics and capabilities of children that are typical or normal for their age group (e.g. the typical size of vocabulary of four-year-olds, the average age of first walking or of understanding numerical concepts). Age norms also provide useful starting points for curriculum planning. Knowledge of age, typical interests, activities and abilities can provide a basis for preliminary planning of a general programme of activities, and the selection of equipment and materials. For example, norms of development provide a basis for assuming that most two-year-olds need daytime naps, most four-year-olds do not understand calendar concepts, or that, typically, most five-year-olds can begin to write their own names, etc. Age norms are also useful for alerting teachers to individual children whose patterns of development depart noticeably from their age group and who warrant close observation by which to ascertain whether special curriculum and teaching strategies are required.

*The dynamic dimension of development* deals with an individual child's progress from immaturity to maturity. This dimension addresses changes over time within an individual and the long-term effects of early experience, rather than the normality of behaviour and abilities of an age group. For example, sequence refers to the order or stages of development through which an individual passes, e.g. in achieving mastery of first language. The curriculum and teaching practices consider what learning and developmental tasks have to be completed before the next learning can occur. Delayed effects refer to the potential positive and negative effects of early experience that may not be manifested at the time of occurrence, but may influence later functioning (e.g. early infant–caregiver attachment may influence later parenting competence).

A developmental approach to curriculum and teaching practices takes into account both dimensions of development. What young children should do and should learn is determined on the basis of what is best for their development in the long term (i.e. the dynamic consequences of early experience) rather than simply what works in the short term.

## How is it best learned?

This question takes us directly to matters of pedagogy, such as consideration of teaching methods, activities, materials and all other practical matters designed to achieve the learning goals, and to take into account what is known about learners' development.

Learning in the four categories of goals is facilitated in different ways. In the case of both knowledge and skills, learning can be aided by instruction as well as by other processes, but dispositions and feelings cannot be learned from direct instruction. Many important dispo-

148                                   www.rtweb.info

sitions are inborn – e.g. the disposition to learn, to observe, to investigate, to be curious, etc. Many dispositions appear to be learned from models, are strengthened by being manifested and appreciated, and are weakened when unacknowledged or ineffective.

Feelings related to school experiences are learned as by-products of experiences rather than from instruction. Both dispositions and feelings can be thought of as incidental learning in that they are incidental to the processes by which knowledge and skills are acquired. To label feelings as incidental is not to belittle them, or to devalue the role of pedagogy in their development; rather, it is to emphasize that they cannot be taught didactically. Children cannot be instructed in what feelings to have.

Recent insights into children's development suggest that, in principle, the younger the child, the more readily knowledge is acquired through active and interactive processes; conversely, with increasing age, children become more able to profit from reactive, passive–receptive pedagogical approaches or instructional processes. In other words, pedagogical practices are developmentally appropriate when the knowledge to be acquired or constructed is related to the child's own first-hand, direct experiences and when it is accessible from primary sources. This is not to say that children do not acquire knowledge and information from such secondary sources as stories, books and films. The extent to which they do so is related to whether young children can connect the materials within the secondary sources to the images and knowledge they already possess. With increasing age and experience, children become more able to profit from second-hand, indirect experiences, and secondary sources.

Thus pedagogical practices are appropriate if they provide young children with ample opportunity to interact with adults and children who are like and unlike themselves, with materials, and directly with real objects and real environments.

However, interactions cannot occur in a vacuum; they have to have content. Interactions must be about something – ideally something that interests the interactors.

What criteria can be used to determine what knowledge or content is appropriate for young children? For example, should young children spend up to ten minutes per day in a calendar exercise? Should young children in southern Florida be making snowflake crystals out of Styrofoam at Christmas time? Should substantial amounts of time be allocated to observance of public holidays and festivals? Why? And why not? What factors, data or other matters should be taken into account in answering questions such as these? One way to approach these questions is to derive principles of practice from what is known about the nature of children's intellectual development.

In principle, a substantial proportion of the content of interaction should be related to matters of actual or potential interest to the children served by the programme. Since not all of children's interests are equally deserving of attention, some selection of which interests are the most worthy of promotion is required. Current views of children's learning and their active construction of knowledge suggest that those interests most likely to extend, deepen and improve their understanding of their own environments and experiences are most worth strengthening during the early years.

## READING 8.5

# Teaching a subject

## John Wilson

> From the developmentalism of the previous reading, we now switch priorities and consider the claims of the subject. John Wilson's challenging philosophical approach asserts the inevitability of engaging in subject matter when teaching. Further, he offers an analysis of four different 'forms of thought', based on philosophical analysis. Interestingly, these articulate quite closely with the curriculum areas to be found in Scotand and Northern Ireland, although some of the subjects of the curriculum in England and Wales are harder to place.
>
> Can the claims of developmentalism (Reading 8.4) and subject study be reconciled? It would be a pity if we were to continue to swing from one to the other.
>
> Edited from: Wilson, J. (2000) *Key Issues in Education and Teaching*, London, New York: Cassell, 48–52

If we are going to do anything we could seriously call educating children (rather than just being nice to them), we will be concerned that they should have some kind of knowledge, or abilities, or skills, or types of competence. But we cannot give them knowledge or competence in general: it is bound to be knowledge of something or competence at something; it is bound to be some kind, or different kinds, of knowledge and competence. For instance, a child can learn to play football and/or chess and/or badminton, but cannot learn to play them all at the same time because they are different games. Similarly, you can teach children about animals and plants or about geology and rock formations, or introduce them to the beauties of the countryside, but you cannot do all these at exactly the same time because they are different kinds of knowledge and experience. You might or might not want to bring them all under one subject title, like perhaps 'nature study' or 'the natural environment', but they would still be different.

This difference is a matter of logic and has nothing to do with wanting to break down subject barriers or any other educational idea. It just is the case that some kinds of interests and questions are different to others. Being interested in why birds migrate is different to being interested in how rocks are formed, and still more different from being interested in what makes a beautiful landscape or what sort of houses would spoil it. Of course, there may be connections between these interests, but they are still different.

These differences are what make 'subjects' inevitable. Suppose you take some children to see a church. Sooner or later, whatever your views about 'subjects', they are going to be interested in it in different ways. Some children will be interested in how it is built or how the spire manages to stay up when it is so tall – that is the start of 'mechanics' or part of 'architecture'. Other children will be interested in who built it and why, how it got to be there, and who wanted it – the start of 'history'. Others may want to know what it is for and what goes on in it – 'religion' or perhaps 'sociology'. And so on. It is inevitable that you should cater for these different interests in different ways simply because they are different. If a child asks, 'How does the spire manage to stand up?' and you reply, 'Yes, isn't it beautiful? It cost £5000 and was built in 1876', you will not be able to educate that child at all; what the child wants to know, now anyway, is something about stresses and structures and building.

So we have to make 'subjects' fit different interests. This is a long and difficult business because many subjects have grown up in a rather haphazard way, not necessarily because of the differences in the particular angles from which people might be interested in things but for quite other reasons. Some of the reasons have to do with our history: for instance, when science becomes important we began to do less Latin, Greek and theology, and more tradition or inertia. This gives us a very mixed bag of subject titles. But what we have to do is not to try to scrap the lot but to look much more closely and carefully at all of them, so that we can find out what we are trying to do. Before we start some major operation that we might call 'changing the curriculum', we have to be clear about what we are doing now, and this brings us inevitably back to questions like 'What is it to teach such-and-such?'.

It would obviously be useful to compile a list of the disciplines: that is, a list of the various angles from which pupils can be interested in things, of the kinds of questions and answers and knowledge that apply to different aspects of them. This is not easy because it is not easy to know just how to chop up different kinds of human knowledge and experience. But certainly one of the more promising lists has been made by Hirst (Hirst and Peters, 1970), and it is worth looking at it to see how the disciplines or 'forms of thought' (as he calls them) might relate to subject titles as they appear in school curricula.

*Logic/mathematics*    This kind of knowledge is not about the world of our sense experience at all but about logical derivations from certain rules or axioms. In some ways, it is like playing a game. You start with the axioms of Euclid or rules about the meaning of certain signs and symbols, and then you derive further knowledge from these. We all have a fairly clear idea what sort of operation this is, and the school subjects that come under the general title 'mathematics' are clear examples of it.

*Science*    This kind of knowledge is about the physical world, about causes and effects in nature, why things fall downwards, why planets move in ellipses and so on. Again, this is pretty clear, and we can identify this discipline in subjects entitled 'chemistry', or 'physics', or 'biology'.

*Personal knowledge*    This is more difficult. But you can see that when we ask questions about why *people* do things (not why planets or light waves do things), it is a different sort of study. People have intentions, purposes and plans, which planets do not have. So 'Why did he . . .?' means something very different from 'Why did it . . .?'. And, as we would expect, the sort of evidence with which we need to work is different: for people we need evidence about what goes on in their heads – about their intentions and designs. The clearest case of a subject title that uses this discipline is 'history', which is surely about why people did things in the past. (If we were interested in why eclipses or earthquakes happened in the past, that would be more like science.) Some aspects of what goes on under title like 'psychology', or 'sociology' may be also concerned with personal knowledge, though other aspects may be more like science: it all depends what sort of answers and knowledge we are after.

*Morality, aesthetics and religion*    These are more difficult still. We lump them together partly because it is not clear what ground each of the three words cover, and there may be some overlap. (Thus for some people 'morality' is part of 'religion', or at least importantly connected with it.) But it seems plausible to say that there are questions about what is morally right and wrong, which are different from questions about what is beautiful, or ugly, or dainty, or elegant ('aesthetics'), and perhaps different again from questions about what one should worship or pray to ('religion'). Philosophers have been working on these areas, trying to help us get clearer about them, but even now we can see that some subject titles include some of the disciplines. Thus if under the title of 'English' I try to get children to appreciate the elegance or effectiveness of a poem or a play, that looks like 'aesthetics' – and it is similar to (the same sort of discipline as) what the French teacher might do with a French poem or what the music teacher might do in musical appreciation classes.

It is worth noting here, incidentally, that not being as clear as we ought to be about these disciplines holds up all possible progress in some cases. The most obvious example is RE. We have the subject title 'RE' (or 'RI' or 'scripture' or 'divinity' or anything we like to choose), but it does not help unless we know what sort of knowledge, what discipline is involved in teaching RE. We can sidestep the problem by, say, teaching church history in RE periods, but that is the discipline of history or personal knowledge and might well be left to the history teachers; or we can encourage children to appreciate the beauty of biblical language, but that is the discipline of aesthetics or literary appreciation and might well be left to the English teacher. Religious people at least will feel that there is something missing if that is all we do. The problem for such people is to point out a special kind of discipline, with a special kind of knowledge, that should go on under 'RE'.

This kind of list is very useful to bear in mind when we are considering rather vaguely entitled new subjects, as perhaps 'social studies' or 'the environment' or 'sex education'. For we at once want to know what disciplines are going to be involved, and the list allows us to raise the question against a useful background.

---

### 📖 READING 8.6

# A perspective on teacher knowledge

## Lee Shulman

> This important reading on curriculum is not about its organization and content, but about the forms of teacher knowledge which are required to teach a curriculum effectively. It is derived from Shulman's classic paper in which he identifies three forms of teacher knowledge: subject content, pedagogic and curricular. This thinking has been extremely influential in teacher training, provision for continuous professional development and conceptualizing the role of curriculum 'consultants' in primary schools.
>
> Thinking of your own curricular strengths, can you identify these three forms of knowledge in yourself? And regarding subjects about which you feel less secure, what forms of knowledge, particularly concern you?
>
> Edited from: Shulman, L. S. (1986) 'Those who understand: knowledge growth in teaching', *Educational Researcher*, **15**, 9–10

How might we think about the knowledge that grows in the minds of teachers, with special emphasis on content? I suggest we distinguish between subject matter content knowledge, pedagogical content knowledge and curricular knowledge.

## Content knowledge

This refers to the amount and organization of knowledge *per se* in the mind of the teacher.

To think properly about content knowledge requires going beyond knowledge of the facts or concepts of a domain. It requires understanding the structures of the subject matter in the manner defined by such scholars as Joseph Schwab (1978).

For Schwab, the structures of a subject include both the substantive and the syntactic structures. The substantive structures are the variety of ways in which the basic concepts and principles of the discipline are organized to incorporate its facts. The syntactic structure of a discipline is the set of ways in which truth or falsehood, validity or invalidity, are established.

When there exist competing claims regarding a given phenomenon, the syntax of a discipline provides the rules for determining which claim has greater warrant. A syntax is like a grammar. It is the set of rules for determining what is legitimate to say in a disciplinary domain and what 'breaks' the rules.

Teachers must not only be capable of defining for students the accepted truths in a domain. They must also be able to explain why a particular proposition is deemed warranted, why it is worth knowing, and how it relates to other propositions, both within the discipline and without, both in theory and in practice.

Thus, the biology teacher must understand that there are a variety of ways of organizing the discipline. Depending on the preferred text, biology may be formulated as: a science of molecules from which one aggregates up to the rest of the field, explaining living phenomena in terms of the principles of their constituent parts; a science of ecological systems from which one disaggregates down to the smaller units, explaining the activities of individual units by virtue of the larger systems of which they are a part; or a science of biological organisms, those most familiar of analytic units, from whose familiar structures, functions and interactions one weaves a theory of adaptation. The well-prepared biology teacher will recognize these and alternative forms of organization and the pedagogical grounds for selecting one under some circumstances and others under different circumstances.

The same teacher will also understand the syntax of biology. When competing claims are offered regarding the same biological phenomenon, how has the controversy been adjudicated? How might similar controversies by adjudicated in our own day?

We expect that the subject matter content understanding of the teacher be at least equal to that of his or her lay colleague, the mere subject matter major. The teacher need not only understand that something is so; the teacher must further understand why it is so, on what grounds its warrant can be asserted, and under what circumstances our belief in its justification can be weakened and even denied. Moveover, we expect the teacher to understand why a given topic is particularly central to a discipline whereas another may be somewhat peripheral. This will be important in subsequent pedagogical judgements regarding relative curricular emphasis.

## Pedagogical content knowledge

A second kind of content knowledge is pedagogical knowledge, which goes beyond knowledge of subject matter *per se* to the dimension of subject matter knowledge for teaching. I still speak of content knowledge here, but of the particular form of content knowledge that embodies the aspects of content most germane to its teachability.

Within the category of pedagogical content knowledge I include, for the most regularly taught topics in one's subject area, the most useful forms of representation of ideas, the most powerful analogies, illustrations, examples, explanations and demonstrations – in a word, the ways of representing and formulating the subject that make it comprehensible to others. Since there are no single most powerful forms of representation, the teacher must have at hand a veritable armament of alternative forms of representation, some of which derive from research whereas others originate in the wisdom of practice.

Pedagogical content knowledge also includes an understanding of what makes the learning of specific topics easy or difficult: the conceptions and preconceptions that students of different ages and backgrounds bring with them to the learning of those most frequently taught topics and lessons. If those preconceptions are misconceptions, which they so often are, teachers need knowledge of the strategies most likely to be fruitful in reorganizing the understanding of learners, because those learners are unlikely to appear before them as blank slates.

Here, research on teaching and on learning coincide most closely. The study of student misconceptions and their influence on subsequent learning has been among the most fertile topics for cognitive research. We are gathering an ever-growing body of knowledge about the misconceptions of students and about the instructional conditions necessary to overcome and transform those initial conceptions. Such research-based knowledge, an important component of the pedagogical understanding of subject matter, should be included at the heart of our definition of needed pedagogical knowledge.

## Curricular knowledge

The curriculum is represented by the full range of programmes designed for the teaching of particular subjects and topics at a given level, the variety of instructional materials available in relation to those programmes, and the set of characteristics that serve as both the indications and contraindications for the use of particular curriculum or programme materials in particular circumstances.

The curriculum and its associated materials are the *materia medica* of pedagogy, the pharmacopoeia from which the teacher draws those tools of teaching that present or exemplify particular content and remediate or evaluate the adequacy of student accomplishments. We expect the mature physician to understand the full range of treatments available to ameliorate a given disorder, as well as the range of alternatives for particular circumstances of sensitivity, cost, interaction with other interventions, convenience, safety, or comfort. Similarly, we ought to expect that the mature teacher possesses such understandings about the curricular alternatives available for instruction.

How many individuals whom we prepare for teaching biology, for example, understand well the materials for that instruction, the alternative texts, software, programmes, visual materials, single-concept films, laboratory demonstrations, or 'invitations to enquiry?' Would we trust a physician who did not really understand the alternative ways of dealing with categories of infectious disease, but who knew only one way?

 READING 8.7

# The role of the subject coordinator

Lucy O'Hara and Mark O'Hara

> The development of subjects within the primary school curriculum has gone a long way in recent years, particularly in England and Wales. Among the potential advantages is an increase in subject progression through succeeding years of curriculum teaching. The whole-school role of the subject coordinator is crucial in working with colleagues to bring this about. This reading reviews this role by taking history as an example.
>
> How are such roles fulfilled in the schools you know best?
>
> Edited from: O'Hara, L. and O'Hara, M. (2001) *Teaching History 3–11: The Essential Guide*. London, New York: Continuum, 178–82

The introduction of the National Curriculum in England and Wales in 1989 placed new pressures on primary school teachers in terms of their subject expertise. Teachers were faced with the task of developing their understanding and capabilities across a broad range of subjects. Subsequent developing foundation stage may have a similar impact on teachers of the 3–5 age range. In many primary schools, the response to these developments since 1989 has been to appoint curriculum coordinators for specific areas, including subjects such as history. The idea of curriculum coordinators was not new in 1989–90. It had, however, been an underdeveloped idea (Bentley and Watts, 1994) and developments in primary education since 1989 have done much to accelerate the process of reappraising what the role involves. This reappraisal has resulted in a move away from seeing coordination posts as rewards for general competence, resulting from long service and experience, towards much more precise definitions of the role involving specific curriculum responsibilities. The intention is to enable nurseries and schools to capitalize upon the collective subject strengths amongst their staff (Alexander *et al.*, 1992, p. 21) by giving coordinators responsibility for curriculum planning in their subject areas, for the organization of resources and for leading staff development. All teachers are now expected to shoulder some degree of curriculum responsibility. Titles vary and include curriculum coordinator, post holder and subject leader.

For many primary school teachers the skills and knowledge associated with curriculum coordination would appear to have been caught not taught (Webb, 1994, p. 64). If the potential of curriculum coordinators for the quality of teaching and learning is to be realized fully this state of affairs must be altered. Many newly qualified teachers have to take on the increasingly complex and accountable role of curriculum coordination early on in their careers and preparation for it is needed during initial training. In small schools, staff often have to take a lead in more than one subject area and in other situations staff are asked to take on subject areas for which they have only a minimal subject background even though they may be very experienced as coordinators in other contexts.

We can consider the role of history coordinators as an example. A job descripton might suggest the following:

General duties as class teacher:

- To take responsibility for a Year 2 class. This responsibility includes:

   the planning, preparation, delivery and assessment of a varied and relevant curriculum;

   ensuring a stimulating, active learning environment for pupils through good classroom organization and display;

   motivating children by personal influence and by awareness of needs.

- To work as part of the staff team, adhering to the school's behaviour policy, showing consideration to colleagues, assisting in curriculum development and involvement in extra-curricular activities.

Specific responsibilities as subject coordinator for history:

- To be responsible for the development of the history curriculum across the school to ensure breadth and balance, progression and continuity.

- To develop and maintain the history policy, guidelines and schemes of work.

- To keep up to date with local and national developments in the history curriculum.

- To liaise where appropriate with other curriculum coordinators.

- To lead staff development in history.

- To support teaching and learning in history across the school.

- To be responsible for monitoring and purchasing resources for history across the school.

Although at first glance the job description above may appear straightforward, the reality can be very different. Some subjects, including history, had not been well defined in primary schools prior to 1989–90, or had been part of something else. In the case of history this often involved being subsumed into broader environmental and/or local studies topics. Nor has the appearance of documentation outlining the content and nature of history (DFE, 1995; QCA,

1999a) led to a sudden and coherent upsurge of teaching in this area. The introduction of literacy and numeracy strategies has had a significant impact on the opportunities for teaching and learning in the foundation subjects generally. Similarly, parallel changes to the priorities for initial teacher training (DfEE, 1998a) are also likely to impact upon the preparedness of some newly qualified teachers to deliver quality teaching in history and other foundation subjects in years to come. The introduction of the Desirable Outcomes for Children's Learning (SCAA, 1996) and the Early Learning Goals (QCA, 1999b) have added further dimension to the need to develop progression and continuity in this area. National documentation alone cannot overcome the varied preconceptions concerning the nature of a subject like history, although it may go some way towards addressing the lack of subject knowledge amongst some teachers. Overcoming this problem is likely to constitute one aspect of the history coordinator's role.

Managing resources and the production of school documentation for the subject (e.g. policy statements, schemes of work and guidance for colleagues) are two more areas which are the responsibility of the coordinator. These are also areas where curriculum coordinators have already made an impact in primary schools (Alexander *et al.*, 1992; Webb, 1994). Such work is important in laying some of the foundations for good practice in teaching history. The establishment of OFSTED in 1992 and the stated intention to inspect all primary schools on a four-yearly basis have given an added impetus to ensuring that school documentation is in place. Curriculum organization and delivery also form part of the coordinator's management and planning responsibilities. Alexander *et al.* (1992, pp. 16–19) drew a distinction between curriculum conception and curriculum organization and the history coordinator will be expected therefore to take a lead in discussions over the integration of subjects, as well as teaching approaches, techniques and methods.

Central to the role of the history coordinator is their responsibility to in the quality of teaching and learning within the subject area across the whole school. The work of Alexander *et al.* (1992) emphasized the importance of 'curricular expertise' as a precursor to quality in teaching and stressed the need for coordinators to possess such expertise. Curricular expertise includes knowledge and understanding of the subject, an understanding of the factors which promote effective learning and the possession of the skills needed to teach a subject successfully. Subject expertise needs to be developed across two broad areas. The first should relate to knowledge and practice outside the school; the second should relate to knowledge and practice outside the school, at local, national and, at times, international levels (Bentley and Watts, 1994). History specialists will have a degree of expertise upon which to build becoming practising teachers. Once in post there will be the opportunity to develop expertise in the first area, within his or her own schools, through practical experiences gained while working with pupils and alongside other colleagues. Support in developing the second, wider area of expertise might be offered through local in-service provision but such opportunities are limited and may not be available in some authorities.

History coordinators charged with promoting quality teaching and learning across the school not only have to update their own subject expertise but also have to be capable of disseminating such expertise to others. School-based dissemination could involve working alongside colleagues in their classrooms or conducting curriculum development meetings. Such dissemination ought to be based, at least in part, upon the coordinator's own school-based assessment and evaluation. Coordinators, therefore, need to consider their role as educators, advisors and facilitators (Bentley and Watts, 1994) as the educating, advising and facilitating component of the coordinator's role brings interpersonal skills sharp relief alongside subject expertise.

As an educator you will have to help your colleagues to develop their own subject knowledge and understanding in history. Inspiring and motivating colleagues has to be underpinned by an ability to empower and enskill those colleagues. Insufficient attention to the latter can undermine attempts to inspire and motivate by reinforcing feelings of inadequacy, both real and imagined, amongst staff.

- As an advisor you will need to have an eye to future developments in the teaching of history and be able to communicate not only with colleagues but also with parents and governors and the headteacher in the school.

- As a facilitator you will need to create a climate of trust and openness in which change can occur. To be effective as a leader you have to become effective as a supporter.

(Bentley and Watts, 1994, pp. 159–60)

Curriculum coordination, therefore, has become an increasingly complex task. It requires the incumbent not only to concentrate on their subject expertise but also, and crucially, upon their interpersonal skills and their ability to motivate and lead colleagues. In service training can only go part way towards developing subject expertise. Curriculum coordinators will have to underpin such training opportunities that do exist by developing autonomous strategies to promote and enhance their subject expertise through self-directed research. In addition, curriculum coordinators are becoming increasingly accountable as a result of parallel developments in education (Webb, 1994); not least teacher appraisal and OFSTED inspections.

 **READING 8.8**

# The curriculum for a learning society

## The Labour Party

The Labour Party document from which this extract has been edited was compiled in 1994, when it was opposing the Conservative government of the day. It is interesting to look back on it in the light of more recent developments. At the time, the introduction of the National Curriculum was going rather badly, with teachers feeling extremely overloaded by prescription and regulation. Many would have agreed then with the Labour Party's characterization of the National Curriculum as 'a block of facts'. However, the main purpose of the document was to open up a new debate about the aims of the curriculum, with an important emphasis on issues such as motivation, rights, global and critical understanding and multi-level partnerships for lifelong learning.

Considering the list offered below, how many of these issues are still important? Have any been resolved? How many remain as challenges?

Edited from: The Labour Party (1994) *Consultative Green Paper: Opening Doors to a Learning Society*. London: The Labour Party, 26–8

At the heart of effective learning and teaching is the quality of the curriculum.

The Labour Party has long supported the need for a national curriculum and welcomed its introduction. Discussion of what was variously described as a common core, compulsory or national curriculum took place under Labour in the 1970s via discussion with parents' organizations, heads, teachers, HMI, local education authorities [LEAs], unions and others.

By the end of the 1970s there was broad agreement that a common curriculum for all pupils should focus on knowledge and understanding of five or six disciplines. There was also some agreement that the limited school subjects most children studied discouraged breadth and balance; were unsuited to the needs of many pupils; were irrelevant to the needs of many employers; took no account of modern technologies; encouraged early overspecialization and had few links with post-16 education, training and employment. Labour supported the introduction of a common examination at 16, the GCSE and the proposals put forward in *Better Schools* (DES, 1985) for a common curriculum. This document now stands as a model of calm appraisal, highlighting the role of LEAs for 'the priority they had given to the formulation of curriculum policies'.

In 1987, however, came the introduction of a ten-subject national curriculum that suspiciously echoed the model laid down by the 1904 Board of Education regulations. The government ignored an emerging consensus that all pupils should have equal access to a broad relevant education with nationally agreed objectives and guidelines, but with content the product of debate between educational partners. Instead, a prescriptive, outdated content-specific national syllabus with no agreed principles and objectives has been imposed.

The present national syllabus concentrates on the timetabled curriculum and ignores the wider curriculum that arises from a school's own ethos and values. It uses testing to drive the content of education and to encourage a climate of failure. It reduces teachers to the status of 'technicians' who 'deliver' a service. It has been subject to endless ministerial tinkering, dangerous political interference, and the influence of unelected and unaccountable, politically motivated right-wing groups and individuals. It has developed into an overassessed, conceptually arid, bureaucratic nightmare, epitomized by a myriad of orders, circulars, amendments, booklets, folders, ring-binders and instructions.

No reason has been given as to why the curriculum prescribed by the government is subject based; indeed, its overprescriptive nature has denied the first principle in the 1988 Act which merely says that the school curriculum must be 'balanced and broadly based', and promote 'the spiritual, moral, cultural, mental and physical development of students at school and society'. The HMI report of the early 1980s advised that the curriculum be defined as areas of study. There is a great deal of concern at the move away from the HMI suggestions of 'areas of study' and a belief that this is one of the reasons that the National Curriculum is so overprescribed.

If there is to be agreement on a framework for a national curriculum there must first be agreement upon its purpose.

The view of education as a block of facts to be learned between the ages of 5 and 16 will lead to a prescriptive national syllabus. The view of education as a means of understanding one's self and society requires the achievement of confidence, skills and independent thought and these can be developed through many avenues.

As a step in opening up the debate we suggest the following as the purpose of a national framework curriculum.

It must be based on a vision of the future that recognizes that adults may change their jobs several times and may have more recreation and leisure than previous generations. They will need imagination, flexibility and drive if they are to play their part as full citizens.

The curriculum must promote success, rather than identify and reinforce failure. It must be a framework within which all children and young people want to strive for higher levels of knowledge, understanding, skill and opportunity – it must motivate children.

It must have a clear defensible set of aims linked to the personal achievements of individuals and to civil and economic needs and expectations.

It must also be preparation for lifelong learning. It must offer fair opportunities to all and be a right for all with no rationing or exclusion on grounds of class, race, gender, disability or 'special need' and it must encourage a culture of respect between young people.

Its content and assessment arrangements must fit together in a coherent way and ensure a measure of common agreed experiences for all children.

It must ensure that the pupil has a clear understanding of national and international relationships, a global dimension which is becoming more difficult to incorporate given the current pressures on the curriculum.

It must involve parents, teachers, governors, local communities, and local and central partnership who will facilitate learning and encourage the 'learning person'.

It must encourage a critical understanding of social, political and economic arrangements and not become an instrument of indoctrination.

It must include measures to continually assess and monitor quality and ensure high standards.

It must apply to all schools, including those in the independent sector.

The pressures now leading to a narrowing of the curriculum and the school experience of our young people are extremely worrying. The demands of the prescriptive curriculum and cutbacks in local authority services mean that children today are not always able to enjoy the breadth of experiences to which they should be entitled.

## READING 8.9

# Good practice: more than a mantra?

Robin Alexander

In 1991 Robin Alexander's report on primary education in Leeds became a 'political football' in a fast-moving national debate about pupil standards, classroom practice, teacher beliefs and the role of LEAs. The book from which this reading is drawn brings together the main findings of Alexander's initial report and presents some major challenges to primary school teachers. In particular, the notion of 'good primary practice' is incisively investigated and analysed.

Does the idea of 'good practice' simply obscure forms of teaching which are routinized, unthinking and untenable in modern schools and classrooms? How do the National Literacy and National Numeracy Strategies stand up to this sort of analysis? How might teaching be conceptualized more securely?

Edited from: Alexander, R. J. (1992) *Policy and Practice in Primary Education*. London: Routledge, 174–91

The ubiquitous phrase 'good primary practice' begs questions nearly every time it is uttered. Consider these quotations (those unattributed are from the Leeds research reported in Alexander, 1992):

We apply all the basic principles of good practice here – a stimulating environment with high quality display and plenty of material for first hand exploration; a flexible day in which children can move freely from one activity to the next without the artificial barriers of subjects; plenty of individual and group work.

Children spend more time with paint pots than mastering the three Rs, said Schools Minister Michael Fallon . . . They should get back to basics and teach the whole class in an organised way . . . (*Daily Mail*, 2.11.91)

The successful candidate will be familiar with good primary practice. A belief in a child-centred approach is essential.

If you don't have drapes and triple mounting, you won't get on here.

Child-centred education ... part of a deliberate political project to undermine the respect the young should have for the achievements of those who went before them. (Anthony O'Hear in the *Daily Telegraph*, 12.2.91)

The children ... spread into the hall, the corridors and the playground. The nursery class has its own quarters and the children are playing with sand, water, paint, clay, dolls, rocking horses and big push toys under the supervision of their teacher. This is how they learn ... Learning is going on all the time, but there is not much direct teaching ... The class of sevens to nines had spread into the corridor and were engaged in a variety of occupations. One group were gathered round their teacher for some extra reading practice, another was at work on an extraordinary structure of wood and metal which they said was a sputnik, a third was collecting a number of objects and testing them to find out which could be picked up by a magnet and two boys were at work on an immense painting of St Michael defeating Satan. They seemed to be working harmoniously according to an unfolding rather than a pre-conceived plan. (CACE, 1967, The Plowden Report, pp. 103–5)

Look on your works, Lady Plowden, and despair. (*Daily Telegraph*, 7.11.91)

Plowden is still my Bible, whatever the government or any airy-fairy academics say. They are not the practitioners – I am!

There is a crisis in primary education ... In France, Holland, Denmark, Germany and Japan, young children learn to read, write, add up and speak another language ... Those countries believe in whole-class teaching, learning facts by heart, children sitting behind desks ... Teachers here seem to have ideological opposition to these ideas, but they must be required to change their ways. (Centre for Policy Studies Director Tessa Keswick, in *Daily Telegraph*, 26.1.96).

The research evidence demonstrates that the level of cognitive challenge provided by the teacher is a significant factor in the child's performance. One way of providing challenge is to set pupils demanding tasks. But, equally, it is important for teachers to organise their classrooms so that they have the opportunity to interact with their pupils: to offer explanations which develop thinking, to encourage speculation and hypothesis through sensitive questioning, to develop, above all, a climate of interest and purpose ... Teachers need to be competent in a range of techniques in order to achieve different learning outcomes ... They need the skills and judgement to be able to select and apply whichever ... is appropriate to the task in hand ... The judgement ... should be educational and organisational, rather than, as it so often is, doctrinal ... The critical notion is that of fitness for purpose. (Alexander *et al.* 1992, pp. 30–1)

When we say of teaching which we do, see or commend 'this is good practice', what are we really asserting? There seem to be four main possibilities:

This teaching is in line with what x defines as good practice and the status of x is such that his/her views must be heeded.

This teaching works, in as far as the children seem to be appropriately and gainfully occupied.

This teaching leads to specific and recognizable kinds of learning and a causal relationship between the teaching and learning can be demonstrated.

This teaching is consistent with my/our values and beliefs about the proper purposes and conduct of education.

Though there is inevitable overlap between the statements their status is nevertheless somewhat different. Thus, the first, being about the exercise of power, is a political statement. The second is essentially a pragmatic statement. The third, being grounded in experience and observation and being concerned with verification, is an empirical statement. The fourth is evaluative in the sense of expressing, and being explicitly validated by, values and beliefs. All four are illustrated in the collage of quotations above.

This classification begins to unravel the 'good' in 'good practice': it is anything but the absolute many claim or wish. What of the notion of 'practice' itself? Is it reasonable to assume that when we speak of good primary practice we are all talking of the same phenomena, and the only problem concerns the basis on which we rate them as good, bad or indifferent? Though we readily acknowledge that 'education' is a pluralist concept, is 'teaching' significantly less so?

The quotations above suggest that it is not. The problem with many everyday accounts or definitions of good practice is that not only do they leave unexplored vital questions of justification, but they also focus in a frequently arbitrary way upon particular aspects of practice which are then elevated to the status of a complete and coherent 'philosophy'. More often than not, they are mere philosophical fragments or preliminary clearings of the throat.

In order to judge the adequacy of a good-practice claim, therefore, we need not only to examine the criteria by which practice is judged to be good, but also to be clear about which aspects of practice are defined in this way and which aspects are ignored. There is of course no reason why a good-practice statement should not be selective and sharply focused, for it is difficult to talk meaningfully with teaching unless we engage with its specifics. The problem comes when over time, or within a statement purporting to stand as a complete educational rationale, some aspects of practice are consistently emphasized while others are consistently ignored. The underlying message of such selectivity is that what is emphasized is all that matters, whether it be – to draw on contrasting selections – display, group work, thematic enquiry, whole-class teaching or the basics.

Figure 8.9.1 attempts to provide a framework for approaching this aspect of the good-practice question in a more rounded way. The two main dimensions reflect a view of teaching as educational ideas in action, or as classroom actions and events which both manifest and are informed by ideas, values and beliefs. The seven aspects of teaching so defined arise from observation of teaching as it happens and from analysis of ideas about teaching which have been articulated by practitioners. The resulting categories are of course not discrete, but are presented separately for analytical purposes. Similarly, the two dimensions, here presented as a sequential list, interact; each aspect of practice is to a greater or lesser extent informed by one, two or all of the areas of ideas, values and assumptions. Armed with such a framework we can return to any good-practice statement, test its emphasis and scope, and examine the thrust and genealogy of the ideas, values and beliefs in which it is rooted.

To take stock: 'good-practice' statements come in different forms. Some are statements of value or belief; some are pragmatic statements; some are empirical statements; some are political statements; most combine more than one of these characteristics, which are themselves neither discrete nor one dimensional; and all presuppose a concept of practice itself. Pursuing our quest for good primary practice in this way, therefore, we can see that while in a physical sense it resides in primary schools and classrooms, in order to know what we are looking for and to begin to understand how we might define and judge it, we need to recognize that it lies, conceptually, somewhere at the intersection of the five considerations or dimensions which have been identified so far: evaluative, pragmatic, empirical, political and conceptual. Figure 8.9.2 represents this relationship.

The quest for good primary practice, then, is as much a conceptual as a physical one. However, the point at which the various overlapping considerations meet is an arena of conflict as much as of resolution. Primary practice – any educational practice – requires us to come to terms with and do our best to reconcile competing values, pressures and constraints. It is about dilemma no less than certainty (Alexander, 1995, Chapter 2). If this is so of

| | ASPECTS | | CENTRAL EDUCATIONAL QUESTIONS |
|---|---|---|---|
| OBSERVABLE PRACTICE | CONTENT | whole curriculum subjects/areas | WHAT should children learn? |
| | CONTEXT | physical interpersonal | |
| | PEDAGOGY | teaching methods pupil organization | HOW should children learn and teachers teach? |
| | MANAGEMENT | planning operation assessment of learning evaluation of teaching | |
| IDEAS VALUES BELIEFS | CHILDREN | development needs learning | WHY should children be educated in this way? |
| | SOCIETY | needs of society needs of the individual | and |
| | KNOWLEDGE | children's way of knowing culturally evolved ways of knowing | What is an educated person? |

**Figure 8.9.1**   Educational practice: a conceptual framework

practice in general, it must also be the case, *a fortiori*, with practice we wish to define as 'good'.

However, there has to be a qualitative difference between practice and good practice if the latter notion is not to become redundant. Or is it the case that good practice is no more than the best we can do in the circumstances? Is our quest for educational quality to run into the morass of relativism? I believe not. Though in Figure 8.9.2 the five considerations or dimensions appear to have equal weight, the pursuit of good practice has to move beyond a mere balancing of competing imperatives. There have to be superordinate reasons for preferring one course of action to another, reasons which will enable education to rise above the level of the merely pragmatic. For education is inherently about values: it reflects a vision of the kind of world we want our children to inherit; a vision of the kinds of people we hope they will become; a vision of what it is to be an educated person. Whatever the other ingredients of good practice may be, they should enable a coherent and sustainable value position to be pursued. Values, then, are central.

Yet, in teaching, values have to be be made manifest rather than merely held or voiced. They are manifested as learning contexts, tasks and encounters. While, clearly, such activities must be congruent with the values they seek to realize, such congruence is of itself no guarantee of success in terms of the specific learning goals which give the broader vision practical meaning. We need to go one step further, therefore, and to couple with the

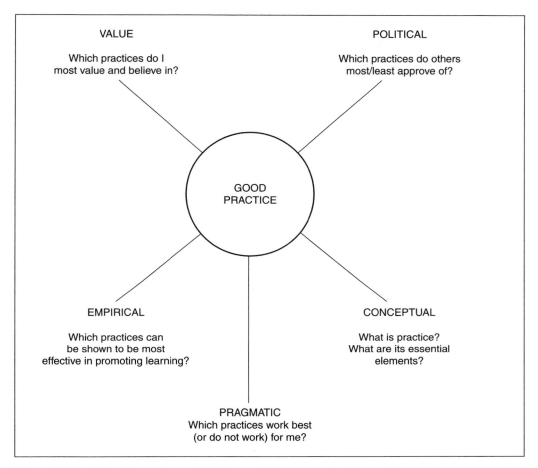

**Figure 8.9.2**    What is good practice? Reconciling competing imperatives

commitment to values and value congruence a clear awareness of evidence, published or experiential, concerning the strengths and weaknesses of the various teaching strategies open to us, in order that we can construct, ideally, learning tasks and contexts which are not just consistent with the values but will also translate them into meaningful learning for the child. It is for this reason that the empirical dimension is so critical an adjunct to matters of value, belief and purpose.

It is also clear that the pursuit of 'effectiveness' *per se*, a currently popular quest among educational researchers and policy-makers, can produce versions of good practice which are incomplete or untenable in the same way that value statements detached from empirical understanding may be inoperable. Those who presume that the inconveniently untidy value problems in the good-practice question are resolved at a stroke by talking of 'effective' practice (or the effective teacher/effective school) are engaging in mere sleight of hand; practice, we must ask, which is effective in relation to what? In relation, of course, to a notion of what it is to be educated. Good practice, then, justifies its approbation by being both intrinsically educative and operationally effective. In the educational arena, effectiveness as a criterion existing on its own is meaningless.

We are now in a position to sum up. Figure 8.9.2 represents good practice as existing at the intersection of the five considerations and as a matter of reconciling competing

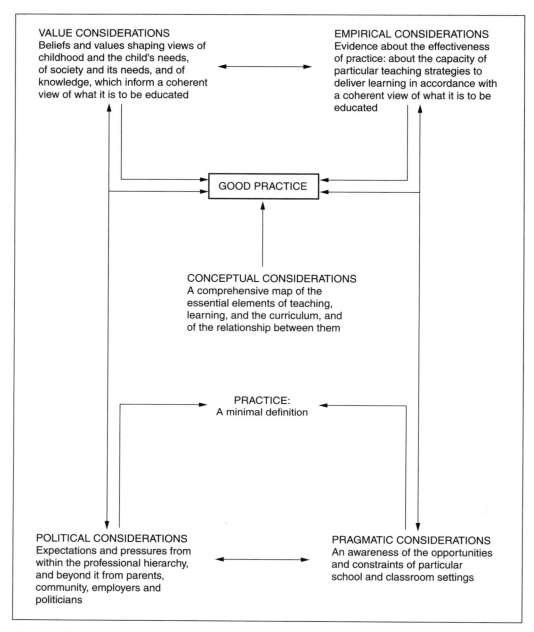

**Figure 8.9.3** What is good practice? Beyond relativism

imperatives. However, I then suggested that this approach does not take sufficient note of what the 'good' in 'good practice' might dictate, and that although all the considerations are important, they are not equivalent. The pursuit of good practice sets the considerations in a hierarchical relationship with evaluative and empirical questions pre-eminent, and with both dependent on a prior conceptualization of the nature of educational practice itself. This alternative relationship, a development of the initial idea, is shown in Figure 8.9.3

## CHAPTER 9

# Planning. How are we implementing the curriculum?

The eight readings in this chapter address key issues in curriculum planning.

First, we have a classic HMI analysis of key characteristics of any curriculum (9.1). This is extremely important, since it offers a conceptual framework for thinking about, and evaluating, curriculum provision.

The issues raised by HMI are well illustrated by examples of policy documents from Scotland and Wales. The Scottish Executive (9.2) sets out its requirements for 'structure and balance' in the curriculum and for the development of appropriate learning dispositions, whilst the Curriculum and Assessment Authority for Wales (9.3) affirms the role of experience, play and appropriateness in the early-years curriculum. Meanwhile, drawing on research in England, Dadds (9.4) worries about the consequences of what she calls the 'hurry-along' curriculum. 'Will it ever slow down?', she wonders.

The reading by Bennett (9.5) moves us into the more practical area of how to actually implement the curriculum in the classroom. He suggests how to structure a session in four parts, working from constructivist principles. Similarly, the readings by Bearne (9.6) and Montgomery (9.7) throw light on the very challenging issue of how to provide adequate differentation within the classroom. How can we match tasks and targets to the existing understandings of each of the children? Not at all easy, but we hope that these readings may offer some ideas for further consideration in your situation.

In Reading 9.8, Kennelwell, Parkinson and Tanner offer principled advice on how to plan for appropriate incorporation of ICT within the curriculum.

The parallel chapter of *Reflective Teaching* moves through successive levels of curriculum planning. It begins with whole-school planning and policies, before moving to focus on the structuring of schemes of work. Short-term planning, for lessons, activities and tasks are then considered, including a section on differentiation. As usual, there are suggestions for 'Key Readings' and *RTweb* is available to provide additional, and regularly updated, ideas.

## READING 9.1

# Characteristics of the curriculum

## Her Majesty's Inspectors

HMI's *Curriculum Matters* series of the 1980s, and the pamphlet entitled *The Curriculum from 5–16* from which this reading is edited, was an attempt to offer a non-statutory framework for a national curriculum. The 5–16 pamphlet identified nine 'areas of learning and experience' (related to subject areas), four 'elements of learning' (knowledge, skills, concepts and attitudes), and five 'characteristics of curriculum', which are discussed below.

It is interesting to see the importance of 'relevance' here for, whilst the other 'characteristics' were emphasized, it was to disappear from the official documents of the 1990s.

What do you see as the relevance of 'relevance'?

Edited from: Department of Education and Science (1985) *The Curriculum from 5–16, Curriculum Matters 2.* London: HMSO, 10–48

The curriculum provides a context for learning which, as well as providing for the progressive development of knowledge, understanding and skills, recognizes and builds on the particular developmental characteristics of childhood and adolescence. Active learning, and a sense of purpose and success, enhance pupils' enjoyment, interest, confidence and sense of personal worth; passive learning and inappropriate teaching styles can lead to frustration and failure. In particular, it is necessary to ensure that the pupils are given sufficient first-hand experience, accompanied by discussion, upon which to base abstract ideas and generalizations.

If the opportunities for all pupils to engage in a largely comparable range of learning are to be secured, certain characteristics are desirable.

## Breadth

The curriculum should be broad. The various curricular areas should reinforce one another: for example the scientific area provides opportunities for pupils to learn and practise mathematical skills. Breadth is also necessary within an area and within its components: thus in the linguistic and literary area pupils should read a variety of fiction and non-fiction myths, legends, fairy tales, animal stories, stories based on family life, adventure stories, historical fiction, science fiction, reference books, factual accounts, documents, directories and articles.

Class teachers in primary schools are in a strong position to arrange the interplay of the various aspects of learning since, as *Primary Education in England* (DES, 1978a) pointed out:

The teacher can get to know the children and know their strengths and weaknesses; the one teacher concerned can readily adjust the daily programme to suit special circumstances; it is simpler for one teacher than for a group of teachers to ensure that the various parts of the curriculum are coordinated and also to reinforce work done in one part of the curriculum with work done in another.

This does not mean that the class teacher can or should be expected to cover the whole curriculum unaided, especially with the older pupils. He or she should be able to call on the support of teachers who, as well as having responsibilities for their own classes, act as consultants in particular subjects or areas of the curriculum.

Primary schools generally offer a broad curriculum in the sense that all the areas of learning and experience are present to some extent. However, care is needed to ensure that breadth is not pursued at the expense of depth since this may lead to superficial work.

## Balance

A balanced curriculum should ensure that each area of learning and experience and each element of learning is given appropriate attention in relation to the others and to the curriculum as a whole. In practice this requires the allocation of sufficient time and resources for each area and element to be fully developed. Balance also needs to be preserved within each area and element by the avoidance, for example, of an undue emphasis on the mechanical aspects of language or mathematics, or on writing predominantly given over to note taking and summarizing. There should also be a balance in the variety of teaching approaches used: didactic and pupil initiated; practical and theoretical; individual, group and full-class teaching.

Balance need not be sought over a single week or even a single month since in some cases it may be profitable to concentrate in depth on certain activities; but it should be sought over a period of, say, a term or a year.

## Relevance

The curriculum should be relevant in the sense that it is seen by pupils to meet their recent and prospective needs. Overall, what is taught and learned should be worth learning in that it improves pupils' grasp of the subject matter and enhances their enjoyment of it and their mastery of the skills required; increases their understanding of themselves and the world in which they are growing up; raises their confidence and competence in controlling events and coping with widening expectations and demands; and progressively equips them with the knowledge and skills needed in adult working life. Work in schools can be practical in a number of ways. First, it can be directly concerned with 'making and doing'.

Second, pupils at all stages need to work and enjoy working with abstract ideas and to come to an understanding of them by drawing on their own concrete experience, observation and powers of reasoning and, whenever possible, by testing out and reinforcing their learning by reference to real examples.

Third, all that pupils learn should be practical, and therefore relevant, in ways which enable them to build on it or use it for their own purposes in everyday life. For example being read to, reading, hearing music, or taking part in a discussion, all have both a specific and a cumulative effect on the individual, especially if teachers use opportunities to relate what is being learned to pupils' interests, to contemporary realities and general human experience.

Fourth, the more that knowledge and skills learned in school can be developed within and applied to activities that have real purpose and place in the wider world, the more clearly their relevance will be perceived by the pupils.

## Differentiation

As stated in HMI's discussion document *A View of the Curriculum* (DES, 1980):

> The curriculum has to satisfy two seemingly contrary requirements. On the one hand it has to reflect the broad aims of education which hold good for all children, whatever their capabilities and whatever the schools they attend. On the other hand it has to allow for differences in the abilities and other characteristics of children, even of the same age . . . If it is to be effective, the school curriculum must allow for differences.

A necessary first step in making appropriate provision is the identification of the learning needs of individual pupils by sensitive observation on the part of the teacher. This may indicate a need for smaller, more homogeneous groups, regrouping for different purposes, or the formation of subgroups for particular activities. Individual work and assignments can be set to allow for different interests, capabilities and work rates so long as this does not isolate pupils or deprive them of necessary contact with other pupils or the teacher. Finally, there should be differentiation in the teaching approaches: some pupils need to proceed slowly, and some need a predominantly practical approach and many concrete examples if they are to understand abstractions; some move more quickly and require more demanding work which provides greater intellectual challenge; many have a variety of needs which cannot be neatly categorized.

## Progression and continuity

Children's development is a continuous process and schools have to provide conditions and experiences which sustain and encourage that process while recognizing that it does not proceed uniformly or at an even pace. If this progression is to be maintained there is a need to build systematically on the children's existing knowledge, concepts, skills and attitudes, so as to ensure an orderly advance in their capabilities over a period of time. Teaching and learning experiences should be ordered so as to facilitate pupils' progress, with each successive element making appropriate demands and leading to better performance.

The main points at which progression is endangered by discontinuity are those at which pupils change schools; they also include those at which children enter school, change classes or teachers, or change their own attitudes to school or some aspect of it. Not all change is for the worse, however, and many pupils find a new enthusiasm or aptitude in new situations. Nevertheless, curricular planning within and between schools should aim to ensure continuity by making the maximum use of earlier learning.

Primary schools have to build on and allow for the influences to which children entering school have already been exposed and to take account of what will be expected of them in the schools to which they will transfer in due course. Continuity within schools may best be achieved when there are clear curricular policies which all the staff have been involved in developing and which present a clear picture of the range of expectations it is reasonable to have of individual pupils. If the goals are as clear as possible, progress towards them is more likely to be maintained.

### 📖 READING 9.2

# The nature and purpose of the curriculum 5–14

## Scottish Executive

The curriculum in Scotland is impressive for its grounding in secure principles of curriculum planning and for its attention to the structure and balance of the curriculum as a whole. As in Northern Ireland, it identifies five broad 'areas of learning', rather than specifying particular subject requirements as in England and Wales.

In this reading, the rationale for this approach is explained.

Edited from: Scottish Executive (2000) *The Structure and Balance of the Curriculum: 5–14 National Guidelines.* Edinburgh: Learning and Teaching Scotland, 3–6, 9

Schools, parents and society care that young people succeed in terms of attaining the knowledge, skills and, in time, the qualifications required for a personally rewarding life, productive employment and active citizenship. Equally, they care that young people develop into healthy, fair-minded, considerate and responsible human beings. The school experience should play a major role in this development. If schools are to succeed in this, they must pay close attention to the nature and structure of the curriculum and how it is put into practice.

Children entering primary school at around five years of age have already become successful learners with a remarkable potential for learning. Their experiences of family, friendships, pre-school groups and the local community have begun to shape and guide to a considerable extent their intellectual and social development. The pre-school curriculum has already offered them a wide range of learning experiences. Entry into primary school, with its variety of more formal curriculum structures and arrangements, presents new and rich opportunities for learning, which should acknowledge and build on what children have already learned about themselves and their world.

A curriculum that offers a breadth of experience and a balance of opportunity for learning is the entitlement of every pupil. From the outset, the 5–14 curriculum should provide clear pathways across the range of areas of learning. These provide a basis for personal growth and for further learning in the different structures of primary, secondary and special schools. The curriculum should build on pupils' experience and learning and be responsive to their needs. It should relate to events and facets of their everyday lives. It should help them develop intellectually, aesthetically, socially, emotionally, spiritually, imaginatively and physically. It should prepare them to face the challenges of life in a rapidly changing society. It should help guide them through the transition from childhood to adulthood.

Pupils thrive on activities that stimulate them, experiences that engage them and in relationships that affirm and nurture them. Through this they become well-rounded people and effective learners. They develop personally and socially. Their individual and collective sense of who they are and of their role in the world around them grows and takes shape. The curriculum should be inclusive and promote equality of opportunity for all. It should help develop in children the knowledge, skills, capabilities and dispositions that they will require in order to gain the best from school and from life. It needs therefore to build progressively on what they learn, offering challenge, rewarding success and celebrating achievement.

The 5–14 curriculum provides a structured continuum of learning for all pupils in which they progressively learn about the world and learn from their experience of it. This will involve pupils in a systematic study of language, mathematics, environmental studies, expressive arts, religious and moral education, ICT, health, and personal and social development (PSD).

More generally, the 5–14 curriculum should help pupils acquire and develop:

- dispositions;

- core skills and capabilities;

- knowledge and understanding.

## Dispositions

Dispositions are ways pupils think and feel about themselves and the world. They help guide pupils in making decisions and taking action. The following dispositions are generally regarded as a fundamental basis for a personally rewarding life and an effective contribution to society. They are of equal importance and clearly interrelate. The 5–14 curriculum should look to foster young people who are positively disposed to:

- *A commitment to learning:* Throughout schooling and to equip them for adult life, children need both to acquire new information and skills and to make new connections and meanings in what they have learned. Learning becomes an exciting and rewarding lifelong process.

- *A respect and care for self:* A sense of self-worth brings a capacity for autonomy and motivation. It is the basis from which care for others grows. It is strongly linked to achievement and attainment.

- *Respect and care for others:* Recognizing that we are interdependent helps pupils develop qualities of cooperation, mutual support and respect for the diversity of people, cultures and beliefs.

- *A sense of social responsibility:* An awareness of positive social attitudes, principles and skills will help pupils become competent and positively disposed to participate in society. A commitment to the environment will be engendered.

- *A sense of belonging:* Being part of and committed to the life of the school is achieved when pupils feel valued, knowing that their opinions count and their concerns are addressed.

Opportunities to develop these dispositions are embedded in programmes and learning experiences across the whole curriculum. They will also find expression in the contexts in which their learning is structured and in the relationships that encompass both their learning environment and the wider life of the school.

## Core skills and capabilities

The curriculum must offer young people opportunities to acquire core skills and to develop the capability to use them in the various contexts they meet in their learning and in their lives. Core skills foster personal and social development and are widely recognized as essential for a healthy lifestyle, responsible citizenship and, in time, employment and successful lifelong learning. The core skills include:

- personal and interpersonal skills including working with others;
- language and communication skills;
- numeracy skills;
- ICT skills;
- problem-solving skills;
- learning and thinking skills.

These skills lay the foundation for those specific core skills that are developed and validated in the later stages of secondary school.

## The acquisition of knowledge and the development of understanding

The curriculum and the way in which it is taught should help pupils acquire important knowledge in each of its main areas. It must also ensure that pupils make connections between what they learn and what they see in the wider world around them. Such knowledge and understanding are acquired and developed within and, just as importantly, across curriculum areas.

Well-designed programmes of study highlight learning links for pupils. Pupils need help opportunities to connect, integrate and apply what they have learned in ways that are creative, thoughtful, sensitive and which promote emotional maturity.

The 5–14 curriculum is based on a set of principles applicable to all pupils: breadth, balance, coherence, continuity and progression.

- *Breadth* ensures the coverage of a sufficiently comprehensive range of areas of learning.

- *Balance* ensures that appropriate time is allocated to each area of curricular activity and that provision is made for a variety of learning experiences.

- *Coherence* emphasizes links across the curriculum so that pupils make connections between one area of knowledge and skills and another.

- *Continuity* ensures that learning builds on pupils' previous experience and attainment and prepares them for further learning.

- *Progression* provides pupils with a series of challenging but attainable goals.

## READING 9.3

# Desirable outcomes for young children's learning

Curriculum and Assessment Authority for Wales

This reading from the official document that structures early-years education in Wales is a clear expression of a developmental approach to curriculum provision (see Katz, in Reading 8.4). In particular, it asserts the importance of play, experience, flexibility and 'appropriateness' – together with the start of induction into Welsh language and culture. It is unusual, but refreshing, for an official document to begin with a poem.

Edited from: Curriculum and Assessment Authority for Wales (1996) *Desirable Outcomes for Children's Learning Before Compulsory School Age*, Cardiff: ACAC, 4–6

Pan feddwn dalent plentyn
I weld llais a chlywed llun
(when I had a child's talent to see a voice and hear an image . . .)

In the opening lines of his epic poem *Afon* (River), Gerallt Lloyd Owen longs for the magic of early childhood. It is the time when the world is there to be explored and the adventure of discovery is all around. He has evoked the very essence of childhood.

That essence is the foundation of early childhood education. It is understanding, appreciating and rejoicing in the extraordinary ability that young children have to search systematically for knowledge, to negotiate relationships, to decode and acquire languages, to agree on symbolic meaning, to respond to challenging adults. It is the imperative to learn.

## Principles

In Wales, good-quality education of nursery age children adheres to the following principles:

- it contributes to the all-round growth and development of every child;

- it provides a springboard for learning through both structured and spontaneous play;

- it ensures active involvement and relevant first-hand experiences in an environment rich with possibilities;

- it values the contribution which parents or carers make to their child's education and encourages a working partnership;

- it ensures that equal opportunities are offered to girls and boys, to children with special learning needs and to those from different cultures;

- it provides experiences and opportunities for young children to become aware of the distinctiveness of Wales, its language and culture.

Adults concerned with nursery age children have a particular responsibility for their care, safety, protection and well-being.

## The context for learning

The early-years curriculum is about the child. It is concerned not only with the content but also with the context of the learning. The process is as important as the outcome.

## The importance of play

Well-structured and purposeful play activities enhance and extend children's learning. For the child, play can be and often is a very serious business. It needs concentrated attention. It is all about perseverance, attending to detail, learning and concentrating – characteristics usually associated with work. Play is not only crucial to the way children become self-aware and the way in which they learn the rules of social behaviour; it is also fundamental to intellectual development.

Young children learn most effectively when they are actively involved in first-hand experiences. Educational provision for young children is centred on the child. It is about adults understanding, inspiring and challenging the child's talent to learn, with adult involvement in children's play being of vital importance. Good early-years educators are there to help children, to guide their play, to offer choices, to challenge children with care and sensitivity, to encourage them and to move their learning along.

## The principle of appropriateness

Appropriateness must underpin education for children of nursery age. Young children vary in the rate and timing of their growth and development. A curriculum designed for them must acknowledge this. Accomplished early-years educators understand that age-appropriate and development-appropriate activities do not always match. The developmental norm will encompass a wide range. Some four-year-olds will barely speak in comprehensible language, whereas others will be reading confidently. Some will have difficulty in completing a simple jigsaw and others will be constructing complex water carriers out of Meccano, buckets, wood off-cuts and string.

Four-year-old children will move along a continuum. This will not be a steady or uniform progression. It can often be erratic, unpredictable and can sometime be regressive. The same child may have needs and skills at both ends of the continuum at almost the same time, for example:

- within minutes a child can be both dependent and independent, depending on changes in environment or adult expectations;

- a young child will need a stable, predictable environment, but will also enjoy challenges and surprises.

## Special needs

Most children, at some time, will have particular needs which educators will need to recognize, consider, understand and cater for appropriately. All children, whatever their needs, have the same entitlement to an invigorating and enriching play curriculum. Children in their early years can have special educational needs with will, in many cases, be temporary. With vigorous and planned intervention these needs can be addressed. Other needs will be permanent and long-term planning will be needed in order to meet them properly. Nursery educators should be alert observers. They should recognize, evaluate, understand and respond to the needs of the individual child. They should take appropriate action if children are not progressing.

## Welsh and the Curriculum Cymreig

When children reach compulsory school age, they will learn Welsh as part of the National Curriculum. All nursery age children can be given opportunities to hear about Wales, about their locality, about customs, about names, about stories and legends, about people and events. These experiences form part of a rewarding and lively learning experience for children to enhance their lives in Wales.

 **READING 9.4**

# The 'hurry-along' curriculum

## Marion Dadds

In this reading, Marion Dadds reflects on the cumulative effect of present requirements in England regarding curriculum coverage and teaching methods. She worries about its overall effects on teachers' capacity to respond to particular pupil needs and interests, and about their motivation and commitment to learning. The dilemma between offering society's curriculum and responding to individual children faces all teachers.

How, when implementing your curriculum, do you try to manage this dilemma to enhance learning and the quality of pupil experience?

Edited from: Dadds, M. (2001) 'Politics of pedagogy: the state and children', *Teachers and Teaching: Theory and Practice*, 7 (1), 49–53

One major effect of central reforms in primary schools in the past ten years has been an increase in the 'hurry-along curriculum' (Dadds, 1994). 'Coverage' has become a more dominant planning and teaching issue for teachers than learning itself (Pollard *et al.* 1992; Dadds, 1994; Warharn and Dadds, 1998; Pollard and Triggs 2000). The effects of this have been at least twofold.

First, the hurry-along curriculum has diminished the frequency of responsive teaching in which teachers take cues for their pedagogical moves from the responses of children. Under the pressure of curriculum delivery, many have reported moving children too quickly through curriculum material, knowing that understanding suffers in the process (Pollard *et al.*, 1992; Warham and Dadds, 1998). Even the children themselves 'have a sense of time as a scarce resource' (Triggs and Pollard, 1998, p. 112). This dilemma between coverage and understanding that has been generated in the past ten years, has led to an overemphasis on convergent teaching led by predetermined objectives. There is extensive documentation and debate in the literature of some of the pedagogical consequences of an overemphasis on convergent teaching (for example, Barnes *et al.*, 1969; Hull, 1985; Dadds, 1994; Black and William, 1998). Here

I review, an illustrative example from a secondary lesson (Barnes *et al.*, 1969) that highlights the nature of the pedagogical problem. In this, we see a teacher's sights set so firmly on the learning objective in the science lesson that he cannot hear the clues the children are giving him about their constructivist learning strategies:

| | |
|---|---|
| Teacher: | You get the white . . . what we call casein . . . that's . . . er . . . protein . . . which is good for you . . . it'll help to build bones . . . and the white is mainly the casein and so it's not actually a solution . . . it's a suspension of very fine particles together with water and various other things which are dissolved in water . . . |
| Pupil: | Sir, at my old school I shook my bottle of milk up and when I looked at it again all the side was covered with . . . er . . . like particles and . . . er . . . could they be the white particles of milk . . .? |
| Pupil 2: | Yes, and gradually they would sediment out, wouldn't they, to the bottom . . .? |
| Pupil 3: | When milk goes very sour though it smells like cheese, doesn't it? |
| Pupil 4: | Well, it is cheese, isn't it, if you leave it long enough? |
| Teacher: | Anyway, can we get on? . . . We'll leave a few questions for later. |

In trying to make sense of the new idea, the children try to link it to what is known and familiar in good constructivist fashion. It is to the teacher's credit that he allows the discussion to move around the children, rather than keeping tight control of every response. Yet he misses the opportunity to reinforce the validity of the children's learning strategy by moving towards his objective prematurely. He could, alternatively, have taken a little more time to travel round a learning loop to help the children anchor their thinking more effectively to their previous knowledge. The hurry-along curriculum for information could, thus, have been transformed into a wait-a-while curriculum for reflection and understanding. In the event, however, there is a conflict between a pedagogy for delivery and a pedagogy for learning. Under the pressure of coverage, learning is sacrificed for teaching.

What will be the long-term effects of a hurry-along pedagogy on children's understanding? Does it affect their attitudes towards their learning and towards a sense of their own ability to participate thoughtfully in learning discussions? Evidence on teacher wait-time (Budd-Rowe, 1974; Black and William, 1998) suggests that this may be so. When teachers slow down their response time to children's questions and answers, benefits begin to emerge. Children who are slower to respond begin to participate more effectively. Teachers' questions and responses become more thoughtful and more complex, as do the children's. Teachers' concepts of the less able children are transformed as time and space allow these children to offer more of themselves in learning events. The self-esteem of less able children is enhanced through their increased participation (Budd-Rowe, 1974). 'What is essential is that any dialogue should evoke thoughtful reflection in which all pupils can be encouraged to take part' (Black and William, 1998, p. 12). The time created in wait-time pedagogy seems to shift the balance of power in the participation stakes and leads to these improvements in quality teaching and learning.

Yet nothing of these politics of wait-time pedagogy appear in current central initiatives. Indeed, when Black and William published their research early in 1998, it was met with public scorn and derision by aspects of the national press and Her Majesty's Chief Inspector. One cannot help wondering whether the notion of 'pace' and predetermined objectives that are prominent features of the literacy hour pedagogy (DfEE, 1998b) will contribute further to the difficulties of the hurry-along curriculum, encouraging teachers, yet once more, to prioritize coverage over understanding. This is not to say that many children will not benefit from more briskness and pace in teaching and from the clarity that predetermined objectives sometimes bring. But we may need a broader, more complex, debate about whose pace and objectives are appropriate in whole-class teaching contexts. It may also be appropriate to revisit Eisner's (1977) distinction between instructional and expressive objectives, which allows teachers to distinguish between intended and unintended learning outcomes. The current narrow focus on instructional objectives and predetermined outcomes may prevent curriculum designers from seeing as valuable or worthwhile any learning that was not initially intended.

As a second effect, the hurry-along curriculum has minimized the opportunities for teachers to draw children's own interests and questions firmly into curriculum planning and teaching. When central agencies have a strong and heavily loaded sense of what children should be learning, then there may be little time to consider what children themselves feel they would be interested to learn (Pollard and Triggs, 2000). Children are fortunate today if their interests map onto the school's rolling curriculum programme for the year. If they do not, those interests may go forever unkindled. In an action research study I supported, the teacher researchers decided to investigate children's views of what would make an interesting curriculum for them. One teacher researcher, working with five- to seven-year-olds, discovered that young children were consistently able to articulate their own interests and the topics that they would like to see represented in the curriculum. Five-year-old Alex, for example, had a clear sense of his own learning interests in the face of his daily directed experiences:

| | |
|---|---|
| I would like to hav. | I would like to have |
| a topicke theat is. | a topic that is |
| birds bicos I like. | birds because I like |
| birds and bicos. | birds and because |
| birds ar intresti | birds are interesting |
| and bicos birds can fly. | and because birds can fly |
| bicos we crant do maths | because we can't do maths |
| and riting all the time | and writing all the time |

What surprised Alex's teacher was not only that Alex had strong desires that were not being fulfilled, but that he perceived his learning experiences to be dominated so much by 'the basics'. For Alex, mathematics and writing were, the teacher later concluded, taking on the hue of penal servitude. What lessons do children learn about the value and status of their own questions and interests if these are never acknowledged within the curriculum; if they never form the basis for serious learning in schools? What do they learn about the politics of knowledge in these circumstances? Is there a danger that others' knowledge and questions will forever seem to be superior to one's own? Under these conditions, classroom experiences are certainly not leading children 'to develop the skills and attitudes associated with being the kind of lifelong learners that we are told will be characteristic of the next century' (Pollard and Triggs, 2000). This should be warning enough not to continue down this particular pedagogical road, for Alex's experience was not isolated. There is accumulated evidence that the self-directed pupil learning can lead to quality learning outcomes of an astonishing kind, and to high levels of independence in thought and action (for example, Bissex, 1980; Calkins, 1983; Graves, 1983; Dadds, 1986; Fraser, 1987; Drummond, 1993; Hart, 1996). Teachers who have retained the courage to diverge from preset objectives to follow children's interests may have something powerful to offer.

It is in the nature of teaching that tensions and dilemmas have to be confronted (Berlak and Berlak, 1981). In particular, the tension between learning processes and coverage of curriculum content has been witnessed in other teaching contexts. Yet it seems to be the case that these tensions have been magnified for teachers in England under the pressure of curriculum reform. They may be magnified further under the pressure to pace lessons more briskly within the literacy and numeracy hours, and to achieve politically defined targets and standards. So, in the face of the pace, objectives, targets and tables that have become part of the dominant linguistic and conceptual discourse of education reform in England (Fielding, 1994), we might wonder how confident good divergent teachers will be to stray from preset paths for better pastures. We might wonder what the absence of divergent teaching will mean, in the longer term, for children's motivation and interest in their learning experiences.

# Managing learning in the primary classroom

Neville Bennett

This reading summarizes the four elements of Bennett's model of classroom teaching: planning and preparation, presentation, implementation and assessment.

Drawing on research and challenging many established classroom practices, he suggests ways of improving teaching and learning. His constructivist starting point is clearly foregrounded – and this illustrates how fundamental assumptions about learning should feed through to curriculum implementation. This reading was written before the introduction of the national strategies for literacy and numeracy in England, and they clearly represent one response to some of the issues Bennett raises.

Would you find this model useful in planning and reviewing your curriculum?

Edited from: Bennett, N. (1992) *Managing Learning in the Primary Classroom*. Stoke-on-Trent: ASPE

A constructivist view of learning perceives children as intellectually active learners already holding ideas or schemata which they use to make sense of their everyday experiences. Learning in classrooms involves the extension, elaboration or modification of their schemata. This process is one in which learners actively make sense of the world by constructing meanings. Learning is believed to be optimized in settings where social interaction, particularly between a learner and more knowledgeable others, is encouraged, and where cooperatively achieved success is a major aim. The medium for this success is talk, which is now widely accepted as a means of promoting pupils' understandings, and of evaluating their progress.

The classroom implications of the above conceptions of children's learning can now be considered. For this purpose a simple model of a teaching cycle is used as shown in Figure 9.5.1.

The cycle begins with the teacher planning and preparing tasks and activities for children which are then presented in some way, for example, through discussion, an experiment, a TV programme, and so on. The children then engage with their work within a classroom management system set up by the teacher: for example, individuals working on individual tasks; mixed-ability groups in an integrated day arrangement; the whole class working in small cooperative groups on the same technology task, and so on. Once this work has been completed, it would be expected that teachers would assess or diagnose it, using that information to feed back to pupils, and to feed forward to inform their next round of planning.

## Planning and preparation

A crucial part of planning is the selection or design of tasks, with associated materials, appropriate to children's capabilities. There are two aspects of this – choosing appropriate content, and the appropriate level, both of which assume an understanding by the teacher of the children's conceptions.

Choosing the content relies heavily on the teacher's knowledge of the subject unless there is a set scheme or textbook which is to be followed. Even here, however, teachers need to choose these carefully. Research on primary school texts in history (Beck and McKeown, 1988) indicates that they fall to enable many pupils to develop a coherent representation or

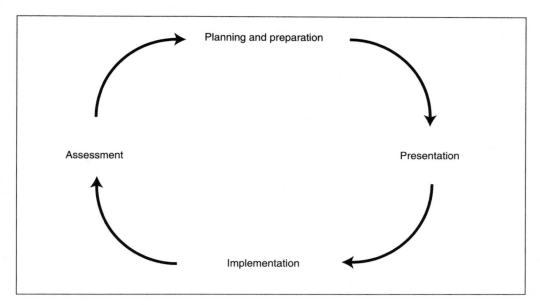

**Figure 9.5.1**    A teaching cycle

theme for a sequence of events. The major deficiency in these texts was that they made inadequate or unfounded assumptions about pupils' background knowledge. Another aspect of content selection is clearly the appropriate choice of content from National Curriculum programmes of study to fulfil particular statements of attainment.

Choosing the appropriate level of a task in relation to individual pupils means avoiding 'the twin pitfalls of demanding too much or expecting too little' (Plowden, 1967) (see also Readings 9.6 and 9.7). HMI have long expressed concern about poor levels of matching, particularly in areas like science and project work. They have argued that the level of demand, and pace of work, is most often directed towards children of average ability in the class, and that high attainers in the class tend to be underestimated and low attainers overestimated. These professional judgements of the Inspectorate are borne out by research studies (Bennett *et al.*, 1984, 1987).

In this context, the notion of the zone of proximal development is also important (see Readings 7.3 and 13.2). This is based on the view that optimal learning is that which involves the acquisition of cognitive skills slightly beyond the child's independent grasp in a cooperative setting. This conception of matching is not common in current practice and its implementation has implications both for teachers' planning and for classroom management.

## Presentation

It is becoming increasingly clear how crucial presentation is in terms of children's learning. The presentation of bits of knowledge or fragmented information supplied either by text or by teachers is not likely to encourage pupils to construct new understandings. Similarly, learners are much more likely to make sense of new input if it is clearly structured and organized (see Reading 13.4). Two aspects of contemporary practice bear on this: the manner in which tasks are specified, and the nature of teacher questions.

Recent studies have shown that although teachers are very good at telling children what to do, they very rarely tell them why they are doing it. Thus, although the immediate task may be clear, the overall purpose, or curricular sequence within which the task is located, is unknown to them. Although teachers in general are good at specifying tasks, about one in six tasks are poorly presented. These create problems for teachers and learners because the manner in which a task is specified confers importance on certain aspects of it, and ignores others. A simple example will suffice. A reception class teacher had the intention of helping children to think logically, and to give them the idea of direction. The task she chose to fulfil this intention was picture sequencing, integral to which was the colouring of each picture to add interest. However, the task was presented to the children with the words 'now we are going to do some colouring and cutting'. Observing and talking to these children after they had finished their activity made it abundantly clear that they had done what they had been asked to do – colouring in. No picture sequencing took place. The teacher's presentation had dictated the children's activity, thereby subverting the teacher's own intentions (Bennett and Kell, 1989).

Another important aspect of presentation is teacher questioning (see Reading 13.5). It is often argued (Edwards and Mercer, 1987) that 'it is essentially in the discourse between teacher and pupils that education is done, or fails to be done'. Studies of teacher–pupil talk (Galton *et al.*, 1988; Tizard *et al.*, 1988; Alexander, 1990) have presented pictures of the pattern, nature and quality of this discourse. Not surprisingly, there appears to be a marked asymmetry in teacher–pupil interaction. Teachers typically spend most of their time talking to, and with, pupils, whereas any individual pupil talks with the teacher for only a very small proportion of his or her time. Most often the individual pupil experiences being talked to, by the teacher, as a member of a group or class, rather than being talked with. From the child's point of view, therefore, although individual work is common in primary schools, individual teaching is not.

With regard to the nature of teacher talk, PRINDEP (Alexander, 1990) classified interactions into five categories – work, monitoring, routine, disciplinary and other. Over a third of the interactions were about the content of the tasks which had been set, about a fifth were concerned with checking, marking and monitoring progress. Routine matters accounted for just over a quarter of the interactions, and discipline and control about 10 per cent. However, of most importance in considering the impact of teachers' presentation of children's learning is the quality of that interaction. The fostering of children's capabilities to talk and listen emerged as a particular issue, and supported the view of HMI (DES, 1990) that 'Where the work is less effective than it should be, it is the development of oracy that is often impoverished and given too little time'.

## Implementation

The Plowden Report (1967) advocated individualization of learning, but recognized a practical difficulty. If all teaching were on an individual basis, only seven or eight minutes a day would be available for each child. The report therefore advised teachers to economize by 'teaching together a small group of children who are roughly at the same stage'. Further, these groups should change in accordance with children's needs, the implication being that the class would be organized flexibly, with groups forming and reforming according to children's needs and activities. Various advantages were perceived for group work. For example, it was expected that it would help children to collaborate together and realize their own strengths and weaknesses, and to make their meaning clearer to themselves by having to explain it to others. It was hoped that apathetic children would be infected by the enthusiasm of a group, while able children would benefit by being caught up in the thrust and counterthrust of conversation in a small group of children similar to themselves.

Unfortunately, research on classroom grouping practices provides little support for this rosy picture. In arguing that children in the group should be 'roughly at the same stage', the Plowden Report was, in modern parlance, calling for ability grouping – and that is what tends to happen. Three-quarters of classes are grouped according to ability for maths, and for reading two-thirds of seven-year-olds and over one-half of nine-year-olds are grouped this way (DES, 1978a). When the focus has been narrowed to observe what actually happens in such groups some sobering findings have been reported, particularly in junior classes. A major finding is that although most children sit in groups, for the great majority of the time they work as individuals on their own, individual, tasks. In other words, pupils work in groups, but not as groups. Further, whilst working in groups the amount of task-related talk is low, interactions tend to be short, and the opportunity to cooperate is slim. Finally, there appears to be a clear sex effect in interaction. The great majority of talk is between pupils of the same sex, even in mixed-sex groups (Galton *et al.* 1980).

What seems to have happened is that teachers have taken note of Plowden's views in having children work in groups, but have preferred to retain individualization rather than to introduce cooperation in that context. The unfortunate outcome of that is a high level of low-quality talk and a dearth of cooperative endeavour. These outcomes could have serious implications both for children's learning and for the fulfilment of National Curriculum attainment targets.

## Assessment

That pupils bring schemata of their own to bear on any given topic, and that some of these will be shared and others idiosyncratic, has to be taken into account by teachers in their planning of classroom tasks. In order to take these schemata adequately into account a clear understanding of what they are is necessary; that is, it requires the teacher to take on the role of diagnostician. A useful metaphor for gaining access to children's conceptions is that of creating 'a window into the child's mind'. To draw back the curtains of that window often needs far more than a rudimentary look at a child's work. It demands a sophisticated combination of observation and careful questioning, and this is likely to need a great deal of time.

However, any individual child spends very little time interacting with the teacher, so how is effective diagnosis happening? Evidence suggests that this is often accomplished by teachers concentrating on what children produce (for example, a page of completed sums), rather than on how it has been achieved. Yet both are necessary for diagnosis. Poor diagnosis has serious implications. No teacher can decide on the next optimal step for a child or children without a clear view of where they are now. It is not possible to extend or modify schemata without knowledge of those schemata.

For teachers effectively to diagnose children's conceptions, to plan appropriate classroom tasks, to present quality explanations and demonstrations and to make curricular choices, requires knowledge and understandings of subject matter. Research indicates that teachers have a better chance of being able to help their pupils develop flexible understandings of subject matter if they understand it well themselves. Moreover, such understandings enable teachers to develop a variety of ways of representing their understanding to pupils, who bring very different experiences and knowledge with them (see Chapter 14).

READING 9.6

# Key issues in classroom differentiation

Eve Bearne

This reading is structured in three parts: identifying the range of learners; considering support for diversity within the school and classroom environment; and reviewing the process of learning. A broad view of differentiation is thus taken. However, the focus on the process of learning moves to the level of tasks and makes a number of important points. Provision of classroom difference for academic purposes is hard enough but, of course, a further consideration is the protection of the self-esteem of all pupils. In this respect, Reading 15.2 is closely connected to Eve Bearne's reading.

How do you provide for differentiation in learning needs?

Edited from: Bearne, E. (1996) *Differentiation and Diversity in the Primary School*. London, New York: Routledge, 246–55

## Identifying the range of learners

Differentiation to ensure progression rests on being able to offer diversity in classroom approaches. It is therefore essential to have a clear view of the range of learning styles, experiences and behaviours which children bring with them to school. Discussion of the range usually starts with identifying children whose progress is worrying. Reasons might vary, from social and emotional factors to being understimulated. Observation and identification are important, and for those children who come within the special education Code of Practice, steps towards providing statements of need are firmly in place in most schools. However, there may not be established practices for identifying those who are achieving very highly.

It may be useful to consider a general description of a range of learners. What kinds of readers and writers inhabit our classrooms? For example, a group of teachers from Suffolk put together a list of characteristics of children in relation to reading. This included children who:

- return to the same book again and again;
- like to read to others;
- prefer to read pictorial text;
- always want to read whatever the teacher has just read to them;
- always read with friends;
- enjoy reading plays;
- almost always read either fiction or fact;
- can read detailed pictorial text with ease;
- prefer an adult to read to them;
- read to escape from everyday reality;
- pretend to read – as rehearsal for reading verbal text; from fear; from idleness!
- are over-ambitious in their choices of books;
- don't yet know how to choose successfully;

- know when to leave a book which they don't like;
- are series/serial readers;
- love Enid Blyton;
- read comic strips;
- choose to read *TV Times*/*Radio Times*;
- read interest magazines;
- are avid readers;
- like a 'slow' read;
- see progress in reading as status;
- read mostly poetry;
- prefer to read extracts than whole texts;
- are reluctant to read;
- like the security of the reading scheme;
- love reading although they find it difficult.

As is apparent from the list above, the teachers found that the range of children's interests and abilities was wide, including some children who might be seen as 'covertly able'. A similar activity could be done in any other area of the curriculum. How might the range of developing mathematicians be described? Or what would 'struggling' in science, art or physical education mean? Identifying some details of the range of learners and learning styles leads naturally towards questions of how their learning needs are catered for. The next move after looking at the range of learners might be to identify the range of contexts and opportunities for learning which are already on offer and which seem to be working well.

## Considering the school and classroom environment

A quick audit of the school and the classroom as contexts for diversity might be a starting point. How 'hospitable to diversity' is the physical setting of the school? It does not take long to go round a school looking at the notices, for example, and asking if they are sufficiently accessible to children and adults who read pictorial texts more readily than print – or the reverse. What about different languages – are the languages of the community represented properly in the school, not just with a token multilingual notice on the office door, but in languages reflecting the specific school context? Is there access for people whose mobility is hampered – do doors open wide enough and are there ramps for wheelchairs, for example? These aspects of differential provision may seem peripheral but they are, in fact, a reflection of the general approach to diversity which will operate in the provision of learning, too. More 'learning-focused' questions in terms of the school environment might be to do with the value given to children's contributions to the life of the school: how is children's work presented and displayed? Is there only 'the best' – or everyone's? And what about resources? How accessible is the library or resource centre and what provision has been made for differentiation here? Does it have books of maps and photographs, technical magazines and manuals . . .? How does the school shape up as an environment for mathematics, geography, science, technology, music . . .? Is children's work in maths, science, design and technology displayed as much and as frequently as art work and written work, for example?

An audit of the classroom might start with the simple question: 'What messages about diversity does my classroom give?' As Avril Dawson points out (1996), it's worth looking at the walls as a good indicator of attitudes; is the work or display material all teacher selected and mounted? What messages about, for example, gender might be signalled by the home corner and dressing up box? What images of boys/girls or different cultures are represented in the books and pictures? Is there a variety of materials to work with? Are there special areas for listening to tapes? Making things? Working on the computer? Reading quietly as well as with friends? Researching, trying out ideas, tackling problem-solving activities? The environment for learning is a powerful factor in making a classroom hospitable to diversity, and exchanges of ideas between colleagues after a classroom audit can be a useful way to focus discussions about differentiation.

Perhaps the most obvious area for discussion of good practice, however, comes in examining teaching methods and the management of learning – how groups are constituted and how they are varied [these issues are considered further in Readings 10.4 and 10.5].

## The process of learning

If differentiation is to do with organizing teaching and learning to accommodate and stimulate future learning, then much of the evidence of differentiation is seen in the process of teaching and learning. For certain activities, differentiation is unnecessary, although attention to diversity will be important. Storytime is one familiar example of this. Much of the time, however, teachers consciously and automatically make decisions about how best to adapt the presentation of ideas to suit the range of learners. The commonly acknowledged areas for differentiation are explained below.

*Input* What decisions are made about factual information, the concepts and the vocabulary which will be used to help learners grasp content and ideas? At this point it's useful to find out what the learners already know, in order to build on existing knowledge. How is this done? Acknowledgement of the diverse experiences brought to an activity (or series of activities) can signal the value given to home or cultural knowledge. At the same time, there is the chance to identify what new information or concepts individuals and the group as a whole might now be introduced to.

*Tasks* This has often meant providing different tasks within an activity to cater for different levels of 'ability' (often judged on literacy). In its worst manifestation it is represented by three, or so, different worksheets: one with mostly pictures and few words; one with more words more densely packed and one picture; and a third with lots of words and no pictures. It is not difficult to imagine the messages this kind of practice gives to all the learners in the classroom. While recognizing that such practices are implemented with the best intentions in the world to support children who experience difficulties, it is clear that some who have difficulties with literacy are perfectly capable or working at a high conceptual level on tasks involving practical application of ideas or talk. The challenge to the teacher is to find ways of framing tasks which can not only genuinely stretch all the learners, but which might provide for the variety of ways in to learning. This is likely, also, to involve an element of choice in order to encourage increasing independence in learning as well as providing for different paces of work. How are tasks differentiated? It might be useful to select one activity – possibly from the term's theme or agreed school scheme of work – and, with a colleague, list how tasks are – or might be – successfully differentiated without suggesting a 'sheep and goats' view of the children.

*Resources* These might be part of the answer to the challenge. While it is important to identify a range of material resources which do not depend on developed literacy – for example, tape recorders, videos, pictures, photographs, maps, diagrams – it is also important to acknowledge and use the range of human resources available in the classroom, school and home.

*Support* This might use some of the human resources available, but it might also mean use of information technology or other tools for learning. Perhaps the most critical element in considering this area of provision for diversity concerns teacher time. There is never enough time to give the individual support that a teacher almost inevitably and continuingly wants to offer. What methods are used for supported learning? What strategies and activities have been identified to help in time management?

*Outcome and response* Outcomes can be both tangible and intangible. Products like information sheets for younger children, newspapers, mathematics games or activities, maps, models, tape recordings, diagrams and instructions provide opportunities for assessing children's capabilities across a range of areas and kinds of abilities. Intangible outcomes are equally open to observation and assessment – increased confidence, ability to carry out a particular operation or to present ideas orally, new-found enthusiasm or the articulation of concepts which have been understood. What range of outcomes might be expected in the activity selected for discussion? The end points of learning are often used to determine how well children have achieved. This kind of summative assessment has its place, but if assessments are to inform future teaching and learning, then there may be a need for diversity of kinds of assessments and variation in times when those assessments are carried out.

Response to the outcomes of learning, by teachers and children, make the process of learning explicit and acknowledge diverse abilities. Response also encourages learners themselves to evaluate their work and leads towards future progress. What kinds of responses are – or might be – made at the end of a learning process or activity in your class?

## READING 9.7

# Curriculum strategies for able pupils

Diane Montgomery

This reading focuses on the needs of 'able' pupils, who may sometimes be overlooked when busy teachers attend to children with difficulties. The reading focuses on three strategies for organizational or curriculum adjustment – acceleration, enrichment and differentiation. Examples are drawn from across the age phases, and not all will be appropriate for young children. However, the principles for adjusting the curriculum to specific needs are certainly applicable. Three forms of differentiation are identified: by task input, by task outcome and through collaborative groupwork.

Do you have children in your class who might benefit from acceleration, enrichment or further differentiation in the curriculum?

Edited from: Montgomery, D. (1996) *Educating the Able*. London: Cassell, 65–73, 81–6

## Acceleration

Acceleration means that the student moves through lower levels or sections of the standard curriculum at a much faster rate than age-matched peers. It is probably the cheapest and simplest form of curriculum provision for able learners. Some typical examples of accelerated provision are as follows.

- *Early entry*: into a new phase of education: nursery, infant, junior, secondary, college.

- *'Grade skipping'*: promotion by usually one or sometimes two years over age-matched peers.

- *Subject acceleration:* joining students in older age groups for particular subject areas, such as mathematics or music, matching knowledge and skills competencies.

- *Vertical grouping*: entry into classes which have students of, for example, five- to seven-years of age, enabling the able five-year-old to work at the level of the six- or even seven-year-olds in the same classroom for all or part of the curriculum, usually language or mathematics.

- *Extra-curricular studies and clubs*: able students join special groups such as NAGC (National Association for Gifted Children), explorers groups and summer schools. Able students are often identified by the large range of extra-mural studies in which they are involved.

- *Concurrent studies:* at the same time as the normal primary curriculum is being studied, the student may be pursuing a study of secondary-school curricula.

- *Telescoping studies*: students follow the normal programme but the studies are compacted into a much smaller time span, perhaps one-third of the usual length.

- *Self-paced and/or self-organized instruction*: students design their own programmes of studies and follow them, often whilst waiting for the rest of the class to catch up.

- *Mentoring*: students, however young, are introduced to and work with an 'expert' in the field of interest on a regular basis. Class teachers or parents may come in to mentor, and schools can be linked to local universities to provide a range of mentors.

- *Correspondence courses*: these can be followed by a student whilst pursuing ordinary school studies during normal school hours.

In the post-war period, acceleration, particularly 'grade skipping', was the major form of differentiation offered to meet the needs of able students. Selective education and acceleration were strongly opposed by those who regarded the concept of giftedness as both élitist and a myth established to maintain the class system and a 'two-nations' philosophy (Benn, 1982). Acceleration was criticized on the grounds that it would damage academic progress and create socioemotional problems in those who were accelerated.

Freeman (1979), writing on the education of the gifted in Britain, was able to conclude that most able children could be well educated in mixed-ability settings and that too much emphasis on the academic side of education could harm socioemotional development. This reflected the move away from acceleration towards enrichment and improved teaching strategies for including and challenging all students.

## Enrichment

In a general sense, all forms of adjustment for the able are forms of enrichment. Passow (1992a) suggested four strategies for the development of enrichment programmes:

- modification of the curriculum to provide additional breadth or depth of coverage;

- modification in the pace of presentation – speeding up the rate of progress through the curriculum to suit the individual's need;

- modification of the nature of the material which was presented, to take account of needs and interests;

- development of process skills such as those of creative and critical thinking, heuristics and problem solving, and affective and interpersonal communication and social skills.

As can be seen, at least two of these strategies would be in accord with the views of progressive educators and would draw criticisms from traditionalists. Progressive educators would, however, regard enrichment as a necessary part of all children's education, not just that of a talented élite.

Similar approaches can be observed in many of the hundreds of enrichment packs available in Britain. Such enrichment packs and materials present subjects which are outside the main curriculum areas, and are truly extension projects. They broaden and deepen pupils' knowledge of an area. The intention of most of those who prepare the packs is that teachers who have individual or small groups of able pupils may give the package as it is to the learners and more or less leave them to organize themselves and work on it. Good literacy skills are demanded by these types of material, and there is a wide range available.

Able pupils in our case studies have nearly always found both these types of study package interesting and useful. The materials are used when the able individuals have completed all the assignments set by their class teacher and are running far ahead of the rest. Giving them their own project, which is structured and has all the supplementary materials included, enables the pupils to opt to work on the 'project' rather than waste time waiting for others to catch up, doing extra examples, reading around interest topics, annoying and distracting others and daydreaming.

## Differentiation

When students of different abilities and needs are integrated within the ordinary classroom, it is recommended that the work which is provided for them should offer substantial differentiation. This can mean:

- the setting of different tasks at different levels of difficulty suitable for different levels of achievement: differentiation by inputs;

- the setting of common tasks which can be responded to in a positive way by all pupils: differentiation by outcomes.

Either of these responses would prove somewhat better than the traditional way of teaching to the middle, which can leave a third of the class unmotivated and uninvolved. However, there are problems with both.

If teachers adopt differentiation by levels of input, then they will be creating a potentially stigmatizing situation in which students doing work of an easier nature can begin to feel lower in ability and value than the rest, for they will be doing recognizably easier work. This can in the long run prove academically handicapping, for these students come to expect that they can never achieve a high standard in any sphere of activity and cease to try, so that they compound their difficulties and begin to fall further and further behind. The able students in this system begin to feel special, for they are doing the 'clever' work; they can develop inflated opinions of themselves and their abilities and begin to look down on the other children, even poking fun at them. All of these attitudes are destructive and wasteful, so that none of the groups is motivated to develop its abilities and talents to the full. Only those with great strength of character or individualism, can survive these social pressures and develop freely, and these pupils are few.

The second view of differentiation, where all students can participate in the same task, is advocated as one of the ways in which all students can have access to the full curriculum without being academically and socially downgraded during the teaching process. However, at the assessment stage or during continuous assessment processes the differences may become clear to the students and their peers, and thus this is becoming a less-favoured option. It too can be discriminatory in an unhelpful way. When able students are set the same task as all the rest, unless the task is itself demanding but not demoralizing for the pupils, the able are quite capable of regularly underfunctioning. Differentiation by outcomes thus often gives very disappointing results.

Differentiation in either of these forms is thus too simple a view. Each brings further difficulties and thus the concept needs to be further developed. In research in the Learning Difficulties Project, a third definition of differentiation was developed:

- the setting of common tasks to which all students can contribute their own knowledge and experience in collaborative activities and so raise the level of output of all the learners.

In order to attain this form of differentiation, it was found necessary to adapt the teaching methods. Rather than change inputs and output mechanisms, the process of collaborative problem solving and other group activities created a form of internal, authentic differentiation [see Readings 13.7 and 13.8].

The definition of an appropriate curriculum for particularly able children thus centres upon the development and use of higher-order thinking skills; exploration; complex in-depth and integrated studies; and the development of self-managed and autonomous learning.

---

### 📖 READING 9.8

# ICT in the primary classroom

## Stephen Kennelwell, John Parkinson and Howard Tanner

This reading derives from a research and development project on the use of information and communication technologies (ICT) in primary schools. It builds on a strong model of teaching and learning and an appreciation of the strengths and weaknesses of ICT within the curriculum as a whole. From this base, specific advice on planning, structuring and monitoring the use of ICT is offered – with emphasis too on how to draw on children's ICT experiences from home and elsewhere. The key point is that successful ICT work requires careful thought as part of a whole school strategy combined with specific, structured classroom preparation.

How systematic is your ICT planning?

Edited from: Kennelwell, S., Parkinson, J. and Tanner, H. (2000) *Developing ICT in Primary Schools*. London, New York: RoutledgeFalmer, 68–87

## Planning for ICT within the curriculum

In our ITCD project, it was found that schools commonly used a planning grid to help ensure a balance of coverage across the curriculum and to maintain coherence and continuity. Typical headings were:

- year-group;

- date;

- theme/topic context;

- description and purpose of activity;

- ICT strand and learning objectives;

- subject learning objectives;

- assessment criteria;

- resources.

Other schools successfully used a termly forecast for medium-term planning, sometimes combined with a planning grid. Each of the subject areas was addressed in turn, providing detailed information about aims and objectives, intended practice and resource requirements.

Primary teachers are faced with a quandary when planning an ICT-based activity. They must ensure that pupils have the support they need for developing their ICT capability, while providing them with contexts that stimulate learning in other subjects as well. This is a challenge that requires clear thinking, and teachers should consider:

1. What is the educational purpose of the activity – to develop ICT capability, to support learning in another area of the curriculum, or both?
2. Will the children need to be monitored to identify opportune moments for teacher intervention to enhance their skills?
3. Does it provide children with experience of using ICT as a tool?
4. Are there opportunities to assess children's ICT competence?
5. Will the children work cooperatively or collaboratively? How will this be introduced and supported?
(Bennett, 1997, p. 65)

Schools found this highly detailed approach very useful for subject areas with which a teacher is unfamiliar or lacking in confidence – which was often the case with ICT work.

There are some changes in adopting a 'ready-made' plan, as opposed to developing a plan for the particular curriculum of the school and the needs of its teachers. However, this can easily lead to an ICT curriculum that is divorced from the learning of other subjects. The QCA (1998) scheme, for instance, is ICT led rather than theme or subject led, in order to exemplify progression in ICT concepts and processes. For example, units in the modelling-control strands include:

- understanding instructions and making things happen;

- routes – controlling a floor turtle;

- exploring simulations;

- modelling effects on screen;

- graphical modelling;

- introduction to spreadsheets;

- controlling devices;

- spreadsheet modelling;

- control and monitoring – what happens if . . .?

The most successful teachers had carried out further development work on these units to relate them to schemes of work for other subjects, to incorporate their own ideas and to add detail of how they would work in their own classrooms.

Plans for ICT activities have a limited lifespan, in any case, and teachers in successful schools recognized the need to replace some of the activities they had used for years in order to take advantage of new resources and research. For instance, the advent of the Internet affords the free exploration of remote information sources. Pupils can visit sites that would otherwise be inaccessible, and this can stimulate the reading of text and the writing of e-mail messages by pupils reluctant to engage in traditional literary forms. Paradoxically, we found that this degree of emancipation increased the need for planning. Web research can lead to pupils becoming frustrated, and there is no value in pupils simply downloading quantities of information without understanding the content. It is thus important for teachers to structure the work and preview relevant pages to ensure that pupils have a chance of success. When effectively managed, pupils can develop higher order skills of independent learning and research (DfEE, 1999c).

All teachers face the same challenges, and most successful schools formed planning teams (either formally or informally) for a particular year group or topic. These teams often enlisted the support of the ICT coordinator to advise them or provide ideas for ICT-based activities that built into a progressive scheme of work for the whole school. We found that where teachers' knowledge and confidence in ICT were low, individual discussion with the ICT coordinator helped them to understand the role of the computer in learning and to identify where the learning of ICT could be recognized and supported.

## Building on pupils' use of ICT at home

An increasing number of pupils in today's primary classrooms are confident, competent and regular users of computers in their own homes. Yet schools' inspectors in Wales note that in around half of primary schools 'teachers often underestimate what pupils can do and much of the work lacks sufficient challenge' (OHMCI, 1999, p. 3). Indeed, Downes (1998) found that pupils preferred their ICT work at home to that carried out in school. In order to gain most from their ICT work in school, it is important that pupils' activities are interesting to them and structured in such a way as to engender understanding that may be difficult for them to achieve unaided. In planning these activities, it is thus important for teachers to appreciate the extent and the nature of children's computer work at home.

Downes (1998) identifies specifically that, in contrast to the short periods of time for which pupils were able to use ICT in school, children work on the computer at home in an uninterrupted fashion for as long as they need. This helps to build their confidence. Furthermore, many of the children regularly engaged in writing and drawing activities, and used information-based programs for leisure as well as school-related work. This reveals some gaps in the expressive use of ICT, however, which schools should attempt to fill by teaching pupils to construct databases, models, hypertexts and multimedia presentations, and by setting relevant homework.

Downes also warns us of the potential inequities produced by an over-reliance on home activities in pupils' learning, and recommends the adoption of strategies to provide opportunities, inside and outside of lesson time, for those pupils who do not have home access to good ICT facilities (Downes, 1999). In the ITCD project, however, we found that extra-curricular provision was quite rare in primary schools, and what there was tended to be provided by ICT enthusiasts for pupils who were already the most ICT capable.

We found that it was these most capable pupils who made the greatest use of ICT in lessons, too. It is thus essential that schools should consider how they can make ICT facilities available outside of lesson time for those who are currently missing opportunities to learn.

## Stimulating and structuring learning

In order to build on informal use at home, the more formal learning in school should be based on clear objectives, involve structured activities and have high expectations of all pupils, with an appreciation of the problems likely to be experienced by pupils and planned strategies to deal with them.

Our ITCD project found that the most successful teaching methods were similar to those recommended for literacy and numeracy teaching. In particular, the following sequence was used effectively:

1. Whole class briefing on the context and activity.
2. Detailed explanation to each group when they were ready to work on the activity.
3. Careful choice of pairs to work on the computer in turn.
4. A review of key points with the group afterwards.

The most successful teachers thus worked with the whole class or group beforehand to clarify their expectations, focus their attention on what they were going to do, generate ideas on how they might go about it and demonstrate any new techniques involved. They identified when it was helpful for pupils to plan their work first on paper so that they had a clear view, for example, of the layout of a document or the structure of a database. In other situations, such as the writing of a book review, pupils were expected to use the computer immediately to draft ideas and then develop them on screen.

Many teachers overestimated the extent to which pupils could develop understanding merely by working on tasks themselves. Important learning activities need to be introduced by explanation and questioning of pupils, and concluded by further questioning and a clear summary of what has been learned.

## Monitoring progress and intervening to help pupils learn

The most effective teaching seen in the ITCD project was both well planned and capable of responding to the *ad hoc* opportunities that arose to stimulate learning at important moments. Pupils benefited from the praise, feedback and support that included guidance on how to improve. The timely intervention of the teacher had a beneficial effect on the development of children's technical skills and knowledge of ICT, and was used to help develop children's higher-order thinking skills. Children seemed to make more rapid progress and become independent more quickly when teachers provided assistance at critical moments. It is thus important to monitor pupils' work frequently in order to make decisions about when intervention will be effective. This is particularly important with ICT for two reasons:

- it is common for pupils to appear to be usefully occupied with the task when in fact they are working very inefficiently and failing to exploit the potential of ICT;

- because of the richness of the resource, pupils may divert from the intended task without it being obvious from their behaviour.

# CHAPTER 10

# Organization. How are we managing the classroom?

The seven readings in this chapter address some of the practical issues which have to be faced if effective teaching and learning is to be provided.

We begin with two complementary readings on how to establish and manage a classroom to directly support teaching and learning. Moyles (10.1) reviews issues concerned with the context, routines, resources, behaviour and forms of communication. Clegg and Billington (10.2) augment this discussion and also draw attention to the messages given through classroom displays.

A reading from Pate-Bain and colleagues on class size is included (10.3). This reports evidence from the largest study of the issue yet completed, the STAR project. Irrespective of class size, further readings consider teaching strategies in relation to whether pupils are taught individually, as a whole class or in groups. In Reading 10.4, McNamara suggests using flexible forms of classroom layout, so that it is possible to switch strategies relatively easily. The reading from Reason (10.5) sets out the rationale for how group work has developed. Croll and Moses (10.6) focus on how classroom teachers can best support children with special educational needs. They challenge conventional, individualized practice and raise issues which are certainly cause for reflection.

Finally, Thomas (10.7) addresses how to manage other adults in classrooms.

The parallel chapter of *Reflective Teaching* addresses similar issues and suggests activities to increase the effectiveness of classroom organization. The first section discusses the classroom environment, including the use of space, resources and time. Section 2, concerns managing children, parents, support staff and records. It includes extensive discussion on individual, group and whole-class organization. The emphasis is on achieving coherence between learning aims and the selected form of classroom organization, and then working towards consistency between the various organizational elements. The chapter concludes with suggestions for 'Key Readings'. Of course, *RTweb* offers further ideas and activities.

## READING 10.1

# Managing the classroom as an environment for learning

Janet Moyles

This reading provides a useful overview of important issues in classroom management. Helpfully, Janet Moyles combines a clear focus on learning objectives with a number of practical suggestions. The five issues she identifies are a useful checklist for evaluating the management of any classroom. How does yours measure up?

Edited from: Moyles, J. (1995) 'A place for everything? The classroom as a teaching and learning context', in Moyles, J. (ed.) *Beginning Teaching: Beginning Learning in Primary Education*. Buckingham: Open University Press, 35–40

To children and teachers alike, the classroom represents 'home' for five or more hours of each weekday during term times. Its prime function is provide a kind of 'workshop' context which supports the crucial interactions between them. The teacher must translate knowledge of children and pedagogy into classroom organisation and management structures to everyone's benefit – no mean feat! The vital elements which must be considered are:

- the physical context;
- structures and routines;
- resource management;
- behaviour;
- communication.

## The physical context

The classroom or class base is part of a larger school building which was built in a particular time in history under the philosophies of education which existed at the time. Very early state elementary schools, for example, had large halls where large numbers of children were taught en masse to read, write and do basic number activities. Schools built in the 1920s to 1930s show a growing emphasis on outdoor activities for children, being characterized by having open-air quadrangles (often containing gardens and outdoor play areas) around which long draughty corridors spawn individual classrooms, with up to 50 children in each! Designs of schools built in the 1960s and 1970s reflect a belief in the interactive and collaborative nature of children's learning and are often open plan, where two or more classrooms are merged together and teachers are intended to function as a team. Whatever the building, teachers must operate current ideologies and practices, making the most of whatever circumstances they have inherited.

Take a moment to turn to the classroom plan in Figure 10.1.1. It reflects a very typical kind of layout for a Reception classroom and contains direct 'clues' as to the activities of the children and, therefore, the practices of the teacher. Many areas of curriculum, including subjects, are represented within the layout, for example language and social skills (the home corner café), literacy (the book corner), design technology (constructional toys and 3-D models), art (painting table), science (water play) and sorting and puzzles (mathematics). It is likely that children will be given some choice of the activities they undertake, albeit choosing from those activities provided by the teacher in specific areas of the room.

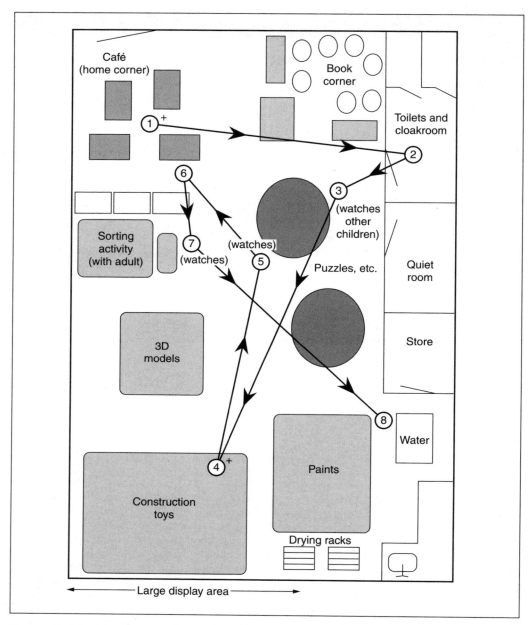

**Figure 10.1.1** The layout of an infant classroom (including tracking of a child's activity choices)

Contrast this with another classroom (perhaps for older children) where group work tables are undesignated in terms of activity. This suggests that the teacher may well direct children's specific activities and may provide expositional or instructional teaching from a central position. On the other hand, the provision of a carpet area suggests that there may be occasions when children work at floor level or perhaps have quiet reading opportunities or gather together in a large social group for story or discussion. What a lot there is to be gleaned by interpreting different classroom layouts! What this reveals is that, whatever the nature of the physical classroom space, the teacher's ideology becomes superimposed to produce a particular way of working for that teacher and the children. Such aspects are worth noting on your next visit to a classroom.

There is also much to learn from the way in which teachers organize seating arrangements. People whose ideology lie in a child-centred type of education can be quite horrified at the sight of rows of desks and chairs which tends to signify whole-class teaching. However, the organization of the desks or tables needs to be contingent upon the type of activities which are taking place – the 'fitness for purpose' notion (see Alexander *et al.* 1992). Collaborative group work requires tables to be organized in such a way that cooperation and interaction between children can take place, for example, that they can all see each other's faces and share resources. Such arrangements, however, can positively hinder children attempting to undertake concentrated, individual work or hinder the teacher in trying to give a demonstration to a whole class. Carpet areas are excellent for bringing a cosy 'togetherness' to shared events in the classroom, be it a story, children telling their 'news' to others, discussion or singing together. They may not be so useful for older children (physically large eleven-year-olds can find sitting on a carpet cross-legged rather demeaning) or for a teacher's detailed exposition on a special topic.

When considering a classroom in which you are going to work, it is advisable to make a layout plan as this both helps to fix the area in your mind and also offers the opportunity of reflecting on it when planning future learning activities.

## Structures and routines

The term 'structures' refers to the way the classroom operates so that children are clear what they are doing and do not need to expend time and energy in constantly finding out where things are and what they must do. Routines represent the order in which things happen and are usually related to the daily and weekly timetable for the class.

Timetables are usually determined at a whole-school level, at least in outline, with several sessions being 'fixed times', for example, hall periods or assemblies (or times for implementation of the National Literacy or Numeracy Strategies). Teachers have the task of deciding on the best time within what is left either individually or in year groups. Making good use of children's and teacher's time is vital as there is always so much to fit in with the subject and broader curriculum implementation. If observation reveals that children are spending much of their time waiting for teacher attention, this may be because the daily structures and routines are inappropriate. Perhaps children are too dependent upon the teacher for resources or tasks, or are given insufficient guidance on what to do when they need help. For instance, advice such as to 'ask another child', 'look in a book' or 'do another task until the teacher can see you', can quickly alleviate this problem even with young children.

Routines are helpful though you must guard against them becoming boring. A little deviation from routine sometimes helps to keep children and teacher alert and interested. For example, if you normally have storytime at the end of the morning or afternoon, try switching it to after morning playtime instead. On that occasion, it could be used as the basis for further learning activities. Among the most important routines are those involved in children entering and leaving the classroom, or in tidying up after a session. Do these things happen smoothly or do the children fidget and tussle with each other? Often, children and teachers simply get overly familiar with a situation and what should be dealt with quickly then becomes a constant thorn in everyone's side. Routines are useful but familiarity can breed contempt!

## Resource management

Regarding classroom resources, it is important to demand appropriate responsibility from the children by, for example, ensuring that they are responsible for the access and maintenance (e.g.: 'We need *all* the pieces in a jigsaw!'). In this way, they begin to become independent of the teacher. However, this means that resources and materials should be located and labelled very carefully. Older children can do this in negotiation with the teacher and even the youngest children can become involved, though location may be the teacher's decision. Train and trust the children! Expect them to behave appropriately in all matters and most of them will. A quality classroom is likely to be one where there is a place for everything and everything mainly in its place! You should not use precious time at the end of each day in sorting out the classroom when there is marking, preparation, display, records and a wealth of other tasks upon which your time is more profitably spent.

## Behaviour

Children and teachers have a right to the best possible classroom experiences – and that also means behaving appropriately towards each other. Issues should be discussed, the responsibilities of each party determined and ground rules established. Both should feel able to raise issues which mean they cannot work effectively in the classroom. For example both teachers and children are affected by noise – constant shouting or nagging will usually make this situation worse, whereas discussion about alleviating the situation can result in a quiet working atmosphere being maintained by the children. As a general rule, children should be given responsibility for going to the toilet without asking, though this may be dependent upon the school layout. A sensible rule which children will readily accept is 'one at a time'. Whatever the rule, it should be established quickly, with firmness and consistency as the chief qualities (see Cullingford, 1991). If, for any reason, changes to the rules are required, these should be communicated, renegotiated, written up and read out for all to see and hear and firmly put into place as efficiently as possible (see Calderhead 1984).

It would be trite to suggest that if you get the classroom organization management sorted out there will be no behaviour problems. You have, however, only to think about the number of times there is a fuss and disagreement over quite minor incidents – a child tripping over another, arguments over resources – to realize that many behavioural issues are at least related to classroom structures and management. Bored children also tend to misbehave, so achieving work at an appropriate standard relieves some problems. Most primary children enjoy school, appreciate the relationship they have with teachers and want to be a part of the stimulating activities. Many behavioural problems are contained within acceptable boundaries once teacher and child have 'got the measure of each other' and a working relationship agreed. This happens when the teacher makes time to work with individuals, knows their names and responds to their needs. Treating children as people and giving them the appropriate respect means that many children will respond with appropriate levels of responsibility and care for others.

## Communication

Primary teachers usually excel at explaining to children what to do and how to do it. Communication, however, breaks down because teachers fail to tell children why they are undertaking certain activity and what they are expected to know and do as a result. So much is taken for granted in the primary classroom and yet children often have a very different level of understanding to adults. In such circumstances, they need explicit guidance (see Edwards and Mercer, 1987).

There will be many different levels at which you communicate with children requiring different classroom groupings. For example, talking to the whole class would be appropriate to establish the groundwork for something to which all children will contribute or for demonstrating a new technique. Grouping by ability for some activities will mean that you can work to stretch the abler children or give closer attention to a group requiring additional help. Grouping by task will be helpful where resources are perhaps limited and only a few children at a time can have access to, for example, science equipment. With younger children, groupings are commonly by friendship and there may also be occasion where sex groupings might be used, particularly where the teacher is attempting to encourage boys to use the home-corner provision or girls to become more adventurous with constructional materials.

Communication with other adults is also an important skill. As a student on a teacher education course, there will be many occasions on which you will work with others as part of learning about classroom practice. In fact, students sometimes feel like 'piggy-in-the-middle' when they receive regular, if sometimes conflicting advice, from a range of tutors and class teachers. Regular communication with a more experienced teacher such as a mentor, can ensure that adversity is kept in perspective and the classroom runs as smoothly as possible – time needs to be set aside for mentoring. These types of communication happen with less frequency as one becomes a teacher with full responsibilities for the class – in fact it can be quite an isolated job in a typical closed classroom situation. You may well have help from nursery nurses (if you work within the early years) and ancillaries, parents, further education students, sixth formers, and professionals whose advice is sought about particular children. You must help them to help you and the children. Be clear before they arrive what their role is and what support is needed. Unless it is vital to the activity that they sit and listen to the story, for example, request their help in preparing the next batch of materials, repairing books, labelling materials or working with individuals.

One level of communication which is often forgotten is that of communicating with yourself – reflecting on your experiences and needs. What did you do today? How did you feel about it? What skills have you used and what needs do you have for tomorrow or next week? Take time out to reflect upon your beliefs about teaching and learning and talk to others about your successes and occasional disasters.

📖 READING 10.2

# Classroom layout, resources and display

## David Clegg and Shirley Billington

In this reading Clegg and Billington offer further practical advice on the organization and use of classroom space, on the management of resources and on display. Like Moyles in the previous reading, they maintain a clear focus on the contribution which these factors can make to the processes of teaching and learning for which the teacher aims.

Do you feel you have the best possible layout and system for resource management in your classroom? And what is the balance of celebrating, stimulating and informing in your display work?

Edited from: Clegg, D. and Billington, S. (1994) *The Effective Primary Classroom: Management and Organization of Teaching and Learning*. London: David Fulton, 123–5

The way classrooms are organized and managed is fundamental to achieving success. We are not simply discussing how we can make a classroom attractive, but how to create an environment which is specifically designed as a place where a teacher's ideas about teaching and learning will bear fruit. In that sense, how the classroom is set up will demonstrate a teacher's ideas about teaching learning will bear fruit. In that sense, how the classroom is set up will demonstrate a teacher's experiences, values and attitudes. The classroom is able to open or close opportunities for children, it will give them messages about a teacher's expectations, and will indicate to them explicitly how they should conduct themselves. It is not hard to think of some common examples. If art materials are left dirty and untidy in a corner of the room, what message is that giving? A book area full of tatty books, poorly displayed, with a threadbare piece of carpet covering the floor is conveying attitudes and values about reading and books. If the teacher's attention must be attracted every time a pupil needs a piece of equipment, what does that say about opportunities for children to make their own decisions? The examples are endless, but the idea is simple – a classroom says a great deal about the teacher, to colleagues, to children and, increasingly, to parents. A teacher's classroom is becoming an open arena, as the public face of the education system, and that is a major reason for ensuring it is the result of careful planning.

Classrooms are not passive environments in which teaching and learning happens to take place – they should be designed to promote and enhance learning. They should motivate and stimulate, and they should be planned to make the most efficient use of the most important resource – namely the teacher.

There is no one way to organize and run classrooms. All we are saying is that the way they are set up and managed should be just as much a part of a teacher's pedagogy as curriculum planning, teaching strategies or assessing learning.

## Classroom layout

When thinking about how classrooms are organized and managed most teachers will begin by considering how the furniture is laid out. However, this is a much more complex process than simply fitting all the furniture in, and making sure that everyone has a seat.

Depending on their approach to teaching and learning, teachers have broadly three options in terms of layout. The first of these options is to create a series of working areas within the classroom. These could include a reading area, a writing area, science area and maths area, and possibly others depending on the age of the children. Within these working areas children would have easy access to an appropriate range of resources and materials. There are some clear advantages to this type of layout. It is easy for children to understand, and by providing a specific area designated for a particular activity pupils can be motivated and develop a sense of purpose. Resources and materials can be carefully matched to learning experiences, and will introduce children to the idea of specific resources relating to specific activities. This kind of layout, however, has some drawbacks. Very few teachers will have enough space to create a sufficient number of areas that will represent the full range of activities they would wish to offer. The availability of resources can be limited to the group of children working within a particular area, and it can operate against making links across the curriculum. This kind of layout may be most appropriate for teachers who have a range of different activities going on at the same time. Typically a group of children could be engaged in a science experiment, others could be working with some construction material and so on, with anything up to five or six different activities.

The second and third options concerning classroom layout have a different focus. Rather than limiting resources to specific areas they look to organizing the classroom in a more holistic way. Essentially, the choice is between putting the resources and materials around the outside of the room, with children working in the middle, or putting the resources in the middle and children round the edges. The former is the more predominant pattern, but has the disadvantage of creating potentially more movement around the room. In the latter option, the theory is that all children have equal access to resourcing.

If we consider all three of these options, the reality is that many teachers opt for a mixture.

Most classrooms have some designated areas, most commonly for wet or practical work, and a reading area. Other resources are usually stored around the edges of the room.

The ways in which teachers wish to operate will also have a bearing on how pupils are arranged. The teacher who, when talking at length to the whole class, prefers children sat together in a carpeted area, and then disperses the children to a variety of areas, with a variety of working partners, may not see the necessity for every child to have his or her own place. If one group will always be working on an activity that does not require desks or table space, then there is no need to have a place for every pupil. When space is limited this could be an important factor. When children are older, and sitting on the floor is less comfortable, or when there are an increasing number of occasions when everybody needs some desk or table space, then clearly this must be provided. The important message is to maintain a degree of flexibility. Modern furniture enables most teachers to provide a range of options. Putting tables together can save space, and enable a group of six or eight children to work together. Similarly the same tables arranged differently can provide space for individual or paired work.

For different reasons, many teachers are beginning to question whether they need a teacher's desk. The large desk which years ago invariably dominated classrooms no longer seems appropriate, and doing without it can save space. In the end it will be a question of teaching style. It would not be difficult for a teacher to monitor how often he or she sits at the desk, then to ask whether it is necessary to be sitting at a desk and then to form some decisions. Those teachers who choose to keep a desk, should think carefully about where to place it. Should it be part of the working environment? Should it form a barrier between teachers and children, or should it be tucked away discreetly in a corner?

The lack of space is often most apparent when people are moving around the classroom. Most teachers will have experienced the exasperation of trying to reach over to a pupil, having to ask other pupils to 'just move over a bit'. It is equally frustrating for children when they are forced to squeeze past other children to collect equipment, or to get from one side of the room to the other. All this is very familiar, and in some classrooms some of this may be unavoidable. The sad fact is that there are sill some classrooms that are too small for the number of pupils, but it is also a fact that some careful thought can begin to alleviate some problems. Planning a classroom layout is rather like creating a painting – sometimes it's the spaces left behind that are important. Organizing routes around the classroom is important. Children need to be able to get from one part of the room to another, and this access should be planned. Observation will help in showing where congestion points occur. Resources that are in regular or constant demand could be placed strategically around the room rather than in one place. It is rarely the case that a teacher needs to be able to walk around four sides of a desk, or a group of tables. Space can be saved by grouping furniture together and by careful positioning around the room.

As previously indicated the main factor when planning a classroom is to keep a degree of flexibility. It should not be thought of as a once-a-year activity but should be something that is open to development and evolution through trial and error. Often classrooms carefully planned and arranged during the holidays look very different when the children actually take over. Many teachers are increasingly involving pupils in planning the layout and design of their room. This can be very effective and beneficial and will often provide some startling insights into how pupils actually see things. Even the youngest children can be involved in making decisions about where things are put, and how the tables are arranged. The ways in which children experience the classroom will be very different from the ways in which the teacher does. The wise teacher will tap into that experience and involve them in making some decisions. It is also perhaps worth remembering that redesigning the layout can motivate and stimulate both teacher and children.

## Managing classroom resources

The following are key issues for consideration by every teacher when thinking about the organization of resources in the classroom.

*Quality* This is a far more important element than quantity. Teachers are natural hoarders, and loathe to discard items which may have outlived their usefulness, but there is little point in shelf space being taking up by outdated or tatty books (which children will avoid using) or cupboards being full of games or jigsaws with pieces missing. The quality of the resources will affect the quality of the learning.

*Appropriateness* Is there a variety of equipment suitable for the planned curriculum, and for the range of abilities within the class? If the school has a policy on centralized resources it may be important to think in terms of a basic equipment list for each classroom and planning activities which will make use of centralized resources at specific times.

*Storage* Resources and materials should be appropriately stored so that a system is evident to the children. Resource areas (not necessarily work areas) can be established, so that all the equipment for a particular subject is collected in a clearly defined location. Colour coding for drawers, and storage boxes with pictorial labels for younger children can help with efficient use of equipment by pupils.

*Accessibility* The more that children can organize resources for themselves the less time should be spent by a teacher on low-level tasks such as giving out paper. Children need to be clear about what they have immediate access to, and what can only be used with permission or under supervision. However, the vast majority of materials in a classroom should be available for children to select for appropriate use.

Consideration should be given to providing basic equipment for continual use such as pots of pencils, a variety of types of paper, and to organizing other materials for ease of access. In order to do this is some classrooms, it may be necessary to remove cupboard doors to provide open shelving, or to purchase some inexpensive and colourful storage such as stackerjacks or plastic baskets.

If children are to make good use of the facilities available in a classroom, they need to be clear about the system which operates. They may need to be clear about the system which operates. They may need to be trained in making appropriate use of resources, and in selecting materials for a particular task. They can play a role in managing classroom resources, and it may be useful to involve them in preliminary planning when organizing the equipment for a particular curriculum area. Sometimes, if the system is not working effectively, they can have some useful observations to make on why things go wrong!

Giving children responsibility for ensuring that the resource system works well is an important aspect of developing independence from the teacher. They should be able, or if young be trained, in the collection, use, return and replacement of materials with minimal reference to the teacher. Where equipment is limited, they can be encouraged to negotiate with other children over the use of a particular resource. Negotiation and sharing equipment are important elements in planning tasks.

## Display in the classroom

The business of display is much more than brightening up dull corners, covering cracks and double mounting: it is another important factor in ensuring classrooms are places in which effective learning can take place.

Display has three distinct uses: it can celebrate, stimulate and inform. How display is used to promote these three functions will also transmit values and messages to children, parents and colleagues. For example, what you choose to celebrate will begin to give messages about what is valued or who is held in high esteem. How you begin to stimulate and inform through display will illustrate some clear ideas about how you regard children and their learning. The transmission of values and attitudes is a dimension that touches all aspects of display, but it is worthwhile thinking about each of the three ways display can be used.

*Celebration* Enjoying and acknowledging children's achievement is an important aspect of any classroom. Displaying those achievements is just one way of demonstrating the regard in which their work is held, but there are many others. One of the restrictions of displaying pupils' work has been that it has led to an over emphasis on the product or outcome, at the expense of the process. It is not too difficult to redress this imbalance. If we consider for a moment the way modern libraries and museums have been eager not only to display authors' and artists' finished items, but to acquire the notebooks, jottings, sketch pads and rough drawings to demonstrate the development of the works, we can perhaps begin to see how schools can also start to acknowledge the process. As teachers who are concerned with process and outcome, it is important that we place equal value on each. Efforts at drafting can be displayed alongside the finished stories, sketches and jottings shown next to the completed art work. This gives clear messages, not least that behind good outcomes, there is usually a great deal of hard work, and that hard work is worth acknowledging and displaying.

There are other, perhaps more fundamental, considerations about displaying work. Display is one way of promoting children's self-image, and giving them a sense of worth. The converse is also true. Failing to display some pupils' work may go some way to alienating those children from the classroom. This is an area where teachers must use their judgement. It is important that all children have work displayed (not all at the same time!) but it is equally important that such work is worthy of display, and is of some significance. Display can also demonstrate the achievements of groups of pupils working towards a common end, as well as the achievements of individuals.

The most effective displays of children's work pay some regard to basic aesthetic consider-ations. The most attractive displays are the result of some thought concerning shape, colour, form and texture. This not only boosts children's confidence in seeing their work promoted in this way, but, perhaps more importantly, it provides an opportunity to discuss these features, as well as some guidance for children when they begin to set up their own displays.

*Stimulation* What is displayed in classrooms can form part of the learning process. A good dramatic, thought-provoking display can provide great stimulation for learning. There are countless ways in which children can be motivated by something they can see, observe, smell, touch or hear. Science investigations can start with a display which challenges through effective questioning, and promotes the development of skills (for example, 'Use the magnify-ing glass to observe, record what you see . . .', 'What do you think will happen if . . .?') all of which can begin to make children think, discuss, predict and hypothesize. Similarly, display can stimulate an aesthetic or artistic response through careful use of colours, textures and forms. In the humanities, a collection of artefacts can be the starting point for enquiry and investigation. The most effective displays are often those which not only stimulate and motivate, but also show the results. These uses of display to celebrate, stimulate and inform are not mutually exclusive and they will often be interlinked.

*Informing* The notion that display within the classroom can support young children's learning is the aspect that is least recognized. Stimulation and motivation are starting points for learning, but display can provide support once children have embarked upon their work. What is actually stuck up on the walls, or stood in a corner, or displayed on a table can act as a resource for the learner. This will vary from classroom to classroom, but it could include such items as current wordlists, key phrases to reinforce an ongoing activity, the display of resource material alongside guidance on how to use it, or simple instructions about what to do in particular circumstances.

The possibility of displaying the process alongside the outcomes can provide a source of support for other pupils and a focus for discussion.

Display makes a very significant contribution to the classroom climate. It is by its very nature a public statement which is there for children, colleagues and parents to see. As it is a significant factor in creating classroom atmosphere it is vital that we do not fall into the trap of 'surface rather than substance' (Alexander, 1992), and that requires thought and consideration about how good display contributes to effective learning rather than simply making the room look nice.

---

 **READING 10.3**

# Class size does make a difference

Helen Pate-Bain, Charles Achilles, Jayne Boyd-Zaharias and Bernard McKenna

The issue of class size has attracted great attention in recent years, with teachers and parents being convinced of its importance. However, many policy-makers, perhaps with an eye on costs, insist that it is less important than teaching strategies.

There is very little secure research evidence on the relationship between class size and attainment, but the most thorough is the STAR project, from Tennessee, which this reading describes.

Do you think class size makes a difference to your teaching? If you had smaller classes, how would you adjust your teaching strategies?

Edited from: Pate-Bain, H., Achilles, C., Boyd-Zaharias, J. and McKenna, B. (1992) 'Class size does make a difference', *Phi Delta Kappan*. November, 253–5

Dissatisfied with earlier research and wishing to have conclusive results, Tennessee's state legislature funded a $12 million, four-year study of class size. Project STAR (student–teacher achievement ratio) analysed student achievement and development in three types of classes: small classes (13–17 students per teacher), regular classes (22–25 students) with a teacher and a full-time teacher aide. An important characteristic of the study was its longitudinal nature: Project STAR followed students from kindergarten in 1985–6 through third grade in 1988–9. In order to assess the effects of class size in different school locations, the project included 17 inner-city, 16 suburban, 8 urban and 39 rural schools. Students and teachers were randomly assigned to class types.

The main focus of the study was on student achievement as measured by three devices: appropriate forms of the Stanford Achievement Test (K-3), STAR's Basic Skills First Criterion Tests (Grade 3). The study's most important finding was that students in the small classes made higher scores (the difference in scores was both statistically and educationally significant) on the Stanford Achievement Test and on the Basic Skills First (BSF) Test in all four years (K-3) and in all locales (rural, suburban, urban, inner city). Other relevant findings include the following:

- the greatest gains on the Stanford were made in inner-city small classes;

- the highest scores on the Stanford and BSF were made in rural small classes;

- the only consistent positive effect in regular classes in order with a full-time aide occurred in first grade;

- teachers reported that they preferred small classes in order to identify student needs and to provide more individual attention, as well as to cover more material effectively;

- the importance of the economic background of students was underscored by the finding that, in every situation, those students who were not economically eligible for the free lunch programme always outperformed those students who were in the free lunch programme.

## Benefits of small classes

To determine whether small classes had a cumulative effect, the top 10 per cent of STAR classes for each year were categorized by class type. The number of small classes in the top 10 per cent of STAR classes increased each year from kindergarten through third grade. In kindergarten, small classes made up 55 per cent of the top-scoring 10 per cent of STAR classes. By third grade, small classes made up 78 per cent of the top 10 per cent. This finding strongly suggests a cumulative and positive effect of small classes on student achievement in grades K-3.

During the course of the study more than 1000 teachers participated in year-end interviews. Their comments revealed a number of ways that instruction benefited from small class size:

- basic instruction was completed more quickly, providing increased time for covering additional material;

- there was more use of supplemental tests and enrichment activities;

- there was more in-depth teaching of the basic content;

- there were more frequent opportunities for children to engage in first-hand learning activities using concrete materials;

- there was increased use of learning centres;

- there was increased use of practices shown to be effective in the primary grades.

A common benefit cited by teachers in small and regular-plus-aide classes was that they were better able to individualize instruction. These teachers reported increased monitoring of student behaviour and learning, opportunities for more immediate and more individualized teaching, more enrichment, more frequent interactions with each child, a better match between each child's ability and the instructional opportunities provided, a more detailed knowledge of each child's needs as a learner, and more time to meet individual learner's needs using a variety of instructional approaches.

## Lasting Benefits study

Project STAR proved that reduced class size in grades K-3 significantly enhanced student achievement. To determine if those positive benefits continue for the STAR students as they progress through the higher grades, the Tennessee State Department of Education appointed the Centre of Excellence for Research in Basic Skills at Tennessee State University to conduct a Lasting Benefits study (LBS).

All students who participated in Project STAR third-grade classes were eligible for Lasting Benefit observation in the fourth grade. This fourth-grade sample contained 4320 students in 216 classes and the Lasting Benefit analysis yielded clear and consistent results.

Students who had previously been in small STAR classes demonstrated significant advantages on every achievement measure over students who had attended regular classes. Further, these results favouring small classes were found to be consistent across all school locations. The positive effects of involvement in small classes are pervasive one full year after students return to regular size classes.

## Effective teachers

In order for educators to make the best use of class-size reductions, they must be aware of what constitutes effective teaching. STAR researchers observed and interviewed 49 first-grade teachers whose classes had made the greatest gains. These teachers consistently displayed similar affective behaviours and characteristics. Their enthusiasm was obvious as they engaged in 'acting', demonstrating and role-playing activities. The teachers frequently expressed positive attitudes toward children, emphasized positive behaviour, praised success, and used humour to promote learning and to motivate students. A love of children seemed to permeate their professional repertoires.

The most effective teachers engaged their students through the use of creative writing, hands-on experiences, learning centres and maths manipulatives. They provided immediate feedback. They practised assertive discipline or some variation of it and made it clear that they had high expectations for their students. They maintained good communication with parents.

In addition to these common behaviours and characteristics, class size appeared to have been a contributing factor to the success of the most effective teachers. Only eight of the 49 (16 per cent) taught regular classes of 22–25 students. Twenty-three (46 per cent) taught small classes of 13–17; seven (14 per cent) taught classes of 18–21; and 12 (24 per cent) had full-time instructional aides in regular-sized classes.

## READING 10.4

# Classroom organization for flexible teaching

David McNamara

> David McNamara suggests that grouping children is often based on 'ability' with the aim of making differentiated instruction easier for teachers. This could be seen as being discriminatory and certainly demands certain social skills from the children. This leads McNamara to suggest a horse-shoe arrangement as a new, flexible way of organizing the children in the classroom.
>
> How do you think your class would respond to McNamara's ideas. Are they worth trying?
>
> Edited from: McNamara, D. (1994) *Classroom Pedagogy and Primary Practice*. London: Routledge, 64–7

The policy of grouping children in the primary classroom has probably reached the status where for many primary teachers it is accepted as characteristic of good primary practice. It is seen as the way to organize children, usually so that they can be allocated to ability groups. Often the groups will move from one activity to another during the day and group composition may change from time to time depending upon the nature of the learning and area of the curriculum. In mixed-ability classrooms it may be appropriate to group children according to aptitude if teaching is to be matched to their ability. Before deciding to group it is important to consider carefully whether this is necessarily good practice and weigh the benefits and costs. For instance, it does not follow that in order for the teacher to provide differentiated learning, pupils have to be physically grouped within the classroom. The groups can, as it were, exist in the teacher's mind and learning activities can be provided for children of different abilities who are randomly distributed throughout the class.

When children are grouped in class, it is usually so that the teacher can form homogeneous groups for learning. However, it is important to remember that to group children according to one characteristic, say, their reading ability, does not get over the fact that they may still be very different on other characteristics – such as mathematical ability, motivation, or the social adaptability necessary to work effectively in groups. Moreover, grouping children according to ability may mean that the groups are alike in terms of social-class background, ethnicity or gender. This could expose the teacher to the charge that discrimination or partiality has influenced group formation (this problem can be worse if children are grouped according to friendship choices). The issue should also be considered with reference to streaming. One of the important reasons for abandoning the practice of streaming children in separate classes according to academic level, and for creating mixed-ability classes in their place, is to overcome the social problems and stigma attached to labelling children. But grouping children within classrooms according to ability, and this is the most common method of grouping, does not disguise the fact that the children are still being organized according to their ability. Indeed the kudos of able children may be enhanced within the unstreamed class because less able children can turn to them as a resource for advice and help when the teacher's attention is elsewhere. If the teacher's aim is to disguise differences in ability it is probably preferable to disperse children randomly throughout the class. The evidence suggests that it is necessary to prepare and train children if they are to work effectively in groups; pupils must be taught to cooperate and provided with appropriate skills if they are to work together. The irony is that classroom studies report that children work best in groups when they receive clear-cut assignments that are closely monitored by the teacher. The notion of children working cooperatively together on creative- or discovery-orientated tasks is not supported by the available evidence; in fact, creative work is probably more likely to be found during whole-class instruction. The evidence also indicates that homogeneous ability grouping may be detrimental to the learning of children in low-ability groups; it is able children who are more likely to be able to cope with and prosper in group settings where pupils are less likely to be under the eye of the teacher.

In sum, there are sound reasons for grouping children in primary classrooms but there are equally convincing reasons for not doing so and for engaging in class teaching. Grouping places a particular burden upon the teacher in terms of the management and organization of the class and the problem of sustaining order may become paramount, resulting in the teacher having less time to attend to teaching and learning. The teacher should not assume that grouping is a prerequisite for good primary practice; whole-class teaching has an equal claim to the teacher's attention.

The practical pedagogic problem facing the class teacher is that she is likely to want to adopt different forms of classroom arrangement from time to time and switch from one to another. A recent report on primary education proposes that it is necessary to strike a balance between the organizational strategies of whole-class teaching, group work and individual teaching (Alexander *et al.*, 1992). In order to strike a balance the teacher must ask, 'What is a good balance and how is the classroom to be organized so as to enable the smooth transition from one organizational form to another?'. Advice available to teachers tends to fall silent when these awkward practical questions are posed. One possible solution is to arrange the desks in a square or horseshoe figuration as the basic form of organization and switch from this to individual, group and whole-class teaching as desired. The square or horseshoe pattern allows the teacher to see every child and every child to see the teacher during class lessons.

Desks are arranged around the sides of the classroom with children facing into the middle of the room. This method has the following advantages:

- children can see each other and are more inclined to listen to each other's contributions than when seated in rows with their backs to colleagues, or in groups where eye contact and audibility are difficult;

- a large space is available in the middle of the room for stories, large pieces or artwork and so on;

- children are able, when required, to work in pairs or threes, which are group sizes that are productive and unlikely to exclude people;

- the teacher can see, at a glance, what every child is doing and reach those with problems quickly;

- desks can quickly be formed into tables of four when required.

This approach allows flexibility and enables a variety of teaching methods to be employed. Class teaching should be successful because children are facing the teacher and are not able to conceal themselves behind others, as they can be when sitting in rows which all face the front of the classroom. Group work can be employed easily, with group sizes determined by the task rather than by the number of children who fit around a table. In addition, some children can work in groups while others work individually.

There are, in sum, possible managerial solutions that make it possible to switch from one form of classroom organization to another and accommodate the advantages of both whole-class teaching and group work.

## READING 10.5

# 'Good practice' in group work

## Rea Reason

In this reading, Rea Reason defends the use of group work against its critics by expressing the psychological rationale on which it is based. She identifies the idea of 'scaffolding learning', the need to attend to individual differences and the importance of social and interactive learning. However, the practical dilemmas faced by teachers are also clear, and Reason urges the development of more genuinely collaborative group work.

How would you develop collaborative group work in your classroom? (see also Reading 13.7).

Edited from: Reason, R. (1993) 'Primary special needs and National Curriculum assessment', in Wolfendale, S. (ed.) *Assessing Special Educational Needs*. London: Cassell, 73–5

Education in British primary schools is founded on a set of prescriptive assumptions about children's learning referred to as 'good practice'. This shorthand phrase encapsulates a range of organization arrangements and teaching methods which include group work, curriculum integration, a learning environment strong on visual impact, an 'exploratory' pedagogy and thematic enquiry (Alexander *et al.*, 1989; Alexander, 1992)

Children typically sit in groups around tables or move from one activity area to another.

In the study of primary schools in London undertaken by Mortimore *et al.* (1988), only one-tenth of the classrooms had tables or desks arranged in rows. In the study by Alexander *et al.* in Leeds none of the classrooms observed had such formal arrangements. Both studies described a wealth of wall displays which included both teacher-prepared stimulus materials and examples of the children's own work.

Classrooms following a timetable based on the notion of 'the integrated day' used to have a number of different activities happening in parallel, each taking place in a designated area of the classroom or focusing on a particular group of children. These could include any aspect of the curriculum combined into particular themes or topics, or taught as separate subjects such as mathematics, where different kinds of mathematical activities took place concurrently.

It is important to mention the psychological and educational basis for the methods of teaching, learning and assessment that are considered to be 'good practice'. These are no 'modern orthodoxies', as suggested by Alexander (1992), but a long and respectable theoretical pedigree. It is the demands they make on teachers that may be considered excessive or impractical.

Three kinds of theoretical influence can be distinguished. The first comes from the notion of 'scaffolded learning' described, for example, by Edwards and Mercer (1987) [see also Reading 13.2]. The teacher is regarded as supporter and facilitator of the children's own ways of making sense of their experiences. The teacher's task is then to provide appropriate learning opportunities, ask open-ended questions and generally guide the child in becoming a self-directed and enquiring learner. The emphasis is more on the processes than the products of learning. Many aspects of National Curriculum documentation, in particular the programmes of study and the non-statutory guidance, reflect this way of thinking.

A second theoretical focus is on individual differences. As children learn at different rates and in different ways, teachers will as far as possible make their plans of instruction tailor-made for each of them. Formative assessment is based on this notion: information of what the child already knows, understands and can do determines what the child might learn next [see Readings 14.3, 14.4 and 14.5].

The third psychological influence regards learning as essentially social and interactive, not only for the children but also for their teachers and parents. Children make their meanings clearer to themselves by explaining them to others. Their understanding is extended through 'debating' observations and ideas with other children sharing the task (CACE, 1967; Bruner, 1986) [see Readings 7.8 and 7.9].

Class teachers may now combine these three theoretical perspectives in the following way:

- children are seated round tables to foster interaction;

- each child has her or his own learning task;

- the teacher moves from child to child offering individual support.

These kinds of arrangements have been criticized on many grounds (Bennett *et al.*, 1984, Galton, 1989; Alexander, 1992). In a class of some 30 children, the quality of the support or advice given to each individual child becomes so brief and superficial that it does not meet its aims of assessing and exploring the child's understanding. Individual work cards or textbook exercises may result in something akin to 'correspondence course' rather than individual tuition. In these circumstances formative assessment becomes very difficult. As children with special needs require even more attention, how can teachers find the time?

Grouping children round tables, as an organizational device, enables teachers to control their own time more effectively. It is easier to think of, say, five groups of children rather than 30 individuals with different needs. The following, taken from interviews with a skilled and experienced teacher, illustrates that approach:

I try to have a clear idea of the children's individual achievements based on my own observations and the records I keep. I decide in advance not only who will work together and on what but which groups or individuals will receive more teacher time. I think in terms of three stages of learning: the 'concept' stage where children are learning new understanding and require much teacher time; the 'development' stage where children need intermittent teacher time; and the 'reinforcement' stage where the activity should be self-sustained. At any one time only a small number of children can be engaged at the 'concept stage'. This planning enables me to manage my time so that all children in turn receive more intensive attention. This is obviously essential for the purposes of assessment and record keeping.

Even for teachers as competent and well organized as this, the dilemma still remains. The more time the teacher devotes to extended interactions with some children, the less demanding on them as teachers must be the activities they give to the rest who may be seen to be marking time. But the more accessible teachers seek to make themselves to all their pupils as individuals, the less time they have for extended and challenging interaction with any of them. Either way critics can argue that time is being wasted.

So why not seat the children in rows and teach them all together as one class? According to the press, the Leeds Primary Needs Programme (Alexander *et al.*, 1989; Alexander, 1992) recommended a return to such 'traditional' methods. Their work was grossly misrepresented. Having questioned 'modern orthodoxy' in its apparent disregard for the preferences of teachers trying to reconcile the considerable demands made on their time, the authors argue that different teaching purposes require different kinds of classroom arrangements. Not surprisingly, whole-class teaching becomes important for some purposes. But the authors also focus on the development of cooperative group work in the classroom. They argue that task and setting should as far as possible be consistent. Just as collaborative activity is difficult in a traditionally arranged classroom, so the concentration needed for individualized tasks may be difficult within groups.

Referring back to the psychological rationales for seating children round tables, the main purpose was to enable them to learn together from the interaction that takes place. The practice of grouping children for organization purposes and then giving them individual tasks does not take that into account. There is indeed a paradox in children sitting together facing each other and then asking them to concentrate on predominantly individualized learning tasks and the collaborative setting in which children were expected to undertake them. Much greater prominence needs to be given to the potential of genuine pupil–pupil collaboration and less to low-level writing, reading and drawing tasks.

READING 10.6

# Meeting special needs in the primary school classroom

Paul Croll and Diana Moses

This reading poses a very serious dilemma for primary school teachers. What is the most effective way of providing for children with special educational needs? Concluding the most comprehensive recent survey of primary school provision, Croll and Moses note that our present broad definitions continue to suggest that one in five children have some form of special need. In the classroom struggle to provide individual support for these children, it is possible that those with the most serious needs may not get the attention they really deserve? Should we, they suggest, rethink and refocus our efforts?

Edited from: Croll, P. and Moses, D. (2000) *Special Needs in the Primary School: One in Five?*. London: Cassell, 151–6

Underlying the provision for pupils with special educational needs there are two main trends that lead in contradictory directions and are not easily reconciled. One emphasizes the uniqueness of individuals and their need for differentiated provision, while the other concentrates on the similarities between learners and, at primary school, the similarity of educational goals, while recognizing that there are going to be a small number of exceptions.

The first approach stresses that all learners are unique and should be so treated; in effect advocating a version of individual education plans for all. Underpinning this idea is that, at the same time as we are unique beings, we are also all the same in that we are all different and require different things. If everyone is treated differently, then the distinction between those who receive the same or very similar provision to each other and those who receive very different provision is diminished. As there is no emphasis on the grouping together of individuals who may be experiencing similar problems and everyone is treated as an individual, there is no reason why all needs cannot be met in the same location.

This idea of the uniqueness of individuals is not, of course, new but has been present for some time in work in the special educational needs context and more generally. Hegarty and Pocklington (1981) and Hodgson *et al.* (1984) argued that the approach more frequently found in special educational needs provision of the highly individualized variety could profitably be used much more widely. This basic position is elaborated by Ainscow (1993). They all start with the issue of what is required to satisfy special educational needs and then move on to conclude that it is the type of provision that should be more generally available in schools.

The desirability of individualized learning for all is also argued for in a totally different context. Bentley (1998) has suggested that a combination of advances in learning theory and the increasing sophistication and availability of information technology will soon result in a totally different approach to all aspects of learning, education and schooling. Although there is no special reference made here to people with learning and other difficulties, the extreme individuality of the approach to learning does automatically apply to all. Although coming from very different starting points and, for the most part, concentrating on different issues, they end up at much the same place with a high level of individualization of provision accompanied by considerable personal choice.

In very marked contrast there are numerous studies on the connection between teaching style, approaches to classroom learning and pupil performance that suggest that, at least for most pupils, increased individualization is not the way ahead. Findings from the ORACLE studies, for example, point to the benefits of whole-class teaching in the primary school (Galton *et al.*, 1980). This was again brought to prominence more recently in the studies of international comparisons of educational standards which indicated that high standards at primary school level are strongly associated with whole-class teaching; all pupils in the class learning the same things at the same time (Reynolds and Farrell, 1996). In these studies no particular attention was directed at those students with the most severe difficulties; instead overall standards in mainstream schools were the focus of attention. However, as the proportion of pupils with special needs is so high, and the vast majority of these children have learning difficulties, issues relevant to overall educational standards must also be relevant to these pupils.

As with the first group of studies discussed, the implications for practice of this second group of studies are also that there should be less distinction between special educational needs and other provision, but here the similarity ends. Instead of all students having individualized work plans, all students, or nearly all students, at least in the primary school, would do the same work, the argument being that despite their all being unique individuals, they all share the same educational needs. All pupils, for instance, need to learn to read and any improvement in methods of teaching reading will benefit all, or nearly all, children and possibly prevent difficulties from arising. In many ways this is a compelling argument and is well backed up by research, the problem with this approach centring around the proviso already made about its application to 'nearly all' rather than absolutely all children. If overall standards are to be raised by treating children in the same way then, it is difficult to escape the conclusion that a small number of children have needs too different to be accommodated within this common framework. This would not, of course, mean that they could not be educated in mainstream schools, but it would mean that they would not share all the same classroom experiences.

These are all issues that seriously affect not only the type of provision that schools make for pupils currently regarded as having special educational needs, but also for all other pupils. On the one hand they can go for ever increasing differentiation, heading in the direction of truly individualized learning that accommodates all students. On the other hand schools could opt for a 'whole-class' approach, emphasizing a shared experience and shared goals, while making special provision for the small number of pupils who cannot benefit from this strategy. In practice, strict adherence to either of these approaches would be regarded as extreme and in virtually all schools different elements of policy and provision will reflect these different approaches. However, the two approaches are so different that attempts to use bits of one and bits of the other are bound to result in unresolved tensions. Current government policy displays these tensions; for instance, the Literacy and Numeracy Hours emphasize commonality of experience, while the requirement to write Individual Education Plans for large numbers of pupils emphasizes individualization and differentiation.

Gerber sees basically the same conflicts present within the wider education system (Gerber, 1996). He argues that special education and mass public education conflict in a fundamental way. Mass public education is based on the notion of providing equality of opportunity; that is, providing access so that advantage can be taken of what is provided. To achieve its ambitious aim of universality, Gerber argues, public schooling largely ignores individual differences that contribute to variable instructional outcomes. On the other hand, special education has been concerned mostly with individuals and how they might be accommodated by institutional transformations. 'In many ways, special education's explicit concern for individual differences has been the source of its moral strength, but also its fatal political weakness' (p. 157). When the two systems are brought together, conflicts are likely to arise, particularly over differential funding and organizational upheaval. These areas of conflict were apparent in the study schools and LEAs, especially in relation to resourcing. Many schools felt that both the overall level of funding for special educational needs provision that they received was inadequate and also that the procedures required were inefficient and burdensome. From the LEA's point of view an ever-increasing amount of professional time and energy is spent in contriving ways in which to prevent the special educational needs budget from spiralling out of control.

The development of an appropriate framework for meeting children's educational needs is a complex and demanding enterprise. The teachers and head teachers we talked to in our survey were highly committed and professional in their attempts to meet the needs of the children for whom they were responsible. Within the Code of Practice and other aspects of current procedures for managing special needs provision, it is almost inevitable that the concerns of teachers will lead to even greater pressure for more statements, for children to be regarded as having special educational needs. Our survey of provision suggests that this is not the best way forward. Policies which pay attention to the common needs of children and ways of meeting them in schools, and which lead to fewer children needing to be formally identified as having special educational needs, would help to give a clearer focus to special needs provision.

 **READING 10.7**

# The teacher and others in the classroom

Gary Thomas

> This reading is based on the idea of 'room management' in which a team of adults work together in a classroom, with clearly understood roles. Research shows this to be remarkably effective and, with the increasing use of classroom assistants of various sorts, ways of using such significant resources in the most beneficial ways have to be developed.
>
> How do you work with other adults in your classroom?
>
> Edited from: Thomas, G. (1989) 'The teacher and others in the classroom', in Cullingford, C. (ed.), (1989) *The Primary Teacher: The Role of the Educator and the Purpose of Primary Education*. London: Cassell, 59–70

A quiet revolution has taken place in the primary classroom. It is now the exception rather than the rule to find teachers who always work on their own. There are fundamental changes in the atmosphere of the class when other adults move into the territory of the teacher and her children.

Some of the possible problems may be categorized as follows.

## Role ambiguity

As increasing numbers of people are involved in the execution of any task, the possibility for misunderstanding amongst them is magnified. With a highly complex task such as teaching, the potential for confusion about role definition is high when more than one person is present.

## Diminishing returns

It has for a long time been realized that personal effectiveness may be reduced when tasks are shared. People will unintentionally obstruct each other, or duplicate the other's effort. The extent to which this occurs depends greatly on the nature of the task and the number of people contributing. While many of the tasks which are being undertaken in the shared classroom would be carried out autonomously, thus reducing many of these effects, there are nevertheless bound to be certain problems to do with sharing the same physical space.

## Confusion amongst children

There is the possibility that children may 'play off' one adult against another, thus diminishing the effectiveness and the credibility of each. Being used to having only one adult in the classroom, children may not fully understand how they should respond to the additional person or people. They may ascribe imaginary weightings to the importance of the various adults who are present and this may serve to accentuate distinctions which the class teacher would wish to minimize; it may on the other hand undermine the position of the teacher.

How does effective teamwork take place without invoking all the problems to which I have just referred? A number of things may be done. We can aim to limit role ambiguity by specifying what each person will be doing; we can aim to reduce loss of effectiveness due to diminishing returns by establishing clear rules of working and identifying areas of work. We can also aim to make clear to the children in the class how the various adults will be operating.

There are limitless ways in which people's time and activity might be organized in the classroom. However, research has indicated that highly significant improvements in children's engagement may be achieved when a 'room management' system of classroom organization is employed as a basis for the structure of the activity of adults in the class.

At the core of the room management lies the activity period, a specific period of time, usually of about an hour, when specific roles are allocated to the various people within the class. It suggests three separate roles are fulfilled: an individual helper; an activity manager; and a mover.

- *The individual helper(s)* concentrates on taking individual children for short periods of teaching. Her work with those children will have been planned beforehand and she will work with a rota of children over the activity period.

- *The activity manager(s)* looks after the work of the rest of the children in the class, who are typically arranged into groups, with the aim of keeping the children engaged on the task in hand. This aim is facilitated through the planned activity of the children, which should be on areas of the curriculum that have already been covered though not necessarily mastered; children will therefore to a greater or lesser degree be consolidating on material and should require little individual help from the activity manager. Such a pattern of work amongst most children will enable the activity manager to effect a series of rapid contacts with this large body. There is a large number of findings on the effective use of teacher attention in reducing inappropriate behaviour and increasing children's overall engagement. In line with suggestions from these, the activity manager aims to maximize her contacts with those children who are working appropriately while prompting with the minimum attention those who are not.

- *The mover* aims to maintain flow in the class by relieving the activity manager and the individual helper from distraction. She will, for instance deal with interruptions, move equipment and sharpen pencils.

Considering classroom dynamics and the learning needs of children who might be experiencing difficulty, we can see that this model has a number of attractions. In its method of providing individual help, it takes account of children's need for learning in short frequent doses. In its method of 'activity management' it says something about type of activity, both of children and adult, which will help if we are thinking primarily about the engagement of the group, and in the role of 'mover' we see someone who will be able to keep the flow going in a session.

There is room for wide adaptation of the system in such a way that the particular people participating in a class develop a unique solution to a unique set of circumstances. As children become more independent there is less need for the function of mover and some of her functions may be delegated to children within the group. If three people were available to work in, say, an upper junior classroom it may be possible to think of a configuration of two activity managers, each responsible for the work of certain groups, and one individual helper. Alternatively, those people may be arranged such that there are two individual helpers and one activity manager. The precise arrangement will depend on the needs of the class.

## CHAPTER 11

# Behaviour. How are we managing the class?

The eight readings in this chapter are concerned with the particular issue of managing behaviour.

Doyle (11.1) analyses the complexity of classrooms and Galton and Holt (11.2 and 11.3) suggest how the tasks which children often experience can create uneasiness and boredom.

The next group of readings move the focus onto class management and discipline. Laslett and Smith (11.4) review four basic 'rules' for effective management. Hargreaves and colleagues (11.5) draw attention to how teachers respond to pupils. Do you provoke or calm them? The reading by Kounin (11.6) draws on his classic research on the behavioural and class management and is well worth detailed study and practise! Merrett and Wheldall (Reading 11.7) offer a different approach to behaviour management, this time based on careful reinforcement of desired behaviours. There is a wealth of practical ideas in this set of readings.

Finally, Reading 11.8 comes from the Elton Committee Report, *Discipline in Schools*. It provides an overview of the many factors that influence behaviour, many of which stem from beyond the classroom.

The parallel chapter of *Reflective Teaching* has a section reviewing key management skills. It then focuses on strategies for managing common classroom episodes – beginnings, transitions, endings, the unexpected and recurring challenges. It concludes with a section on whole-school issues, including behaviour policies. This section draws on the Elton Report. There are suggestions for 'Key Readings' and these are supplemented on *RTweb*.

READING 11.1

# Learning the classroom environment

Walter Doyle

This reading from Doyle highlights some of the reasons why classroom teaching is so difficult to do well, and gives some useful pointers to making it easier. In his view, classroom environments are highly complex and events often unfold simultaneously in ways which cannot be forseen. Doyle believes that teachers develop strategies and skills for reducing some of this complexity, and identifies five ways in which this is done.

Does your classroom sometimes feel complex in the ways which Doyle describes? How helpful are the skills which he suggests?

Readings 11.4 and 11.6 are also particularly relevant to these issues.

Edited from: Doyle, W. (1977) 'Learning the classroom environment: an ecological analysis', *Journal of Teacher Education*, 28 (6), 51–4

Deliberation about the nature of teaching skills has generally centred on the teacher's ability to manage subject matter – to explain content, formulate questions and react to student answers. Naturalistic studies of classrooms suggest, however, that knowing how to manage subject matter sequences represents only a small part of the skill necessary to be a teacher.

## Salient features of classrooms

The most salient features of the classroom for the student teachers in my study were multidimensionality, simultaneity and unpredictability. The following brief discussion of these categories will clarify the nature of environmental demands in classrooms.

Classrooms were multidimensional in the sense that they served a variety of purposes and contained a variety of events and processes, not all of which were necessarily related or even compatible. In classrooms, student teachers confronted groups with a wide range of interests and abilities as well as a diversity of goals and patterns of behavior. In addition, they faced a multiplicity of tasks that included such matters as processing subject matter information, judging student abilities, managing classroom groups, coping with emotional responses to events and behaviours, and establishing procedures for routine and special assignment, distribution of resources and supplies, record keeping, etc. These tasks also interacted in the sense that ways of dealing with one dimension (e.g. distributing resources and supplies) had consequences for other dimensions (e.g. managing classroom groups) and in the sense that procedures at one point established a precedent that restricted options at a later time. It was not uncommon to find student teachers initially overwhelmed to some degree by the sheer quantity of activities, many of which were seen to interfere with their primary interest in managing subject matter.

In addition to the quantity of dimensions in classrooms, many events occurred simultaneously. In a discussion, for instance, teachers needed to attend to the pace of the interaction, the sequence of student responses, fairness in selecting students to answer, the quality of individual answers and their relevance to the purposes of the discussion, and the logic and accuracy of content while at the same time monitoring a wide range of work involvement levels and anticipating interruptions. While giving assistance to individual students, teachers also had to remember to scan the rest of the class for signs of possible misbehaviour or to acknowledge other students who were requesting assistance. Examples such as these can be easily multiplied for nearly any set of classroom activities.

The simultaneous occurrence of multiple events, together with the continuous possibility of internal and external interruptions, contributed to an unpredictability in the sequence of classroom events, especially for student teachers who had not yet learned to anticipate consequences. Student teachers often found it difficult to predict student reactions to a set of materials or to judge how much time it would take to complete an activity. They were also frequently frustrated by changes in the normal schedule, breakdowns in equipment and interruptions. The fact that classrooms can go in many different directions at any given point in time often complicated the task of enacting lesson plans in intended ways.

## Strategies and skills for reducing complexity

Analysis of induction sequences indicated that all teachers developed strategies that could be interpreted as attempts to reduce the complexity of the classroom environment There appeared to be considerable variations, however, in the success of different strategies.

In cases labelled 'unsuccessful', student teachers appeared to attempt to reduce classroom complexity by ignoring the multiplicity and simultaneity of the environment. In many instances, this method of reducing complexity involved (a) localizing attention to one region of the classroom; and (b) being engrossed in one activity at a time.

Successful strategies tended to be more congruent with the multiplicity and simultaneity of the environment. A preliminary attempt to codify these skills produced the following categories:

- chunking, or the ability to group discrete events into large units;

- differentiation, or the ability to discriminate among units in terms of their immediate and long-term significance;

- overlap, or the ability to handle two or more events at once (Kounin, 1970 [Reading 11.6]);

- timing, or the ability to monitor and control the duration of events; and

- rapid judgement, or the ability to interpret events with a minimum of delay.

Discussions with cooperating teachers during the three-year course of the present research suggested that these categories represent a part of the tacit knowledge experienced teachers have about the way classrooms work.

The first two skills, chunking and differentiation, suggest that student teachers undergo a concept formation process during which they learn to classify and interpret classroom events and processes in ways that are relevant to the demands created by multidimentionality, simultaneity and unpredictability. In describing pupils, for instance, successful student teachers tended to classify individuals in terms of their potential for disruption, skills in classroom tasks, inclinations to participate in lesson activities, etc. They seemed to know that the movement of some students around the room to secure supplies or sharpen pencils could be ignored whereas the movement of other students required careful monitoring. Similarly, successful teachers learned to judge content in terms of how students would react to it and how difficult it would be to implement in the classroom, in contrast to those who retained purely academic criteria for content adequacy. In sum, successful student teachers transformed the complexity of the environment into a conceptual system that enabled them to interpret discrete events and anticipate the direction and flow of classroom activity. In addition they learned to make rapid judgements about the meaning and consequences of events and to act decisively.

The skills of overlap and timing supplement the interpretive strategies of chunking, differentiation and rapid judgement in ways that enable successful student teachers to regulate classroom demands to some degree. The need for overlap was a continuing condition in classrooms. Successful teachers were able to divide attention between several simultaneous dimensions of classroom activity structures. They were also easily distracted by changes in sound or movement in the classroom. Hence they were in a position to react to developing circumstances as necessary. During the course of the observations, timing also emerged as an especially salient skill for managing classroom demands, one that operated on several levels. It was apparent, for example, that timing was related to the effectiveness of directives to individual students (e.g. 'Stop talking and get back to work!'). Successful managers tended to pause and continue to gaze at the target student for a brief period after issuing such a directive. The target student typically returned to work immediately after receiving the directive, but looked up again in one or two seconds. If the teacher was still monitoring the student, there was a greater likelihood that the directive would be followed. Unsuccessful managers, on the other hand, tended to issue directives and continue as if compliance had been achieved. Over time, this latter pattern seemed to result in directives being ignored and, therefore, reappeared more frequently with less effect.

 **READING 11.2**

# Ambiguity and learning

Maurice Galton

This reading focuses on the ways in which pupils perceive the tasks which are set for them. Research has show that children are often unaware of teachers' academic intentions but are often very conscious of behavioural expectations. These factors tend to produce a sense of ambiguity and uncertainty combined with a weak sense of ownership and low involvement in the learning activity.

Maurice Galton illustrates this theory and uses it to explain why 'progressive practice' never really developed in schools. However, the issues are even more far reaching: how can children be encouraged to fully engage with their learning?

Edited from: Galton, M. (1987) *Teaching in the Primary School*. London: David Fulton, 120–42

The final explanation for the failure fully to implement progressive or informal practice can be termed the 'ambiguity' theory. A crucial stage of this concerns the setting or negotiating of new tasks and activities. As Doyle (1979, 1986) points out, when setting tasks in the classroom teachers have in mind a variety of purposes, based partly on their perception of the needs of individual children. The more complex the task, the greater the possible range of purposes and therefore the greater the ambiguity, with the risk that the child will misinterpret the teacher's intention. For example, in a recent observation of creative writing, a teacher encouraged the children to draft and redraft stories using the approach recommended by Graves (1983). When the stories were finally completed the children were allowed to use the word processor to produce a final version for inclusion in a book of stories. Seen from the pupils' eyes, the teacher displayed a remarkable degree of inconsistency. Some children, having produced pages of writing, were made to redraft it further, while others who produced six lines were allowed to use the computer. The teacher was able in each case to justify these decisions in terms of the pupils' special needs. One child who had written several pages was at a stage where the teacher felt 'she needed to develop her ideas further, they were becoming stereotyped', while the child who wrote six lines 'had concentrated well, which was unusual for him and had also worked well with the other children in his group'. The children, however, were not party to these deliberations. When asked by the observer how they knew when their work was ready to be published, they replied 'we take it to the teacher and he tells us'.

There is considerable evidence that tasks, such as story writing, do indeed appear to be carried out more successfully if the children can feel that they have ownership over their ideas (Cowie, 1989). However, in taking on this ownership, children have to accept the risk of having their ideas evaluated critically. This risk can be reduced if the child has some idea of the criteria being used for this evaluation. During the Effective Group Work in the Primary Classroom project it was very noticeable how repeatedly children complained about not understanding why teachers made certain decisions. As one pupil put it:

> If I could see what it was learning me I could do it but I don't see what it's learning me. I am not really bothered because I want to know what it's learning me. One teacher, Miss Preston, did say that if you don't like what we are giving you come and tell us about it but I think lots of people are frightened to do that.

Teachers would emphasize the importance of the processes rather than the product of the learning, but rarely tried to explain to children why they were being asked to do certain activities at times when there was a need to direct the learning or to introduce a new topic. Indeed some teachers made a point of saying that they thought that 'children of this age don't need to understand why they do things'. In one example children were investigating various ways of measuring time, using an assortment of materials such as sand, water and plastic bottles. Both teachers under observation began by emphasizing the importance of time and gave very precise instructions about how the children were to proceed with the task and how they were not to worry too much about results because what mattered was their ideas. As the children began to assemble the apparatus, it was noticeable that almost every pupil had on their wrist a cheap digital watch; to some of them, at least, it must have seemed strange that they should need to engage in an attempt to measure time in a variety of crude ways when a more accurate method was immediately to hand. With hindsight it would have been relatively easy for the teacher to explain that the main purpose of the exercise was not to measure time but to provide a problem-solving exercise where certain science skills could be developed. However, in the earlier example of developing children's writing skills through publishing, it would have been less easy for the teacher to explain the reasons for what appeared to be unfair treatment of some children as compared to others, without embarrassing the child who was allowed to publish only six lines. None the less, the pupils have eventually to face up to their limitations. The pupil who was allowed to publish six lines told the observer:

> When we have finished we have to read each other's stories. I watch what the others are reading but no-one reads mine.

An even greater ambiguity in setting classroom tasks stems from the fact, as Doyle (1983) points out, that tasks have not only an academic content but also a behavioural purpose. The teacher's main purpose during a question and answer session may be to tease out the children's ideas so that the lesson may be shaped in terms of the pupils' concerns rather than the teacher's. At any one time a question may also be used to see if a child is paying attention. The pupil therefore has to work out what kind of question they are being asked. Is it the kind where a speculative answer will be praised or where a wrong answer will be seized upon as evidence of inattention? This sort of dilemma offers another excuse for pupils to adopt a strategy of avoidance – they leave someone else to make the initial responses until the purpose behind the teacher's questions becomes clear. Similarly, when writing it may not always be clear to the pupil what the difference is between redrafting and being made to do corrections.

Rowland (1987) argues that in negotiating ownership with children one removes the need to exercise authoritarian control over behaviour. Nias (1988) is more cautious and admits uncertainty about the causality of this process. It may be, therefore, that the form of the control exercised over the pupils' behaviour by the teacher largely determines whether pupils perceive the teacher's interventions as collaboration or as a 'take-over'. Thus, when children regard control of the classroom organization and of their behaviour as primarily the teacher's responsibility, then, because they are unable to distinguish easily between the teacher's role as 'policeman' and as 'negotiator', they play safe and seek to hand back responsibility for the learning to the teacher.

 **READING 11.3**

# Learning to be 'stupid'?

John Holt

> John Holt's writing has a direct and challenging style which is, at the same time, grounded and empathic. In this reading he proposes that many children 'learn to be stupid' in schools, because of what he believes to be the routinized and 'boring' nature of much of their experience. This reading is thus about the relationship between children's motivation and the ways in which learning tasks are presented and managed. It is closely connected to the previous reading (11.2).
>
> How can classrooms and tasks be managed in ways which tap children's interests and enthusiasms, whilst still satisfying the requirements of curriculum plans?
>
> Edited from: Holt, J. (1982) *How Children Fail.* London: Penguin, 262–5

Children are subject peoples. School for them is a kind of jail. Do they not, to some extent, escape and frustrate the relentless, insatiable pressure of their elders by withdrawing the most intelligent and creative parts of their minds from the scene? The stubborn and dogged 'I don't get it' with which they meet their teachers – may it not be a statement of resistance as well as one of panic and flight?

To a very great degree, school is a place where children learn to be stupid. A dismal thought, but hard to escape. Infants are not stupid. Children of one, two, or even three throw the whole of themselves into everything they do. They embrace life, and devour it; it is why they learn so fast and are such good company. Listlessness, boredom, apathy – these all come later. Children come to school curious; within a few years most of that curiosity is dead, or at least silent. Open a first or third grade to questions, and you will be deluged; fifth-graders say nothing. They either have no questions or will not ask them. They think, 'What's this leading up to? What's the catch?'. Curiosity, questions, speculation – these are for outside school not inside.

Boredom and resistance may cause as much stupidity in school as fear. Give a child the kind of task he gets in school, and whether he is afraid of it, or resists it, or is willing to do it but is bored by it, he will do the task with only a small part of his attention, energy and intelligence. In a word, he will do it stupidly – even if correctly. This soon becomes a habit. He gets used to working at lower power, he develops strategies to enable him to get by this way. In time he even starts to think of himself as being stupid, which is what most fifth-graders think of themselves, and to think that his low-power way of coping with school is the only possible way.

It does no good to tell such students to pay attention and think about what they are doing. I can see myself now, in one of my ninth-grade algebra classes in Colorado, looking at one of my flunking students, a boy who had become frozen in his school stupidity, and saying to him in a loud voice, 'Think! Think! Think!'. Wasted breath; he had forgotten how. The stupid way – timid, unimaginative, defensive, evasive – in which he met and dealt with the problems of algebra were, by that time, the only way he knew of dealing with them. His strategies and expectations were fixed. He couldn't even imagine any others. He really was doing his dreadful best.

The attention of children must be lured, caught, and held, like a shy wild animal that must be coaxed with bait to come close. If the situations, the materials, the problems before a child do not interest him, his attention will slip off to what does interest him, and no amount of exhortation or threats will bring it back.

A child is most intelligent when the reality before him arouses in him a high degree of attention, interest, concentration, involvement – in short, when he cares most about what he is doing. This is why we should make schoolrooms and schoolwork as interesting and exciting as possible, not just so that school will be a pleasant place, but so that children in school will act intelligently and get into the habit of acting intelligently. The case against boredom in school is the same as the case against fear; it makes children behave stupidly.

 READING 11.4

# Four rules of class management

## Robert Laslett and Colin Smith

The voice of experience speaks clearly through the apparently simple injunctions contained in this reading – 'get them in'; 'get them out'; 'get on with it' and 'get on with them'. In their discussions of these topics, Robert Laslett and Colin Smith succeed in highlighting the key practical issues in classroom management in a very accessible way. Although initially written in relation to secondary school context, their advice remains valuable in relation to any school classroom.

How do you cope with the four rules of class management?

Edited from: Laslett, R. and Smith, C. (1984) *Effective Classroom Management: A Teacher's Guide*. London: Croom Helm, 1–10

The skills of successful classroom management can be reduced to 'four rules', attention to which should enable all teachers to improve efficiency and harmony in their classrooms.

## Rule one: get them in

The first rule requires attention to planning the start of each lesson. The process of beginning a lesson smoothly and promptly involves greeting, seating and starting.

*Greeting* Simply by being present before the class arrives, the teacher establishes his role as host, receiving the class on his territory and, by implication, on his terms (Marland, 1975). Apart from the vital practical advantage of being able to check that the room is tidy, materials are available, displays are arranged and necessary instructions or examples are written on the blackboard, being there first allows the teacher to underline quietly his authority by deciding when the class comes into the room.

*Seating* Just how seating is arranged must depend on the type of lesson to be taught, and the type of classroom furniture. Whether using traditional serried ranks of desks or less formal group tables, each teacher needs to establish who sits where.

*Starting* Every lesson should start with some activity that keeps each child quietly occupied in his own place. What type of activity depends very much on the age and ability of the child and the nature of the lesson. Ideally, the work should involve reinforcement of previously acquired skills, particularly those required for the lesson which is about to be taught. Establishing a routine will require setting specific tasks and providing detailed verbal and written instruction. Having settled the class to work in this way, the temptation to leave them at it must be avoided.

## Rule two: get them out

However, before considering the content of the lesson, the second rule which needs to be mastered is how to conclude the lesson and dismiss the class. If this seems a strange order of priorities, it is worth remembering that if most disciplinary problems arise from a poor start to the lesson, hard-won control is most frequently lost and learning wasted at the end of lessons.

*Concluding* Learning that has taken place during a lesson can often be wasted if an opportunity is not taken to reinforce what has been taught by a summary and brief question session. It is no use trying to do that over the heads of children who are still working or who are busy collecting exercise books. So at three minutes before the presumed end of the lesson, 'as precisely as that' (Marland, 1975), or at whatever time is judged necessary, work should stop, leaving an opportunity for the collection of materials, putting books away and some revision and recapitulation of the lesson.

*Dismissing* Once the bell does go, there is need for an established, orderly routine which ensures that the class gets beyond the door without the teacher having to spend time clearing debris from the floor or readjusting the lines of desks. If this can be done without recourse to sending out one section or row at a time, such informality is welcome. Traditional verbal prompting, 'arms folded, sitting up straight', may still have its place, however.

It is also important to remember that classes are never just leaving one place, they are going on to another. Children need to be cued in to their next activity.

## Rule three: get on with it

'It' refers to the lesson itself – its content, manner and organization. Momentum is the key to determining the content of a lesson, its variety and pace.

*Content* Variety is needed within a lesson to maintain interest, curiosity and motivation. Activities planned for the start and finish, as suggested above, will go some way towards achieving these aims. However, there is also a need to plan for some variety within the main body of the lesson. Alternating preferred activities with more boring ones, mixing familiar work with new learning, and balancing quiet individual work with more active group tasks can all help keep a lesson moving (Sloane, 1976). It is essential, however, that variety should not become confusion. Each activity should be clearly specified and the teacher's expectations clarified so that each child knows what he should be doing and when he should be doing it.

Pace is also helped by breaking up a topic into several smaller units of learning. It can also help to have as a target the intention that every child should have something finished, something marked in every lesson. Though often unattainable, such an aim does direct attention to the importance of immediate feedback and reinforcement in helping children to learn (Stott, 1978).

The momentum or flow of classroom industry is of great importance to discipline, as interruptions lead to loss of energy and interest on the part of pupils and teachers (Tanner, 1978; Rutter *et al.*, 1979).

*Manner* Classroom atmosphere is a term frequently used, but rarely analysed. Here again, however, what might at first be thought to result from 'personality' can be described as a series of skills. Similarly, positive interaction between teacher and class can be traced to the way in which they communicate with each other. The skills involved in creating a good classroom atmosphere are really a series of mechanisms to regulate what goes on in the classroom.

Behaviour does seem to be better and atmosphere brighter where ample praise is used in teaching (Hopkins and Conrad, 1976). Praise needs to be natural and sincere and should never become dull and routing. It is a good idea to try to think of at least six synonyms for 'good' and to use them appropriately. 'Great', 'superb', 'fine', 'splendid', 'remarkable' are some examples, or use more colloquial expressions such as 'ace', 'knockout' or 'cracker', if they come naturally. Similarly, 'nice' is a word so often used, when children would surely be more stimulated to know that their work was 'delightful', 'imaginative', 'beautiful', 'interesting', 'original' or 'fascinating'.

The way the teacher talks to the class reflects his attitude to them not only in what is said, but how it is said. Facial expression and tone of voice are as important to communication as making sure that attention is gained, by getting the class to stop work and listen carefully to what has to be said. It follows that what has to be said should be clear, simple and important enough to merit stopping the lesson.

The old adage, 'quiet teacher, quiet class' contains good advice, but should be followed with some reservation; 'inaudible teacher, insufferable class' may also be true. Adequate volume is an essential to being understood and it may help if teachers assume that in any class there is very likely to be at least one child with some hearing loss.

Emphasizing the importance of using your eyes to communicate, is recommended by Marland (1975). Two or three sentences on a theme should be addressed to one child in one part of the room. As another idea is developed, the teacher shifts his gaze to another child in another part of the room, then focuses on a third for the next theme. This approach should help develop a 'feel' for what is going on in the different areas of the classroom. This is how to develop the traditional teacher's eyes in the back of the head.

*Organization* In any given subject, every class is a mixed-ability group. Whether dealing with high flyers or low achievers, teachers must allow for the fact that some children will work more rapidly and accurately than others. On the way to the ideal of individualizing educational programmes for all their pupils, teachers can start by splitting their class into groups. The amount and difficulty of work demanded from each group can then be related to their abilities in that particular subject. There are three ways of doing this – by rota, quota or branching.

Rota, as in rotation of crops, refers to groups moving round the classroom from one activity to another. The development of learning centres is essential to this approach. These are areas of the classroom using alcoves, bookshelves or simply tables arranged to provide an environment for the accomplishment of a particular instructional purpose (Lemlech, 1979). They can be used for the practice of particular skills, gathering further information, extending experience or for instructional recreation.

Quota, similarly requires the teacher to work out an appropriate amount of work to be completed during a session by each group. Each child has an assignment card or booklet, which becomes a record of work completed as it is checked by the teacher. This system can be simply an extension of the rota system with individual requirements, such as reading to the teacher, handwriting or spelling practice being added.

Branching, involves starting all the class together on a particular activity, doing an exercise from the board or working together from a textbook, then, as this is completed, 'branching' groups into different activities or areas of the room. For the quicker workers, who are likely to finish the common activity first, there may need to be a number of further pieces of work.

## Rule four: get on with them

The temptation to misbehave is lessened where teachers and children get on well together. Many of the points already mentioned will help build a good pupil–teacher relationship, based on skilful, confident teaching geared to children's specific needs (Wallace and Kauffman, 1978). To further develop mutual trust and respect, the teacher also needs to show an awareness of each child as an individual and a sensitivity to the mood of the class as a whole. The teacher needs to know who's who and what's going on.

*Who's who?* Once a child's name is known, discipline is immediately easier because requests or rebukes can be made more personal. Recognition also implies interest on the part of the teacher. It is easy to learn the names of the best and worst children, but less easy to remember those who do not attract attention to themselves. The attention is needed just as much, and sometimes more.

A daily chat, however brief, about something not connected with lessons can be a source of insight as well as a way of establishing rapport. It might be said that a chat a day, keeps trouble at bay! As with praise, personal interest must be natural and genuine, not merely assumed.

*What's going on?* Few classes of children are likely to be so purposefully malevolent as to set out on a planned campaign of disruption. Group misbehaviour is more likely to build up from a series of minor incidents. It is necessary therefore for teachers to acquire a sensitivity to group responses. 'The key to developing this talent lies in a combination of monitoring, marking and mobility' (Brophy and Evertson, 1976).

Frequently scanning the class, even while helping one individual should enable the teacher to spot the first signs of trouble quickly and intervene firmly but quietly. Often, merely moving to the area from which louder voices are indicating some distraction can refocus attention on the work in hand. The mild personal rebuke addressed to an individual can be far more productive than a formal public warning.

Marking work in progress is not only a good way of giving immediate feedback, it is also a natural form of contact. Rather than reprimanding the child who is not concentrating on his work, offering help and advice may be the best way to return his attention to the task in hand.

Mobility is needed to avoid teachers becoming desk-bound by queues waiting for attention, which can screen inactivity elsewhere in the classroom and themselves become social gatherings and a potential source of noise and distraction. It is essential to develop a routine, which enables children to find help from each other if the teacher is occupied, or which provides them with alternative purposeful activities while waiting for advice or correction. This will free the teacher to move around the room, sharing his time and interest, adding all the time to his awareness of personalities and problems.

It is this combination of activities that enables the responsive teacher to judge correctly the times for serious endeavour or light-hearted amusement.

# READING 11.5

# Provocative and insulative teachers

David Hargreaves, Stephen Hestor and Frank Mellor

This is a relatively simple but very important reading which highlights the importance of the disposition and initial reaction of teachers in response to deviance by pupils. Thinking of classroom interaction as an ongoing process, Hargreaves and his colleagues suggest that, whatever a pupil's initial action, the response of the teacher may either exacerbate or calm the situation. It is suggested that these responses are characteristic of 'provocative' or 'insulative' teachers.

What is your initial reaction to a child's deviant act? And would your more considered reaction be any different?

Edited from: Hargreaves, D., Hestor, S. and Mellor, F. (1975) *Deviance in Classrooms*. London: Routledge, 260–2

The study of Jordan (1974) is a symbolic interactionist examination of the perspectives of a group of deviant boys and of their teachers. Jordan outlines two types of teachers which we might term as 'deviance-provocative' and 'deviance-insulative'. The first type of teacher finds that the deviant pupils behave in highly deviant ways in his classroom and his handling of them serves to exacerbate their deviance. The second type of teacher finds that the same pupils present relatively few problems in his classroom and his handling of them serves to inhibit their deviance.

The deviance-provocative teacher believes that the pupils he defines as deviant do not want to work in school and will do anything to avoid it. He thinks it is impossible to provide conditions under which they will work; if they are ever to work then the pupils must change. In disciplinary matters he sees his interaction with these pupils as a contest or battle – and one that he must win. He is unable to 'de-fuse' difficult situations; he frequently issues ultimatums and becomes involved in confrontations. He considers these pupils to be 'anti-authority' and is confident that they are determined not to conform to the classroom rules. The deviants are neglected in lessons and punished inconsistently, whereas overtly preferential treatment is accorded to the conformist pupils. He expects the pupils to behave badly and makes many negative evaluative comments upon them, both to them as well as to colleagues in the staffroom. The pupils are referred to a higher authority when they refuse to comply. The derogation of and laughing at pupils is common, and he is highly suspicious of them because his experience has shown that they cannot be trusted. He avoids contact with such pupils outside the classroom The pupils are blamed for their misconduct. Since he believes the pupils are resistant, hostile and committed to their deviance, they are seen as potential saboteurs and he refuses to believe that any signs of improvement are authentic.

The deviance-insulative teacher believes that these pupils, like all pupils, really want to work. If the pupils do not work, the conditions are assumed to be at fault. He believes that these conditions can be changed and that it is his responsibility to initiate that change. In disciplinary matters he has a clear set of classroom rules which are made explicit to the pupils. He makes an effort to avoid any kind of favouritism or preferential or differential treatment; he also avoids confrontations with pupils. He rarely makes negative evaluative comments on pupils who misbehave. When he punishes deviant conduct, he allows the pupils to 'save face'. He does not derogate them in the classroom – or in the staffroom where he often springs to the defence of a deviant pupil who is being discussed. He is highly optimistic, in contrast with the fatalism of the deviance-provocative teacher, and confidently assumes that pupils will behave well and cooperate with him. He perceives all the pupils as potential contributors to the lesson and sees the unpredictability of the deviant pupils as a potential source of change. He encourages any signs of improvement. Whereas the deviance-provocative teacher dislikes the deviant pupils and considers himself unfortunate in having to teach them, the deviance-insulative teacher claims to like all children and considers it a privilege to work with any pupil. He respects and cares about the deviant pupils and tells them so. He enjoys meeting them informally outside the classroom, where he can joke with them and take an interest in their personal problems. He trusts them.

The difference between the two types of teacher is not merely that one is more open to the possibility of type transformation than the other. That, to the deviance-insulative teacher, deviant pupils never become stabilized deviants in the first place is the outcome of a different common-sense knowledge of classroom deviance and a different set of wider assumptions about human nature and education – a different 'philosophy of life' and a different 'philosophy of education'.

## READING 11.6

# Discipline and group management in classrooms

Jacob Kounin

> Kounin's book on group management is a classic text which has been of enormous influence in the analysis of classroom management. Based on careful study of videotapes of US classrooms, Kounin's insights are well grounded in observation of teacher actions and pupil response. Amongst the attractions of the work are the amusing names which Kounin gave to some of the patterns which he identified: when did you last do a 'dangle', or subject your class to a 'slowdown'? Do not be deceived or put off by the language of this reading, for it has immensely practical implications. The term 'recitation' describes a whole-class, teacher-directed teaching session.
>
> Edited from: Kounin, J. (1970) *Discipline and Group Management in Classrooms*. New York: Holt, Rinehart and Winston, iv, 74–101

The planned and unplanned realities of a classroom necessitate a teacher having skills that go beyond curricular planning and managing individual children. These skills pertain to group management – to what a teacher plans and does in a classroom that is aimed at more than one child and that affects more than one child.

An analysis of real classrooms reveals that there are concrete techniques of managing classrooms that relate to the amount of work involvement and misbehaviour in learning situations. Study of videotapes showed that there were specific categories of teachers' behaviour that correlated with their managerial success as measured by pupil work involvement, deviancy rate, contagion of misbehaviour and effectiveness of desists. Some of the dimensions of teachers behaviours that made a difference in the behaviour of pupils were, as we termed them: withitness (demonstrating that she knew what was going on); overlapping (attending to two issues simultaneously); transition smoothness (absence of dangles, flip-flops and thrusts); slowdowns (where momentum is lost); and maintaining group focus.

## Withitness

Withitness was defined as a teacher's communicating to the children by her actual behaviour that she knows what the children are doing, or has the proverbial 'eyes in the back of her head'. What kinds of teacher behaviours, and in what circumstances, provide cues to pupils as to whether the teacher does or does not know what is going on? It is not adequate to measure what a teacher knows in order to obtain a score for the degree of her withitness. It is necessary to measure what she communicates she knows. The children, after all, must get the information that she knows or doesn't know what they are doing.

Desist events are examples of incidents where a teacher does something that communicates to the children whether she does or doesn't know what is happening. In desist events a child is doing something and the teacher does something about it. Does she pick the correct target and does she do it on time? Or, does she make some kind of mistake that communicates the information that she doesn't know what is happening?

## Overlapping

Overlapping refers to what the teacher does when she has two matters to deal with at the same time. Does she somehow attend to both issues simultaneously or does she remain or become immersed in one issue only to the neglect of the other? These kinds of 'overlapping' issues occur in both desist events and in child intrusion events.

An overlapping issue is present at the time of a desist event when the teacher is occupied with an ongoing task with children at the time that she desists a deviancy. Thus, if she is in a recitation setting with a reading group and she notes and acts upon a deviancy occurring in the seatwork setting, she is in an overlapping situation.

Considering the results of both Videotape Studies, one may conclude that both the withitness and the overlapping of teachers have a significant bearing upon their managerial success but that the effects of withitness are greater than the effects of overlapping. Throughout, the correlations of withitness with both work involvement and freedom from deviancy scores are higher than the correlations between teachers' overlapping scores and children's behaviour. Both Videotape Studies, however, show that overlapping and withitness are significantly related to each other. To reiterate, teachers who show signs of attending to more than one issue when there is more than one issue to handle at a particular time, are likely to pick correct deviancy targets and do something about the deviancy on time – before the deviancy becomes more serious or begins to spread to other children. On the other hand, teachers who become immersed in one issue only when there is more than one issue to handle, are more likely to act upon an incorrect deviancy target or act upon the deviancy too late – after the misbehaviour becomes more serious or spreads to other children. And handling the correct deviant on time is evidently more important than the method used in handling the deviancy.

How might one interpret the relationship between withitness or overlapping? One interpretation is that broadening one's scope of active attending, as manifest in overlapping, enables a teacher to receive more information about what is going on. This knowledge is necessary to achieve withitness. However, overlapping is not adequate unless it leads to some behaviour that communicates to the children. Children probably do not categorize an overlapping dimension or even perceive it. What they do see, categorize in some way, and react to, is what the teacher does. They do see her pick on the wrong person or do it too late, in which case they form a judgement, however, explicit or implicit, that she doesn't know what is going on. However, if she acts promptly and on the correct deviant then they see her as having 'eyes in the back of her head'. And, if the children perceive her as knowing what is going on she is more likely to induce worklike behaviour and restrain deviancy than if they see her as not knowing what is going on. Thus, overlapping correlates to withitness (enables withitness to occur) but does not, in and of itself, relate to managerial success, whereas withitness does.

Regardless of the type of theoretical linkage between overlapping and withitness, the reality of classrooms dictates that both are essential for managerial success. Unless some other technique is available to obtain knowledge about what is going on except by attending, one can safely recommend that teachers engage in both manifest overlapping and demonstrated withitness.

## Transition smoothness

A teacher in a self-contained classroom must manage considerable activity movement: she must initiate, sustain and terminate many activities. Sometimes this involves having children move physically from one part of the room to another, as when a group must move from their own desks to the reading circle. At other times it involves some psychological movement, or some change in props, as when children change from doing arithmetic problems at their desks to studying spelling words at the same desks.

How do teachers go about initiating and maintaining activity flow in a classroom? Are there sizeable differences among teachers in this respect, and if so, do these differences relate to differences in the amount of work involvement or deviancy of children? Is it possible to delineate concrete behaviours of teachers that one can use to constitute measures of movement management? Or, must one resort to impressionistic judgements or ratings having to do with 'smoothness', 'jerkiness', 'dragginess' or 'really moving'? There are two major categories of movement mistakes. First are behaviours producing jerkiness. These are actions of teachers that interfere with the smoothness of the flow of activities. The second category of movement mistakes is of teacher behaviours producing slowdowns that impede the momentum of activies.

*Jerkiness* The categories associated with jerkiness in transitions are stimulus-boundedness, thrusts, dangles and flip-flops. Stimulus-boundedness may be contrasted with goal-directedness. Does the teacher maintain a focus upon an activity goal or is she easily deflected from it? In a stimulus-bound event, a teacher behaves as though she has no will of her own and reacts to some unplanned and irrelevant stimulus as an iron filing reacts to a magnet: she gets magnetized and lured into reacting to some minutia that pulls her out of the main activity stream. A thrust consists of a teacher's sudden 'bursting in' on the children's activities with an order, statement or question in such a manner as to indicate that her own intent or desire was the only determinant of her timing and point of entry. That is, she evidenced no sign (pausing, looking around) of looking for, or of being sensitive to, the group's readiness to receive her message. A thrust has a clear element of suddenness as well as an absence of any observable sign of awareness or sensitivity to whether the target audience is in a state of readiness. A dangle was coded when a teacher started, or was in, some activity and then left it 'hanging in mid-air' by going off to some other activity. Following such a 'fade away' she would then resume the activity. For example: the teacher is engaged in checking the children's previous seatwork. Children are taking turns reading their answers to the arithmetic problems. The teacher said 'that's right' after Jimmy finished reading his answer to the third problem. She then looked around and said, 'All right, Mary, read your answer to the fourth problem'. As Mary was getting up, the teacher looked around the room, and said, 'My now. Let's see. Suzanne isn't here, is she? Does anyone know why Suzanne is absent today?'. Flip-flops were coded only at transition points. A transition entails terminating one activity (put away spelling papers) and starting another (take out your workbooks and turn to page 190). In a flip-flop a teacher terminates one activity, starts another, and then initiates a return to the activity that she had terminated. An example: the teacher says, 'All right, let's everybody put away your spelling papers and take out your arithmetic books'. The children put their spelling papers in their desks, and, after most of the children had their arithmetic books out on their desks, the teacher asked, 'let's see the hands of the ones who got all their spelling words right'.

*Slowdowns* Slowdowns consisted of those behaviours initiated by teachers that clearly slowed down the rate of movement in a recitation activity. Slowdowns refer to movement properties that may or may not be smooth and unidirectional but which clearly impede or produce friction in the forward momentum of an activity. Their effect is to hold back and produce dragginess in the progress of an activity. Two major categories of slowdowns are overdwelling and fragmentation. Overdwelling was coded when the teacher dwelled on an issue and engaged in a stream of actions or talk that was clearly beyond what was necessary for most children's understanding or getting on with an activity. Overdwelling would produce a reaction on the part of most children of: 'All right, all right, that's enough already!'. Overdwelling could apply to either the behaviour of children or to the task. A fragmentation is a slowdown produced by a teacher's breaking down an activity into sub-parts when the activity could be performed as a single unit.

Movement management, including both smoothness and momentum is a significant dimension of classroom management. Within this dimension it is more important to maintain momentum by avoiding actions that slow down forward movement than it is to maintain smoothness by avoiding sudden starts and stops. And techniques of movement management are more significant in controlling deviancy than are techniques of deviancy management as such. In addition, techniques of movement management possess the additional value of promoting work involvement, especially in recitation settings.

## Maintaining group focus

A classroom teacher is not a tutor working with one child at a time. Even though she may work with a single child at times, her main job is to work with a group of children in one room at one time. Sometimes the group is the entire class and sometimes it is a subgroup or subgroups (as when she is at the reading circle with one group while another subgroup or other subgroups are at seatwork). Given this partial job analysis, it may be fruitful to see what techniques teachers use in recitation sessions to maintain group focus.

*Group alerting* This refers to the degree to which a teacher attempts to involve children in the task, maintain their attention, and keep them 'on their toes' or alerted. Positive group alerting cues were:

- any method used to create 'suspense' before calling on a child to recite: pausing and looking around to 'bring children in' before selecting a reciter, saying 'Let's see now, who can . . .' before calling on a reciter;

- keeping children in suspense in regard to who will be called on next; picking reciters 'randomly' so that no child knows whether he will be called on next or not;

- teacher calls on different children frequently or maintains group focus: intersperses 'mass unison' responses; says, 'Let's put our thinking caps on; this might fool you'; asks group for show of hands before selecting a reciter;

- teacher alerts non-performers that they might be called on in connection with what a reciter is doing; they may be called on if reciter makes a mistake; presignals children that they will be asked about recitation content in the immediate future;

- teachers presents new, novel or alluring material into a recitation (a high-attention value prop or issue).

Negative group alerting cues were:

- the teacher changes the focus of her attention away from the group and becomes completely immersed in the performance of the reciter; or directs a new question and subsequent attention to a single new reciter only, without any overt sign of awareness that there is a group;

- the teacher prepicks a reciter or performer before the question is even stated;
- the teacher has reciters perform in a predetermined sequence of turns.

*Accountability* Accountability refers to the degree to which the teacher holds the children accountable and responsible for their task performances during recitation sessions. This entails her doing something to get to know what the children are actually doing and to communicate to the children in some observable manner that she knows what they are doing. The degree to which she goes out to obtain this knowledge and to communicate it, is the degree to which she holds the children in the group accountable for their performances. The most usual means of securing information is for the teacher to require children to produce or demonstrate work that is being done in the current setting and to check these demonstrations. Thus, the following are the kinds of behaviours associated with accountability.

- The teacher asks children to hold up their props exposing performances or answers in such a manner as to be readily visible to the teacher.
- Teacher requires children to recite in unison while the teacher shows signs of actively attending to the recitation.
- Teacher brings other children into the performance of a child reciting. (Teacher says: 'Jimmy, you watch Johnny do that problem and then tell me what he did right or wrong'.)
- Teacher asks for the raised hands of children who are prepared to demonstrate a performance and requires some of them to demonstrate.
- Teacher circulates and checks products of non-reciters during a child performance.
- Teacher requires a child to demonstrate and checks his performance.

Our findings show that teachers who maintain group focus by engaging in behaviours that keep children alerted and on their toes are more successful in inducing work involvement and preventing deviancy than are teachers who do not. This aspect of teacher style is more significant in recitation settings than in seatwork settings.

*Satiation* This important further issue is concerned with the nature of the activities programmed in the classrooms. What are the groups of children required to do – what is the teacher moving them into and out of? Does the nature of the classroom activity programme relate to work involvement and deviancy? Answers entail an analysis of the curriculum. Indeed, even within the same grades of the same school, teachers do vary in what they emphasize, in how they sequence the activities, and in what they do beyond the school's basic curricular commonalities.

Does a teacher do anything beyond the usual routine in a recitation session that would be likely to produce either a clear feeling of repetitiousness or a clear feeling of progress in an academic activity? In our research, the code for progress cues consisted of three categories. 'Routine' was coded when the teacher engaged in ordinary and usual kinds and amounts of behaviour relating to progress or repetition: she did nothing special to induce feelings of progress nor did she impose special repetitiousness during recitations. 'Positive cues' were noted whenever a teacher did something beyond the immediate call of duty to get a child or group to feel that they were making progress and accomplishing something in the activity. 'Negative cues' were coded whenever a teacher repeated an explanation or demonstration beyond what was necessary for clarity, or when she had a child or children repeat a performance when it was already correct.

## Conclusion

It is possible to delineate concrete aspects of teacher behaviour that lead to managerial success in the classroom. These techniques of classroom management apply to emotionally disturbed children in regular classrooms as well as to non-disturbed children. They apply to boys as well as to girls. They apply to the group and not merely to individual children. They are techniques of creating an effective classroom ecology and learning milieu. One might note that none of them necessitate punitiveness or restrictiveness.

This focus upon group management techniques in classrooms is intended to go beyond simplified slogans such as 'create rapport' or 'make it interesting'. Neither does this focus entail a preoccupation with such characteristics as 'friendly', 'warm', 'patient', 'understanding', 'love for children', and similar attributes of people in general. These desirable attributes will not manage a classroom. Rather, the business of running a classroom is a complicated technology having to do with developing a non-satiating learning programme; programming for progress, challenge and variety in learning activities; initiating and maintaining movement in classroom tasks with smoothness and momentum; coping with more than one event simultaneously; observing and emitting feedback for many different events; directing actions at appropriate targets; maintaining a focus upon a group; and doubtless other techniques not measured in these researches.

The mastery of classroom management skills should not be regarded as an end in itself. These techniques are, however, necessary tools. Techniques are enabling. The mastery of techniques enables one to do many different things. It makes choices possible. The possession of group management skills allows the teacher to accomplish her teaching goals – the absence of managerial skills acts as a barrier.

The focus upon group management skills is not opposed to a concern for individual children. The mastery of group management actually enables the teacher to programme for individual differences and to help individual children. If there is a climate of work involvement and freedom from deviancy, different groups of children may be doing different things, and the teacher is free to help individual children if she so chooses. One might say that a mastery of group management techniques enables a teacher to be free from concerns about management.

### READING 11.7

# Positive teaching in the primary school

Frank Merrett and Kevin Wheldall

This reading provides advice on achieving and maintaining class discipline and task engagement from a behaviourist perspective, and it might thus be read in conjunction with Skinner's work (Reading 7.1). The emphasis is on changing pupil behaviour using positive reinforcement in a controlled, skilful and managed way, rather than becoming negative, as can all too easily happen when discipline problems arise in classrooms. The use of such techniques may seem to jar with some aspirations for classroom relationships, but in one form or another they contribute to the repertoire of many experienced teachers.

Are you able to manage positive reinforcements consistently?

Edited from: Merrett, F. and Wheldall, K. (1990) *Identifying Troublesome Classroom Behaviour*. London: Paul Chapman Publishing, 11–22

There are five principles of positive teaching.

1. Teaching is concerned with the observable.
2. Almost all classroom behaviour is learned.
3. Learning involves change in behaviour.
4. Behaviour changes as a result of its consequences.
5. Behaviours are also influenced by classroom contexts.

These five principles sum up what we mean by positive teaching. The main assumption is that pupils' behaviour is primarily learned and maintained as a result of their interactions with their environment, which includes other pupils and teachers. Consequently, behaviour can be changed by altering certain features of that environment. As we have said, the key environmental features are events which immediately precede or follow behaviour. This means that classroom behaviours followed by consequences that the pupils find rewarding will tend to increase in frequency. Similarly, certain changes in behaviour may be brought about merely by changing the classroom setting.

One way of thinking about positive teaching is in terms of the ABC in which:

A refers to the antecedent conditions, i.e. the context in which a behaviour occurs or what is happening in that environment prior to a behaviour occurring.

B refers to the behaviour itself, i.e. what a pupil is actually doing in real physical terms (not what you think he or she is doing as a result of inferences from his or her behaviour).

C refers to the consequences of the behaviour, i.e. what happens to the pupil after the behaviour.

Let us look at consequences in a little more detail.

A major concern within positive teaching is with the identification of items and events which pupils find rewarding and to structure the teaching environment so as to make access to these rewards dependent upon behaviour which the teacher wants to encourage in class.

Consequences may be described as rewarding punishing. Rewarding consequences, which we call positive reinforcers, are events which we seek out or 'go for', whilst we try to avoid punishing consequences. Neutral consequences are events which affect us neither way. Behaviours followed by positive reinforcers are likely to increase in frequency. Behaviours followed by punishers tend to decrease in frequency whilst neutral consequences have no effect. In positive teaching, infrequent but appropriate behaviours (for example, getting on with the set work quietly) are made more frequent by arranging for positive reinforcers, such as teacher attention and approval, to follow their occurrence. This is called social reinforcement.

Undesired behaviours may be decreased in frequency by ensuring that positive reinforcers do not follow their occurrence, i.e. a neutral consequence is arranged. Occasionally it may be necessary to follow undesired behaviours with punishers (for example, a quiet reprimand) in an attempt to reduce the frequency of behaviour rapidly but there are problems associated with this procedure. Punishment plays only a minor and infrequent role in positive teaching, not least because sometimes what we believe to be punishing is, in fact, reinforcing to the pupil. Pupils who receive little attention from adults may behave in ways that result in adult disapproval. Such pupils may prefer disapproval to being ignored and will continue to behave like this because adult attention, in itself, whether praise or reprimand, is positively reinforcing. This is what some people call attention-seeking behaviour.

We should note that terminating a punishing consequence is also reinforcing and can be, and often is, used to increase desired behaviours. This is known as negative reinforcement. Again this has problems associated with its use since pupils may rapidly learn other, more effective, ways of avoiding the negative consequence than you had in mind. For example, some teachers continually use sarcasm and ridicule with their pupils. They cease only when their pupils behave as they wish. However, another way for pupils to avoid this unpleasant consequence is to skip lessons or stay away from school.

Finally, one can punish by removing or terminating positive consequences (for example, by taking away privileges). This is known as response cost, but again there are similar problems associated with this. Pupils may find alternative ways of avoiding this unpleasant consequence. Lying, cheating and shifting the blame are common strategies employed. These are all behaviours we would wish to discourage but by creating consequences which we believe to be aversive we may be making them more likely to occur.

When we want to teach pupils to do something new, or to encourage them to behave in a certain way more frequently than they normally do, it is important that we ensure that they are positively reinforced every time they behave as we want them to. This normally leads to rapid learning and is known as continuous reinforcement. When they have learned the new behaviour and/or are behaving as we want them to do regularly, then we may maintain this behaviour more economically by reducing the frequency of reinforcement.

Another important reason for wanting to reduce the frequency of reinforcement is that pupils may become less responsive if the positive reinforcer becomes too easily available. Consequently, once pupils are regularly behaving in an appropriate way we can best maintain that behaviour by ensuring that they are now reinforced only intermittently. Intermittent reinforcement can be arranged so that pupils are reinforced every so often (i.e. in terms of time) or, alternatively, after so many occurrences of the behaviour. These different ways of organizing the frequency of reinforcement are known as reinforcement schedules.

It should be emphasized that positive teaching is not about creating robots who just do as they are told, mindlessly following the teacher's instructions. Rather, positive teaching is about helping children to become effective, independent learners. Positive teachers should, in effect, like all good teachers, have the ultimate aim of making themselves redundant.

---

## 📖 READING 11.8

# Discipline in schools

The Committee of Enquiry on Discipline in Schools (The Elton Report)

---

The Elton Committee conducted a major enquiry into the factors which influence the conditions in which learning takes place. They drew important conclusions for classroom teachers but also highlighted the vital contribution of many other partners in education. This point is illustrated by this summary of their report, which highlights the complexity of factors which influence discipline in schools – many of which are beyond the remit of the classroom teacher.

Thinking of a school in which you work or have worked, what do you think are the greatest influences on pupil behaviour?

Edited from: The Committee of Enquiry on Discipline in Schools (1989) *Discipline in Schools: Report of the Committee of Enquiry chaired by Lord Elton*. London: HMSO, 11–17

---

## The enquiry

Our task was to recommend action to the government, local authorities, voluntary bodies, governors, head teachers, teachers and parents aimed at securing the orderly atmosphere necessary in schools for effective teaching and learning to take place. We find that most schools are on the whole well ordered. But even in well-run schools minor disruption appears to be a problem. The relatively trivial incidents which most concern teachers make it harder for teachers to teach and pupils to learn. Our recommendations would secure a real improvement in all schools.

## Teachers

The central problem of disruption could be significantly reduced by helping teachers to become more effective classroom managers. We see the roles of initial and in-service training as crucial to this process. Our evidence suggests that the status of teachers has declined in recent years and that it may have reduced their authority in the eyes of pupils and parents. We ask the Secretaries of State to clarify the legal basis of teachers' authority. We emphasize the serious implications that any teacher shortages would have for standards of behaviour in schools, and the need for their pay and conditions of service to be such as to ensure the recruitment, retention and motivation of sufficient teachers of the required quality.

## Schools

We draw attention to the growing body of evidence indicating that while other factors such as pupils' home backgrounds affect their behaviour, school-based influences are also very important. The most effective schools seem to be those that have created a positive atmosphere based on a sense of community and shared values.

We recommend that head teachers and their senior management teams should take the lead in developing school plans for promoting good behaviour. Such plans should ensure that the school's code of conduct and the values represented in its formal and informal curricula reinforce one another; promote the highest possible degree of consensus about standards of behaviour among all staff, pupils and parents; provide clear guidance to all three groups about these standards and their practical application; and encourage staff to recognize and praise good behaviour as well as dealing with bad behaviour. Punishments should make the distinction between minor and more serious misbehaviour clear to pupils, and should be fairly and consistently applied.

We see the head teacher's management style as a crucial factor in encouraging a sense of collective responsibility among staff, and a sense of commitment to the school among pupils and their parents.

We point out the links between the content and methods of delivery of the school curriculum and the motivation and behaviour of pupils, particularly those who are not successful academically. We emphasize the importance of the Secretaries of State ensuring that the National Curriculum offers stimulating and suitably differentiated programmes of study for the full ability range, and that the national assessment system is supportive and not threatening. We urge schools to achieve the best possible match between the needs and interests of individual pupils and the curriculum which they are required to follow.

We stress the importance of personal and social education as a means of promoting the values of mutual respect, self-discipline and social responsibility which underlie good behaviour, and we recommend that personal and social education should be strengthened both inside and outside the National Curriculum.

We emphasize the importance of the pastoral role of class teachers and form tutors and the need for schools to maintain regular contact with the education welfare service and other support agencies rather than calling them in as a last resort.

We draw attention to evidence indicating links between the appearance of school premises and the behaviour of pupils. We stress the need for appropriate building design. We urge all schools to develop policies to deal with litter, graffiti and other damage, and to follow the good example set by the best primary schools in displaying pupils' work.

We highlight the problems that many schools are experiencing during the lunch break.

We draw attention to evidence indicating that the most effective schools tend to be those with the best relationships with parents. We urge heads and teachers to ensure that they keep parents well informed, that their schools provide a welcoming atmosphere which encourages parents to become involved, and that parents are not only told when their children are in trouble but when they have behaved particularly well.

We recommend that schools' policies on discipline should be communicated fully and clearly to parents. If children are excluded from school for an indefinite period, the school should readmit them only after an agreement setting out the conditions under which they will be allowed to return has been signed by their parents.

## Parents

We highlight the crucial role parents play in shaping the attitudes which produce good behaviour in school. Parents need to provide their children with firm guidance and positive models through their own behaviour. Not all parents appreciate the degree of commitment and consistency required to provide such guidance. We think schools have an important part to play in preparing pupils for the responsibilities of parenthood. We therefore recommend that education for parenthood should be fully covered in school personal and social education programmes, and that the government should develop a post-school education strategy aimed at promoting socially responsible parenthood.

We recommend that parents should take full advantage of all formal and informal channels of communication made available by schools, and that parent–teacher associations should ensure that their activities are accessible and rewarding to as many parents as possible.

We conclude that there is a need to increase parental accountability for their children's behaviour. We ask the government to explore the possibilities for imposing civil liability on parents for damage or injury done by their children in school.

## Pupils

We draw attention to evidence indicating that pupils tend to behave more responsibly if they are given responsibilities. We recommend that schools should create opportunities for pupils of all ages to take on appropriate responsibilities, and that they should recognize pupils' non-academic achievements. We welcome the government's support for the development of records of achievement as a means of promoting a sense of responsibility among pupils.

We stress the need for the rapid assessment of the special educational needs of pupils with emotional and behavioural difficulties by all LEAs. We urge schools and LEAs to ensure that failure to identify and meet the learning needs of some pupils is not a cause of their bad behaviour.

Our evidence indicates that, while all LEAs make alternative provision for the most difficult pupils, its pattern tends to be a more or less improvised response to needs and difficulties. We recommend that all LEAs should review their alternative provision and, in determining its future pattern should aim to provide adequate, appropriate and cost-effective support services for schools and individual pupils. We suggest that the most effective provision is likely to be based on support teams of specialist teachers working in mainstream schools with access to places in on-site units and, in exceptional cases, off-site units.

We highlight the strong concerns expressed to us about the effect that violent television programmes may be having on childrens' attitudes and behaviour. We emphasize the need for careful regulation and monitoring of this aspect of broadcast, cable or video material, and the responsibility of parents for restricting their children's access to antisocial images. We recommend that broadcasters should take full account of their educational responsibilities for all television programmes.

## Attendance

Our evidence indicates that, while overall attendance rates seem to have remained relatively stable for many years, there are significant differences in the rates for individual schools which cannot always be explained by differences in their catchment areas. We encourage heads and teachers to take action to minimize unauthorized absence and internal truancy.

## Police

We encourage head teachers to develop clear understandings with local police forces about how intruders in their schools should be dealt with. We emphasize the value of school–police liaison projects and, in particular, the contribution that the police can make to education for responsible citizenship.

## Governors

We identify two major areas in which governors can help to promote good behaviour in schools. One is the positive contribution that they can make to developing and monitoring their school's policy on discipline. The other is through the decisive part that they play in the appointment of staff, especially the head teacher. We emphasize the importance of governors looking for the personal qualities required for managing of a school or a classroom effectively, and for working as part of a team.

## Local Education Authorities

We urge LEAs to develop their management information systems so that they can target their consultancy and support services on schools in difficulty. We stress the need for them to provide more effective consultancy services, particularly in the areas of school management and institutional change, and to ensure that the guidance and support systems which they provide for schools are coherent and properly coordinated.

## Government

We point out that most teachers see smaller classes as an important contribution towards reducing the problem of classroom disruption, but that it is difficult to identify relationships between class size and pupils' behaviour. We recommend that the Secretaries of State should commission research to investigate these relationships.

# CHAPTER 12

# Communication. What are its classroom characteristics?

There are seven readings in this chapter and they address a wide range of issues concerning the use of language in school contexts.

We begin with Wells (12.1) to establish the first important principle, that communication is about the creation of meaning with others. His examples come from work with young children, but the principle applies in any situation, as does his argument about the limitations of transmission forms of teaching. The latter is extended in Reading 12.2, by Barnes's classic work contrasting 'transmission' and 'interpretation' views of education. However, Edwards and Mercer (12.3) show how difficult it is for teachers and pupils to build knowledge together in classrooms, for there is always a tension between control of the class and responsiveness to each learner. Whoever said that classroom communication was easy?

Davies, in Reading 12.4, helps us to work though the competing claims of those who demand standard English and those who emphasize the appropriateness of language use. Meanwhile, Blackledge (12.5) shows how the cultural and linguistic backgrounds of bilingual learners can be used as a rich resource for classroom learning. In Reading 12.6, Collins draws attention to the quiet children who are often overlooked in classrooms. Why do they withdraw from communication, and what should we do about it?

Finally, we conclude with a powerful analytic framework by Webster, Beveridge and Reed (12.7). This enables systematic comparison of teaching–learning activities and analysis of the structure of communication. Just who is in control? And who, in such circumstances, feels engaged?

The parallel chapter of *Reflective Teaching* considers the major characteristics of classroom communication: the quantity, balance of participation and the content of talk. There is a section on language and inclusion, dealing with standard English, bilingualism, diversity and the plight of those children who find it hard to join in with classroom communication. 'Key Readings' provides ideas for taking the issues further, and *RTweb* remains as an additional resource if you need it.

📖 READING 12.1

# Conversation and the reinvention of knowledge

Gordon Wells

Gordon Wells and his collaborators produced an important study of the ways in which young children acquire language and 'make meaning' as they develop through home and school. This extract focuses on the conditions which facilitate high-quality conversation and learning. In particular, Wells sees this as 'the guided reinvention of knowledge' – a view which he contrasts with the transmission mode which many adults adopt in their interaction with children (see Reading 12.2).

How was your 'reinvention of knowledge' guided when you were young?

Edited from: Wells, G. (1986) *The Meaning Makers*. Oxford: Heinemann Educational, 216–22

When I communicate with other people, whether it is to inform, request or persuade, what I have in mind is an idea – an event, action or outcome – that I intend they should understand. However, this idea arises from my mental model of the world, which is in itself the product of my unique personal biography. Nobody else has exactly the same mental model of the world, since nobody else has had exactly the same experience. It follows, therefore, that nobody can have exactly the same ideas as I have.

Even if my listener were able to form the same ideas as I have, however, I still am not able to transmit my ideas directly to him or her in all their simultaneity and multifaceted particularity, since language, the most effective means of communication available, requires that I select and arrange what I mean in an ordered sequence that is compatible with the possibilities of syntax and vocabulary. Furthermore, while my ideas are personal and particular, the categories of language, in terms of which I now have to represent them, are public and general. It is simply not possible, therefore, to convey the ideas that I have in mind in a form that does full justice to their simultaneous complexity and specificity.

In normal conversation between mature adult members of the same culture, this does not normally cause a problem. Their past experience, both of language and of the world to which it refers, is sufficiently similar for there to be a considerable overlap between them in the idea they might wish to communicate. Furthermore, in speech at least, there are strategies available for negotiating over the intended meaning if a mismatch is suspected. Finally, where conversational meaning is jointly construed over successive turns, there are opportunities to amplify or modify what one has said in the light of the feedback received in subsequent contributions. Although participants in a conversation never know for sure what the other meant by a particular utterance, over the conversation as a whole there are sufficient opportunities for each to calibrate his or her interpretation of what is meant against that of the other for a consensus to be reached that is usually adequate for most communication purposes.

On the other hand, where the conversational participants come from different cultural backgrounds, or where they differ greatly in their level of cognitive and linguistic maturity – as is the case in interactions between children and their parents or teachers – the possibility of misunderstanding is both substantial and ever present. And unless they – or at least the more mature of the participants – take the necessary steps, the meanings that they construct on the basis of their differing mental models and linguistic resources are likely to become increasingly divergent.

When considering the ways in which adults can facilitate their children's language development, four principles were suggested:

- to treat what the child has to say as worthy of careful attention;

- to do one's best to understand what he or she means;

- to take the child's meanings as the basis for what one says next;

- in selecting and encoding one's message, to take account of the child's ability to understand – that is, to construct an appropriate interpretation.

Where these principles are followed by both participants, it is possible for minds to make contact – even when they are separated by wide differences in maturity and experience.

Conversation may not be perfect as a means of information exchange, therefore, but when engaged in collaboratively, it can be an effective medium for learning and teaching. In any case, since there is no better alternative, we must do the best we can.

If the argument above is correct, it follows that the conception of teaching as 'transmission' must be a mistaken one. First, it is not possible, simply by telling, to cause students to come to have the knowledge that is in the mind of the teacher. Knowledge cannot be transmitted. It has to be constructed afresh by each individual on the basis of what is already known and by means of strategies developed over the whole of that individual's life both outside and inside the classroom. On both these counts there are bound to be substantial differences between the individuals in any class of students and, hence, a wide variation in the interpretations that are put upon the teacher's words. Unless students are given opportunities to formulate the sense they make of new topics in their own way, using their own words, an important means of gaining understanding is lost. In addition, the teacher loses the opportunity to discover what meanings the students bring to the topic and so is unable to make his or her contributions contingently responsive.

Second, a unilateral definition of what is to count as worthwhile knowledge and of how it is to be constructed undervalues the contributions that students can make in terms of their own experience, interest and methods of inquiry, thereby impoverishing the learning experience. Furthermore, to override their natural predisposition to attempt to construct their own knowledge is to force them into a relatively passive role, with a consequent reduction in their commitment to the endeavour and an increase in the likelihood that what is learned will not be integrated into their action-oriented model of the world and so will soon be forgotten.

In sum, what is wrong with the transmission model is that it places the teacher or textbook at the centre of the educational enterprise and focuses almost exclusively on the input, in the mistaken belief that, to obtain the desire outcomes, what is most important is to ensure that the input is well selected, sequenced and presented in terms of the educated adult's understanding of what is to be learned.

However, once we give due recognition to the fact that knowledge can only be constructed by individual knowers and that this occurs most effectively when they have an active engagement in all the processes involved, it becomes clear that a different model of education is required – one that is based on a partnership between students and teachers, in which the responsibility for selecting and organizing the tasks to be engaged in is shared.

To urge that classrooms should be placed in which the curriculum is negotiated – where students are encouraged to take the role of expert when they are able to do so, and where they have a part in determining the goals to be aimed for and the procedures to be followed – may seem to be reducing the importance of the role of the teacher. However, this is very far from being the case. What is required, though, is a different conception of the relationship between teacher and students – one in which the teacher aims to facilitate learning rather than to direct it. This is not to deny the teacher's greater expertise and experience, but to argue that it will be of much greater value to students if it is offered collaboratively rather than being imposed.

Nor am I suggesting that the teacher should relinquish the overall responsibility for setting directions, proposing specific content or evaluating achievement. On the contrary, final decisions on these matters require informed judgement that can only be gained through professional training and experience. Nevertheless, in fulfilling these responsibilities, the teacher should explain the criteria on which decisions are based so that, within the limits of their capabilities, students can share in the day-to-day planning of learning activities to an increasing degree. The aim, therefore, should be to foster the development of students' ability to take control of their own learning so that eventually they can assume these responsibilities for themselves.

Following these principles, teaching can no longer be seen as the imparting of information to relatively passive recipients and then checking to see that they can correctly reproduce it. Instead, it is more appropriately characterized as a partnership in learning. The tasks of the partners are necessarily different as a result of their differing levels of expertise, but the goal is the same for students and teacher alike. Without too much exaggeration, it can be described as the guided reinvention of knowledge.

We are the meaning makers – every one of us: children, parents and teachers. To try to make sense, to construct stories, and to share them with others in speech and in writing is an essential part of being human. For those of us who are more knowledgeable and more mature – parents and teachers – the responsibility is clear: to interact with those in our care in such a way as to foster and enrich their meaning making.

## READING 12.2

# Knowledge, communication and learning

Douglas Barnes

> *From Communication to Curriculum* has been an extremely influential book on language use in schools. In this brief extract, Douglas Barnes represents some of the issues discussed by Wells in the previous reading and offers a model of classroom communication in which the 'transmission' of official school knowledge is contrasted with the 'interpretation' of everyday action knowledge. There are clear resonances here with the contrasting views of learning within Chapter 6 and the same issue is addressed in Reading 18.5 in a discussion of the struggle for teachers' understanding of learning when the National Curriculum was being implemented.
>
> How does this model relate to the teaching of subject knowledge in your classroom?
>
> Edited from: Barnes, D. (1975) *From Communication to Curriculum*. London: Penguin Books, 146–9

Figure 12.2.1 is intended to have the status of a hypothesis regarding the relationship between transmission and interpretation and the distinction between 'school knowledge' and 'action knowledge'.

The strong vertical lines represent four dimensions of classroom communication which I hypothesize will vary together. The horizontal broken lines represent this relationship, and in explaining the diagram I shall read across the upper line first.

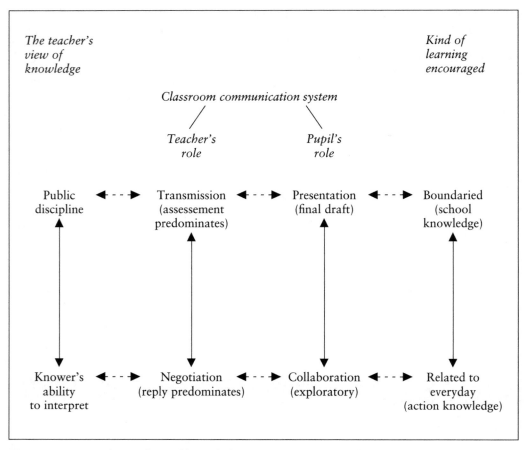

**Figure 12.2.1** Relationships of knowledge, communication and learning

If a teacher sees knowledge as existing primarily in a public discipline he will set up classroom communication so that transmission and assessment predominate. This will compel pupils to adopt a mainly presentational performance in which speech and writing perform 'final draft' functions. This will encourage boundaried learning in which the new knowledge is not brought into relationship with the learner's purposes and interests.

If a teacher sees knowledge as existing primarily in the knower's ability to interpret, he will emphasize the reply aspect of his classroom role, thus making possible a negotiation between his knowledge and his pupils' knowledge. This will open to them a collaborative approach in which the exploratory functions of speech and writing predominate. This will encourage pupils to relate new knowledge to their existing purposes and interests.

If knowledge is regarded as 'content', the valued possession of a group, teaching becomes a package deal. The teacher offers his own values and habits of mind wrapped up inextricably with his subject matter; his pupils are faced with a take-it-or-leave-it. If we wish to encourage pupils to be able to adapt to new problems, and to take responsibility for their own actions rather than to follow custom, then a passive view of learning will not do. In making the ethical decision to prepare pupils for choice and responsibility, teachers implicity choose also an interpretation view of learning. What is of practical interest is that a large proportion of teachers who would publicly assert their ends to be a world of self-responsible and flexible people do not in fact will the means which are required. That is, they see teaching primarily as an act of transmitting existing knowledge, minimizing the part actively played by pupils. This puts a premium upon routine performances. School learning becomes a special form of activity which need not impinge upon the pupil's life outside school and the values which inform it. Teaching in which transmission predominates is the negation of 'education for living'.

To advocate an interpretation view of education is not to argue that teachers should never present knowledge to their pupils, but rather to imply that certain patterns of communication should follow the presentation, as pupils negotiate their own ways of grasping the knowledge thus presented.

 READING 12.3

# Classroom discourse and learning

## Derek Edwards and Neil Mercer

> This extract is from the conclusion of *Common Knowledge*, a book which reports detailed research using video recordings of lessons and analysis of teacher–pupil language interaction and associated learning. In a sense, it constitutes a further, and particularly constructive, exploration of the tension between 'transmission' and 'interpretive' modes of language learning. The role of the teacher is highlighted in the creation of 'joint understandings' and 'cognitive socialization through language' (see also Reading 7.3 by Vygotsky, several other readings in Chapter 7 and, in particular, Reading 13.2).
>
> Think of a short linguistic interaction between yourself and a pupil. How do Edwards and Mercer's three conclusions relate to your example?
>
> Edited from: Edwards, D. and Mercer, N., (1987) *Common Knowledge: The Development of Understanding in the Classroom.* London: Methuen, 156–68

Our findings suggest three main conclusions about the educational processes we have observed.

- *Experiential learning and teacher control:* Despite the fact that the lessons were organized in terms of practical actions and small-group joint activity between the pupils, the sort of learning that took place was not essentially a matter of experiential learning and communication between pupils. The role of the teacher was crucial throughout, both in shaping the general pattern and content of the lesson, and in producing the fine-grained definition of what was done, said and understood.

- *Ritual and principle:* While maintaining a right control over activity and discourse, the teacher nevertheless overtly espoused and attempted to act upon the educational principle of pupil-centred experiential learning, and the importance of pupils' engagement in practical activity and discovery. This led to the pupils' grasp of certain important concepts being essentially 'ritual', a matter of what to do or say, rather than 'principled', i.e. based on conceptual understanding. Particular sorts of classroom discourse that appeared to underlie the creation of such procedural knowledge included a heavy reliance on 'cued elicitation', together with an overriding concern to conduct the lessons in terms of getting through the set of planned activities, rather than, say, making sure that a planned set of concepts were understood by everyone.

● *Language and the socialization of cognition:* The overriding impression from our studies is that classroom discourse functions to establish joint understandings between teacher and pupils, shared frames of reference and conception, in which the basic process is one of introducing pupils into the conceptual world of the teacher and, through her, of the educational community. To the extent that the process of education can be observed taking place in the situated discourse of classrooms, it is on our evidence essentially a process of cognitive socialization through language.

The relation of power and control to the creation of joint understandings in both problematic and of great importance. An inherent part of education is an asymmetry of roles between teacher and learner. Much of the process remains mysterious. In however friendly and informal a manner, they are frequently asked to do things, learn things, understand things, for no apparent reason other than that it is what the teacher wants them to do. The goals and purposes of the lesson are not revealed. Indeed, neither often are the concepts that the lesson may have been designed to 'cover'.

However, the asymmetry of teacher and learner is essential to the 'zone of proximal development', and so also is the notion of control. Children do not simply acquire knowledge and vocabulary. They acquire at the same time the capacity for self-regulation. Just as verbal thought originates as social discourse, so self-regulated behaviour begins with the regulation of one's behaviour by other people. The successful process involves a gradual handover of control from teacher to learner, as the learner becomes able to do alone what could previously be done only with help. In formal education, this part of the process is seldom realized. For most pupils, education remains a mystery beyond their control, rather than a resource of knowledge and skill with which they can freely operate.

There appears to be a fundamental dilemma for our teachers – that of balancing the conflicting demands of, on the one hand a child-centred ideology of learning and on the other hand, an essentially socializing role as the society's agents of cultural transmission in the context of a system of compulsory education.

## READING 12.4

# 'Correct' or 'appropriate' language?

Chris Davies

This reading addresses the issue of 'correctness' in the use of English, and in the teaching of English. The role of the National Literacy Strategy in England is considered in terms of how to balance correct and appropriate language. Ultimately, it is argued, children have a right to effective literacy – which includes much more than simple correctness, important though that may still be.

Edited from: Davies, C. (2000) '"Correct" or "appropriate"? Is it possible to resolve the debate about which should be promoted in the classroom', in Davison, J. and Moss, J. (eds) *Issues in English Teaching*. London, New York: Routledge, 110, 113–6.

At most levels within the profession, it is likely that there is general agreement about the need for teachers of English to treat the fragile confidence of learners with considerable care. This is particularly so if the children become conscious that their own forms of language do not match the language registers of formal education. At a basic level, this requires that teachers show sufficient patience and restraint to balance the identification of errors, whether in writing or speech, with the identification of the linguistic achievement. Sometimes that merely means simply not marking every error in red pen, or interrupting a speaker in mid-flow, but in more positive terms it entails the conscious effort by teachers to recognize and acknowledge what has actually been achieved in novice attempts at literacy.

Sensitivity to the anxieties of learners is not the whole story, of course. We also owe them a firm conceptual framework upon which to develop their own capacities with language. English teachers would, for the most part, view the notion of appropriateness as providing this, in a far more powerful way than the rather more simplistic notion of correctness. This, it must be understood, constitutes no more than a starting point for helping children to develop the literacy and oracy skills and understandings that will carry them through their education and out into the adult world, but it is one that possesses sufficient conceptual coherence to provide a useful foundation for thinking about language use.

The notion of appropriateness recognizes the simple linguistic truth that there is always more than one way of saying anything – and that is the job of any mature language user to choose what will work best for their particular purpose. This is the case whether writing an academic essay, a love letter, an analysis of investment possibilities, or a note on the fridge door for your mum. Decisions about tone of voice, level of formality, tentativeness versus assurance, humour versus solemnity, etc., all come down to decisions about what kinds of vocabulary and syntax – what register – will be most appropriate in order to communicate whatever it is you must communicate to the listener or to the reader.

The crucial point here is that, underlying all such decisions, the notion of correctness is never abandoned – indeed, it is always central. But the question is less likely to be 'is this correct or not?', as if there was only one permitted way of saying or writing anything, but 'what would be correct in the case of this particular register?'. In effect the central question to be asked in relation to any task involving speaking or writing is: 'what language will work best in order to achieve this particular goal?'. Conceptualizing speaking or writing tasks in terms of appropriateness does not mean indifference to whether the job has been done correctly – rather, it means thinking about what constitutes 'correct' in any particular context. Thus, when we concern ourselves with the question of what is appropriate in language, we are also implicitly concerned with questions of correctness.

The current government is enacting a strong commitment to the improvement of children's language use, in the form of its National Literacy Strategy. The emphasis in this goes far beyond the enforcement of correctness. It is interesting, indeed, that – despite the immense amount of detailed grammatical work contained in the learning proposed for the daily Literacy Hour – the prescriptive teaching of correct English is not explicitly emphasized:

> Through Key Stage 2, there is a progressive emphasis on the skills of planning, drafting, revising, proof-reading and presentation of writing. The range of reading and writing increases and, with it, the need for pupils to understand a wider variety of texts, their organisation and purposes. Of course, pupils also need to continue to work on autonomous strategies for spelling and correcting their own mistakes. (DfEE, 1998c, p. 5)

The Strategy does, though, require the teaching of a vast amount of knowledge about language which will, it is hoped, provide a firm foundation upon which children can learn to develop their own language resources. The spirit of this guidance attempts to be non-prescriptive, with its emphasis on helping children to develop autonomous literacy strategies, and to correct their own writing. It is too early to say whether this really represents a satisfactory balance between prescription and the provision of support for the learner.

Reports of its implementation suggest that the Literacy Hour itself has introduced a marked degree of relentless seriousness into the early literacy experiences of young primary school children. It does, though, constitute a radically new approach to the whole issue, and may develop into something very important when the practical efforts of working primary school teachers have perhaps succeeded in eliminating some of its excesses.

At the same time, educational policy-makers seem now to be trying hard to address the issue of Information and Communications Technology, which has, until now, had relatively minor impact upon formal education. Sooner or later, this technology will take upon itself most of the difficulties and decisions that writers currently face in writing accurate, standard English. Even now, word-processors offer guidance on spelling and grammar, which, with every upgrade, becomes both more competent and more intrusive. There is a real problem of homogenization implied in progress of this kind. It could be that stylistic variation will be sacrificed, or regularized, in the interests of painless text production, which will potentially have a reductive effect on the range of choices available both when writing or speaking.

Equivalent reductions in the variability of speech are already underway as a result of the explosion in mass communication, over satellite and cable TV, the Internet, and as a result of the role of English as an overwhelmingly dominant world.

Although schools will experience these changes only gradually, the identification of this trend is important for the way that it focuses our attention on the longer-term question of what should be the central priorities of literacy teaching in the future. English teaching has, in fact, moved a very long way from the passionate but inward-looking concerns of creative/expressive writing in the 1960s. Nowadays – as initiatives such as the National Literacy Strategy demonstrate inescapably – we have learned to view literacy as a basic right of all young people, and something that is considerably more sophisticated than the notion of unvarying correctness could ever permit us to contemplate:

> The great divide in literacy is not between those who can read and write and those who have not learned how to. It is between those who have discovered what kinds of literacy society values and how to demonstrate their competencies in ways that earn recognition. (Meek, 1991, p. 9)

As the National Literacy Strategy also emphasizes, literacy is above all about the autonomous capacity to manage complex language resources in one's own interests.

## READING 12.5

# Language, culture and story in the bilingual primary school

## Adrian Blackledge

This reading draws attention to the diversity of languages is the UK and to the rich resource they provide for language learning. In particular, Adrian Blackledge draws on his classroom experience to show how bilingual children can develop their confidence and enhance their learning when drawing on their home languages and cultures. Story is shown to be an important means for connection and affirmation.

There is a more general point here about the valuing of home languages. Is there more that could be done in relation to the language of your pupils?

Edited from: Blackledge, A. (1994) 'Language, culture and story in the bilingual primary school', in Blackledge, A. (ed.) *Teaching Bilingual Children*. Stoke-on-Trent: Trentham books, 43–7, 55–7

Children in British schools speak more than 200 languages. As many as 500,000 children learn to speak a language other than English at home before they encounter English at school. It has long been recognized that children's primary learning medium is their first language. Yet at policy-making level there has been scant recognition of these other languages of Britain, of their immense value as a resource, or of the crucial part they have to play in the education of bilingual children. Still less have governments encouraged teachers to promote the development of children's languages in the classroom, preferring to turn a deaf ear to the voices of more than half a million children.

As a teacher in a multilingual primary classroom I became aware that bilingual children's work would sometimes improve dramatically when they used their home language. This was particularly evident when children were telling stories to each other in their own languages.

In a large, multilingual school in Birmingham, children from Year 6 told stories to children from Year 3 in homogeneous linguistic groups. During a series of weekly storytelling sessions, stories were told in Sylheti, Mirpuri and Malay. Some groups of bilingual children were asked to tell their stories in English. All children were then asked to write one of their stories in English. It soon became clear that most of the children telling stories in their first language were relating tales which originated in the narrative wealth of their home culture. In the course of this work children discussed their experiences of telling and listening to stories. The following is a transcript of part of a conversation with four Mirpuri-speaking girls in Year 6.

Teacher: Where do your stories come from?
Shakila: No, it doesn't matter. It depends who I am telling it to I suppose. If I was telling it to a teacher, or to Saima, I would use English. If I was telling it to my little brother, he's four and doesn't know English really yet, I would use Mirpuri.
Teacher: But you don't think you tell the story better in Mirpuri, even though it is told to you in Mirpuri?
Shakila: No, it's just who I'm talking to.
Teacher: What about you two – do you prefer to tell stories in English or Mirpuri?
Noreen: I think English, because I can explain them better in English.
Sabrina: Yes, I think so, too. You can explain the stories better in English.
Teacher: Even if the stories are told to you in Mirpuri?

Sabrina:     Yes, even when my aunt or grandma tells me a story in Mirpuri, I can tell it better in English, because I usually hear more stories in English.

Teacher:     What about you, Saika, which language do you prefer to use to tell stories?

Saika:       I don't know, it doesn't matter. I can tell it the same in both.

Teacher:     You don't think, like Noreen and Sabrina, that you tell stories better in English?

Saika:       No I don't think so.

Teacher:     The story you told today, where did you first hear it, and in which language?

Saika:       My grandma told it to me in Mirpuri. She doesn't speak English.

Teacher:     Is it just as easy to tell that story in English as in Mirpuri?

Saika:       Yes, it's the same.

Savva (1990) reminds us that 'bilingual children's language experience is not the same: each of them has a different linguistic background'. The four girls in this conversation apparently have very similar linguistic histories: each born in Britain to Mirpuri-speaking parents and educated at the same school from the age of four, yet they have different perceptions of their abilities to tell sophisticated stories in their first language. While Saika and Shakila feel that they have equal narrative facility in Mirpuri and English, Noreen and Sabrina have a different view of their storytelling skills in the two languages. Noreen and Sabrina both feel that they are better able to 'explain' their story in English than in Mirpuri. This perception of their language preferences raises an important question: are Noreen and Sabrina's narrative skills (and therefore, by implication other language skills) being replaced by the skills they are learning in English? Levine (1990) emphasizes the importance of a dialectical relationship between the languages children already know and their becoming adept in the new one:

It is our hope, and what we work for, that English will become an *additional*, not a displacing language in our pupils' lives.

If English is to replace rather than add to the languages of the children we teach, we must ask what is the effect of such a programme on their cultural identity, their self-esteem and sense of their place in the community.

The monolingual teacher can do much to encourage an additive rather than a subtractive bilingual environment; that is, a classroom environment in which children are adding a new language to their existing skills rather than replacing their first language with that of the school. A bilingual education programme will be successful if the school actively promotes the value and use of children's languages. The curriculum need not be taught through those languages. If children are encouraged to use their languages at their convenience, and these languages are accorded genuine value in the classroom, it is likely that existing and new languages will develop side by side.

Cummins and Swain (1986) provide evidence from a range of bilingual education programmes to show that experience with either first or second language can promote development of the linguistic proficiency underlying both languages. Skills learned in one language will transfer readily to another. Thus if children speak in their home language for part of the curriculum they are not wasting time that could be spent 'learning English'. In fact their development of skills in the home language enables them to learn English more proficiently and with greater sophistication. Children are able to add a new language to their existing skills when their first language is strongly reinforced by a committed bilingual education programme in the school.

Most of the 50 children in my study were aware of using languages at the mosque which they rarely used elsewhere, e.g. Urdu for instruction, Arabic for reading the Quran. All of the children said they used English and the home language at school; many added that they used English in the classroom, and the home language mainly in the playground. Although most of the children said they hear stories in English and the home language, a majority said they prefer to tell stories in English. However, almost all of the children qualified this by saying, as Shakera (Sylheti) does, that their language of narrative depends on their audience.

> If I tell it to someone who speaks my language I would tell it in my language because they won't understand the words that are hard for that person. So it would be easy in my language for them.

When encouraged to use their home language for storytelling, bilingual children will bring to the classroom the narrative riches of their culture. Of the bilingual children telling stories in their home language as part of our project, the vast majority told a story which originated in their home culture. Of those bilingual children telling stories in English, fewer than half told a story which originated in their home culture. The majority of children working in English wrote stories drawn from experiences in their own domestic lives in Birmingham. In general, the stories originating in the home culture were more sophisticated then those of local origin. Shakila's story of 'The King and his Seven Wives', told in Mirpuri, was based in the rich narrative tradition of the Indian sub-continent; Saima's story, 'Three Wishes, No More!' was set in Pakistan, an adaptation of a tale she first heard in Mirpuri. She told the story in Mirpuri and wrote it in English. The children's stories originating in the home culture tended to have folk/fairy-tale characteristics, while stories set in local contexts tended to be more mundane accounts of daily life. Umar's Malaysian folk-tale of 'The Elephant and the Ants' provided a further example of a story told in home language, then written in English.

Children and their families hold a wealth of learning opportunities. The stories they tell, which have perhaps never been written down before they write them; the chance to share part of their culture, and for that to be valued by other children; their knowledge of language use in different contexts; the opportunity to accord status to a variety of languages by making authentic use of them in the curriculum – all of these valuable resources are easily overlooked. If bilingual children are to use their whole linguistic repertoire in schools, they must be confident that their languages have a genuine role to play in all areas of the curriculum and in all areas of school life.

By these means schools will begin to provide an additive orientation to bilingual education, developing in children the ability, confidence and motivation to succeed.

---

### READING 12.6

# Pupils silenced by anxiety

Janet Collins

> In this reading, Janet Collins draws attention to the needs of those children who are often overlooked in busy classrooms – the 'quiet' children. Such children, she argues, may actually have significant needs which teachers need to be sensitive to.
>
> In your classroom, which children get most of your attention? And which get least?
>
> Edited from: Collins, J. (1996) *The Quiet Child*. London, New York: Cassell

Based on my work with pupils who rarely speak in class and who find it difficult to collaborate with peers, I am convinced that habitually quiet and non-participatory behaviour in school is detrimental to personal development and learning. To illustrate what I mean by quiet non-participatory behaviour I will refer to two of the pupils I observed as they worked with teachers and pupils in mainstream classroom settings during the last two years of primary school and the first year of secondary school. These observations are supported by data from one-to-one interviews carried out with the pupils, their teachers and their parents. It is important to note that these are mainstream pupils who are not identified as having special educational needs of any kind.

In all my observations of Diana working with her class teachers she rarely spoke in class except to answer direct questions with short or monosyllabic answers. However, in an interview Diana connected talk with the formulation and expression of good ideas. To her, good talkers are, 'people that come out with good ideas'. Moreover, she admitted that she has her fair share of good ideas at home. The reason why she is reluctant to share her ideas in school is revealed when she describes the behaviour of a fellow pupil. Diana begins by describing Rasheeda but soon changes the 'she' to 'you' thus, perhaps unconsciously, including herself in the group of people who find it difficult to volunteer answers in class.

> . . . she never even says owt, probably because she's too shy because sometimes they think of good things and think 'No people might think it's daft' and you're worried about what other people're thinking but then say he asks someone else a question and they say the answer that you thought of Mr T——— says it's not daft, but you're always worried about what other people'll think rest of the time.

A lack of confidence and a fear of other people's scorn prevent Diana from answering the teacher's questions. Her frustration when she finds that she had the right answer is clear. Thus opportunities for dialogue with the teacher are limited by her concern for what other people might say. If, as Diana suggests, some pupils are inhibited in this way, this calls into question the value of whole-class discussions especially if such discussions constitute the major part of pupil–teacher dialogue.

More worrying still is Diana's assumption that she is somehow outside the group of those who are being taught. When asked if she talked to the teacher she said yes. However, her account of such an exchange suggested how limited such a dialogue might be.

> . . . when I am stuck he has to help me . . . work and everything but most of the time he's like talking his self like doing things on the board and things so you can't really talk to him when he's trying to learn children.

'Most of the time', Diana feels that she cannot talk to the teacher because he is teaching the children. For her, teaching seems to involve a transmission of knowledge from teacher to pupils who act as passive recipients. There is no indication here that Diana, or indeed her teacher, regards education as a collaborative search for knowledge through genuine dialogue. Moreover, Diana precludes herself from the group of children being taught. It seems that there needs to be a change of attitude and practice before Diana, and pupils like her, can actively engage in the learning process. I believe that closer relationships between pupils and teachers are central to this development. A difficulty in collaborating with peers in some circumstances certainly seemed to be at the root of some of Roxana's difficulties in school.

According to my observations, Roxana's behaviour in school was erratic, as she appeared to swing from quiet confidence to total despair. Whilst at times her behaviour seemed to be the epitome of confident self-assurance, at others she seemed to come psychically 'undone' at the mere thought of working with other pupils. The following examples illustrate how quickly and dramatically her behaviour changed in response to specific events.

The first occasion occurred during Roxana's final year in primary school. During a tape-recorded interview Roxana was asked how she would improve the small-group discussions in which she took part. She appeared to have given some thought to the subject and spoke passionately about the need for an opportunity to work as a member of mixed-sex groups. She saw this as a positive way to break down barriers of communication between the boys and girls in the class. In the context of the interview we explored the idea and tried to anticipate how such cooperation might be achieved. However, a few days later, when the opportunity came for her to work in mixed-sex groups Roxana refused to participate. What separates her inability to take part from a simple case of 'cold feet' is the seemingly total despair that she exhibited. She stood at the edge of the room physically shaking and seemed extremely close to tears. It was almost as if working with individuals who were not her close and trusted friends somehow threatened her very existence.

The speed with which Roxana appeared to shift from confidence to total despair is illustrated by a second incident, which occurred during her first year at secondary school. The lesson was music, her favourite. During the first part of the lesson Roxana appeared to be a confident and able pupil. Looking happy and self-assured, she moved easily from instrument to instrument, carrying out the teacher's instructions. Moreover, she taught other pupils, both boys and girls, how to play. Indeed her confidence seemed to grow as her suggestions as to how the music should progress were accepted by the teacher.

However, as the composition of the music neared completion and the class prepared for a 'performance' in front of another class Roxana's behaviour suddenly changed. Her countenance became sullen and unhappy. She fidgeted nervously with her fingers, and seemed prepared to become part of the audience. After an irritable comment from her teacher that she was 'being silly' she consented to take part, which amounted to nothing more than unenthusiastic tapping of a tambourine. Throughout the rest of the lesson she stood close to the classroom wall attempting to hide behind her fringe, seemingly on the verge of tears. Whatever had prompted the change of behaviour, it is not too dramatic to describe the effect as devastating.

A striking feature of this incident was the teacher's obvious irritation at Roxana's violent and seemingly wilful change of mood. When she opted out of the music lesson the teacher responded with annoyance, bordering on anger that an obviously talented musician should choose to become temperamental at a time when he was under pressure himself. If such behaviour is seen as wilful defiance, this is clearly challenging to the teacher's authority.

However, if pupils like Roxana are to be educated in mainstream school and have access to the full curriculum and social life of the school her seemingly erratic behaviour needs to be understood, not merely tolerated. Observations of Roxana over several years and in a variety of situations suggests that Roxana's sudden withdrawal was not wilful defiance but rather a defence mechanism to protect herself from being overwhelmed by what she perceived to be external threats. In many respects Roxana's frequent and dramatic shifts of mood in response to relatively minor events illustrate a need to 'preserve her existence' in the face of overwhelming anxieties.

These case studies would suggest that before pupils like Roxana can play an active and consistent role in their own education they need to:

- be made aware of their anxieties;

- learn to put their anxieties in perspective and thus reduce the incidence of anxiety;

- learn strategies that will help them to avoid or overcome anxiety.

For pupils silenced in the classroom by acute and often irrational anxieties, personal development involves learning new, more positive and secure ways of being. Where will they learn these if not at school? Attachment theory (e.g. Bowlby, 1988; Barrett and Trevitt, 1991) would suggest the need for anxious or insecure pupils to be able to rely on relationships with key members of staff to act as a 'secure base' from which they gradually learn increased independence. Where teachers are unable or unwilling to fulfil such a role professional counselling staff may be needed to provide temporary support for anxious pupils like Roxana.

## 📖 READING 12.7

# Who holds the initiative in classroom interaction?

## Alec Webster, Michael Beveridge and Malcolm Reed

This reading derives from a study of literacy development in primary and secondary schools. The research began by involving large numbers of teachers in the construction of a framework for describing and analysing key differences in classroom and communication, and this framework is described below. The model was used for detailed observational purposes, but it is also extremely useful as a more general way of reflecting on classroom practice. It is important to note that the model is not prescriptive. Indeed, it recognizes the potential 'fitness for purpose' of teaching methods and forms of communication which might be placed in each of the four quadrants.

Thinking of some of your favourite teaching strategies and lessons, how would you characterize them in terms of this framework?

Edited from: Webster, A., Beveridge, M. and Reed, M. *Managing the Literacy Curriculum: How Schools Can Become Communities of Readers and Writers*. London, New York: Routledge, 36–42

In our study, we needed a way of examining teaching and learning, whilst also accommodating some of the complexities of classroom reality. Ideally, as well as generating descriptors which could be used to quantify aspects of the teaching process, our schema would also provide signposts for professional development, for improving teaching encounters and remaking literacy within the curriculum. Not surprisingly, such a framework was not easy to come by.

As our research developed, ideas were tested out amongst teaching colleagues and in workshops held in the schools where data were to be collected. Importantly, any thoughts that we presented at this stage had to be user-friendly, look as though it might work in practice, and make links with what teachers already knew about teaching and learning. The final version of our framework, having been ratified by teachers and incorporating their ideas, is shown in Figure 12.7.1.

Two continua provide the structure for the framework. The horizontal axis is concerned with the degree of initiative, engagement and active involvement of the pupils in learning. The vertical axis is concerned with the level of management, control and mediation exercised by the teacher. Using these fundamental dimensions, we are then able to describe a wide range of classroom conditions. These include: the nature of interactions between teacher and taught; the way exercises are set and problems tackled; the quality of questioning and the nature of assessment; how process issues are discussed or reviewed; and the relative emphasis on activities such as rote drilling compared with discovery learning or free choice.

In effect, the model reflects different images of the roles of teacher and pupil which influence how the business of learning in the classroom might operate. The two continua provide a clear summary of what can be valued in any teacher's professional activity.

The model also highlights different zones of interaction: above the horizontal axis is essentially the teacher's domain, characterized by high adult management and control, whilst the area below this axis characterizes the pupil's domain, where learning is mostly managed by pupils themselves or is dependent on resources.

The framework is not intended to be a precision instrument, but a way of looking, of gauging relative emphasis. We would not expect that all that transpires in a classroom could be encapsulated by our model, or that individual teachers or pupils could be located precisely

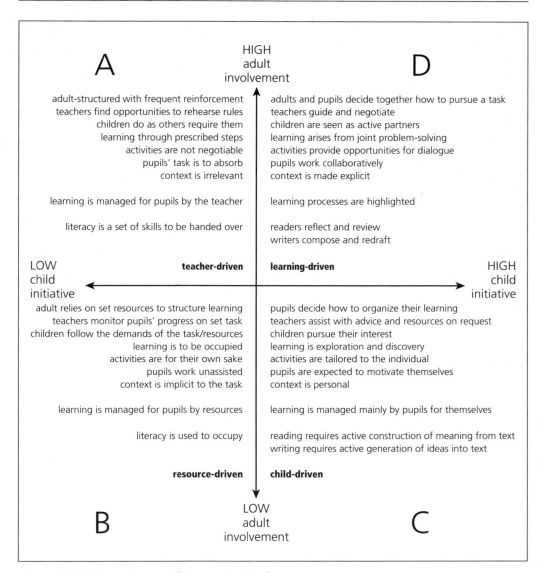

**Figure 12.7.1**   Teacher–pupil interaction in classrooms

within it. The intention is to identify predominant kinds of teaching and learning styles, how they overlap or emerge, and the possible consequences for pupils' experience.

Although our major concern was to develop a useful framework for description at this stage, teachers drew their own conclusions about how and why they worked in certain ways rather than others. We initially provided the framework without judgements attached regarding the quality or merits of the separate quadrants defined by the two axes. There are some accounts of classroom environments which suggest that, for most teachers, establishing and maintaining order and cooperation are the highest priority (see, for example, Doyle, 1986). We would expect some teachers to spend some time with some groups of pupils, in didactic mode, managing learners rather than learning. We also know, from research such as that carried out by Bennett *et al.* (1984), that strong emphasis is placed by many teachers on the practice of routine tasks and consolidating learning, perhaps using occupier resources or activities. At other times pupils may be encouraged to research problems for themselves with little direction, to pursue their own pathways and make their own discoveries or mistakes. Opportunities may also be designed for collaborative tasks which emphasize joint planning, partnership and the weighing of process issues.

In such ways, teachers are adaptive to the conditions in which they operate and which prevail at any moment in time. Volatile teaching groups, where demanding tasks are difficult to sustain, may have to be managed by coercion and a high degree of structure and control. In order to deal with some of the business of the day, teachers may require some pupils to work unaided without requesting help. Group work and experiential learning are higher-risk activities requiring more cooperation and preparation. Some tasks demand more closely supervised practical experience than others in which rote practice may be essential, such as learning tables in mathematics.

What teachers do is constrained by the nature of the learning, the resources available, levels of pupil interest and cooperation, together with a myriad of other factors which impinge on the social context of the classroom. Effective learning may or may not be high on the agenda. The types of experience characterized in the four quadrants of the model enable us to describe the dynamics of a particular teaching context in terms of adult–pupil proximation and to understand how aspects of literacy are embedded within these contexts. Our use of the term quadrant is not to imply a quasi-scientific rigour, but to indicate a teacher's sense of direction, emphasis or orientation.

## Quadrant A: teacher-driven

Quadrant A in the framework is characterized by high teacher management and didactic styles, rote teaching and prescription with little negotiation, where the pupil is assigned the role of passive recipient. All the teachers who have worked with the model recognize this image of the adult as a purveyor of knowledge, where pupils are viewed as empty vessels, some more receptive than others. In this domain, literacy teaching is seen as a set of skills to be handed over and drilled. Learning would typically progress through a sequence of adult-controlled steps, largely decontextualized, with relevance and meaning more apparent to the teacher than the learner. Learning is viewed as a matter of building, through direct teaching, from simple to complex, from smaller to larger skill sequences.

## Quadrant B: resource- or occupier-driven

In contrast, Quadrant B is characterized by lack of explicit theory, adult or child initiative, and a limited amount of management, direction, modelling, adult or child initiative. In this domain, literacy may be used mainly to occupy pupils. For example, pupils may be simply supervised in a library area without any specific reason for being there other than for those who can get on independently with their own reading.

## Quadrant C: child-driven

Quadrant C draws on child-centred models of teaching and learning, and the view that pupils are basically the architects of their own understanding. The image of the pupil is one of a self-motivated individual or mini-scientist, whilst the teacher's role is to provide a wealth of materials to furnish a rich and stimulating environment. The pupil takes much of the initiative in determining a learning pathway, and is encouraged to pursue an interest but with little guidance, structure or management.

## Quadrant D: learning-driven

Finally, Quadrant D ascribes active roles to both teachers and pupils in a learning partnership. The emphasis is on learning which is facilitated, but not controlled, by the adult. Learning is viewed as a complex process, more than just the sum of a number of small sub-skills. In fact, the smaller units of a task are seen as more readily acquired within the context of a meaningful whole. Essential to effective learning are opportunities to take risks and make mistakes in collaboration with partners who contribute different perspectives and understandings: learning is a social enterprise which draws on the immediate resources of participants.

## CHAPTER 13

# Teaching. How are we developing our strategies?

This chapter begins with a reading, from Galton and colleagues (13.1) establishing the principle that teaching strategies must be linked to learning objectives. This may seem uncontroversial, but it should not be taken for granted. Comfortable routines of teaching often seem to creep in even when alternative methods might be more effective. Of course, the key principle is 'fitness for purpose'.

Tharp and Gallimore (13.2) summarize the Vygotskian underpinning of much modern teaching with their concept of learning as 'assisted performance'. Their four-stage model is worth study and reflection. For instance, can you apply it to aspects of your own learning, and what was the role of the teaching of 'more capable others' in that? In Reading 13.3, Moyles offers an example of a teaching episode and of teaching skills intended to support 'active learning'. She identifies eight issues to consider in planning a session and these, of course, represent techniques for 'assisting performance'.

The next group of readings are more directly concerned with teaching skills. We begin with a reading from Muijs and Reynolds (13.4) who advise on the most effective techniques for 'direct instruction' – the basis of the literacy and numeracy strategies in England. Perrot (13.5) then provides an analysis of questioning skills and strategies and Phillips (13.6) focuses on ways of structuring classroom discussion. There are then two readings on group work. Bennett and Dunne (13.7) advise on the structured management of group tasks and Biott and Eason (13.8) suggest key issues for the promotion of collaborative learning.

Finally, Osler and Starkey (13.9) provide a provocative check by reviewing the pedagogic principles that are suggested by the UN Convention on the Rights of the Child. How far do you manage to fulfil these principles in your classroom work?

The associated chapter of *Reflective Teaching* has sections covering key aspects of individual, group and whole-class teaching. First, it considers class and individual dialogue, dealing with explanations, questioning, discussion and listening. The second section focuses on group activity and how best to facilitate this. At the end of the chapter, 'Key Readings' makes many helpful suggestions, amplified and updated as usual by those on *RTweb*.

READING 13.1

# Towards an appropriate theory of pedagogy

Maurice Galton, Linda Hargreaves, Chris Comber and Debbie Wall, with Anthony Pell

This reading tries to link the types of knowledge that children need to learn, with the forms of pedagogy that are most likely to bring this learning about. It identifies three forms of knowledge and three associated types of pedagogy – thus making the point very clearly that teachers need to develop a repertoire of teaching strategies. The reading draws on a major US review and the findings of two decades of research in UK primary schools.

Edited from: Galton. M., Hargreaves, L., Comber, C. and Wall, D., with Pell, A. (1999) *Inside the Primary Classroom: 20 Years on*. London, New York: Routledge, 185–9

In building up a set of pedagogic principles, we need to start with the nature of children's learning. What are the knowledge demands made upon the learner? A useful initial answer is the typology developed by Patricia Alexander and her colleagues (Alexander, P. *et al.*, 1991). They reviewed a large number of articles in journals of education and psychology, to arrive at a classification of different types of knowledge. In relation to teaching and learning in the primary school there appear to be three key elements of knowledge: procedural, conceptual and metacognitive. Each of these has implications for pedagogy.

## Procedural knowledge

Alexander, P. *et al.* (1991) define procedural knowledge as being concerned with the acquisition of information (knowing this or that about something) and the rules of acquisition or use of information (knowing how to use something). The idea of a procedure, therefore, encompasses not only the knowledge of facts but also knowing where such facts would be applicable.

Such a definition, for example, fits well with the growing use of ICT (information and communication technology) within schools. In a project that was part of the government's Superhighways Initiative, primary-aged children were engaged in various topics and were required not only to locate the relevant information on the pages of the World Wide Web (i.e. knowing about something), but to download it into their own research folders. They edited it to extract relevant information and then made use of the thesaurus within the word-processing package on the computer in order to ascribe familiar meanings to unfamiliar words (knowing how to use something). More straightforward examples would include learning and applying various algorithms in mathematics and understanding their application, or the rules of grammar and their use in appropriate language settings.

There is a clear consensus among researchers, both here and in the US, that teaching explicit procedures of this kind is best done by direct instruction (Rosenshine, 1987 [see also Reading 13.4]). This view is echoed by Charles Desforges (1995, p. 129) who states that, 'direct instruction is best used for knowledge transmission, for showing, telling, modelling and demonstrating. It is never on its own sufficient to ensure deeper understanding, problem solving, creativity or group work capacities'.

## Conceptual knowledge

The second broad classification in the typology used by Alexander, P. *et al.* is conceptual knowledge. This is knowledge of ideas and the understanding of principles, which includes defining elements, or classifying objects, and recognition of instances of belonging and not belonging to given classes. Encompassed within this definition is domain and discipline knowledge, because in order to process the vast amounts of information which defines a given class, we need to group information into sub-categories or domains. As a concept becomes a part of a formal system of learning or central to a specialized field of study, it develops into a sub-category of a discipline. As well as enabling us to order information, part of this conceptual understanding also includes what Alexander, P. *et al.* (1991) term discourse knowledge, that is knowledge about language and its uses. One element of this discourse enables us to convey our understanding of a principle or an idea to another person. To do this, we need to understand how to combine words appropriately to convey meaning in prepositional statements, which Alexander *et al.* call syntactic knowledge. The same process also involves rhetorical knowledge which has to do with an understanding of the appropriate register for the audience to whom the language is directed or, more simply, the available styles of verbal and written communication.

Constructivist views of learning have tended to concentrate on conceptual understanding and how this is enhanced. It is precisely because the process of construction and reconstruction of ideas is mediated through discourse that, as Bennett (1992) argues, social interaction is so important. Hence, while some more simple concepts can be taught in sequence as a collection of procedures, more complex activities – such as mathematical problem solving, discussion of social issues, hypothesizing in science, creative writing – should all involve some degree of cooperative activity, either with adults or with peers. Again, there is strong research support (Slavin, 1986; Bennett and Dunne, 1992; Galton and Williamson, 1992) for the argument that the successful application of cooperative group work in classrooms leads to improved achievement. Moreover, as pupil involvement increases so too does the development of such valued social outcomes as enhancing self-esteem and better understanding between different races and cultures.

## Metacognitive knowledge

The third and final major element in the scheme put forward by Alexander, P. *et al.* (1991) concerns the development of metacognitive knowledge, that is knowledge of one's cognitive processes. It embodies not only strategic knowledge but self-knowledge – that is, knowledge of ourselves as learners, including the appropriate control mechanisms required to ensure success, such as the ability to identify our own errors and monitor our own thinking.

Because metacognition requires learners to be able to regulate their own thinking, it is essentially an individual process – something that one acquires through experience while being helped and supported in the process by others more knowledgeable than oneself. Various writers, including Brown (1990) in the US and Wood (1988) in the UK, refer to this support as scaffolding. Where the teacher helps to regulate the pupil's behaviour, the scaffold, or framework, is often a simple set of key elements which allow the student to implement a procedure to solve a problem. Giving the rules for the order of multiplication where brackets are present, to enable students to carry out complex algebraic calculations, would be one example. Helping young pupils to write descriptions of familiar objects by providing cue-cards with size, shape, colour printed on each, with an instruction to write at least three lines under each heading, provides another instance.

Where pupils are learning to regulate their own thinking, the capacity to interrogate and interpret sources of evidence becomes crucial, or to put it in simpler terms, pupils need to be able to ask the right questions. The processes involved in this kind of thinking are essentially the same whether the learning is regulated by adults, peers or oneself. When pupils have the capacity to regulate their own thinking they are, therefore, able to solve problems by talking to themselves rather than with a teacher or another pupil (Brown and Palinscar, 1986). They learn to engage in the most effective forms of dialogue, particularly questioning, by modelling these internal conversations on those previously held with teachers and peers. However, as

Robin Alexander's (1991) Leeds study clearly demonstrated, occasions where children ask questions of the kind that help them to regulate their own thinking have been found to be quite rare in primary classrooms.

Scaffolding this questioning process is a central concern of what Brown and Palinscar refer to as reciprocal teaching (Rosenshine and Meister, 1994). This is primarily a process of teaching students to use specific cognitive strategies, particularly question generation and summarization. Reciprocal teaching was first used for improving reading comprehension. In this earlier study, Palinscar and Brown (1984) gave students a passage of exploratory material to read paragraph by paragraph. During this reading the pupils practised the use of four comprehension strategies: generating questions, summarizing, clarifying word meanings, and predicting what might appear in the next paragraph. During the early stages of reciprocal teaching, Brown and Palinscar recommend that the teacher assumes the major responsibility for instructing by explicitly modelling the process. The students then practise the strategies on the next section of text, and the teacher supports each student's participation through specific feedback, additional modelling, coaching, hints and explanation. In the early reading programmes reciprocal teaching often took place with individual pupils, but in more recent studies the learning is scaffolded within a cooperative learning framework where peers are invited to initiate discussion and react to other students' statements.

## Conclusion

If standards are to rise in primary schools, the previous paragraphs suggest that a very different framework is required from the simple promotion of whole-class teaching. We can now build upon Robin Alexander's framework (1995) by subdividing his discourse category into:

- direct instruction, which instructs pupils in what to do, how to do it and which checks their progress;

- enquiry, which poses problems by asking challenging questions and by offering alternative explanations; and

- scaffolding, which is mainly concerned with the development of support for pupils so that they learn to 'think for themselves'.

It is important to emphasize that those seeking to develop a theory of teaching should continually stress Gage's (1985) definition of pedagogy as 'the science of the art of teaching'. This implies that the effective teacher will always try to ensure that within given provision there are opportunities for children to display their own individuality.

READING 13.2

# Teaching as the assistance of performance

Roland Tharp and Ronald Gallimore

This reading is an elaboration of Vygotsky's ideas (see Reading 7.3), and sets out with particular clarity a four-stage model of learning in which different types of assistance in performance are characteristic: support from others; from self-regulation; from internalization; and where performance declines and new learning is necessary.

The concept of 'scaffolding' the development of understanding is illustrated by Janet Moyles in Reading 13.3 and by Gordon Wells in Reading 12.1. However, it has been found to be hard to achieve in busy classrooms. The idea of self-regulation is closely linked to pupil self-assessment (see Reading 14.5).

How does Tharp and Gallimore's four-stage model relate to your own learning? Think, for instance, about how you learned to swim, ride a bicycle or speak a new language. How does it relate to your classroom teaching?

Edited from: Tharp, R. and Gallimore, R. (1988) *Rousing Minds to Life: Teaching, Learning and Schooling in Social Context*. New York: Cambridge University Press, 28–39

To explain the psychological, we must look not only at the individual but also at the external world in which that individual life has developed. We must examine human existence in its social and historical aspects, not only at its current surface. These social and historical aspects are represented to the child by people who assist and explain, those who participate with the child in shared functioning:

Any function in the child's cultural development appears twice, or in two planes. First it appears on the social plane, and then on the psychological plane. First it appears between people as an interpsychological category, and then within the child as an intrapsychological category. This is equally true with regard to voluntary attention, logical memory, the formation of concepts, and the development of volition. (Vygotsky, 1978, p. 163)

The process by which the social becomes the psychological is called internalization: the individual's 'plane of consciousness' (i.e. higher cognitive processes) is formed in structures that are transmitted to the individual by others in speech, social interaction, and the processes of cooperative activity. Thus, individual consciousness arises from the actions and speech of others.

However, children reorganize and reconstruct these experiences.

Indeed, the child is not merely a passive recipient of adult guidance and assistance; in instructional programmes, the active involvement of the child is crucial (Bruner, 1966).

In summary, the cognitive and social development of the child proceeds as an unfolding of potential through the reciprocal influences of child and social environment. Through guided reinvention, higher mental functions that are part of the social and cultural heritage of the child will move from the social plane to the psychological plane, from the socially regulated to the self-regulated. The child, through the regulating actions and speech of others, is brought to engage in independent action and speech. In the resulting interaction, the child performs, through assistance and cooperative activity, at developmental levels quite beyond the individual level of achievement. For skills and functions to develop into internalized, self-regulated capacity, all that is needed is performance, through assisting interaction. Through this process,

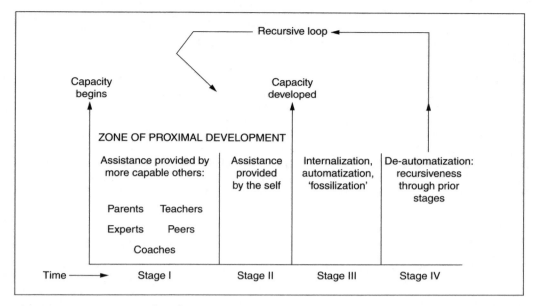

**Figure 13.2.1** Genesis of performance capacity: progression through the ZPD and beyond

the child acquires the 'plane of consciousness' of the society and is socialized, acculturated, made human.

Assisted performance defines what a child can do with help, with the support of the environment, of others, and of the self. For Vygotsky, the contrast between assisted performance and unassisted performance identified the fundamental nexus of development and learning that he called the zone of proximal development (ZPD).

The development of any performance capacity in the individual thus represents a changing relationship between self-regulation and social regulation. We present progress through the ZPD in a model of four stages. The model focuses particularly on the relationship between self-control and social control.

## Stage I: Where performance is assisted by more capable others

Before children can function as independent agents, they must rely on adults or more capable peers for outside regulation of task performance. The amount and kind of outside regulation a child requires depend on the child's age and the nature of the task: that is the breadth and progression through the ZPD for the activity at hand.

Such assistance of performance has been described as scaffolding, a metaphor first used by Wood *et al.* (1976) to describe the ideal role of the teacher.

During Stage I, we see a steadily declining plane of adult responsibility for task performance and a reciprocal increase in the learner's proportion of responsibility. This is Bruner's fundamental 'handover principle' – the child who was a spectator is now a participant (Bruner, 1983, p. 60). The developmental task of Stage I is to transit from other-regulation to self-regulation.

## Stage II: Where performance is assisted by the self

If we look carefully at the child's statements during this transition, we see that the child has taken over the rules and responsibilities of both participants in the language-game. These responsibilities were formerly divided between the adult and child, but they have now been taken over completely by the child. (Wertsch, 1979, p. 18)

Thus, in Stage II, the child carries out a task without assistance from others. However, this does not mean that the performance is fully developed or 'automatized'.

During Stage II, the relationships among language, thought and action in general undergo profound rearrangements. Control is passed from the adult to the child speaker, but the control function remains with the overt verbalization.

The phenomenon of self-directed speech reflects a development of the most profound significance. According to Vygotsky, and his follower Luria, once children begin to direct or guide behaviour with their own speech, an important stage has been reached in the transition of a skill through the ZPD. It constitutes the next stage in the passing of control or assistance from the adult to the child, from the expert to the apprentice. What was guided by the other is now beginning to be guided and directed by the self.

## Stage III: Where performance is developed, automized and 'fossilized'

Once all evidence of self-regulation has vanished, the child has emerged from the ZPD into the developmental stage for that task. The task execution is smooth and integrated. It has been internalized and 'automatized'. Assistance, from the adult or the self, is no longer needed. Indeed 'assistance' would now be disruptive. It is in this condition that instructions from others are disruptive and irritating; it is at this stage that self-consciousness itself is detrimental to the smooth integration of all task components. This is a stage beyond self-control and beyond social control. Performance here is no longer developing; it is already developed. Vygotsky described it as 'fossilized', emphasizing its fixity and distance from the social and mental forces of change.

## Stage IV: Where de-automatization of performance leads to recursion back through the ZPD

The lifelong learning by any individual is made up of these same regulated, ZPD sequences – from other-assistance to self-assistance – recurring over and over again for the development of new capacities. For every individual, at any point in time, there will be a mix of other-regulation, self-regulation and automatized processes. The child who can now do many of the steps in finding a lost object might still be in the ZPD for the activities of reading, or any of the many skills and processes remaining to be developed in the immature organism.

Furthermore, once children master cognitive strategies, they are not obligated to rely only on internal mediation. They can also ask for help when stuck or during periods of difficulty. Again, we see the intimate and shifting relationship between control by self and control by others. Even for adults, the effort to recall a forgotten bit of information can be aided by the helpful assistance of another so that the total of self-regulated and other-regulated components of the performance once again resembles the mother and child example of shared functioning. Even the competent adult can profit from regulation for enhancement and maintenance of performance.

Indeed, a most important consideration is that de-automatization and recursion occur so regularly that they constitute a Stage IV of the normal developmental process. What one formerly could do, one can no longer do. The first line of retreat is to the immediately prior self-regulating phase. A further retreat, to remembering the voice of a teacher, may be required, and consciously reconjuring the voice of a tutor – is an effective self-control technique.

But in some cases no form of self-regulation may be adequate to restore capacity, and a further recursion – the restitution of other regulation – is required. Indeed, the profession of assisting adults (psychotherapy) is now a major Western institution. In all these instances, the goal is to reproceed through assisted performance to self-regulation and to exit the ZPD again into a new automatization.

## READING 13.3

# Teaching to promote active learning

## Janet Moyles

In this reading, Janet Moyles illustrates teacher skills in assessing a classroom situation and responding to it by scaffolding learners' understandings. In this case, the learners are age 10 and the teacher both models a way of learning and, through authentic discussion, draws the children into the problem solving and leaves them in control of the process. This principle of positioning the learner 'in control' is important in active, experiential learning approaches (Rowland, 1984). It seems to work because new knowledge that has been personally discovered is often more easily appropriated into previous thinking. This key principle of 'active learning' applies with learners of any age, but is particularly significant in work with young children.

Moyles offers a number of helpful ideas for use in developing active learning techniques within a repertoire of teaching strategies.

Edited from: Moyles, J. (2001) 'Just for fun? The child as active learner and meaning-maker', in Collins, J., Insley, K. and Soler, J. (eds) *Developing Pedagogy: Researching Practice* London: Paul Chapman Publishing, 18–23

The teacher sits down beside a group of four 10-year-old children who are attempting to design and make a pulley system from a range of different materials. The children have been having some difficulty in making their pulleys work, and concentration has begun to wane. The teacher, without speaking, manipulates the various pieces of wood, pulley wheels and string under the watchful eye of the children. One child approaches and asks her what she is doing. The teacher replies that she has a problem in trying to make her pulley work and wonders if the child can think of a way of doing so. The rest of the children gather round and make various suggestions, all of which the teacher tries until one achieves the desired result and the pulley is made to work. The children analyse with the teacher how success has been achieved and evaluate the outcome, then they quickly return to their own efforts and consult with each other on producing the desired outcome. The teacher leaves the technology table, returning around ten minutes later to find a series of different pulleys being eagerly discussed and experimented with by the children.

In this incident, the actions of the teacher enabled the children to be successful in their learning outcomes and to retain the ownership and control of their own play and active learning. This is surely at the heart of good teaching. For children to achieve learning goals set by others and to add to their existing schema, they need adults who can 'scaffold' their attempts (Bruner, 1973). This must enable them to use first-hand experiences within what Vygotsky terms 'the zone of proximal development' – the gap between what the child can currently do alone and what he or she could do with support [see Reading 7.3]. Alternatively, of course, the teacher could have approached the children with questions about what they were doing or, indeed, have given directions as to what they should do to achieve the desired outcome. This approach could have left the children with the feeling that only someone outside of themselves could provide the answer to their problem, rather than the answer coming from within the children's own intellect and experiences.

With the adult operating both as model and as facilitator of their own thinking and questioning, the children were challenged to provide their own solutions rather than generating a dependency upon the teacher. The latter has been shown by researchers to create impossible situations in classes of 30 and more children, who are then all potentially dependent upon the teacher for their learning. As Darling (1994) argues:

> Once children see education as something that other people do to them, they lose the ability to take any initiative or responsibility for their own learning. In particular the kinds of enquiry that children naturally pursue are not reflected in the way traditional schooling categorises knowledge into different 'subjects'. It is this lack of correspondence which accounts for children's low motivation. Child-centred educational theory suggests that we could and should have classrooms where learning is largely self-motivated and the atmosphere is fairly relaxed. (pp. 4–5)

A model that perceives children as having a central role in their own learning also has to acknowledge teachers as learners themselves, rather than as general purveyors of existing knowledge. This means a fundamental shift in some teachers' thinking and in the strategies they apply to children's learning. Dweck and Legett (1988) emphasize, like Bruner and Vygotsky, children's need for support as they struggle to understand and make sense. One might also add the children's need to be trusted to negotiate, discuss and understand their own learning needs and be responsible for some of the outcomes. This requires practitioners who have a clear view of their own role. For example, in planning for learning sessions, teachers might wish to consider the factors below. This will lead to the active learner retaining some control over the learning activities and having opportunities to reflect on their own cognitive processes. The order can be adjusted according to the task.

1. *Entering strategy*
   What will be your starting point(s)? Introduction?

2. *Exploration model*
   What exploration will the children undertake? What materials/resources need to be available? How/by whom would they be set up?

3. *Contents*
   What do you intend the children should learn? Subject and/or processes and/or skills?

4. *Ownership and responsibility*
   How/at what point will it be possible for the practitioner to withdraw and allow the children ownership? How will the children know what they are supposed to learn through their active involvement?

5. *Adult value strategies*
   What will the practitioner role be? How will you interact/intervene in the learning and sustain/extend it? What level of support will the children require?

6. *Evaluation and analysis*
   How/when will you observe to see what children were learning in relation to concepts covered?

7. *Reflection*
   What opportunities will you provide for children to reflect on their learning and be part of the evaluation/analysis of processes and outcomes?

8. *Justification*

What kind of outcomes will you expect? How will the value of these be communicated to others?

This model is readily applied to a range of teaching and learning situations and links with the kind of teacher action shown in the cameo at the start of this reading. The teacher's entering strategy was to model the kind of actions undertaken by the children in order to enable them to understand not only the processes of their own learning but the content of the technological activity. The children could see from the teacher's actions what they were intended to learn and had opportunities to reflect on her outcomes and evaluate them in terms of their own potential achievement. The adult valued and trusted the children, giving them the responsibility and ownership of their task by leaving them to complete it, having scaffolded their attempts. She valued and evaluated the active processes of their learning equally with the outcomes. This is what could be termed 'the learning relationship'.

Teachers face several dilemmas when making this kind of learning provision for children: large class sizes, the dictates of imposed curricula, pressures from others (including parents) to provide paper evidence of children's learning, to mention but a few. Practitioners should consider, however, the outcomes of not providing appropriate experiential learning. The result is often demotivated children, who can 'perform' and conform to adult requirements but who often have little understanding of learning intentions and little responsibility for themselves as learners (Bennett and Kell, 1989). An example would be the young child who can readily count to ten and beyond but has no concept of the 'fiveness' of five, or what constitutes '5 + 1'. Hughes (1986) has shown clearly that, when adults allow children to manipulate the numbers in concrete terms through having the objects to handle and move, they are capable of much greater levels of understanding, not only of numbers but of their own metacognitive processes.

The practitioner's sensitivity and empathy with children as they work to make sense of learning opportunities is vital, for, as Willig (1990) suggests:

Teaching is about negotiation of meanings between teachers and pupils. Skilled teachers encourage pupils' contributions and look for links between the knowledge children bring to the situation and the new experiences to which they are being introduced. The act of learning then becomes an exchange of viewpoints where the learner works hard on the new material, grafts it on to existing learning and comes out of the experience with fresh insights. (p. 184)

## READING 13.4

# The main elements of effective direct instruction

Daniel Muijs and David Reynolds

Direct instruction has had significant influence in recent years through the English National Literacy and Numeracy Strategies, though it has many other applications. This reading indicates some of its significant features and research underpinnings. The reading also includes a brief account of 'weaknesses and limitations', and this may be of particular interest to teachers of younger children. Some teachers are critical of direct instruction for failing to take account of developmental needs and the interests of children (see Katz in Reading 8.4, or Dadds in 9.4).

What, for you, are the advantages and disadvantages of this approach to teaching? Can you overcome the problems?

Edited from: Muijs, D. and Reynolds, D. (2001) *Effective Teaching: Evidence and Practice*. London: Paul Chapman Publishing, 3–16

It is not enough merely to teach the whole class in order to have a lesson involving effective direct instruction. A number of conditions need to be met in order to maximize the effectiveness of these. Five will be discussed here.

## Clearly structured lessons

The lesson should have a clear structure, so students can easily understand the content of the lesson and how it relates to what they already know. Many researchers recommend starting the lesson with a review and practice of what was learned during the previous lesson, for example by going over homework, as this will allow the teacher to find out to what extent students have grasped the content of previous lessons, and therefore to what extent this content will need to be retaught.

The objectives of the lesson should be made clear to students from the outset, with examples such as 'today we are going to learn about . . .', or through writing the objectives on the board or on a flipchart. During the lesson the teacher needs to emphasize the key points of the lesson, which may otherwise get lost in the whole. A certain amount of repetition will do no harm here. At the end of the lesson the main points should once again be summarized either by the teacher, or preferably by the students themselves, e.g. through asking them what they have learned during the lesson. Sub-parts of the lesson can usefully be summarized in the same way during the course of the lesson. Teachers must also clearly signal transitions between lesson parts such as the start of a new topic or practice of the previous topic. All this not only ensures that students will remember better what they have learned, but will help them to more easily understand the content as an integrated whole, with recognition of the relationships between the parts.

## Clear, structured presentations

Within this overall structure, it is recommended that material should be presented in small steps pitched at the students' level, which are then practised before going on to the next step. This allows students to gain a sense of mastery over the content and will stop them getting bored or losing the thread of the lesson. Information should be presented with a high degree of clarity and enthusiasm. Teachers need to focus on one point at a time, avoid digressions and avoid ambiguity.

There are a number of ways to enhance the clarity of presentations. Two traditional models of presenting a topic are the deductive model and the inductive model. In the deductive model, the presentation starts with general principles or rules and goes on to more detailed and specific examples. An example of this is teaching comparative democracy. One could start with the general principle of what democracy means, and then attempt to apply this to the political system of a variety of countries. In the inductive model, the presentation starts with (real-life) examples and moves on to general rules or principles. Using the same examples, one could look at the system of government in a number of different countries, and then work out some general principles of what makes for democratic government.

## Pacing

Pacing of the lesson is an important, but not wholly uncontroversial part, of effective direct instruction. Initially, researchers suggested that lessons need to be fast paced. The advantages of this were seen to lie in maintaining momentum and interest of students, and in allowing a relatively large amount of content to be processed. However, it has been found that while this seems to be the best way to teach lower-level basic skills and younger students, in higher grades and for more demanding content the pacing needs to be slower to allow students more time to develop understanding. It is recommended that lessons designed to teach basic skills are paced in such a way that during weekly or monthly reviews students are able to respond correctly in 90–95 per cent of cases.

## Modelling

A useful procedure to follow when teaching certain topics is to model explicitly a skill or procedure. Modelling means demonstrating a procedure to learners. This can be more effective than using verbal explanations, especially with younger learners or those who prefer a visual learning style. Modelling follows this sequence: the teacher (or another person who is perceived to be an expert) demonstrates the behaviour by doing it, linking the behaviour to skills or behaviours that learners already possess. She or he needs to go through the different parts of the behaviour in a clear, structured and sequential way, explaining what she or he is doing after each step. Then learners need to memorize the steps seen, and imitate them (Ausubel, 1968).

## Use of conceptual mapping

A strategy that can help to structure the lesson in students' minds is the use of conceptual mapping. A conceptual map is a framework that can be presented to students before the topic of the lesson is presented, providing the student with an overview linking different parts of a topic and with a ready-made structure (or schema). This helps students to store, package and retain the concepts, and to link different lessons to one another. This is especially useful for more complex topics, which take several lessons to cover. An example of this is the conceptual map for a history topic in Figure 13.4.1.

## Interaction and individual/group practice

Two other crucial parts of the direct instruction lesson are interactive questioning and individual or group practice [see Readings 13.5, 13.6 and 13.7].

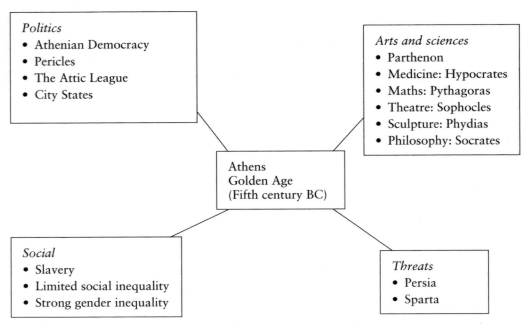

**Figure 13.4.1**   Conceptual map: the Golden Age of ancient Athens

## Some examples of direct instruction

One of the most ambitious applications of direct instruction models is currently taking place in England, in the form of the National Literacy and National Numeracy Strategies. These were developed as a result of worries about the performance of English students in these two subjects, and have been strongly inspired by research showing the effectiveness of direct instruction. Figure 13.4.2 illustrates the structure of the 'Literacy Hour', a daily hour of teaching reading and writing that all English primary schools are recommended to use.

As can be seen in the figure, this lesson plan follows a typical direct instruction model, starting with two whole-class sessions, followed by individual and group practice, with a whole-class review section at the end. This is a highly prescriptive model, and it has to be remarked that there is no research evidence to support an exact time spent on whole-class teaching and individual/group work in each lesson.

The English National Numeracy Strategy, for the teaching of primary mathematics likewise was inspired by the direct instruction model, but takes a less prescriptive approach, outlining general teaching strategies rather than setting out a strictly delineated time for each part of the lesson.

The advice to teachers given in this strategy, however, clearly shows the influence of direct instruction. Thus, on the education ministry website, teachers are advised to 'spend as much time as possible in direct teaching and questioning of the whole class, a group of students, or individuals'. It is further stated that: 'direct teaching and good interaction are as important in group work and paired work as they are in whole-class work but organizing students as a "whole class" for a significant proportion of the time helps to maximize their contact with you so that every child benefits from the teaching and interaction for sustained periods' (DfEE, 1999).

The examples above are essentially 'three-part lessons' – starting with a whole-class session, followed by individual/group practice and a final whole-class session at the end of the lesson.

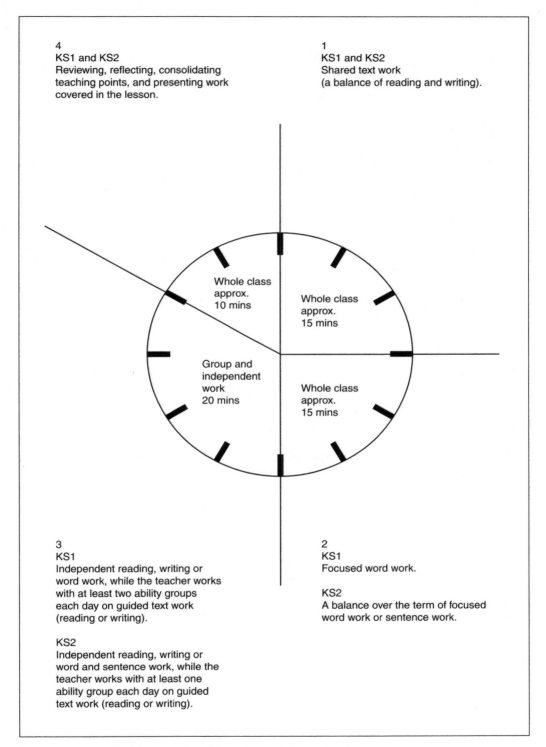

4
KS1 and KS2
Reviewing, reflecting, consolidating
teaching points, and presenting work
covered in the lesson.

1
KS1 and KS2
Shared text work
(a balance of reading and writing).

Whole class
approx.
10 mins

Whole class
approx.
15 mins

Group and
independent
work
20 mins

Whole class
approx.
15 mins

3
KS1
Independent reading, writing or
word work, while the teacher works
with at least two ability groups
each day on guided text work
(reading or writing).

KS2
Independent reading, writing or
word and sentence work, while the
teacher works with at least one
ability group each day on guided
text work (reading or writing).

2
KS1
Focused word work.

KS2
A balance over the term of focused
word work or sentence work.

**Figure 13.4.2** The Literacy Hour in English primary schools

This is not the only model possible in direct instruction. Alternatives have been developed, such as short whole-class presentations followed by individual practice, which is followed by the next short whole-class session, etc. There is no evidence that this is either more or less effective than the three-part lesson strategy.

## Weaknesses and limitations of direct instruction

While direct instruction may be one of the most effective teaching strategies available, it is not necessarily the best strategy to use in all circumstances (see Reading 13.1). Direct instruction has been found to be the best method to teach rules, procedures and basic skills, especially to younger students (Brophy and Good, 1986). However, when the goals of the lesson are more complex or open-ended (e.g. developing students' thinking skills, or discussing the merits of different electoral systems), the structured and teacher-directed approach that characterizes direct instruction is not the most effective model. More open-ended models may be more appropriate for achieving these goals (Joyce and Weill, 1996).

The effectiveness of direct instruction also seems to depend on the characteristics of the students taught. The highly structured approach seems to be particularly effective for students from disadvantaged backgrounds, or students starting from a low level of achievement in a particular subject. For example, in a recent study in England and Wales, relationships between student achievement and direct instruction-style teacher behaviours were twice as high in schools with a high or average percentage of students from deprived backgrounds. This suggests that these students are more in need of explicit teaching. However, it must be remarked that positive relationships were also evident in low-deprivation schools (Muijs and Reynolds, 2000).

A further problem with direct instruction is that the role of students may become too passive, leading to overdependence on the teacher and underdevelopment of independent learning skills (Gipps and McGilchrist, 1999). Additionally, it is entirely possible to use effective direct teaching strategies to teach undemanding and unchallenging content, or to teach in a way that does not suitably connect material. Finally, in some cases direct instruction can degenerate into ineffective lecture-style ('chalk and talk') lessons with little interaction with students.

Finally, we need to acknowledge that the evidence on direct instruction is skewed towards primary age students and the subjects of mathematics and English. More research in other subjects and in secondary schools is needed to see whether this method is supported in those settings as well.

📖 READING 13.5

# Using questions in classroom discussion

Elizabeth Perrot

This is a detailed reading on the various skills and strategies involved in the use of questions in classroom discussion. This is an essential part of any teaching repertoire. Perrot considers how to use questioning to improve both the quality of children's thinking, particularly with reference to 'higher-order thinking' and the extent of their participation. Finally, she reviews some of the most important issues in the development of an effective overall questioning strategy.

Questioning is one of the most important techniques of teaching, and taping a session when using questioning is always revealing. What does Perrot's analysis of skills offer to you?

Edited from: Perrot, E. (1982) *Effective Teaching: A Practical Guide to Improving Your Teaching*. London: Longman, 56–91

Research studies carried out in many parts of the world have shown that the majority of teacher's questions call for specific factual answers, or lower cognitive thought. But higher cognitive questions, which cause pupils to go beyond memory and use other thought processes in forming an answer, have an important role. While both types of questions have their part to play in teaching, a heavy reliance on lower-order questioning encourages rote learning and does little to develop higher-order thinking processes.

Teaching skills associated with helping pupils to give more complete and thoughtful responses are: pausing, prompting, seeking further clarification and refocusing a pupil's response.

Teaching skills associated with increasing the amount and quality of pupils' participation are: redirecting the same question to several pupils, framing questions that call for sets of related facts, and framing questions that require the pupil to use higher cognitive thought.

Such teaching skills are a means to an end (pupils' behaviour). Therefore, you must have clearly in mind the particular end you wish to achieve. Additionally you must become a careful observer of pupils' behaviour, since their reactions can give you valuable clues about the effectiveness of your own performance.

## Helping pupils to give more complete and thoughtful responses

*Pausing*: If the teacher's object is to sample what the class knows within a relatively short time and to elicit brief answers, 'rapid-fire' questioning is an appropriate skill. On the other hand, if the teacher's objective is to provide an atmosphere more conducive to discussion, in which pupils will have time to organize longer and more thoughtful responses, he must adopt a more appropriate questioning procedure. One skill that may be used to encourage longer and more thoughtful responses is to pause for three to five seconds after asking a question, but before calling on a pupil. The use of this skill should eventually result in longer responses because your pupils will be able to discriminate between pausing behaviour and your 'rapid-fire questioning'.

However, they will not automatically give longer answers when you first begin using pausing in your discussions. Depending upon their previous classroom experiences, relatively few pupils may respond appropriately. Some may begin to daydream, hoping they will not be called on; others may raise their hands without first thinking. Therefore, when you first start using pausing behaviour, you should help the pupils learn what you want them to do.

Immediately after the question, verbal prompts can be presented, such as, 'Please think over your answer carefully', 'When I call on you, I want a complete answer', then pause for three to five seconds before you call on someone. Success lies in using questions which require longer and more thoughtful responses, pausing to allow ample time to organize those responses and reinforcing pupils for such responses.

If the pupil's response does not come up to the level you are seeking, you must be prepared to help him to develop a better answer. Good ideas, however, should not be rejected simply because you did not previously consider them. You should always be prepared to evaluate and accept good answers, and to reinforce the pupil for them.

*Prompting* This strategy is based on a series of questions containing hints that help the pupil develop his answer. Sometimes a single prompt will be sufficient to guide the pupil to a better answer. More commonly, it is necessary for the teacher to use a series of prompts which lead the pupil step by step to answer the original question. Teacher prompts may be in the form of intermediate questions, clues or hints, that give the pupil the information he needs to arrive at a better answer. If the initial response is partly correct, first reinforce the correct part by telling the pupil what was right. Then begin by modifying the incorrect part. The exact questions used in a prompting sequence cannot be specified in advance, since each depends on the pupils's previous response. However, you should always have in mind the criterion response. Equally important, you should praise the final answer as much as if the pupil gave it at the beginning.

*Seeking clarification* In some instances, a pupil may give a response which is poorly organized, lacking in detail or incomplete. Here you face a situation in which the pupil is not wrong, but in which his answer still does not match the response you seek. Under these circumstances you can use the probing skill of seeking clarification. Unlike prompting, seeking clarification starts at a different point on the response continuum. The teacher is not adding information; he is requesting the pupil to do so.

*Refocusing* There are numerous occasions when the teacher receives a response that matches the one he wants. Refocusing may then be used to relate the pupil's response to another topic he has studied. The skill is used to help the pupil consider the implications of his response within a broader conceptual framework. He is asked to relate his answer to another issue. Refocusing is the most difficult form of probing since the teacher must have a thorough knowledge of how various topics in the curriculum may be related. You will be able to refocus more effectively if you study the content of your planned discussion beforehand, and note relationships with other topics the class has studied.

## Improving the amount and quality of pupils' participation

*Redirection* In using the technique of redirection, the same question is directed to several pupils. The question is neither repeated nor rephrased even though more than one pupil responds. To use redirection effectively, you must choose a question which calls for an answer of related facts or allows a variety of alternative responses. A poor question for redirection is one requiring only a single answer, such as 'What is the capital of France?' In this case, the first correct response effectively shuts off further questioning.

The first result of redirection is that you will talk less and the pupils will participate more. A second gain, which can be used to advantage later, is that by requiring several pupils to respond to the same question you can begin encouraging pupils to respond to each other.

*Questions calling for sets of related facts* You undoubtedly encounter pupils in your classes who respond to almost any type of question as briefly as possible; that is, they answer 'yes' or 'no', or use only short phrases. Before you blame the pupils for not achieving more, be sure

| Function | Skill | Participant |
|----------|-------|-------------|
| To increase readiness to respond | Pausing<br>Handling incorrect responses<br>Calling on non-volunteers | Class<br>Individual<br>Individual |
| To increase quantity of participation | Redirecting questions<br>Calling for sets of related facts | Class |
| To improve quality of response | Asking higher-order questions<br>Prompting<br>Seeking clarification<br>Refocusing | Individual<br>Individual<br>Individual<br>Individual |
| To increase quantity of participation while improving quality of response | Redirecting higher-order questions | Class |

**Figures 13.5.1**   The relationships between functions and skills

you are not at fault. You may be using types of questions associated with short answers that are not recognizable by their stem. When you ask, 'Isn't the purpose of your local police force the protection of life and property?' you are actually seeking a simple 'yes' or 'no' response. The question is so phrased that confirmation by the pupil is an acceptable answer. If on the other hand, you want discussion, you should phrase the same questions as follows: 'What are the duties of our local police force?' A 'yes' or 'no' response will not suffice here. But what if you have good questions and the pupils are still not responding adequately? Where do you start? As we have suggested, the question itself is only part of the story. Pupils previously allowed to respond briefly or to give memory-type responses are not likely to respond to your expectations at first. Praise the pupil for what he has stated and ask him to contribute more. Success lies in using questions which require longer and better responses and in reinforcing the pupils for their successively longer and better responses.

*Higher-order questions*   Besides encouraging pupils to give longer responses you should also try to improve the quality of their responses. Indeed, the kinds of questions the teacher asks will reveal to the pupil the kind of thinking which is expected of him. Since different kinds of questions stimulate different kinds of thinking, the teacher must be conscious of the purpose of his questions and the level of thinking they evoke.

An effective questioning sequence is one that achieves its purpose. When your purpose is to determine whether pupils remember certain specific facts, ask recall questions, such as: 'What is the capital of Canada?', 'When did Henry VIII become King of England?'.

When your purpose is to require pupils to use information in order to either summarize, compare, contract, explain, analyse, synthesize or evaluate ask higher-order questions. For instance: 'Explain the kinds of problems caused by unemployment'. 'How did life in the eighteenth century differ from life today?'

## Developing an overall questioning strategy

In order to be effective, skills must be appropriately incorporated into a questioning strategy planned to achieve particular learning objectives. Figure 13.5.1 indicates the relationships between functions and skills.

A common problem in questioning sequences is a lack of emphasis on higher-order questions. This may be due to failure in planning a strategy where the primary objective is the improvement of the quality of thought. It may also be related to the fact that questioning is taking place in a group situation where the teacher is concerned with the quantity of pupil participation. In his effort to increase the quantity of pupil participation a teacher might rely on redirecting a disproportionate number of multiple-fact questions. Such tactics tend to emphasize recall and decrease the time available for asking higher-order questions and probing.

A second problem relates to the teacher's failure to refocus. A primary task of the teacher is to help pupils relate what they are presently learning to what they have previously learned. Perhaps an even more significant task is to help pupils to understand that the ideas which they are studying are often relevant to other situations. Refocusing is probably the most difficult probing skill. Although the use of this skill depends on the preceding answer of the pupil, teachers who have clearly in mind the conceptual content of their lesson can plan for questioning sequences which enable them to use refocusing.

A third problem arises from the teacher's failure to have clearly in mind criteria for evaluating pupil responses. As previously mentioned, skills provide a means to an end. Only by specifying a particular end can a teacher determine which means are appropriate. To increase the quality of pupils' answers teachers should:

- carefully plan questions which require higher-order responses;

- have in mind the criteria for an acceptable answer;

- identify previously learned facts which are essential to the initiation of the higher-order questions;

- review for essential information to determine what the pupils know;

- frame questions that can be used systematically to develop the original pupil response and meet the higher-order criteria.

## READING 13.6

# Talking and learning in the classroom

Terry Phillips

Phillips considers the vexed question of how to encourage task-focused and cognitively challenging classroom talk amongst pupils in Key Stage 2 classrooms. He is critical of the dominance of teachers in overuse of whole-class teaching, and of just allowing children to 'chatter' in groups. Rather, he argues that activities should be carefully structured to facilitate language development and to expose children to a range of different forms of language use.

Is there a place for more structured language development activities in your classroom?

Edited from: Phillips, T. (1985) 'Beyond lip-service: discourse development after the age of nine', in Wells, G. and Nicholls, J. (eds.) *Language and Learning: An Interactional Perspective*. London: Falmer Press, 386–8

Teachers of older children sometimes feel guilty because although they realize that extensive use of class discussion can have a negative effect upon the children's language if they employ mainly closed questions, they find it difficult to teach without using them. They are aware that they talk twice as much as all the children put together, but they also know that you can't hold a discussion with twenty or more children without exercising some leadership. Perhaps that is why, in the 1970s, many teachers responded to the call to give talk greater recognition by 'permitting' children to chatter whilst they worked, and by encouraging them to discuss things in small groups. Ironically, however, the increase in the quantity of talk in school turned attention away from a consideration of the overall quality of the talk, especially its appropriateness for particular educational purposes. It was almost as if such teachers believe that talk *per se* would promote the range of cognitive processes demanded of children as they moved towards and through secondary schooling.

There has since been a reaction and many more teachers have reverted totally to class teaching because as they put it, 'at least you know where you're going' and 'it's the simplest way to teach the basics'. The frustrations of trying to cope with the nearly impossible have become too much for them and, rather than merely pay lip-service to the idea of children learning through undifferentiated group talk, they have opted for the simple alternative. Although research has shown that there is a range of writing styles, within which one style is more appropriate for a particular function than another (Britton, 1971; Wilkinson *et al.*, 1979; Bereiter and Scardamalia, 1985) there is a trend towards paring back the range of options for talk. But there are probably as many styles of talking as there are styles of writing, each one fostering a different kind of cognitive process. So what might teachers do instead of going 'back to basics'? How might they take children 'forward to fundamentals' in terms of such fundamental life skills as: being able to argue in a way which is rational and does not confuse the argument with its proponent; being able to reflect upon and evaluate ideas and experiences; and being able to adopt a style of language which is appropriate for the purpose it is intended to serve?

A curriculum which brings children more and more into contact with organized bodies of knowledge demands that we use the school day efficiently. If we aim to facilitate spoken language development and, with it, cognitive processes, we must be selective about the kinds of conversation we encourage; and we must also structure the talk. I don't mean that we should prescribe rules for this kind of talk or that kind of talk, only that we should take account of what is known about styles of discourse and their relationship which will help the talk, where appropriate, to be an instrument for higher-order cognitive activity. In view of what has been said about the mode of talk that accompanies much practical activity, for instance, it would seem worthwhile to organize the activity so that there is a planning stage when discussion takes place away from the materials to be used, then an activity stage, followed by a withdrawal for further discussion in which group members can reconsider their initial ideas and fashion modified ones, then a second activity stage, and a final report back stage. It would not be too difficult to establish such a routine for practical activities right across the curriculum, activities such as solving a mathematical problem, constructing a model or designing a layout, or carrying out a scientific experiment. The biggest advantage of such a procedure would be that it would accustom children to the fact that they can interrupt the flow of operational language at any point to do some thinking. In time it might be possible to draw the children's attention to what has been happening, and then invite them to interrupt, themselves, when they perceive the moment to be right.

To take a second example – in this case the language of argument/discussion – it might be beneficial to frame discussion topics in ways which invite speculation and leave conclusions open, instead of requiring children to reach a decision. The kind of topic which involves selecting what to include and what to exclude from a list would then be a first stage, to be followed by a discussion in which children make explicit the reasons for their selection. At that stage of development they can be encouraged to explain why they are rejecting someone else's suggestion before they give reasons for their own.

If, through the middle years, children are encouraged to listen to as many different models of spoken language as possible, at the secondary stage they will be ready to work out, with their teachers, how speakers achieve their purposes. Taped interviews, radio and television broadcasts, and film are excellent sources for such studies. In media studies it has been realized for quite a while that it is important to study the visual component of such materials and it can only be beneficial to give prominence also to the study of the spoken text.

It would be possible to continue with a list of 'for instances' for a long time, but I shall conclude by drawing out the main principles upon which they were formulated. Spontaneous spoken language development does not stop the moment the child leaves the first school, but the nature of later schooling means that we cannot rely on there being sufficient opportunity for spontaneous classroom conversation to guarantee that the development which does occur will be adequate for a wide range of educational purposes. Teachers have to be ready to structure opportunities for talk in a way which takes cognizance of the fact that different styles of talk are suited to different forms of mental activity.

### 📖 READING 13.7

# A rationale for cooperative group work

Neville Bennett and Elizabeth Dunne

This reading illustrates an application, to cooperative group work, of Neville Bennett's influential model of teaching and learning. As is made clear in the extract, language is used by teachers and pupils for slightly different purposes at each stage of the teaching cycle. This calls for particular consideration by teachers in developing an appropriate repertoire of linguistic skills for clarifying intentions, offering high-quality presentations and support for implementation, and engaging in assessment activity. For instance, among the major skills which may be called for, we might identify explaining, discussion and questioning.

Can you relate this model to your own classroom practice?

Edited from: Bennett, N. and Dunne, E., (1992) *Managing Classroom Groups*. Hemel Hempstead: Simon and Schuster Education, 188–94

Here we draw threads together in order to present a summary. A useful framework for these purposes is the model of the teaching cycle modified for a group task, as in Figure 13.7.1.

The teacher's intention was for the group to work cooperatively on a story plan, the story to be based on a beach scene. The task was presented or introduced via an actual walk on the beach where children explored its features prior to a discussion with the teacher. This discussion is continued in the group in order to develop the story plan. The teacher observes that the children work cooperatively, with Laura taking a lead and helping other members of the group. She nevertheless considers that the group process could have been improved by building more on each other's ideas, and by encouraging all children in the group to participate. The teacher's observations and assessments led her to the decision that the task had been appropriate, but that she must consider ways of improving the manner in which the group works together.

Utilized in this way, the model is a valuable aide-memoire for the teacher and, used over time, can give a clear picture of progress in terms of group functioning.

In the following, each element of the model is considered in turn, leading, in each case, to

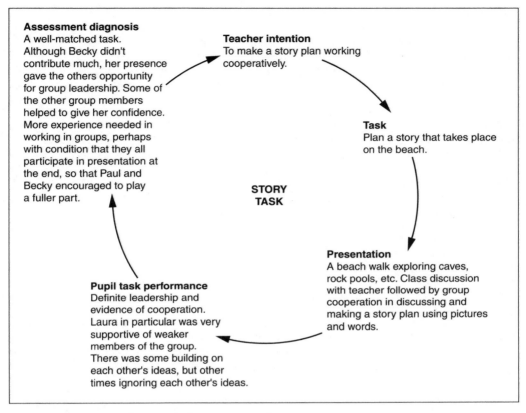

**Assessment diagnosis**
A well-matched task.
Although Becky didn't
contribute much, her presence
gave the others opportunity
for group leadership. Some of
the other group members
helped to give her confidence.
More experience needed in
working in groups, perhaps
with condition that they all
participate in presentation at
the end, so that Paul and
Becky encouraged to play
a fuller part.

**Teacher intention**
To make a story plan working
cooperatively.

**Task**
Plan a story that takes place
on the beach.

**STORY
TASK**

**Presentation**
A beach walk exploring caves,
rock pools, etc. Class discussion
with teacher followed by group
cooperation in discussing and
making a story plan using pictures
and words.

**Pupil task performance**
Definite leadership and
evidence of cooperation.
Laura in particular was very
supportive of weaker
members of the group.
There was some building on
each other's ideas, but other
times ignoring each other's ideas.

**Figure 13.7.1**   A teaching cycle for a group task

a set of 'action questions' designed to guide the teacher through the decision points necessary to setting up and implementing effective cooperative groups.

## Teacher intentions

Transforming intentions into appropriate tasks requires consideration of:

● the interaction between social and cognitive intentions;

● the type of task required;

● the match of appropriateness of the task to children in the group.

Whether the teacher's planning starts with curriculum content or with a single, or a group of, attainment targets, it is necessary to distinguish between the social and cognitive demands of the tasks. The cognitive demand relates to the curriculum content of the task, whereas the social demand relates to the type and amount of cooperation required and thus to decisions about the model of group to be chosen

Action questions at this planning stage include: on which curriculum area are you going to base the task(s)? With which attainment targets are you dealing? With which specific statement of attainment are you concerned? Which model of cooperative group is to be used?

With regard to the type of task planned, cooperative group work is not a panacea for children's social and cognitive development, it is one option or approach in the teacher's repertoire which must sit alongside other approaches such as individual and whole-class work. We believe it has particular value in problem-solving and applications work. It is in such types of task that abstract talk ought perhaps to predominate, if the task is designed well. However, it is worth recalling that virtually no abstract talk was apparent in the maths, science and technology tasks we observed and recorded. This does not mean that the nature of these curriculum areas precludes abstract talk; it is an issue of task design. There is thus a major challenge for teaches to develop tasks in these curriculum areas that incorporate demands for abstract talk and thought.

Our findings in this area support those of Margaret Donaldson (1978) who found that abstract talk is more difficult for children to generate, and is less fluent than talk relating to action. Teachers need to be aware of this since early attempts at abstract talk may be hesitant and less coherent. It should, nevertheless, be encouraged.

Action questions here are: what kind of task is required to fulfil your intention – problem-solving, discussion, production? Will your demand be 'tight' or 'loose'? Will this task generate the kind of talk you desire?

The third aspect of transforming intentions into tasks is the 'match' or appropriateness of task demands to children's capabilities. Typically, the concept of matching has focused on the individual child and the extent to which tasks have been matched to that child's ability, or have overestimated or underestimated it. However, Vygotsky's notion of the zone of proximal development shifts the focus on the individual child acting in cooperating with others (Vygotsky, 1962). In this context, match is achieved by the mediation of others through the medium of talk. This shift in focus has implications for the teacher's role. No longer does it become necessary to fine-tune matching; matching can be considered more broadly, as long as the task is appropriate for cooperative groupwork. In these circumstances, matching will be achieved when children in the group make sense of task demands through their talk. As we have seen in this study, and as has been reported elsewhere, it can occur to the benefit of all children irrespective of their level of attainment.

Action questions of relevance here are: what is the actual task chosen? Is it suitable for cooperative working? Does it fit the group model chosen? Are the cognitive demands reasonably appropriate to the children's capabilities?

## Presentation and implementation

These two aspects of the model are considered together since decisions about presentation (e.g. whether to introduce a task by means of a walk on the beach, or a discussion, or a television programme, etc.) are closely tied up with the way in which the class and the groups are managed and supported. They have common implications for the teacher's role.

Foremost among these is the nature of the teacher's own language. As HMI (1989) recently argued in their report on primary maths, 'It was the quality of the exposition and dialogue with the teacher that enabled the children to reflect upon and think through mathematical problems and ideas. This factor, more than any other, marked the difference between good and mediocre work'.

Of particular relevance to group work has been the continuing debate about the extent and nature of teacher intervention with groups. Some researchers and commentators feel that the teacher ought to operate a 'hands-off' approach, whereas others argue the opposite. The National Oracy Project has, for example, argued (National Oracy Project, 1990) that one of the major roles for teachers is to model effective and supportive use of talk in their own behaviour. With specific regard to group work they argue that it is better to be involved fully with one group than try to spend a few minutes with each. This is the best way to create planned intervention that may extend children's thinking, to introduce a new aspect, or to give the teacher more information about individuals, while the other groups are responsible for their own success. Joining in activities, they argue, rather than supervising them, extends the possibilities for dialogue.

Although published in 1990, the above recommendations clearly have their genesis in the Bullock Report published fifteen years earlier. It set out its advice as follows:

> The teacher's role should be one of planned intervention, and his purposes and the means of fulfilling them must be clear in his mind. Important among these purposes should be the intention to increase the complexity of the child's thinking, so that he does not rest on the mere expression of opinion but uses language in an exploratory way. The child should be encouraged to ask good questions as well as provide answers, to set up hypotheses and test them, and to develop the habit of trying out alternative explanations instead of being satisfied with one.

> It is important that the teacher should spend time with each of the small groups to guide the language into fulfilling its purpose. 'Guidance' is not used here in the sense of dominant intervention; indeed receptive silence is as much a part of it as the most persuasive utterance. The teacher has first to be a good listener, letting his genuine interest act as a stimulus. His questions will encourage the pupils to develop or clarify points in their thinking, or take them beyond it into the contemplation of other possibilities. We must not give the impression, however, that this is a simple matter and that there are no problems.

> The teacher must devise situations in which the pupils will naturally adopt the kind of behaviour he wants to encourage. In other words, he must structure the learning so that the child becomes positively aware of the need for a complicated utterance, and is impelled to make it. In this way the teacher's skilled and carefully controlled intervention is a valuable means of extending his pupils' thinking and making new demands upon their language. (DES, 1974, pp. 10, 11)

Although we respect the above advice, we have no evidence to present from our own studies to support this type of approach. We utilized a 'hands-off' study so far as teachers were concerned because of our wish to ascertain how children in groups worked without teacher input, and how they dealt with devolved responsibilities for pupil requests.

An issue linked with the National Oracy Project advice about dealing in depth with one group at a time is that of discipline and control. Losing and maintaining control are always high on the list of teacher concerns, and are certainly criteria that teachers consider when asked to change their practice. Our experience is that anxieties of this kind are unfounded, and similar findings are reported elsewhere. Cohen (1986), for example, writing from her research in American classrooms, argues:

> From the teacher's point of view, groupwork solves two common discipline problems. It helps with the problem of the low-achieving student who is often found doing anything but what he or she is supposed to be doing. Moreover, it helps to solve the problem of what the rest of the class should be doing while the teacher works intensively with one group. The most typical strategy is to have the rest of the students working with pencil and paper at their seats. However, this produces all kinds of discipline problems. If the rest of the class has been trained to work independently in groups, the teacher will be free to give direct instruction to one small group.

The final aspect of presentation and implementation considered here is the composition of classroom groups. Our findings are clear – mixed-ability groups of about four children provide a good environment for effective group work. Helping behaviour in the form of knowledge sharing and the provision of explanations tends not to happen in ability groups of low- and average-attaining children. Importantly, high attainers do not suffer in mixed-ability groups. Sex differences are also apparent, and our provisional findings indicate that groups in which boys outnumber girls could depress language experience for the latter.

Questions to guide action in the area of presentation and implementation are: how will the task be presented/introduced? What expectations have you for group behaviour and co-operation? How will the children be informed? Will the responsibility for pupil requests be devolved to the groups? What is your strategy for intervening in the groups? How will you compose your groups?

## Assessment

Assessment is not a discrete teacher activity. Much of it takes place during the implementation stage, through teacher observations and questions. Assessment serves several different purposes, for which different techniques are required. Assessment of group processes, through which teachers gain understanding of the nature and quality of pupil interaction, is best achieved in our experience through the use of a tape recorder. Children soon ignore the machine even if there is some initial 'microphone talk'. Not only does the teacher gain an insight into the talk used, but also into interaction patterns, the development and changes in leadership roles and early indications of forms of group malfunctioning.

The quality of these processes will reflect in the quality of group outcomes, the assessment of which requires different techniques. We have highlighted several of these including interviewing individual, or groups of, children in order to access their understanding or schema. Short written assessments can also be used for this purpose. Class discussions can also draw out contrasts in group thinking and approaches.

Some of these techniques require time to carry out and record. Nevertheless, this is time well spent. Better understanding of children's attainment and developing schema should feed forward into better planning of future tasks.

Action questions here are: what are you going to assess? How are you going to assess it? How are you going to feed back to pupils and groups? How are you going to record your assessments? How are you going to use this information in planning future tasks?

---

### 📖 READING 13.8

# Promoting collaborative learning

## Colin Biott and Patrick Easen

> Biott and Easen have analysed some key issues which must be faced in promoting collaborative learning. They highlight the risk taking which is involved as the 'self' and capabilities of each child become exposed within the group. Thus the power relationships and the collective sense of meaning held by the children are vital to the success of collaborative group activity. The teacher can help in two ways: by creating favourable conditions, and by fostering appropriate skills.
>
> Collaborative learning has been strongly advocated as a practical means of implementing social constructivist ideas in classroom situations, and yet it is not easy to implement. Could you develop collaborative group work in your classroom using Biott and Easen's practical suggestions?
>
> Edited from: Biott, C. and Easen, P. (1994) *Collaborative Learning in Staffrooms and Classrooms*. London: David Fulton, 203–9

Collaborative learning is essentially about the development of the self in a social context. This implies that collaborative learning has both personal and contextual features which are closely interwoven. Through working and learning together, both children and teachers develop a sense of who they are and what they can or cannot do. They learn about their own and each others' strengths and weaknesses as they are revealed in particular circumstances and contexts. For this reason, acts of collaboration may be perceived as involving various degrees of anxiety and risk for those involved.

The meaning of the collaborative activity for those involved, then, is crucial and it is important for participants in a collaborative activity to retain a feeling of control. Activities perceived as having 'performance goals' and as being 'challenging', therefore, may be seen as presenting a high degree of risk to the self. The same activities, of course, may be perceived quite differently by another participant.

The concepts of 'power' and 'meaning' are inseparable in collaborative learning. There are times when having the strategies and skills to create these meanings through collaboration are insufficient without the strategies and skills to handle any power issues that may arise during it. Hence our emphasis on trying to understand the place of conflict in collaborative relationships.

There are two main ways in which a teacher may encourage the development of collaborative learning. These are concerned with: creating favourable conditions; and teaching encouraging and fostering skills.

## Creating favourable conditions for collaborative learning

There is more to improving collaborative learning than organizing children into groups and setting certain tasks. In addition, it is necessary to create favourable classroom conditions, so that children value working together and have opportunities to give and experience help, support and challenge in their relationships with each other. Teachers who create these conditions:

- Offer opportunities for children to learn social competences in situations where they can make, and act upon, shared understandings of how to be both cooperative with others and assertive for themselves. The teachers convey, to the children, that collaboration may be unstable and unpredictable, that it is not based simply upon obedience and compliance and that conflict and disagreements can be constructive. The children learn that working with others can be both enabling and constraining.

- Provide a wide range of paired and group activities and also encourage children to consider working with a partner on some occasions when they are completing the same individual tasks so that they can compare and talk about what they are doing.

- Expect that all children will be able to contribute, in different ways, to the quality of activities, and they do not stress leadership in ways which give status to superior knowledge or bossiness.

- Spend time listening to children when they are working collaboratively and give children time both to find ways to work together and to develop ideas.

- Model a collaborative approach in their interactions with children. They listen and discuss disagreements, interpret some conflicts and difficulties in children's relationships in positive ways, and do not expect everyone to be able to get everything right first time. They spend some time wondering about things with children, seeking alternatives and showing themselves to be uncertain, rather than always being concerned about knowing answers and being correct.

- Organize space, time and resources to allow some flexibility for some parts of each day. They provide a variety of possibilities for different kinds of purposeful activities in specific parts of the room.

- Do not rely solely on impressions of surface behaviour and snatches of overheard conversations when judging whether, or how well, children are learning collaboratively.

- Work, through systematic enquiry, towards understanding the most favourable ways to group children, when setting formal group assignments, taking into account sex, gender racial and ability differences. They experiment to find helpful ways to prepare their children for collaboration; they think about different ways to start a group activity and how to participate once a group has started its work. Most importantly, they review how their approach affects children's sense of control over what they are doing and how learning ensues.

## Teaching, encouraging and fostering skills of collaborative learning

How children learn to work together, and what they learn about doing it, can be haphazard, fragmented, inconsistent, ambiguous and sometimes contradictory. Children's capacity to work well with other children may not necessarily match their attainment in other fields. We have seen evidence of poor collaborative skills and strategies from children who are adept at private, individual work, and been surprised by the exceptional capabilities of some who have been much less accomplished in written work.

Helpful teachers:

- Make their expectations about working together clear to the children and teach them how to collaborate.

- Give consistent feedback which embraces emergent as well as imposed collaboration. Feedback of this nature is concrete and focused, seeking also to explore children's perceptions of what is going on, rather than being judgemental. This helps children to understand processes of collaborative work so that they are not put off by challenge and disagreements and learn to develop strategies and skills to handle conflict constructively. Feedback, then, helps to maintain and enhance the collective as well as individual self-esteem of children.

- Take action if they notice that a child is vulnerable to domination or rejection by other children, intervening in a way which has positive effects upon the child's social identity and enhances future relationships.

- Encourage children to make contributions to collaborative activities by showing them how to listen, question and respond. They teach helping skills and techniques such as peer tutoring, including how to record what their partners like to do and how they learn best. They model, through their own actions, and teach, that some questions will be more helpful than others when children are responding to other children's ideas.

Many of the ideas embodied above may have as much relevance to the staffroom as they do to the classroom. Collaboration is multi-layered and pervasive, and learning may be carried over from one area of a teacher's professional life to another.

## READING 13.9

# Pedagogic principles derived from human rights

Audrey Osler and Hugh Starkey

Schooling can be seen by pupils as something that is done 'to them', rather than 'with them', and sometimes the pressure on teachers to enhance performance reinforces this problem. Occasionally therefore, it is worthwhile to pause and reflect on the broader picture. This reading reviews principles embedded within the UN Convention on the Rights of the Child (UNCRC) to raise two questions: 'What is the quality of the children's experience?' and 'How might pupils' school experience affect their development as future citizens?'.

These are enormously significant questions, but how might they be answered in your classroom? How can we create virtuous teaching strategies so that we can confidently expect greater pupil participation and engagement to produce enhanced performance – as well as improving opportunities for citizenship and the overall quality of pupil experience?

Edited from: Osler, A. and Starkey, H. (1998) *Teacher Education and Human Rights*. London: David Fulton Publishers, 153–7.

When we examine the relevance to schools of the UN Convention on the Rights of the Child, it is apparent that the 'principle of participation' has wide-ranging implications for classroom organization, curriculum and pedagogy. Indeed, the rights enacted in the Convention suggest a number of specific principles that we should apply to the processes of teaching and learning (see Figure 13.9.1).

## Dignity and security

The student's right to dignity implies a relationship between teacher and student that avoids abuse of power on the part of the teacher, including the avoidance of sarcasm. In this relationship the teacher's own right to dignity should not be forgotten. Teachers need to establish, with their students, a classroom atmosphere in which name-calling and mockery are

| Pedagogic principles | Article(s) of the UNCRC |
|---|---|
| dignity | preamble, 28 |
| security | 19, 23, 29 |
| participation | 12, 13, 14, 15, 31 |
| identity | 7, 8, 16 |
| inclusivity | preamble, 2, 23, 28, 29, 31 |
| freedom | 12, 14, 15 |
| access to information | 13, 17 |
| privacy | 16 |

**Figure 13.9.1**   Articles of the UNCRC applicable to teaching and learning

unacceptable. It is the teacher's responsibility to ensure that those who are most vulnerable are protected from bullying and have the opportunity to learn in a secure environment.

## Participation

The principle of participation which runs through the Convention has a particular application in the classroom, and an appropriate pedagogy will be responsive to the needs of individual students and to the group as a whole. Students should be given opportunities to exercise choice and responsibility in decisions which affect them at classroom level, for example in the planning and organization of their own work. It is noteworthy that approaches based on choice, responsibility and negotiation that are regularly developed with very young children are often abandoned as they grow older. It is, of course, the case that interdisciplinarity and a certain flexibility is built into the primary curriculum in the sense that the same teacher is likely to be responsible for several if not all areas of the curriculum. Although limitations on the choices open to older students are frequently explained in terms of curriculum constraints and subject specialization, they may also be closely related to teacher beliefs about the extent of children's autonomy and teacher control.

## Identity and inclusivity

The preservation and development of identity, including the recognition of the multiple identities which the individual may adopt is, a key right within education, yet one which is perhaps the most easily violated. Teachers need to ensure that they meet certain basic requirements, such as correct use and pronunciation of the child's name. Respect for individual children, their cultures and families is critical. This requires us to value diversity in the classroom and to recognize that diversity and hybridity are essential characteristics of all human communities. It means seeing children's characteristics, whether cultural, emotional or physical, as attributes to be built upon, rather than deficiencies. Education systems, schools and classrooms that deny or marginalize diversity are likely to discriminate against those who do not match the presupposed norm. Children whose social and cultural backgrounds are different from those of their teachers, and those with learning difficulties or disabilities, are particularly disadvantaged in such systems.

## Freedom

Pedagogy needs to permit maximum freedom of expression and conscience. The exercise of the rights of freedom of expression, freedom of conscience and religion, and freedom of association and peaceful assembly all require a range of skills which need to be developed in the classroom. The right of children to have their opinion taken into account in decisions made about them similarly requires a pedagogy which promotes skills of expression and decision making. Teaching and learning need to be based on student–teacher dialogue. It assumes a model of learning and development in which the learner will often be the person best suited to identifying her or his own needs. The model assumes that the teacher is continually developing his or her own teaching skills and is also open to learn from the students. Freedom of expression will have certain limitations, as we have seen, in order to protect the freedoms, security and dignity of others.

## Access to information

The exercise of the right of freedom of expression is at least partially dependent on access to information and ideas, including information from the mass media and from a diversity of national and international sources. Teachers have a responsibility to ensure that the child not only has skills of reading and writing to gain access to information but is able to interpret visual images critically, in newspapers, video and other media. Skills involved in the development of visual literacy include questioning, recognition of bias and discrimination and those skills associated with the design and production of visual materials, for example a photo sequence or video. An appropriate pedagogy will permit students to identify issues about which they wish to learn more, analyse the mass media, encourage creativity, imagination, criticism and scepticism, and arrive at their own judgements. The selection and range of sources of information in the classroom is usually determined by teachers, within the confines of available resources. While the teacher is responsible for ensuring that the child is protected from materials injurious to his or her well-being, there is also an obligation to develop a pedagogy whereby children have access to information on a need-to-know basis and are encouraged to identify and express their needs.

## Privacy

The right to privacy that is jealously guarded by so many adults is as often disregarded when we are dealing with children in the context of the school, the staffroom and the classroom. Pedagogy should respect the child's right to privacy, with regard to family and home, and schools need safeguards, in the form of guidelines, to protect the child's reputation when sharing information about individuals. While recognizing that we often ask personal questions of children in order to build upon their own experiences, cultures and identities, as teachers we need to remember that there exists a power relationship between teacher and student which may sometimes cause children to reveal more than they might wish to do. The teacher should consider the context, and avoid situations where children may be asked to reveal personal information in public, as for example in a whole-class discussion. If the principle of the child's best interests is consistently applied as a primary consideration, this should not prevent teachers seeking information designed to protect a child judged to be vulnerable in some way.

In summary, the Convention on the Rights of the Child can help us to elaborate pedagogical principles by which the implementation of the school curriculum can become an education of democratically minded citizens.

## CHAPTER 14

# Assessment. How are we monitoring learning and performance?

The seven readings in this chapter provide clarification of the many types of assessment and indications of the positive, and negative, roles that it can fulfil in teaching and learning.

In the first group of readings, definitions and applications of different types of assessment are discussed. Reading 14.1, by Harlen and colleagues, reviews assessment purposes. Black (14.2), an early contributor to the construction of the national assessment system in England and Wales and a policy adviser in many countries, poses key questions about the pros and cons of assessment deriving from his experience.

Four readings concern the development of formative assessment. The first of these concern day-to-day classroom feedback to children – perhaps the most sustained element of assessment. Burrell and Bubb (14.3) illustrate the application of a typology of different forms of feedback, proving that it is difficult to do. However, in Reading 14.4 Clarke offers excellent practical advice to take things forward. Pupil self-assessment is the particular focus of Muschamp (14.5) and she offers practical suggestions drawn from extensive classroom action research. Meanwhile, Drummond (14.6) appeals for assessment to be cast as an attempt to 'understand' children's perspectives rather than simply as a way of judging them.

Finally, Filer and Pollard (14.7) challenge the use of national assessments for summative purposes of accountability and comparison by arguing that such categoric judgements or assessments are likely to be insecure. Drawing on a sociological analysis of teacher–pupil interaction, they offer three reasons why the notion of the objectivity of assessment is a myth.

The parallel chapter of *Reflective Teaching* also begins with significant sections on formative 'assessment for learning' and summative 'assessment of learning'. These sections provide both information and practical advice. It then addresses some key issues in assessment: the effect on class relationships, manageability, validity and reliability, curriculum distortion and the impact on children. There is then a section on record keeping and on reporting to parents. Finally, the chapter turns to the use of assessment information for curriculum planning, tracking progress, performance management and school improvement.

There is a useful list of 'Key Readings' and useful, updated sources for further study are available in 'Notes for Further Reading' on *RTweb*. The website also offers a number of other resources on assessment, including further Reflective Activities.

READING 14.1

# Assessment purposes and principles

Wynne Harlen, Caroline Gipps, Patricia Broadfoot and Desmond Nuttall

Perhaps the single most important source of confusion regarding assessment stems from misunder-standings about the purposes of different forms of assessment. There are many types of assessment, but each is suited to particular purposes and cannot safely be used in other ways. This reading provides an excellent overview of assessment purposes, key principles and four of the most important types of assessment.

Assessment purposes have often been conflated by policy-makers, but what type would be most helpful to you in your work?

Edited from: Harlen, W., Gipps, C., Broadfoot, P. and Nuttall, D. (1992) 'Assessment and the improvement of education', *Curriculum Journal.* 3 (3), 217–25

Assessment in education is the process of gathering, interpreting, recording and using information about pupils' responses to an educational task. At one end of a dimension of formality, the task may be normal classroom work and the process of gathering information would be the teacher reading a pupil's work or listening to what he or she has to say. At the other end of the dimension of formality, the task may be a written, timed examination which is read and marked according to certain rules and regulations. Thus assessment encompasses responses to regular work as well as to specially devised tasks.

All types of assessment, of any degree of formality, involve interpretation of a pupil's response against some standard of expectation. This standard may be set by the average performance of a particular section of the population or age group, as in norm-referenced tests. Alternatively, as in the National Curriculum context, the assessment may be criterion-referenced. Here the interpretation is in terms of progression in skills, concept or aspects of personal development which are the objectives of learning, and the assessment gives direct information which can be related to progress in learning. However, the usefulness of criterion-referenced assessment depends on the way in which the criteria are defined. Too tightly defined criteria, while facilitating easy judgement of mastery, require an extensive list which fragments the curriculum. On the other hand, more general criteria, which better reflect the overall aims of education, are much less easily and reliably used in assessing achievement.

The roles of assessment in education are as follows:

- as the means for providing feedback to teachers and pupils about ongoing progress in learning, has a direct influence on the quality of pupils' learning experiences and thus on the level of attainment which can be achieved (formative role);

- as the means for communicating the nature and level of pupils' achievements at various points in their schooling and when they leave (summative role);

- as used as a means of summarizing, for the purposes of selection and qualification, what has been achieved (certification role);

- as providing part of the information used in judging the effectiveness of educational institutions and of the system as a whole (evaluative or quality control role).

There is an unavoidable backwash on the curriculum from the content and procedures of assessment. The higher the stakes of the assessment, the greater this will be. Multiple-choice and other paper-and-pencil tests provide results which are easily aggregated and compared but their use encourages teachers to ignore much of what pupils should learn as they 'teach to the test'.

Not all assessment purposes are compatible. Strong evidence from experience in the US, combined with that now accumulating in England and Wales, indicates that information collected for the purposes of supporting learning is unsuitable and unreliable if summarized and used for the purposes of quality control, that is, for making judgements about schools, and its use for this purpose severely impairs its formative role.

There is likely to be a trade-off between, on the one hand, cost and quality and, on the other, effectiveness. The cheapest assessment techniques, such as multiple-choice, machine-markable tests, may be convenient instruments to use but provide poor-quality information for the purposes of communication and little or no support for the learning process itself.

## Key principles

These issues concerning the purposes of assessment are borne in mind in proposing the following set of principles to inform policy-making on assessment:

- assessment must be used as a continuous part of the teaching–learning process, involving pupils, wherever possible, as well as teachers in identifying next steps;
- assessment for any purpose should serve the purpose of improving learning by exerting positive force on the curriculum at all levels. It must, therefore, reflect the full range of curriculum goals, including the more sophisticated skills and abilities now being taught;
- assessment must provide an effective means of communication with parents and other partners in the learning enterprise in a way which helps them support pupils' learning;
- the choice of different assessment procedures must be decided on the basis of the purpose for which the assessment is being undertaken. This may well mean employing different techniques for different assessment purposes;
- assessment must be used fairly as part of information for judging the effectiveness of schools. This means taking account of contextual factors that, as well as the quality of teaching, affect the achievement of pupils;
- citizens have a right to detailed and reliable information about the standards being achieved across the nation through the educational system.

## Formative assessment

A major role identified for assessment is that of monitoring learning and informing teaching decisions on a day-to-day basis. In this role, assessment is an integral part of the interactions between teacher, pupil and learning materials. Because of this relationship, some teachers, who practise formative assessment well, may not recognize that what they are doing includes assessing.

What is required from a formative assessment scheme is information that is: gathered in a number of relevant contexts; criterion-referenced and related to a description of progression; disaggregated, which means that distinct aspects of performance are reported separately; shared by both teacher and pupil; a basis for deciding what further learning is required; the basis of an ongoing running records of progress.

A scheme of formative assessment must be embedded in the structures of educational practice; it cannot be grafted on to it. Thus there are implications in the foregoing for the curriculum, for teachers, in terms of required supporting materials and pre-service or in-service training, and for record-keeping practice.

## Summative assessment

Summative assessment is similar to formative assessment in that it concerns the performance of individual pupils, as opposed to groups. In contrast with formative assessment, however, its prime purpose is not so much to influence teaching but to summarize information about the achievements of a pupil at a particular time. The information may be for the pupils themselves, for receiving teachers, for parents, for employers or for a combination of these.

There are two main ways of obtaining summative information about achievements: summing up and checking up (Harlen, 1991). The former is some form of summary of information obtained through recording formative assessments during a particular period of time and the latter the collection of new information about what the pupil can do at the end of a period of time, usually through giving some form of test. The nature and relative advantages and disadvantages of these are now briefly reviewed.

*Summing up* provides a picture of current achievements derived from information gathered over a period of time and probably used in that time for formative purposes. It is, therefore, detailed and broadly based, encompassing all the aspects of learning which have been addressed in teaching. To retain the richness of the information it is best communicated in the form of a profile (i.e. not aggregated), to which information is added on later occasions. Records of achievement (RoA) provide a structure for recording and reporting this information, combining some of the features of formative assessment with the purposes of summative assessment in that they involve pupils in reviewing their own work and recognizing where their strengths and weaknesses lie.

*Checking up* offers no such additional benefits as an approach to summative assessment. It is generally carried out through providing tests or tasks specially devised for the purpose of recording performance at a particular time. End of year tests or examinations are examples, as are the end of module tests for checking performance in modular programmes and external public examinations.

Checking-up and summing-up approaches have contrasting advantages and disadvantages. Tests used for checking up are limited in scope unless they are inordinately long and so are unlikely to cover practical skills and some of the higher-level cognitive skills. On the other hand, they do provide opportunities for all pupils to demonstrate what they have learned. Summative assessment which is based only on formative assessment depends on the opportunities provided in class for various skills and understandings to be displayed and, further, may be out of date in relation to parts of work covered at earlier points and perhaps not revisited.

This suggests that a combination of these two approaches may be the most appropriate solution. There are several advantages to having test materials available for teachers to use to supplement, at the end of a particular period, the information they have from ongoing assessment during that time. The emphasis is on 'test materials' and not tests. These would ideally be in the form of a bank from which teachers select according to their needs. The items in the bank would cover the whole range of curriculum objectives and the whole range of procedures required for valid assessment. This provision would also serve the purposes of the non-statutory Standard Assessment Tasks (SATs).

The main advantages are that the availability of a bank of test material would provide teachers with the opportunity to check or supplement their own assessment in a particular area where they felt uncertain about what pupils can do. This would ensure that all aspects of pupils' work were adequately assessed without requiring extensive testing. Checking their own assessments against those arising from well-trialled and validated tasks would also build up teachers' expertise and lead to greater rigour in teachers' assessments.

## Assessment for evaluative and quality assurance purposes

Information about pupils' achievement is necessary in order to keep under review the performance of the system as a whole – the quality assurance role of assessment. In the absence of such information it is possible for rumour and counter-rumour to run riot. For example, the argument about the levels of performance of seven-year-olds on reading (prior to the national assessment data) would never had been possible had there been a national survey of reading performance at the age of 7.

To serve this purpose, assessment has to be carried out in a way which leads to an overall picture of achievement on a national scale. It requires measures of achievement of a large number of pupils to be obtained and summarized. For this purpose, testing in controlled conditions is necessary. However, if every pupil is tested, this leads to adverse effects on both teaching practice and on the curriculum and an overemphasis on formal testing generally. Further, surveys which test every pupil cannot provide the depth of data required to provide a wide-range and in-depth picture of the system. Thus, testing every pupil at a particular age is not appropriate for assessing performance at the national level.

To serve the evaluative role, assessment at the national level does not need to cover all pupils nor to assess in all attainment targets those who are included. The necessary rigour and comparability in assessment for this purpose can be provided by the use of a sample of pupils undertaking different assessment tasks. Following the pioneering work of the APU [Assessment of Performance Unit], it would be possible to obviate the 'excessively complicated and time consuming' approach of the SATs and still provide the comprehensive coverage of every subject area across a satisfactorily large sample of particular age groups of pupils.

## Assessing school effectiveness

It is well established that the attainment of an individual is as much a function of his or her social circumstances and the educational experiences of his or her parents as it is of the effectiveness of the school or schools attended. To judge the effectiveness of a school by the attainment of its pupils is therefore misleading and unfair. What is wanted is a model that disentangles the effect on attainment of the school from that of the pupils' background. The value-added approach, that looks at the gain in achievement while the pupils is at a particular school (that is, the progress he or she makes there) offers a way forward and is, indeed, the basis of school effectiveness research such as that reported in *School Matters* (Mortimore *et al.*, 1988; see also McPherson, 1992).

The assessments of attainment used (both on entry to the school and on leaving) should be as broad as possible to ensure that school effectiveness is not reduced to efficiency in teaching test-taking skills but reflects the full range of the aims of the school.

To counter the narrowness of outcomes implied by test results, even when shown in value-added form, it is suggested that schools should publish detailed reports covering such areas as: the aims of the schools; details of recent inspection reports (if any); particular areas of expertise offered; cultural and sporting achievements; community involvement; destinations of leavers. In short, the school should show its test results as part of its record of achievement.

READING 14.2

# Assessment: friend or foe?

Paul Black

In this reading, Paul Black offers insights based on many years of experience of assessment policy and practice across the world. He highlights the dilemmas that assessment poses for teachers. But he also indicates why assessment is an enduring concern that we cannot avoid and thus have to learn to manage.

A key point is to try to ensure that all forms of assessment are consistent with learning objectives. How far are you comfortable with that idea, in relation to your classroom practices and any assessment requirements you face?

Edited from: Black, P. (1998) *Testing: Friend or Foe? Theory and Practice of Assessment and Testing*. London: Falmer Press, 154–9

Is assessment a 'friend' or a 'foe'? The answer to this question is likely to be a mixed one. The alternatives can be examined in relation to the three main purposes that assessment serves. First, as an essential element of any learning programme, formative assessment must be a friend. Second, because anyone with educated capabilities requires proof of their achievements, summative individual assessment will always be essential, but the effort required for its attainment may strain any affection for the process. Finally, since the public good requires accountability, this function is also inescapable – although we may have no more love for its necessity than we have for paying taxes.

Altogether then, the best attitude to assessment that might be achieved lies between affection and indifference.

However, if the system as a whole is ill-designed, hostility may be the only option. Assessment and testing will inevitably be areas of contention. The main reasons for this are:

- Assessment and testing are important guard posts on the boundary between the internal work of schools and the public interest in control of that work.

- Assessment issues are not marginal features of education they are central.

- The assessment and testing practices which any of us experience are a product of our particular historical and social contexts: this insight might help us to understand them better, but it will also warn us that the practices cannot easily be changed.

- Assessment practices cannot stand still they are driven by social changes and can be used to promote or resist those changes. A notable case is the need to move from higher education for an élite to mass higher education, with the consequent erosion of the dominance of special interests, whether or university entrance, or of particular professions, or of other social élites.

- At the same time, there are other professional pressures to change. These include moves towards criterion-referencing and away from norm-referencing, towards achieving a better match between learning aims and testing realities, towards assessing an increasingly broad range of outcomes and personal qualities, and towards giving teachers an enhanced role in assessment.

- The structure of assessment and testing policies is a complex one, involving the intersection of aspects of psychology, pedagogy, curriculum, statistics, professional competence and status, budgets and competing public and political priorities.

Thus there are strong drives for change, but policy cannot simply 'cruise down a broad, smooth road'. The appropriate metaphor is rather of 'negotiating a mountain pass'. Perhaps using this metaphor, evoking negotiation of tight bends, the risk of precipitous falls, the juggernaut coming the other way, seems a little dramatic. But if it is justified, this is because any policy faces several obstacles and dilemmas, all of which are difficult to overcome or resolve. Seven of the main obstacles may be summarized as follows.

## No educational system can move too far and too fast from its starting point

Even if we can be freed from old assumptions and can think ourselves into new frame-works, we are still constrained by history and tradition, for all studies of educational change show that attempts to move quickly are counterproductive. If they fail, they give reform a bad name.

## The different purposes are bound to be in tension

A strong drive for accountability can undermine good practices for certification, for example by requiring a uniformity that inhibits change and by emphasizing reliability at the expense of validity. Policies focused on the accountability and certification functions that pay no heed to their effect on classroom learning will inevitably damage formative assessment. The difference purposes, pursued in isolation, pull in contrary directions, not least because they involve debate between those whose interests are bureaucratic, those caring for the pro-fessional status and conditions of teachers, and those whose concerns are centred on the strengthening of the pupil. Optimum resolutions are hard to find, but must be pursued.

## Validity is central yet hard to attain

Achieving information of a quality which will justify the inferences and actions which must be based upon it, i.e. valid information is notoriously hard to achieve. If this information is to be generated cheaply, we have to use test situations that are so bizarrely unlike those in which people have to use their learned competencies that the task seems almost impossible. Yet it is hard to prove that hallowed practices are both strange and harmful, even harder to justify the cost of doing better. Even without such constraints far more work is needed to explore the extent to which any known assessment practices can in fact be justified in the light of the way the results are to be expressed, in the way they are to be understood as meaningful indicators of performance, and in the way they are to be used, both to influence teaching and learning and to select or predict for students' futures. Such justifications are notably lacking at present.

## A wide variety of assessment methods is available, but can we afford to use them?

All methods have their advantages and disadvantages. A system that uses a range of methods can give a rich picture of pupils that, with careful interpretation, can be robust against various sources of random error and of bias. However, such richness has a high cost, which raises the question of priorities. How much are we prepared to pay for better assessment?

## Teachers and schools need the freedom of diversity, but society needs uniformity

Teachers are the key to any change, and assessment practices cannot improve unless teachers can be supported by programmes to develop their assessment expertise. Given such programmes, more can be achieved if the status of teachers can be recognized and their expertise trusted. However, this cannot go far if they do not have freedom of manoeuvre, so a tension will arise between imposed uniformity and local autonomy, a tension which will inhere in matters of curriculum, assessment criteria, assessment standards and the currency of qualifications.

## Pupils' expectations are crucial to the learning society

Building up the capability of pupils is the ultimate goal in education, and assessment is more than a useful adjunct for this task. Much of current thinking is about the future of social, business and industrial organizations is moving away from centrally controlled and unchanging structures to 'flat management' structures, which are more adaptable because they can learn quickly and in which responsibility is increasingly delegated to those 'on the ground'. If pupils are to be prepared for such a society, responsibility for their own learning, and self-assessment so that they can monitor and so control and improve their work outside the protective and supportive framework of the school, will be aims deserving increased priority. Yet to focus on this type of enhancement of pupils' learning takes time and new pedagogy, and less of the content curriculum will be covered. How can teachers be brave enough to do this, and how can external high-stakes assessment support them?

## Public concerns about standards can be fuelled and misled by simplistic interpretations of test scores

Raw score data cannot give meaningful and trustworthy comparisons unless they are judged in the contexts of comprehensive data on the many factors that affect such scores, and sophisticated analysis upon which careful evaluations of the data can be based. A particularly salient feature here is the variation in the extent to which different societies feel able to trust and support teachers in playing an important part in assessments for pupil certification and for accountability.

Improved learning requires thoughtful reflection, discussion, interaction between teachers and taught, formative feedback. It follows that reform of curriculum, of pedagogy and of formative assessment all have to go together. Reform of assessment cannot proceed on its own. Certification and accountability policies should be as consistent with and as supportive of such a reform as possible, yet the fact that all countries seem to compromise in trying to reconcile different purposes and functions is a sure sign that there are no easy solutions. It is hard to proceed by small steps, yet too risky to try to change everything at once.

Any significant improvement in assessment practices must be supported, if not initiated, by political policies and one strategic priority of such policies must be to achieve optimum consistency between the curriculum, pedagogy and the different purposes which assessment should serve. Thus, reform has to be systemic in design, even if it may be piecemeal in implementation. Political strategies are bound to be affected by the understanding of assessment issues, on the part both of politicians and of the general public to whom they must appeal. The following quotation by Shepard talking about the need for reform of assessment policies in the US could well apply to most other countries.

If they are unaware of new research findings about how children learn, policy makers are apt to rely on their own implicit theories which were most probably shaped by the theories that were current when they themselves attended school . . . Some things that psychologists can prove today even contradict the popular wisdom of several decades ago. Therefore, if policy makers proceed to implement outmoded theories or tests based on old theories, they might actually subvert their intended goal – of providing a rigorous and high quality education for all students. (Shepard, 1992, p. 301)

## READING 14.3

# Teacher feedback in the Reception class

## Andrew Burrell and Sara Bubb

This reading takes some of the big issues in assessment and grounds them in classroom practice. It reports on a small-scale study that focused on the nature of the feedback given to two children, Richard and Jane, in a Reception class. Teacher feedback was observed and categorised using a typology developed by Caroline Gipps and her colleagues (1996). This is thus also a nice example of the application of research for professional reflection.

Are there any significant patterns in the forms of feedback that you offer the children in your class?

Edited from: Burrell, A. and Bubb, S. (2000) 'Teacher feedback in the Reception class', *Education 3–13*, 28 (3), 59–63.

Children in school need to feel secure and happy in order to meet the challenges presented to them through the school curriculum, particularly learning to read and write. The class teacher and other adults are likely to play a particularly important part in achieving this. One aspect of their interaction with the children concerns the kind of feedback given. Such feedback might contribute to the children's emotional and social adjustment. Moreover, it may affect their attitude and behaviour in response to the intellectual demands that are made on them.

Research conducted by Gipps *et al.* (1996) observed the process of feedback to children by primary teachers. It was suggested that the feedback serves three functions. First, as part of the classroom socialization process. This would seem to be particularly important in the child's first year in school. Second, it serves to encourage the children and maintain motivation and effort. Finally, it identifies specific aspects of attainment or good performance in relation to a specific task. Through their research, Gipps *et al.* (1996) were able to generate a typology of teacher feedback. Details of this typology are provided in Figure 14.3.1.

We conducted a small-scale study to examine the nature and frequency of verbal feedback in the reception class in relation to adjustment to school. The class teacher was asked to nominate two children, one who they thought had adjusted poorly to school and the other who they considered had adjusted very well. This required her to make a personal judgement based on her own construct of 'adjustment'. In the case study, Jane was considered by her class teacher to be very well adjusted to school. In contrast, Richard was considered to be poorly adjusted to school. These two children were in a class of 27 pupils, 15 of whom were full-time from September. The data were collected using a form of semi-structured observational event sampling. This required the observer to focus on the two children throughout the day and to record the types of feedback that each received. The observation was divided into five-minute intervals, in which significant events were recorded.

The structured observations were then considered in relation to the typology of feedback suggested by Gipps *et al.* (see Figure 14.3.2). Striking differences can be observed. In terms of

| | Type A | Type B | Type C | Type D | |
|---|---|---|---|---|---|
| **1**<br>**Positive**<br>**feedback** | A1<br>Rewarding | B1<br>Approving | C1<br>Specifying<br>attainment | D1<br>Constructing<br>achievement | **1**<br>**Achievement**<br>**feedback** |
| | rewards | positive personal expression; warm expression of feeling; general praises; positive non-verbal feedback | specific acknowledgement of attainment/use of criteria in relation to work/behaviour; teacher models; more specific praise | mutual articulation of achievement; additional use of emerging criteria; child role in presentation; praise integral to description | |
| **2**<br>**Negative**<br>**feedback** | A2<br>Punishing | B2<br>Disapproving | C2<br>Specifying<br>improvement | D2<br>Constructing<br>the way<br>forward | **2**<br>**Improvement**<br>**feedback** |
| | punishing | negative personal expression; reprimands; negative generalizations; negative non-verbal feedback | correction of errors; more practice given; training in self-checking | mutual critical appraisal | |

**Figure 14.3.1**    Teacher feedback typology: a summary

positive feedback, Jane, who is considered by her class teacher to be well adjusted, received feedback that is both rewarding and approving. In contrast, Richard, the child considered by his class teacher to be poorly adjusted, receives no positive feedback from any of the adults he comes into contact with in the classroom during the course of the day. If we consider negative feedback, the poorly adjusted child receives a high proportion of feedback which can be regarded as 'disapproving'. In addition to this, there were also two occasions of feedback in which the child was punished. The well-adjusted child received no such negative feedback.

Richard, the poorly adjusted child, did receive feedback of the 'improvement' kind (C2). This was mainly in the form of descriptive feedback whereby the teacher specified how something being learned could be corrected. Feedback of this kind is specific to a particular task or aspect of behaviour and is focused on where mistakes lie. Both children received feedback which prompted and supported them to examine their work and to make comparisons with their previous performance. This was usually in the form of a dialogue between the teacher and child.

Overall, tracking the children over the course of the day provided only one example of feedback of the 'constructing achievement' kind. This was targeted to Jane, the child who was

|  | Type A | Type B | Type C | Type D |  |
|---|---|---|---|---|---|
| 1<br>**Positive feedback** | A1<br>Rewarding | B1<br>Approving | C1<br>Specifying attainment | D1<br>Constructing achievement | 1<br>**Achievement feedback** |
| Richard<br>Jane | 0<br>3 | 0<br>4 | 0<br>0 | 0<br>1 |  |
| 2<br>**Negative feedback** | A2<br>Punishing | B2<br>Disapproving | C2<br>Specifying improvement | D2<br>Constructing the way forward | 2<br>**Improvement feedback** |
| Richard<br>Jane | 2<br>0 | 14<br>0 | 7<br>0 | 2<br>2 |  |

**Figure 14.3.2**   Frequency of teacher feedback

considered by the class teacher to be well adjusted. It is interesting to note the absence of feedback that was concerned with attainment and achievement.

The child's first year at school marks for most children the transition from home into a school setting. Research supports the need for an early positive adjustment to school and the benefits this has on future learning. Teacher feedback has a crucial role in such adjustment. In our child-focused observations, sharp differences existed in the kinds of feedback given to those children who had, according to the class teacher, adjusted very well to school and those who had not. We might speculate that if this was representative of the feedback they received on a daily basis there would either be an upward spiral or, of more concern, a downward one in their attitudes towards school and learning.

## READING 14.4

# Reinforcing learning intentions through oral feedback

Shirley Clarke

Shirley Clarke offers a simple but extremely powerful insight in this reading. She draws attention to the tendency for teacher feedback to focus on secondary, surface features of pupils' work, rather than on the main learning objectives. Clarifying learning intentions with children, combined with maintaining that focus through consistent feedback, is undoubtedly extremely effective.

Could you improve the feedback that you offer the children in your class?

Edited from: Clarke, S. (2001) *Unlocking Formative Assessment: Practical Strategies for Enhancing Pupils' Learning in the Primary Classroom.* London: Hodder & Stoughton Educational, 50–3

This reading deals with two aspects of feedback: oral and written, including marking. It focuses mainly on feedback from teacher to child, but this develops to include children's feedback to each other.

Various research studies have concluded that feedback is most useful when it focuses on the learning intention of the task, rather than other features of the work. However, research also shows that most teachers give feedback to children about four other features of their work before, or even instead of, the learning intention of the task. The four issues that interpose are:

- presentation (handwriting/neatness);

- surface features of writing (full stops, capital letters and especially spelling);

- quantity;

- effort.

It is easy to see why this happens: those aspects are most noticeable in children's work at first sight. They are also relatively straightforward to deal with. Ironically, these are the very things teachers accuse parents of focusing on at parents' evenings.

For an example of what can happen, consider the following classroom episode:

The children have been asked to cut out, order and then glue muddled-up pictures of a story onto a piece of paper. Learning intentions and success criteria are displayed prominently, as follows:

*We are learning to:* Order stories.
*How will we know we've done this:* The pictures will be in the same order as the story we read.

- As the children start to work, the teacher notices that one child already has glue all over his trousers. She goes to the child and speaks to him, getting him to go quickly to the washroom to clean up. The rest of the group starts to fuss about glue. One child rushes to get a cloth as she notices glue on her table and the whole class starts to chat about glue or anything else.

- The teacher notices a child having difficulty cutting out and goes over to help her hold the scissors correctly, talking about how much better she is getting at this. One child tells the teacher that she's been able to cut out properly for a year now. Some children, having roughly cut out two of their pictures are now going back to them and cutting them out more neatly, because they don't want the teacher to criticize their cutting. They had not cut out neatly in the first place because they thought the emphasis was on ordering.

- The teacher passes a child who has, at last, written her name on the paper with a capital letter at the beginning of her name. She praises the child enthusiastically. Some of the children now cross out their names on their sheets, because they realize they had also forgotten to do this.

- The teacher congratulates one child who is working industriously, saying how pleased she is to see her working so hard. The children sit up straighter to get some praise themselves.

At this point, the class knows that the learning intention and success criteria are a lie. The teacher has made clear by her words that what she is looking for is not the ordering, but presentation, surface features, effort and cutting skills.

Alternatively, consider the following strategy for giving feedback focused around the learning intentions:

- As the children start to work, the teacher notices that one child already has glue all over his trousers. She goes to the child and first says something about the learning intention: 'Well done, I can see you've got the first picture in place. Now what happened next in the story, after the Little Red Hen had dug the ground?' Some of the children quietly call out 'planted the seeds' and continue with their ordering. The teacher then whispers to the child, 'You've got glue on your trousers. Go and clean up quickly'.

- The teacher notices a child having difficulty cutting out. She moves to her and congratulates her on cutting out all the pictures first: 'That's a very good strategy. You have cut out all the pictures first so that you can shuffle them around and change your mind'. Some of the children are now peeling off their stuck-down pictures, because they agree that it is a very good strategy. The teacher then whispers to the child about holding the scissors.

At this point, the class knows that the learning intention and success criteria are the truth. The teacher has made clear by her words that what she is looking for is ordering.

This technique has been received very powerfully by teachers, who realize how often they have fallen into the trap of focusing on other features and distracting the class from the prime focus of their learning. One teacher said:

> I recognized things in myself like commenting about the handwriting and spelling, when I should be commenting on the learning intention. It's been a real revelation to me. I'm aware of it all the time now and when I hear myself starting to say 'You've left a capital letter out there', I stop really quickly now and go back to talking about the learning intention.

It takes a while to get into the habit, but the strategy is simple. We need to learn to make sure that something about the learning intention is mentioned first, whilst holding onto the thought about the secondary feature. Indeed, mention the glue or handwriting, if it is necessary, in a whisper. The class will retain their focus on the learning intention, which will be apparent in their improved work.

---

## READING 14.5

# Pupil self-assessment

Yolande Muschamp

---

Yolande Muschamp and a team of seconded teachers spent two years working with colleagues in 24 classrooms to develop practical ways of encouraging pupil self-assessment in primary school classrooms. One product of this action research study was this reading. It contains practical advice, based around the negotiation and use of 'targets'. The idea of pupil self-assessment is closely related to Vygotsky's conception of self-regulation (see Reading 7.3 and 13.2).

Do you see a role for self-assessment in your classroom?

Edited from: Muschamp. Y. (1991) 'Pupil Self-Assessment', *Practical Issues in Primary Education*, No. 9. Bristol: National Primary Centre (South West), 1–8

---

Our discussions with teachers revealed a strong commitment to, 'ongoing assessment, that could be built upon every day'. Teachers wanted to support children's learning through careful use of formative assessment. What is more, many felt that children should themselves be involved in their own assessment. As one teacher put it:

We are now more conscious about making children independent and responsible for their own learning. It is fascinating to see how they view their role and work, and want to look back.

This was not a new idea. Involving children in self-appraisal had been suggested, for example, by HMI as a way of motivating children and the introduction of records of achievement was also based on this principle. However, we wanted to take this involvement further to see whether particular assessment strategies could lead to the children taking a greater responsibility for their learning and progress.

Working alongside children we were initially able to record the evaluations that they made of their work. We also asked them to comment on the work of other children presented to them in a folder. This showed that children were making assessments, but in a relatively limited way. For instance, we asked children what, specifically, made a piece of work 'good'. Although we received a wide range of answers the comments which predominated related to presentation.

The writing must be neat.

The letters are very big, I think the 'g' is the wrong way round.

Without exception the children commented on how neat or tidy they felt each piece of work to be; how large the letters were; or how accurately drawings had been coloured. Often this was given as the only reason for the work to have any worth. When questioned further, some children were able to explain some of the specific features that made a piece of work satisfactory:

The answers are all right.

You mustn't repeat things like 'and then' and you must put in a lot of details and describing words.

The lines don't go over the edges.

However, when asked why they thought they were doing a particular activity, very few children understood the specific aims of their teacher. Their comments were often very general:

So when we grow up we will know how to write.

To help you get a good job.

As a group we shared our findings and decided to see if extending children's understanding of the purpose of activities, would widen the range of comments that they made. We hoped that children would develop a fuller picture of the progress they made if more aspects of the learning aims were shared with them. It was agreed that, in each of the classes, children would be encouraged to move through three stages.

## Stage 1: Sharing aims and using targets

Teachers felt that by introducing plans at the beginning of the year, and then monthly or half termly, children were provided with an overview or context for their work. Three parts to this strategy emerged.

The first was establishing learning objectives in which children were given, or helped to plan, clear learning objectives. The skills, knowledge and understanding that activities were designed to develop were discussed. These were presented to even very young children in such ways as, 'learning how to . . .' and 'learning all about . . .'.

Second, was selecting a focus. Here we found it was important to be very precise and explicit about what it was the children were going to do. Within activities we selected one or two specific areas to focus on, for example, 'good beginnings for stories', 'measuring accurately to the nearest centimetre' and 'concentrating on the sequence of an account'.

Finally, we made decisions on forms of learning support. For instance, children did not always have the technical language to talk about their work and rarely had considered which method to use. Introducing a few helpful terms and discussing the range of methods available became part of the sharing of aims. These might have included words such as, 'description', 'design', 'fair test', 'account'. The methods might include, 'looking closely and drawing', 'taking notes', 'using an index' and 'drafting'.

Once a child had a clear idea of what it was they were trying to do, then planning targets became much easier.

The targets were particularly important because, when matched closely to the activities that had been planned, they allowed children to decide when the activity had been successfully completed and to monitor what they had learned. We found that it was helpful to plan the targets as questions that the children could ask themselves. Thus, when learning a skill, the child could ask: 'What will I be able to do?'. When the learning objective was finding out or acquiring knowledge, the child could ask: 'What do I know now?'. When the objective was to develop understanding, the child could ask: 'Can I explain?'.

However, children did not always learn what was planned. Indeed, despite following a carefully planned curriculum, many teachers were reluctant to lose opportunities for learning that presented themselves almost by chance. We thus found it important to allow time to discuss what else the child had learned during the activities.

In some activities it was very difficult for pupils to decide if any learning had taken place at all, even though teachers were confident that the activities had been of value. There were particular types of activities that fell into this category: practice, art, enjoyment and religious education. Practice and reinforcement activities did not always lead to any new learning. Many physical actions, for example, throwing and catching, did not always show any short-term improvement. It was hard for pupils to identify the specific learning in some forms of artistic self-expression or expression of points of view. Learning that took place around art activities, such as learning to mix paint, share equipment or clear away, was easier to identify. Enjoyment experienced in many activities, for example reading or watching a dramatic performance, seemed to make children uncertain about what they had actually learned. A similar difficulty existed here with regard to religious education. It became very complex when children and teachers tried to assess benefits beyond just the factual information that had been learned.

We tried several ways of getting around these difficulties and found one simple, but by no means perfect solution. We added new targets which would only reflect the completion of a task: 'I will/have read . . .', 'we will/have visited . . .' and 'I have/will created . . .'. These were supplemented with the child's account of their enjoyment or interest in the activities. As these comments accumulated over the year, long-term changes, for example in the enjoyment or developing interest in music, could be detected.

Having planned the targets, assessing them became relatively straightforward. Children were encouraged to refer to their targets alongside their work. One pleasing effect was that children often kept on course and did not become bored with the assessments. There were also noticeable improvements in the pacing of work. The following approaches were used:

- *Teacher assessment:* with the targets planned and documented, teachers found it effective to assess them in a short discussion with a child. A child could be asked to perform, explain or give an account of a topic. This was supplemented by an open question about unexpected outcomes and general questions about activities that the child had enjoyed or taken a particular interest in.

- *Peer assessement:* working in groups, children soon found it easy to discuss and assess their targets with their friends. Many teachers were surprised at how sophisticated the questioning of each other became. In a few schools this led to the development of pupil-designed questionnaires for self-assessment.

- *self assessment:* the children's initial comments were rather basic, such as, 'this is good, for me'. Some targets were simply ticked with no comment. However, with encouragement, children soon illustrated how targets had been met and moved quickly on to planning new ones, 'I have counted threes with Daniel. I went up to 39. My next pattern is sixes'.

## Stage 2: Reviewing, 'feeding forward' and recording

The main purpose of the review stage was for the child to stand back and assess the progress that they had been making over a few weeks, a month or a term. This stage also included selecting documentation to record this progress, looking back and editing old records. A valuable outcome was the creation of a basis for reporting to parents, transferring to a new class and planning for the future.

Many different ways of reviewing were tried. The most successful often reflected the way the classrooms already operated and did not therefore appear unusual or artificial to the children. For example:

- *Conferencing:* in which time was put aside for the teacher and pupil to talk together about how targets had been met, what should be followed up and 'fed forward' into future planning. The children were already used to reading with the teacher in a one-to-one situation. A card index was used to keep track of whose turn it was to talk with the teacher. Notes for future planning were written on the cards.

- *Quiet time:* was provided to allow children to look through their work alone or with a partner. They were encouraged to take notes for planning and development activities.

- *Questionnaires:* were designed by the teacher and by the children as a basis for review. Some were adapted so that they could be used to annotate any work chosen to be stored as a record.

Although we found teachers continuously responding to, and advising children, it was felt that a lot of good ideas for future action were still being lost or forgotten at the review stage. Several ways of developing a system for managing this 'feed forward' were tried and proved successful. For instance:

- *Ideas box:* at a class level many ideas for future investigations were collected and stored on cards for all to use. This system operated rather like the floor book.

- *'How to' books:* children wrote up things that they had learnt to do in a class book for others to use. However more was often learned by children during the writing up than by other children reading the books. They were very popular and of great interest to other children.

- *Notebooks:* a small notebook or a page set aside in a larger book, folder or profile were used in some classes for children to record their own plans, areas for development and interests. These were often used to complete planning sheets.

Two particular challenges faced us at the recording stage. First, how could the recording that the children did themselves become part of everyday classroom life? Many solutions were determined by what was already happening in the classrooms. For instance, loose-leaf records were selected and moved to a profile or record of achievement folder; photocopying or photography were used where schools felt able to afford them, and were already using them for other purposes; children's comments were written down for them by an older child or adult in schools where this sort of shared activity was encouraged.

Second, on what basis should a selection for a record be made? The reasons for selection varied from school to school, reflecting the policies that had been developed for similar areas such as the selection of work for displays or the participation in assemblies. In many schools children were encouraged to select their 'best work' as a record of their achievement, whereas another school decided to select 'before and after' pieces, such as, a first draft and a final desktop-published version of a story; or a list from a brainstorming and a drawing of the final result of an investigation in science. The idea of 'significance' was introduced in some classes, so that children were helped to identify pieces of work which had a special meaning or association for them. Additionally, sampling by subject or over time was tried. This was often done as a 'snap-shot' exercise but could be used as a carefully scheduled system.

## Stage 3: Helping to report on progress

An exciting highlight of the self-assessment strategies that we were developing occurred when the children were given the opportunity to share their assessments with their parents or carers. This worked most successfully where this was part of an overall policy for home–school liaison. Schools where parents were already fully involved in classroom activities found it easier to encourage children's involvement in the reporting process. The children's role in this process varied enormously. For instance:

- *helping in the preparation of reports* occured when children were encouraged to write a short report of their progress and thoughts about school based on the reviews that they had carried out. Teachers and the parents then added their comments.

- *playing host* was a role undertaken when parents and carers visited the school during an ordinary day. The children took them on a tour of specially prepared displays; showed them the work they were doing; and shared their profiles or records of achievement with them.

- *preparing for parent interviews* was an important role for children in lots of different ways, such as putting out a display of their work or taking their profiles home to share before a parent–teacher interview. Some accompanied their parents, or actually organized a parents' afternoon themselves.

It is always hard to evaluate development projects, for what may be proved to be possible in the short term may not be sustained over a longer period. However, we can record teacher opinion that the encouragement of pupil self-assessment through the use of targets had a very worthwhile effect on teaching and learning processes in the classrooms in which we worked. Furthermore, everyone – teachers, parents and pupils themselves – seemed to enjoy working in this way.

📖 READING 14.6

# Trying to understand

## Mary Jane Drummond

In this powerful reading, Mary Jane Drummond leads us to consider some of the fundamental questions in assessment though a consideration of the thinking of kindergarten children. In particular, she demonstrates how assessment must be connected to understanding of pupils' perceptions if it is to have value in informing teaching–learning processes.

Reviewing the assessment evidence available to you about pupils, to what extent does it enable you to understand them and their learning needs?

Edited from: Drummond, M. J. (1993) *Assessing Children's Learning*. London: David Fulton, 70–188

In assessing learning, the act of seeing gives way to the act of understanding; the process of collecting evidence is followed by attempts to make the evidence meaningful. In this part of the practice of assessment, the assessors strive to make sense of what they have seen and remembered.

The work of Vivian Gussin Paley (1981), an American kindergarten teacher, provides many instructive examples of the educator 'seeing children as (s)he wishes them to be'. Or rather, seeing them at first in this way; Paley records her detailed evidence and sets it against her wished-for interpretation. Time and again, the educator's perspective, the educator's intentions, do not match the evidence. Time and again, Paley is forced to reconsider, to reconstruct the framework within which she makes meaning. In the following incident (Paley, 1981, pp. 57–8), the five-year-old children in Paley's kindergarten class have planted lima beans in individual milk cartons, but after three weeks no green shoots have appeared. Wally discovers that his beans have disappeared.

'They're gone!' he yelled, bringing me his carton. 'Gone! I looked through the whole dirt!'
'Can I look in mine?' asked Rose.
'You might as well,' I answered. 'They don't seem to be coming up.'
There was a rush to the planting table. Everyone began digging into cartons or dumping their contents on the newspaper-covered table. The conversation unfolded:

| | |
|---|---|
| Andy: | Where are the beans? |
| Wally: | They're invisible. |
| Andy: | Impossible. They came from a store. Someone took them out. |
| Teacher: | Who? |
| Andy: | A robber. |
| Eddie: | When it was dark a criminal took them. |
| Teacher: | Why would he do it? |
| Jill: | Maybe someone came in and said, 'Oh, there's nothing growing. We must take some of them out'. |
| Eddie: | I think a robber broke in and said, 'They don't need to plant those beans'. |
| Teacher: | Why would a robber want them? |
| Wally: | To sell them. |
| Andy: | Or cook them. |
| Ellen: | No, maybe to fool people with. See, he could plant them in his garden and when flowers came up people would think he's nice. |

Teacher:    If I were a robber I'd take a record player.

Eddie:    Not if you wanted to plant seeds.

Here we see two ways of understanding the world at work. The children account for the missing beans with imaginary robbers; the teacher is intent on the logical connections, as she sees them, between a real robber and what he would be likely to steal. The children do not consider that the robber's imaginary theft needs any further explanation: stealing is what robbers do. If there are beans to steal, and a robber about, then the robber will certainly steal them. Trying to understand her pupils' thinking, Paley talks to another kindergarten class about the decaying Halloween pumpkin that they are observing (Paley, 1981, pp. 59–60).

Teacher:    Why does your pumpkin look like this?

Tim:    It's full of mold.

Carter:    It's moldy. Plants are growing inside.

Julia:    Little vines.

William:    They make the top fall in.

Kevin:    Dead plants and animals get mold.

Tim:    Old pumpkins get moldy.

Julia:    It's going to become dust.

Teacher:    How does that happen?

Julia:    It'll get so dry you won't even see it.

Teacher:    By the way, we have a problem in class. We planted lima beans and after a long time nothing came up. We looked in the dirt to see if any roots had grown and we couldn't find the beans. They were gone.

Kevin:    Was the window open? The wind blew them away.

Teacher:    They were deep down in the dirt.

Candy:    A squirrel could have took them.

Teacher:    We didn't see a squirrel in the room.

Candy:    It could have hid somewhere.

Teacher:    Our windows are locked at night. How could the squirrel have gotten back out?

William:    He could scratch a hole in the window.

Kevin:    Or in the door.

Carter:    May a robber stepped in. They can get in windows very easily.

Teacher:    Why would he want the beans?

Carter:    For his garden.

Julia:    Or to cook them. Somebody has a key to your windows, I think.

There was no further talk of squirrels once the robber theory was suggested. I was so surprised by this change of opinion after talking about a rotting pumpkin that I presented my question to the third kindergarten. One child said a bird might be the culprit, another suspected worms. However, when a third mentioned robbers, everyone immediately agreed that the beans had been removed by a human intruder to plant, eat or sell.

The children use 'robbers', Paley comes to see, as a powerful explanatory theory for all missing items. Mislaid coats, beans, rugs and sweaters are all attributed to robbers. These children's theory satisfies their need to account for missing objects, by drawing on one single attribute of robbers – their propensity to rob. All other aspects of a robber's behaviour are left out of the account; the teacher's attempts to make the supposed robber's behaviour consistent in adult terms are rejected out of hand, not because they threaten the children's explanation but because they are simply irrelevant. The children's implicit syllogism is too pure and simple to be contaminated with the teacher's irrelevancies. Their argument seems to go:

Robbers steal things.
The beans have disappeared.
Therefore robbers stole the beans.

Paley's account of her pupils' thinking is deeply rewarding, since it enables the reader to follow in her footsteps as she comes, little by little, to understand and respect the role that illusion and fantasy play in the minds of five- and six-year-olds. They have, she concludes, 'become aware of the thinking required by the adult world,' but are not yet 'committed to its burden of rigid consistency' (p. 81).

Paley is not dismayed or destroyed by the necessity of reshaping her interpretations of children's thinking; she is, rather, humbled by what the children have taught her to see, and grateful for the opportunity to learn from them. For Paley, as for all of us, 'knowledge is always from a position'. The new 'position', from which she applies her knowledge of children's minds, may in turn be reformed and renewed; in the meantime there is no weakness in her understanding, but a strength, in that as she strives, in her daily work, to understand what she has seen, she also constantly and critically reviews this very process of coming to understand.

There are three crucial questions that teachers and other educators must ask themselves as they set about assessing children's learning. When we look at learning:

- What is there to see?

- How best can we understand what we see?

- How best can we put our understanding to good use?

We would be deluding ourselves if we thought that these questions could ever be answered once and for all, or that assessment is a practice that can ever be perfected. Children's learning is so complex and various that the task of trying to understand it is necessarily complex too. The task entails trying to see and understand the whole, as well as the minutest parts; it requires us to appreciate the past, and analyse the present, as well as envisage and welcome the future; it obliges us to look for and attend to differences as well as similarities, individuals as well as groups, the unexpected as well as the intended outcome, absence as well as presence. It demands a broad vision and a narrow focus.

Above all, effective assessment requires educators to make choices, in the interests of children, that are based on a coherent set of principles, which are themselves an expression of each educator's core values. As these choices are made, and translated into daily classroom practice, teachers are exercising their responsibility for children's learning, their right to act in children's interests, and their power to do so wisely and well.

# The myth of objective assessment

## Ann Filer and Andrew Pollard

This reading highlights the social factors that inevitably affect school assessment processes, pupil performance and the interpretation of assessment outcomes. The consequence, it is argued, is that National Curriculum Assessment procedures cannot produce 'objective' evidence of pupil, teacher or school performance. Whilst much assessment evidence may have valuable uses in supporting learning, it is thus an insecure source of comparative data for accountability purposes.

How do circumstances affect performance and assessment in your school?

Edited from: Filer, A. and Pollard, A. (2000) *The Social World of Pupil Assessment: Processes and Contexts of Primary Schooling*. London: Continuum.

The assessment of educational performance is of enormous significance in modern societies. In particular, official assessment procedures are believed to provide 'hard evidence' on which governments, parents and the media evaluate educational policies and hold educational institutions to account; pupil and student learners are classified and counselled on life-course decisions; and employers make judgements about recruitment.

Underpinning such confident practices is a belief that educational assessments are sufficiently objective, reliable and impartial to be used in these ways. But is this belief supported by evidence? Can the results of nationally required classroom assessments be treated as being factual and categoric?

Our longitudinal, ethnographic research (Filer and Pollard, 2000) focused on social processes and taken-for-granted practices in schools and homes during the primary years and beyond. In particular, it documented their influence on three key processes: the production of pupil performance, the assessment of pupil performance and the interpretation of such judgements. On the basis of this analysis we argue that, despite both politicians' rhetoric and the sincere efforts of teachers, the pure 'objectivity' of assessment outcomes is an illusion. More specifically, we suggest that:

- individual pupil performances cannot be separated from the contexts and social relations from within which they develop;

- classroom assessment techniques are social processes that are vulnerable to bias and distortion;

- the 'results' of assessment take their meaning for individuals via cultural processes of interpretation and following mediation by others.

Our argument thus highlights various ways in which social processes inevitably intervene in assessment.

In this reading we confine ourselves to describing and selectively illustrating the core analytic framework which we have constructed. In particular, we identify five key questions concerned with assessment. These are set out in Figure 14.7.1.

## Who is being assessed?

The key issue here concerns the pupil's personal sense of identity. Put directly, each pupil's performance fulfils and represents his or her sense of self-confidence and identity as a learner.

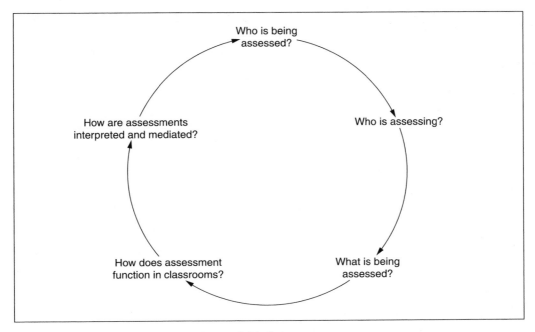

**Figure 14.7.1**   Questions concerning social influences on assessment

We see self-perceptions held by individuals and judgements made about individuals as being inextricably linked to the social relationships through which they live their lives. Of course, there certainly are factors that are internal to the individual in terms of capacities and potentials, but realization of such attributes is a product of external social circumstances and social relationships to a very significant extent (see Pollard with Filer, 1996). Amongst these are school assessments, of various forms, which constitute formalized, partial, but very powerful social representations of individuals. In our full account (Filer and Pollard, 2000), we provide extensive case study examples of such influences on the development of children's identities – for instance, through the story of Elizabeth and her primary school career.

In the autumn of 1988, five-year-old Elizabeth entered Mrs Joy's reception class with about 27 other children and began her schooling at Albert Park. She was a physically healthy, attractive and lively child and assessments made during that first year relate to such characteristics, as well as to her intellectual and linguistic competence. Teacher records recorded a range of Elizabeth's communication, physical and intellectual skills:

Vocabulary good – a clear ability to express herself – confident – can communicate with adults. Can concentrate and talk about her observations.

Good language and fine motor skills – reading now enthusiastic – writing good.

Can organise herself, is able to take turns.

(Profile for Nursery and Reception Age Children, Summer 1989, Reception)

However, Mrs Joy perceived Elizabeth's classroom relationships in a more negative light, as her records from the time also show:

Elizabeth is loud during class activity time – she never looks particularly happy unless doing something she shouldn't be. Elizabeth is a loud boisterous child who needs constant correction of negative behaviour. When corrected she often cries and becomes morose for a short period. Elizabeth doesn't mix well with the girls and disrupts them at any given opportunity. (Teacher records, Reception, 1988–9)

Elizabeth's mother described herself as 'strict' and 'watchful' and was concerned for Elizabeth's behaviour and safety from the earliest age. She was particularly sensitive to the ways in which her daughter behaved in school. At home, in interview, she gave her views on parental responsibilities in this respect:

It's the school's responsibility to *teach* the children, but as for behavioural – I mean, that still belongs to the parent. What a child is taught *before* it goes to school shows up when it's *at* school. I say if the parents let the child run riot before they go to school and don't show any discipline whatsoever, how can they expect that child to behave itself when it goes to school? (Eleanor Barnes, parent interview with Ann Filer, July 1994, Year 5)

Other expectations of Elizabeth's mother related to Elizabeth's identity as a girl and a wish that she was 'more dainty' and, in the opinion of her Year 2 teacher, a wish that she could have 'a neat, quiet child'. Certainly, Eleanor Barnes held gendered expectations regarding the learning styles of girls and boys. Though, of course, she certainly wished for Elizabeth to do well at school, she revealed in many of her conversations in interview an expectation for a physical and intellectual passivity in girls that Elizabeth did not conform to. For instance:

. . . I mean, in some ways I think she should have been a boy because she's got so much *energy*, and she just wants to know about *everything* – How does this work? Why does it work like that? What do you do with this? – I mean, probably that is *her*. That is her personality. She wants to know everything and she wants to know what everybody else is doing. (Eleanor Barnes, parent interview with Ann Filer, July 1995, Year 6)

Even these brief illustrative snippets of data convey the interaction between the evolving identity of children and the views and actions of significant others in their lives. The data demonstrates just how diverse, complex and enduring such influences can be. However, variability in such social support for children is likely to be echoed by variability of their performance – with the result that this may not reflect their true potential. Performance is thus, in part, a social product that reflects self-belief and circumstances.

## Who is assessing?

Having argued that pupil identity can only be understood in context, we clearly need to focus on teachers – since they are undoubtedly the most powerful classroom participants with whom pupils must interact.

In particular, we need a sociological conception of pedagogy and its link to each teacher's own sense of personal identity. For this, we have used the concept of 'coping strategy' and traced how satisfying role expectations and the constant pressures of teaching must be balanced with maintaining sense of personal integrity and fulfilment. In the immediacy of classroom dynamics, this can be seen as teachers juggle to resolve endemic dilemmas. At the level of the school, it is played out through negotiation between different interest groups and the formation of taken-for-granted institutional assumptions. In *The Social World of Pupil Assessment* (Filer and Pollard, 2000), we relate such issues to the context of the early 1990s in which the National Curriculum and new assessment requirements were introduced. A case study of Marie Tucker and her classroom practice demonstrates the detailed application of this analysis, showing how her coping strategies, classroom organization and associated pedagogies produced particular contexts which satisfied her, but within which pupils such as Elizabeth then had to learn and perform. It also documents how Mrs Tucker began to perceive and assess pupils in terms of their actions in relation to her personal criteria.

Teachers thus mediate national policy, and this is likely to be a constructive process as requirements are adapted to particular classroom and pupil circumstances. However, whatever the settlement achieved by the teacher, the pupil has to respond to that situation and accept assessment in terms of his or her teacher's interpretation. This, we argue, will reflect both standard national requirements and local, or personal, adaptions.

## What is being assessed?

An official answer to such a question might point to the subject content of a test, or to listed criteria of judgement, and would draw conclusions in terms of the 'attainment' of pupils. More colloquially, inferences about the particular 'abilities' of children may be legitimated by faith in the objectivity and categoric techniques of 'standardized assessment'. However, we argue that such confident conclusions are misplaced, because pupil knowledge, skills and understandings are embedded in particular sociocultural understandings and further conditioned by factors such as gender, ethnicity and social class.

To put the problem simply, to what extent does National Curriculum Assessment measure the inherent capability of a pupil, and to what extent the influence of socio-economic and cultural factors on a child? Would we be assessing Elizabeth's performance as a distinct entity, or must we also recognize the circumstances that enable or restrict her capabilities? This could lead into an analysis of the material, cultural and social capital available to families, and the extent to which children embody such advantages or disadvantages and are thus more, or less, able to cope with the school curriculum. Similarly, at the level of the peer group, we could focus on the ways in which cultural factors can enable or constrain performance. Whilst the school performance of some children may be enhanced by being with a 'good group of friends', a well understood influence is also that of an anti-learning culture. In many comprehensive schools this is a very serious problem, through which 'swots', 'ear-oles' and 'keeners' are denigrated. Sadly, we also found signs of it in the primary schools we studied, with some children wanting to avoid achievement because 'it's so embarrassing when you get praised by everybody'.

Thus, whilst pupils' subject knowledge, skill or understanding may seem to be 'objectively' revealed by the neutral, standardization technique of a test or assessment procedure, test results also reveal the facilitation or constraint of sociocultural influences and forms of understanding. In *The Social World of Pupil Assessment* we illustrated the latter through a detailed analysis of a Year 3 'news' session at Albert Park Primary School. In particular, we showed how classroom meanings were created through interaction of circumstances, strategies and identities, and how language was used to satisfy pupil agendas as well as in response to teacher-led instruction.

Assessment, this analysis suggests, can never tap pure knowledge or capability – any result will also always reflect the wider sociocultural circumstances of its production. Beyond the formal subject matter, what else is being assessed?

## How does assessment function in classrooms?

To really try to understand classroom assessment, we felt that we needed to trace the links between assessment and other sociologically important influences on classroom life – ideology, language and culture.

As a whole, these factors are played out through particular power relations between teachers and pupils, and have significant consequences for social differentiation. We have explored these ideas drawing on some of Basil Bernstein's work (1975) to analyse how assessment and other classroom processes are bound together in patterns of authority and control. We contrasted ways in which particular forms of assessment give rise to patterns of teacher–pupil relationships and interactions in the teaching process, and patterned goals for learning. In particular, we analysed ways in which testing and other assessment practices associated with 'performance goals' can act to polarize pupil attainment and thus, unwittingly, can promote 'learned helplessness' in some children. Additionally, we considered ways in which contrastive forms of teachers' assessment language can act to promote or inhibit pupils' responses. This highlights the ways in which classroom language is conditioned by patterns and forms of control, which are embedded in teachers' routine, everyday practices.

The consequence of this analysis, we would argue, is that it is not possible for teachers to be 'neutral' in their impact on pupil performance or in their assessment of pupil performance. Irrespective of intentions, each teacher's assessment practices generates a particular set of evaluative circumstances within which interaction with each child takes place. Elizabeth's experience was particular – it was not entirely shared by her classmates, nor was it consistent from year to year. The scope for variability in the overall effect of assessment practices is enormous.

## How is assessment interpreted and mediated?

In following through the assessment process, we needed to consider the various 'audiences' for assessments, with particular reference to families and, to a lesser extent, peers. How do they react to the assessment judgements that are made, and what effect does their reaction have?

For pupils such as Elizabeth, parents, siblings, families and peers are important 'significant others'. We traced their influence throughout our case study children's lives from age 4 to age 11, and found that their response to seemingly official assessment results was particularly important. Most specifically, in *The Social World of Pupil Assessment* we analysed how families interpret, mediate and give meaning to assessment outcomes so that their impact on their child is shaped and filtered. Whilst a few parents appeared to take assessment results at face value, far more engaged in supportive conversations with their children. Knowing their children very well, they were able to explore the test outcomes in relation to their previous experiences, aptitudes and future interests. In this way, the personal meaning and significance of the tests was negotiated, endorsed and concluded as the latest episode in the family narrative of each pupil's childhood. Such meanings and conclusions were crucial for future self-confidence and engagement with new learning.

Once again, then, we would argue that the outcomes of assessment cannot be seen as categoric and direct in their consequence. Rather, their meaning is malleable and is drawn into existing frames of reference, relationships and patterns of social interaction. For each learner, this is an extremely important process in the development of further phases of their personal narrative and in the construction of identity.

## Conclusion

Overall, then, in relation to each of the five major questions set out in our cyclical model, we emphasize the influence of social factors on assessment. In particular, learner, assessor, focus, process and interpretation are all embedded in particular sociocultural contexts and caught up in webs of social relationships.

In such circumstances, we believe that the technical 'objectivity' of assessment is a myth too far. Certainly, it is an insecure foundation on which to base categoric and high-stakes measures of performance for teacher, school and LEA comparison. Indeed, we would go further and argue that because of these, and other, sociological factors, presently established assessment practices are likely to yield patterns and systematic effects which are fundamentally divisive. As a consequence, policy-makers' attempts to configure the education system to meet the demands of international competition, may also unwittingly reinforce social divisions and widen the life-chance gaps which many children already face. The relationship between performance and circumstances cannot be removed or wished away.

## CHAPTER 15

# Social inclusion. What are the consequences of classroom practices?

There are eight readings in this chapter and they reflect the prolific research that exists concerning inequalities and differential life chances within our societies.

We begin Maden's argument (Reading 15.1) that education policy should not ignore the reality of the social circumstances beyond school that affect the lives of children. Such variations are significant and must be taken into account in considering school, teacher or pupil performance.

In Reading 15.2, Pollard draws on a range of social research to offer an integrative model for analysing processes of differentiation and polarization within schools, and this provides a conceptual framework for the readings that follow.

Ireson and Hallam (15.3) bring the latest research on 'ability grouping' – a practice that has shown significant growth in recent years. Echoing much previous research, they suggest that, whilst it can have positive academic effects in the short term, it can also have significant unintended consequences. This is an excellent example of the interaction of academic differentiation and pupil polarization, and of its dangers. Given the need to meet individual needs in school, then some forms of differentiation are both necessary and inevitable. However, Thorne (15.4) provides ideas on how, with particular reference to gender, to avoid divisive effects and promote cooperative classroom relationships.

Roaf and Bines (15.5) focus on special educational 'needs' (SEN) and suggest that it would be more appropriate to think in terms of rights and opportunities. Reading 15.6, by Murphy, focuses on the attainment of girls and boys – a popular media topic in recent years. She shows how pupils' learning and performance is affected by gender identity. Racism is the topic of the readings by Epstein (15.7) and Troyna and Hatcher (15.8). Both show how pervasive it is, the former through the application of some of Foucault's ideas and the latter through a study of child cultures in mostly white primary schools.

The parallel chapter of *Reflective Teaching* considers the social consequences of children's school experiences in school. It begins with a review of the major influences on children's attitudes to others and to themselves, and there is then a major section on six dimensions of difference – disability and SEN, gender, race, social class, age and sexuality. The chapter then moves to address the reinforcement and polarization of difference through pupil culture. Challenges to teachers in avoiding social differentiation are then posed. These concern the official curriculum, class management, language, relationships, expectations, assessment and the hidden curriculum. Finally, suggestions are made for developing inclusive classroom policies and practices.

There are Reflective Activities for classroom investigation and suggestions for *Key Readings* at the end of the chapter. The resources on *RTweb* extend this.

## READING 15.1

# Social circumstances in children's experience of exclusion

## Margaret Maden

In this reading, Margaret Maden argues that education policy should take greater account of the challenging social factors that affect the lives of many children and young people in the UK. She is particularly concerned with those who are disadvantaged, and this argument could be augmented with data on those who are economically and culturally advantaged. How, she asks, can public policy be shaped to enhance the opportunities for *all* our children? Implicitly, she draws attention to the danger that pressure for enhanced performance can actually *create* social exclusion.

Edited from: Maden, M. (1999) 'The challenge of children in the education system', in Tunstell, J. (ed.) *Children and the State: Whose Problem?* London, New York: Cassell, 73–6, 90

Schools represent, transmit and sometimes challenge a dense and complex conflation of social and educational history, as well as current expectations and norms. Schools are where society's hopes and fears are concentrated and synthesized into a detailed set of daily transactions involving all our children. To quantify the matter, most children spend around 15,000 hours in school between the ages of 4 and 16, the statutory ages between which school attendance is a legal requirement in England and Wales. However, this amounts to less than 15 per cent of children's lives, or some 23 per cent of their waking hours.

It is important then, that the influences and forces acting on children's education outside the boundaries and capability of schools are not ignored. However, in their eagerness to reform and improve schools, governments frequently marginalize these wider forces. This is partly because over the past two decades academic studies in the UK and elsewhere have persuaded governments that the effect and impact of schools working with very similar children are dissimilar. Life chances (measured and described mainly through academic scores and outcomes) are thus observably affected by the particular school attended, irrespective of its budget, the age and condition of its buildings or, it appears, the experience and qualifications of its teachers. Pressure, then, is exerted on schools to improve rather than there being an emphasis on strategies which might improve the wider context of children's lives.

A huge literature is now available on 'school effect' and its less well understood or documented progeny, 'school improvement'. In most of this we should note that as energetic activity and centralized prescription increase, so, simultaneously, does an almost wilful dislocation and decoupling occur between the lived experiences and habitats of children and the directions taken in education policy. Thus it is that what is taught in schools, and increasingly, how it is taught are determined by central government, but in arriving at such decisions – affecting seven million pupils in 25,000 primary and secondary schools in England and Wales – little or no reference is made to the wider experiences and lives of children.

No one should doubt governments' determined commitment to raising educational standards and to the importance ascribed to schools in securing the UK's success in the global economy. Within this there is an assumed and implicit concern for children, but there is no articulation of policy in relation to an analysis of their changing lives, needs and desires.

Who then are these children in the final years of this second millennium? What do we know about them, both inside and outside school? Some key UK statistical indicators (OPCS, 1993; Childline, 1997; NCH, 1998; Leffert and Petersen, 1995; Ghate and Daniels, 1997) include the following:

- The number of children living in families dependent on basic welfare benefit has doubled.

- In the past ten years. The value or spending power of these benefits has fallen.

- Children in benefit-dependent families change school more often, lose more days of schooling through illness and are more likely to truant than their peers whose families are in paid employment.

- In families with dependent children, 60 per cent of couples are both in paid employment, with most women being in part-time jobs.

- The percentage of children under age 16 being brought up by lone parents has increased from 8 per cent in 1972 to 21 per cent in 1994.

- In 1995 some 3000 ten-year-olds contacted Childline. Bullying and physical abuse accounted for 20 per cent of the concerns, followed by family tensions and conflicts. Half said they had unsuccessfully tried to obtain advice and support elsewhere.

- In a survey of eight- to fifteen-year-olds carried out by the National Society of the Prevention of Cruelty to Children (NSPCC), 44 per cent of the older children in this group said that their greatest source of anxiety was their academic work. More generally, over 20 per cent said they felt they had 'no one to turn to' about their worries.

- In the same survey, over three-quarters of children said their grandparents were important people in their lives, particularly so when (which was the case in a quarter of all homes surveyed) there was an absent parent.

- Nearly 40 per cent of eleven- to sixteen-year-olds have part-time jobs and these include one in four under-thirteens (who are, by law, barred from any kind of paid employment).

- One in five girls under age 16 claim to have experienced sexual intercourse, compared to almost one-third of boys.

- Sixty per cent of eleven-year-olds express 'considerable concern' about their employment prospects and two-thirds express concern about 'the environment'.

- Among fifteen- and sixteen-year olds, the reported use of drugs between 1989 and 1996 increased from 15 per cent to 40 per cent (cannabis), 2 per cent to 20 per cent (glues and solvents), 0.5 per cent to 1 per cent (heroin) and from 1 per cent to 13 per cent (amphetamines).

- Sixty per cent of twelve- to fifteen-year-olds report themselves as having had at least one alcoholic drink in the previous week, but over the past decade the percentage of 'regular teenage drinkers' has declined.

- A quarter of fourteen- and fifteen-year-old boys and a third of girls are 'regular cigarette smokers'.

- Criminal convictions, mainly for theft and handling stolen goods, among ten- to thirteen-year-old boys fell from 3.8 per cent in 1985 to 2.6 per cent in 1994, but for girls rose from 1.1 per cent to 2.3 per cent.

- Eighty per cent of children reported bullying at school and had already been the victim of at least one crime outside school.

- A third of eleven- to fifteen-year-olds have played truant at least once, but only 3 per cent regularly abscond.

- More than 75 per cent of school-leavers who have been in the care of local authorities (around 8000 per annum) have no academic qualifications and most will be unemployed and not in education or training. More than half of school pupils in care regularly truant.

- In LEAs with the highest levels of social and economic disadvantage, 20 per cent of sixteen-year-olds left school with no graded examination results, compared with an English average of 9 per cent.

Of course, these snatched and disconnected glimpses of social factors in the lives of a significant proportion of UK children cannot tell us enough about our chosen subject. For this we need some closely observed studies, probably from a latter-day Turgenev or George Eliot. However, whether by means of social attitude surveys or through the experienced and empathetic eye of a good teacher or imaginative novelist, we need a properly grounded knowledge of children before we implement wholesale, large-scale educational reforms. The waves of such reform, year on year, from 1987 through to 1998 and beyond were not, however, characterized by any such knowledge.

What we do not yet have is a public strategy that rests on empirically based knowledge of children and their real lives, or ways of learning which treat children as more than potentially fractious dependants. In other words, public policy in education still has to acknowledge and use the knowledge that exists concerning children's lives, their multiple intelligences and the variable, flexible structures which are most likely to maximize learning outcomes. Such outcomes are more than academic, as are the conditions which are needed if continuous and successful learning is to be nourished in all, not just some of, our young people.

# Social differentiation in primary schools

Andrew Pollard

This reading provides one way of taking stock of issues associated with the provision of equal opportunities in primary schools. Initially, the reasons why teachers differentiate amongst pupils and also the possible unintended consequences of doing so are considered. Criteria of judgement for facing this major dilemma are then offered, together with a model for thinking about school processes and social consequences. Could this reading provide a framework for synthesizing some of the other readings in this chapter concerning processes and consequences?

Edited from: Pollard, A. (1987) 'Social differentiation in primary schools', *Cambridge Journal of Education*, 17 (3) 158–61

'The act or process of distinguishing something by its distinctive properties' – that is how my dictionary defines differentiation and, of course, it is a process in which we all engage as we go about our daily lives. Indeed, we could make a few effective decisions without recourse to judgements about the particular qualities of people and things. However, serious responsibilities and potential problems are introduced when 'processes of distinguishing' are applied by those with a degree of power and authority to the qualities and lives of other people; for instance, as applied by us regarding the children in our classes at school. Further importance accrues if it can be shown that some of the judgements of differentiation, on which practices are based, are often inaccurate and may thus lead to injustices occurring. In such circumstances, the issues raised inevitably extend beyond the practical ones of the moment, which may have provided an initial impetus for distinctions to be drawn, to encompass personal, ethical and moral concerns.

Of course, it can reasonably be argued that differentiation is both necessary and inevitable in classrooms. Classroom life is characterized by complexity, and rapid decisions certainly have to be made by teachers. As an exercise in information processing the challenges are considerable. Perhaps it is thus inevitable that teachers develop ways of thinking about children that make it possible both to anticipate potential difficulties before they arise and to interpret circumstances and events so that effective action can be taken. To this extent, differentiation may be seen as the product of a range of strategies that enable teachers to 'cope' with the demands of classroom life.

There seem to be three particular areas around which teacher knowledge of pupil differences tends to accumulate. The first relates to the issue of control and discipline, for teachers know very well that the maintenance of classroom order provides an infrastructure without which many essential activities cannot take place. The second concerns the interpersonal relationships that are developed with children – who is 'good to have in the class' and who is 'difficult to get on with' – and, of course, 'good relationships' have been a much prized quality of classroom life for many years and seen as one vital source of fulfilment and security for both teachers and children. Finally, and by no means unimportantly, there is teacher knowledge about children's learning achievements, needs and capacities.

Differentiation of children can thus be seen partly as a response to the practicalities of classroom life and partly as a necessary attribute of forms of 'good teaching' in which responsiveness to individuals is made a priority.

On the other hand there is a great deal of sociological and historical evidence, collected in many countries and with different age groups, that demonstrates socially divisive effects when patterns in differentiation practices evolve in settings such as schools and classrooms. The most obvious criteria around which such patterns occur are those of 'race', social class, sex, academic ability, age and physical disability.

Of course, to varying degrees that one might want to discuss, these criteria represent 'objective' attributes that may call for different treatment. Yet, at the same time they are applied to people who share certain fundamental freedoms and human rights. Thus, if it can be shown that such rights are denied or adversely affected by patterns in social practices then a cause for concern certainly exists.

Differentiation thus poses some severe dilemmas. Is it to be seen as an evil or a good? On the one hand one can argue that to fail to differentiate is to deny individuality and the unique qualities and needs of people. On the other hand, it can be argued that differentiation is iniquitous, for in making distinctions of any sort some children may be advantaged over others.

How then should we, as teachers, face such dilemmas? Perhaps dilemmas can only be resolved by making reflective judgements of appropriateness and of worthwhileness for specific situations. However, such judgements need to be supported both by principled criteria and by social awareness of what actually happens – for instance, as highlighted by available research on the topic. I will discuss each of these elements in turn.

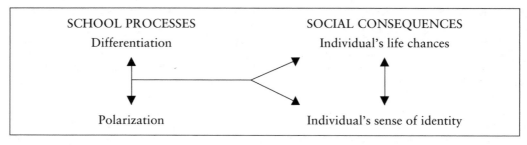

**Figure 15.2.1**   The differentiation–polarization process and its consequences

## Criteria of judgement

On this point one cannot avoid facing the issue of value commitments and beliefs about the basic purposes of education. As an example, and in full recognition of my own commitments and of the rights of others to make different choices, I offer the following educational priorities which might be adopted with regard to children: to foster children's intellectual growth; to facilitate children's personal and social development; to maximize children's opportunities in life; and to prepare children to exercise rights and accept responsibilities as individuals and as future citizens.

If these four educational priorities are accepted for the moment, then we can consider the effects of differentiation in terms of them. For instance:

- *Intellectual growth:* Does differentiation depend on children's thinking or lead to superficiality? Does differentiation open horizons or lead to closure?

- *Personal and social development:* Does differentiation facilitate children's growth or stunt it?

- *Opportunities:* Is differentiation enabling or disabling?

- *Rights and responsibilities:* Does differentiation enfranchise or disenfranchise, increase social awareness or decrease it?

To answer such questions we need to consider the second ingredient – awareness and knowledge of the types and processes of differentiation which may occur in schools.

## Awareness of differentiation processes

I am not going to attempt a review of all the research that is relevant to this issue – that would take volumes. In any event, on this matter the detail is arguably less important than principles which might be applicable to a range of situations and practices. I will therefore simply attempt to set up and discuss the relatively concise analytical model in Figure 15.2.1.

## Differentiation

Differentiation refers here to any way in which individual children are distinguished, one from another, by teachers. I thus use the term explicitly to describe processes of distinction that children have relatively little control over. There are various aspects of this at a classroom level and I offer some examples below:

There are those to do with the content and form of the curriculum – e.g. how are girls, the disabled and black people represented in reading books? Are the positions of children on a maths scheme taken as an indicator of a status which children wish to acquire?

There are aspects of differentiation that are related to classroom management – e.g. do children line up by sex? Are the 'second years' and the 'third years' regularly dismissed at different times?

Some aspects of differentiation are particularly explicit such as when it is reflected in classroom organization – e.g. to what extent are children ability grouped in your school? How often is gender used as an organizational device in activities?

Powerful forms of differentiation can also occur through the language which is used in school which may, or may not, be equally meaningful and appropriate to all social groups. This, of course, is crucial because language is the medium through which much of school life and individual academic progress is manifested – e.g. how are the needs of those for whom English is a second language catered for? Do some children understand the register and vocabulary of the teachers better than others?

Another rather subtle but powerful form of differentiation concerns interpersonal relationships. Are there differences in the quality of the rapport that is established with different children? Are some children 'told off' more than others have specific expectations of individual children formed so that one acts in particular ways towards them? Are there differences in the number of times boys and girls, younger and older children, 'good' and 'naughty' children have contact with and get the attention of the teacher?

Closely related to the above is the question of expectations that research suggests can effect the way children are treated. For instance to whom are challenging questions directed? Which children are regularly asked to take responsibilities? On hearing a disruptive noise, are there children to whom one looks first?

Another issue concerns reinforcement and the differential valuing of children's efforts. Are merit points or other extrinsic rewards given and, if so, is there a pattern in who gets them? Whose work is on the walls? Who 'shows things' and performs in assemblies? Is any particular social group overrepresented?

For each aspect of differentiation there are hundreds of such questions and, of course, it is not my purpose to suggest that all such forms of differentiation are, in some inevitable way, 'wrong'. The question which has to be asked though is whether there are patterns of differentiation that might represent a less than just and fair treatment of the individual attributes and rights of each child and each social group.

## Polarization

The issue and phenomenon of polarization is closely related to that of differentiation. Polarization refers to actions and processes that children initiate rather than teachers. In simple terms, polarization can be seen as a response by children to the differentiation which they experience. The effect of polarization is thus to multiply, amplify and compound the social consequences of the initial differentiation. This can be seen to work in the studies of children's social relationships and perceptions. For instance, friendship groups are often related to academic status as well as to criteria such as race and sex and they may even reveal the influence of seat places where these are dictated by the organization of the classroom. Status and popularity within child culture can also be seen to depend partly on the relationship of each child with the teacher. Children who find it hard to succeed in school, or who get into trouble a lot, may develop relatively antagonistic attitudes to school and may act in conjunction with others in similar positions. On the other hand, children who are successful in school, who are well trusted by their teachers and stimulated by the form and content of the curriculum may well feel very positive about it. Status in child culture is often obtained by demonstrating that one can cope with school life, that one is strong, able enough and independent enough. Polarization thus occurs every time a child is teased because he is, she is 'only on red-level books' or when, say 'John's gang' develops its reputation for 'mucking about' and is contrasted with the quieter groups who 'just walk around' and 'do what the teacher says'.

Another way of approaching this is to see children in school as having to cope in two social spheres at the same time. They have to cope with the formal requirements of teachers and normally have to accept the judgements which may be made of them. They also have to cope with the social world of the playground and of their peers. In both contexts they have to retain their dignity as individuals. The result of this is that, if they are treated in particular ways in class, then in the playground they are likely to either play on the prestige they have gained or try to recoup some of the dignity they may have lost. In any event, the effects of the initial differentiation is likely to be increased by the polarization which then follows.

The model above postulates that these two processes exist in interaction together. For instance, the effect of polarization of attitudes and of peer group association could well lead to increased differentiation as teachers respond to them. The danger is thus that the two processes mesh together to produce a vicious circle in which, in the midst of everyday school life, the overall differentiation effect is steadily increased.

## But what are the social consequences of these processes?

I would suggest that social consequences of two main sorts result. The first concerns the self-image and sense of identity which each child develops – how do they see themselves? How much self-confidence do they have? The second concerns life chances more directly – what range of options are open to children as they go through their school careers? How are future possibilities for each child being affected by school processes and experiences?

The self-image and identity of individuals is constructed through social interaction with others. We thus come to 'know' ourselves gradually and continuously throughout life. At any point, though, we 'present' our self to others in particular ways – usually in ways which we feel are appropriate for the situation as we perceive it and in ways which support our existing image of 'who we are'. Schools have a very significant role to play in this process of identity formation for they are, for most children, the first formal organization that they will have experienced. In a sense therefore, school life provides the primary medium through which the public identities of each child are created, explored, tested, evolved and adopted. Children take forward a particular sense of self and act upon it as they experience new situations. In turn, others then react to the presentation of this identity. It does not take much imagination to see that the prospects for children who have developed a sense of failure and dissatisfaction in school are likely to be very different from those of children who have had their efforts praised, valued and reinforced.

To take the argument about life chances further, because of the links between education, assessment, credentialism and employment, schools play a very important gate-keeping role through their influence on the long-term prospects of children. Indeed, the processes of differentiation and polarization, which may be identified in the classrooms of even very young children, may well manifest themselves in terms of income, housing, occupation and status 30 years on.

This seems to me to be the major challenge of socially aware teaching, with any age of child. One is certainly not solely concerned with the intellectual or expressive development of individuals. In ways from which one cannot withdraw, one is also inevitably concerned with issues involving rights.

## READING 15.3

# The effects of ability grouping

Judith Ireson and Susan Hallam

This reading is drawn from a carefully researched study of 'ability' grouping (referring, of course, to present attainment rather than fixed capacity). The evidence is in two parts and links to Pollard's analysis in Reading 15.2. First, Ireson and Hallam confirm that differentiated classroom groupwork can enhance attainment if it is used appropriately. Second, however, they demonstrate the polarizing effect of teasing and other peer-group activity that can lead pupils to develop negative self-images and low dispositions to learn. This can affect both low- and high-attaining children. Abiltity grouping may thus have an effective short-term role in differentiated teaching, but it can also have unintended, negative social consequences.

How is this dilemma managed in your school?

Edited from: Ireson, J. and Hallam, S. (2001) *Ability Grouping in Education*. London: Paul Chapman Publishing, 25–8, 35, 58–62

There are two main questions of interest when we consider whether ability grouping within schools has an impact on pupil attainment. The first is whether it raises the attainment of all pupils and the second is whether it raises the attainment of particular groups of pupils at the expense of others. On both these questions the evidence is mixed, but as a whole, the picture from the research is that ability grouping has little or no effect on average attainment. The impact on particular groups is variable and influenced by a wide range of local factors, making it difficult to draw any firm conclusions. However, more rigid grouping, such as streaming, disadvantages pupils in the lower groups.

## Ability grouping and attainment

Streaming was used in the majority of large primary schools until the 1950s, but was largely phased out following the demise of the eleven-plus examination. During the 1960s and 1970s several research studies were completed, demonstrating that streaming had little impact on attainment. The most comprehensive research study in England and Wales was by Barker Lunn (1970), who compared the achievement gains of students in 36 streamed and 36 unstreamed junior schools matched on social class. There were no meaningful differences in achievement between the pupils in the streamed and unstreamed schools. The size and quality of this study provides particularly strong evidence that ability grouping is not by itself a major factor affecting achievement at primary level. Similar findings were reported by Daniels (1961) who compared achievement in streamed and unstreamed schools over a four-year period. He concluded that lower ability pupils made better progress in unstreamed schools, while the higher ability pupils were not held back. Blandford (1985) found a greater spread of achievement in streamed schools, with the higher ability pupils performing better but the lower ability pupils performing worse. Lower ability children performed better in unstreamed schools. Douglas (1964) examined the progress through primary school of 5000 pupils born in 1946. Children in the lower streams made much less progress relative to those in the top stream. Several of the studies referred to above also found very little movement of pupils between streams. The research demonstrated that middle-class children occupied the top stream while the working-class children populated the middle and lower streams. These findings were influential in the destreaming of primary schools.

Slavin (1987) reviewed the international research and concluded that, across the fourteen studies he reviewed (which included the Barker Lunn study referred to above), the effects of ability grouping were essentially zero. Among the American studies, one by Goldberg *et al.* (1966) stands out as providing particularly strong evidence. This involved 86 Grade 5 classes in New York elementary schools. Pupils were assigned to classes on the basis of IQ scores according to fifteen different grouping patterns that varied in homogeneity. They remained in those classes for two years. Most comparisons of achievement showed no difference according to the type of grouping and, where there were differences, it was the pupils in the more heterogeneous groupings that performed better than those in homogeneous classes.

In the United Kingdom, primary teachers implement a variety of grouping strategies in the classroom. Within class ability, grouping is widely utilized, particularly by schools that are too small to implement setting or streaming. Some schools group pupils from more than one year group or age group to enable regrouping. In the United Kingdom, the recent introduction of literacy and numeracy hours as part of the National Literacy Strategy has been accompanied by recommendations to group pupils by ability in these areas of the curriculum for certain activities. Some teachers group pupils by ability within the classroom for most of the day.

Meta-analyses of the research on within class ability grouping (Lou *et al.*, 1996) and cross-age grouping (Kulik and Kulik, 1992) in primary schools indicate that, when implemented appropriately, they can lead to positive academic effects. Cross-grade grouping can produce positive effects on achievement when it is used for targeted teaching. For example, the Joplin plan is a system of teaching reading in which several year groups are regrouped for reading instruction according to their attainment in reading. Kulik and Kulik (1992) reviewed fourteen studies in which children were formed into cross-age groups on the basis of their attainment in a particular subject, typically reading. The overall effects were positive.

The research on ability grouping in primary schools suggests that whereas streaming does not provide gains in attainment overall, other types of grouping have positive academic effects. In particular, groupings that are formed to enable teachers to target specific aspects of the curriculum can raise attainment, providing they are implemented appropriately.

## Abiltity grouping and social consequences

Our research also explored pupils' experiences of learning within different types of grouping. Previous research has indicated the stigmatization of pupils in the lower streams as a problem created by streaming. Pupils in higher ability groups are also the subject of naming and teasing, but the language used to refer to high and low ability children has a different quality. Derogatory terms are often used to refer to lower ability pupils, whereas terms such as 'boffin' or 'brainy' are used when referring to those of high ability. Both groups of pupils can be victims of teasing that may be malicious in intent. This occurs at primary and secondary level and with pupils at both ends of the ability spectrum.

> I don't like it when people poke fun. It doesn't happen that often . . . not quite a lot, but a couple of weeks ago, people laughed at me and sometimes they call you thick. (Primary pupil)

> People say like 'You're silly' and all that . . . it makes me feel sad. (Primary pupil)

> I get teased a lot at the bottom end of the school I get beaten up and kicked . . . they throw pebbles and sand at me and call me fatso and all that. (Primary pupil)

> Some children in the top sets are show offs and they say 'Oh, I'm brainier than you'. (Below average ability, primary)

> Mixed ability classes are better because you could learn more things from other people and other people won't take the mick out of you. (Secondary pupil in a set school)

I get teased and called the professor because I'm one of the clever ones . . . it bothers me. (Primary pupil)

Sometimes people might say things but they're not really being nasty . . . they say things to make you laugh like you've got a really good brain . . . it's so big it's popping out through your ears. (Primary pupil)

I'm in set 3 and I'd like to move to set 2 because it isn't too hard but you still have to be pretty intelligent. You don't get teased as much as in the top set. (Secondary pupil in a set school)

Primary-aged pupils sometimes reported the teasing to teachers who generally took action to resolve the situation.

Joan sometimes says that I can't do anything . . . I tell the teacher and she sometimes puts her in detention. (Year 3 average ability, primary)

Sometimes they say 'You don't know what to do and you're a baby . . . you've got to tell them to go to Mrs B' . . . I tell the teacher and she tells them off sometimes. (Year 4, below average ability, primary)

Teachers are not always perceived as being supportive and in some cases may also make comments.

I prefer mixed ability classes as no one gets the mickey taken out of them and teachers can't make their horrid remarks. (Secondary set school)

Some pupils are very aware of the sensitivities of the situation.

I think mixed ability is best because it would be embarrassing if you were in the bottom group or set. (Mixed ability school)

Over 40 per cent of pupils interviewed from the six primary schools reported either having been teased or having witnessed teasing that was related to grouping practices or academic ability. For some, the teasing was interpreted as 'playful', particularly for those children in the higher ability groups, but many found it upsetting.

Overall, our research suggests that ability grouping has an impact on pupils' self-esteem, academic self-concept and their emotional responses to school. However, this relationship is not entirely straightforward, as many different factors are interrelated. When considering the impact of school organization, it is important to take account of the multiple facets of students' self-perceptions, social disadvantage, developmental changes and gender differences. Our research indicates that, in the lower secondary years, socially disadvantaged pupils and girls have less positive self-esteem than socially advantaged pupils and boys. When students' academic self-perceptions are considered, however, gender differences remain, while social disadvantage is not an important factor. Boys have much more positive views of themselves in mathematics and science, even when attainment is taken into account, while girls have more positive views of themselves in relation to English, although the difference is smaller. These findings are consistent with previous research and perhaps reflect more general perceptions of mathematics and science as 'masculine' subjects. However, the gap between the self-perceptions of girls and boys, particularly those of high attainment, is of some concern, especially as emotional factors may influence their choice of subjects in later years of education.

Overall pupils in schools with more structured grouping feel less positive about school. Pupils in the schools with less structured grouping had more positive relationships with the school and their teachers. The differences are small but consistent. Teasing is one factor that contributes to pupils' feelings about school. Pupils of all abilities may be teased, but for those in lower ability groups, teasing can reinforce pupils' negative views of their academic attainment. Taken together, the evidence indicates that pupils have lower self-esteem in schools that have higher levels of ability grouping. In such circumstances, the children feel less positive about their school as a whole.

Positive attitudes towards learning and positive self-concepts are important elements fostering a disposition to learn in the future. While the emphasis in previous research has been on the negative impact of ability grouping on lower attaining pupils, our research indicates that structured ability grouping may also have a negative effect on more able pupils' self-concepts. It is thus important for schools to beware of becoming too seduced by a technical approach to ability grouping. They should ensure that all pupils are supported and encouraged to develop positive learning dispositions.

 **READING 15.4**

# How to promote cooperative relationships among children

Barrie Thorne

> Barrie Thorne's book *Gender Play* is well worth reading as a study of how boys' and girls' identities are formed. In this extract, she considers the practical implications of her work and offers advice to teachers on promoting cooperation among children. She particularly considers the classroom management of groups, reinforcing cooperative behaviour, providing opportunities and challenging stereotyping.
>
> This advice is applicable to all forms of differentiation. Is it helpful in thinking about how your class interacts together, and in considering how you could influence this.
>
> Edited from: Thorne, B. (1993) *Gender Play: Girls and Boys in School.* Buckingham: Open University Press, 157–67

In my ethnographic study of children's daily lives in school, I have sought to ground and develop, with detailed substance and a sense of process and activity, the claim that gender is socially constructed. I have argued that kids, as well as adults, take an active hand in constructing gender, and that collective practices – forming lines, choosing seats, teasing, gossiping, seeking access to or avoiding particular activities – animate the process.

Thus, I showed how kids construct 'the girls' and 'the boys' as boundaried and rival groups through practices that uphold a sense of gender as an oppositional dichotomy. But I also examined practices that have the effect of neutralizing, or, as in situations of 'crossing', even challenging the significance of gender.

Some of these practices have been developed by teachers and researchers trying to challenge racial separation and inequality and in this brief review I will try to encompass some of the interactive dynamics of race and gender. The ideas may also apply to the handling of other differences, such as religion or disability.

## In grouping students, use criteria other than gender or race

When teachers and aides divide girls and boys into competing teams or tell them to sit at different tables, they ratify the dynamics of separation, differential treatment, stereotyping and antagonism. Organizing students on other grounds, such as random sorting, and using terms of address like 'class' or 'students' rather than the ubiquitous 'boys and girls' will help undermine gender marking.

This suggestion raises a basic dilemma. When granted autonomy and left on their own, kids tend to separate by gender and sometimes also by race. Should school staff determine all seating, even in lunchrooms? Should playground aides bustle into situations kids have set up and urge girls and boys to play together? Obviously this is neither practical nor desirable. Kids do not flourish when they are perpetually watched and controlled; they need, and will struggle to claim, at least some independence from adults.

On the other hand, when adults form mixed-gender groups, I have observed that some kids look a little relieved: the adult action takes away the risk of teasing and makes girl–boy interactions possible. One boy told me: 'You get to talk to kids you usually wouldn't get to know'. When they do choose to form groups, for whatever purpose, I believe that school staff should try, consciously to maximize heterogeneity.

## Affirm and reinforce the values of cooperation among all kids regardless of social categories

A teacher recently told me about her efforts to undermine 'girl–boy staff' and foster more cooperative cross-gender relations among her students. 'We're one class, not boys and girls; we're going to get together as a class', she repeatedly told them. By emphasizing 'the class', she affirmed a more inclusive basis of solidarity.

To be effective, affirmation of the value of mixed-gender and mixed-race interaction may need to be explicit and continual. Lisa Serbin and her colleagues (who found extensive gender separation among children in a pre-school), trained the teachers to positively reinforce cooperative cross-gender play, for example with comments like 'John and Cathy are working hard together on their project'. This behaviour-modification effort lasted for two weeks, during which the amount of cross-gender play increased significantly. But when the programme was discontinued, the children returned to the earlier pattern.

## Whenever possible, organize students into small, heterogeneous and cooperative work groups

Unfortunately, we can't lessen the crowding of most schools, but small-group instruction may create pockets of less public and thus, perhaps, more cooperative interaction. Indeed, social psychologists who study the dynamics of intergroup relations have found that when people from different racial or gender groups interact in smaller groups focused on a shared goal requiring interdependence, they are more likely to see one another as individuals rather than through the lens of 'us-versus-them'.

Elliot Aronson and his colleagues entered the desegregated classrooms and organized small multiracial groups to work together on reports, studying for quizzes, and other collaborative tasks. They called this a 'jigsaw classroom', referring to the principle of a jigsaw puzzle in which each person has pieces of information the entire group needs to complete the task. The result was a de-emphasis on racial divisions and in increase in friendships among African-American, Chicano and white students.

## Facilitate kids' access to all activities

In many activities, especially on playgrounds and even in classrooms, girls and boys may not have equal access to particular activities, for example in some classrooms boys have been found to have more access than girls to computers.

To broaden access to gender-typed activities school staff can make a point of teaching the skills to everyone and, if possible, setting an example by challenging stereotypes.

School staff might consider introducing playground games, like handball, that have the potential to increase the amount of cross-gender play. A playground rule that would-be players cannot be 'locked out' of a game unless there are already too many players can also lessen opportunities for exclusion and may embolden more kids to join activities stereotypically associated with the other gender. By introducing new activities and teaching relevant skills in a gender-neutral way, teachers and aides can create conditions in which kids themselves may more often form mixed-gender groups. The transformative elements of play – a sense of the voluntary and of control over the terms of interaction – can be drawn on to facilitate social change.

## Actively intervene to challenge the dynamics of stereotyping and power

Proximity does not necessarily lead to equality, as critics of the philosophies of assimilation and integration have long pointed out. Boys and girls and kids of different racial and ethnic backgrounds my be encouraged to interact more frequently, but on whose terms? Groups may be formally integrated, but tensions and inequalities may persist. In the de-segregated middle school where Schofield observed, the teachers by and large affirmed a neutral or colour-blind ideology, trying to ignore the presence of race divisions, though teachers more readily marked gender in their interaction with students. But the students often divided and sometimes hassled one another along lines of both race and gender, and there was persistent mistrust and fear between black and white students. The teaching staff were so intent on pretending that race made no difference that they did little to help white and black students learn how to interact with one another or explore the nature and meaning of cultural difference and the dynamics of racism. In some situations, it may be important for teachers to deal openly with rather than ignore social divisions.

My observations of antagonistic mixed-gender interactions suggest that the dynamics of stereotyping and power may have to be confronted explicitly. Barbara Porro and Kevin Karkau engaged their classes in discussions about gender stereotyping, persistent separation between girls and boys, and the teasing ('sissies', 'tomboys', 'you're in love') that kept them apart. Porro explained sexism to her students by finding terms that six-year-olds could understand; the class began to label sexist ideas (e.g. that women could not be doctors, or men could not be nurses) as old-fashioned.

Such accounts suggest ways in which teachers can engage in critical thinking about and collaborative ways of transcending social divisions and inequalities.

## READING 15.5

# Needs, rights and opportunities in special education

Caroline Roaf and Hazel Bines

The field of special educational needs has always generated controversies of principle and definition, and perhaps this is inevitable as the tension between needs and resources is played out. In this readin, Roaf and Bines interrogate some key terms and consider how they have been applied. They identify various problematic aspects of the concept of 'needs' and suggest an alternative discourse of 'opportunities' and 'rights'.

How would consideration of 'opportunities' and 'rights' affect the ways in which you think about special education in relation to your school?

Edited from: Roaf, C. and Bines, H. (1989) 'Needs, rights and opportunities in special education', in Roaf, C. and Bines, H. (eds.) *Needs, Rights and Oportunities*. London: Falmer Press, 5–15

The development of special education during the last hundred years has traditionally focused on handicap and needs. It has involved efforts to expand provision for children and young people whose impairments or difficulties are not adequately catered for in ordinary schools or who may need additional help to cope with the demands of mainstream curricula and schooling. Such growth has been seen as the best means of focusing and securing special resources and expertise. Progress has also largely been measured in terms of expansion of the range, as well as the amount, of special provision available for children and young people in order to cater for an increase in number and a wider range of handicaps and difficulties or needs.

Nevertheless, there have been a number of changes in the ways in which this development of special needs provision and curricula has been viewed and secured. In particular, the language and categories of handicap have been replaced by the more generic and flexible concept of special educational need. This new concept, as developed by the Warnock Report (DES, 1978b) and incorporated into the 1981 Education Act represented an attempt to remove formal distinctions between handicapped and non-handicapped students and to replace categories through an expanded and more flexible definition of special need. This could potentially incorporate one-fifth of the whole school population, including children and young people in both ordinary and special schools. It also reflected a shift in emphasis from medical or psychological criteria of assessment and placement towards an educational, interactive and relative approach which would take into account all the factors that have a bearing on educational progress (DES, 1978b, para 3.6).

However, the emphasis on needs may have obscured other aspects in the development of special education, such as the degree to which equality of opportunity has been a significant dimension of debate and policy. There has, for example, been considerable concern about the issue of equal access to education, notably in regard to children with severe and multiple difficulties. Similarly, debate over segregation and placement in special schooling has been related to lack of equal educational opportunity. The increasing focus on integration as the model of good practice thus represents not just a new approach to fulfilling needs but also an intention to secure equal access to a common schooling for all children.

'Special educational need' remains a very difficult and complex concept in practice. It has the appearance of simplicity and familiarity, yet the greatest care is required in evaluating needs, in prioritizing them and in being clear in whose interest they are being stated.

First, the term 'needs' is often used in relation to the development and learning of all children. Given their individuality and idiosyncrasy, defining what constitutes a 'special' educational need in any particular case can be difficult. However, if special eduction is to be used as a basis for special resource allocation, the difference between special and other educational needs would seem to have to be acknowledged. Although the 1981 Act emphasizes the relationship between learning difficulty and special educational need, learning difficulty in the past has largely been used in relation to remedial provision. Since this has been somewhat separate from other special education, its more general use for all forms of special needs is ambiguous. In addition, although 'special educational needs' is now the generic term, the number of specific descriptive categories has not been reduced. Indeed, the Warnock Report and 1981 Act, while attempting to remove differences between handicapped and non-handicapped students, did not take special education out of the realm of handicap. Instead, more students have been brought within its brief under the much broader and ill-defined category of learning difficulty, and further divisions have emerged, particularly between students who are subjects of statements and those who are not.

Second, the relativism of needs as currently understood can lead to haphazard and unequal provision. 'Special educational need' is a legal and administrative term as well as an educational and descriptive one thus taking on different meaning according to the context in which it is used. Such relativism is also a feature of the legislative definitions within the 1981 Education Act.

Needs are a matter of professional and value judgement The moral and political basis of such judgements are usually neglected because we still focus on the receiver – the individual or group with needs. Yet hidden within these conceptions of needs are social interests, for example, to make the disabled productive or control troublesome children, together with a range of assumptions about what is normal (Tomlinson, 1982). When we focus on needs and particularly when we take our assumptions about the nature of those needs for granted, we do not ask who has the power to define the needs of others. We do not enquire why it is professionals who mostly define needs as opposed to parents or the students themselves. Nor do we fully explore the normative nature of our assumptions, for example, that they are grounded in conceptions of 'normal' cognitive development or behaviour whether such assumptions are informally operated, by teachers in the classroom, or more formally operated, by normative testing. We focus on what seem to be the genuine needs of the individual who lacks something and who have a need. However, we do not consider how needs may be generated by valuing certain aspects of development and attainment more than others. For example, if we did not value certain cognitive skills, would there be the needs currently identified as 'special' in schools? (Hargreaves, 1983).

The term 'needs' has now become a euphemism for labelling individuals as 'special'. The idea of having a difficulty suggests something can be done about it and tends to focus on individuals as a bottomless pit of problems to be overcome or filled up. The concept of needs remains deficit-based, despite attempts to relate it to context, with a pronounced tendency to slippage back towards individuals and their problems.

Given that needs is a problematic concept, 'opportunity' would seem to offer a better approach to special education. There is a much more explicit focus on context: opportunity raises questions of system rather than individual failure. When linked with equality, to make 'equality of opportunity', it also raises issues of discrimination and disadvantage. Equality of opportunity is also a widely known and understood rationale. Therefore it may be easier for the majority of teachers and policy-makers to relate to opportunity rather than needs or at least to see the educational, social and political implications of requiring that equal opportunity be extended to those with impairments and difficulties.

'Rights' as a basis for developing special education policy and practice would also seem to have a number of advantages. As Kirp (1983) has suggested, comparing British and American special education policies and legislation, thinking about special education in terms of political and legal rights makes us reappraise resource allocation, relationships among the affected parties, the level and amount of dispute and the very conception of handicap. In respect of resource allocation, for example, the American structure of rights does not formally treat resource limits as constraining what can be provided. Whereas the British approach weighs the interests of special and ordinary children, the American orientation on rights places the burden of adjustment on the ordinary school. The greater disputes engendered by a rights approach, including increased litigation, may make for a more dynamic policy and lead school authorities to offer more than would otherwise have been provided. In respect of the disabled themselves, rights should encourage a stronger definition and assertion of self and interests, reducing professional power and paternalism. When rights legislation is explicitly linked with other civil rights, special education also becomes part of the larger struggle for equity. Race or gender dimensions of being 'special' can then also be raised.

Taken separately, therefore, there are advantages but also limitations to needs, rights and opportunity. In searching for the best way forward we suggest the following starting points.

'Needs statements' in themselves should not be regarded as a sufficient basis for developing policy and practice, because of the tendency to reinforce individualized, deficit-based approaches. Instead, needs should be tied to entitlement of rights and opportunity, in order to emphasize a systems approach and to strengthen and assert the interests and equity of those considered to have such needs. This would also remove some of the burden of guilt and stigma which is still associated with having special educational needs. To be entitled to something is very different and more positive than to need it, since it gives both validity and value to the claim.

Needs should also be seen in terms of what constitutes a relevant difference. Instead of trying to hide differences under a catch-all generic term, it might be more useful to explore whether and when differences matter and should or should not be considered. The discourse of opportunity and rights could be particularly helpful.

## READING 15.6

# Gendered learning and achievement

Patricia Murphy

This reading explores differences in boys' and girls' attainment in maths, English and science. It highlights the ways in which gender influences shape learning opportunities and are thus reflected in assessed outcomes. The reading draws on cultural models of learning (see Reading 7.8) and reinforces the suggestion (in Reading 14.7) that national assessments cannot be seen as being entirely 'objective'. Significantly, however, they do represent an official form of differentiation – in this case, on the basis of gender.

Do the boys and girls in your class perform differently and can you identify cultural influences? If so, is there anything you can do to offer more opportunity?

Edited from: Murphy, P. (2000) 'Gendered learning and achievement', in Collins, J. and Cook, D. *Understanding Learning*. London: Paul Chapman Publishing, 109–21

How we understand the influence of gender on children's learning, and how this in turn affects the way they understand and respond to assessments, depends on our perceptions of the ways children make sense of their worlds. Current views of assessment reflect a 'processing' model of mind. The task of assessment being 'how to read out the stored knowledge of the learner in the most accurate and reliable way' (Roth, 1997, p. 9). It is assumed here that information is 'given' and that tasks are therefore stable across learners, i.e., children perceive and interpret them in the same way. A cultural view of learning, on the other hand, views mind as shaped by culture. As Bruner puts it: 'although meanings are "in the mind" they have their origins and their significance in the culture in which they are created' (Bruner, 1996, p. 3). One of these ways of making sense draws on cultural beliefs about what it is to be a girl and a boy.

Culturally defined stereotypes and expectations of girls and boys are evident at all levels of socialization. From birth, girls and boys experience different socialization processes. Parents' expectations differ for boys and girls. These different expectations are reflected in the activities and toys parents provide and in their reactions to their children. Consequently boys and girls engage in different hobbies and pastimes from an early age, and their interests continue to diverge with age. An outcome of different socialization patterns is that children develop different ways of responding to the world and making sense of it, ways which influence how they learn and what they learn. In this way children learn to value those activities, traits and behaviours associated with their gender and, consequently, gender becomes a self-regulating system. The more children engage in gendered activities, the more they develop the skills and understandings associated with them, understandings which emerge as gender-related ways of being in the world.

## Gendered achievement

In national assessments of mathematics in England and Wales, overall similarities in girls' and boys' performance are reported. However, evidence from international surveys show that girls and boys differ in the way they achieve their scores in tests. Girls' superior performance is associated with computation, whole number and estimation and approximation, as well as algebra. Boys' superior performance is associated with geometry, particularly three-dimensional diagrams, measurement and proportional thinking. National surveys in the USA and in England and Wales also found boys outperformed girls on the use of measuring instruments but only where boys had more experience of using them outside school. These achievement differences can therefore be understood in terms of children's opportunity to learn rather than their ability to learn.

International surveys show that girls outperform boys in reading and writing across the 5–16 range. However, at age 6–7 years it mattered if the text was story- or information-based. The performance gap in favour of girls was reduced on questions drawing on information texts, and boys were found to outperform girls on some multiple-choice questions. Girls' performance was enhanced on questions to do with feelings and motivation, boys where reasons for actions were sought. What the task was about mattered, for example, if it was about a girl's viewpoint or a boy's viewpoint. Girls performed better on the former and boys better on the latter. At the older ages (10–11) more girls achieved the expected level than boys (76 per cent compared with 65 per cent). Boys' superior performance was associated with questions drawing on information with short or multiple-choice responses. Girls' superior performance was associated with open-ended questions requiring extended responses involving interpretation and explanation. Girls tended to do better than boys when questions involved imagery and poetic language. In writing tasks, girls were ahead of boys at both ages. Girls spell significantly better than do boys, though the size of the difference declines with age. Girls also use punctuation more and structure and organize their work better than boys (QCA, 2000). Boys do better when questions required short responses or right/wrong answers, as in multiple choice, and overall writing competence was not required.

These gender differences in English persist through school even when there is no evidence to suggest they reflect differences in innate linguistic ability (OFSTED, 1993b). An argument to explain this is again related to gendered choices and learning.

In science, as in mathematics, overall performance shows little difference between boys and girls of primary age. However, it is again apparent that girls and boys achieve their scores in different ways. Girls' and boys' interests in science-related topics vary. In national surveys of science, systematic content effects were observed for both primary and secondary pupils (DES, 1988a; 1989a). Questions that involved health, reproduction, nutrition and domestic and social situations showed girls performing at a higher level than boys. The converse occurred with 'masculine' contents, e.g., traffic, building sites, submarines, space flight, etc. In physics assessments, 'masculine' contents dominate and there is often use made of diagrams to represent phenomena. Girls tend to have less experience of such contents, consider them to be gender inappropriate and so lack confidence in their approach to them.

Other gender differences relate to children's different views of salience. For example, when given the choice, girls and boys focus on different aspects of phenomena. Girls pay more attention than boys to colour, sound and smells. Boys on the other hand pay attention to structure and movement more than girls (Murphy and Elwood, 1998). In both cases these differences link closely to those noted in the play of pre-school and infant pupils. However, these views of salience often go unobserved and emerge later in assessments as achievement differences (Kimbell *et al.*, 1991).

Recent observations of Year 6 children (age 10–11) in design and technology showed the self-regulating nature of gender development in operation, but in ways unremarked and therefore unchallenged by teachers. The children had to design a vehicle of their choice. The issues for learning were to do with the design and make aspects of the task. What vehicle was made and, therefore, what aesthetic issues if any obtained were irrelevant. Typically, boys made sports cars, army vehicles, rocket carriers and the occasional train. Girls' vehicles were related to the transport of food, e.g. pizzas, circus animals, families and the occasional stretch limousine. The finish of the product therefore engaged the children in different details but it was the quality of the finish rather than the details that were noted by the teacher. This is another example of differences in opportunity to learn that needs to be taken into account to inform interpretations of assessment outcomes.

If we consider overall test results, gender differences in achievement may appear to be an issue only in relation to boys' achievement in English. This is far from the case. For example, the pattern of achievement in maths and science is not equally distributed for boys and girls. Boys typically are represented in greater numbers in the highest and lowest levels of achievement compared with girls. This pattern appears to hold across schooling and has been associated with the differential expectations of teachers and pupils. Feedback is critical in shaping pupils' perceptions of themselves in relation to subjects and schooling generally. Assessment plays a key role in this. One concern is the way that affective characteristics often acquired through schooling become understood as cognitive abilities. Thus girls' conformity can be understood as intellectual timidity and lack of flair, and some boys' disruptive behaviour as lack of ability, and others' independence and risk-taking as brilliance. Patterns of achievement which see girls typically clustered in the middle levels and boys spread more and at the extremes begins to make sense seen in this light. Differences in the distribution of boys and girls across levels and grades in assessment may also arise when the selection of achievements in subject tests reflect those skills and understandings they acquire through their gendered choices and ways of interacting in the world. As we have seen, there is evidence of this across the core subjects.

If we adopt a cultural approach to learning, then assessment cannot be viewed as objective. It can, however, aim to be more just. To achieve this, children need to be given opportunities to show what they know and interpretations of scores need to recognize and distinguish between a lack of achievement and a lack of opportunity.

Gender differences increase with schooling as we unwittingly build on children's strengths and fail to recognize the limitations that gendered learning can create. Assessment has the ability to inform and misinform, to liberate and to control. Attention to children's ways of knowing is essential if its benefits for learning are to be realized.

 **READING 15.7**

# Social relations, discourse and racism

Debbie Epstein

> This reading begins with an exceptionally clear account of how Foucault's post-structuralism has been applied to education, and the use of the concepts of 'discourse' and 'positioning' in the analysis of social relations (see also Reading 15.8). Debbie Epstein applies this theoretical framework to the issue of race and racism to show how they are socially constructed in relation to power at political, institutional and interpersonal levels.
>
> To what extent can you identify with this powerful analysis of racism? And what are its implications?
>
> Edited from: Epstein, D. (1993) *Changing Classroom Cultures: Anti-racism, Politics and Schools*. Stoke-on-Trent: Trentham Books, 9–16.

## Social relations and discourse

Social relations are organized through a number of institutions and social structures, of which the education system is one (others include the family, the law, the political system, and so on). Within each of these social institutions there are a number of different possible ways of behaving and of understanding the nature of the institution. These different versions of the particular institution are in competition with each other for dominance and, at different times and in different places, different versions will be more or less successful. Indeed, contradictions and conflict are part of the network of social relations with which we all live. If we take the example of education, we can see that the different sides of current struggles around teaching methods (for example, over the use of 'real books' to teaching reading) represent a struggle between different understandings of what it means to teach and to learn and different notions of what schooling is for and about.

These competing understandings are expressed through language and through the ways in which institutions like schools are actually organized. The French philosopher, Michel Foucault, used the terms 'discourse' (taken from the field of linguistics) and 'discursive practices' to describe these understandings and their expression through language, organization forms and ways of behaving. The various discourses which are available in relation to particular social institutions and structures provide us with different possible ways of behaving and understanding the world as well as limiting (but not determining) what can be done and said. We are positioned in various discourses as well as taking up positions ourselves. For example, we identify ourselves and are identified as heterosexual, lesbian or gay and could not do so if categorizing discourses of sexuality did not exist. In this limited sense, we can be said to be 'produced' by discourses and discursive practices.

In *Discipline and Punish* (1977), Foucault discusses the ways in which schools have arisen as a site of discipline and surveillance of children, saying that:

A relation of surveillance, defined and regulated is inscribed at the heart of the practice of teaching, not as an additional or adjacent part, but as a mechanism that is inherent to it and which increases its efficiency. (p. 176)

Following Foucault, Valerie Walkerdine (1985) argues that discourses in schooling both regulate and produce the child as a 'rational, independent, autonomous (individual as a quasi-natural phenomenon who progresses through a universalised developmental sequence towards the possibility of rational argument' (p. 203). In this context, she suggests that schooling not only 'defines ... what knowledge is but also defines and regulates what "a child" is' (pp. 207–8). Schools, then, are sites of struggles, not only about knowledge, but also about ideologies of childhood, about what it means to be a teacher and to be gendered. Consequently, there are, within schooling, a number of different, sometimes contradictory, discourses available through which teachers and children are produced and produce themselves.

It is possible, for example, to imagine teachers behaving in a number of different ways in relation to students, and these ways may come from a number of different discourses. The most obvious discourse of teaching might be called the 'instructional discourse'. Within it, teachers pass on information, demonstrate how to do things, and so on. Within this discourse it would be impossible to imagine a teacher knowing less than pupils in her/his class about a topic being taught. However, teachers also operate, especially in the early years of schooling, within what might be called a 'mothering discourse'. In this context, teachers might offer comfort to children who are distressed or look after them in physical ways, such as changing their undergarments if they have 'wet' themselves.

It would not, however, be open to a teacher to undertake all the functions of mothering and remain in the role of teacher, and even very young children are aware of the differences in expected behaviours. One little girl, when she was six and a pupil in the school where her mother taught, resolved the conflict of discourses by regularly calling her mother 'Mrs Mummy' when at school. There are, of course, many other discourses within which teachers can and do operate – for example, those of social work, policing and so on.

The question of which discourses are dominant is not a natural one, for the social meanings given to different discursive practices will vary according to one's position within a particular set of social relations. What seems like common sense will, in general, represent the interests of dominant groups in society, while what seems 'biased' or 'extreme' may well be those discourses which seek to oppose those interests (although subordinated groups develop their own versions of common sense). In education, for example, it may seem perfectly reasonable to assume that it is desirable to give a 'balanced' view of controversial and political questions and this is often argued against anti-racist and anti-sexist education. However, subjects which are controversial change over time. For example, until relatively recently the teaching of evolutionary theory rather than the creation story as given in Genesis was considered both subversive and controversial. Furthermore, the demands of 'balance' seem rather different depending on one's position in relation to the issue.

## Race and racism

There are a number of discourses around issues of race and racism in education and other social structures. One of our most widespread common-sense understandings is that 'race' exists as an objective social fact.

One of the characteristics of Western science is that it categorizes, and the post-Darwinian assumption has been that people can be categorized in similar ways to chemical elements, plants, animals and so forth. In the process of categorization, it has been assumed that particular groups of people have certain essential characteristics, which are (usually) biologically determined. Thus, for example, in certain racist discourses African-Caribbean men and women are assumed to be naturally 'physical', while South Asian women are assumed to be naturally 'passive'. It has been further assumed that when someone has been categorized, or has categorized him or herself, according to one of a number of types of categories, which include race, gender, sexuality, ability and so on, then everything important which can be said about this person has, in fact, been said. In this way, social identities such as those of race are constructed. Such social identities are not simply about how we are seen or categorized They are also important in how we ourselves experience and understand the world.

In terms of race, it is assumed, in keeping with the essentialist processes of categorization discussed above, that certain kinds of people are 'black' and other kinds of people are 'white'. This is the basis of racism directed against black people. The concepts race and racism are mutually dependent. This is not a static situation, but a dynamic process in which racist discourses feed on the concept of race, and in which the concept of race is constantly re-articulated and reproduced through racist discourses in a symbiotic relationship.

I would suggest that racism can be best understood in terms of process – or, perhaps, those processes which result in the disadvantage for particular groups of people defined through racist discourses. In British society and its historical context, the people against whom racist processes work are most often black, but at other times and in other places, other groups, such as the Irish or Jews, have been the chief butt of different forms of racism and it should be noted that anti-Irish racism in Britain, and anti-Semitism more generally, continue to be active and, indeed, seem to be on the increase.

Because racism is a process, which changes over time and place and varies with macro- and micro-political conditions, it is not possible to give a simple, straightforward definition to the word. Racism cannot be reduced to a simple formula, such as the often quoted equation 'racism equals power plus prejudice'. Certainly both prejudice and power play a part in the construction of racism. However, power is more complicated than such a formula allows for and personal prejudice is not necessarily a component in every situation in which black people are disadvantaged. If, for example, an oversubscribed school offers places first to those children who have had a sibling there (even if the sibling has left), which is very common, this is likely to disadvantage black children in areas where there have been relatively recent influxes of black people. It is unlikely that such a practice would have originated from the prejudiced intention of reducing the numbers of black pupils, but this will be the effect. It is practices such as these which are defined as 'indirect racism' in the Race Relations Act 1976. The operation of the 'market' in education under the Education Reform Act (1988), will also disadvantage black pupils disproportionately. However, it was instituted at the behest of new-right economic ideology rather than directly by racism.

Racism involves a variety of processes and institutional arrangements which are socially constructed. These processes take place both at macro-levels, involving national and even global politics, and at micro-levels, in the organization of particular institutions like schools and in the relationships between individuals.

As pointed out above, one of the processes involved in the construction of racism is the acceptance, as common sense, of racial categories. However, racism cannot be combated simply by refusing to accept racial categories. The adoption of slogans such as 'One race the human race', while it may be an important aim, does not recognize that racism makes a real difference in the material world to people's life chances and experiences (Henriques, 1984) and may even be a form of racism itself in its refusal to recognize difference.

There are many racisms, not just one. What they have in common is the outcome of black disadvantage in housing, employment, education, and many other areas of everyday life.

📖 READING 15.8

# Racism in children's lives

## Barry Troyna and Richard Hatcher

> Troyna and Hatcher carried out a detailed study, in two 'mainly white' primary schools, of pupil culture and of the attitudes of the children towards race. This reading is from the conclusions of their book. The analysis is challenging for teachers, for it reveals the embeddedness of racist conceptions within the cultures of the children in the schools and the particular importance of the stance that is taken by teachers towards racist incidents. Although most children lacked a sense of the social structure within which racism develops, many children were committed to the principle of equal opportunities.
>
> Are your pupils aware of and offended by inequalities? If so, could you build on this to increase their understanding of issues such as racism?
>
> Edited from: Troyna, B. and Hatcher, R. (1992) *Racism in Children's Lives: A Study of Mainly-white Primary Schools*. London: Routledge, 196–204

The schools that we studied are similar to many hundreds of primary schools in urban areas, located in streets of Victorian terraces or new estates on the outskirts. They are similar, too, in containing a minority of black children, perhaps two or three, or half a dozen, in each class. A visitor in the classroom and playground will observe children working together and playing together, black and white, with no sign that 'race' is a significant feature of their lives as children. It is unlikely that such a visitor would overhear a racist remark or witness any other form of racist behaviour. It would be easy to conclude that racism among children is not an issue that such schools need to devote much attention to. These schools seem to confirm the validity of the 'contact hypothesis' that racial prejudice and discriminatory practices are dispelled by the positive experience of white and black children being together in school.

Our evidence does not appear to support this view. On the contrary, it reveals that 'race', and racism, are significantly features of the cultures of children in predominantly white primary schools. By far the most common expression of racism is through racist name-calling. There is a wide variation in black children's experiences of racist name-calling. For some it may be almost an everyday happening. For others it is less frequent, with occurrences remembered as significant events whose recurrence remains a possibility in every new social situation. For all, it is in general the most hurtful form of verbal aggression from other children.

The variation in the experiences of black children are not explicable in terms of differences of ethnic group, or of gender. Differences between schools seem to be mainly the consequence of the effectiveness of the stance that teachers, non-teaching staff, and in particular the head teacher, take towards racist incidents, but there is also a wide variation in the experiences of black children in the same school, which is mainly a function if differences in the characteristic patterns of social interaction that black children are involved in and in particular the level of conflict within them.

Many black children also have experiences of racism outside school. In some cases these are of harassment by other, perhaps older, children. School policies on racist behaviour may suppress it within the school but have no effect on the behaviour of some of the white pupils once they leave the school premises. In addition, many black children have experiences of racism in the adult word: disputes with neighbours, arguments in shops, conflict in the community. These experiences, and the roles taken up by black adults within them, provide a context for their experiences in school, their understanding of them and their responses to them, that other children, and school staff, may be unaware of.

Children's cultures can be analysed in terms of the interplay of processes of domination and equality. Elements of elaborated and common-sense ideologies, both racist and anti-racist, deriving from family, television and community, enter into and circulate within children's cultures. Here they interact with common sense understandings generated by everyday social interaction among children. Social processes of dominance and conflict may become racialized in various ways to legitimize forms of racist behaviour. But interaction among children also gives rise to a strong egalitarian dynamic, which may be generalized to issues of 'race' and link up with anti-racist ideologies. Relationships of friendship between white and black children reinforce this egalitarian dynamic, but do not necessarily lead to its generalization to all black children.

There is a wide variation among white children in their knowledge, attitudes and beliefs about 'race', both within children's culture and in the wider society. Some children are largely ignorant of processes of racial discrimination in society, but the majority of white children have quite an extensive knowledge base and set of interpretive frameworks through which they make sense of issues such as immigration, racial violence, South Africa, and relations between black and white people in their own community. The principal sources outside the school are parents and other adult relatives, television, and their direct experiences in the community. These make available a range of contradictory messages about 'race', and in any case children do not passively receive them but actively select and reinterpret.

The attitudes and beliefs of white children range from those who make use of racist frameworks of interpretation to those who are committed to well-developed notions of racial equality. Many children display inconsistent and contradictory repertoires of attitudes, containing both elements of racially egalitarian ideologies and elements of racist ideologies.

The curriculum needs to not only address the real experience that children bring with them to the classroom, it needs to offer them the conceptual tools to interpret it. These are two related elements in how the children in our study thought about 'race' that are pertinent here.

The first is their limited understanding of notions of social structure. Many had little or no understanding of how 'race' was socially structured by, for example, the economy and the state. This is a symptom of a general absence of political education in the primary curriculum. Yet it is clear that children of ten and eleven years are capable of understanding such ideas, even with little help from the curriculum. The consequence of the lack of 'sociological' concepts was that children tended to use concepts derived from their own experiences of interpersonal interaction to explain phenomena at the level of society. So, for example, lacking concepts of ideology based on material interests, many children explained racist behaviour in society in terms of personal motivations of 'jealousy', transferring a concept that was central to experiences of conflict in their own relationships.

The second conceptual limitation concerned the notion of inequality that children used. For many children, white and black, this as a powerful principle capable of organizing a consistent anti-racist perspective. But for others, it stumbled at the idea that to achieve equality for the unequal may require unequal treatment, particularly if the inequality is not just at the level of interpersonal relations but is socially structured in ways that the child is not aware of. The curriculum can make an important contribution towards helping children to develop the principle of equality that is so important in their personal lives into a more complex and encompassing concept of social justice.

Finally, we want to stress the two strands that run through the culture of children. We have demonstrated how significant racism is in the lives of white children. We have also been made award of the strength of anti-racist attitudes and behaviour. The frequent presence of racially egalitarian elements in the thinking even of children who engage in racist behaviour is a crucial factor on which teachers can build. In doing so, the existence in every class of children who have a clear anti-racist commitment is potentially the most powerful resource, if they can be helped to gain the confidence, the skills and knowledge to express it, both in the curriculum and the interpersonal interaction.

# PART 3

# Beyond classroom reflection

## CHAPTER 16

# Learning as a newly qualified teacher

The readings in this chapter are intended for both newly qualified teachers and school mentors.

We begin, in Reading 16.1, with Smith and Coldron challenging NQTs (newly qualified teachers) to review their long-term aims. 'What sort of a teacher', they ask, 'do you want to be?'. Kempe and Nicholson (16.2) are concerned with the continuity of learning from initial training to the first year of teaching. They focus on taking stock of strengths and weaknesses and the development of a professionally constructive career entry profile.

Carré, in Reading 16.3, offers three short case studies of newly qualified teachers in school illustrating some of the factors affecting success. These include, allowing time for skill development, the quality of support within the school and remaining calm when facing problems.

Finally, Moyles, Suzchitzky and Chapman (16.4) provide a reading more explicitly for mentors. They review key roles and issues to be addressed.

In *Reflective Teaching*, the parallel chapter is in three parts. First, principles of induction for newly qualified teachers are considered, using provision in England as a particular example. There is then a section on 'mentoring as reflection', making explicit links to reflective practice and to the significance of mentoring conversations for constructive professional support and challenge. Finally, the third section analyses the induction mentor's role in extending NQTs' knowledge, skill and confidence. 'Key Readings' are suggested, and there are additional, updated ideas on *RTweb*.

📖 **READING 16.1**

# Thinking about the sort of teacher you want to be

## Robin Smith and John Coldron

This reading poses some direct questions about how a newly qualified teacher might approach her or his career. It encourages reflection on two points in particular: the process of improving and consolidating one's skills; and the challenge of sustaining oneself as a 'thoughtful teacher'. The point made about finding personal fulfilment through such development is also important.

What sort of teacher do you want to be?

Edited from: Smith, R. and Coldron, J. (1998) 'Thoughtful teaching', in Cashdan, A. and Overall, L. (eds) *Teaching in Primary Schools*. London: Cassell, 63–7

During initial training you come into contact with many experienced teachers. As you watch them teach, listen to the way they talk to individuals, deal with disputes and talk about teaching, you use them as models. Sometimes you are lucky enough to meet a person who is inspiring in every aspect of the profession, more often it will be someone who is good in many respects but not in others – and of course you also meet those who exemplify for you everything you think is bad about teachers! These models are crucial in helping you to reflect on your own identity as a teacher – 'I want to teach like her'; 'I like the way he does that, but not this'; 'I will never become that sort of teacher'. When you use models like these, you can identify aspects of teaching that are sometimes very difficult to make clear in any other way. Thus, seeing and using examples furthers your thinking about teaching. Teachers who are striving to improve constantly check themselves against such models and try to be more and more discriminating about what they like and don't like about what they see: 'I want to teach like her, because . . .'; 'If I could do what he does in those circumstances, then I would achieve . . .'; 'That way of relating to children is wrong'.

Unfortunately, once training is finished and you are in a post, this way of thinking about your teaching can, for a number of reasons, be more difficult to do well. One reason is that, although based in school, you have far fewer opportunities to observe how other teachers really work in the intimacy of their own classrooms. A second reason is that in order to make as good a job as you can of the first year, you focus on your immediate practice and do not notice so much what others are doing, or you may only look for what will help with narrow, but urgent, practical concerns. Another danger is that as you become more confident from year to year in your way of doing things, it is tempting to relax and enjoy the relative ease compared with your first year and not to seek alternative models of practice.

Having constructed your identity, what need have you for further building blocks? Well, looking at the way others are doing it should be not only an initial stimulus but also a source of continuing challenge. As a thinking teacher you should therefore take every opportunity to observe others and to talk with them about their aims and style. Team teaching is an excellent means of doing this. School management can also help by using in-service days to allow teachers to go to other schools or to observe each other in a planned way. Reading descriptions of other teachers' practice is a good substitute for actual observation, since the best accounts give a real flavour of the teaching and classroom atmosphere.

Here is an extract from Woods (1990), in which some Year 6 children described their teacher's way of establishing a classroom atmosphere where their views were relevant:

> She talks to the whole group together and then we just tell her our ideas, and other people comment on them and suggest this and that and then we put it all together. She lets us talk

about it more than other teachers. She lets us have our own conversations and arguments and then gets us back to the point. She lets us speak, she lets us vote although we're not 18 . . . She lets us breathe more. Most of all she listens, unlike other teachers who jump to conclusions. (Woods, 1990, p. 76)

You will inevitably think about day-to-day details of classroom practice, such as 'What is the most effective way to give children access to the art materials?'. What is harder is to reflect on issues of style and relationships; for example, 'Does my humour suit all the children in my class?' and 'Do I allow my children to be independent in the classroom?'. It is almost impossible to find time, or the company, in which to ask the more fundamental questions: 'What do I mean by education?', or 'Why are schools the best places to educate children?'. When you are immersed in the urgency of daily practice, questions like this can seem at best a luxury and at worst an irrelevant indulgence.

But, in fact, consideration of these questions has the potential to develop your practice more radically than do those that seem more directly relevant. Think of a house: the type and quality of the rooms and facilities are dependent on the foundations. To change these will inevitably change the living space and what is possible in that space. The pressures to be unthinking are very powerful. The urgency of day-to-day concerns, the culture of the school and the social position of teachers conspire to make you accept the status quo. It is therefore necessary to force yourself to think about the more fundamental questions in order to keep a critical perspective on your own current practice and to develop and improve.

Much of what you do as a teacher is determined by the need to survive in a reasonably dignified way from day to day. Survival is always set in a specific context. It means particular children and their parents, a particular head teacher, perhaps with her own view of how you should be teaching, a particular community of school colleagues and support staff who over the years have built up a school identity in a specific building and community, with a way of doing things, an approach best described as an ethos, with all its overtones of territorial identity. These things exert powerful social forces on you, which makes questioning them very difficult, but they do need to be questioned. Schools can develop ways of working that help the school but are not good for children. For example, control and discipline are central concerns of headteachers, teachers and parents because without a calm, harmonious atmosphere schools cannot work. But in striving for control, teachers can forget that it is a means to an end, not an end in itself.

Similarly, the National Curriculum and the increasing prescriptions as to teaching method, because they come from central government, have immense power to affect what you do; but this does not mean that you should not, in the interests of the children, consider the rights and wrongs of what you are being asked to do. We do not mean a knee-jerk rejection, but a coming to a professional judgement.

A powerful way of enabling yourself to question the way things are is to work at more than one school. Our advice to young teachers is to spend from two to three years in one school, then to move on and do the same in another. By working for that length of time in three schools you will have gained a critical perspective on ways of doing things and not be confined by the horizons of a single school community.

So what do these points add up to? You need to be able to think beyond the confines of your own classroom needs, the school's habits, the community setting and the apparently all-powerful dictates of government. This means being committed to learning continually about teaching, education, children, and yourself as a teacher. Student teachers often express envy at what seems to be the unassailable confidence of the experienced teacher. For reflective teachers it is not like that. Yes, you are comfortable with your craft in that you know how to survive and at the same time to deliver what is asked of you. As a successful, experienced teacher you will have immense skill and ability. But as the problems of survival fade, so experience gives you new insight into your failings. Because your aim is no longer set merely on getting through, you become only too aware of how far your practice falls short of your more considered ideals.

Uncomfortable questions crowd in on you: 'Do I do enough in my class of 30 for the low attainers *and* the high attainers?'; 'Do I teach more to deliver knowledge rather than for understanding to be achieved?'; 'How can I teach better to lead someone to real understanding?'; 'Do I handle the children with humour and affection?'; 'Despite all of my and my colleagues' efforts, have we only played the school's part in allocating most children to their preordained place in society rather than giving them opportunities for self-fulfilment or betterment?'.

A teacher who is continuing to develop is someone who enjoys the challenge of being creative in practice and thoughtful about theory. She enjoys the tension between what actually happens, what she thinks ought to happen to children in her classroom, and the constraints imposed by the education system of which her classroom is a part. By theory, we mean what you gain from all the ways of being thoughtful about teaching described in this chapter – deepening subject knowledge, using models offered by others as a means of discriminating your own preferred style, discussing educational questions with colleagues, gaining a critical perspective on the school's ethos and 'common sense', being determined to ask and to answer impartially how far what is imposed by others (from the head teacher to the Secretary of State for Education and Employment) are in the best interests of children.

One way of engaging with theory is by teachers acting as researchers. Traditionally, there has been an apparently unbridgeable gulf between classroom practitioners and educational researchers. At the time of writing there is a determined effort to encourage teachers to identify research questions about classroom practice, to read and analyse educational research that addresses those questions and to engage in small-scale research projects themselves in pursuit of the answers. It is an initiative that has great potential and is aimed at enabling teachers to be more reflective.

We have been writing this for teachers who are at the beginning of their careers. However, it is worth noting that the approach we advocate can make teaching more creative and fulfilling throughout a career. Thoughtful, creative teachers have much to offer their pupils, but also much to gain in their professional lives.

## READING 16.2

# Developing a Career Entry Profile

Andy Kempe and Helen Nicholson

> The transition from trainee to full-time teacher can sometimes be challenging, but important steps have been taken in recent years to make it easier. Among the most significant is the development of Career Entry Profiles. These are designed to improve the continuity and targeting of mentoring when newly qualified teachers begin their first post. In principle, therefore, mentors for NQTs should be able to pick up on previously established professional development needs. In this way, teaching performance in the first years of teaching should be significantly enhanced.
>
> Edited from: Kempe, A. and Nicholson, H. (2001) *Learning to Teach Drama 11–18*. London: Continuum, 214–6

In recent years, the practice of profiling professional development has become an established part of teaching. Profiles play an increasingly important role in appraisal. For example, they are used to counsel teachers on how to progress in their careers and to give new employers insights into their interests, skills and achievements.

Towards the end of their initial teacher training, student teachers need to consolidate what they have achieved and identify what they yet need to develop in order to become established as teachers. Committing these observations to paper is the first step towards creating a profile of professional development.

In England and Wales student teachers will, at the end of their initial teacher training, complete a formalized Career Entry Profile (CEP) as part of the requirements for qualification. In Scotland and Northern Ireland a similar form of profiling is strongly recommended as good practice but it is not statutory. In any event, student teachers should make sure that what they state on this first important entry in their career profile is honest and accurate. Indeed, at the end of initial training it is important to look forward to the induction period as a way of building on achievements and drawing on the support systems available to address necessary aspects of practice. Compiling CEPs gives student teachers an opportunity to set out clearly what they want and need from their first job. As the DfEE express it, a CEP: 'supports new teachers as they make the transition from ITT [initial teacher training] to becoming established in the profession and helps schools to provide the support and monitoring which each individual NQT needs from the outset of their career'.

The Career Entry Profile is an official document against which standards of professional competence achieved by NQTs may be measured. However, as a prelude to compiling their official CEP, student teachers sometimes find it useful to think about their strengths and areas for development in more personal terms. For this, trainees may find it helpful to plot their 'strengths, weaknesses, opportunities and threats' in a SWOT activity. For example, a SWOT might cover:

- *Strengths:* In subject knowledge, classroom practice, experience.

- *Weaknesses:* More usefully recognized as areas for further development. These may relate to a number of gaps in teaching experience, subject knowledge or practice.

- *Opportunities:* How is the first year of teaching perceived in terms of new areas of learning? What openings do new teachers see for their professional development? Those that have already secured employment before completing their training course may wish to consider the role they will undertake.

- *Threats*: What is there at the philosophical, ideological, national and local levels that may make the first years of teaching difficult? This may involve clarifying aims and values, and some people may wish to consider personal issues here that might present particular challenges.

An example is given in Figure 16.2.1 of how a trainee might use this type of analysis at the end of his or her training.

Over the course of initial training, trainees will have a huge amount of valuable experience and achievements on which to draw as a professional, and the process of completing a SWOT and then working on a CEP will help in recognizing this. Looking at the statements on the SWOT chart above a trainee might want to identify those that are personal and keep them private. However, he or she should also identify those that might usefully serve as a benchmark against which progression in the published standards and competences might be made. How, for instance, might the illustrative statements be rephrased to show how they link with the required NQT standards and competences?

Compiling a Career Entry Profile productively involves student teachers trying to put themselves into the shoes of the school mentors who will be responsible for their induction as newly qualified teachers. This involves helping NQTs fulfil their strengths while facilitating opportunities to address those areas in which they have identifiable gaps or omissions. Induction tutors and mentors will be concerned about the personal welfare of an NQT but,

| Strengths | Weaknesses |
|---|---|
| Make a summary list here all of the things you are good at that will help you as a teacher. | Summarize here what you feel your gaps are. |
| • Bags of enthusiasm.<br>• Extensive subject knowledge.<br>• Ability to enthuse children.<br>• Setting clear and purposeful tasks which lead to progression.<br>• Good personal organization and IT skills. | • Tend to take on too much, then worry about inability to manage it all.<br>• Limited classroom management skills.<br>• Timing lessons – still try to cram too much in.<br>• Sometimes pitch lessons too high – lower ability groups get bored. |
| **Opportunities** | **Threats** |
| When considering the first year of full-time teaching, what sort of opportunities will you look forward to taking? | When considering the first year of full-time teaching, what sort of pitfalls will you need to watch for? |
| • Involvement in whole-school initiatives.<br>• Planning progression for a whole year.<br>• More work on subject specialism. | • Taking on too much – getting too tired to do things properly.<br>• Professional support networks.<br>• Discipline problems with some groups. |

**Figure 16.2.1**   Example of a SWOT analysis for a trainee teacher

at the end of the induction year, it is the NQT's professional capability that must be assessed. This assessment will determine whether or not they may proceed with their teaching career.

Student teachers may expect their placement schools and training institutions to scrutinize, agree upon and sign a copy of the Career Entry Profile. The NQT's first school must be presented with a copy of the profile. Schools will then be able to keep the profiles on record and use them to inform the NQT's induction programme and serve as a baseline against which to judge progression in the first year of teaching.

In writing any kind of CEP a balance does need to be struck between the idealistic and the realistic. It is particularly crucial for student teachers to identify as accurately as possible what areas there are for further development in terms of subject knowledge, planning, classroom management and monitoring and assessment. However, student teachers who have already secured a post before compiling an entry profile should consider the particular situation of their new school.

## READING 16.3

# Case studies from the first year of teaching

Clive Carré

> This reading is drawn from an extensive study of the experience of trainees during initial teacher education programmes. Focusing on students on a PGCE course, their experience was tracked from the start of their training and on into their first appointments as newly qualified teachers. The study traced the ways in which the craft knowledge of experienced teachers is gradually acquired.
>
> In this extract, we see how NQT experiences in the first year of teaching can be extremely variable from school to school and person to person, but there are also some important commonalities. Amongst these, needing time to work things out, a supportive environment and a calm, constructive approach to problems are particularly important.
>
> Edited from: Carré, C. (1993) 'The first year of teaching', in Bennett, N. and Carré, C. (eds) *Learning to Teach*. London, New York: Routledge, 208–10

Among two most important factors contributing to professional development in teacher induction programmes are support and specific feedback. However, even when these are provided, new teachers require 'time to develop the complex repertoires of behaviour necessary to succeed in classrooms' (Spingfield and Wolfe, 1990). Data from our study suggest that the rate at which development takes place varies with the individual, but progress was often limited or accelerated because of school influences. Detailed examination of the progress of individuals illustrated different patterns of development. For example, we offer below summary profile sketches of three beginning teachers who taught nine- to ten-year-olds. Each was in a school where staff were friendly and helpful.

## Sonia – steady improvement

Sonia settled in quickly, having organized her classroom before school started and prepared plans of work to half-term. The head teacher had provided detailed information about the school and children she was to teach. The picture was one of competent preparedness on both sides.

She was confident and gradually learned not to overorganize. She explored different teaching strategies and balancing whole-class teaching, group work and individual work. She was a thinking person and willing to learn through trial and error which approaches were best for her and the children. As she became less 'flustered and panicky to get everything sorted out', her relationship with the children improved and she no longer needed to nag them!

Her relationship with staff was good. Her mentor was supportive and she received well-informed feedback throughout. At no time had there been any problems; the headteacher thought she had shown gradual improvement and was much more professionally aware at the end of the year.

## Anthony – downhill progress

Anthony felt exhausted and stressed at the end of the first week. On the first day he realized that his efforts of planning and collecting resources had been in vain. Not only had the school not communicated the topic he was to teach but he had no general school information, school policies or curriculum outlines. He had serious problems settling in, exacerbated by the conflict between what the school wanted and his complying with those expectations. For example, his idealistic views about teaching maths for meaning, were in conflict with the school's insistence on 'a clear focus on National Curriculum requirements and evidence in children's books'.

He was confident, enjoyed the children but found 'an awful lot of pressure from different directions'. There were expressions of concern about organization and control and his naive views on theory and practice. Feedback about his performance was minimal; his facade of confidence made people reticent to help. He said 'my self-esteem went down and down, as I got more and more busy'. His good days were good and his bad days were 'real black bits'. The school indicated that he had 'improved radically in his display work and relationships with children'. He realized that he had to get a lot right in teaching subject matter, especially getting children to understand mathematical ideas.

## Felicity – slow to start, rapid acceleration

It is hard to dismiss the real difficulties which Felicity had to establish herself on equal terms with her experienced team teacher. She had planned conscientiously before term started, along guidelines given by the school. Her problem was to try to establish herself alongside a teacher who was set in his ways and could handle any disciplinary problem with ease, when she was facing, 'the worst class in the school . . . rowdy lot of little devils with attitude problems'.

Unintentionally, her team teacher, also her mentor, inhibited her from making her mark and she felt superfluous. She said 'really he's the teacher and I hardly say a word'. After the second term the picture changed dramatically. She became more confident, took advantage of the mentor's modelling to learn more about matching, management and control. In the third term they shared ideas in planning, she was frequently in sole charge of the 60 children and she introduced and established music as an important part of the curriculum. It was thought by the head teacher that they had, over the year, forged a productive working relationship and that Felicity with determination 'had developed a strong professional awareness'.

## Conclusion

It was clear from the study as a whole that the arrangements made before taking up appointments varied widely, though in general the reaction to the newly qualified teachers on arrival was warm and supportive. The NQTs shared a perception of the year as an intense learning period, exhaustingly hard work, demanding but in retrospect enjoyable. Associated with feelings of increasing confidence were their improved control of children, often through getting to know them better. This in turn enabled them to try out different teaching strategies and to take more risks. Classroom organization improved and with it the planning for progression. They got better at handling subject knowledge, representing ideas, making judgements about the appropriateness of tasks, diagnosing successes (or otherwise) and planning accordingly.

# The challenges of effective mentoring

Janet Moyles, Wendy Suschitzky and Linda Chapman

This reading comes from an interesting research project on the challenges of mentoring in primary schools. The workload implications are seen to be real, but the reading also clearly shows the need for training and support of mentors themselves. Maintaining appropriate professional challenge and critical friendship is by no means easy, but it is an important skill to support our collective professional development.

Is the importance of mentoring and of mentoring skills recognized and provided for in your school?

Edited from: Moyles, J., Suschitzky, W. and Chapman, L. (1998) *Teaching Fledglings to Fly . . .? Mentoring and Support Systems in Primary Schools*. London: Association of Teachers and Lecturers

One of the overwhelming features that struck us during our research was the diversity and great variation in practice between schools, heads and mentors. This reflects the very individuality of those being mentored and those mentoring, and the special relationships that are likely to be formed in some learning partnerships. The extent of the mentoring role also reflects the generally overwhelming nature of primary pedagogy, as Alexander states:

> We may now have to acknowledge that the main reason why it is becoming increasingly difficult to train someone adequately for the class teacher role is that the role itself has become an impossible one to train for. (Alexander, 1992, p. 202)

The job is so diverse that the skills of mentors need to be equally diverse in order that they can advise on the many facets needed by the new entrant to teaching. There are, we believe, questions to be asked as to whether, with limited financial and human resources, primary schools have the time for the kind of mentoring that is required to develop high-quality practitioners. There is no doubt they have the skills as 'expert practitioners' but we believe that training is vital if mentors are to understand newly qualified teachers' developing needs across training and into their first years of teaching.

We were concerned throughout the research that NQT mentors and some student mentors (and, to a certain extent, the heads of schools) were somewhat 'satisfied' that their role is to ensure that the new entrant 'survives' rather than 'develops'. It seems that an invisible barrier is often erected between mentors and NQTs in the name of collegiality which prevents the mentoring from doing more than ensuring the day-to-day survival and 'comfort' of the NQT. We feel this is inappropriate in a professional context where discussion of the strengths and weaknesses of practice are such a key feature of potential development alongside the identification of specific needs of individual teachers for continual professional development.

This concern reminded us of the model of mentoring outlined by Maynard and Furlong (1995) in which they express the learning relationship between mentor and new entrant in terms of apprenticeship, competency and reflection.

**Apprenticeship** (new entrants will do as you do or as you tell them)

**Competency** (new entrants will show you that they can do this and/or this)

**Reflection** (new entrants know why they are doing this or this)

Maynard and Furlong emphasized that this is not a linear model and we would concur with this. Development of new skills often requires some 'input' at the apprenticeship-type level, which must be followed by new entrants showing a level of competence in that skill before they can begin to reflect on their practices and deepen their understanding and underpinning rationale. At the first level, newly qualified teachers are likely to need support and training if they are to acquire new skills without losing confidence and to show their competency. If they are to evaluate their own competences and reflect on practice they will need their mentors to adopt an educator role. This process will spiral both as an individual teaching practice progresses and in the development from one practice to another and the continuation into the NQT year offering a continuous 'loop' between the three modes that Maynard and Furlong identify. During the first year, mentors will need to assist NQTs in the continuous development of new skills and competences. They will seek to extend and enrich practice through reflective evaluation and this, in itself, will lead to the identification of other skills to be acquired. Clear documentation of priority setting and action planning will enable progress to be monitored over the NQT year.

In a later study by Maynard (1997) mentors were asked to suggest their own order of priority of strategies for supporting students. They offered the following:

- supporter

- model

- giver of feedback

These mentors, in the same way as those involved in our study, failed to mention 'challenger' as part of their support strategies.

Our research also found that the mentoring needs of newly qualified teachers are likely to be more in the area of generic teaching skills than in subject mentoring. This is so despite recent initiatives showing that the government perceives the latter to be a vital feature of new entrants' training and, therefore, an important feature of the mentor's role. However, no one within our research, in relation to the comments made during interviews or from video material analysis, felt that subject knowledge was a key feature of mentoring roles (see Richards *et al.*/ATL Report, 1997). Edwards and Collison (1996) also found that subject mentoring did not feature as a student/mentor concern. We would tentatively suggest that primary teachers' 'instinct' still appears to be towards child-centred, rather than subject-centred, practices. This is not surprising, given that most NQTs need considerable support in developing their understanding of handling classroom organization and child management issues, as well as attempting to ensure understanding of aspects such as differentiation. That said, it appeared very difficult to highlight in primary classrooms the difference between mentoring for subject knowledge and mentoring about management of learning in that subject. They are both concerned with pedagogy at their root and one can be a vehicle for the other.

We saw little evidence of action planning or target setting either by mentors with new entrants, or by NQTs with support from their mentors. Indeed, mentors tended to leave 'up-in-the-air' ideas about what might be done, and did not then translate these into specific actions or targets for which the new entrant could aim. New entrants themselves might suggest something they could do, but these did not appear to be confirmed or written down at the time of the mentoring discussion by either of the learning partners. This consequentially meant that there was no way in which they could form targets or form a basis for the evaluation of progress or achievement.

We began to speculate that, as the new entrant develops greater confidence and competence, it may be most appropriate for the mentor to suggest and negotiate a specific focus for attention and to ensure that the new entrant makes their own action plans for step-by-step improvement. This would involve both of them thinking through what was needed in the short, medium and long term. We trailed this idea on a group of 30 NQT mentors at a recent training session. When confronted with the following 'action plan' outline, they had significant difficulty in responding to some aspects.

- What is your new entrant currently doing well?

- What is s/he not currently doing so well?

- What identified needs therefore does s/he have?

- What are the priorities in dealing with these needs?

- Why are these priorities?

- When will these need to be done? Which of these are short-term, medium-term and long-term priorities?

- What will you need to do to help her/him? How and with what support? Can you make an action plan?

- What skills will you need to have to fulfil your role? How will you acquire these? What help do you need?

- How will you evaluate success? What will be your success criteria for the new entrant? For yourself?

Identifying needs was accomplished relatively easily and mentors were quickly able to make lists of things at which the NQT succeeded or with which s/he needed help of some kind. However, when then asked to identify priorities, they were less sure of how to proceed. Most floundered when it came to considering these priorities in terms of timescale and rationale and most had given little thought to what was needed to support their own actions and needs in enabling the NQT to move forward (rather than merely 'cope'). Success criteria had not been considered. We believe this gives an insight into the nature of the kind of support and training mentors themselves need if they are to promote development of new entrants to the profession.

Effective mentoring carries some responsibility for the assessment of the new entrant, if mainly at the formative (rather than summative) level. This is mainly acceptable to, and accepted by, student mentors (increasingly so as first competences and now Standards for Career Entry have emerged). NQT mentors, on the other hand, avoid this role and there is clear discomfort with applying any obvious assessment procedures or even taking a 'critical colleague' role. Teachers feel it is a reflection on their own capabilities and professionalism if their new entrant does not 'perform' to a perceived standard, which in itself is dominated by the ethos of the school. In theory, TTA [Teacher Training Agency] standards (if they are made workable) could contribute significantly to schools' understanding of what demands can and should be made on students and NQTs. Poorer new entrants are arguably less likely to slip through the net. Only one of our NQTs was perceived to have any potential problem and these were minimized by the mentor and the school.

Most new entrants indicated that they expected more constructive criticism than most of them received from their mentors or others, which may have served to alleviate the weaker NQTs' difficulties. Schools and teachers will need significant support from LEAs and possibly HE institutions to learn to apply standards and give clear and specific constructive criticisms to NQTs. Teachers perceived their role to be more critical in terms of students and were more at ease in this role than NQT mentors all of whom perceived NQTs (even though they were only a few weeks from the end of their ITT course) as being peers.

Finally of course, there are considerable professional development gains available to mentors, as they themselves pointed out to us, by analysing teaching and learning in the way that is required when they adopt a role as 'critical colleague'.

## CHAPTER 17

# School improvement and continuing professional development

The five readings in this chapter address a wide range of whole-school issues concerning teacher culture, school development planning, accountabilty to the market, to parents and to governors, and the efficacy of school inspection.

In Reading 17.1, MacBeath and Mortimore review what has been learned from the focus on school improvement of recent years. They identify eight points, beginning with important recognition that schools cannot compensate for society and concluding that we need to develop deeper understanding of learning.

Southworth, Nias and Campbell (17.2) report on the key features of the 'culture of collaboration' which has been an important characteristic of many English primary schools. They point, in particular, to the important relationship between personal and collective commitments.

Continuing professional development is vital for personal fulfilment and for developing the quality of educational provision. Solomon and Tresman (17.3) provide an analysis of how the two may interconnect around value commitments and 'professional identity'.

Two readings follow on inspection and accountability. In Reading 17.4, Barber asserts the achievements of 'New Labour' education policy. With particular reference to OFSTED and other accountability measures, he provides an overview of the system that has been created. Richards (17.5), on the other hand, analyses OFSTED procedures and concludes that 'it claims more than it can justifiably claim' and that 'its judgements are more partial and subjective than it acknowledges'. There is a tension here, then, between the confident momentum of the system, and professional concern that it is all too crude and inaccurate. Perhaps we need to go back to MacBeath and Mortimore's conclusion and build a new system based on what we know about learning itself?

The parallel chapter of *Reflective Teaching* addresses a wide range of significant issues. The first three sections offer substantial accounts of what is known about school effectiveness, school improvement and learning organizations. Section 4, is on evaluating schools and addresses self-evaluation, performance and target-setting and external inspection. Continuing professional development is the subject of the final section. This is seen in relation to school cultures, school improvement planning and performance management. There are 'Reflective Activities' for investigating aspects of school practices and, at the end of the chapter, there are suggestions for 'Key Readings'. *RTweb* extends the choice of such resources.

# What have we learned about school improvement?

John MacBeath and Peter Mortimore

This short reading takes stock of knowledge about how to improve the performance of schools and also offers some reflection on the relationship between research and public policy. In recent years, school improvement has been a very successful field of both research and policy. Whilst MacBeath and Mortimore point out the limitations of knowledge, they are also able to highlight some important principles on which professional commitment and practice could be based.

What issues are raised for policy and practice in the school in which you teach?

Edited from: MacBeath, J. and Mortimore, P. (2001) 'School effectiveness and improvement: the story so far', in MacBeath, J. and Mortimore, P. (eds) *Improving School Effectiveness*. Buckingham: Open University Press, 1–2

We have entered a new millennium with sophisticated science and spectacular technology but still without the knowledge of how to educate all our children. We have discovered how to engineer the blueprint of living beings but we are still searching for an environment in which children can learn with enjoyment and effect.

School has been entrusted with the educational task and been accepted from generation to generation as fulfilling its remit honestly and ethically. Alternatives to school have been tried and, for the most part, have enjoyed a brief life. Schooling has become such an integral feature of the social and economic landscape that it is almost impossible to conceive of different approaches to educating children, at least in their pre-adolescent years.

Politicians and policy-makers have a specific interest in the here and now and are constrained to work within the boundaries of what their constituents expect of an educational system. So, having promoted education to the forefront of policy they have to make schools work, to make them work more effectively and within a political lifetime. 'Raising standards' has retained its pre-eminent place in the transition from the second to the third millennium, proof of which has to be demonstrated within the parameters of school, school curriculum and school assessment. Seeking evidence to support their policies, governments have had a rich fund of effectiveness research on which to draw, not only in the United Kingdom but on a worldwide basis.

From the researchers' viewpoint, it is a matter of concern that policy-makers do not draw deeply enough on the well, nor with the caution and circumspection that the data demand. From the policy point of view this appears as ambivalence and equivocation when what is needed is clear-cut answers to straightforward policy questions. In reality, school effectiveness research has contributed massively to policy formation, but the challenge to governments and educational gatekeepers is to have the courage to listen more intently to what researchers in this field are saying and where the research is leading us. While impolitic for those in seats of government openly to change their mind, it is the first moral imperative for the researcher when presented with evidence, new frames of reference and alternative paradigms.

This counterpoint of policy conviction and research caution has been characteristic of the movement of ideas in school effectiveness nationally and internationally over the last two decades. School effectiveness research has been charged by its critics with being defensive and precious, a charge to which we must on occasion plead guilty. It has at times set in opposition a school effectiveness 'camp' and a school improvement 'camp', as if these two were not integrally and umbilically related. Researchers have too often talked to one another rather than to teachers or parents and their language has often been impenetrable and self-referring. But the movement has also been open to robust critique and has learned from its critics. It has grown in complexity and sophistication. It has expanded its boundaries, widened its thinking, challenged its own premises. In short, we have learned:

- that school education cannot compensate for society and that in making high demands of teachers and raising our expectations of schools we must have scrupulous respect for the evidence on socio-economic inequality and the changing nature of family and community life;

- that schools can make a difference and that being in an effective as against a less effective school is a crucial determinant of life chances for many individual young people;

- that 'effects' are complex and multilayered and that, while schools of themselves can make a difference, there are even more significant effects at the level of department and classroom;

- that children experience schools differently; that achievement is not a simple linear progression but subject to ebbs and flows over time and in response to the influence of the peer group and pupils' own expectations on the basis of gender, race and social class;

- that the context of national culture is a powerful determinant of parent, student and teacher motivation and that school improvement requires more than simplistic borrowing of remedies from other countries;

- that we are learning, and still have a lot to learn, about how schools improve and what kind of support and challenge from external sources is most conducive to their effective development;

- that a salient dimension of school improvement is helping schools to be more confident in the use of their own and other data; more self-critical and more skilled in the use of research and evaluation tools;

- that we will only make dramatic advances in educational improvement, in and beyond schooling, when we develop a deeper understanding of how people learn and how we can help them to learn more effectively.

## READING 17.2

# The culture of collaboration

Geoff Southworth, Jennifer Nias and Penny Campbell

This reading derives from an influential research project which established the concept of 'collaborative culture'. Working alongside teachers in six primary schools that had been selected for having 'good staff relationships', the research team were gradually able to understand and analyse the social processes and dynamics of interaction through which trust was built up. One particular feature is the way in which the staff achieved individual fulfilment through the development of the school as a whole.

Have you experienced a 'collaborative culture' in your career as a pupil, trainee teacher or teacher?

Edited from: Southworth, G., Nias, J. and Campbell, P. (1992) 'Rethinking collegiality: teachers' views', mimeo presented to the American Educational Research Association, New Orleans, 1–12

Those who advocate collegiality do so on the basis of prescription rather than description. What conditions in a school facilitate collegiality? Is it 'force-fed' or can it occur 'naturally'? What do teachers and head teachers think about collegiality?

At the outset of the Primary School Staff Relationships (PRSS) project, the research team were conscious that advocates of collegiality had not shown what this phenomenon looked like in practice. These researchers therefore took a limited view and set out to provide first-hand accounts of how head teachers, teachers and other staff behaved when they 'worked together'. It was decided to limit the team's enquiries to schools where, in very loose terms, 'things were going well'.

The enquiry was limited to five schools with between five and twelve teaching staff (including the head teacher), a secretary and at least one ancillary worker. The enquiry was ethnographic with team members acting as participant observers.

The main concept to emerge from the five studies is that of 'organizational culture' where culture is loosely defined as 'the way we do it here', that is, as a set of norms about ways of behaving, perceiving and understanding. A culture is, however, underpinned by jointly held beliefs and values and symbolized for members of the culture by objects, rituals and ceremonies. Each of the five project schools had its own culture that embodied strongly held beliefs about the social and moral purposes of education and about the nature of effective educational practice. These beliefs originated with the head teachers. In three of the schools the head had worked for a long time in each school over ten years to develop and sustain an organizational culture the project team describe as a 'culture of collaboration'. This, it was felt, enabled the teaching and ancillary staff to work closely together in a natural, taken-for-granted way. In the other two schools the heads were endeavouring to develop a culture of collaboration but were impeded by conflicting values held by long-established staff members. Over the course of the year's fieldwork some key individuals (e.g. deputy head teacher, curriculum leaders) left each of these schools and this enabled the new and developing culture to become more firmly established, not least because in both schools it already existed in sub-groups.

The culture of collaboration was built on four interacting beliefs: individuals should be valued but, because they are inseparable from the group of which they are part, groups too should be fostered and valued; the most effective ways of promoting these values are through a sense of mutual security and consequent openness. We will briefly look at each.

## Valuing individuals – as people and for their contribution to others

In the schools where a culture of collaboration existed, even the most mundane and apparently insignificant details of staff behaviour were consistent with its values. Respect for individuals occurred in many guises. There were few status distinctions, all staff used the staffroom and joined in conversations and humour. Newcomers felt free to speak and valued, as one novitiate teacher said:

> They [the staff] treat me as an individual, here to do a job, not to be looked down upon or anything like that. I'm like anybody really.

Everyone who came to the schools was made welcome. A recently appointed teacher commented:

> They make everybody very welcome. It's marvellous and I like the way they've got time for parents and involve the parent a lot in the school . . . they care and that's what came across to me.'

In addition to respecting and nurturing others as individuals in their own right, heads, teachers and ancillaries in the collaborative schools perceived the differences between them as a mutually enriching source of collective strength, as one teacher said:

> Working in a team doesn't mean that everybody's the same and everybody's so busy saying yes, yes, yes to one another that nothing happens. That deadens it. You've got to have different personalities and different ideas to spark other people off, but it can be done without aggression.

Everyone's contribution to the school was valued. Gratitude and appreciation were regularly and openly expressed:

> It's never taken for granted and it's never left to just one teacher – all staff make the point of expressing their appreciation to whoever they are thanking.

## Valuing interdependence – belonging to a group and working as a team

Individual staff members at three of the schools valued one another as people, each with his/her own identity, personality, interests, skills, experiences and potential. Yet they also appreciated the diversity which this brought to the school. Likewise, interdependence has two aspects. Together the members of each staff made a group that was valued because it provided a sense of belonging. At the same time they accepted a collective responsibility for the work of the school so creating a sense of team in which staff helped, encouraged and substituted for one another:

> There's a great deal of warmth between us and it's almost like a family that closes ranks against outsiders when it's being attacked by a piece of gossip or an occasion of vandalism.

Whilst group membership was effectively satisfying, it was not the whole story since in the three collaborative schools staff also felt a sense of collective responsibility for their work and saw themselves as a 'team'. One head wrote in a school document:

> We feel that the consideration and closeness which characterizes relationships between adult members pervades the school as a whole. Thus issues like infant–junior department liaison are less important than the sense of the school as a whole.

Being a 'team' meant to recognize and value the unique contribution of each member to a joint enterprise. It did not necessarily mean doing the same job nor working in the same teaching space but it did mean working to the same ends.

The sense of collective responsibility showed itself in many ways. Most noticeable was the habitual way in which everyone advised, supported and helped one another. A teacher reported:

> If you say 'I'm doing such and such, I haven't got any good ideas', there will be six or seven different ideas thrown at you instantly. Or if you get halfway through doing something and you happen to say 'Oh, it's not working', or 'It's going wrong', there's always someone who is willing to help in any sort of situation. And in dealing with the children you never feel, if you have a problem, that you're cut off, there's always somebody else who is willing to help you. It's often the case [in other schools that] there is someone around who is capable of helping, but not always that they will help, but in this school that doesn't seem to be so. Everyone seems very ready to help.

## Valuing security

This belief and the next are linked. Security is a condition for the growth of openness and openness is the best way of simultaneously fostering the individual and the group. They are connected by a notion of interdependence which means mutual constraint as well as enrichment. To accept as all the staff did that one is dependent on everyone else is to admit that there are limits to one's autonomy. Limits operated in various ways, spoken and unspoken, but, whatever their nature or extent, acceptance of them was mandatory:

> To work here you'd have to be prepared to work as part of this team. If you persisted in not being part of a team you could exist here but you wouldn't be happy. You could make it but not in any satisfying sense . . . If you're not prepared to submit, in the Biblical sense, you're not going to be an effective team member. But once you can see it's in the best interests of the children, it's easy.

Though to submit is to accept another's power over oneself, when all members of a team do so their power over each other is evenly balanced and becomes influence instead. So, within a situation of agreed interdependence, as one teacher said: 'We're all influencing each other, I'm quite convinced of that'. However, an exception to this was the head teacher since staff in the collaborative schools deferred to their heads. In part this can be explained by the fact that the beliefs underlying that 'culture of collaboration' emanated from and were exemplified by the heads of the three schools. Since all staff agreed with these beliefs the heads enjoyed a degree of personal authority that transcended that of other staff.

The fact that the heads' responsibility for the main policies in their schools was virtually unchallenged and that staff exercised a good deal of mutual influence over one another made the collaborative schools very secure places in which to work.

## Valuing openness

Many of the day-to-day attitudes and actions of the staff demonstrated the value they attached to openness. Heads, teachers and ancillaries were ready to admit publicly to a sense of failure:

> In the other schools I've taught in you *didn't* fail. If you did you kept it very quiet. It took me a good four months when I came here to realize that . . . when you had problems you didn't hide them away, you voiced them and you got them sorted out instantly instead of taking them home and worrying about them.

Staff were also ready to display other negative emotions, such as guilt, anxiety and anger. And it was regarded as normal for individuals to voice irritation or dissent directly to one another. Disagreements were accepted as part of life:

> Differences of opinion do emerge but we're all very open, straightforward. If we don't agree with someone we do say so. You know, you just state that you didn't agree and that you thought such and such . . . it doesn't need to be argument.

The heads developed and sustained the culture via their own sense of example (e.g. teaching, taking assemblies, dealing with staff), positive reinforcement and careful selection of staff when opportunities to recruit arose. The heads were also keenly aware of what was happening daily in 'their' schools and demonstrated a 'dedicated obsessiveness' (Coulson, 1978) with all aspects of the school's life and work. Moreover, because they were frequently touring the school and present in the staffroom, talking, listening, joining in with the teaching and planning, they were members of the staff group. They could simultaneously occupy two positions, leader and member, and this prevented them from being aloof and isolated from the staff.

Although there was an asymmetrical distribution of power between the head and staff, just as with teachers and pupils in classrooms, to be less powerful is not to be powerless. Heads and staff negotiated a 'working consensus' (Pollard, 1985) which involved some degree of accommodation to each other's interests. Thus, it was no surprise that the heads negotiated – both explicitly and implicitly – and sought compromises. However, the heads were only prepared to compromise on some things. They would not, for instance, alter their most deeply and strongly held beliefs. This would, presumably, have been too injurious to the head's professional identity. Therefore, negotiation occurred within the parameters of each head's professional convictions. Similarly, compromises were reached in order to preserve the self-image of individual staff. Negotiations were often subtle, coded and tacit, and 'truces' were sometimes struck. The heads also had to be skilled in keeping negotiations 'open' so that fresh compromises could be later reached as and when circumstances allowed.

It would be simplistic to say the heads in the collaborative schools controlled what happened there but they certainly exerted a great deal of influence and occasionally used their power directly. Since this influence was transacted through one-to-one contacts, formal and informal meetings, and negotiations, the heads more noticeably than others revealed a micro-political dimension to the notion of collegiality. Obvious as this may seem, given recent work and the idea that schools are arenas of struggle where notions of hierarchy and equality, democracy and coercion coexist in close proximity (Ball, 1987, pp. 15 and 19), the micro-political aspects need emphasizing since those who promote collegiality appear to be unaware of their existence.

READING 17.3

# A model for continuing professional development

Joan Solomon and Sue Tresman

This reading provides an opportunity to stand back and consider the nature of continuing professional development. It begins with a brief review of the accountability challenges that have faced many professions, including teaching, in recent years. However, if excellence in the quality of public services is to be sustained, then the personal needs and commitment of professionals should be understood too. Solomon and Tresman highlight the significance of 'professional identity' and suggest crucial links for teachers between identity, values, knowledge and beliefs. The most enduring form of continuing professional development is thus a process of coming to know oneself, and one's strengths, weaknesses and commitments as a teacher.

Edited from: Solomon, J. and Tresman, S. (1999) 'A model for continued professional development' *Journal of In-service Education*, **25** (2), 307–8, 310–1, 315–6

We set great store by the idea of professionalism despite the present climate of contestation from many sides. In a recent book, *Teachers' Professional Lives* (Goodson and Hargreaves, 1996), almost every contributed chapter begins by deconstructing the whole notion. But then professionalism has been under increasing attack for a very long time, not just by politicians, but by journalists and the public. This applies to social workers, doctors, engineers, scientists and lawyers, as well as teachers, although to different extents. Two qualities used to be thought to specify professional status: the possession of esoteric knowledge and the ideals of high service. However, in this information age no communicable knowledge can remain esoteric. Service to others, once the hallmark of the professionals, is now a public right. This means that, in our fiercely egalitarian times, professional quality is subject to continual monitoring on behalf of the recipients, as well as by the providers. At first, this resulted in little more than a decline in prestige, and then in trust. In the medical profession, this downward progression could be seen very clearly in the growing public resort to litigation instead of doctor–patient trust. More recently, the doctors are fighting not only for their professional freedom to prescribe and treat as they think fit, but also their right to maintain and regulate their own standards of quality in the performance of operations and patient recovery. However, in education both these battles may appear to have been already lost. Teachers have become tightly managed by the team of senior teacher/managers, by the powerful board of governors and by OFSTED inspectors. The latter body has recently taken to recommending even the preferred style of teaching. 'Failing teachers' are identified not by a professional body like the promised General Council of Teachers, but by non-teaching bureaucrats. All of this allows little room for the activities of the traditional professionals and challenges us to look far more deeply into the nature of professionalism.

## Exploring the development of professional identity

Modern social psychology has long acknowledged the existence of multiple identities. The varied social and professional worlds to which each of us belong stimulate different value or moral positions, different beliefs and different actions in different contexts. Indeed, philosophers as different as Dennett (1981), Ziman (1978) and Popper (1972), have all agreed that it is in the very nature of actions that they are brought about by beliefs and nor just by knowledge alone. The underlying values or moral positions can rarely be made explicit, but beliefs are more dynamic. As even Karl Popper, a positivist philosopher of science much concerned with the nature of knowledge, wrote with emphasis – 'We can act on our beliefs' (Popper, 1972). These distinctions between values, knowledge, belief and action are valuable for thinking about how teachers react to new challenges. Handal and Lauvas (1987) have written interestingly on what they call teachers' 'practical theory', which is dynamic, a basis for action, and yet also subject to change as the teacher experiences new situations and new knowledge, in much the same vein as the work of Schön and Kuhn. They add to this a valuable perspective on the private and personal:

> The practical theory (of teachers) refers to a person's private, integrated but ever-changing system of knowledge, experience and values which is relevant to teaching practice at any particular time. (Handal and Lauvas, 1987, p. 79)

Rom Harré (1983) has generalized and extended this argument into the realm of one's sense of identity in a social situation like school teaching. He writes:

> Thought and action, as necessary conditions for having an idea of myself as a person, are also . . . embedded in all kinds of social practices . . . So the acquisition of the idea of personal identity for oneself is at least in part a consequence of social practices (actions). (p. 211)

For a teacher these social practices arise as they take part in the 'community of practitioners' within the school situation (Lave and Wenger, 1991). This happens in the early years of being a teacher. Gradually, the image of oneself as a professional develops out of stories of classroom incidents and reflection upon them. As Harré says, self-knowledge becomes a kind of continuously changing autobiography, a narrative that organizes memories and values into a collage image of the self that makes sense of ones actions, if only retrospectively!

## A model of continued professional development

To be a professional is to hold values about the teaching to be done that transcend, but also inform the detailed items of daily practice, and may even be more important than the subject knowledge that was the cornerstone of '20-day' designated GEST provision and remains a priority for TTA INSET funding. Values may be hard to put into words, but we have collected considerable research evidence that teaching is a kind of professional action that has to be built upon values, beliefs and knowledge. We also know that it is reflection on this action that slowly constructs a self-image based on reconstructions of previous episodes, a process that is not dissimilar to writing an autobiography. This circular process establishes a professional identity upon which the teacher's very 'honour', to use Rom Harré's term, as well as values are dependent. This is the kind of reflection-in-action that helped Donald Schön's 'reflective practitioners' (Schön, 1983) to develop a deeper understanding of their daily work. Later authors, e.g. Schön, (1992) and Edwards and Brunton (1993), developed Schön's ideas to examine reflective practice within the teaching profession. Figure 17.3.1 shows in a simplified way, this normal, within-school cycle on the left side of the drawing.

Many teachers also have goals and ambitions beyond the immediate confines of the classroom, although still related to their professional identity. They consider in-service education, curriculum criticism, implementation and development, as well as prestige study courses for a postgraduate degree, as part and parcel of their professional development, despite conflicts with the pressure of work from which they often suffer in these days of anxiety and classroom stress. This is represented on the right-hand side of Figure 17.3.1. This time, the action is new in the sense that covers new material, which might be new content, to be taught or related to curriculum innovation. We have highlighted the action aspect of this because it provides an opportunity to reflect, as a practitioner, on what happened and on how

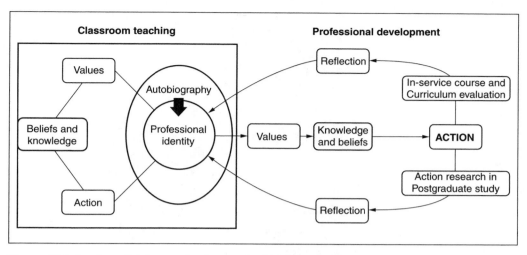

**Figure 17.3.1** A model for continuing professional development

this related to the teacher's values and beliefs. Did her pupils' knowledge and understanding grow in valuable ways?

It follows that providers of professional development courses need to help these teachers, not just to learn new skills and content knowledge, but also to offer them effective and imaginative ways of reflecting on the application of their learning in the context of the classroom.

## READING 17.4

# A new context for accountability and inspection

## Michael Barber

Michael Barber was a major architect of New Labour education policy from 1997 to 2001. In this reading, he reviews some of the most significant features of policy for 'system-wide improvement' and reveals the integrated elements of the accountability and inspection system in England. Of course, what Barber sees as a 'framework for continuous improvement' has been seen by others as an overbearing system to generate narrow performance gains (see, for example, Readings 9.4 or 17.5). However, his text does convey a sense of the development of the system, and suggests the welcome return to an important element of school-based self-evaluation. Such activity should now be 'informed' both by performance evidence and by professional judgement. The role of reflective teachers will remain as central as ever.

Edited from: Barber, M. (2001) 'A new context for accountability and inspection', *Education Review.* **14** (2), 4–8

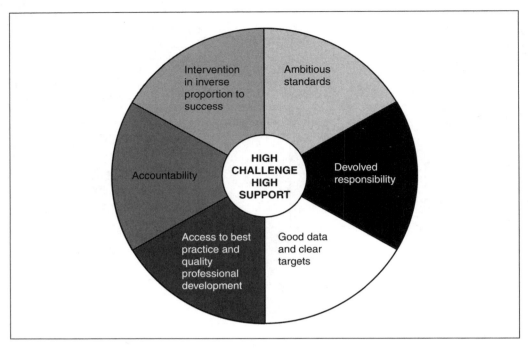

**Figure 17.4.1** A framework for continuous development

Over the last decade the education service has put in place an approach to system-wide improvement. This framework for continuous improvement can be illustrated as shown in Figure 17.4.1).

This framework is designed to make continuous improvement for all schools in all circumstances a reality.

- The National Curriculum sets the standards.

- More funding is devolved to schools than in any other country, with additional funding, through programmes like Excellence in cities, being targeted to those facing the greatest challenge.

- All schools set targets and measure their performance on the basis of excellent comparative data.

- They can easily access best practice information, for example through the Standards site and the National Grid for Learning.

- They have increasing opportunities for professional development of staff.

- They have increased resources and many more support staff in classrooms.

- They are held to account through inspection and the published performance tables.

- Intervention is in inverse proportion to success. Schools that are underperforming are the subject of an intervention tailored to their specific circumstances; a successful school may be subject to shorter inspections and has opportunities to lead the service, for example through becoming a beacon school.

All the evidence suggests that this framework is bringing higher standards and will continue to do so. The remarkable progress at primary level, the incremental progress at secondary level and the steady reduction in the extent of failure in the system are all testimony to its effect, as is the evidence from places such as Texas, Kentucky, North Carolina and Singapore which apply similar approaches.

This context is important because the inspection process is a vital part of an overall strategic approach. Any discussion of inspection in isolation would miss the point.

It is also important to emphasize the powerful benefits to education of a vigorous inspection system. It is not just that it has contributed to improved focus on school improvement than in the past, important though these gains are. There are other strengths that are sometimes forgotten:

- Some American accountability systems tend to be driven by data from test scores. Although these are important, they do not provide insight into the quality of teaching or leadership that bring about improved test scores. In other words, external inspection enables a deeper understanding of success and the evidence for refined intervention where there is underperformance.

- Accountability systems which depend solely on test outcomes inevitably emphasize academic or vocational outcomes to the exclusion of all others. While, of course, academic and vocational success is a key goal for publicly provided education, no one believes it is the only outcome. Enabling young people to become well-rounded, self-reliant, creative and capable of working with others is also important. An inspection system can bring these wider goals within the scope of the accountability system, ensuring they are given a priority they would not otherwise receive and gathering evidence of the factors that enable schools to achieve these goals.

- An inspection system provides an effective means of gathering feedback on major government strategies as they are implemented. The series of reports OFSTED has produced on literacy and numeracy, for example, have made a major contribution to the success of the programmes. I hasten to add that OFSTED reports are not an alternative to academic evaluation. We need both.

In all these ways, quite apart from the clear public accountability case and the value to parents of the reports, the OFSTED system has made a major contribution to progress. Moreover, as we refine our accountability systems, each of these justifications needs to be borne in mind.

Taken together, they make an overwhelming case for maintaining an independent external inspection system. Establishing that, however, is not to say that the current model of inspection is necessarily right for all time. In a rapidly changing world the inspection process, like everything else, needs to seek continuous improvement.

There have been some major refinements in the OFSTED process in the last few years: varying the length of the cycle, depending on the previous inspection report and schools' results; the growing involvement of teachers and heads in inspection teams; OFSTED's growing emphasis on and training for school self-evaluation; and, most radically, the introduction of the new 'short' or 'light-touch' inspections for successful schools.

These and other changes have generally been welcomed and had beneficial outcomes. Meanwhile, a number of profound changes have occurred in the education service as a whole since OFSTED inspections began. Further radical shifts can be anticipated. Combined, these developments are altering the context for inspection and suggest, therefore, ways in which it might evolve:

- The National Curriculum and its assessment have become firmly embedded. The standards set by the curriculum, the content in the programmes of study and the national tests have become central to policy and practice at every level.

- The data provided by national testing increasingly drives the system. Whether they draw on the Autumn Package, data provided by the LEA or analysis from programmes such as ALIS and YELLIS, teachers are firmly focused on data about pupil performance. This has been one of the most dramatic changes in the last decade.

- Target-setting, based on the analyses of data, has also become embedded. In the Learning from Success consultation conferences, target-setting was shown to be one of the most popular policy developments in recent years. Ask teachers why and they talk about the focus it places on each pupil and what he or she needs to learn next. Indeed, target-setting has become crucial to the achievement of continuous improvement and an important factor in ensuring that education is tailored to the talents and aspirations of each individual.

- The new data system being developed nationally, the Common Basic Data ASet, will ensure further improvements in the data. Once this is in place (from 2002) it will allow pupil mobility to be taken into account in the national data and enable system-wide value-added analysis based on prior attainment.

- There are many more means than ever before of identifying and disseminating best practice. Reformed LEAs, beacon schools, teacher research networks, the National college for School Leadership and the new research centres are among them. The Standards website, for example, received over 70 million hits in the calendar year 2000 and the hit rate is still rising.

- Moreover, the growing investment in professional development related to national, school and individual priorities makes it possible for teachers to learn the skills necessary to adopt successful practice.

- The introduction of performance management this year will enable every teacher to secure the opportunities necessary to improve their practice and give their school greater capacity to meet its objectives.

The combination of these factors greatly enhances the potential of rigorous school self-evaluation. Even the more promising school self-evaluation approaches before the mid-1990s had serious flaws. Too often, they lacked the access to comparative data which makes hard-edged analysis possible. Moreover, those at school level undertaking them were too often unaware of developments in practice elsewhere that, had they known about them, might have led them to question their practice more readily. These weaknesses can now be remedied. As a result, in may schools self-evaluation which links targets, practice, performance management and professional development is driving improvement.

At the same time, as more powerful self-evaluation is becoming possible, so is much closer collaboration between schools in the search for progress. Whether it is through Excellence in Cities, Education Action Zones, Beacon networks, modernized LEAs, new partnerships or collaboratives such as the Bedfordshire Upper School Improvement Partnership, collaboration is now the name of the game.

Increasingly what this means is that, while each school is seeking to achieve their core goals to a high standard, it is also making a wider contribution to the system as a while. In short, an entirely different culture is emerging. As the culture changes, the key to success will be trust in the informed professional judgement of teachers. This concept is crucial to the resolution of two long-standing debates in the education service.

In the early 1990s, the introduction of the National Curriculum prompted a debate about national prescription and professional judgement. The problem for the teaching profession in defending professional judgement was the lack of hard evidence about its impact and the lack of any capacity in the system to ensure that when teachers reached judgements they did so on the basis of the data and recent professional development in relevant best practice.

The concept of 'informed professional judgement' offers a way through. The increased availability of research and data as well as access to best practice and professional development is strengthening teachers' capacity to act as effective professionals. It empowers them.

The second debate has been about the relationship between self-evaluation and inspection, what Americans call internal and external accountability. As so often in the heated debates in education, the answer is not one or the other but both. Trust and accountability are co-evolutionary.

The way forward for inspection needs to be examined in this context. No doubt both the new chief inspector and the government will want to continue the evolutionary development of inspection in the months ahead. A number of questions will be worth considering as part of that process. They include the following:

1. Self-evaluation is already successfully playing a highly significant part in light-touch inspections. What are the lessons of this for the inspection system as a whole?
2. The new collaborative monitoring programme for the 560 secondary schools in challenging circumstances, involving OFSTED and the Standards and effectiveness Unit is, following extensive consultation with the schools involved, proving both successful and supportive. What are its implications for the relationship between inspection and follow-through, school by school?
3. Are there ways that OFSTED can further reduce the bureaucratic burdens that schools feel inspection brings?
4. Can OFSTED build on the work it has already begun to give schools the option of determining in part the focus of an inspection, so that it can help head teachers and governors to address their own priorities?
5. How can OFSTED give greater attention to the importance of ethos in a school?
6. Standards in many kinds of service, education included, are increasingly benchmarked across international boundaries in the modern world. What, if anything, does this imply for an inspection system?

Each of these qualities is worth debating as the education service considers how it can continue its impressive progress.

## READING 17.5

# School inspection in England: a reappraisal

## Colin Richards

Colin Richards, a former senior HMI, has been one of the most trenchant critics of the school inspection system in England, particularly during the period in which it was led by HMCI Chris Woodhead. This reading is a summary of his reappraisal of OFSTED, in which he argues that it simply claims far more than it can deliver in terms of insight, accuracy and fairness. We should note that, when he wrote in 2001, evidence was available to underpin most of his claims. However, OFSTED procedures are often reviewed. Do you feel that the problems identified by Richards can be, or have been, overcome? Or should the whole system be reconceptualized?

Edited from: Richards, C. (2001) *School Inspection in England: A Re-appraisal*, Impact No. 9, Philosophy of Education Society of Great Britain, 1–4

The Office for Standards in Education (OFSTED) was created almost ten years ago as an instrument of accountability through the 1992 Education Act. The second and more controversial of its chief inspectors resigned late in 2000. The time is propitious for a reappraisal of the OFSTED system of inspection.

Summed up briefly, my argument is that the OFSTED inspection system promises more than it can deliver. It claims more than it can justifiably claim. Its judgements are inevitably more partial and subjective than it acknowledges.

## Inspections and aims

OFSTED employs inspectors to *inspect* schools but what is the nature of inspection? OFSTED never satisfactorily addresses the basic issue. I argue that inspection involves more than observing, gathering evidence and reporting it orally or in writing. Inspectors are not simply a human form of camera, neutrally capturing what goes on in schools. They have to make judgements, not measurements; they have to interpret, not just record; they have to make judgements about whether what they are observing or scrutinizing is worthwhile; they can only make those judgements against a background of aims and values. But what are those aims and values? OFSTED is silent on such issues. Its inspectors should not make such overall judgements about 'effectiveness' or 'quality' in the absence of explicit aims and values. When and because they do so, OFSTED promises more than it can deliver.

## Inspection language

Quite rightly, OFSTED expects its inspectors to report using 'everyday language,' but people use and understand words in different ways. This means that OFSTED reports are never, and can never be, absolutely clear, precise or unambiguous; they are inevitably going to be interpreted in different ways by different people. The judgements they report in 'everyday language' are, at best, inspectors' professional judgements, inevitably value laden and inevitably subjective to a degree. Readers of inspection reports (and OFSTED itself!) need to be aware of the danger of treating inspection judgements as more definitive or precise than they can possibly be.

## Inspection of standards

Strictly speaking, 'standards' are benchmarks or norms against which the quality of a particular activity or process is evaluated. Strictly speaking, OFSTED does not report on such 'standards' but on schools' or pupils' performance in relation to them. The standards of pupils' attainment reported by OFSTED are embodied in National Curriculum level descriptions or in GCSE and A/AS grade descriptors. These are contentious: not everyone agrees on their worth or appropriateness. Also, since they are expressed in everyday language, they can be, and will be, interpreted somewhat differently by inspectors and the teachers being inspected in a particular school. This does not mean that inspectors cannot or should not make judgements in relation to level or grade descriptions but it does mean that they should do so only in a rough-and-ready, tentative way and that their judgements may quite properly be challenged by teachers whose work is being inspected.

When reporting standards, OFSTED gives priority to the reporting of performance data, particularly in the core subjects in Key Stages 1–3. OFSTED's uncritical use of performance data fails to acknowledge that there are fundamental disagreements over their reliability, their validity and the uses to which they are put. Tellingly, OFSTED places far more emphasis on performance data as so-called 'measures' of standards than it does on the judgements of its own registered and team inspectors.

Again, in reporting on standards of attainment OFSTED promises more than it can deliver. Its reporting is partial, potentially flawed and far from incontrovertible or uncontentious.

## Inspection of teaching and learning

OFSTED makes much of its claim to be able to evaluate 'the quality of teaching, judged in terms of its impact on pupils' learning and what makes it successful or not'. In reality there are considerable limitations on its inspectors' ability to make such judgements.

In relation to learning, inspectors are limited largely to commenting on pupils' *observable* responses. They can comment, for example, on whether pupils appear interested, whether they seem to be concentrating on their work, whether they actively contribute to a lesson, and so on. I argue that, except in a minority of cases, inspectors cannot assess the extent of children's learning in lessons.

Inspectors' ability to judge the 'impact' of teaching on learning is equally limited. Expect in certain cases, inspectors cannot evaluate the effectiveness of teaching in bringing about learning in the lessons they observe. Inspectors can, however, comment legitimately and valuably on the way lessons are conducted. What inspectors appear to be doing increasingly is judging how far the lessons they see conform to 'accepted' models of 'good' teaching promulgated by central government. But 'good' in this sense does not necessarily mean 'good' in the sense of 'enhancing children's learning'.

As before, OFSTED claims too much when it makes a strong, unequivocal statement about the quality of teaching and learning in schools nationally or in particular schools.

## Inspection of progress and improvement

I also argue that OFSTED inspectors are not in a position to evaluate and report on pupils' progress either in particular lessons, or over longer periods of time, and therefore cannot comment on schools' contributions to that progress. Likewise, they cannot evaluate the extent of a school's improvement from one inspection to the next. The necessary evidence and other conditions to make valid comparisons and judgements of improvement are simply not available. Again, OFSTED promises too much and schools may be judged unfairly as a result.

## Possibilities

Assuming at least some of the arguments are sound, where does that leave OFSTED inspection? Should the OFSTED inspection process be modified, be radically overhauled or be dispensed with altogether? Certainly the limitations I have outlined imply that the OFSTED process is in need of urgent review.

I can go on to suggest several uses for school inspection which take account of the criticisms I have raised. I believe these to be valuable in informing educational policy and practice, but they are much more limited than the claims OFSTED itself makes for inspection.

## CHAPTER 18

# Reflective teaching and society

The five readings in this chapter all address the issue of how education relates to society.

Archer begins (Reading 18.1) with an analysis of how education systems develop and change over time in response to an evolving interplay of pressures and constraints.

But what should an education system be designed to achieve? Freire (18.2) devoted his life to a radical view of education as a form of emancipation, and the reading here illustrates this. He challenges top-down, transmission models of teaching and learning and argues that they act as a form of 'oppression'. Rather, education should build on the consciousness and activity of the learner so that they can 'more wisely build the future'. In that context, it is interesting to read the Council of Europe's Memorandum on teaching and learning about human rights in schools (Reading 18.3).

The two final readings concern the ways in which education policy is formed. Bowe, Ball and Gold (18.4) begin with an analysis of the contexts of macro-political influence, text construction by government agencies and actual practice in LEAs, schools and classroom. They show how policy-making is open to shaping and challenge at each stage. Indeed, our final reading, by Pollard and his colleagues (18.5), characterizes recent history in primary education in terms of struggles over values, understanding and power.

What influence can individuals, such as teachers, have over social structures, such as the education system? And what influence should they have?

The parallel chapter of *Reflective Teaching* begins with a review of the aims of education in relation to social development. It identifies and discusses wealth creation, cultural reproduction and social justice as particular goals. In a section on 'classroom teaching and society' it highlights the value issues which reflective teachers face when they recognize the ways in which their actions contribute to the future identities and life chances of pupils. Reflective teaching is then related to the democratic process and to the importance of teachers contributing their professional voice to policy debates and public decision making on educational topics. Of course, there is a list of suggested 'Key Readings', and more support is available from *RTweb*.

📖 READING 18.1

# Thinking about educational systems

Margaret Archer

This reading comes from the introduction to Margaret Archer's impressive analysis of the ways in which educational systems form, develop and change through time. She argues that such systems reflect the priorities and conceptions of those who have power. However, such power is likely to be contested and, in any event, those in a position to make policy must also relate their ambitions to the constraints of practical realities.

To what extent can you relate Archer's model, as expressed here, to the recent history of changing educational policy?

Edited from: Archer, M. (1979) *The Social Origins of Educational Systems*. London: SAGE Publications, 1–3

How do educational systems develop and how do they change?

This first question about the characteristics of education can be broken down into three subsidiary ones: 'Who gets it?'; 'What happens to them during it?' and 'Where do they go to after it?'. These enquiries about inputs, processes and outputs subsume a whole range of issues, many of which have often been discussed independently. They embrace problems about educational opportunity, selection and discrimination, about the management and transmission of knowledge and values and about social placement, stratification and mobility. At the same time they raise the two most general problems of all, namely those about the effects of society upon education and about the consequences of education for society.

The fundamental question here is, 'Why does education have the particular inputs, processes and outputs which characterize it at any given time?'. The basic answer is held to be very simple. Education has the characteristics it does because of the goals pursued by those who control it. A second question asks, 'Why do these particular inputs, processes and outputs change over time?'. The basic answer given here is equally simple. Change occurs because new educational goals are pursued by those who have the power to modify previous practices. As we shall see, these answers are of a deceptive simplicity. They are insisted upon now, at the beginning because, however complex our final formulations turn out to be, education is fundamentally about what people have wanted of it and have been able to do to it.

The real answers are more complicated but they supplement rather than contradict the above. It is important never to lose sight of the fact that the complex theories we develop to account for education and educational change are theories about the educational activities of people. This very basic point is underlined for two reasons. First, because however fundamental, much of the literature in fact contradicts it and embodies implicit beliefs in hidden hands, evolutionary mechanisms and spontaneous adjustments to social change. There education is still seen as mysteriously adapting to social requirements and responding to demands of society not of people. Second, and for the present purposes much more importantly, our theories will be about the educational activities of people even though they will not explain educational development strictly in terms of people alone.

The basic answers are too simple because they beg more questions than they solve. To say that education derives its characteristic features from the aims of those who control it immediately raises problems concerning the identification of controlling groups, the bases and processes upon which control rests, the methods and channels through which it is exerted, the extensiveness of control, the reactions of others to this control, and their educational consequences. Similarly, where change is concerned, it is not explained until an account has been given of why educational goals change, who does the changing, and how they impose the changes they seek. To confront these problems is to recognise that their solution depends upon analysing complex forms of social interaction. Furthermore, the nature of education is rarely, if ever, the practical realization of an ideal form of instruction as envisaged by a particular group. Instead, most of the time most of the forms that education takes are the political products of power struggles. They bear the marks of concession to allies and compromise with opponents. Thus to understand the nature of education at any time we need to know not only who won the struggle for control, but also how: not merely who lost, but also how badly they lost.

Second, the basic answers are deceptively simple because they convey the impression that education and educational change can be explained by reference to group goals and balances of power alone. It is a false impression because there are other factors which constrain both the goal formation and goal attainment of even the most powerful group – that is, the group most free to impose its definition of instruction and to mould education to its purposes. The point is that no group, not even for that matter the whole of society acting in accord, has a blank sheet of paper on which to design national education. Conceptions of education are of necessity limited by the existing availability of skills and resources. Another way of stating this is to say that cultural and structural factors constrain educational planning and its execution. Since this is the case, then explanations of education and educational change will be partly in terms of such factors.

Moreover, only the minimal logical constraints have been mentioned so far, in practice, educational action is also affected by a variable set of cultural and structural factors that make up its environment. Educational systems, rarities before the eighteenth century, emerged within complex social structures and cultures and this context conditioned the conception and conduct of action of those seeking educational development. Among other things, the social distribution of resources and values and the patterning of vested interests in the existing form of education were crucially important factors. Once a given form of education exists it exerts an influence on future educational change. Alternative educational plans are, to some extent, reactions to it (they represent desires to change inputs, transform processes, or alter the end products); attempts to change it are affected by it (by the degree to which it monopolizes educational skills and resources); and change is change of it (which means dismantling, transforming, or in some way grappling with it).

READING 18.2

# Challenging the 'banking' concept of education

Paulo Freire

Freire was committed to emancipatory education for the poor of Brazil. His ideas, whilst radical, are now internationally respected for the way in which they explicitly recognize the relationships between education, knowledge and power. In this excerpt from his classic book (first published in 1970), he argues that a traditional, transmission pedagogy can be a form of oppression in which alien knowledge has to be 'banked'. A more 'emancipatory' education would build on the knowledge resources and agency of learners, and of their communities.

Reading beyond the polemical style, what challenges does this reading offer for education systems within the UK?

Edited from: Friere, P. (1999) *Pedagogy of the Oppressed*. New York: Continuum, 52–5, 60, 64–5

A careful analysis of the teacher–student relationship at any level, inside or outside the school, reveals a narrating subject (the teacher) and patient, listening objects (the students).

The teacher talks about reality as if it were motionless, static, compartmentalized and predictable. Or else he expounds on a topic completely alien to the existential experience of the students. His task is to 'fill' the students with the contents of his narration – contents which are detached from reality, disconnected from the totality that engendered them and could give them significance. Words are emptied of their concreteness and become a hollow, alienated and alienating verbosity.

Education thus becomes an act of depositing, in which the students are the depositories and the teacher is the depositor. Instead of communicating, the teacher issues communiqués and makes deposits that the students patiently receive, memorize and repeat. This is the 'banking' concept of education, in which the scope of action allowed to the students extends only as far as receiving, filing and storing the deposits. They do, it is true, have the opportunity to become collectors or cataloguers of the things they store. But in the last analysis, it is the people themselves who are filed away through the lack of creativity, transformation and knowledge in this (at best) misguided system. For apart from inquiry, apart from the praxis, individuals cannot be truly human. Knowledge emerges only through invention and re-invention, through the restless, impatient, continuing, hopeful inquiry human beings pursue in the world, with the world and with each other.

In the banking concept of education, knowledge is a gift bestowed by those who consider themselves knowledgeable upon those whom they consider to know nothing. Projecting an absolute ignorance onto others, a characteristic of the ideology of oppression, negates education and knowledge as processes of inquiry. The teacher presents himself to his students as their necessary opposite; by considering their ignorance absolute, he justifies his own existence. The students, alienated like the slaves, accept their ignorance as justifying the teacher's existence – but, unlike the slave, they never discover that they educate the teacher.

The *raison d'être* of libertarian education, on the other hand, lies in its drive towards reconciliation. Education must begin with the solution of the teacher–student contradiction, by reconciling the poles of the contradiction so that both are simultaneously teachers and students.

The capability of banking education to minimize or annul the students' creative power and to stimulate their credulity serves the interests of the oppressors, who care neither to have the world revealed nor to see it transformed. The oppressors use their 'humanitarianism' to preserve a profitable situation. Thus they react almost instinctively against any experiment in education which stimulates the critical faculties and is not content with a partial view of reality but always seeks out the ties which link one point to another and one problem to another. Indeed, the interests of the oppressors lie in 'changing the consciousness of the oppressed, not the situation which oppresses them', for the more the oppressed can be led to adapt to that situation, the more easily they can be dominated.

Those truly committed to liberation must reject the banking concept in its entirety, adopting instead a concept of women and men as conscious beings, and consciousness as consciousness intent upon the world. They must abandon the educational goal of deposit-making and replace it with the posing of the problems of human beings in their relations with the world. 'Problem-posing' education, responding to the essence of consciousness – intentionality – rejects communiqués and embodies communication. It epitomizes the special characteristic of consciousness: being conscious of, not only as intent on objects but as turned in upon itself in a Jasperian split – 'consciousness as consciousness' of consciousness. Liberating education consists in acts of cognition, not transferrals of information.

In problem-posing education, people develop their power to perceive critically the way they exist in the world with which and in which they find themselves. They come to see the world not as a static reality, but as a reality in process, in transformation. Although the dialectical relations of women and men with the world exist independently of how these relations are perceived, it is also true that the form of action they adopt is, to a large extent, a function of how they perceive themselves in the world. Hence, the teacher–student and the students–teachers reflect simultaneously on themselves and the world without dichotomizing this reflection from action, and thus establish an authentic form of thought and action.

Once again, the two-educational concepts and practices under analysis come into conflict. Banking education attempts, by mythicizing reality, to conceal certain facts which explain the way human beings exist in the world; problem-posing education sets itself the task of demythologizing. Banking education resists dialogue; problem-posing education regards dialogue as indispensable to the act of cognition which unveils reality. Banking education treats students as objects of assistance; problem-posing education makes them critical thinkers. Banking education inhibits creativity and domesticates (although it cannot completely destroy) the intentionality of consciousness by isolating consciousness from the world, thereby denying people their ontological and historical vocation of becoming more fully human. Problem-posing education bases itself on creativity and stimulates true reflection and action upon reality, thereby responding to the vocation of persons as beings who are authentic only when engaged in inquiry and creative transformation. In sum: banking theory and practice, as immobilizing and fixating forces, fail to acknowledge men and women as historical beings; problem-posing theory and practice take the people's historicity as their starting point.

Problem-posing education affirms men and women as beings in the process of becoming – as unfinished, uncompleted beings in and with a likewise unfinished reality. Indeed, in contrast to other animals who are unfinished, but not historical, people know themselves to be unfinished; they are aware of their incompletion. In this incompletion and this awareness lie the very roots of education as an exclusively human manifestation. The unfinished character of human beings and the tranformational character of reality necessitate that education be an ongoing activity.

Problem-posing education is revolutionary futurity. Hence it is prophetic (and, as such, hopeful). Hence, it corresponds to the historical nature of humankind. It affirms women and men as beings who transcend themselves, who move forward and look ahead, for whom immobility represents a fatal threat, for whom looking at the past must only be a means of understanding more clearly what and who they are so that they can more wisely build the future.

# Memorandum on teaching and learning about human rights in schools

## Council of Europe

The beginning of this reading reflects its legal origins as a Statute of the Council of Europe, but it goes on to list six areas of practical action in schools which are intended to develop childrens awareness of human rights. This reading clearly represents the long-standing concern that education should promote social justice and, given the complexity and diversity of the societies across Europe, it is not surprising that this should be an important issue for the European Union.

How high a priority do you place on teaching and learning about human rights and the development of social justice?

Edited from: Committee of Ministers of the Council of Europe (1985) *Appendix to Recommendation No. R (85) 7, Memorandum on teaching and learning about human rights in schools*, Strasbourg: Directorate of Human Rights, Council of Europe

The Committee of Ministers, under the terms of Article 15.b of the Statute of the Council of Europe:

considering that the aim of the Council of Europe is to achieve a greater unity between its members for the purpose of safeguarding and realizing the ideals and principles which are their common heritage;

reaffirming the human rights undertakings embodied in the United Nations Universal Declaration of Human Rights, the Convention for the Protection of Human Rights and Fundamental Freedoms and the European Social Charter;

having regard to the commitments to human rights education made by member states at international and European conferences in the last decade;

recommends that the governments of member states, having regard to their national education systems and to the legislative basis for them:

encourage teaching and learning about human rights in schools in line with the suggestions contained in the appendix hereto;

draw the attention of persons and bodies concerned with school education to the text of this recommendation.

## Human rights in the school curriculum

The understanding and experience of human rights is an important element of the preparation of all young people for life in a democratic and pluralistic society. It is part of social and political education, and it involves intercultural and international understanding.

Concepts associated with human rights can, and should, be acquired from an early stage. For example, the non-violent resolution of a conflict and respect for other people can already be experienced within the life of a pre-school or primary class.

Opportunities to introduce young people to more abstract notions of human rights, such as those involving an understanding of philosophical, political and legal concepts, will occur in the secondary school, in particular in such subjects as history, geography, social studies, moral and religious education, language and literature, current affairs and economics.

Human rights inevitably involve the domain of politics. Teaching about human rights should, therefore, always have international agreements and covenants as a point of reference, and teachers should take care to avoid imposing their personal convictions on their pupils and involving them in ideological struggles.

## Skills

The skills associated with understanding and supporting human rights include:

intellectual skills, in particular:

skills associated with written and oral expression, including the ability to listen and discuss, and to defend one's opinions;

skills involving judgement, such as: the collection and examination of material from various sources, including the mass media, and the ability to analyse it and to arrive at fair and balanced conclusions: the identification of bias, prejudice, stereotypes and discrimination;

social skills, in particular:

recognizing and accepting differences; establishing positive and non-oppressive personal relationships: resolving conflict in a non-violent way; taking responsibility; participating in decisions; understanding the use of the mechanisms for the protection of human rights at local, regional, European and world levels.

## Knowledge to be acquired in the study of human rights

The study of human rights in schools will be approached in different ways according to age and circumstances of the pupil and the particular situations of schools and according to age and circumstances of the pupil and the particular situations of schools and education systems. Topics to be covered in learning about human rights could include:

the main categories of human rights, duties, obligations and responsibilities;

the various forms of injustice, inequality and discrimination, including sexism and racism;

people, movements and key events, both successes and failures, in the historical and continuing struggle for human rights;

the main international declarations and conventions on human rights such as the Universal Declaration of Human Rights and the Convention for the Protection of Human

Rights and Fundamental Freedoms.

The emphasis in teaching and learning about human rights should be positive. Pupils may be led to feelings of powerlessness and discouragement when confronted with many examples of violation and negations of human rights. Instances of progress and success should be used.

The study of human rights in schools should lead to an understanding of, and sympathy for, the concepts of justice, equality, freedom, peace, dignity, rights and democracy. Such understanding should be both cognitive and based on experience and feelings. Schools should, thus, provide opportunities for pupils to experience affective involvement in human rights and to express their feelings through drama, art, music, creative writing and audio-visual media.

# The climate of the school

Democracy is best learned in a democratic setting where participation is encouraged, where views can be expressed openly and discussed, where there is freedom of expression for pupils and teachers, and where there is fairness and justice. An appropriate climate is, therefore, an essential complement to effective learning about human rights.

Schools should encourage participation in their activities by parents and other members of the community. It may well be appropriate for schools to work with non-governmental organizations which can provide information, case studies and first-hand experience of successful campaigns for human rights and dignity.

Schools and teachers should attempt to be positive towards all their pupils, and recognize that all their achievements are important – whether they be academic, artistic, musical, sporting or practical.

# The training of teachers

The initial training of teachers should prepare them for their future contribution to teaching about human rights in their schools. For example, future teachers should:

be encouraged to take an interest in national and world affairs;

have the chance of studying or working in a foreign country or a different environment;

be taught to identify and combat all forms of discrimination in schools and society and be encouraged to confront and overcome their own prejudices.

Future and practising teachers should be encouraged to familiarize themselves with:

the main international declarations and conventions on human rights;

the working and achievements of the international organizations which deal with the protection and promotion of human rights, for example through visits and study tours.

All teachers need, and should be given the opportunity, to update their knowledge and to learn new methods through in-service training. This could include the study of good practice in teaching about human rights, as well as the development of appropriate methods and materials.

# International Human Rights Day

Schools and teacher training establishments should be encouraged to observe International Human Rights Day (10 December).

## READING 18.4

# Three contexts of policy making

Richard Bowe and Stephen Ball, with Ann Gold

The authors of this reading provide a framework for thinking about the policy-making process. They describe policy as a 'discourse' and as 'a set of claims about how the world should be and might be' and see it as contested by different social groups. Three contexts in which this takes place are identified, including the context of practice in which practitioners mediate, interpret and recreate the meaning of policy texts.

How does the analysis relate to the latest national policy to affect schools?

Edited from: Bowe, R. and Ball, S., with Gold. A. (1992) *Reforming Education and Changing Schools*. London: Routledge, 13–23

We approach policy as a discourse, constituted of possibilities and impossibilities, tied to knowledge on the one hand (the analysis of problems and identification of remedies and goals) and practice on the other (specification of methods for achieving goals and implementation). We see it as a set of claims about how the world should and might be, a matter of the 'authoritative allocation of values'. Policies are thus the operational statements of values, statements of 'prescriptive intent'. They are also, as we conceive it, essentially contested in and between the arenas of formation and 'implementation'.

We envisage three primary policy contexts, each context consisting of a number of arenas of action, some public, some private. These are: the context of influence, the context of text production and the context of practice (see Figure 18.4.1).

The first context, the context of influence, is where public policy is normally initiated. It is here that policy discourses are constructed. It is here that interested parties struggle to influence the definition and social purposes of education, what it means to be educated. The private arenas of influence are based upon social networks in and around the political parties, in and around government and the legislative process. Here, key policy concepts are established (e.g. market forces, National Curriculum, opting out, budgetary devolution); they acquire currency and credence and provide a discourse and lexicon for policy initiation. This kind of discourse forming is sometimes given support, sometimes challenged by wider

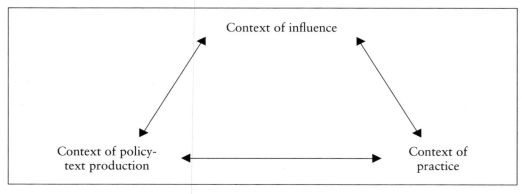

Figure 18.4.1   Three contexts of policy making

claims to influence in the public arenas of action, particularly in and through the mass media. In addition there are a set of more formal public arenas, committees, national bodies, representative groups, that can be sites for the articulation of influence. Clearly, in trying to understand the education policy-making of the last three conservative governments it is important to be aware of the considerable 'capture' of influence by the new-right think tanks that operated in and around the Conservative Party. But it is also vital to appreciate the ebb and flow in the fortunes of and the changes in personnel of the DES, and to recognize the increasing 'ministerialization' of policy initiation. As we noted earlier, this contrasts starkly with the virtual exclusion of union and local authority representatives from arenas of influence and the much diminished and discredited contribution from the educational establishment.

This context of influence has a symbiotic but none the less uneasy relation to the second context, the context of policy-text production. Because, while influence is often related to the articulation of narrow interests and dogmatic ideologies, policy texts are normally articulated in the language of general public good. Their appeal is based upon claims to popular (and populist) common sense and political reason. Policy texts therefore represent policy. These representations can take various forms: most obviously 'official' legal texts and policy documents; also formally and informally produced commentaries which offer to 'make sense of' the 'official' texts, again the media is important here; also the speeches by and public performances of relevant politicians and officials; and 'official' videos are another recently popular medium of representation. Many of those towards whom policy is aimed rely on these second-hand accounts as their main source of information and understanding of policy as intended. But two key points have to be made about these ensembles of texts which represent policy. First, the ensembles and the individual texts are not necessarily internally coherent or clear. The expression of policy is fraught with the possibility of misunderstanding, texts are generalized, written in relation to idealizations of the 'real world', and can never be exhaustive, they cannot cover all eventualities. The texts can often be contradictory, they use key terms differently, and they are reactive as well as expository (that is to say, the representation of policy changes in the light of events and circumstances and feedback from arenas of practice). Policy is not done and finished at the legislative moment, it evolves in and through the texts that represent it, texts have to be read in relation to the time and the particular site of their production. They also have to be read with and against one another – intertextuality is important. Second, the texts themselves are the outcome of struggle and compromise. The control of the representation of policy is problematic. Control over the timing of the publication of texts is important. A potent and immediate example of struggle in arenas of text production is that which goes on in relation to National Curriculum working party reports. Groups of actors working within different sites of text production are in competition for control of the representation of policy. Most of these struggles go on behind closed doors but occasional glimpses of the dynamics of conflict are possible. What is at stake are attempts to control the meaning of policy through its representation.

Policies then are textual interventions but they also carry with them material constraints and possibilities. The responses to these texts have 'real' consequences. These consequences are experienced within the third main context, the context of practice, the arena of practice to which policy refers, to which it is addressed.

The key point is that policy is not simply received and implemented within this arena, rather it is subject to interpretation and then 'recreated'.

Practitioners do not confront policy texts as naive readers, they come with histories, with experience, with values and purposes of their own, they have vested interests in the meaning of policy. Policies will be interpreted differently as the histories, experiences, values, purposes and interests which make up any arena differ. The simple point is that policy writers cannot control the meanings of their texts. Parts of texts will be rejected, selected out, ignored, deliberately misunderstood, responses may be frivolous, etc. Furthermore, yet again, interpretation is a matter of struggle. Different interpretations will be in contest, as they relate to different interests, one or other interpretation will predominate although deviant or minority readings may be important.

The policy process is one of complexity, it is one of policy-making and remaking. It is often difficult, if not impossible to control or predict the effects of policy, or indeed to be clear about what those effects are, what they mean, when they happen. Clearly, however interpretations are not infinite, clearly also, as noted already, different material consequences derive from different interpretations in action. Practitioners will be influenced by the discursive context within which policies emerge. Some will have an eye to personal or localized advantage, material or otherwise, which may stem from particular readings of policy texts. But to reiterate, the meanings of texts are rarely unequivocal. Novel or creative readings can sometimes bring their own rewards.

## READING 18.5

# Values, understanding and power

## Andrew Pollard, Patricia Broadfoot, Paul Croll, Marilyn Osborn and Dorothy Abbott

This final reading is drawn from the conclusion of the first book from the PACE project, which researched the impact of the Education Reform Act 1988 on primary education in the 1990s. Changes and continuities were each documented, and this was interpreted in terms of a struggle between teachers and government based on differences in values, educational understanding and forms of power. Perhaps this was a particularly rapid and challenging period of change, but the basic issue of the relationship between the commitments of the teaching profession and the policies of government remains vital to constructive educational development.

To what extent do you now feel able to contribute, as a respected partner and with a shared commitment, to government strategies for the improvement of the quality of education?

Edited from: Pollard, A., Broadfoot, P., Croll, P., Osborn, M. and Abbott, D, (1994) *Changing English Primary Schools? The Impact of the Education Reform Act at Key Stage One.* London: Cassell, 231–40

Three analytic themes emerged as central to our attempt at interpretation, and we identified these themes as values, understanding and power.

## Values

Values lie at the heart of all educational decisions. At their most general, these concern the broad commitments which inform educational and social aims and the moral foundations of educational provision.

Such values are fundamental to decisions about curriculum, teaching approaches and the sorts of outcomes which are intended from educational processes. Messages about educational values are either given explicitly in statements of educational aims or are implied by decisions about curriculum, assessment and pedagogy. The feelings and perspectives of teachers and children about their experiences in schools also reflect value positions. Teachers' conceptions about what it is to be a teacher and about the nature of the teaching profession are the cornerstones of their professional ideologies and are inevitably heavily value laden. Children's responses to classroom situations may also be considered in value terms as they begin to absorb the beliefs and commitments of their families, culture and society. Value considerations may thus be used to describe the changing orientations of participants to educational situations and to explain their feelings and perspectives.

We sketched out the historical background to the debate about the nature of English primary schooling, and the way in which changing social, economic and political movements, trends and struggles have impacted on issues concerning the nature and content of that provision. We described the long-established traditions of elementary schooling in this country which are rooted in the mass state educational provision of the nineteenth century – and fed by concerns over social order and the perceived need for international competitiveness. This tradition emphasizes the inculcation of basic skills and a moral order through tight central control of curriculum and assessment arrangements, and hence, of teachers and schools. By contrast, the equally long-standing 'developmental' tradition is rooted in the work of major educational philosophers such as Rousseau and Dewey and of influential practitioners such as Maria Montessori and Charlotte Mason. It emphasizes the importance of responding to the needs and interests of the individual child and helping them to 'develop' to their full potential. As we also saw, these differences in values have resonances with the analysis of 'education codes' which has been so powerfully advanced by Bernstein (1975, 1987).

Into this long-running debate impacted a new market ideology in education which, as in other parts of state provision, brought with it an emphasis on competition and consumerism. Policies rooted in this philosophy have starkly polarized the values of most teachers against those of government. However, of all the sectors of the education profession, it is arguably primary teachers who have experienced these tensions the most sharply for they had most thoroughly embraced the implication of the developmental tradition. In addition, the emergent professionalism which had been developing in the 1980s was strongly supportive of collaboration between schools, teachers and pupils as a form of learning and collective development. The contrast in value positions could hardly have been more stark.

Teachers initially supported the National Curriculum because of the entitlement to broad and structured experiences which it offered. In this sense, it embodied egalitarian values. Such values had been reflected in relatively undifferentiated curriculum provision in primary schools. However, the National Curriculum and assessment procedures emphasized the need for curriculum differentiation for different pupils. Government and parental concern for academic standards reinforced this, but teachers were nervous about its effects, particularly if it led towards forms of streaming or setting.

## Understanding

Understanding is a concept which highlights the representation of what is to count as educationally valid knowledge. Linked to this are assumptions about the nature of teaching and of teachers' roles and about various more specific features of practice such as assessment. The key issue in the contrast between an understanding of education as the inculcation of established knowledge versus its definition as a process of helping learners to construct their own insights and understanding.

Knowledge has traditionally been viewed as an established body of fact which, with associated skills and attitudes, can and should be taught. This view was articulated by the right-wing pressure groups which contributed to the Education Reform Act and was reflected in the subject specification and much of the content of the National Curriculum. An alternative, Piagetian perspective placing emphasis on the ways in which learners construct knowledge from experience, was superseded in the emergent professionalism of the 1980s by a new approach. This approach, influenced by Vygotskian psychologists, informed many curriculum development projects. It drew attention to the importance of experience and instruction and to the nature of the social context in which learning takes place and the support which needs to be available from more knowledgeable others. Both these theories of learning and of the curriculum were reflected in National Curriculum documents. Indeed their uneasy coexistence was the basis for a good deal of the controversy that surrounded the generation of the different subject curricula.

The net effect of this was that, whilst teachers had been gradually evolving one view of knowledge and learning through the 1980s, much of the National Curriculum, and certainly its assessment procedures, required them to act in ways which derived from quite different assumptions. Whilst the former emphasized the teacher's professional skills, judgement and understanding in promoting learning, the latter tended to devalue the professional pedagogic skills of the teacher by implying that the 'delivery' of the curriculum was largely unproblematic. This was well illustrated in the government's 1993 proposal that non-graduate teachers should be accepted for work with young pupils.

Differing ways of understanding knowledge and learning also have implications for different perspectives on curriculum organization and teaching method. Over the period of the research reported here, considerable pressure was applied to schools to get them to consider introducing more subject specialist teaching, rather than using forms of integrated topic work. This pressure had a strong effect, though it was regretted by many teachers. Similarly, we documented how classroom pedagogy has been changing as new ways of understanding teaching and new educational priorities are put forward.

Understanding of the purpose and capacity of assessment also relates to views of knowledge and learning. Government attention in the early 1990s focused on standardized testing in the hope of providing attainment information for parents and for published school league tables. This strategy assumed that it was both possible and desirable to treat assessments as providing reliable categoric evidence. Teachers had a rather different view. Thus teachers saw the ways in which teacher assessment could feed, formatively, into teaching–learning processes and many embraced this as part of their professional repertoire. Assessment information was treated as provisional evidence, reflecting the continuous learning process. The gap in understanding between teachers and government on this specific issue was very considerable, but it stood as an indicator of a far wider range of differences in perception. This brings us to the issue of power.

## Power

Issues of power pervade any consideration of the introduction of educational reform in the early 1990s. Like other major changes, the introduction of the National Curriculum not only involved the direct application of power, but also revealed power relationships which in other times had been hidden or so taken for granted that little attention had been paid to them (Lukes, 1974).

The most obvious power struggles involved in the introduction of the National Curriculum were those between central government imposing or requesting changes and the educational service (LEAs, schools, teachers) implementing, mediating or resisting them. The changes introduced in the 1988 legislation were widely interpreted as a shift in the relations of power between central government, local providers of education and the teaching profession. However, as well as demonstrating power over the educational system at governmental and policy-making level, the changes associated with the legislation also had implications for the operation of power within schools. Thus there were changes in the implementation of relationships between governors, heads, teachers and parents. Changes in school practices also affect changes in classroom practices and, as we have seen, the relative power of teachers and pupils to influence classroom events has begun to change as teachers attempt to 'deliver' the National Curriculum.

However, whilst power is typically conceived as a means of control and source of constraint, it may also be manifest in more positive ways. Changes may, in principle, also be empowering – for instance, if they allow people to work together in more effective pursuit of agreed goals. Unfortunately, there have been few signs of this over the period of our study.

Head teachers in particular faced enormous pressures at the internal–external interface of their schools. They become directly accountable to governors for implementing central policies, but they did not always agree with these nor feel that it was possible to deliver them. Having formally had considerable autonomy in their role, they now felt immensely constrained. In response to this, some head teachers used their power in more managerial ways.

We have also described how classroom teachers were often required to act in ways with which they fundamentally disagreed and considered to be educationally unsound. This was particularly true in relation to the perceived overloading of the curriculum, the pressure for change in pupil–teacher relationships and what was regarded as the inappropriateness of summative assessment procedures.

Teacher responses to this broad but consistent trend varied between compliance, mediation and resistance. Initially, many welcomed the National Curriculum and sought to incorporate it into existing practices. Some drew very constructively on the 'practical theorizing' which had underpinned the emergent professionalism of the 1980s. They attempted to maximize positive aspects of change, such as formative assessment, curriculum progression, the use of subject knowledge and whole-school planning. In so doing, they were, in a sense, recreating their source of professional power in 'expertise'. Other teachers simply tried to survive in the context of rapidly imposed and changing requirements. Workloads, stress levels and demoralization became very high and teachers began to consider forms of collective action to assert a countervailing power to that of the government. The most telling example of this was provided in 1993 when resistance over assessment requirements led to reporting procedures being boycotted in many schools.

The pressure on head teachers, teachers and pupils was reflected in changes in classroom practices. In particular, teachers used their power over pupils in that context to tighten classroom organization and to increase direction of pupil tasks.

There can be no doubt that, overall, the trends for head teachers, teachers and pupils in terms of power were all in the direction of increased constraint.

## Conclusion

The picture we are left with from the first phase of the PACE research reveals change and resistance; commitment and demoralization; decreasing autonomy but some developments in professional skills. Is it possible to make any sense out of these apparently contradictory findings?

Certainly a broad consensus in English primary schools has emerged on the structural benefits of having a national curriculum. It is seen as providing for progression and continuity and, with careful design, it is seen as a potential source of coherence. Organizational benefits for teacher training and supply, continuous professional development, curriculum development, parental participation, teacher accountability and national monitoring of educational standards are accepted.

Unfortunately, though, the introduction of the National Curriculum into England was seriously compromised because of the ways in which professionally committed teachers were alienated. The Education Reform Act brought enormous changes for teachers. However, rather than providing a legislative framework through which they could offer and fulfil their professional commitment, the reforms introduced constraint and regulation into almost every area of teachers' work. Yet it seems most unlikely that education standards can rise without the whole-hearted commitment of teachers, working to support pupils' learning.

Having said that, it is also clear that professional commitment has not yet been entirely dissipated. Ironically, collegiality has developed within many schools as a response to the reforms. Unprecedented levels of cooperation are often manifest in schools, between schools and between teacher associations, but these have often been used to defend the quality of the education service against government policies rather than to work in partnership with government towards shared goals.

Our final conclusion then must be one which records, with sadness, the many lost opportunities of this period of change. The amount of legislative time, of financial resources, of public debate and of teacher energy devoted to the innovations was unprecedented. Yet so much was destructive or wasted because of the ideological clash between the government and teachers. Nor are the struggles surrounding the implementation of the Education Reform Act and its supplementary legislation yet over; this is certainly a time in which history is being made.

# BIBLIOGRAPHY

ACAC (Curriculum and Assessment Authority for Wales) (1996) *Desirable Outcomes for Children's Learning Before Compulsary School Age*. Cardiff: ACAC.

Acker, S. (1995) 'Carry on caring: the work of women teachers', *British Journal of Sociology of Education*, **16** (1), 21–36.

Acker, S. (1999) *The Realities of Teachers' Work: Never a Dull Moment*. London: Cassell.

Ainscow, M. (1993) *Towards Effective Schools for All: A Reconsideration of the Special Needs Task*. Tamworth: NASEN.

Alexander, R. (1990) *Teachers and Children in PNP Classrooms*. Primary Needs Independent Evaluation Project Report 11. Leeds: University of Leeds.

Alexander, R. (1991) *Primary Education in Leeds*. Twelfth and final report from the Primary Needs Independent Evaluation Project. Leeds: University of Leeds.

Alexander, R. (1992) *Policy and Practice in Primary Education*. London: Routledge.

Alexander, R. (1995) *Versions of Primary Education*. London: Routledge.

Alexander, R. J. (2000) *Culture and Pedagogy*. London: Blackwell.

Alexander, R., Willcocks, J. and Kinder, K. (1989) *Changing Primary Practice*. London: Falmer Press.

Alexander, R. J., Rose, J. and Woodhead, C. (1992) *Curriculum Organization and Classroom Practice in Primary Schools: A Discussion Paper*. London: HMSO.

Alexander, P., Schallert, D. and Hare, V. (1991) 'Coming to terms: how researchers in learning and literacy think about knowledge', *Review of Educational Research*, **61** (3), 315–43.

Allatt, P. (1993), 'Becoming pivileged: the role of family processes', in Bates, I. and Riseborough, G. (eds), *Youth and Inequality*, Buckingham: Open University Press, and D. J. Smith (eds), *Psycho-social Disorders in Young People: Time Trends and their Causes*. Chichester: Wiley.

Anderson, B. (1983) *Imagined Communities*. London: Verso Press.

Anderson, G. L. and Herr, K. (1999) 'The new paradigm wars: is there room for rigorous practitioner knowledge in schools and universities?' *Educational Research*, **28** (5).

Andrews, G. R. and Debus, R. L. (1978) 'Persistence and the causal perceptions of failure: modifying cognitive attributions', *Journal of Educational Psychology*, **70**, 154–66.

Archer, M. (1979) *The Social Origins of Educational Systems*. London: SAGE Publications.

Aries, P. (1962) *Centuries of Childhood*. Harmondsworth: Penguin.

Arnot, M., David, M. and Weiner, G. (1996) *Educational Reforms and Gender Equality in Schools*. London: Equal Opportunities Commission.

Ausubel, D. P. (1968) *Educational Psychology: A Cognitive View*. New York: Holt, Rinehart and Winston.

Ball, S. (1981) *Beachside Comprehensive*. Cambridge: Cambridge University Press.

Ball, S. (1987) *The Micropolitics of Schooling*. London: Routledge.

Banks, M., Bates, I., Breakwell, G., Bynner, J. Emler, N. Jamieson, L. and Roberts, K. (1992) *Careers and Identities*. Buckingham: Open University Press.

Barber, M. (2001) 'A new context for accountability and inspection', *Education Review*, **14** (2), 4–8.

Barker Lunn, J. C. (1970) *Streaming in the Primary School*. Slough: NFER.

Barnes, D. (1975) *From Communication to Curriculum*. London: Penguin.

Barnes, D., Britton, J. and Rosen, H. (1969) *Language, the Learner and the School*. Harmondsworth: Penguin.

Barrett, G. (1986) *Starting School: An Evaluation of the Experience*. Final Report to AMMA. CARE. Norwich: University of East Anglia.

Barrett, M. and Trevitt, J. (1991) *Attachment Behaviour and the Schoolchild*. London: Routledge.

Barth, R. (1990) *Improving Schools from Within*. San Francisco, CA: Jossey-Bass.

Bassey, M. (1978) *Practical Classroom Organization*. London: Ward Lock.

Bassey, M. (1990) 'Creating education through research', *Research Intelligence*, autumn, 40–4.

Baumrind, D. (1971) 'Current patterns of parental authority', *Developmental Psychology Monographs*, **4**, 99–103.

Beard, R. (1999) *National Literacy Strategy: Review of Research and Other Related Evidence*. London: DfEE.

Beck, I. L. and McKeown, M. G. (1988) 'Toward meaningful accounts in history texts for young learners', *Educational Researcher*, **17**, 31–9.

Bell, R. Q. (1979) 'Parent, child and reciprocal influences', *American Psychologist*, **34**, 821–6.

Bellack, A. A., Kliebard, H. M., Hyman, R. T. and Smith, F. L. (1966) *The Language of the Classroom*. New York: Teachers College Press.

Bendix, R. (1964) *Nation-Building and Citizenship*. New York: Wiley.

Benn, C, (1982) 'The myth of giftedness. Part 2', *Forum*, **24**, 78–84.

Bennett, N. (1992) *Managing Learning in the Primary School*, Association for the Study of Primary Education. Chester: Trentham Books.

Bennett, N. and Dunne, E. (1992) *Managing Classroom Groups*. Hemel Hempstead: Simon and Schuster.

Bennett, N. and Kell, J. (1989) *A Good Start? Four Year Olds in Infant Schools*. Oxford: Blackwell.

Bennett, N., Desforges, C., Cockburn, A. and Wilkinson, B. (1984) *The Quality of Pupil Learning Experiences*. London: Lawrence Erlbaum Associates.

Bennett, N., Roth, E. and Dunne, R. (1987) 'Task processes in mixed and single age classes'. *Education* 3–13, **15** 43–50.

Bentley, D. and Watts, M. (1994) *Teaching and Learning in Primary Science and Technology*. Buckingham: Open University Press.

Bentley, T. (1998) *Learning Beyond the Classroom*. London: Routledge.

Bereiter, C. and Scardamalia, M. (1985) 'Children's difficulties in learning to compose', in Wells, G. and Nichols, J. (eds) *Language and Learning*. London: Falmer.

Berger, P. L. (1963) *Invitation to Sociology*. New York: Doubleday.

Berger, P. L. and Luckmann, T. (1967) *The Social Construction of Reality: A Treatise in the Sociology of Knowledge.* Harmondsworth: Penguin.

Berlak, A. and Berlak, H. (1981) *Dilemmas of Schooling.* London, Methuen.

Berliner, D. (1984) 'The half-full glass: a review of research on teaching', in Hosford, P. (ed.) *Using What We Know about Teaching.* Alexandria, VA: Association of Supervision and Curriculum Development.

Bernstein, B. (1971) 'On the classification and framing of educational knowledge', in Young, M. F. D. (ed.). *Knowledge and Control.* London: Collier Macmillan.

Bernstein, B. (1975) *Class, Codes and Control: Towards a Theory of Educational Transmissions,* **3.** London: Routledge and Kegan Paul.

Bernstein, B. (1987) *Pedagogy, Symbolic Control and Identity.* London: Taylor & Francis.

Bernstein, B. (1990) *The Structure of Pedagogic Discourse.* London: Routledge and Kegan Paul.

Beyer, L. (1988) *Knowing and Acting: Inquiry, Ideology and Educational Studies,* Basingstoke, Falmer Press.

Bissex, G. (1980) *GYNS at Work.* Harvard MA: Harvard Press.

Black, P. and Atkin, J. M. (eds) (1996) *Changing the Subject: Innovations in Science, Mathematics and Technology Education.* London: Routledge.

Black, P. and William, D. (1998) *Inside the Black Box: Raising Standards Through Classroom Assessment.* London: Kings College.

Blandford, J. S. (1985) 'Standardized tests in junior schools with special reference to the effects of streaming on the constancy of results', *British Journal of Educational Psychology,* **28,** 70–3.

Blenkin, G. and Kelly, A. (1994) *The National Curriculum and Early Learning: An Evaluation.* London: Paul Chapman.

Bliss, L., Askew, M. and Macrae, S. (1996) 'Effective teaching and learning: scaffolding revisited', *Oxford Review of Education,* **22** (1), 37–61.

Blyth, W. A. L. (1967) *English Primary Education,* Vol. II. London: Routledge and Kegan Paul.

Blyth, W. A. L. (1984) *Development, Experience and Curriculum in Primary Education.* London: Croom Helm.

Board of Education (1926) *Education of the Adolescent, Report of the Consultative Committee (Hadow Report).* London, Board of Education.

Borich, C. (1996) *Effective Teaching Methods.* 3rd edn. New York: Macmillan.

Bowe, R. and Ball, S. J. with Gold, A. (1992) *Reforming Education and Changing Schools.* London: Routledge.

Bowlby, J. (1951) *Maternal Care and Mental Health.* London: HMSO.

Bowlby, J. (1988) *Secure Base.* London: Routledge and Kegan Paul.

Bredo, E. (1994) 'Reconstructing educational psychology', *Educational Psychologist,* **29,** 1.

Brighouse, T. (1994) 'Magicians of the inner city', TES/Greenwich Lecture, *Times Educational Supplement,* 22 April, Section 2, 1–2.

Brigley, S. (1991) 'Education accountability and school governors,' in Golby, M. (ed) *Exeter Papers in School Governorship, No 3.* Tiverton: Tiverton Publications.

Britton, J. (1971) What's the use – a schematic account of language function', *Educational Review,* **23** (3), 205–19.

Broadfoot, P., Osborn, M., Planel, C. and Sharpe, K. (2000) *Promoting Quality in Learning: Does England Have the Answer?* London: Cassell.

Brophy, J. (1992) Probing the subtleties of subject matter teaching. *Educational Leadership*, **49** (7), 4–8.

Brophy, J. and Good, T. (1974) *Teacher/Student Relationships: Cause and Consequences.* New York: Holt, Rinehart and Winston.

Brophy, J. E. and Evertson, C. M. (1976) *Learning from Teaching: A Developmental Perspective.* Boston: Alleyn and Bacon.

Brophy, J. E. and Good, T. L. (1986) 'Teacher behaviour and student achievement', in Wittrock, M. C (ed.) *Handbook of Research on Teaching.* New York: Macmillan.

Brown, A. (1990) 'Domain-specific Principles Affect Learning and Transfer in Pupils', *Cognitive Science* **14** (1), 107–33.

Brown, A. and Palinscar, A. (1986) *Guided Cooperative Learning and Individual Knowledge Acquisition.* Technical Report 372, Cambridge, MA: Bolt, Beranak and Newham Inc.

Brown, P. (1991) 'The "third wave": education and the ideology of parentocracy', *British Journal of Sociology of Education*, **11**, 65–85.

Brown, P., (1995), 'Cultural Capital and Social Exclusion: Some Observations on Recent Trends in Education, Employment and the Labour Market', *Work, Employment and Society*, **9**, 29–51.

Brown, S. and McIntyre, D. (1993) *Making Sense of Teaching.* Buckingham: Open University Press.

Browne, N. and Ross, C. (1991) 'Girls' stuff, boys' stuff: young children talking and playing', in N. Browne (ed.), *Science and Technology in the Early Years.* Milton Keynes: Open University Press.

Bruner, J. S. (1966) *Towards a Theory of Instruction.* Cambridge, MA, Harvard University Press.

Bruner, J. (1973) *Beyond the Information Given.* London: Allen and Unwin.

Bruner, J. (1980) *Under Fives in Britain.* London: Grant McIntyre.

Bruner, J. (1983) *Child Talk.* London: Oxford University Press.

Bruner, J. (1986) *Actual Minds-Possible Worlds.* Cambridge, MA: Harvard Educational Press.

Bruner, J. (1990) *Acts of Meaning.* Cambridge, MA: Harvard University Press.

Bruner, J. (1996) *The Culture of Education.* Cambridge, MA: Harvard University Press.

Buchmann, M. (1984) 'The priority of knowledge and understanding in teaching', in Katz, L. and Raths, J. (eds.) *Advances in Teacher Education*, Vol. 1. Norwood, NJ: Ablex.

Budd-Rowe, M. (1974) 'Wait-time and rewards as instructional variables, their influence on language, logic and fate control', *Journal of Research in Science Teaching*, **11** (2), 81–94.

Burns, S. and Lamont, G. (1995) *Values and Visions: Handbook for Spiritual Development and Global Awareness.* Hodder and Stoughton.

Burrell, A. and Bubb., S. (2000) 'Teacher feedback in the Reception class', *Education 3–13*, **28** (3), 59–63.

CACE (1967) *Children and their Primary Schools* (The Plowden Report). London: HMSO.

Calderhead, J. (1984) *Teachers' Classroom Decision Making.* London: Holt, Rinehart and Winston.

Calderhead, A., (1994) 'Can the complexities of teaching be accounted for in terms of competences? Contrasting views of professional practice from research and policy', mimeo produced for an ESRC symposium on teacher competence.

Calkins, L. (1983) *Lessons From a Child*. New Hampshire, CT: Heinemann.

Campbell, J. (1998) 'Primary teaching: roles and relationships', in Richards, C. and Taylor, P. H. (eds) *How Shall We School our Children?* London: Falmer.

Campbell, J. (1999) 'Recruitment, retention and reward: issues in the modernization of primary teaching'. *Education 3–13*, **27** (3), 24–31.

Campbell, J., Evans, L., Neill, S. R. St J. and Packwood, A. (1991) *The Use and Management of Infant Teachers' Time: Some Policy Issues*. Coventry: University of Warwick, Policy Analysis Unit.

Campbell, R. J. (1993) 'The National Curriculum in primary schools: a dream at conception, a nightmare at delivery', in Chitty, C. and Simon, B., *Education Answers Back: Critical Responses to Government Policy*. London: Lawrence and Wishart.

Campbell, R. J. and Neill, S. R. St J. (1994) *Curriculum Reform at Key Stage 1 – Teacher Commitment and Policy Failure*. Harlow: Longman.

Campbell, R. J., Evans, L., Packwood, A. and Neill, S. R. St. J. (1991) *Workloads, Achievement and Stress: Two Follow Up Studies of the Use of Teacher Time at Key Stage 1*, London: Assistant Master and Mistresses Association.

Carre, C. (1993) 'The first year of teaching', in Bennett, N. and Carre, C. (eds) *Learning to Teach*. London, New York: Routledge.

Chaudhary, V. (1998) 'Blunkett attacks negligent parents', *Guardian*, 17 April, 7.

Chazan, M. (2000) 'Social disadvantage and disruptive behaviour in schoo'l, in T. Cox (ed.) *Meeting the Needs of Vulnerable Children*. London: Falmer Press.

Childline (1997) *Beyond the Limit: Children Who Live with Parental Alcohol Misuse*. London.

Clark, C. (1988) 'Asking the right questions about teacher preparation: contributions of research on teacher thinking', *Educational Researcher*, **17** (2), 5–12.

Claxton, G. (1990) *Teaching to Learn*. Oxford: Blackwell.

Claxton, G. (ed.) (1997*) Hare Brain, Tortoise Mind. Why Intelligence Increases When You Think Less*. London: Fourth Estate.

Claxton, G. (1999) *Wise Up: The Challenge of Lifelong Learning*. Stoke on Trent: Network Press.

Claxton, G. (forthcoming) *Get Smarter: How to Have More Good Ideas*.

Cohen, E. (1986) *Designing Groupwork: Strategies for the Heterogeneous Classroom*, New York: Teachers' College Press.

Cohen, E. (1994) 'Restructuring Classrooms: Conditions for Productive Small Groups', *Review of Educational Research*, **64**, 1–35.

Cole, M. (1992) 'Culture in development', in *Developmental Psychology*. Hillsdale, NJ: LEA.

Collins, J. (1996) *The Quiet Child*. London, New York: Cassell.

Collins, R., Hunt, P. and Nunn, J. (1997) *Reading Voices*. Plymouth: Northcote House.

Committee of Ministers of the Council of Europe (1985) *Appendix to Recommendation No. R (85) 7, Memorandum on teaching and learning about human rights in schools*. Strasbourg: Directorate of Human Rights, Council of Europe.

Connell, R. W., Ashden, D. J. Kessler, S. and Dowsett, G. W. (1982) *Making the Difference: Schools, Families and Social Division*. Sydney: Allen and Unwin.

Connell, R. W., Johnston, K. and White, V. (1992) *Measuring Up*, Canberra: Australian Curriculum Studies Association.

Cooley, C. H. (1902) *Human Nature and the Social Order*. New York: Charles Scribner's Sons.

Cooper, B. and Dunne, M. (2000) *Assessing Children's Mathematical Knowledge Social Class, Sex and Problem-Solving*. Buckingham: Open University Press.

Corno, I. (1989) 'Self-Regulated Learning', in Zimmerman, B. J. and Schunk, D. H. (eds) *Self-regulated Learning and Academic Achievement: Theory, Research and Practice*. New York: Springer-Verlag.

Cortazzi, M. (1990) *Primary Teaching, How It Is: A Narrative Account*. London: David Fulton.

Coulson, A. A. (1978) 'Power and decision-making in the primary school', in Richards, C. (ed.) *Power and the Curriculum: Issues in Curriculum Studies*. Driffield, Nafferton Books.

Cowie, M. (1989) 'Children as writers', in Hargreaves, D. (ed.) *Children and the Arts*, Milton Keynes: Open University Press.

Croll, P. (ed.) (1996) *Teachers, Pupils and Primary Schooling*. London: Cassell.

Cruickshank, D. (1987) *Reflective Teaching*. Reston, VA: Association of Teacher Educators.

Cullingford, C. (1991) *The Inner World of the School: Children's Ideas about Schools*. London: Cassell.

Cullingford, C. (1999) *The Causes of Exclusion*. London: Kogan Page.

Cummins, J. and Swain, M. (1986) *Bilingualism in Education*. Harlow: Longman.

Cunningham, P. (1999) *Being a Primary Teacher in the Twentieth Century*. Coventry: CREPE, University of Warwick.

Cyster, R., Clift, P. S. and Battle, S. (1979) *Parental Involvement in Primary Schools*. Slough: NFER.

Dadds, M. (1986) 'Whose learning is it anyway?' in Conner, C. (ed.) *Topic and Thematic Work in the Middle and Primary Years*. Cambridge: Cambridge Institute of Education.

Dadds, M. (1994) 'The changing face of topic work in the primary curriculum', *The Curriculum Journal*, 4 (2), 253–66.

Dadds, M. (1994) 'Working the child's curriculum: in adversity'. Paper.

Dadds, M. (2001) 'Politics of pedagogy: the state and children', *Teachers and Teaching: Theory and Practice*, 7 (1), 49–53.

Damarin, S. (1990) 'Gender and the learning of fractions'. Paper presented to the American Educational Research Association, Boston, MA, April.

Damerell, R. (1985) *Education's Smoking Gun: How Teachers' Colleges have Destroyed Education in America*. New York: Freandlich Books.

Daniels, J. C. (1961) 'The effects of streaming in the primary schools: II. Comparison of streamed and unstreamed schools', *British Journal of Educational Psychology*, 31, 119–26.

Darling, J. (1994) *Child–Centred Education and its Critics*, London: Paul Chapman.

Darling-Hammond, L., Ancess, J. and Falk, B. (eds) (1995) *Authentic Assessment in Action Studies of Schools and Students at Work*, New York: Teachers College Press.

David, M. (1993) *Parents, Education and Gender Reform*. Cambridge: Polity Press.

Davie, R., Butler, N. and Goldstein, H. (eds) (1972) *From Birth to Seven.* Harlow: Longman.

Davies, B. (1982) *Life in the Classroom and Playground.* London: Routledge.

Davies, B. (1987) 'The accomplishment of genderedness in pre-school children', in Pollard, A (ed.) *Children and their Primary Schools. A New Perspective.* London: Falmer Press.

Davies, C. (2000) ' "Correct" or "appropriate"? Is it possible to resolve the debate about which should be promoted in the classroom?' in Davidson, J. and Moss, J. (eds) *Issues in English Teaching.* London, New York: Routledge.

Davies, J. and Brember, I. (1995) 'Attitudes to school and the curriculum in Year 2, Year 4 and Year 6: changes over four years'. Paper presented at the European Conference on Educational Research, Bath, England, 14–17 September.

Dawson, A. (1996) ' "You think I'm thick, don't you?" Children's reading histories', in E. Bearne (ed.) *Differentiation and Diversity in the Primary School.* London: Routledge.

Denbo, S. (1988) *Improving Minority Student Achievement: Focus on the Classroom,* Washington, DC: Mid-Atlantic Equity Center Series.

Dennett, D. (1981) 'True believers: the intentional strategy and why it works', in A. F. Heath (Ed.) *Scientific Explanation.* Oxford: Clarendon Press.

Department for Education (1995) *Key Stages 1 and 2 of the National Curriculum.* London: DFE.

Department for Education and Employment (1997) *Excellence in Schools.* London: HMSO .

Department for Education and Employment (1998a) *Circular 4/98: Teaching: High Status, High Standards.* London: DfEE.

Department for Education and Employment (1998b) *The National Literacy Strategy: Literacy Training Pack.* London: DfEE.

Department for Education and Employment (1998c) *The National Literacy Strategy: A Framework for Teaching.* London: DfEE.

Department for Education and Employment (1999a) *NLS Fliers 1 and 2* (based on NLS Teaching and Learning Strategies training module). London: DfEE.

Department for Education and Employment (1999b) *The Structure of the Literacy Hour.* http: //www.standards.dfee.gov.uk/ literacy/literacy hour.

Department of Education and Science (1974) *A Language for Life* (The Bullock Report). London: HMSO.

Department of Education and Science (1978a) *Primary Education in England.* London: HMSO.

Department of Education and Science (1978b) *Special Educational Needs* (The Warnock Report). London: HMSO.

Department of Education and Science (1980) *Education 5–9.* London: HMSO.

Department of Education and Science (1981) *The School Curriculum.* London: HMSO.

Department of Education and Science (1985) *Better Schools.* London: HMSO.

Department of Education and Science (1986) *English from 5 to 16.* London: HMSO.

Department of Education and Science (1987) *Mathematics from 5–16.* London: HMSO.

Department of Education and Science (1988) *Science at Age 11 – A Review of APU Survey Findings.* London: HMSO.

Department of Education and Science (1989a) *Science at Age 13 – A Review of APU Survey Findings.* London: HMSO.

Department of Education and Science (1989b) *Aspects of Primary Education: the Teaching of Mathematics*. London: HMSO.

Department of Education and Science (1990)*The Implementation of the National Curriculum in Primary Schools*, London: HMSO.

Department of Education and Science (1992) *Reform of Initial Teacher Training: A Consultation Document*. London: Department of Education and Science.

Desforges, C. (1995) *An Introduction to Teaching*. Oxford: Blackwell.

Dewey, J. (1916) *Democracy and Education*. New York: Free Press.

Dewey, J. (1933) *How We Think: A Restatement of the Relation of Reflective Thinking to the Educative Process*. Chicago: Henry Regnery.

DiMaggio, P. and Powell, W. (1983) 'The iron cage revisited', *American Sociological Review*, 48 (2), 147–60.

Donaldson, M. (1978) *Children's Minds*. Glasgow: Fontana/Collins.

Douglas, J. (1964) *The Home and School*. London: Macgibbon and Kee.

Doyle, W. (1979) 'Classroom tasks and student abilities', in Peterson, P. and Walberg, H. J. (eds.) *Research on Teaching: Concepts, Findings and Implications*. Berkeley, CA: McCutchan.

Doyle, W. (1983) 'Academic work', *Review of Educational Research*, 53 (2), 159–99.

Doyle, W. (1986) 'Classroom organization and management', in Wittrock, M. (ed.), *Handbook of Research on Teaching* (3rd edn). New York: Macmillan.

Doyle, W. (1990) 'Classroom knowledge as a foundation for teaching, *Teachers' College Record*, 91, 347–60.

Drummond, M. J. (1993) *Assessing Children's Learning*. London: Fulton.

Duckworth, E. (1987) *The Having of Wonderful Ideas*. New York: Teachers College Press.

Dunn, J. (1993) *Young Children's Close Relationships*. Sage: Newbury Park, California.

Dunne, E. and Bennett, N. (1990) *Talking and Learning in Groups*. London: Macmillan.

Duveen, G. (1999) 'Representations, identities, resistance', in K. Deaux and G. Philogene (eds) *Social Representations: Introductions and Explorations*. Oxford: Blackwell.

Dweck, C. S. and Leggett, E. (1988) 'A social–cognitive approach to motivation and personality', *Psychological Review*, 95 (2), 956–73.

Dweck, C. S. (1975) 'The role of expectations and attributions in the alleviation of learned helplessness', *Journal of Personality and Social Psychology*, 31, 674–85.

Dweck, C. S. (1986) 'Motivational processing affecting learning', *American Psychologist*, October, 1040–6.

Dweck. C. S., Davidson, W., Nelson, S. and Emma, B. (1978) 'Sex differences in learned helplessness: the contingencies of evaluative feedback in the classroom', *Development Psychology*, 14, 268–76.

Eccles, J., Midgley, C. and Alder, T. (1984) 'Grade-related changes in the school environment: effects of achievement motivation', in J. G. Nicholls (ed.) *Advances in Motivation and Achievement. Vol. 3: The Development of Achievement Motivation*. London: JAI Press.

Edmunds, R. (1979) 'Effective schools for the urban poor', *Educational Leadership*, 37 (3) 15–27.

Edwards, A. and Brunton, D. (1993) 'Supporting reflection in teachers' learning', in J. Calderhead and P. Gates (eds) *Conceptualizing Reflection in Teacher Development*. London: Falmer Press.

Edwards, A. and Collison, C. (1996) *Mentoring and Developing Practice in Primary Schools: Supporting Student-teacher Learning in Schools*. Buckingham: Open University Press.

Edwards, A. and Knight, P. (1994) *Effective Early Years Education: Teaching Young Children*. Buckingham: Open University Press.

Edwards, C., Gandidi, L. and Forman, G. (eds) (1993) *The Hundred Languages of Children. The Reggio Emilia Approach to Early Childhood Education*. Norwood, NJ: Ablex.

Edwards, D. and Mercer, N. (1987) *Common Knowledge: The Development of Understanding in the Classroom*. London: Methuen.

Eisner E. (1977) 'Instructional and expressive objectives', in M. Golby (ed.) *Curriculum Design*. Buckingham: Open University.

Epstein, D. (1993) *Changing Classroom Cultures: Anti-racism, Politics and Schools*. Stoke on Trent: Trentham Books.

Feiman-Nemser, S. (1990) 'Teacher preparation: structural and conceptual alternatives', in Houston, W. R. (ed.) *Handbook of Research on Teacher Education*. New York: Macmillan.

Fielding, M. (1994) 'Delivery, packages and the denial of learning', in Bradley, H., Conner, C. and Southworth, G. (eds) *Developing Teachers, Developing Schools*. London: Fulton.

Filer, A. (1993) Contexts of assessment in a primary classroom. *British Education Research Journal*, **19** (1), 95–108.

Filer, A. (ed.) (2000) *Assessment: Social Process and Social Product*. London: Falmer Press.

Filer, A. and Pollard, A. (2000) *The Social World of Pupil Assessment*. London: Continuum.

Firestone, S. (1979) 'Down with childhood', in Hoyles, M. (ed.) *Changing Childhood*. London: Readers and Writers.

Fogel, A. (ed.) (1993) *Developing through Relationships: Origins Of Communication, Self and Culture*. Hemel Hempstead: Harvester Wheatsheaf.

Foucault, M. (1977) *Discipline and Punish: The Birth of the Prison*. London: Penguin.

Fraser, A. (1987) 'A child-structured learning context', *Cambridge Journal of Education*, **17** (3), 146–52.

Freeman, J. (1979) *Gifted Children: Their Identification and Development in a Social Context*. Lancaster: MTP Press, and Baltimore, MD: University Park Press.

Friere, P. (1999) *Pedagogy of the Oppressed*. New York: Continuum.

Fuhrer, U. (1993) 'Behaviour-setting analysis of situated learning: the case of newcomers', in Chaiklen, S. and Lave, J. (eds) *Understanding Practice: Perspectives on Activity and Context*. Cambridge: Cambridge University Press.

Fuller, F. and Bown, O. (1975) 'Becoming a teacher', in Ryan, K. (ed.) *Teacher Education*, 74th Yearbook of the National Society for the Study of Education, Part 2. Chicago: University of Chicago Press.

Furlong, J. and Maynard, T. (1995) *Mentoring Student Teachers: The Growth of Professional Knowledge*. London: Routledge.

Gage, N. (1985) *Hard Gains in the Soft Sciences: The Case for Pedagogy*. CEDR Monograph, Bloomington, IN: Phi Delta Kappa.

Galloway, D., Rogers, C., Armstrong, D. and Leo, E., with Jackson, C. (1998) *Motivating the Difficult to Teach*. London: Longman.

Galton, M. (1989) *Teaching in the Primary School*. London: David Fulton.

Galton, M. and Williamson, J. (1992) *Group Work in the Primary Classroom*, London: Routledge.

Galton, M., Hargreaves, L., and Comber, C. (1998) 'Classroom practice and the National Curriculum in small rural primary schools', *British Educational Research Journal*, **24** (1), 43–61.

Galton, M., Hargreaves, L., Comber, C., Wall, D and Pell, A. (1999) *Inside the Primary Classroom – 20 years on*. London: Routledge.

Galton, M., Simon, B. and Croll, P. (1980) *Inside the Primary Classroom*. London: Routledge and Kegan Paul.

Gardner, H. (1983) *Frames of Mind: The Theory of Multiple Intelligences*. New York: Basic Books.

Gardner, P. and Cunningham, P. (1999) '"Saving the nations' children": teachers, wartime evacuation in England and Wales and the construction of national identity', *History of Education*, **28** (3), 327–37.

Geertz, C. (1968) 'Religion as cultural system', in Cutler, D. (ed.) *The Religious Situation*. Boston, MA: Beacon Press.

Geertz, C. (1973) *The Interpretation of Cultures*. New York: Basic Books.

Gerber, M. (1996) 'Reforming special education: beyond inclusion', in Christenson, C. and Rizvi, F. (eds) *Disability and the Dilemmas of Education and Justice*. Buckingham: Open University Press.

Ghate, D. and Daniels, A. (1997) *Talking About My Generation*. London: NSPCC.

Gilborn, D. and Youdell, D. (1999) *Rationing Education: Policy Reform and School Inequality*. Buckingham: Open University Press.

Gipps, C. (1992) *What We Know About Effective Primary Teaching*. London: Tufnell Press.

Gipps, C. and McGilchrist, B. (1999) 'Primary school learners', in P. Mortimore (ed.) *Understanding Pedagogy and its Impact on Learning*. London: Paul Chapman Publishing, 52–5.

Gipps, C. and Murphy, P. (1994) *A Fair Test? Assessment, Achievement and Equity*. Buckingham: Open University Press.

Gipps, C., McCallum, B. and Brown, M. (1996) 'Models of teacher assessment among primary school teachers in England'. *The Curriculum Journal*, 7 (2), 167–83.

Glaser, R. (1991) 'The maturing of the relationship between the science of learning and cognition and educational practice', *Learning and Instruction*, **1** (2).

Goffman, E. (1961) *Asylums*. New York: Anchor Books, Doubleday.

Goldberg, M. L. (1965) *Research on the Talented*. New York: Teachers College, Columbia University.

Goleman, D. (1996) *Emotional Intelligence – Why it Matters More than IQ*. London: Bloomsbury.

Goleman, D. (1998) *Working with Emotional Intelligence*. London: Bloomsbury.

Good, T. L., Grouws, D. A. and Ebmeier, D. (1983) *Active Mathematics Teaching*. New York: Longman.

Goodson, I. and Hargreaves, A. (1996) *Teachers' Professional Lives*. London: Falmer Press.

Gordon, D. *et al.* (2000) *Poverty and Social Exclusion in Britain*. York: Joseph Rowntree Foundation.

www.rtweb.info

Gracey, H. (1972) *Curriculum or Craftsmanship: Elementary School Teachers in a Bureaucratic System.* Chicago: University of Chicago Press.

Graves, D. H. (1983) *Writing: Teachers and Children at Work.* London: Heinemann.

Greenfield, S. (1997) *The Human Brain: A Guided Tour.* London: Weidenfeld and Nicolson.

Gregg, P., Harkness, S., and Machlin, S. (1999) *Child Development and Family Income.* York: York Publishing Services.

Griffin, G. A. and Barnes, S. (1986). 'Using research findings to change school and classroom practice: results of an experimental study', *American Educational Research Journal,* **23** (4), 572–86.

Halsey, A. H., and Young, M. (1997) 'The family and social justice', in A. H. Halsey, H. Lauder, P. Brown, and A. S. Wells (eds) *Education, Culture, Economy and Society.* Oxford: Oxford University Press.

Handal, G. and Lauvas, P. (1987) *Promoting Reflective Teaching: Supervision in Action.* Buckingham: Open University Press.

Hargreaves, A. (1978) 'The significance of classroom coping strategies', in L. Barton and R. Meighan (eds) *Sociological Interpretations of Schooling and Classrooms.* Driffield: Nafferton.

Hargreaves, A. (1994*) Changing Teachers, Changing Times: Teachers' Work and Culture in the Postmodern Age.* London: Cassell.

Hargreaves, D. (1983) *The Challenge for the Comprehensive* School. London: Routledge and Kegan Paul.

Hargreave, D., Hestor, S. and Mellor, F. (1975) *Deviance in Classrooms.* London: Routledge.

Harlen, W. (1991) 'National Curriculum assessment: increasing the benefit by reducing the burden', in *Education and Change in the 1990s, Journal of the Educational Research Network of Northern Ireland,* **5**, February, 3–19.

Harré, R. (1983) *Personal Being.* Oxford: Clarendon Press.

Hart, S. (1996) *Beyond Special Needs.* London: Paul Chapman.

Harter, S., Rumbaugh Whitesell, N. and Kowalski, P. (1992) 'Individual differences in the effects of educational transitions on young adolescents' perceptions of competence and motivational orientation', *American Educational Research Journal,* **29**, 777–807.

Hayes, D. (2001) 'Professional status and an emerging culture of conformity among teachers in England', *Education 3–13,* **29** (1), 43–9.

Head, J. (1996) 'Gender identity and cognitive style', in Murphy, P. and Gipps, C. (eds) *Equity in the Classroom: Towards Effective Pedagogy for Girls and Boys.* London: Falmer Press.

Hegarty, S. and Pocklington, K., with Lucas, D. (1981) *Educating Pupils with Special Needs in Ordinary Schools.* Windsor: NFER-Nelson.

Helsby, G. (1999) *Changing Teachers' Work.* Buckingham: Open University Press.

Helsby, G. and McCulloch, G. (eds) (1997) *Teachers and the National Curriculum.* London: Cassell.

Henriques, J. (1984) 'Social psychology and the politics of racism', in Henriques, J., Hollway, W., Urwin, C., Venn, C. and Walkerdine, V. *Changing the Subject: Psychology, Social Regulation and Subjectivity.* London: Methuen.

Her Majesty's Inspectorate (1989) *Aspects of Primary Education. The Teaching of Mathematics.* London: HMSO.

Her Majesty's Inspectorate (1992) *Provision for Highly Able Pupils in Maintained Schools.* London: HMSO.

Hirst, P. H. and Peters, R. S. (eds) (1970) *The Logic of Education*. London: Routledge and Kegan Paul.

Hodgkin, R. A. (1985) *Playing and Exploring: Education through the Discovery of Order*. London: Methuen .

Hodgson, A., Clunies-Ross, L. and Hegarty, S. (1984) *Learning Together: Teaching Children with Special Educational Needs in the Ordinary School*. Windsor: NFER-Nelson.

Holt, J. (1982) *How Children Fail*. London: Penguin.

Hopewell, B. (1996) 'The Intelligence Advantage – Organizing for Complexity', book review of McMaster, M. (1995), *Long Range Planning*, **29** (6), 902–04.

Hopkins, A. (1978) *The School Debate*. Harmondsworth, Penguin.

Hopkins, B. L. and Conrad, R. J. (1976) 'Putting it all together: super school' in Haring, N. G. and Schiefelbush, R. C. (eds.) *Teaching Special Children*. New York: McGraw Hill.

Howe, C. (1999) *Gender and Classroom Interactions*. Edinburgh: Scottish Council for Educational Research.

Hoyle, E. (1980) 'Professionalization and deprofessionalization in education', in Hoyle, E. and Megarry, J. (eds.) *World Yearbook of Education 1980: Professional Development of Teachers*. London: Kogan Page.

Hoyle, E. (1982) 'The micropolitics of educational organizations', *Education, Management and Administration*, **10**, 87–98.

Huberman, M. (1993) *The Lives of Teachers*. London: Cassell.

Hughes, M. (1986) *Children and Number*. Oxford: Basil Blackwell.

Hughes, M., Desforges, C. and Mitchell, C., with Carr, C. (2000) *Numeracy and Beyond: Applying Mathematics in the Primary School*. Buckingham: Open University Press.

Hughes, M., Wikeley, F. and Nash, T. (1994) *Parents and Their Children's Schools*. Oxford: Basil Blackwell.

Hull, R. (1985) *The Language Gap.* London: Methuen.

Hutt, S. L., Tyler, S., Hutt, C. and Christopherson, H. (1989) *Play, Exploration and Learning. A Natural History of the Pre-School*. London: Routledge.

Ireson, J. and Hallam, S. (2001) *Ability Grouping in Education*. London: Paul Chapman Publishing.

Jackson, C. (1997) 'Self-concept, social comparison and gender in the classroom: a case for an integrated theoretical approach', unpublished PhD thesis. Lancaster: Lancaster University.

Jackson, C. and Warin, J. (2000) 'The importance of gender as an aspect of identity at key transition points in compulsory education', *British Educational Research Journal*, **26** (3), 375–88.

Jackson, P. W. (1977) 'The way teachers think', in Glidwell, J. C. (ed.) *The Social Context of Learning and Development*. New York: Gardner Press.

Jackson, P. W. (1968) *Life in Classrooms*. New York: Teachers College Press.

James, W. (1890) *Principles of Psychology*, Vol. 1. New York: Henry Holt.

Jeffrey, B. and Woods, P. (1998) *Testing Teachers: The Effects of School Inspection on Primary Teachers*. London: Falmer.

Jensen, A. (1967) 'The culturally disadvantaged: psychological and educational aspects', *Educational Research*, **10**, 4–20.

John–Steiner, V. (1997) *Notebooks of the Mind: Explorations of Thinking*. Oxford: Oxford University Press.

Jones, E. and Reynolds, G. (1992) *The Play's the Thing: Teachers' Roles in Children's Play*. New York: Teachers' College Press.

Jordan, B., Redley, M. and James, S., (1994) *Putting the Family First: Identities, Decisions, Citizenship*. London: UCL Press.

Jordan, J. (1974) 'The organization of perspectives in teacher–pupil relations: an interactionist approach', unpublished M.Ed. thesis. Manchester: University of Manchester.

Joyce, B. and Weil, M. (1996) *Models of Teaching*. 5th edn. Boston: Allyn and Bacon.

Kanter, R. M. (1974) 'Commitment and social organization', in Field, D. (ed.) *Social Psychology for Sociologists*. London: Nelson.

Karrby, G. (1989) 'Children's perceptions of their own play', *International Journal of Early Childhood*, **21** (2), 49–54.

Katz, L. G. (1998) 'A developmental approach to the curriculum in the early years', in Smidt, S (ed.) *The Early Years: A Reader*. London, New York: Routledge, 11–16.

Kemmis, S. (1985) 'Action research and the politics of reflection', in Boud, D., Keogh, R. and Walker, D. (eds.) *Reflection: Turning Experience into Learning*. London: Croom Helm.

Kempe, A. and Nicholson, H. (2001) *Learning to Teach Drama 11–18*. London: Continuum.

Kimbell, R., Stables, K., Wheeler, T., Wosniak, A. and Kelly, V. (1991) *The Assessment of Performance in Design and Technology*. London: Schools' Examination and Assessment Council.

King, R. (1978) *All Things Bright and Beautiful?* London: John Wiley.

Kirp, D. (1983) 'Professionalization as policy choice: British special education in comparative perspective', in Chambers, R. G. and Hartman, W. T. (eds) *Special Education Policies*. Philadelphia: Temple University Press.

Koerner, J. (1963) *The Miseducation of American Teachers*. Boston: Houghton Mifflin.

Kounin, J. (1970) *Discipline and Group Management in Classrooms*. New York: Holt, Rinehart and Winston.

Krasner, S. D. (ed.) (1983) *International Regimes*. Ithaca, NY: Cornell University Press.

Kulik, J. A. and Kulik, C.-L. C. (1992) 'Meta-analytic findings on grouping programs', *Gifted Child Quarterly*, **36** (2), 73–7.

Kuykendall, C. (1989) *Improving Black Student Achievement*. Washington, DC: The Mid-Atlantic Equity Center Series.

Labour Party, the (1994) *Consultative Green Paper: Opening Doors to a Learning Society*. London: The Labour Party.

Lacey, C. (1976) 'Problems of sociological fieldwork: a review of the methodology of Hightown Grammar', in Hammersley, M. and Woods, P. (eds.) *The Process of Schooling*. London: Routledge and Kegan Paul.

Lacey, C. (1977) *The Socialization of Teachers*. London: Methuen.

Laslett, R. and Smith, C. (1984) *Effective Classroom Management: A Teacher's Guide*. London: Croom Helm.

Lave, J. and Wenger, F. (1991) *Situated Learning: Legitimate Peripheral Participation*. Cambridge: Cambridge University Press.

Lawrence, D. (1987) *Enhancing Self-esteem in the Classroom*. London: Paul Chapman Publishing.

LeDoux, J. (1996) *Emotional Brain*. New York: Simon and Schuster.

Leiberman, A. and Miller, L. (1984) *Teachers: Their World and Their Work*. Alexandria, VA: Association for Supervision and Curriculum Development.

Lemlech, J. K. (1979) *Classroom Management*. New York: Harper and Row.

Leont'ev, A. N. (1981) *Problems of the Development of Mind*. Moscow: Progress Publishers.

Levine, J. (1990) *Bilingual Learners and the Mainstream Curriculum*. London: Falmer Press.

Lewin, N., Lippitt, R. and White, R. K. (1939) 'Patterns of aggressive behaviour in experimentally created social climates', *Journal of Social Psychology*, 10, 271–99.

Light, P. and Butterworth, G. (eds) (1992) *Context and Cognition: Ways of Learning and Knowing*. Hemel Hempstead: Harvester Wheatsheaf.

Lortie, D. (1975) *School Teacher: A Sociological Study*. Chicago: University of Chicago Press.

Lou, Y., Abrami, P. C., Spence, J. C., Poulsen, C., Chambers, B., and d'Apollonia, S. (1996) 'Within-class grouping: a meta-analysis', *Review of Educational Research*, 66 (4), 423–58.

Louis, K. S. and Miles, M. B. (1992) *Improving the Urban High School: What Works and Why*. London: Cassell.

Lukes, S. (1974) *A Radical View of Power*. London: Macmillan.

Lyotard, J. F. (1984) *The Post-modern Condition: A Report on Knowledge*. Manchester, Manchester University Press.

MacBeath, J. and Mortimore, P. (2001) 'School effectiveness and imrovement: the story so far', in MacBeath, J. and Mortimore, P. (eds) *Improving School Effectiveness*. Buckingham: Open University Press.

MacGilchrist, B., Myers, K and Reed, J. (1997) *The Intelligent School*. London: Paul Chapman Publishing.

Macleod, D. and Meikle, J. (1994) 'Education changes "making head quit"', *Guardian*, 1 September.

Maden, M. (1999) 'The challenge of children in the education system', in Tunstall, J. (ed.) *Children and the State: Whose Problem?* London, New York: Cassell.

Maher, F. and Rathbone, C. (1986) 'Teacher education and feminist theory: some implications for practice', *American Journal of Education*, 94 (2), 214–35.

Maitland, S. (1991) *Three Times Table*. London: Virago.

Marland, M. (1975) *The Craft of the Classroom: A Survival Guide*. London: Heinemann.

Marshall, T. H. (1948) *Class, Citizenship and Social Development*. Garden City, NJ: Doubleday.

Martin, C. L. and Halverson, C. E. (1981) 'A schematic processing model of sex-typing and stereotyping in children', *Child Development*, 52, 1119–34.

Maylor, U. (1995) 'Identity, migration and education', in Blair, M. and Holland, J. (eds) *Identity and Diversity*. Clevedon: Multilingual Matters, 39–49.

Maynard, T. (2001) 'The student teacher and the school community of practice: a consideration of learning as preparation', *Cambridge Journal of Education*, 31 (1), 44–9.

Maynard, T. and Furlong, J. (1993) 'Learning to teach and models of mentoring', in McIntyre, D., Hagger, H. and Wilkin, M. (eds) *Mentoring: Perspectives on School-based Teacher Education*. London: Kogan Page.

McAuley, H. (1990) 'Learning structures for the young child: a review of the literature', *Early Child Development and Care*, 59, 87–124.

McGarrigle, J. and Donaldson, M. (1974) 'Conservation accidents', *Cognition*, **3**, 341–50.

McMaster, M. (1995) *The Intelligent Advantage: Organizing for Complexity*. Knowledge Based Development Co. Ltd.

McNamara, D. (1994) *Classroom Pedagogy and Primary Practice*. London: Routledge.

McPherson, A. (1992) *Measuring Added Value in Schools*, National Commission on Education Briefing No. 1. London: National Commission on Education.

Meadows, S. (1993) *The Child as Thinker*. London: Routledge.

Meadows, S. (1996) *Parenting Behaviour and Children's Cognitive Development*. Hove: Psychology Press.

Meek, M. (1991) *On Being Literate*. London: Bodley Head.

Mercer, N. (1995) *The Guided Construction of Knowledge*. Clevedon: Multilingual Matters.

Merrett, F. and Wheldall, K. *Identifying Troublesome Classroom Behaviour*. London: Paul Chapman Publishing.

Merton, R. (1968) *The Self-Fulfilling Prophecy, Social Theory and Social Structure*. London: Collier MacMillan.

Meyer, J. W. (1980) 'The world polity and the authority of the nation-state' in Bergesen, A. (ed.) *Studies of the Modern World-System*. New York: Academic Press.

Mills, C. W. (1959) *The Sociological Imagination*. New York: Oxford University Press.

Montgomery, D. (1996) *Educating the Able*. London: Cassell.

Morrison, A. and McIntyre, D. (1969) *Teachers and Teaching*. Harmondsworth, Penguin.

Mortimore, P. (1993) 'School effectiveness and the management of effective learning and teaching', *School Effectiveness and Improvement*, **4** (4), 290–310.

Mortimore, P. and Mortimore, J. (1986) 'Education and social class', in R. Rogers (ed.) *Education and Social Class*. London: Falmer Press.

Mortimore, P., Sammons, P., Stoll, L., Lewis, D., and Ecob, R. (1988) *School Matters: The Junior Years*, Wells, Sommerset: Open Books.

Moyles, J. (1995) 'A place for everything? The classroom as a teaching and learning context', in Moyles, J. (ed.) *Beginning Teaching: Beginning Learning in Primary Education*. Buckingham: Open University Press.

Moyles, J. R., Suschitzky, W. and Chapman, L. (1998) *Teaching Fledglings to Fly . . .? Mentoring and Support Systems in Primary Schools*. London: Association of Teachers and Lecturers.

Mroz, M., Hardman, F. and Smith, F. (2000) 'The discourse of the Literacy Hour', *Cambridge Journal of Education*, **30** (3), 379–90.

Muijs, R. D. and Reynolds, D. (2000) 'Effective mathematics teaching: year 2 of a research project'. Paper presented at the International Conference on School Effectiveness and School Improvement. Hong Kong, 8 January.

Munn, P. and Schaffer, H. R. (1993) 'Literacy and numeracy events in social interactive contexts', *International Journal of Early Years Education*, **1** (3), 61–80.

Murphy, P. (1997) 'Gender differences – messages for science education', in Harnquist, K. and Burgen, A. (eds), *Growing up with Science: Developing Early Understanding of Science*. London: Jessica Kingsley.

Murphy, P. (2000) 'Gendered learning and achievement', in Collins, J. and Cook, D. (eds) *Understanding Learning*. London: Paul Chapman Publishing, 109–21.

Murphy, P. F. and Elwood, J. (1998) 'Gendered experiences, choices and achievement – exploring the links', *International Journal of Inclusive Education*, **2** (2) 85–118.

Muschamp, Y., Pollard, A. and Sharpe, R. (1992) 'Curriculum management in primary schools', *The Currculum Journal*, **3** (1), 21–39.

National Assessment of Educational Progress (NAEP) (1983) *The Third National Mathematics Assessment*. Denver, CO: Education Commission of the States.

National Curriculum Council (1993) *The National Curriculum at Key Stages 1 and 2*. York: National Curriculum Council.

National Oracy Project (1990) *Teaching, Talking and Learning in Key Stage 1*. York: National Curriculum Council.

Newman, D., Griffin, P., and Cole, M. (1989) *The Construction Zone: Working for Cognitive Change in School*. Cambridge: Cambridge University Press.

Nias, J. (1988) 'Informal education in action: teachers' accounts', in Blyth, A. (ed.) *Informal Primary Education Today*. London: Falmer Press.

Nias, J. (1989) *Primary Teachers Talking: A Study of Teaching at Work*. London: Routledge.

Nias, J. (1997) 'Would schools improve if teachers cared less?' *Education 3–13*, **25** (3), 11–22.

Nias, J. (1999) 'Primary teaching as a culture of care', in Prosser, J. (ed.) *School Culture*. London: Paul Chapman.

Nias, J., Southworth, G. and Yeomans, R. (1989) *Staff Relationships in the Primary School: A Study of Organizational Cultures*. London: Cassell.

Nunes, T., Schliemann, A. and Carraher, D. (1993) *Street Mathematics and School Mathematics*. Cambridge: Cambridge University Press.

O'Hara, L. and O'Hara, M. (2001) *Teaching History 3–11: The Essential Guide*. London, New York: Continuum.

Office for Standards in Education (1993) *Curriculum Organization and Classroom Practice in Primary Schools – A Follow Up Report*. London: DFE.

Office for Standards in Education (1993a) *Access and Achievement in Urban Education*. London: HMSO.

Office for Standards in Education (1993b) *Boys and English*. London: DFE.

Office for Standards in Education (2000) 'Literacy and numeracy are key to higher standards in all schools, says chief inspector', OFSTED press release, 8 February.

Osborn, M. (1986) 'Profiles of a typical French and English primary teacher', mimeo, Bristol, University of Bristol.

Osborn, M. (1996a) 'Identity, career and change: a tale of two teachers', in P. Croll (ed.), *Teachers, Pupils and Primary Schooling*. London: Cassell.

Osborn, M. (1996b) 'Teachers as adult learners: the influence of the national context and policy change', Paper given at the International Conference on Education and Training. Warwick, March.

Osborne, M., McNess, E. and Broadfoot, P., with Pollard, A. and Triggs, P. (2000) *What Teachers Do: Changing Policy and Practice in Primary Education*. London, New York: Continuum.

Paley, V. G. (1981) *Wally's Stories*. Cambridge, MA: Harvard University Press

Palinscar, A. and Brown, A. (1984) 'Reciprocal teaching of comprehension-fostering and comprehension-monitoring activities', *Cognition and Instruction*, **2**, 117–75.

Parker-Rees, R. (1997) 'Making sense and made sense: design and technology and the playful construction of meaning in the early years', *Early Years*, **18** (1), 5–8.

Parker-Rees, R. (1999) 'Protecting playfulness', in Abbott, L. and Moylett, H. (eds) *Early Education Transformed: New Millennium Series*. London, New York: Falmer Press, 64–6.

Passow, A. H. (1990) 'Needed research and development in educating high-ability children', *European Journal of High Ability*, **1** (4), 15–24.

Perrone, V. (1989) *Working Papers: Reflections on Teachers, Schools and Communities*. New York: Teachers College Press.

Piaget, J. (1961) 'A genetic approach to the psychology of thought', *Journal of Educational Psychology*, **52**, 151–61.

Pilling, D. and Pringle, M. K. (1978) *Controversial Issues in Child Development*. London: Paul Elek.

Plowden Report, the (1967) *Children and their Primary Schools*. London: HMSO.

Pollard, A. (1982) 'Towards a model of coping strategies', *British Journal of Sociology of Education*, **3** (1), 19–37.

Pollard, A. (1985) *The Social World of the Primary School*. London: Cassell.

Pollard, A. (1987) 'Social differentiation in primary school', *Cambridge Journal of Education*, **17** (3), 158–61.

Pollard, A. (1990) 'Towards a sociology of learning in primary schools', *British Journal of Sociology of Education*, **11** (3), 241–56.

Pollard, A. (1997) *The Basics and an Eagerness to Learn: A New Curriculum for Primary Schooling*. SCAA: International Conference London, June.

Pollard, A., Broadfoot, P., Croll, P., Osborn, M., and Abbott, D. (1994) *Changing English Primary Schools? The Impact of the Education Reform Act at Key Stage One*. London: Cassell.

Pollard, A. with Filer, A. (1996) *The Social World of Children's Learning: Case Studies of Pupils from Four to Seven*. London: Cassell.

Pollard, A. and Filer, A. (1999) *The Social World of Pupil Career: Strategic Biographies Through Primary School*. London, New York: Cassell.

Pollard, A., Filer, A. and Furlong, J. (1995) *Identity and Secondary Schooling: A Longitudinal Ethnography of Pupil Career*. Application to ESRC (Grant R000236687).

Pollard, A. and Triggs, P., with Broadfoot, P. McNess, E. and Osborn, N. (2000) *What Pupils Say: Changing Policy and Practice in Primary Education*. London: Continuum.

Pollard, A., Muschamp, Y. and Sharpe, R. (1992) 'Curriculum management in primary schools', *Curriculum Journal*, **3** (1), 21–39.

Poorthuis, E., Kok, L. and Van Dijk, J. (1990) 'A curriculum assessment tool'. Paper presented at the Second Biennial European Conference of the European Council for High Ability (ECHA), Budapest, October.

Popper, K. (1972) *Objective Knowledge*. Oxford: Clarendon Press.

Preece, F. W. P., Skinner, C. N. and Riall, A. H. R. (1999) 'The gender gap and discriminating power in the National Curriculum Key Stage 3 Science Assessments in England and Wales', *International Journal of Science Education*, **21** (9), 979–87, presented at West Glamorgan Headteacher Conference, Newport, February, 'Primary Education'.

Pring, R. (2000) *Philosophy of Educational Research*. London: Continuum.

Putnam, R. (1987) 'Structuring and adjusting content for students: a study of live and simulated tutoring of addition', *American Educational Research Journal*, **24** (11), 13–48.

Qualifications and Curriculum Authority (1999a) *The National Curriculum: Handbook for Primary Teachers in England*. London: DfEE/QCA.

Qualifications and Curriculum Authority (1999b) *Early Learning Goals*. London: DfEE/QCA.

Qualifications and Curriculum Authority (2000a) *Standards at Key Stage 1, English and Mathematics*. London: QCA.

Qualifications and Curriculum Authority (2000b) *Standard at Key Stage 2, English, Mathematics and Science*. London: QCA.

Qualifications and Curriculum Authority/Department of Education and Employment (1999) *The Review of the National Curriculum in England*. London: QCA.

Qvortrup, J. (1993) *Childhood as a Social Phenomenon: Lessons from an International Project* (47). Vienna: European Centre.

Qvortrup, J. (1997) 'Childhood and societal macrostructures'. Paper presented at the Conceptualizing Childhood: Perspectives on Research Conference. Keele: University of Keele.

Reason, R. (1993) 'Primary special needs and National Curriculum assessment', in S. Wolfendale (ed.) *Assessing Special Needs*. London: Cassell, 73–5.

Reay, D. (1998) *Class Work: Mothers' Involvement in Children's Schooling*. London: University College Press.

Reay, D. (2000) 'A useful extension of Bourdieu's conceptual framework? Emotional capital as a way of understanding mothers' involvement in their children's education?' *The Sociological Review*, **48** (4), 568–85.

Reay, D. and William, D. (1999) '"I'll be a nothing": structure, agency and the construction of identity through assessment', *British Educational Research Journal*, **25** (3), 343–54.

Reynolds, D. (1982) 'The search for effective schools', *School Organization*, **2** (3), 215–37.

Reynolds, D. and Farrell, S. (1996) *Worlds Apart? A Review of International Surveys of Educational Achievement Involving England*. London: HMSO.

Reynolds, D. and Muijs, R. D. (1999) 'The effective teaching of mathematics: a review of research'. *School Leadership and Management*, **19** (3), 273–88.

Richards, M. and Light, P. (1986) *Children of Social Worlds*. Cambridge: Polity Press.

Richards, C. (2001) *School Inspection in England: A Re-appraisal*, Impact No. 9. Philosophy of Education Society of Great Britain.

Roaf, C. and Bines, H. (1989) 'Needs, rights and opportunities in special education', in Roaf, C. and Bines, H. (eds) *Needs, Rights and Opportunities*. London: Falmer Press, 5–15.

Robson, S. (1993) 'Best of all I like choosing time. Talking with children about play and work', *Early Child Development and Care*, **92**, 37–51.

Rogers, C. R. (1951) *Client-centred Therapy*. Boston: Houghton Mifflin.

Rosenshine, B. (1987) 'Direct instruction', in Dunkin, M. (ed.) *Teaching and Teacher Education*. Oxford: Pergamon.

Rosenshine, B. and Meister, C. (1994) 'Reciprocal teaching: a review of research', *Review of Educational Research*, **64** (4), 479–530.

Rosenshine, B. and Stevens, R. (1986) 'Teaching functions', in Wittrock, M. C. (ed.) *Handbook of Research on Teaching*. Upper Saddle River, NJ: Merrill/Prentice Hall.

Rosenshine, B., Meister, C. and Chapman, S. (1996) 'Teaching students to generate questions: a review of intervention studies', *Review of Educational Research*, **66** (2), 181–221.

Rosenthal, R. and Jacobson, L. (1968) *Pygmalion in the Classroom: Teacher Expectation and Pupils' Intellectual Development*. New York: Holt, Rinehart and Winston.

Ross, D. and Kyle, D. (1987) 'Helping pre-service teachers learn to use teacher effectiveness research', *Journal of Teacher Education*, **38**, 40–4.

Roth, W.-M. (1997) 'Situated cognition and the assessment of competence in science'. Paper presented at the Seventh Conference of the European Association for Research in Learning and Instruction, Athens, Greece, 26–30 August.

Rowland, S. (1984) *The Enquiring Classroom*. London: Falmer.

Rowland, S. (1987) 'An interpretative model of teaching and learning', in A. Pollard (ed.) *Children and Their Primary Schools*. London: Falmer Press.

Royal Society of Arts (1994) *Start Right* (The Ball Report). London: RSA.

Rutter, M., Maughan, B., Mortimore, P. and Ouston, J. (1979) *Fifteen Thousand Hours: Secondary Schools and Their Effects on Children*. London: Open Books.

Säljö, R. and Wyndhamn, J. (1990) 'Problem-solving, academic performance and situated reasoning: a study of joint cognitive activity in the formal setting', *British Journal of Educational Psychology*, **60** (3), 245–54.

Sallis, J. (1988) *Schools, Parents and Governors*. London: Routledge.

Sammons, P. Hillman, J. and Mortimore, P. (1995) *Key Characteristics of Effective Schools: A Review of School Effectiveness Research*, research commissioned by Office for Standards in Education. London: Institute of education and Office for Standards in Education.

Sarason, S. (1982) *The Culture of the School and the Problem of Change*, 2nd edn., Boston: Allyn and Bacon.

Sarup, M. (1991) *Education and the Ideologies of Racism*. Stoke-on-Trent: Trentham Books.

Savva, H. (1990) 'The rights of bilingual children', in Carter, R. (ed.) *Knowledge About Language and the Curriculum*. London: Hodder and Stoughton.

Schaffer, E. (1997) Interviews with the author. University of Newcastle, autumn.

Schön, D. (1981/1987) *Educating the Reflective Practitioner: Toward a New Design for Teaching and Learning in the Professions*. San Francisco, CA: Jossey-Bass.

Schön, D. (1983) *The Reflective Practitioner. How Professionals Think in Action*. London: Temple Smith.

Schön, D. A. (1992) 'The theory of inquiry: Dewey's legacy to education', *Curriculum Inquiry*, **22**, 119–39.

Schön, D. (1995) *The Reflective Practitioner*. London: Arena.

School Curriculum and Assessment Authority (1996) *Nursery Education: Desirable Outcomes for Children's Learning on Entering Compulsory Education*. London: DfEE/SCAA.

Schwab, J. J. (1978) *Science, Curriculum and Liberal Education*. Chicago: University of Chicago Press.

Scottish Executive (2000) *The Structure and Balance of the Curriculm: 5–14, National Guidelines*. Edinburgh: Learning and Teaching Scotland.

Scribner, S. (1985) 'Vygotsky's uses of history', in Wertsch, J. V. (ed.), *Culture, Communication and Cognition: Vygotskian Perspectives*. Cambridge: Cambridge University Press.

Senge, P. M. (2000) 'Systems change in education', *Reflections*, 1 (3), 58.

Shepard, L. A. (1992) 'Commentary: what policy makers who mandate tests should know about the new psychology of intellectual ability and learning', in Gifford, B. R. and O'Conner, M. C. (eds) *Changing Assessments: Alternative Views of Aptitude, Achievement and Instruction*. Boston and Dordrecht: Kluwer, 301–28.

Shulman, L. (1986) 'Those who understand: knowledge growth in teaching', *Educational Research*, 15, 4–14.

Shulman, L. (1987) 'Knowledge and teaching: foundations of the new reform', *Harvard Educational Review*, 57, 1–22.

Sikes, P., Measor, L. and Woods, P. (1985) *Teacher Careers: Crises and Continuities*. Lewes: Falmer Press.

Skeggs, B. (1997) *Formation of Class and Gender: Becoming Respectable*. London: Sage.

Skinner, B. F. (1954) 'The science of learning and the art of teaching', *Harvard Educational Review*, 24, 86–97.

Slavin, R. (1986) 'Small group methods', in Durkin, M. (ed.) *The International Encylopedia of Teaching and Teacher Education*. London: Pergamon.

Slavin, R. E. (1987) 'Ability grouping and student achievement in elementary schools: a best evidence synthesis', *Review of Educational Research*, 57 (3), 293–6.

Sloane, H. N. (1976) *Classroom Management: Remediation and Prevention*. New York: Wiley.

Smith, A. (1998) *Accelerated Learning in Practice*. Stafford: Network Educational Press.

Smith, D. and Tomlinson, S. (1989) *The School Effect: A Study of Multi-racial Comprehensives*. London: Policy Studies Institute.

Smith, R. and Coldron, J. (1998) 'Thoughtful teaching', in Cashdan, A, and Overall, L. (eds) *Teaching in Primary Schools*. London: Cassell, 63–7.

Smith, T. and Noble, M. (1995) *Education Divides: Poverty and Schooling in the 1990s*. London: Child Poverty Action Group.

Solomon, J. and Tresman, S. (1999) 'A model for Continued Professional Development', *Journal of In-service Education*, 25 (2), 307–16.

Sotto, E. (1994) *When Teaching Becomes Learning*. London: Cassell.

Southworth, G., Nias, J. and Campbell, P. (1992) 'Rethinking collegiality: teachers' views', mimeo presented to the American Educational Research Association, New Orleans.

Stenhouse, L. (1975) *An Introduction to Curriculum Research and Development*. London: Heinemann.

Stobart, G., White, L., Elwood, L., Hayden, M. and Mason, K. (1992) *Differential Performance in Examinations at 16+: English and Mathematics*. London: Schools Examination and Assessment Council.

Stott, D. H. (1978) *Helping Children with Learning Difficulties*. London: Ward Lock Education.

Strulansky, S. and Shefataya, S. (1990) *Facilitating Play: A Medium for Promoting Cognitive, Socio-emotional and Academic Development in Young Children*. Gaithersberg: Psychosocial and Educational Publications.

Suffolk Education Authority (1987) *In the Light of Torches*. London: Industrial Society.

Swilansky, S. (1968) *The Effects of Socio-dramatic Play on Disadvantaged Pre-school Children*. London: Academic Press.

Sylva, K. (1992) 'Conversations in the nursery: how they contribute to aspirations and plans', *Language and Education*, 6 (2, 3 and 4), 147–8.

Sylva, K. (1994) 'The impact of early learning on children's later development', in *Royal Society of Arts, Start Right* (The Ball Report). London: RSA, 84–96.

Tabachnik, R. and Zeichner, K. (eds) (1991) *Issues and Practices in Inquiry-oriented Teacher Education*. London: Falmer Press.

Tanner, J. M. (1961) *Education and Physical Growth*. London: University of London.

Tanner, L. N. (1978) *Classroom Discipline*. New York: Holt, Rinehart and Winston.

Teacher Training Agency (2000) *Improving Standards Through Evidence-based Teaching*. London: TTA.

Tharp, R. and Gallimore, R. (1988) Rousing Minds to Life. New York: Cambridge University Press.

Thomas, G. (1989) 'The aims of primary education in member states of the Council of Europe', in Galton, M. and Blyth, A. (eds) *Handbook of Primary Education in Europe*. London: David Fulton.

Thomas, G., Meyer, J. W., Ramirez, F. O. and Boli, J. (1987) *Institutional Structure: Constituting State, Society and the Individual*. Beverley Hills, CA: Sage.

Thorne, B. (1993) *Gender Play: Girls and Boys in School*. Buckingham: Open University Press.

Tizard, B. and Hughes, M. (1984) *Young Children Learning*. London: Fontana.

Tizard, B., Blatchford, D., Burke, J., Farquhar, C. and Plewis, I. (1988) *Young Children at School in the Inner City*. Hove: Lawrence Erlbaum.

Tobias, S. (1994) 'Interest, prior knowledge and learning', *Review of Educational Research*, 64 (1), 37–54.

Tomlinson, S. (1982) *The Sociology of Special Education*. London: Routledge and Kegan Paul.

Tooley, J. and Darby, D. (1998) *Educational Research: an OFSTED Critique*. London: OFSTED.

Triggs, P. and Pollard, A. (1998) 'Pupil experience and a curriculum for lifelong learning', in C. Richards and P. H. Taylor (eds) *How Shall We School our Children?* London: Falmer.

Troyna, B. and Hatcher, R. (1992) *Racism in Children's Lives: A Study of Mainly-white Primary Schools*. London: Routledge.

Valli, L. (1992) *Reflective Teacher Education: Cases and Critiques*. New York: SUNY Press.

Vulliamy, G. and Webb, R. (2000) 'Stemming the tide of rising school exclusions: problems and possibilities', *British Journal of Educational Studies*, 48 (2), 119–33.

Vygotsky, L. S. (1962) *Thought and Language*. Cambridge, MA: MIT Press.

Vygotsky, L. S. (1978) *Mind in Society: The Development of Higher Psychological Processes*. Cambridge, MA: Harvard University Press.

Vygotsky, L. S. (1981) 'The development of higher mental functions', in Wertsch, J. V. (ed.) *The Concept of Activity in Soviet Psychgology*. Amonk, NY: Sharpe.

Walker, A. and Walker, C. (eds) (1997) *Britain Divided: The Growth of Social Exclusion in the 1980s and 1990s*. London: Child Poverty Action Group.

Walker, R. and Adelmam, C. (1976) 'Strawberries', in M. Stubbs and S. Delamont (eds) *Explorations in Classroom Observation*. Chichester: Wiley.

Walkerdine, V. (1984) 'Developmental psychology and the child-centred pedagogy; the insertion of Piaget into early education', in Henriques, J., Hollway, C., Urwin, C., Venn, C. and Walkerdine, V., *Changing the Subject*. London: Methuen.

Walkerdine, V. (1984) 'Some day my prince will come', in McRobbie, A. and Nava, M. (eds.) *Gender and Generation*. London: Macmillan.

Walkerdine, V. (1985) 'On the regulation of speaking and silence: subjectivity, class and gender in contemporary schooling', in Steedman, C., Urwin, C. and Walkerdine, V. (eds.) *Language, Gender and Childhood*. London: Routledge and Kegan Paul.

Wallace, G. and Kauffman, J. M. (1978) *Teaching Children with Learning Problems*. Columbus, OH: Merrill.

Waller, W. (1932/1961) *The Sociology of Teaching*. New York: Russell and Russell.

Warham, A. and Dadds, M. (1998) 'Hotness explained: children learning in a science lesson', unpublished research paper (in progress). Cambridge: University of Cambridge.

Warin, J. (1998) 'The role of gender in the development of the young child's sense of self within the social context of early school experiences', unpublished PhD thesis. Lancaster: Lancaster University.

Webb, R. (1993a) 'The National Curriculum and the changing nature of topic work', *The Curriculum Journal*, 4 (2), 239–52.

Webb, R. (1993b) *Eating the Elephant Bit by Bit: The National Curriculum at Key Stage 2*. London: Associaton of Teachers and Lecturers.

Webb, R. (1994) *After the Deluge: Changing Roles and Responsibilities in the Primary School*. London: Association of Teachers and Lecturers.

Webb, R. and Vulliamy, G. (1996) *Roles and Responsibilities in the Primary School: Changing Demands, Changing Practices*. Buckingham: Open University Press.

Webb, R. and Vulliamy, G. (2002) 'The social work dimension of the primary teacher's role', *Research Papers in Education*, 17 (2), to be published.

Welch. A. R. (1993) 'Class, culture and the state in comparative education: problems, perspectives and prospects', *Comparative Education*, 29 (1), 7–27.

Wells, G. (1985) *Language at Home and in School*. Cambridge: Cambridge University Press.

Wells, G. (1986) *The Meaning Makers*. Oxford: Heinemann Educational.

Wertsch, J. V, and Tulviste, P (1996) 'L. S. Vygotsky and contemporary developmental psychology', in Daniels, H. (ed.) *An Introduction to Vygotsky*. London: Routledge.

Wertsch, J. V. (1979) 'From social interaction to higher psychological process: a clarification and application of Vygotsky's theory', *Human Cognition*, 2 (1), 15–18.

Wertsch, J. V. (1991) *Voices of the Mind: A Sociocultural Approach to Mediated Action*. London: Harvester Wheatsheaf.

Wertsch, J. V. and Stone, C. A. (1985) 'The concept of internalization in Vygotsky's account of the genesis of higher mental functions', in J. V. Wertsch (ed.) *Culture, Communication and Cognition*. Cambridge: Cambridge University Press.

White, J. (1993) 'What place values in the National Curriculum?', in O'Hear, P. and White, J. (eds) *Assessing the National Curriculum*. London: Paul Chapman.

Whiting, B. B. and Edwards, C. P. (1988) *Children of Different Worlds*. Cambridge, MA: Harvard University Press.

Wigfield, A., Eccles, J., MacIver, D., Reuman, D. A. and Midgley, C. (1991) 'Transitions during early adolescence: changes in children's domain-specific self-perceptions and general self-esteem across the transition to junior high school', *Development Psychology*, **27**, 552–65.

Wilkinson, A., Barnsley, G., Hanna, P. and Swan, M. (1979) 'Assessing language development', *Language for Learning*, **1** (2), 59–76.

Willig, C. J. (1990) *Children's Concepts and the Primary Curriculum*. London: Paul Chapman.

Wise, A. E. *et al.* (1985) 'Teacher evaluation: a study of effective practices', *The Elementary School Journal*, **86**, 61–121.

Walker, R. and Adelma, C. (1976) 'Strawberries', in Stubbs, M. and Delamont, S. (eds) *Explorations in Classroom Observation*. London: Wiley.

Wood, D. (1988) *How Children Think and Learn*. Oxford: Blackwell.

Wood, D. J., Bruner, J. S. and Ross, G. (1976) 'The role of tutoring in problem solving', *Journal of Child Psychology and Psychiatry*, **17** (2), 89–100.

Woodhead, C. (1998) 'Where do you stand?' *Times Educational Supplement*, 5 June, 17.

Woods, P. (1977) 'Teaching for survival', in Woods, P. and Hammersley, M. (eds), *School Experience*. London: Croom Helm.

Woods, P. (1979) *The Divided School*. London: Routledge and Kegan Paul.

Woods, P. (1987) 'Managing the primary teacher's role', in Delamont, S. (ed.) *The Primary School Teacher*. Lewes: Falmer Press

Woods, P. (1990) *Teacher Skills and Strategies*. Lewes: Falmer Press.

Woods, P. (1993) *Critical Events in Teaching and Learning*. London: Falmer Press.

Woods, P. (1995) *Creative Teachers in Primary Schools*. Buckingham: Open University Press.

Woods, P. and Jeffrey, B. (1997) 'Creative teaching in the primary National Curriculum', in Helsby, G. and McCulloch, G. (eds) *Teachers and the National Curriculum*. London: Cassell.

Woods, P. and Wenham, P. (1994) 'Teaching and researching the teaching of a history topic: and experiment in collaboration', *The Curriculum Journal*, 5 (2), 133–61.

Yeomans, R. and Sampson, J. (eds) (1994) *Mentorship in the Primary School*. London: Falmer Press.

Zeichner, K. M. and Gore, J. M. (1990) 'Teacher socialization', in Houston, W. R. (ed.) *Handbook of Research on Teacher Education*. New York: Macmillan.

Zeichner, K. M. and Liston, D. (1990) *Traditions of Reform and Reflective Teaching in US Teacher Education* (Issue Paper 90–1). East Lansing, MI: National Center for Research on Teacher Education.

Ziman, J. (1978) *Reliable Knowledge*. Cambridge: Cambridge University Press.

# PERMISSIONS DETAILS

## Chapter 1

1.1 'Thinking and reflective experience', by John Dewey, edited from *How We Think: A Restatement of the Relation of Reflective Thinking to the Educative Process* (1933), published by Henry Regnery, and from *Democracy and Education* (1916), published by the Free Press

1.2 'Reflection-in-action', by Donald Schön, edited from *The Reflective Practitioner* (1983), published by Temple Smith and reproduced by permission of Ashgate Publishing

1.3 'Dilemmas of schooling', by Ann Berlak and Harold Berlak, edited from *Dilemmas of Schooling* (1981), reproduced by permission of Ann Berlak, Harold Berlak and Routledge

1.4 'Creative meditation and professional judgement', by Marilyn Osborn, Elizabeth McNess and Patricia Broadfoot, edited from *What Teachers Do: Changing Policy and Practice in Primary Education* (2000), reproduced by permission of Continuum

1.5 'Reflections on reflective teaching', by Robert Tabachnick and Kenneth Zeichner, edited from *Issues and Practices in Inquiry-Oriented Teacher Education* (1991), reproduced by permission of Falmer Press

## Chapter 2

2.1 'Analysing the role of mentors', by John Sampson and Robin Yeomans, edited from *Mentorship in the Primary School* (1994), reproduced by permission of Falmer Press

2.2 'Learning through induction into a community of practice', by Anne Edwards and Jill Collison, edited from *Mentoring and Developing Practice in Primary Schools: Supporting Student-teacher Learning in Schools* (1996), reproduced by permission of Open University Press

2.3 'Students' school-based learning', by Trisha Maynard, edited from 'The student teacher and the school community of practice: a consideration of "learning as participation"', *Cambridge Journal of Education*, 31 (1) (2001), reproduced by permission of Taylor and Francis

2.4 'Competence and the complexities of teaching', by James Calderhead, edited from 'Can the complexities of teaching be accounted for in terms of competencies? Contrasting views of professional practice from research and policy' (1994) mimeo, reproduced by permission of James Calderhead

## Chapter 3

3.1 'The teacher as researcher', by Lawrence Stenhouse, edited from *An Introduction to Curriculum Research and Development* (1975), reproduced by permission of the trustees of the estate of Lawrence Stenhouse

3.2 'Action research and the development of practice', by Richard Pring, edited from *Philosophy of Educational Research* (2000), reproduced by permission of Continuum

3.3 'Improving standards through evidence-based teaching', by Teacher Training Agency, edited from *Improving Standards Through Evidence-based Teaching* (2000), reproduced by permission of TTA

3.4 'Three paradigms of educational research', by Michael Bassey, edited from 'Creating education through research', *Research Intelligence*, autumn (1990), reproduced by permission of Michael Bassey

## Chapter 4

4.1 'The sociological imagination', by C. Wright Mills, edited from *The Sociological Imagination* (1959), reproduced by permission of Oxford University Press, Inc.

4.2 'European variations in primary education', by Norman Thomas, edited from *Handbook of Primary Education in Europe*, edited by Maurice Galton and Alan Blyth (1989), reproduced by permission of David Fulton Publishers

4.3 'Primary teaching and "social work"', by Rosemary Webb and Graham Vulliamy, edited from 'The social work dimension of the primary teacher's role', *Research Papers in Education*, 17 (2) (2002), reproduced by permission of Taylor and Francis

4.4 'Childhood and education', by Andrew Pollard and Pat Triggs, edited from *What Pupils Say: Changing Policy and Practice in Primary Education* (2000), reproduced by permission of Continuum

4.5 'Family capital, schooling and social class', by Diane Reay, edited from 'A useful extension of Bourdieu's conceptual framework? Emotional capital as a way of understanding mothers' involvement in their children's education', *The Sociological Review*, 48 (4) (2000)

## Chapter 5

5.1 'Feeling like a teacher', by Jennifer Nias, edited from *Primary Teachers Talking: A Study of Teaching as Work* (1989), reproduced by permission of Jennifer Nias and Routledge

5.2 'Polarities in teacher's thinking', by Martin Cortazzi, edited from *Primary Teaching: How It Is* (1990), reproduced by permission of David Fulton Publishers

5.3 'The self-determination of creative teachers', by Peter Woods, edited from *Creative Teachers in Primary Schools* (1995), reproduced by permission of Peter Woods and the Open University Press

5.4 'The worlds of children and adults', by Bronwyn Davies, edited from *Life in the Classroom and Playground* (1982), reproduced by permission of Bronwyn Davies and Routledge

5.5 'The social world of primary school learning', by Andrew Pollard and Ann Filer, edited from *The Social World of Pupil Career: Strategic Biographies Through Primary School* (1999), reproduced by permission of Continuum

5.6 'The importance of gender identity during school transfer', by Carolyn Jackson and Joanna Warin, edited from 'The importance of gender as an aspect of identity at key transition points in compulsory education', in *British Educational Research Journal*, 26 (3) (2000) reproduced by permission of Taylor and Francis

5.7 'Identity, migration and education', by Uvanney Maylor, edited from 'Identity, migration and education', in *Identity and Diversity*, edited by M. Blair and J. Holland (1995), reproduced by permission of the Open University

## Chapter 6

6.1 'Leadership and the socio-emotional climate in classrooms', by John Withall and W. W. Lewis, edited from 'Social/emotional climate in the classroom' in *Handbook of Research on Teaching*, edited by N. L. Gage (1963), published by the American Educational Research Association

6.2 'Life in classrooms', by Philip Jackson, edited from *Life in Classrooms* (1968), reproduced by permission of Teachers College Press, copyright 1990 of Teachers College, Columbia University

6.3 'Teachers and classroom relationships', by Peter Woods, edited from 'Managing the primary teacher's role, in *The Primary School Teacher*, edited by Sara Delamont (1987), reproduced by permission of Falmer Press

6.4 'Teachers, pupils and the working consensus', by Andrew Pollard, edited from *The Social World of the Primary School* (1985), reproduced by permission of Continuum

6.5 'Establishing a working consensus: teaching styles and pupil types', by Maurice Galton, Linda Hargreaves, Chris Comber and Debbie Wall, with Anthony Pell, edited from *Inside the Primary Classroom: 20 Years On* (1999), reproduced by permission of RoutledgeFalmer

6.6 'Teacher expectations and pupil achievement', by Caroline Gipps and Barbara Mac-Gilchrist, edited from 'Primary school learners', in *Understanding Pedagogy and its Impact on Learning*, edited by P. Mortimore (1999), reproduced by permission of Paul Chapman publishing

6.7 'What is self-esteem?', by Denis Lawrence, edited from *Enhancing Self-esteem in the Classroom* (1987), reproduced by permission of Paul Chapman Publishing

## Chapter 7

7.1 'The science of learning and the art of teaching', by Burrhus Skinner, edited from 'The science of learning and the art of teaching' (1954), published in *Harvard Education Review*, 24

7.2 'A genetic approach to the psychology of thought', by Jean Piaget, edited from 'A genetic approach to the psychology of thought' in *The British Journal of Educational Psychology*, 52 (1961), reproduced by permission of Carfax Publishing Company

7.3 'Mind in society and the ZPD', by Lev Vygotsky, edited from *Mind in Society: The Development of Higher Psychological Processes* (1978), reproduced by permission of Harvard University Press

7.4 'Playful learning', by Rod Parker-Rees, edited from 'Protecting playfulness', in *Early Education Transformed: New Millennium Series*, edited by L. Abbott and H. Moylett (1999), reproduced by permission of Falmer Press

7.5 'The idea of multiple intelligences', by Howard Gardner, edited from *Frames of Mind: The theory of Multiple Intelligences* (1985), published by Paladin Books

7.6 'Motivational processes affecting learning', by Carol Dweck, edited from 'Motivational processes affecting learning', in *American Psychologist*, October (1986), reproduced by permission of the American Psychological Association

7.7 'Learning and the development of "resilience"', by Guy Claxton, edited from *Wise Up: The Challenge of Lifelong Learning* (1999), reproduced by permission of Network Press

7.8 'Cultural Psychology', by Jerome Bruner, edited from *Acts of Meaning* (1990), reproduced by permission of Harvard University Press

7.9 'Culture, context and the appropriation of knowledge', by Neil Mercer, edited from *Context and Cognition: Ways of Learning and Knowing*, edited by Paul Light and George Butterworth (1992), reproduced by permission of Prentice Hall

7.10 'Applying school learning', by Martin Hughes, Charles Desforges and Christine Mitchell, with Clive Carré, edited from *Numeracy and Beyond: Applying Mathematics in the Primary School* (2000), reproduced by permission of Open University Press

7.11 'Learning through the years of schooling', by Andrew Pollard and Pat Triggs, edited from *What Pupils Say: Changing Policy and Practice in Primary Education* (2000), reproduced by permission of Continuum

## Chapter 8

8.1 'Accounting for a world curriculum', by John Meyer and David Kamens, edited from 'Conclusion: accounting for a world curriculum', in *School Knowledge for the Masses: World Models and National Primary Curricular Categories in the Twentieth Century*, edited by John W. Meyer, David H. Kamens and Aaron Benavot, with Yun-Kyung cha and Suk-Ying Wong (1992), reproduced by permission of Falmer Press

8.2 'On the classification and framing of educational knowledge', by Basil Bernstein, edited from *Knowledge and Control: New Directions for the Sociology of Education*, (1971), published by Collier-Macmillan

8.3 'Aspects of children's learning', by the Central Advisory Council for England, edited from *Children and their Primary Schools* (The Plowden Report) (1965), Crown copyright reproduced by permission of the Controller of HMSO

8.4 'A development approach to the curriculum in the early years', by Lilian G. Katz, edited from 'A development approach to the curriculum in the early years', in *The Early Years: A Reader*, edited by S. Smidt (1998) reproduced by permission of Routledge

8.5 'Teaching a subject', by John Wilson, edited from *Key Issues in Education and Teaching* (2000), reproduced by permission of Cassell

8.6 'A perspective on teacher knowledge', by Lee Shulman, edited from 'Those who understand: knowledge growth in teaching', in *Educational Researcher*, February (1986), published by the American Educational Research Association

8.7 'The role of the subject coordinator', by Lucy O'Hara and Mark O'Hara, edited from *Teaching History 3–11: The Essential Guide* (2001), reproduced by permission of Continuum

8.8 'The curriculum for a learning society', by the Labour Party, edited from *Consultative Green Paper on Education: Opening Doors to a Learning Society* (1994), reproduced by permission of the Labour Party

8.9 'Good practice: more than a mantra', by Robin Alexander, edited from *Policy and Practice in Primary Education* (1992), reproduced by permission of Robin Alexander and Routledge

## Chapter 9

9.1 'Characteristics of the curriculum', by Her Majesty's Inspectors, edited from *The Curriculum from 5–16, Curriculum Matters 2* (1985), Crown copyright reproduced by permission of the Controller of HMSO

9.2 'The nature and purpose of the curriculum 5–14', by the Scottish Executive, edited from *The Structure and Balance of the Curriculum: 5–14 National Guidelines* (2000), reproduced by permission of Teaching and Learning, Scotland

9.3 'Desirable outcomes for children's learning', by the Curriculum and Assessment Authority for Wales, edited from *Desirable Outcomes for Children's Learning Before Compulsory School Age* (1996), reproduced by permission of ACAC

9.4 'The "hurry-along" curriculum', by Marion Dadds, edited from 'Politics of pedagogy: the state and children', in *Teachers and Teaching: Theory and Practice*, 7 (1) (2001), reproduced by permission of Taylor and Francis

9.5 'Managing learning in the primary classroom', by Neville Bennett, edited from *Managing*

*Learning in the Primary Classroom* (1992), reproduced by permission of ASPE and Trantham Books

9.6 'Key issues in classroom differentiation', by Eve Bearne, edited from *Differentiation and Diversity in the primary school* (1996), reproduced by permission of Routledge

9.7 'Curriculum strategies for able pupils', by Diane Montgomery, edited from *Educating the Able* (1996), reproduced by permission of Continuum

9.8 'ICT in the primary classroom', by Steven Kennelwell, John Parkinson and Howard Tanner, edited from *Developing ICT in the Primary Schools* (2000), reproduced by permission of RoutledgeFalmer.

## Chapter 10

10.1 'Managing the classroom as an environment for learning', by Janet Moyles edited from 'A place for everything? The classroom as a teaching and learning context', in *Beginning Teaching: Beginning Learning in Primary Education*, edited by J. Moyles, (1995), reproduced by permission of Open University Press

10.2 'Classroom layout, resources and display', by David Clegg and Shirley Billington, edited from *The Effective Primary Classroom: Management and Organization of Teaching and Learning* (1994), reproduced by permission of David Fulton Publishers

10.3 'Class size does make a difference', by Helen Pate-Bain, Charles Achilles, Jane Boyd-Zaharias and Bernard McKenna, edited from 'Class size does make a different', *Phi Delta Kappa*, November (1992), reproduced by permission of Helen Pate-Bain and Phi Delta Kappa

10.4 'Classroom organization for flexible teaching', by David McNamara, edited from *Classroom Pedagogy and Primary Practice* (1994), reproduced by permission of David McNamara and Routledge

10.5 ' "Good practice" in group work', by Rea Reason, edited from 'Primary special needs and National Curriculum assessment', in *Assessing Special Educational Needs*, edited by S. Wolfendale (1993), reproduced by permission of Continuum

10.6 'Meeting special needs in the primary school classroom', by Paul Croll and Diana Moses, edited from *Special Needs in the Primary School: One in Five?* (2000), reproduced by permission of Continuum

10.7 'The teacher and others in the classroom', by Gary Thomas, edited from 'The teacher and others in the classroom' in *The Primary Teacher: The Role of the Educator and the Purpose of Primary Education*, edited by Cedric Cullingford (1989), reproduced by permission of Continuum

## Chapter 11

11.1 'Learning the classroom environment', by Walter Doyle, edited from 'Learning the classroom environment: an ecological analysis' in *Journal of Teacher Education*, **28** (6), (1977), reproduced by permission of the American Association of Colleges for Teacher Education

11.2 'Ambiguity and learning', by Maurice Galton, edited from *Teaching in the Primary School* (1987), reproduced by permission of David Fulton Publishers

11.3 'Learning to be "stupid"?', by John Holt, edited from *How Schools Fail* (1982), reproduced by permission of A. M. Heath on behalf of John Holt

11.4 'Four rules of class management', by Robert Laslett and Colin Smith, edited from *Effective Classroom Management: A Teacher's Guide* (1984), reproduced by permission of Robert Laslett, Colin Smith and Routledge

11.5 'Provocative and insulative teachers', by David Hargreaves, Stephen Hestor and Frank Mellor, edited from *Deviance in Classrooms* (1975), reproduced by permission of David Hargreaves and Routledge

11.6 'Discipline and group management in classrooms', by Jacob Kounin, edited from *Discipline and Group Management in Classrooms* (1970), reproduced by permission of Holt, Rinehart and Winston

11.7 'Positive teaching in the primary school', by Frank Merrett and Kevin Wheldall, edited from *Identifying Troublesome Classroom Behaviour* (1990), reproduced by permission of Paul Chapman Publishing

11.8 'Discipline in schools', by the Committee of Enquiry on Discipline in Schools (the Elton Report), edited from *Discipline in Schools: Report of the Committee of Enquiry chaired by Lord Elton* (1989), reproduced by permission of HMSO

## Chapter 12

12.1 'Conversation and the reinvention of knowledge', by Gordon Wells, edited from *The Meaning Makers* (1986), reproduced by permission of Heinemann Educational

12.2 'Knowledge, communication and learning', by Douglas Barnes, edited from *From Communication to Curriculum* (1975), published by Heinemann, reproduced by permission of Douglas Barnes

12.3 'Classroom discourse and learning', by Derek Edwards and Neil Mercer, edited from *Common Knowledge: The Development of Understanding in the Classroom* (1987), reproduced by permission of Derek Edwards, Neil Mercer and Routledge

12.4 ' "Correct" or "appropriate" language?', by Chris Davies edited from ' "Correct" or "appropriate" language? Is it possible to resolve the debate about which should be promoted in the classroom', in *Issues in English Teaching*, edited by J. Davison and J. Moss (2000), reproduced by permission of Routledge

12.5 'Language, culture and story in the bilingual primary school', by Adrian Blackledge, edited from 'Language, culture and story in the bilingual primary school', in *Teaching Bilingual Children*, edited by A. Blackledge (1994), reproduced by permission of Trentham books

12.6 'Pupils silenced by anxiety', by Janet Collins, edited from *The Quiet Child* (1996), reproduced by permission of Continuum

12.7 'Who holds the initiative in classroom interaction?', by Alec Webster, Michael Beveridge and Malcolm Reed, edited from *Managing the Literacy Curriculum: How Schools Can Become Communities of Readers and Writers* (1996), reproduced by permission of Routledge

## Chapter 13

13.1 'Towards an appropriate theory of pedagogy', by Maurice Galton, Linda Hargreaves, Chris Comber and Debbie Wall, with Anthony Pell, edited from *Inside the Primary Classroom: 20 Years on* (1999), reproduced by permission of Routledge

13.2 'Teaching as the assistance of performance', by Roland Tharp and Ronald Gallimore, edited from *Rousing Minds to Life: Teaching, Learning and Schooling in Social Context* (1988), reproduced by permission of Roland Tharp, Ronald Gallimore and Cambridge University Press

13.3 'Teaching to promote active learning', by Janet Moyles, edited from 'Just for fun? The child as active learner and meaning-maker', in *Developing Pedagogy: Researching Practice*, edited by J. Collins, K. Insley and J. Soler (2001), reproduced by permission of Paul Chapman Publishing

13.4 'The main elements of effective direct instruction', by Daniel Muijs and David Reynolds, edited from *Effective Teaching: Evidence and Practice* (2001), reproduced by permission of Paul Chapman Publishing

13.5 'Using questions in classroom discussion', by Elizabeth Perrot, edited from *Effective Teaching: A Practical Guide to Improving Your Teaching* (1982), reproduced by permission of Longman

13.6 'Talking and learning in the classroom', by Terry Phillips, edited from 'Beyond lip-service: discourse development after the age of nine', in *Language and Learning: An Interactional Perspective*, edited by G. Wells and J. Nicholls (1985), reproduced by permission of Falmer Press

13.7 'A rationale for cooperative group work', by Neville Bennett and Elizabeth Dunne, edited from *Managing Classroom Groups* (1992), reproduced by permission of Simon and Schuster Education

13.8 'Promoting collaborative learning', by Colin Biott and Patrick Easen, edited from *Collaborative Learning in Staffrooms and Classrooms* (1994), reproduced by permission of David Fulton Publishers

13.9 'Pedagogic principles derived from human rights', by Audrey Osler and Hugh Starkey, edited from *Teacher Education and Human Rights* (1998), reproduced by permission of David Fulton Publishers

## Chapter 14

14.1 'Assessment purposes and principles', by Wynne Harlen, Caroline Gipps, Patricia Broadfoot and Desmond Nuttall, edited from 'Assessment and the improvement of education', in *Curriculum Journal*, 3 (3) (1992), reproduced by permission of Wynne Harlen and Routledge

14.2 'Assessment: friend or foe?', by Paul Black, edited from *Testing: Friend or Foe? Theory and Practice of Assessment and Testing* (1998), reproduced by permission of Falmer Press

14.3 'Teacher feedback in the Reception class', by Andrew Burrell and Sara Bubb, edited from 'Teacher feedback in the Reception class', *Education 3–13*, 28 (3) (2000), reproduced by permission of Trentham Books

14.4 'Reinforcing learning intentions through oral feedback', by Shirley Clarke, edited from *Unlocking Formative Assessment: Practical Strategies for Enhancing Pupils' Learning in the Primary Classroom* (2001), reproduced by permission of Hodder and Stoughton Education

14.5 'Pupil self-assessment', by Yolande Muschamp, edited from *Practical Issues in Primary Education*, Issue number 9 (1991), reproduced by permission of Yolande Muschamp and the National Primary Centre (South West)

14.6 'Trying to understand', by Mary Jane Drummond, edited rom *Assessing Children's Learning* (1993), reproduced by permission of David Fulton Publishers

14.7 'The myth of objective assessment', by Ann Filer and Andrew Pollard, edited from *The Social World of Pupil Assessment: Processes and Contexts of Primary Schooling* (2000), reproduced by permission of Continuum

## Chapter 15

15.1 'Social circumstances in children's experience of exclusion', by Margaret Maden, edited from 'The challenge of children in the education system', in *Children and the State: Whose Problem?*, edited by J. Tunstell (1999), reproduced by permission of Continuum

15.2 'Social differentiation in primary schools', by Andrew Pollard, edited from 'Social differentiation in primary schools', in *Cambridge Journal of Education*, **17** (3) (1987), reproduced by permission of Carfax Publishing Company

15.3 'The effects of ability grouping', by Judith Ireson and Susan Hallam, edited from *Ability Grouping in Education* (2001), reproduced by permission of Paul Chapman Publishers

15.4 'How to promote cooperative relationships', by Barrie Thorne, edited from *Gender Play: Girls and Boys in School* (1993), reproduced by permission of Barrie Thorne and Open University Press

15.5 'Needs, right and opportunities in special education', by Caroline Roaf and Hazel Bines, edited from 'Needs, rights and opportunities in special education', in *Needs, Rights and Opportunities*, edited by Caroline Roaf and Hazel Bines (1989), reproduced by permission of Falmer Press

15.6 'Gendered learning and achievement', by Patricia Murphy, edited from 'Gendered learning and achievement', in *Understanding Learning*, edited by J. Collins and D. Cook (2000), reproduced by permission of Paul Chapman Publishing

15.7 'Social relations, discourse and racism', by Debbie Epstein, edited from *Changing Classroom Cultures: Anti-racism, Politics and Schools* (1993), reproduced by permission of Trentham Books

15.8 'Racism in children's lives', by Barry Troyna and Richard Hatcher, edited from *Racism in Children's Lives: A Stud of Mainly-white Primary Schools* (1992), reproduced by permission of the late Barry Troyna, Richard Hatcher and Routledge

## Chapter 16

16.1 'Thinking about the sort of teacher you want to be', by Robin Smith and John Coldron, edited from 'Thoughtful teaching', in *Teaching in Primary Schools*, edited by A. Cashdan and L. Overall (1998), reproduced by permission of Cassell

16.2 'Developing a Career Entry Profile', by Andy Kempe and Helen Nicholson, edited from *Learning to Teach Drama 11–18* (2001), reproduced by permission of Continuum

16.3 'Case studies from the first year of teaching', by Clive Carré, edited from 'The first year of teaching', in *Learning to Teach*, edited by N. Bennett and C. Carré (1993), reproduced by permission of Routledge

16.4 'The challenges of effective mentoring', by Janet Moyles, Wendy Suschitzky and Linda Chapman, edited from *Teaching Fledglings to Fly . . .? Mentoring and Support Systems in Primary Schools* (1998), reproduced by permission of the Association of Teachers and Lecturers

## Chapter 17

17.1 'What have we learned about school improvement?', by John MacBeath and Peter Mortimore, edited from 'School effectiveness and improvement: the story so far', in *Improving School Effectiveness*, edited by J. MacBeath and P. Mortimore (2001), reproduced by permission of Open University Press

17.2 'The culture of collaboration', by Geoff Southworth, Jennifer Nias and Penny Campbell, edited from 'Rethinking collegiality: teachers' views', mimeo presented to the American Educational Research Association, New Orleans (1992), reproduced by permission of Geoff Southworth

17.3 'A model for continuing professional development', by Joan Solomon and Sue Tresman, edited from 'A model for continued professional development' in *Journal of In-service Education*, **25** (2) (1999), reproduced by permission of the National Union of Teachers

17.4 'A new context for accountability and inspection', by Michael Barber, edited from 'A new context for accountability and inspection', *Education Review*, **14** (2) (2001), reproduced by permission of PESGB

17.5 'School inspection in England: a reappraisal', by Colin Richards, edited from *School Inspection in England: A Reappraisal*, Impact No. 9, Philosophy of Education Society of Great Britain (2001), reproduced by permission of the Philosophy of Education Society of Great Britain

## Chapter 18

18.1 'Thinking about educational systems', by Margaret Archer, edited from *The Social Origins of Educational Systems* (1979), reproduced by permission of Sage Publications

18.2 'Challenging the "banking" concept of education', by Paulo Freire, edited from *Pedagogy of the Oppressed* (1999), reproduced by permission of Continuum

18.3 'Memorandum on teaching and learning about human rights in schools', by the Council of Europe, edited from *Appendix to Recommendation No. R. 85 (7) Memorandum on teaching and learning about human rights in schools* (1985), reproduced by permission of Directorate of Human Rights, Council of Europe

18.4 'Three contexts of policy making', by Richard Bowe and Stephen Ball, with Ann Gold, edited from *Reforming Education and Changing Schools: Case Studies in Policy Sociology* (1992), reproduced by permission of Stephen Ball and Routledge

18.5 'Values, understanding and power', by Andrew Pollard, Patricia Broadfoot, Paul Cross, Marilyn Osborn and Dorothy Abbott, edited from *Changing English Primary Schools?* (1994), reproduced by permission of Continuum

# INDEX

Tables and illustrations are indicated by *italics*.